RACE, CLASS, GENDER, AND JUSTICE IN THE UNITED STATES

A TEXT-READER

CHARLES E. REASONS

Central Washington University

DARLENE J. CONLEY

Central Washington University

JULIUS DEBRO

University of Washington

ALLYN AND BACON

Boston • London • Toronto • Sydney • Tokyo • Singapore

Series Editor: Jennifer Jacobson
Editor-in-Chief, Social Sciences: Karen Hanson
Editorial Assistant: Tom Jefferies
Marketing Manager: Judeth Hall
Editorial-Production Service: Omegatype Typography, Inc.
Composition and Prepress Buyer: Linda Cox
Manufacturing Buyer: Joanne Sweeney
Cover Administrator: Kristina Mose-Libon
Electronic Composition: Omegatype Typography, Inc.

Library of Congress Cataloging-in-Publication Data

Race, class, gender, and justice in the United States : a text-reader / [edited by] Charles
E. Reasons . . . [et al.].
    p. cm.
    Includes bibliographical references and index.
    ISBN 0-205-27994-5 (alk. paper)
    1. Discrimination in criminal justice administration—United States.   I. Reasons,
Charles E.

HV9950 .R33   2002
364.973—dc21
                                                     2001046365

Printed in the United States of America
10   9   8   7   6   5   4   3   2   1   06   05   04   03   02   01

CONTENTS

Race, Class, Gender, and Justice in the United States is a text-reader that provides an excellent introduction to the significance of race, class, and gender to the law and the criminal justice system in American society today. Often texts and readers address only one of these issues, such as gender and justice, or race and justice. This book addresses all three issues in an interrelated way so that students can appreciate the importance of each issue and can view them collectively. The readings in this book were selected with three purposes in mind: (1) to analyze race, class, and gender for each major topic addressed; (2) to provide a wide range of materials from different disciplines so students understand that no one discipline is satisfactory to address all of these issues; and (3) to offer readable text to promote students' understanding.

The three authors combine more than 70 years of teaching, work in corrections, research, and legal practice.

DISTINCTIVE FEATURES

The following features are designed to make *Race, Class, Gender, and Justice* an understandable guide for students. The book is divided into six parts. Each part begins with an overview of issues in an area of criminal justice and a critical assessment and discussion of the readings that follow. The introduction to Part One provides a basic theoretical framework and elaborates on the concepts of race, class, and gender that are woven throughout the rest of the book. The topics covered are comprehensive: the causes of crime, the law, policing, courts, and corrections. At the end of each part overview is a reference list for further reading and questions to enhance understanding and critical thinking. The questions should be useful to both students and professors for discussion and subsequent examination. The eighteen interdisciplinary readings cover a wide range of academic and popular sources and topics, such as racial profiling. Four of the readings were written specifically for this book. A wide variety of minority groups are addressed in the readings, including African Americans, Hispanics, and gays and lesbians.

ORGANIZATION

Part One, A New Look at Race, Class, Gender, and Justice, provides a context for the rest of the book. The overview presents a theoretical analysis of the concepts of race, class, and gender and an understanding of their significance for society and justice. The two readings in this section address the issues of race, class, gender, and justice for both the victim and the offender. For example, in the first reading, Chancer looks at three highly publicized cases emphasizing how gender, class, and race of both offenders and victims influence media presentation, public perception, and subsequent legal outcomes. In addition, this reading demonstrates empirical differences in both victimization and crime rates on the basis of gender, class, and race.

In Part Two, Crime Rates and Explanations, the classic criminological question is addressed—What causes crime and criminal behavior? The overview provides an analysis of criminological theory, from classical explanations to personality, environmental, and power-conflict explanations. The readings in this part look at a wide variety of issues from racism and politics and the war on crime, to structured inequality and homicide among Latinos, to violence against gays and lesbians. For instance, Seyfried offers an insightful analysis of stereotypes and their affect on African American males both in the classroom and in their subsequent criminality. Part Two provides several levels of understanding of the causes of crime and criminal behavior.

Part Three, The Law, addresses the nature of race, class, and gender bias in the law—a topic that is often unexplored in criminology and criminal justice texts. The overview provides a theoretical analysis of law, from order to conflict perspectives. Each reading in this section addresses how the law and its operation can reflect differences in power based on race, class, and gender. The historical influence of inequality, race, and gender on the nature of the law and its administration is explored, including their effects on areas ranging from the Constitution and Civil War amendments to the O. J. Simpson trial.

Part Four, Policing, explores the importance of race, class, and gender for social control agents such as the police. The overview gives a history of the emergence of the police force in relationship to class inequality, and the subsequent development of policing in light of race, class, and gender inequality. From the early nightwatch to community policing and racial profiling, the three readings in this part provide insight into how race, class, and gender have influenced policing, and how discrimination can effectively be reduced.

Part Five, The Courts, considers the many ways race, class, and gender impact the courts and judicial decision making. The overview provides a history of the definition and rule of law, as well as an analysis of our dual court system, including both the federal and state levels. The articles in this section examine race, class, and gender and the effects these nonlegal factors have on judges and judicial decision making. While de jure (in-law) discrimination no longer exists, de facto (in-fact) discrimination is still evident from sentencing studies, to court orders, to classification, and sentencing.

Finally, Part Six addresses the issue of corrections. The overview looks at the history of corrections, emphasizing its impact on the underclass and on racial minorities. The readings in this part include an original writing on Black Muslims and the current effects of racism on prisoners. The high rate of minority females being incarcerated and the effect on the children of female African American prisoners is also addressed. The readings in this part also discuss the increase in incarceration in the last two decades, which has weighed most heavily on racial minorities in urban areas, largely due to the failed war on drugs.

ACKNOWLEDGMENTS

We are indebted to each of the authors and scholars whose work makes up this reader. Their expertise and experience make this an important story to be told.

We very much appreciate the efforts of Karen Hanson at Allyn and Bacon who patiently waited for our manuscript. Her dedication helped make this project worthwhile for all concerned.

We would also like to thank those who did a great deal of nitty-gritty work on the manuscript, including copying, typing, and related efforts. These include Barb Demory, Josh Botsford, Tammy Burrier-Green, Nick Davalos, and those working in the editorial department at Allyn and Bacon.

Finally, we are grateful to the following reviewers for their insightful comments and helpful suggestions: Billy R. Close, Florida State University; Zelma Henriques, John Jay College; and Ralph A. Weisheit, Illinois State University.

PART ONE

A New Look at Race, Class, Gender, and Justice

In 1970, Charles Reasons was working on his Ph.D. at Washington State University in Pullman, Washington. During this time he made his first visit to a maximum security prison in Walla Walla, Washington—the Washington State Penitentiary. He knew that Walla Walla was a rural agricultural area from his youth where he had worked in the crops during the summer. However, when he visited the maximum security institution, he was surprised to see that approximately 30 percent of the inmates were nonwhite. In Washington state at that time, only about 4 percent of the population was nonwhite, but the inmates were disproportionately African American, Hispanic, and Native American. This all-male population was also disproportionately from poor and working-class backgrounds. After completing his Ph.D., Reasons worked in Olympia, Washington, where he surveyed educational needs of all inmates in the state of Washington. In this survey completed in 1972, he discovered that Walla Walla was not unique. The inmate population throughout the state was largely male, disproportionately nonwhite, and of lower socioeconomic status. Furthermore, he found that the educational level of inmates was lower than that of persons on the outside. Somewhat surprisingly, Reasons found that two former fellow college football players were incarcerated, one an African American for drug-related offenses, and the other a white for homicide. On reflection, Reasons realized that growing up as a white, working-class youth, he had experienced a fair amount of violence and crime, so this shouldn't surprise him.

This early experience with prisons brought home the point made in many academic sources, that race, class, and gender are integral to understanding law and crime in the United States. In his first book, *Race, Crime and Justice* (written with Jack Kuykendall, 1972), Reasons addressed the racial inequities in the law and the criminal justice system. In 1974 he published *The Criminologist: Crime and the Criminal,* in which he explored the crimes of professionals—white-collar and corporate crime. This book emphasized that white-collar crime represents not only the color of the collar (type of job), but also the color of the skin and the class of the criminal. Thus, white-collar and corporate crime rarely are caught up in the criminal justice system due to issues of power.

Reasons left Washington State in 1972 to pursue a career as a professor, researcher, and lawyer, and later returned to his home state in 1999. A lot had changed during this time in both Washington and in the United States. The race, class, and gender disproportionalities in prison had increased (Modia and Olsen, 2001). This underlines the importance of addressing race, class, and gender in issues of crime and criminal justice (Pallone, 2000).

ON HUMAN SIMILARITIES AND DIFFERENCES

Most humans are more similar, of course, than different. Compared to other animals, we are both physically and mentally different, but all races, classes, and genders share more similarities than differences. Both human similarities and differences are a matter of *ascribed characteristics,* qualities we are born with, and *achieved characteristics,* qualities we gain through the process of socialization. When we talk about the social significance of these various characteristics, we are talking about power.

RACE

Although the concept of race has been around for centuries, it became scientifically important in the 18th and 19th centuries. During this period, which historians call the age of science and enlightenment, humans began to create naturalistic or scientific explanations for what goes on in the world. Prior to this time, the behavior of stars, weather, and human behavior were largely explained by god, religion, and what we would call "otherworldly" or supernatural explanations. With the rise of science, humans started explaining the earth, moon, stars, weather, and other natural phenomena through observation and study, that is, through the scientific method. The typology and classification of humans into subgroups based on race seemed to followed the logic of the typology and classification of plants and other animal life. Although Charles Darwin's *Origins of Species* specifically described plants and nonhuman life forms, the notion of evolution and of inferior and superior forms of life were applied to the human social realm (Gossett, 1963). This became known as *social Darwinism:* Races were not only placed in typologies and classification schemes, but they were also ordered from inferior to superior.

When white men "discovered" the Americas, they found indigenous peoples in what is now Canada, the United States, Mexico, and South America. These people differed from the European explorers in both skin color and culture—language, laws, religion, politics, and family and other social institutions. The massacre and conquering of such peoples and the seizure of their land was much more politically and socially acceptable to majority groups when it could be justified on the basis of innate inferiority. That is, if these people were viewed as inferior races and cultures, it became "white man's burden" to civilize them. This was particularly important for the British empire, which moved from relative obscurity as a nation in the 16th century, to the largest world power in the 18th and 19th centuries, colonizing a large part of the world, including Asia and the Americas. The British crown was largely influenced by the Christian faith. Religious objections to oppressing nonwhites, however, could be quieted by pointing out the "scientific" evidence. This racism—the assumption of physical, moral, intellectual, and social superior and inferiority based on characteristics presumed to be ascribed—became very important in the British Empire and its colonies, including those in the United States and Canada. The British were the first to practice large-scale enslavement of Africans for financial gain; such slavery and racism became particularly important for the North American colonies.

Legal definitions of race arose early in the 17th century and became important in maintaining the subordination of Blacks, Native Americans, Asians, and others. That is, *de jure* racism, or racial distinctions in the law, became very important for both establishing and then maintaining the early colonies and their growing enterprises. As Part Three explains, in the United States, dejure racism and racial distinctions that suppressed non-whites go back more than 400 years. (Bell, 2000). It was not until the 1960s and 1970s that racism in the law was eliminated.

The historical definition of race is quite different from that which exists today. Formerly, there were Nordic, Jewish, German, Italian, Polish, and other "races." Today we call them ethnic groups. If we look at the definition of race today, the census and other statistics reveal that race has come to mean largely skin pigmentation. Of course, there is still a great deal of ambiguity about the actual definition of race, in terms of an example, people of Hispanic origin have differing skin pigmentations and may have different cultures in terms of languages, religions, and so on. Although Hispanics are defined not as a race but as an ethnic group, color plays a major role in their lives. Table 1.1 shows race distribution in the United States, according to contemporary definitions of race. Historically, the "one drop of blood" principle in law stated that a person who has one drop of nonwhite blood in his or her family lineage is not white (Bell, 2000). This was essentially a social definition of race based on skin pigmentation. Most of us have multiple races in our history (for example, Reason's great-grandmother was one-half Choctaw Indian). The absurdity of the one drop of blood theory has to be put in the historical context of notions of racial purity and ways the dominant white group attempted to maintain its racial purity. One method was through laws against racial intermarriage, which were severely enforced with heavy punishment for violations.

A horrific 20th-century example of the attempt to maintain so-called racial purity is Germany's Third Reich's extermination of more than six million Jews, along with homosexuals, gypsies, people with disabilities, and others. Hitler's Nuremberg laws, which discriminated against the Jews, were not unlike early United States laws that discriminated against Jews, Blacks, and other nonwhites. However, Hitler's "final solution"—the extermination of the Jews—was evidence of the horrendous consequences of racist theory (Montagu, 1953), and confirmed the truism that if we believe something is real, then it is real in its consequences. If those in power identify a specific race, gender, class, or other distinction as threatening, then they may attempt to eliminate or reduce that threat, and they may be successful (Newman, 2000). Some examples are the witchcraft trials in England and the early American colonies and the killing of suspected witches, attesting to misogyny—the fear and hatred of women; the lynching of Blacks in the United States, attesting to whites's fear and hatred of Blacks; eugenics in the first half of the 20th

TABLE 1.1   Race of U.S. Population

RACE/ETHNICITY	NUMBERS (IN MILLIONS)	PERCENT OF POPULATION
White	224.1	82.3
Black	34.9	12.9
American Indian, Eskimo, and Aleutian	2.3	0.9
Asian and Pacific Islander	10.8	4.0
Hispanic Origin	30.4	11.2

Source: Borgna Brunner, Ed., *Time Almanac 2000.* Boston: Information Please, 1999.

century—an attempt to address the perceived inferiority of people who were poor, non-white, or had mental or physical disabilities; and finally, the McCarthyism and the purge of alleged communists in the 1950s based on political ideology.

SOCIAL CLASS

Just as people classify others based on race and gender, they also make distinctions based on social class. Social class is both an objective and a subjective status. Objectively, we can determine class by looking at *income*—how much money you make—and *wealth*—how much you have accumulated in material possessions, such as land, houses, cars, stocks, and so on. Social stratification based on social class has existed for centuries; however, social class as we know it today arose with industrial capitalism. Before capitalism, people were divided into classes largely as a caste system. That is, you were born in a certain class, and you remained there. You had no opportunity to move out of that specific class, so class was entirely hereditary. With the emergence of capitalism—and the trilogy of individual rights of property, contract, and individual freedom—came the ability to change one's station in life. This was part of a revolution against the rigid religious, hereditary, political, economic, and social institutions that had existed before.

With the arrival of industrial capitalism, people were forced to leave their land to secure work in factories. As a result, a class structure arose, consisting of the working class, who worked in the factories, and the capitalist class, who owned the factories (Thompson, 1975). Since the early days of industrial capitalism, the nature of the capitalist class and the working class has changed dramatically. Today, for example, occupations in which people earn their livelihood through hourly or monthly wages from an employer range all the way from a gas station attendant to a physicist working for a research laboratory. And more people earn a living by performing professional and technical services than by working in factories. Nonetheless, a high degree of social stratification based on income and wealth still exists.

Income

In 1999, the bottom 20 percent of Americans earned 4.29 percent of all income whereas the top 20 percent of Americans earned 50.4 percent of the income (Brunner, 2000, p. 838). (See Table 1.2.) Income inequality continued to grow in the 1990s, though at a slower rate than in the 1980s. Between 1989 and 1998, the share of total income earned by the bottom 20 percent of households fell 0.4 percentage points, while the share received by the top 5 percent grew from 17.9 percent in 1989 to 20.7 percent in 1998. Income inequality increased even during the boom in the second half of the 1990s: From 1995 to 1998, the real incomes of low-income families, or families in the 20th percentile, grew 1.9 percent each year. But this was a slower rate of growth than the 2.3 percent growth rate for families in the middle (60th percentile), and far slower than the 3.2 percent rate for families at the top (95th percentile) (Brunner, 2000, p. 838).

African Americans and Hispanics made only mixed progress in the 1990s. Over the entire decade, the average income of Black families grew 1.1 percent per year, more than double the rate for whites (0.4 percent per year). During the boom years of 1995 to 1998, however, the growth in Black family earnings (1.9 percent per year) trailed that of whites (2.4 percent per year). For Hispanics, the story was reversed. Over the full decade of the

TABLE 1.2   Average After-Tax Income in 1997 and 1999

INCOME GROUP	1999[1]		1977	
	AVERAGE INCOME	SHARE OF ALL INCOME (PERCENT)	AVERAGE INCOME	SHARE OF ALL INCOME (PERCENT)
Lowest fifth	$ 8,800	4.2%	$ 10,000	5.7%
Second fifth	20,000	9.7	22,100	11.5
Middle fifth	31,400	14.7	32,400	16.4
Fourth fifth	45,100	21.3	42,600	22.8
Highest fifth	102,300	50.4	74,000	44.2
Top one percent	515,600	12.9	234,700	7.3

Note: Figures rounded to nearest hundred dollars. [1]Projected.

Source: Center on Budget and Policy Priorities. www.cbpp.org. (Based on data from the Congressional Budget Office.)

1990s, Hispanic family incomes fell an average of 0.4 percent per year, but Hispanic families did much better than whites during the boom years, when average Hispanic family income grew 4.1 percent per year (Mischel, Bernstein, & Schmitt, 2001). From 1967 to 1996, the number of Blacks earning more than $50,000 rose from 1.7 percent to 7.4 percent. However, the percent of whites making more than $50,000 rose from 10.8 percent to 18.8 percent. The inequities in wages are as wide today as they were thirty years ago. Blacks earned 63 cents for every dollar earned by whites, and the gap has widened with increased economic prosperity. One-third of the country's two million Native Americans live below the poverty line, and Native Americans have a median family income lower than that of Blacks. If we look at Black and Hispanic male earnings as a percentage of white male earnings in Figure 1.1, we find disparities over all, especially among those with a college degree (Brunner, 2000, p. 826).

If we add gender to the picture, we find that in 1996, women who worked full time, year round earned 74 cents for every dollar earned by men. Over a lifetime of work, the average 25-year-old woman who works full time year round until she retires at age 65 will earn $523,000 less than the average working man. In 1996, 70 percent of working women earned less than $25,000 compared with only 48 percent of working men (Levin, MacInnis, Carroll, & Bourne, 2000).

If we look at earnings by both sex and race, we find that there are definite historical and current inequities. (See Table 1.3). Men earn considerably more than women, and white men earn more than Black and Hispanic men. At the bottom of the heap are Black and Hispanic women. The wage gap between men and women narrowed in the 1990s. In 1999, the median income earned by women was 76.9 percent of that earned by men, up from 73.1 percent in 1989 (Mischel, Bernstein, & Schmitt, 2000). However, the racial and ethnic differences remain.

Wealth

When we look at the distribution of wealth in the United States, we even see more glaring disparities. The top 1 percent of wealth holders control 39 percent of total household

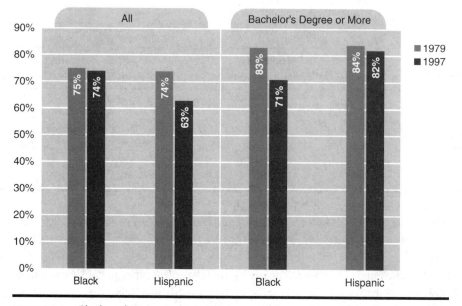

FIGURE 1.1   Black and Hispanic Male Earnings as a Percentage of White Male Earnings

TABLE 1.3   Earnings by Sex and Race, 1948–1997

| | Median Earnings (All Races) | | Earnings as a Percentage of Men's (All Races) | | | | | | | |
| | | | All Races | White | | Black[1] | | Hispanic Origin[2] | |
YEAR	MEN	WOMEN	WOMEN	MEN	WOMEN	MEN	WOMEN	MEN	WOMEN
1997	$25,212	$13,703	54.4%	103.6%	54.7%	71.8%	51.8%	64.3%	40.7%
1996	24,381	13,109	53.8	104.7	54.4	69.2	49.4	64.8	39.8
1995	23,761	12,775	53.8	105.9	54.6	70.9	48.6	65.8	39.6
1994	23,523	12,418	52.8	104.4	53.5	69.0	48.5	66.8	39.7
1993	23,439	12,269	52.3	104.2	53.4	69.2	45.1	64.9	38.4
1988	25,653	12,053	47.0	105.6	48.1	63.7	38.9	68.9	37.0
1983	23,577	10,183	43.2	105.3	43.9	61.3	37.9	77.1	36.9
1978	26,001	9,673	37.2	104.7	37.6	62.7	33.9	76.6	34.6
1973	27,394	9,508	34.7	104.9	35.0	63.5	31.6	77.0	32.9
1968	25,459	8,595	33.8	104.8	34.8	62.2	27.6	—	—
1963	21,742	6,613	30.4	106.5	31.9	55.4	21.3	—	—
1958	19,132	6,011	31.4	106.2	34.2	52.9	20.0	—	—
1953	17,827	6,453	36.2	105.2	40.1	58.1	23.5	—	—
1948	14,678	6,181	42.1	104.8	47.3	56.9	20.5	—	—

Year-round, full-time workers, aged 15 years and over. Income in 1997 dollars. Dash indicates data are not available.

[1]Prior to 1967, data are for black and other races.

[2]Persons of Hispanic origin may be of any race.

Source: Current Population Reports, Series P60, U.S. Bureau of the Census. Web: www.census.gov/hhes/income/histinc/p02.html.

wealth. The share of wealth held by the bottom 80 percent of Americans is only 15 percent of the total wealth. The richest 1 percent of households own 48 percent of financial wealth, and the top 20 percent of households control 94 percent of the total financial wealth in the United States. The average white family has twenty times the wealth of the average nonwhite family. In dollar terms, the average net worth of a white person is $43,800, while the average net worth of a Black person is $3,700. The more income and wealth you have, the more you can accumulate. If we look at each quintile (20 percent) of income earners between 1947 and 1993 (see Figure 1.2), we see that the bottom 20 percent of income earners had the lowest growth between 1947 and 1973, and the bottom 40 percent had negative growth between 1973 and 1993. On the other hand, the top 20 percent grew substantially in later periods. If we look at family net worth, we see extreme disparities here also (Mischel, Bernstein, & Schmitt, 2000).

How do we explain such great disparities in income and wealth in the United States? A significant part of our dominant ideology is that all people are born equal and have equal opportunity to obtain income and wealth. However, we know both income and wealth are mainly hereditary (ascribed), and only partly achieved. That is, the best predictor that you will become extremely rich is whether you were born extremely rich. Likewise, the best predictor that you will be impoverished is whether you were born impoverished. Social scientists call this intergenerational transfer of class; the class we are born into greatly affects our opportunities. First, it has a great impact on *human capital,* or the intellectual and social skills necessary to achieve in society. If one is born into a family with limited income, then it is more likely that fewer learning tools will be available and parents will spend less time facilitating intellectual and social skills. The education we receive is in part based on where we live and the tax base provided. Because we are segregated in society based on income, very poor areas will have reduced learning opportunities. Furthermore,

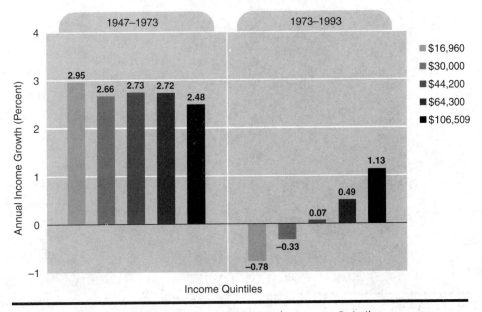

FIGURE 1.2   Annual Individual Income, 1947–1993, by Income Quintiles

our *social capital,* or our connections to role models and career opportunities, are shaped by where we are born. Our ability to network, create contacts, and learn about opportunities are not evenly distributed in society. Although we recognize this, we still cling to the ideology that anybody can become anything he or she wants to be. This may be true in the abstract, but in fact our choices are limited on the basis of where we are born and who we are in terms of social class, race, and gender. These limits on our opportunities are referred to as *structured choices;* that is, we have little influence over the nature of choices we are offered due to the class we are born into. For example, if you are born into poverty (an ascribed status) you are more likely to stay poor because you have limited social and human capital. (Figure 1.3).

International data show that the poor in the United States have fewer opportunities for class mobility than those elsewhere. Among the world's wealthy countries, the United States has both high average incomes and high poverty rates. Recent research by Bruce Bradbury (UNICEF) and Markus Jantti (Abo Akademi University in Finland), for example, found that the United States has more of its population living in poverty (20.7 percent) than does any other advanced economy (Mishel, Bernstein, & Smith, 2001). Poverty rates in most advanced economies were less than half of those in the United States: Spain (10.3 percent), France (9.4 percent), Germany (8.5 percent), the Netherlands (6.5 percent), Belgium (5.7 percent), Denmark (4.9 percent), and Sweden (2.9 percent) (Mischel, Bernstein, & Schmitt, 2000). One popular rationalization is that the higher U.S. poverty rates are not a significant social problem because the United States also offers the poor a greater opportunity to "get ahead" than other countries offer. We may have more poor people at any given time, the argument goes, but the deserving don't remain poor for long.

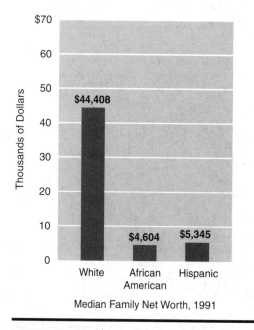

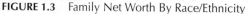

FIGURE 1.3   Family Net Worth By Race/Ethnicity

Percent of the Poor

The data in Figure 1.4, however, suggest that economic mobility is actually lower in the United States than in more-regulated European economies. The figure shows the share of the poor in each country that manage to escape poverty from one year to the next. In the United States, each year about 29 percent of the poor see their incomes increase enough to rise out of poverty—the same percentage as in the United Kingdom. But in all the other countries studied, the poor were more likely to leave poverty than they were in the United States. (Mischel, Bernstein, & Schmitt, 2001). The following list (based on distinctions in Reasons and Perdue, 1981) shows our corporate ideology that we are mainly a classless society, and when class differences do exist, it is due to individual failure. Given these beliefs, you can understand why some people turn to illegal means to obtain their livelihood and survive.

Corporate ideology

1. *Privatism.* Perhaps the hallmark of corporate ideology is an emphasis on personal and private, as opposed to public and social, interests. Expressed commonly in such phrases as "looking out for number one," the "me generation," and "how to be your own best friend," this symbol becomes a stimulus to various industries. For example, insurers commonly remind viewers in their television commercials that the welfare of the survivors of disaster is still largely a personal (not community) responsibility. "Real-life" survivor programs dramatically emphasize this.

2. *Progress.* Corporate ideology presents the idea of progress in the sense of commodity growth. For example, progress in health care is described in terms of costly (and profitable) technology rather than effective, preventive public care. The more consumer goods we have, the better off we are!

3. *Triumph of the will.* According to this common belief, individual determination can remove all obstacles. All social barriers will fall if you believe, work hard, and never say die. In corporate society, tales of heroes overcoming impossible odds become stereotyped media fare. For example, the wonder woman is able to master the roles of career woman, homemaker, and spouse or partner simultaneously. The handicapped

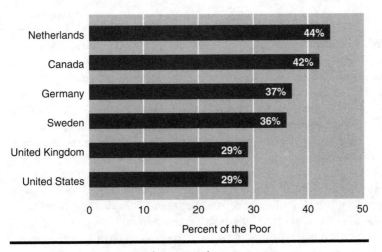

FIGURE 1.4   Average Annual Exit Rate from Poverty

hero is handsome, personable, married, and always gainfully employed (despite being paralyzed from the neck down). An obvious corollary of this belief is, "It's your own fault if you do not succeed."

4. *Commodification of human qualities.* Goods and services available in the marketplace are offered as substitutes for human qualities. Banks become friendly, automobiles are something to believe in, and soft drinks bring people together.

5. *Trickle down.* According to this ideological component, what benefits the private sector (through greater profit) creates benefits for the public sector. For example, reducing corporate taxes is supposed to provide more jobs. However, in an increasingly capital-intensive economy, large-scale technology is valued over labor. Thus, corporate investment in advanced technology is intended frequently to reduce labor costs rather than create a need for more workers. Further, with globalization, large companies are able to export high-paying union jobs for low-paying jobs in undeveloped countries. As Figure 1.2 shows, the profit flows to the top, trickles to the middle, and is cut off for the bottom 40 percent.

6. *Conspicuous consumption.* You are where you live, and what you wear, drive, and eat demonstrate your success. These prime symbols are advanced by a multibillion-dollar advertising industry.

7. *Nuclear familism.* In the corporate order, the small, nuclear family is advanced as the ultimate social unit and reason for being. Primarily a consumptive unit, the "good" family enables its individuals to achieve. The "bad" family, however, is seen as the cause of serious social problems.

8. *Equal opportunity.* Although the title of much antidiscrimination legislation, this prime symbol is the corporate interpretation of fair play. In general, this component of the ideology calls for a place at the starting line for all who wish to race. Equal opportunity is advanced in lieu of questioning why there must be winners and losers, or why it is not possible to improve the conditions of people in general. Furthermore, any advantage to certain groups such as minorities and women, may be attacked as "reverse" racism and sexism. Thus, affirmative action is under attack due to the assumption of a "level playing field."

9. *Chattel relationships.* A sense of property ownership dominates social relationships. Possessive demands intensify as one's circle of intimates grows increasingly smaller.

10. *Expertise.* Corporate ideology includes the belief that important political, economic, and other social decisions should be left to those in power who are in a position to "know." Thus, decisions concerning human values are declared to be matters for scientists, technicians, managers, and specialists.

11. *Economy of scale.* This idea is best described as "big is best." Economic problems are seen as too large and complex to be solved without massive capital investment by those giants who can afford it, or by public–private partnerships, where public funds are used for private interests.

12. *Careerism.* The corporate order is no haven for the Renaissance person. Careerism involves the components of anti-intellectualism, and antitheoreticalism. The emphasis is on solving problems without first understanding them. This ideology component emphasizes the advancement of the manager, technician, and vocational workers. Studies in the liberal arts that raise questions about the existing order may be branded as irrelevant to earning a living.

Our dominant ideology or belief system often explains differences among groups in terms of individual differences. For example, the ideology might state that females and nonwhites don't work as hard as males and whites. This kind of individualistic explanation ignores structural advantages and disadvantages that existed historically and today. That is, in the past, women and nonwhites were not allowed to be educated or work in specific occupations, and thus were unable to own property and accumulate wealth and income. Although de jure (in law) restrictions based on race and gender have been eliminated in the last few decades, it will take many more decades to eliminate the effects of more than 400 years of such restrictions and preferential treatment.

GENDER

One's sex is determined at birth by one's reproductive organs. However, one's gender is determined through the process of learning we call *socialization.* That is, as we grow up, we learn how to think, act, and look male, female, transsexual, homosexual, or some other gender. Sociologists and social psychologists have done numerous studies on how gender socialization occurs and how we learn to become little boys and little girls, and men and women. While the two sexes are needed for procreation (although scientific advancement may someday change this), one's gender—how we look and behave as a male or female— is something we learn.

When it comes to sexuality, we may be heterosexual (attracted to the opposite sex), homosexual (attracted to same sex), or bisexual (attracted to both sexes). Of course, although heterosexual reproduction is needed to maintain the species, homosexuality and bisexuality have a long history. Data on sexual orientation show that 96 percent of men and 97 percent of women in the United States identify themselves as heterosexual, 3.5 percent of men and 2.1 percent of women identify themselves as homosexual, and 0.6 percent of men and 0.9 percent of women identify themselves as bisexual (Brunner, 2000). The ways society and its laws have dealt with sexual orientation have varied over time. There is a long history of de jure discrimination, such as laws persecuting women and barring them from certain occupations, such as witchcraft. In western societies, there is a long history of persecuting homosexuality and bisexuality through prosecution. Although persecution of women is no longer legal in the United States, as we will see, persecution of homosexuality and bisexuality is still legal.

Women have suffered gender discrimination in job opportunities and wages, which becomes particularly damaging when a woman has to raise a family alone. (See Table 1.4). As expected, married couples earn more than single parents do; however, women, particularly minority women, are disadvantaged. This weighs most heavily on minority families because they are more likely to be headed by single parents. (See Table 1.5). Therefore, there are higher poverty rates among minorities and minority children. Despite the economic boom in the second half of the 1990s, the national poverty rate in 1998 was 12.7 percent, just one-tenth of a percentage point less than it was in 1989, and a full percentage point higher than in 1979.

Child poverty has remained stubbornly high. In 1998, 18.9 percent of American children—almost one in five—lived in poverty. This 1998 child poverty rate was an improvement over the 19.6 percent rate for 1989, but still well above the 16.4 percent rate for 1979. In 1998, more than one in four African Americans (26.1 percent) and Hispanics

TABLE 1.4   Median Income of Households with Selected Characteristics, 1997

CHARACTERISTIC	WHITE		BLACK		HISPANIC ORIGIN[1]		ALL RACES	
	As a % of All White Households	Median Income	As a % of All Black Households	Median Income	As a % of All Hispanic Households	Median Income	As a % of All Households	Median Income
Overall		$38,972		$25,050		$26,628		$37,005
Region								
Northeast	20%	41,214	18%	23,312	17%	24,023	19%	38,929
Midwest	25	40,040	18	23,861	7	31,009	24	38,316
South	34	36,681	55	25,074	34	26,207	36	34,345
West	22	39,479	9	29,989	41	27,276	21	39,162
Type of Household								
Family households	69	47,454	67	29,915	81	29,253	69	45,347
Married-couple families	56	52,199	31	45,372	56	34,317	53	51,681
Single-father household	4	38,511	5	28,593	6	28,249	4	36,634
Single-mother household	10	25,670	31	17,962	19	16,393	12	23,040
Nonfamily households	31	22,380	33	17,073	19	16,807	31	21,705
Male living alone	10	25,415	13	17,139	7	16,524	11	23,871
Female living alone	15	15,818	16	13,738	7	9,666	15	15,530
Size of Household								
One person	26	19,288	29	15,258	14	12,222	26	18,762
Two persons	33	40,954	25	26,870	21	26,390	32	39,343
Three persons	17	50,269	19	28,047	20	26,396	17	47,115
Four persons	15	55,819	15	35,529	21	33,053	15	53,165
Five persons	7	52,493	7	36,525	14	31,586	7	50,407
Six persons	2	48,974	3	32,050	5	30,185	2	46,465
Seven persons or more	1	46,044	2	30,799	4	36,088	1	42,343
Number of Earners								
No earners	21	15,324	21	8,172	15	7,842	21	14,142
One	33	31,412	44	21,319	36	20,464	34	29,780
Two	36	55,474	28	44,728	36	37,106	35	54,192
Three	7	68,363	6	57,599	9	47,569	7	67,182
Four or more	2	86,319	1	77,190	4	58,360	2	84,816

[1]Persons of Hispanic origin may be of any race.

Source: U.S. Bureau of Census, *Money Income in the United States 1997.* www.census.gov.

(25.6 percent) lived in poverty, a rate about two and one-half times greater than that for whites (10.5 percent). Racial disparities in poverty rates were even worse for children. In 1998, more than one in three African American (36.7 percent) and Hispanic (34.4 percent) children were growing up in poverty, compared to 15.1 percent of white children (Mischel, Bernstein, & Schmitt, 2001).

PREJUDICE AND DISCRIMINATION

We all have prejudices and discriminate in some manner during our lives. For example, a superficial type of prejudice would be preferring one brand of product without considering any other brands. A prejudice in favor of, say, Sears tools may evidence itself in actual behavior (discrimination) when you shop for a drill. However, if a Sears drill isn't avail-

TABLE 1.5   Families by Type, 1970–1998 (with children under age 18, for selected years 1970–1998)

FAMILY TYPE	1970	1980	1990	1991	1992	1993	1994	1995	1996	1997	1998
Total											
Two parents[1]	85%	77%	73%	72%	71%	71%	69%	69%	68%	68%	68%
Mother only[1]	11	18	22	22	23	23	23	23	24	24	23
Father only[2]	1	2	3	3	3	3	3	4	4	4	4
No parent	3	4	3	3	3	3	4	4	4	4	4
White											
Two parents[1]	90	83	79	78	77	77	76	76	75	75	74
Mother only[1]	8	14	16	17	18	17	18	18	18	18	18
Father only[2]	1	2	3	3	3	3	3	3	4	4	5
No parent	2	2	2	2	2	2	3	3	3	3	3
Black											
Two parents[1]	58	42	38	36	36	36	33	33	33	35	36
Mother only[1]	30	44	51	54	54	54	53	52	53	52	51
Father only[2]	2	2	4	4	3	3	4	4	4	5	4
No parent	10	12	8	7	7	7	10	11	9	8	9
Hispanic[3]											
Two parents[1]	78	75	67	66	65	65	63	63	62	64	64
Mother only[1]	—	20	27	27	28	28	28	28	29	27	27
Father only[2]	—	2	3	3	4	4	4	4	4	4	4
No parent	—	3	3	4	3	3	5	4	5	5	5

[1]Excludes families where parents are not living as a married couple.

[2]Includes some families where both parents are present in the household, but living as unmarried partners.

[3]Persons of Hispanic origin may be of any race.

Note: Data applies to U.S. families.

Source: U.S. Bureau of the Census, *Current Population Reports.*

able, or if the law requires you to consider other drills, then your prejudice may not develop into differential treatment or discrimination.

All societies have prejudice and discriminate in their behavior, as do all individuals. In any given society or nation, some forms of major social institutions are preferred over others. For example, family structures can be nuclear or extended; political institutions can be decentralized, centralized, democratic, republican, or authoritarian; religions can worship a single deity or multiple deities; legal institutions can be rehabilitative, restorative, punitive, or retributive; economic institutions can be collective, individualistic, corporate, agrarian, or competitive. Of course, the institutions we grow up with are what we view as "normal." Different institutions in other societies may not be appreciated, and thus we become *ethnocentric*. Our family, political, religious, legal, and economic institutions are just the normal way of doing things. As the history of colonialism points out, when we meet societies and cultures with institutions different from ours, we may reject them and try to replace them, dominate them, and make them conform to our institutions. Our United States institutions and culture are being transferred and copied throughout the world—what one author refers to as the McDonaldization of the world (Ritzer, 1993).

Just as the imposition of British culture on other societies in the 19th century was called *pax Britainicana,* the second half of the 20th century and the beginning of the 21st century can be labeled *pax Americana,* that is, the dominance of the United States as a world power. Figure 1.5 illustrates how we can be prejudiced, discriminate, or both on the basis of race, class, or gender. This shows the relationship between discrimination and prejudice in terms of race, class, and gender. For example, there may be laws that say you have to discriminate on the basis of race even though you are not prejudiced, or laws, such as those in effect today, that prohibit discrimination even though you are prejudiced.

Since the Civil Rights Movement and the Women's Movement of the 1950s and 1960s, de jure, or legal, racism and sexism has been largely eliminated from the law. This recent revolution marks a radical departure from 400 years of racism, sexism, and classism. Of course, it hasn't eliminated inequality among races, classes, and genders; *de facto* inequality, that is, inequality in fact, still exists. We cannot, of course, pass laws against thought, so we all have the legal right to be prejudiced—to prejudge people on the basis of race, class, and gender. However, we cannot treat them differentially in a public place on the basis of such distinctions. For example, today employers may have prejudices, but they cannot treat people differentially due to those prejudices.

For many centuries the law *required* us to treat people of different races, gender, and classes in different ways. Even if you did not personally hold prejudices, you had to abide by the law by refusing to serve certain people or refusing to hire certain people in certain occupations, for example. In the second half of the 20th century, the United States finally established equality in law as first promised in the U.S. Constitution. This is nothing less than a revolution in the history of the United States, in law, in social institutions, and in ideology (Wong, 1999; MacKinnan, 1987). As we will see in the readings in Part One, race, class, and gender historically and today have a great relevance for the law and criminal justice system (Kendall, 1997).

Prejudice

		Non-Prejudice	Prejudice
No Discrimination		Race	Race
		Class	Class
		Gender	Gender
Discrimination		Race	Race
		Class	Class
		Gender	Gender

FIGURE 1.5   Prejudice

In the first reading, "Gender, Class, and Race in Three High-Profile Crimes," Lynn Chancer analyzes how the media's portrayal of victims and offenders helps to portray a crime, its subsequent public events, and even subsequent policies. The first case study in Reading 1 involves the rape of a woman on a pool table in a bar amid cheering men. This case eventually inspired the movie *The Accused,* portraying how victim-blaming can turn a rape victim almost literally into a defendant.

In the second case study, a young Portuguese woman in New Bedford, Massachusetts, was a victim of rape by Portuguese men in a predominately Portuguese community. Initial news reports were sympathetic toward the young woman, but over time the media found fault with her and started to view her as the cause of the rape. Students of rape point out that according to attribution theory, a rape victim's chances of being blamed for her own victimization increase when she has prior acquaintance with her attackers; there are opportunities to attribute a "bad reputation" to the woman; the rape takes place in a bar, alcohol is present; and the rape occurs in close proximity to the victim's residence. All of these factors were present and contributed to the sexist blaming of the victim.

Another important factor in this case was the media focus on the rapists as Portuguese, not just as male. The emphasis on the ethnicity of the defendants led to increasing prejudice and discrimination toward Portuguese people in general. The Portuguese community saw themselves being labeled negatively and, in response, created defense committees for the defendants and increasingly viewed the victim as the "cause" of the incident. Arguably, there was class bias in addition to gender bias given that the young Portuguese woman was a working-class woman. Historically, however, in a male-dominated society, rape has been hard to prove legally. The significance of the nature of the victim and the extent to which the crime is viewed as serious is emphasized in rape cases. Therefore, in the New Bedford rape case, issues of sexism, classism, and ethnicity became prominent. From the initial support of the victim in the media, there arose over time a portrayal of the victim as unworthy of receiving protection since she "brought it upon herself."

The Central Park jogger case contrasts sharply with the New Bedford case regarding the class and race of the victim and offender. The victim in the Central Park case was a young professional investment banker working in midtown Manhattan and out for a nightly jog. Unlike the victim in the New Bedford case, the Central Park victim was a white, upper-middle-class professional who did not have a "bad reputation" and was a successful contributing member to society. Pre-existing class and ethnic biases were working in the sense that the New Bedford woman was a "welfare mother," whereas the Central Park victim was a successful professional white woman.

Racial differences between victims and offenders are just as important as the class differences between them. The offenders were a group of black teenagers and were described in such terms as a "wolf pack" terrorizing the park. One of the greatest fears of white society, historically and today, is that nonwhites—particularly Blacks—will conquer, rape, and intermarry with white women. Historically, African Americans have been disproportionately executed for rapes compared to whites, and the most important predictor of a prisoner's receiving the death penalty is the race of the victim. In fact, some states such as Georgia had laws providing the death penalty for the rape of a white woman by a Black man, but not for the rape of a Black woman by a white man. Furthermore, it was not until 1977 in *Coker vs. Georgia* that the Supreme Court ruled that the death penalty for rape was cruel and unusual punishment. This ruling was partly due to the fact that Blacks were disproportionately executed for rape of white women. Of the hundreds of men executed in the United States for rape, there has never been a white man executed for the rape of a Black woman. Finally, the atrocities committed through lynching were often justified by alleged rapes of white women by Black men. Therefore, the media portrayal of the rape of a white professional woman of "good character" by a marauding "pack of wolves" who were Black fed on racist presumptions, imagery, and fears.

Finally, the Bensonhurst case involves a young Italian American woman who crossed community racial boundaries by dating both Black and Hispanic men. She thus had a "bad reputation" in the Italian American community, and when her Black boyfriend came to the community, he was murdered for crossing these boundaries and "violating" an Italian American woman. This points out the racism that can exist in minority communities and the fact that the line between ethnic groups can be both rigid and fluid. (The fact that racial and ethnic minorities can be racist themselves is well presented in Spike Lee's classic movie *Do the Right Thing*.) Residential, ethnic, and racial segregation are also highlighted in the Bensonhurst case. We are a highly segregated society in terms of class, race, and ethnicity, historically due to laws of an apartheid nature. An African American youth was perceived as violating the Italian American neighborhood simply by entering the neighborhood, and also as violating the informal norm of dating an Italian American woman. (Interracial boundaries and racial hatred, and the behavior of defending turf and boundaries, is well portrayed by Robert De Niro in the movie *A Bronx Tale*.)

Sexism, in addition to racism, is evident in this case. Blaming the victim was very much a part of the "bad reputation" of the Italian American woman because she dated Hispanics and Blacks. Further, the Italian neighborhood believed itself to be under siege by the media and responded by defending the murderers. The community expressed racism when marchers, half of whom were Black, marched through the streets of Bensonhurst to reclaim the streets of New York City. Racial boundaries and geography are still prevalent in the more recent phenomenon of racial profiling. That is, a person is under suspicion if he or she is a nonwhite in a white community or conversely, a white in a nonwhite community.

These three cases point out not that the media create classism, racism, and sexism, but that they selectively present aspects of cases that feed into existing biases and prejudices. Students of crime know the media distort the nature and extent of crime. For example, they disproportionately emphasize violent crime, although the largest proportion of crime is nonviolent. The media also emphasize stranger violence, although most violence is committed by persons who are acquaintances of the victims, and they present victims disproportionately as white females, although nonwhite females are much more likely to be victimized, as are minority males (Beckett & Sasson, 2000). These distortions occur because the media are a for-profit entertainment business, not objective reporters of the reality of crimes, offenders, and victims (Surette, 1998). Nonetheless, the way the media frame crime and criminal justice issues affects public perceptions, and ultimately public policy (Beckett & Sasson, 2000).

In Reading 2, Judge Arthur L. Burnett provides an insightful analysis of the types of de facto discrimination that occur in the administration of justice. He focuses on race, gender, and national origin discrimination throughout the system, from policing to sentencing. He first discusses police contact with citizens in terms of their use of discretion and the notion of reasonable and articulable suspicion. Under the law, a police officer must be able to articulate specifically the reason for stopping a citizen. In police circles this is called a "Terry stop," after the Supreme Court decision requiring probable cause for arresting or stopping and frisking a citizen. Burnett observes that several nonlegal factors such as a high-crime area, high-unemployment area, or public housing area, may be used as a basis of bias in interfering with rights of citizens. This results in de facto class discrimination, which disproportionately weighs on minority citizens.

Burnett also discusses drug courier profiles, which are used to justify stop, detention, seizure, or arrest decisions by police officers, and may camouflage racial, ethnic, and gender bias. This is particularly pertinent today, given the prevalence of profiling and the fact that the war on drugs is particularly directed at minorities. Police and criminal justice officials hold stereotypes of what "normal" crimes and "normal" criminals are like (Swigert & Farrell, 1977). These images of the crime, the suspect, and the victim are based not only on experience and training, but also on prejudice and bias. These stereotypes can lead to a self-fulfilling prophecy: If, because of stereotyping, all of the drug interventions and arrests are done in minority communities, then officers and statistics reflect disproportionate minority involvement. Consequently, the police continue to give more attention to those areas, there are more arrests, and so on. (An example of bias and stereotypes regarding crime and criminals is evident in the movie *The Usual Suspects,* starring Kevin Spacey.) Burnett notes that what the courts may view as consensual contact and consensual searches in reality may often be coerced. That is, although consent may be given, it is coerced consent because of the nature of the interaction and the situation. For example, if police enter a bus, stand in front of one of the passengers, and ask questions, it is hardly voluntary if the suspect answers the questions, since he or she is confronted by two officers in a confined space. Burnett also points out the class and race bias in focusing on interstate bus transportation, particularly in the war on drugs; only poorer, working-class drug traffickers would use public rather than private transportation.

The final policing issue that Burnett addresses is the frequent use in urban minority communities of observation posts and road blocks as crime and traffic control methods. These practices are legally questionable and are likely to engender more animosity and less cooperation from a law-abiding minority citizen. Burnett notes that the random stop of young black males who drive expensive vehicles is based on prejudice and bias. Unfortunately, as we will see, the Supreme Court of the United States in *Wren v. U.S.* has allowed "pretextual stops" based on traffic violations, which may be used as a basis of subsequent contact and search of the passengers and vehicles. The *Wren v. U.S.* decision has further inflamed the issue of racial profiling on U.S. highways.

Next, Burnett addresses prosecutorial bias. He cites particular legal cases in which prosecutors use race, ethnicity, or national origin in a defamatory way. As we will see in Part Five, prosecutorial discretion in the laying of charges, the nature of charges, plea negotiations, and related matters often weigh heavily against minorities. Burnett addresses the selection and composition of juries, and the fact that peremptory challenges may be a de facto way to eliminate women and ethnic or racial minorities from juries. Although defendants don't generally have an affirmative right to have members of their racial, ethnic, or gender group represented on the jury, they do have the right to a selection process that is free of prejudice and discrimination. Under early English common law and subsequent statutes, minority ethnic defendants had an affirmative right to have half of their juries consist of members of their own ethnic group. These laws arose when anti-Semitism was widespread and there was a great deal of animosity toward Jewish traders and mercantilists. To give them fair treatment, the British crown provided that when Jewish traders were tried for a crime, half of the jury should be Jewish. This law expressly recognized that certain minority groups were viewed negatively and experienced prejudice and discrimination. Although today there is no such affirmative right, certain jurisdictions, such as Minneapolis, Minnesota, require that the jury pool be proportionate to the ethnic and racial composition of the jurisdiction in which the alleged crime occurred.

The last area Judge Burnett addresses is sentencing. As subsequent readings elaborate, mandatory minimum sentencing, particularly related to drug offenses, raises issues of ethnic and racial discrimination. The fact that mandatory minimums for crack cocaine are much higher than those for powder cocaine represents class and racial or ethnic discrimination. Thus, people prosecuted and convicted for crack cocaine offenses are minority members, whereas most people prosecuted and convicted for powder cocaine offenses are white. There are also class differences in these two populations. Although we have eliminated all of the de jure or express racism and sexism in the law, there are still many areas where de facto discrimination occurs. The appearance of justice is as important as the reality of justice, and the appearance of de facto discrimination does not bode well for our justice system.

STUDY QUESTIONS

1. Through examples, distinguish between differences based on race, class, and gender and their impact on inequality.

2. Distinguish between prejudice and discrimination, and between de jure and de facto discrimination. Give examples of each.

3. Discuss how ethnicity, class, and gender affected the way the New Bedford rape case was portrayed in the media.

4. How does the Central Park jogger case show the significance of the class and race of the victim and offender?

5. How did racism and sexism influence the Bensonhurst murder?

6. How do stereotypes create de facto discrimination on the basis of race, gender, and national origin, from policing to sentencing?

REFERENCES

Bell, Jr., Derrick A. (2000). *Race, Racism and American Law*. New York: Aspen Law and Business.

Beckett, Katherine, and Theodore Sasson (2000). *The Politics of Injustice: Crime and Punishment in America*. Thousand Oaks, Cal.: Pine Forge Press.

Brunner, Borgna, Ed. (1999). *Time Almanac 2000*. Boston: Information Please.

Gossett, Thomas (1963). *Race: The History of an Idea*. Dallas: Southern Methodist University Press.

Kendall, Diana (1997). *Race, Class, and Gender in a Diverse Society*. Boston: Allyn and Bacon.

Levin, Jack, Kim MacInnis, Walter Carroll, and Richard Bourne (2000). *Social Problems: Causes, Consequences, Interventions*. Los Angeles: Roxbury Publishing Company.

MacKennan, Catherine (1987). *Terrorism Unmodified: Discourses on Life and Law*. Cambridge, Mass.: Harvard University Press.

Mischel, Lawrence, Jared Bernstein, and John Schmitt (2001). *The State of Working America: 2000/2001.* Ithaca, N.Y.: Cornell University Press.

Modie, Neil, and Lise Olsen (2001). "Disproportionate Number of Blacks in State's Lockups," *Seattle Post-Intelligencer,* July 12, p. B3.

Montagu, Ashley M. F. (1953). *Man's Most Dangerous Myth: The Fallacy of Race,* 3rd ed. New York: Columbia University Press.

Newman, David M. (2000). *Sociology: Exploring the Architecture of Everyday Life.* Thousand Oaks, Cal.: Pine Forge Press.

Pallone, Nathaniel J. (2000). *Race, Ethnicity, Sexual Orientation, Violent Crime: The Realities and the Myths.* New York: Hiawatha Press.

Reasons, Charles (1974). *The Criminologist: Crime and the Criminal.* Pacific Palisades, Cal.: Goodyear.

Reasons, Charles, and Jack Kuykendall (1972). *Race, Crime and Justice.* Pacific Palisades, Cal.: Goodyear.

Reasons, Charles, and William D. Perdue (1981). The Ideology of Social Problems. Palo Alto: Mayfield.

Reiman, Jeffrey (2001). *The Rich Get Richer and the Poor Get Prison,* 6th ed. Boston: Allyn and Bacon.

Ritzer, George (1993). *The McDonaldization of Society.* Thousand Oaks, Cal.: Pine Forge Press.

Surette, Ray (1998). *Media, Crime, and Criminal Justice: Images and Realities,* 2nd ed. Belmont, Cal.: West/Wadsworth.

Swigert, Victoria L., and Ronald A. Farrell (1977). "Normal Homicides and the Law," *American Sociological Review, 42:* 16–32.

Thompson, E. P. (1975). *The Making of the English Working Class.* London: Penguin.

Walker, Samuel (1998). *Sense and Nonsense About Crime and Drugs: A Policy Guide.* 4th ed. Belmont, Cal.: West/Wadsworth.

Wong, Paul (1999). *Race, Ethnicity, and Nationality in the United States.* Boulder: Westview Press.

Gender, Class, and Race in Three High-Profile Crimes

The Cases of New Bedford, Central Park, and Bensonhurst

LYNN CHANCER
Barnard College

INTRODUCTION

Feminist criminology, reflecting developments in feminist theory as a whole, has become increasingly concerned about the complex ways in which prejudices based on gender, class, race, and ethnic discrimination combine to affect and structure social experience. While radical feminists of the contemporary "second wave" first analyzed patriarchy as a social structure affecting *all* women, both feminists and feminist-oriented criminologists are in the process of further refining the paradigm of gender to encompass differences between women.[1] For example, it is obvious that not only gender but class position affects whether and how particular women will be treated within the criminal justice system, as well as within local communities in which they may live. Similarly, sociological factors such as race, ethnicity, and/or sexual preference often further compound the discriminatory effects of gender within American culture.

This [reading] attempts to illuminate these refined feminist concerns by focusing on a specifically criminological question: how is the role of gender in highly publicized instances of violent crime affected when considerations of class, race, and ethnicity are also taken into account? In each of three cases I have selected for purposes of analyzing this question, sexist attitudes were present in a given situation and then either hardened, nourished, or mitigated by the coming together of several factors. In each of the three selected cases, women's sexual freedom was limited either directly and violently, or much more indirectly and subtly. Other factors which were commonly present in each case included: (a) media saturation of a violent crime, meaning that each case was covered on a daily or near-daily basis both when initial incidents occurred and over the course of ensuing trials; (b) prior to the coverage, a pre-existing conflict and potential competition between sexual, ethnic or racial, and class forms of oppression in a given community or urban area; and (c) a felt exigency among community members to respond in some fashion or another to this now highly publicized "event," an event which refers both to an actual crime and a media construction.

First, the New Bedford case with which I begin involved a gang rape of a young woman in a bar that took place in New Bedford, Massachusetts, in March of 1983. The second case, which was just as clearly coercive, was the . . . "Central Park" rape case in which a young woman was attacked by a group of young men while jogging in Central Park on the evening of April 19, 1989. In the last example cited for comparative purposes, the racist killing of young Yusef Hawkins in Bensonhurst, Brooklyn, on August 23, 1989, a gang of white youths shot Hawkins to death because he was allegedly mistaken for a local woman's boyfriend. Although the third case involves homicide rather than rape, a sexual component was nonetheless entailed: the Bensonhurst case involved young men incensed that the local woman in question preferred to date an African-American or Hispanic man over a white in their predominantly Italian-American neighborhood.

As I will try to show, television and newspaper coverage picked up each event and saturated it, devoting front page or top story local TV news attention to the incident for weeks after the crime had actually occurred. In all three instances, social variables came to be pitted against one another. The New Bedford case involved a conflict between two sociological dimensions—sexual and ethnic forms of discrimination (class did not play a noticeable role, since most of the persons in the Portuguese community were either working or lower middle class). The Central Park case entailed the confluence of three biases: class, gender, and race were invoked through the circumstances and media coverage of the case. Lastly, the Bensonhurst case brought all the above variables into play, suggesting not only the presence of sexism and racism but class and ethnic antagonisms as well.

To facilitate this analysis, I used newspaper accounts from both a local and national source. In the New Bedford case, I looked at news coverage in the New Bedford *Standard Times* and *The New York Times* from March 6, 1983 [to] March 22, 1984—the year following the rape until verdicts were reached in the trial. With regard to the Central Park case, I perused all newspaper coverage in *The Daily News* and *The New York Times* from April 19, 1989 (when the incident occurred) until August 1990 (the end of the first Central Park trial). I used the same two newspapers for the Bensonhurst incident, scanning the period between August 23,1989 (the date of the incident) until the end of the first trial in December 1990. I have supplemented newspaper coverage by looking at magazine reportage, particularly weekly news magazines such as *Time* and *Newsweek,* for the three cases. In the Central Park and Bensonhurst cases, more local news coverage as presented

in *The Village Voice* and *Newsday* were also analyzed.

My interest in studying high-profile crimes such as those in New Bedford, Central Park, and Bensonhurst stems from a desire to incorporate contemporary developments in cultural and literary theory of media into criminology (an incorporation I believe to be a much-needed effort). As will become apparent, cases like New Bedford and Bensonhurst suggest that media coverage can become a part, virtually an inanimate "player" in the unfolding of community response to instances of crime. People in a town or city where a "notorious" crime occurred seem to be reacting not only to the crime and their feelings about *it,* but also to how they feel that crime is perceived by *others* given media saturation of the event. (Of course, a semiotically or postmodern-oriented observer might contend these two levels of response frequently cannot be differentiated experientially, even if it is possible to do so analytically.) Even more specifically, I am particularly interested in the implications of highly publicized crimes occurring in communities where, as is frequently the case, the social atmosphere is already divided by sexual, class, ethnic, and racial tensions. Media coverage may harden pre-existing sexist and racist sentiment, or other divisions, by shaping them in particular directions so that one form of prejudice is highlighted at the expense of another as reaction to a case unfolds over time.

NEW BEDFORD, MASSACHUSETTS: A CASE OF GENDER VERSUS ETHNICITY

That I start with the New Bedford case is not accidental. The conclusions of the earlier analysis (Chancer, 1987) may provide a framework of possible insights which can then be expanded to include similarities with, and divergences from, the Central Park and Bensonhurst cases. In the New Bedford, Massachusetts, incident, a young woman was raped on a pool table in a bar of cheering men. While the community's initial reaction was sympathetic toward the rape victim and condemning of the rapists, it changed over the course of the year following the rape into hostility toward the victim and sympathy for the rapists. This sympathy manifested itself in public demonstrations against the latters' conviction and petitions of protest to the local judge signed by as many as 16,000–18,000 people (Chancer, 1987). This shift was apparently inseparable from the fact that the case involved not only sexism and the blaming of a rape victim for her own victimization, but also a long history of discrimination against the Portuguese in the town of New Bedford and neighboring Fall River. The Portuguese were a majority in the town (approximately 60–65%) and were beginning to feel a greater degree of acceptance and economic and political respectability at around the time the rape occurred.

Following the rape, however, people in the Portuguese community began to feel incensed at media descriptions of the "Portuguese" rapists. In fact, media coverage was extremely intense and focused on the horrifying fact of a woman being raped in a bar full of people. Stories abounded in both local and national newspaper and television accounts, and the trial was the first criminal trial to be televised nationally on cable TV. As the publicity reached a saturation level, initially in the immediate aftermath of the rape and then later before and during the trial of the rapists, members of the Portuguese community became concerned that the case was reviving prejudice against the Portuguese population as a whole. Defense committees were formed, and slowly but surely community reaction shifted toward defense of the rapists and, concomitantly, toward condemning the rape *victim* who had allegedly "caused" the incident to occur in the first place. During a large protest march which followed the trial and the conviction of 4 out of 6 indicted men, the two defendants who were not convicted were given a "heroes' welcome" by the crowd.

That the young woman who was raped in New Bedford came to be blamed for her own victimization, however, cannot be viewed entirely as a by-product of anti-Portuguese discrimination. For one thing, neither the press nor the community paid any attention to the seemingly important fact that *the rape victim herself was of Portuguese descent*—why was there so much hostility toward her when she, too, could have been perceived as a member of the Portuguese community in New Bedford? (Her name, Cheryl Araujo, became a matter of public knowledge when she died in a Florida car accident several years after the rape. Publicity of the rape led her to leave New Bedford because of threats she and her family received.) Given this and other suggestive information, ethnic discrimination was a necessary but not sufficient explanation of the sexism which led to the victim herself being blamed (Chancer, 1987). Another factor was the traditional ideology within the community itself about the respective gender roles of women versus men, assumptions the young woman had violated by entering the bar at all when she could have been home with her children. The New Bedford case conforms perfectly to the findings of attribution theory that five criteria increase a rape victim's chances of being blamed for her own victimization: the victim tends to be blamed if (a) this victim had some prior acquaintance with her attackers; (b) a reason can be found to attribute a "bad reputation" or non-traditional behavior to the woman involved; (c) the rape takes place in a bar; (d) alcohol was present; and (e) the rape occurred in close proximity to the victim's residence. If it is true that these factors increase the likelihood that a rape victim will be blamed for her own victimization, then it would not have been surprising if some degree of victim blaming occurred even *without* media saturation and a pre-existing history of anti-Portuguese discrimination in the town of New Bedford.

Nonetheless, it is hard to believe that the tendency for victim blaming within a traditionally oriented community on purely sexist grounds would have manifested itself quite as explosively, nor taken on the highly political dimension it did, were it not for the particular conflict of sexual and ethnic forms of prejudice the case entailed. Thus, a second conclusion reached was that subordinate groups subjected to an invidious legacy of prior prejudice may wish to defensively deny wrongdoings committed by members of their group

(Chancer, 1987). Such defensiveness may be particularly facilitated when the crime in question happens to be a rape, so that the "blame the victim" ideology which has uniquely surrounded prosecution of rape cases in American and other patriarchal cultures comes into play. This reactive tendency, I would argue, is produced by a structural, "no win" situation in which such groups have found themselves embedded. If they acknowledge the actual heinousness of a given crime, they fear reinforcing negative stereotypes about the group as a whole; on the other hand, if they deny the seriousness of a violent act and rationalize the actions of a given perpetrator(s), they find themselves defending criminal acts (and possibly the object of scorn for this latter position as well).

The "media" focus . . . is extremely relevant here insofar as it is newspaper and television saturation of a particular crime which acts as an historically specific catalyst for the accretion of such defensiveness. Without media saturation of the "event," Portuguese residents of New Bedford would have been far less concerned, if concerned at all, about the ethnically discriminatory potential of the case. Provocative references to "Portuguese" rapists angered the community precisely because they were encountered in print and television media, and consequently publicized widely to the larger, dominant culture which was known to have been antagonistic to Portuguese assimilation.

THE CENTRAL PARK JOGGER: INTRODUCING CLASS AND RACE DIFFERENCES

This brief discussion sets the stage for raising several issues of comparison between the New Bedford case and the Central Park rape which took place in April 1989 when a group of youths assaulted a young woman who was out jogging in the park at approximately 10:00 P.M. Three critical differences are immediately apparent, helping to distinguish the latter case from the former. First of all, unlike New Bedford, where ethnicity could conceivably be "cancelled out" on both sides of the equation because both victim and perpetrators

were of Portuguese descent, the woman raped in Central Park was white whereas the seven teenagers arrested for assaulting her were black. Secondly, the Central Park case did *not* involve "victim blaming" to anywhere near the degree (if at all) evident in the New Bedford example. Not only was the young woman jogger not held responsible for her own victimization but she even became something of a folk "heroine" as New Yorkers cheered on and closely followed her—or, more precisely, media accounts of her—recovery.[2] This is quite a marked contrast to the "heroes' welcome" extended the *rapists* in New Bedford, and the threats and hatred to which the rape *victim* there was subjected. The third major divergence is that the black community in New York does *not* seem to have become defensive in such a way that the guilt of the defendants was denied or somehow exonerated. In fact, just the opposite appears to have occurred. According to *The New York Times,* 600 families in the Schomburg Plaza housing project where several of the defendants lived sent flowers to the victim in Metropolitan Hospital in the weeks following the rape. The same group of families invited city residents to a prayer vigil "hoping that the mass display of concern could help defuse any notions that the people of Harlem are not moved by the victim's suffering" (Marriott, 1989). How, if at all, can conclusions reached on the basis of the New Bedford incident help to explain why victim blaming and exoneration of the perpetrators unfolded in one case and not in the other?

Attribution theory may again contribute to an understanding of the lesser degree of victim blaming in the Central Park relative to the New Bedford case. The circumstances of the second rape barely conform to the five criteria previously cited—the woman was not previously acquainted with her attackers and did not live in the same neighborhood as they, nor were alcohol and a barroom setting entailed. While one might contend she was jogging in a park which bordered her own home and therefore could be considered her neighborhood, most New Yorkers would probably agree she had strayed into strange and lonely territory at that deserted hour. Finally, and perhaps most important in this case, the victim did *not* have a "bad reputation." Indeed, she was portrayed as an exemplary person by the standards of upper middle class society.

Consequently, returning to feminist theory and feminist criminology, an extremely important distinction between the New Bedford and Central Park cases involves the different class background of the respective victims. That the young woman in New Bedford was a single mother receiving assistance, while the young woman in Central Park was an upper middle class investment banker, certainly affected whether or not victim blaming began to occur.

Here, not just attribution theory but the way in which media coverage combined with pre-existing attitudes to *represent* a particular picture of the class background of the victim must have been seen as a crucial factor in the way the New York City community began to actually perceive the young woman in the Central Park case. For instance, both the *Daily News* and *The New York Times* immediately began to set up a semiotic connection in readers' minds between the "young woman" and her occupation. The *Daily News* rarely reported on the story without writing comma, "an investment banker" after referring to the "victim" or "the young woman." The *Times'* first coverage of the story on April 21 begins with similar language: " . . . The woman, a 30-year old investment banker" and then goes on to elaborate " . . . who had worked at Salomon Brothers for three years and lives on the Upper East Side, has been an avid runner and bicyclist . . ." (Wolff, 1989). And consider one of the lead stories in the *News* on the same day, in which the young woman is described as living the "way most of us dream. . . ." This American dream theme continues as we are treated to a number of details of the victim's life: that she grew up in Upper St. Clair, Pennsylvania, an affluent suburb of doctors, lawyers, and professionals 10 miles south of Pittsburgh and *far from the steel mills* (my emphasis); that she graduated Phi Beta Kappa from Wellesley, received a masters from Yale's School of Management, and was rated one of the top new hires

at Salomon Brothers, and that " . . . she was much more than a brain . . . in her yearbook photo she appears as a pretty blond in a turtleneck sweater with an engaging smile and eyes gleaming with promise . . ." (Krieger, 1989). Much detail is similarly devoted to information about her family background and the respectable professional occupations of her father and brothers. The comparison with the New Bedford case is telling and sad in that no such complimentary phrases were written about the young woman in the New Bedford case. Cheryl Araujo was described as a "welfare mother" if she was described at all. When a few days later the Sunday *Daily News* headline indignantly told readers that the arrested youths had said of the young woman, "SHE WASN'T NOTHING" (Clark & Landay, 1989) (so that one's sympathies were appropriately directed toward a rape victim and one's anger toward the rapists), they could have been describing the relative invisibility accorded the rape victim by media reporters and the community in the New Bedford case.

This is not to say that no news coverage whatsoever focused on the potentially victim-blaming issue of why the jogger was out alone in Central Park. In fact, a *Daily News* story entitled "Why Jog at Night?" (1989) hints at the "foolishness" of jogging at that hour. But it is to say that the tone is one of gentle concern rather than the harsh condemnation so apparent in the New Bedford instance. The problem here is not the woman but that "These kids have no self-discipline and do what they want without consequences. . . . If they see what they want, they take it" (Clark & Landay, 1989).[3] The young woman, moreover, is represented as part of a joggers' community, one which of course is differentially composed of middle and upper class adherents. Tim Moore, a friend, is quoted as saying " . . . only a jogger would understand . . ." (Clark & Landay, 1989) why it is that people with busy schedules would wish to run at that time if no other was available, and would find the activity compelling and invigorating.

Clearly, then, a major difference between the two cases revolves around class, in two senses: one, that the young woman in the Central Park case was of a higher economic and social status than the young woman in the New Bedford instance; and, secondly, that there was a *class distinction* between her superior status and the relatively lower standing of her attackers. (In the New Bedford case, on the other hand, both ethnicity *and* class could be cancelled out on both sides of the equation. That is, Cheryl Araujo did not have this advantage on her side to potentially ameliorate and mediate the effects of blatant sexism.) News coverage, of course, capitalized upon and promoted this class issue by making it into an American dream story: not only was the jogger's background a success story, but so also was the portrayal of her recovery process.

Nonetheless, to point to the role of class in influencing why the Central Park victim was blamed to a relatively lesser degree, if at all, than was the young woman in New Bedford, is not to deny other specific traits which distinguished the two cases. The fact that a *series* of attacks on people in Central Park took place that night may have also decreased the likelihood of victim blaming. Similarly, it may be the fact that the young woman in the Central Park case was beaten much more severely to the point of near-death, whereas injuries to the young woman in New Bedford were far less physically life-threatening and required less post-traumatic hospitalization. At the same time, I am arguing that the class factor cannot be ignored and that the specific configuration of gender, class, race, and ethnic factors which surround particular instances of violent crimes against women must all be taken into account. In this respect, I am not only in agreement with socialist feminist criminology but even with aspects of the argument made by Herman and Julia Schwendinger (1983).[4]

Nonetheless, yet another unfortunate ramification of this pre-existing class division, magnified by media coverage, between two women otherwise commonly victimized by a violent crime is that in *both cases* the conflict contributes to a demeaning of the rape itself. That victim blaming took place in the New Bedford case meant a loss of much needed community support and sympathy for Cheryl Araujo. That victim blaming did *not* occur

in the Central Park case is far less or not at all immediately problematic for the young woman involved, yet implies that her experience may come to be resented by some persons in the (New York) community who may suspect *they* would not be treated nearly as sympathetically because of their own class or racial background. In both instances, the violent crimes of gang rape come to arouse a second level of hostility aimed at women, albeit in these two cases for important and differing reasons.

This brings me to the second comparative issue raised when we began to analyze the Central Park incident. Why did the black community in New York City *not* respond as vehemently and defensively as did the Portuguese in New Bedford? Why was the culpability of the rapists *not* denied despite the potential for the same structural tendency described earlier to unfold? Several possibilities come to mind, each of which may provide a hint toward an answer. For one thing, as Joyce Williams and Karen Holmes reported in their 1981 study, victim blaming attitudes in rape cases vary directly with traditional or non-traditional attitudes toward sex roles extant in a given community. According to their account of women treated for rape in San Antonio, Texas, who were either "white Anglo," black, or Mexican-American, the first two groups were less likely than the latter to be blaming of rape victims (Williams & Holmes, 1981). To the extent the African-American community in New York City may (similarly) hold less rigidly stereotyped attitudes about sex roles than did the Portuguese community of New Bedford, this factor may form part of the explanation, as may the potentially very powerful influence of the black church in discouraging denial of crimes that cause enormous human suffering.

On the other hand, defensiveness may have existed at a latent level, never becoming manifest in the way evident in New Bedford because of the differing majority/minority, dominate/subordinate relationships in the two cases. As already mentioned, the Portuguese community of New Bedford was a majority population, whereas Black Americans in New York are a large, diverse, but nonetheless minority group in the City, subject to pervasive racism within a predominantly white dominant culture. This suggests that *even* if a similar defensiveness to that which existed in New Bedford was likewise provoked within segments of the Black American community of New York City, it is hard to imagine it taking the visible public form of huge pro-defendant demonstrations in which the arrested youth are hailed as "heroes" and petitions signed on their behalf. Such demonstrations would be perceived (and perceived as capable of being perceived) as further exacerbating racism in the City.

At the same time, and as will be apparent when we turn to the Bensonhurst case, demonstrations of public outrage are not just conceivable but *likely* in instances where black Americans have themselves been the victims rather than perpetrators of crime, and whites the assailants.[5] Yet, it is interesting that in an already alluded to *New York Times* article, Harlem residents expressed their fear

> that the crime and highly publicized arrests of black youths for assaulting a white woman would ignite smoldering racial divisions among black and white New Yorkers. A common concern was that the attack, while not termed racial by the public, would further fuel a misconception that blacks, particularly young males, are to be subjects of fear and scorn. (Marriott, 1989)

Consequently, a potential for defensiveness based on the same structural dilemma operating in the New Bedford case was present, even if not historically enacted for a variety of reasons.

But it was not just differing configurations of class, and the ramifications of this difference, which distinguished the New Bedford and Central Park cases. The fact of the defendants and victim being of different races was highly significant as well. For, indeed, based on newspaper reportage of the Central Park case, there was good reason for members of the local black community to feel defensive. Almost all of the *Daily News* coverage in the two weeks following the incident referred to the group of attackers as a "wolf pack," language rarely used to describe violent crime committed by groups of white teenagers. (For example, it is entirely absent from coverage of the white Bensonhurst defendants.) Again, language reinforces a

highly problematic semiotic connection between being black, committing violent crime in groups, and not existing in human form.[6] This racist allusion to animality, so reminiscent of both social Darwinism and the worst excesses of biologically oriented criminality of the Lombroso/Hooton variety, was initially avoided by *The New York Times* but later picked up in stories quoting others using the terminology (and then eventually dropping the quotes as the story approached its denouement). For instance, note the language of a *Daily News* editorial on the subject:

> There was a full moon Wednesday night. A suitable backdrop for the howling of wolves. A vicious pack ran rampant through Central Park . . . This was bestial brutality . . . The only way to deter these marauding bands is to use the full force of the law against them. The kid gloves have to come off . . . wolf packs have been roaming the subways in increasing numbers. Assaulting and robbing passengers. They've declared the subways their turf. Wednesday's wolves declared Central Park their turf. . . . (Editorial, 1989)

The editorial goes on to illustrate the earlier point about the rape victim remaining relatively impervious from blame. Each New Yorker, we are counselled, must make his or her own individual decision about personal safety, but *as a city* New Yorkers can never accept the principle that some areas are off limits. It is not the *victim's* fault, but the prime responsibility for safety must fall on government to provide

> more police patrols, better lighting, more activities that draw crowds . . . collectively, New Yorkers must claim the streets and the night for themselves. Retreating behind doors [emphasis added] is like telling the wolf pack: Go on, the city is yours. (Editorial, 1989)

Of course, it is interesting to inquire into whether a point of view quite as sympathetic to the victim, and quite as condemning of the city's political and policing establishment, was expressed by the *Daily News* when Yusef Hawkins was killed one evening simply because he was black. That no such analogous editorial appeared—and in fact my research indicates one did not—on the day marchers walked through Bensonhurst to reclaim the streets of the city for all New Yorkers, black and white, points to the substantial role of racism in *both* the victim's ability to remain relatively immune from sexist attribution of culpability *and* the inability of the community to defensively protest racism in this case *even if* such a desire had been present and provoked.

Thus, it is not just the *class* differences between the victim and perpetrator which distinguishes the Central Park from the New Bedford examples but in fact this *racial* element as well. Once again, I would argue that this juxtaposition of mediated circumstances not only feeds upon pre-existing racism in a community where whites remain in a dominant and majority position, but it also reinforces sexist attitudes in an insidious fashion. If one listens closely to the very language employed even in writing *this* account, a "story" which I think accurately portrays the way class and racial discrimination accrued to the benefit of the rape victim, one nonetheless can note an almost inescapable tendency to at once deflect attention from the very real suffering the woman in the Central Park case experienced *regardless of her class or race.* In this respect, a radical feminist treatment of rape such as that found in Susan Brownmiller's (1975) *Against Our Will: Men, Women and Rape* is useful insofar as it calls attention to rape as an act of sexual politics aimed at exercising social control over *all* women. As a violent act of forced sexual intercourse, rape reflects sexual oppression in a society still brimming with patriarchal fear and intimidation. While it may affect women differently depending upon the class and race of the victim, it nevertheless poses a threat to all women. At the same time, that the plight of the Central Park rape victim becomes "compared" with other victims' plights in rape cases must be seen as a structural dilemma bequeathed when sexism, racism, and class-based discriminations co-exist in an explosive and uneasy juxtaposition. The effect of media coverage is often to act as a catalyst amidst this sociological maze, forcing comparisons and competition between these factors to appear as though inevitable by its characteristic lack of analytical precision.

BENSONHURST: SIMILARITIES AND DIFFERENCES IN A HOMICIDE CASE

In turning to my third example, the murder of Yusef Hawkins on August 23, 1989, the sociological maze is raised to yet another level of complexity. New Bedford involved conflicts between gender and ethnic-based discrimination, and Central Park highlighted divisions based on gender, class, and race. Arguably, Bensonhurst suggests the presence of all of the forms of oppression referred to so far—gender, class, race, *and* ethnic. This is so despite the fact that, unlike the first two cases, homicide rather than rape was entailed, Yet, if one were to rely either on media accounts or interpretations of the event presented by public officials in the immediate aftermath of Hawkins' death, gender discrimination would appear to be virtually non-existent as a dimension of the case. Nonetheless, in addition to the case involving a race-motivated murder, the actions of the young men simultaneously amounted to coercive interference with a woman's right to sexual freedom (i.e., a woman's ability to date or sleep with whomever she chose).

In early *New York Times* coverage of the case, then-Mayor Edward Koch and then-Police Commissioner Benjamin Ward described the case as "merely" a case of a spurned lover and mistaken identity. In minimizing the degree of race and gender-based discrimination involved (while absurdly suggesting that somehow the situation would have been improved if the *right* person had been identified), this depiction failed to note the victim-blaming of Gina Feliciano which quickly began to occur among some members of the Italian-American community in Bensonhurst. According to the *Times* on August 31, many residents (including women) believed that "Miss Feliciano's friendships with Black and Hispanic men in the neighborhood increased in the racial tension that the police say erupted in the attack." The article goes on to report one person who lived in the community saying "She provoked everybody . . . it's a sin."[7] On September 1, the *Times* similarly noted that

The fault, in the eyes of much of the neighborhood, lies with Gina Feliciano, who violated the mores

of the Italian-American community by dating black and dark-skinned Hispanic men . . . [Again] "She provoked everybody," said Carmen Mercado. ("Bensonhurst . . . ," 1989) [my brackets]

When the case came to trial, the "cherchez la femme" theme rose even more noticeably to the surface as attorneys explicitly built Feliciano's alleged role into their defense of Joseph Fama, one of the young men on trial for homicide. At the same time, community antagonism toward this young woman continued to mount in a way which is again, sadly, reminiscent of New Bedford.

That another form of gender-based victim blaming occurred in the Bensonhurst example suggests the potential applicability of attribution theory even to cases where overt physical violence has not occurred, and a woman is only secondarily victimized by an actual crime. As did the situation of the young woman in New Bedford, Gina Feliciano's circumstances also conform with attribution theory findings that women are more likely to be blamed if a crime occurs close to their place of residence and if they are acquainted through neighborhood ties with a given group of assailants. In addition, the likelihood that victim blaming will increase if there is evidence of previous "bad reputation" or "non-traditional" behavior on the part of the woman is borne out here by the perception that dating black or Hispanic men violated community mores. On the other hand, the Bensonhurst case can likewise be distinguished from the Central Park case in that Gina Feliciano had no class status to mitigate against, or neutralize, perceptions of her own culpability in the public eye. Early newspaper accounts of the Bensonhurst homicide do not mention Feliciano's occupation or economic status. As in the New Bedford case, class exerts an influence by its very absence and presumed inferiority.

But what about the issue of community response to the murder of Yusef Hawkins, victimized by the ultimate act of violence? For the second time, events in Bensonhurst are so strongly reminiscent of those in New Bedford that one suspects a virtual genre of such high-profile crimes may exist. Perhaps a more general criminological

pattern involving a distinctive mix of media exposure and traditionally oriented subcultural attitudes toward gender, class, and race or ethnicity, takes recurring forms. For just as in the aftermath of the New Bedford gang rape, so *The New York Times* ran similarly formulaic features on the characteristics of Bensonhurst as an Italian-American community in the aftermath of Hawkins' killing. The resentment felt by members of the Portuguese community at the fact that their "Portuguese" identity was being broadcast by the media, and that "Portuguese" defendants were shown wearing headphones they needed for translation, is echoed in a 1989 *Times* story.

This is a closed, insular world, this enclave in Brooklyn where Italian is as likely to be spoken as English, a world of tightknit families and fear and hostility toward the outside. It is a world, too, where the young men who gravitate each night to a specific street corner or candy store to hang out with their friends grow up with a macho code.

But there were blunt expressions of racism, too, a feeling that their neighborhood was being maligned by the news media and, above all, talk of defending their world ("Bensonhurst . . . ," 1989).

The same article described Bensonhurst as a neighborhood of "one- or two-family houses that line the tree-lined streets" where little had changed since *The Honeymooners* was set there in the 1950s.

Similar accounts abounded in the *Daily News,* and the case made national and local television broadcasting on virtually a nightly basis. Preexisting racist sentiment, then, was aggravated and exacerbated by the defensiveness incumbent on such coverage. This defensiveness was based only partially on the community's sense that the social boundaries of its own neighborhood were being invaded (an observation which harks back to social ecology theory). In addition, one suspects that class sensitivities of the kind Sennett and Cobb (1972) astutely described were also stung as predominantly working-class residents of Bensonhurst (or New Bedford, for that matter) were reminded of their lack of upper-class, gentrified status in capitalist America.

Thus, when a group of 60–70 marchers (of whom about half were black) (Bohlen, 1989) marched through the streets of Bensonhurst less than a week after the killing to "reclaim the streets of New York," it is horrifying but not amazing that they were met with an enraged response. A la New Bedford, it was the protesters who became recast as the intruders, the troublemakers, the *victimizers,* while members of the Italian-American community (including, we shall see, the defendants themselves) saw themselves as *victimized*—those who were truly under siege. And so, in a counter-demonstration so redolent with overt racism that some journalists compared it to 1960s Mississippi, local white residents shouted "Niggers, go home," "You savages," and "Long Live Africa," holding up hate-filled signs and watermelons. Simultaneously, and confirming Katz's (1989) phenomenological thesis of how "self-righteous slaughter" comes to be rationalized,[8] the arrested young men were seen as "good boys . . . they were defending the neighborhood"; at the same counter-demonstration, the white crowd shouted "Let the boys from Bensonhurst go!" and "Central Park, Central Park! " Interestingly, the Central Park rape case—a case familiar to the Bensonhurst residents largely by virtue of their exposure to it as a media representation—thereby came to be placed in competition with the murder of Yusef Hawkins, used as yet another vehicle for transforming a sense of collective defensiveness and guilt into collective anger and blaming of the black demonstrators *qua* "other."

Obviously, then, it was not only Gina Feliciano who was blamed for instigating the incident but, by extension of the counter-demonstrators' angry logic, even Yusef Hawkins as well. Ultimately, one suspects many members of the community must have felt that it was *their* neighborhood which had been "invaded," *their* turf which had been exposed. Organized hostility was aimed much more openly, and publicly, at the black and white marchers who protested Hawkins' killing than it was at Ms. Feliciano; after all, it was the former group who dared to collectively protest, just as in New Bedford the young woman who was the object of so much hostility had dared to prosecute her attackers. In both

cases, painful media exposure was produced, and the vulnerability of the community to vestiges of ethnic and class discrimination was re-ignited. Thus, I would argue that the Bensonhurst case did indeed involve multi-layered dimensions based on the intersection not only of gender discrimination, but class, race, and ethnically based prejudices as well.

CONCLUSION

In the New Bedford and Bensonhurst cases, media saturation created a specific variety of community defensiveness that fed into pre-existing sexist and racist sentiment in traditionally oriented communities. In and of itself, this media saturation played a "role" in the unfolding of events to the extent it aroused anger at the community's helplessness and inferiority vis-à-vis its perceived class and ethnic position in the surrounding world. Television and news coverage are uncontrollable, rendering the community powerless. As in both New Bedford and Bensonhurst, they magnified ethnic sensitivities by subjecting these communities to microscopic inspection. However, since no concrete outlet for rage against media exists, it may become displaced toward victims who themselves come to be seen as instead the "real" perpetrators of a given violent crime. In New Bedford, it was the young woman who should not have been in a bar away from her children in the first place. In Bensonhurst, it was Gina Feliciano who ought not to have been bringing in men from outside her neighborhood and race, and demonstrators (symbolically, black persons) who ought not have been crossing the territorial boundaries of the neighborhood. Consequently, media saturation can inflame and give new collective shapes to already existing prejudices.

Secondly, whether a group enacts the potential for defensiveness created by media exposure of violent crime committed by one of its members also depends on particular configurations of dominant/subordinate relationships between a given local community and the larger society of which it is a part. Despite the discriminatory identification made between "wilding" and the activities of young black men, and the racist usage of "wolf pack" language to describe black rather than white teenage group violence, public sympathy for the defendants may be much more difficult in this instance than it was in New Bedford. The extremity of continuing racism in American culture, and the minority status of black Americans in New York City, would raise the fear of public defense reinforcing this form of oppression. At the same time, studies such as that done by Williams and Holmes (1981) suggest that victim blaming in rape cases may not be as severe within the Black community as it would be in Portuguese or Italian-American communities where more rigid gender divisions persist. On the other hand, the Portuguese community in New Bedford was a majority population, while the Italian-American community in Bensonhurst does not face nearly as severe a legacy of continuing discrimination and powerlessness as do blacks in the United States. Consequently, it would not be surprising if protesting racism may be deemed much more socially permissible in cases where blacks have been the *victims* rather than the *perpetrators* of highly publicized violent crimes. (In other words, it may be easier to protest the killings of Eleanor Bumpurs, Michael Stewart, or Michael Griffith than to call attention to racist treatment accorded teenagers out "wilding" or those young black men shot by Bernhard Goetz.)

Finally, with regard to highly publicized rape cases and questions of gender, the young woman raped in Central Park may have managed to escape much of the victim blaming foisted upon the young woman in New Bedford, and Gina Feliciano in Bensonhurst, because of her upper class background. This conclusion verifies and validates the concerns of socialist feminists, and so-

cialist-feminist criminologists (including Herman and Julia Schwendinger, 1983), about taking both class and gender factors into account when trying to understand the full complexity of women's life experiences.

At the same time, this analysis suggests that when highly publicized violent crimes involve the complex intersection of gender simultaneously with dimensions of class, race, and ethnic-based biases, an uneasy potential for competition between these variables is created. In the case of the Central Park incident, this meant that members of New York's black community might secretly resent the young woman for reinforcing stereotypes of young black men, or for the fact that her rape was publicized while stories of minority women's victimization go far less told (if told at all). Or, returning for a moment to the Bensonhurst case, accounts of Gina Feliciano's "victimization" can appear as though measured against the murder of Yusef Hawkins when indeed no comparison can or should have to be made, nor resentment need to be aroused. Yet, the "cherchez la femme" theme continues to be so deeply embedded in patriarchal societies that its presence is sometimes barely noticeable.

In sum, then, one major task of a socialist feminist criminology must be to account for the confluence of gender, class, race, and ethnicity-related factors in the unfolding of crime. But it must also, and at the same time, be scrupulous lest focusing on these other factors would obfuscate the specifically *sexist* nature of victim blaming still so common in American culture. Both dimensions need to be considered if we are to untangle and clarify these complicated layers—as though peeling back the layers of a sociological onion—evoked when the spotlight of high profile media coverage stirs deeply embedded community anxieties.

NOTES

1. With regard to the question of class within socialist feminist thought as a whole, see Eisenstein (1979) and much more recently, Hansen and Philipson (1990). Eisenstein's argument is applied in a particularly explicit fashion to criminology in Messerschmidt (1986).

2. I refer here to a public response, to hostile quotes people were *not* willing to provide reporters as they did in New Bedford, and to the fact that no demonstrations or marches antagonistic to the rape victim initially occurred. I think many people wondered why a young woman would go jogging by herself in as dangerous a place as Central Park at night, but this thought did not translate into *blaming* her or in any way diffusing the responsibility of the rapists.

3. Compare this statement with a quote published in the New Bedford *Standard Times* and attributed to a woman marcher: "I'm also a woman, but you don't see me getting raped. If you throw a dog a bone, he's gonna take it—if you walk around naked, men are just going to go for you" *(Standard Times,* 1984).

4. In *Rape and Inequality,* Herman and Julia Schwendinger (1983) criticize Susan Brownmiller's (1975) radical feminist work *Against Our Will: Men, Women and Rape* for ignoring the historical specificities introduced when rape is placed not only in the context of gender but class and race variables as well. Nonetheless, I think the Schwendingers' work tends to be reductionistic in its eagerness to ignore gender as an autonomous source of oppression. Thus, the Schwendingers have difficulty explaining the persistence of rape and domestic violence against women *across* class lines. This was also taken up in Messerschmidt's (1986) work.

5. This argument may be buttressed by recalling that the highly publicized Bernhard Goetz case did not provoke the expression of ire or become a cause celebre within the black community, despite expressions of racist sentiment which subtly or not-so-subtly surrounded that particular "event." On the contrary, the reported case of Tawana Brawley did lead to public expressions of anger, as did the killings of Michael Stewart and Eleanor Bumpurs.

6. In my research, I have yet to find cases of white teenagers who moved from place to place while committing a series of crimes being similarly described.

7. Virtually identical quotes were mentioned in the *Times'* coverage of the New Bedford case, similarly attributed to both female and a members of the Portuguese community in describing the "culpability" of the young woman who had been raped.

8. See Jack Katz's (1989) account of "self-righteous slaughter." Katz argues that the slaughterer frequently sees himself (or herself?) as defending the "good." I would add to this that *communities' perception* of a killing can be equally defensive.

REFERENCES

"Bensonhurst: A Tough Code in Defense of a Closed World" (1989) *The New York Times* September 1:A1.

Bohlen, C. (1989) "In Bensonhurst, Grief Mixed with Shame and Blunt Bias." *The New York Times* August 28:Al.

Brownmiller, S. (1975) *Against Our Will: Men, Women and Rape.* New York: Simon and Schuster.

Chancer, L. (1987) "New Bedford, Massachusetts, March 6, 1983-March 22, 1984: The 'Before and After' of a Group Rape." *Gender and Society* 1:239–260.

Clark, P. and R. Landay (1989) "Rape Suspects Laugh Over Attack." *Daily News* April 23:3.

Editorial (1989) "Juvenile Delinquency." *Daily News* April 22:11.

Elsenstein, Z. (1979) *Capitalist Patriarchy and the Case for Socialist Feminism.* New York: Monthly Review Press.

Hansen, K. V. and I. J. Philipson (1990) *Women, Class and the Socialist Imagination.* Philadelphia, PA: Temple U. Press.

Katz, J. (1989) *The Seductions of a Crime.* New York: Basic Books.

Krieger, M. (1989) "Lived a Dream Life." *Daily News* April 22:2.

Marriott, M. (1989) "Harlem Residents Fear Backlash from Park Rape." *The New York Times* April 24:B3.

Messerschmidt. J. (1986) *Capitalism, Patriarchy and Crime: Toward a Socialist Feminist Criminology.* Totowa, NJ: Rowman & Littlefield.

Schwendinger, H. and J. Schwendinger (1983) *Rape and Inequality.* Newbury Park, CA: Sage.

Sennett, R. and J. Cobb (1972) *The Hidden Injuries of Class.* New York: Knopf.

Williams, J. E. and K. A. Holmes (1981) *The Second Assault: Rape and Public Attitudes.* Westport, CT: Greenwood.

Wolff, C. (1989) "Youth Rape and Beat Central Park Jogger." *The New York Times* April 21:B1.

Permeation of Race, National Origin, and Gender Issues from Initial Law Enforcement Contact through Sentencing

The Need for Sensitivity, Equalitarianism, and Vigilance in the Criminal Justice System

ARTHUR L. BURNETT
Associate Judge
Superior Court of the District of Columbia

This article takes a close look at the actual operation of the entire criminal justice system with reference to issues of racism, national origin, and gender bias, from the initial police or law enforcement contact with the individual through the final process of sentencing the guilty offender.

What is the remedy when, in the exercise of police discretion, a police officer takes an African-American or Hispanic youth into custody and tells a white youth in an identical situation to "get lost" and to be careful not to get caught again? If a police officer seizes for forfeiture a motor vehicle driven by an African-American, Hispanic or Asian-American youth upon smelling the aroma of marijuana, with some ashes still in the ashtray, but tells the white youngster "to clean himself up" and "go home," is there a problem with the fairness of our criminal justice system? If a prosecution is thus brought against the minority youth and a factual record establishes such invidious discrimination, would a court be justified in dismissing the criminal prosecution or rejecting the forfeitures?

Is there evidence of racial or national origin discrimination when police officers set up "observation posts" in black neighborhoods or in Hispanic neighborhoods, but not in predominantly white neighborhoods? Similarly, consider this scenario: police officers observe through binoculars a hand-to-hand transaction or exchange on a comer between a black male and a black female, and conclude, based on asserted police experience, that they have just seen a narcotics transaction. But, what they saw may well have been a mere exchange of a dollar bill for four quarters to use in a nearby parking meter. Have the officers committed discrimination on the basis of race or national origin? Would the police officers have made the same assumption in a suburban shopping area regarding an exchange between two white individuals? To what extent should the character of the neighborhood influence the specific and articulable suspicion required by *Terry v. Ohio,*[1] with reference to meeting the standards for a stop and frisk, or probable cause required by the Fourth Amendment for an arrest?[2] To what extent are police experience and special expertise in observing narcotics transactions or other types of alleged criminal activity relevant factors in determining articulable suspicion or probable cause? Is this simply a pretext to justify police conduct and to sustain a prosecution at a motion to suppress hearing? To what extent should a judge or a magistrate, in issuing a search warrant based on a police affidavit, be influenced by generalizations about the neighborhood as a "high crime area," a "high unemployment area," or a "public housing area," and thus run the risk of applying a lower standard of probable cause than would be applied to an application for a search warrant for a single family residence in an affluent and predominantly white neighborhood?

Law enforcement officials may use other law enforcement procedures in a manner which reflects either conscious or unconscious racial and national origin bias. To what extent do economic conditions of a neighborhood offset claims of racism or national origin discrimination as an objective, realistic, and justifiable law enforcement consideration?[3] To what extent are "drug courier profiles" used to justify the police officers' stop, detention, seizure or arrest decisions on subtle factors, which may camouflage a bias based on racial and national origin factors, a bias which may have been their primary basis for acting?[4]

Finally, we must stop, pause, and give serious consideration to the reverse of these situations. To what extent do minority defendants attempt to raise bias and discrimination issues as a bar to justifiable criminal prosecution and conviction? Sensitive and responsible criminal prosecutors, defense lawyers, and judges must engage in critical analyses of the facts and evaluations of witness credibility when defendants endeavor to raise issues of racism, national origin discrimination, and gender bias, which may be totally unfounded and merely presented in a criminal prosecution as a means of trying to avoid criminal responsibility.

The purpose of this [reading] is to conduct a journey through the criminal justice system where issues of racism, national origin discrimination, gender bias, and prejudice frequently surface and occur. We need to recognize when such bias and prejudice occur and to sensitize all participants responsible for administering the criminal justice system so that we can effectively eradicate such factors and thus enhance the quality and fairness of our criminal justice system as we apply it to an increasingly diverse and multi-cultural society in the United States of America.

THE INITIAL POLICY CONTACT

Our constitutional jurisprudence recognizes that there can be consensual contacts between law en-

forcement officers and private citizens without any encroachment upon the Fourth Amendment rights of our citizens.[5] But are these "consensual contacts" really voluntary and consensual, or do they violate the civil liberties of suspected criminal offenders? The question is complicated by the fact that the process may never surface in court—where no arrest is made and thus no criminal prosecution is initiated, a court will not hear of it unless the citizen is courageous enough to bring a civil rights civil law suit for money damages.[6]

The case of *People v. Evans*[7] vividly illustrates how application of the legal concept of "consensual contact" can be abused. On December 7, 1989 at about 9:30 P.M., Sergeant Giardina and his partner approached Annette Evans, a nineteen-year-old African-American woman with no prior criminal record, as she was about to board a bus in New York City's Port Authority terminal. After a brief conversation, Sergeant Giardina told Evans he thought she was carrying drugs. A search of her hand luggage revealed several ounces of cocaine in a brown paper bag. After conducting a suppression hearing, the judge concluded: "[T]he picture that emerges is one of discriminatory law enforcement which does incalculable damage to our civil liberties but produces at best questionable results for the war on drugs."[8]

Reviewing the Evans case, Justice Carol Berkman in her findings of fact noted that the police interdiction program at the Port Authority began as a result of intelligence that large amounts of drugs were routed through the terminal. Officers monitoring the terminal were ordered to observe unusual behavior. Berkman noted that Sergeant Giardina was adamant that the program did not use drug courier "profiles" and that he denied any knowledge of the federal "drug profiles." She also noted that Giardina testified that if a person were behaving "unusually," two plainclothes officers would approach and engage that person in conversation. She quoted Sergeant Giardina who stated that, "during [a] conversation you further enhance your own suspicions on whether or not they may or may not be carrying . . . drugs."[9] Sergeant Giardina stated that the next step was to ask whether the person would mind having his or her bag searched. Justice Berkman observed that, contrary to the practice of the Amtrak police, the officers did not explicitly explain to the individual the right to refuse inspection. With reference to the phrase "behaving unusually," she observed: "The Sergeant appeared to be an experienced witness, but unable to articulate, when pressed, the factual bases for his conclusions. He became nervous, somewhat truculent, and inconsistent, when required to detail his asserted observations of unusual behavior or inconsistent responses from the defendant. For these reasons, he was not credible."[10]

Justice Berkman, in her conclusions of law, observed:

> The operations of the Port Authority drug interdiction program, as presented at this hearing, bear every hallmark of being the pedestrian/bus traveler equivalent of a roving roadblock, without any proof that the program operates "in a uniform nonarbitrary and nondiscriminatory manner" or that it is "carried out pursuant to a plan embodying explicit, neutral limitations on the conduct of individual officers."[11]

She continued: "Moreover, no records are required to be kept of stops, so that the Port Authority Police Department (and the courts) will never know with any certainty how many people are stopped, or by whom, or under what circumstances."[12] She then echoed the sentiment of many sensitive and thoughtful judges: "While the problem of the trade in illicit drugs is an extraordinarily serious one, no crime is so serious under our nation's constitutional system as to justify giving the police virtually unfettered discretion in executing searches."[13]

Justice Berkman's incisive observation is of great interest. She writes: "The issue would be easier if the same standard applied to pedestrians as to automobiles. But while stopping a moving vehicle is unquestionably a 'seizure,' stopping a moving pedestrian, even one who is clearly on his way somewhere, does not receive the same constitutional deference."[14] Thus, it appears that people in automobiles under the United States Supreme Court's interpretation of the Fourth Amendment have far greater protection than pedestrians walking on our sidewalks, in our bus and railroad stations, and through our airport concourses. We need merely to look at *United States v. Mendenhall*.[15] Justice Berkman in *Evans* cogently observed, "the question of whether police–citizen encounters such as the one in this case are seizures has confounded the Supreme Court,"[16] and thus she suggested a comparison of *Reid v. Georgia*[17] with *Florida v. Royer*[18] and *United States v. Mendenhall*.[19] She then concluded:

> Although the Justices were unable to reach anything but plurality "agreement" in Mendenhall and Royer, and although Reid appears inconsistent with those cases, it would appear that the PAPD has relied heavily on them for the legal blueprint for its drug interdiction program. This is unfortunate, for if anything can be distilled from these cases, it is that the courts have failed to provide the police with clear, understandable guidelines for their work.[20]

Finally, it is significant to note that the court in Evans observed:

> If police expertise can see criminality where civilians are blind, at least the police should be able to articulate and explain their suspicions and conclusions. . . . The incantation that behavior is "unusual" cannot suffice. . . . Too much deference to police "expertise" is an abdication of judicial responsibility, particularly where, as here, the police officer's own testimony shows that his expertise focuses to a disproportionate extent on Blacks and Hispanics.[21]

A critical reading of the numerous cases addressing the "drug courier profile" concept indicates that law enforcement officers can use it to mask racial and national origin bias and prejudice, and that officers can, and frequently do, engage in post hoc rationalizations to justify their stops and subsequent arrests of suspects and seizures of property.[22] Thus, this "profile" becomes a tool which can be used to cover up racism and national origin discrimination and gender bias. It is also a law enforcement technique which can be used to validate law enforcement action, when the facts standing alone, or in combination, might be viewed as innocent conduct, except for the race, national origin, or gender of the individual involved in the conduct.[23] Conscientious judges, faithful to the concept of equal treatment for all of our citizens, must allow sufficient cross-examination of officers in court proceedings concerning the facts upon which they relied to determine reasonable articulable suspicion and must scrutinize the explanations and the credibility of such officers to assure that race, national origin, and gender factors have not improperly influenced the initial police encounter.

A review of Supreme Court precedent and federal courts of appeals decisions suggests that federal courts may be demanding too much of the "mythical" reasonable person in situations in which two or three law enforcement officers confront a young and unsophisticated African-American or Hispanic person. Are we placing the standard of what the reasonable person would do far too high and are we convicting people who do not really feel free to ignore the police and go about their business, especially when that person is a national origin minority young adult in America today?

Some protectors of constitutional rights and civil liberties would urge that we need judges with a "reality orientation" who will act as the Pennsylvania Supreme Court recently did:

> *Applying the test to the facts of the instant case, we find under the totality of the circumstances, the police conduct would have communicated to a reasonable person that the person was not free to leave. It is not our intention to single out the fact that the Appellants were confronted by four police officers as dispositive of our inquiry, but the nature of the confrontation demonstrated a show of authority which constituted a restraint of the Appellants' liberty. We hold that a seizure occurred in this case.*[24]

This case is distinguishable from *United States v. Sokolow,*[25] which involved a defendant who flew from Hawaii to Florida with no luggage; who paid $2,100 for two airplane tickets from a roll of $20 bills that appeared to contain a total of $4,000; whose flight had a turnaround time of 48 hours; and who gave a name different from that in the telephone listing. The Pennsylvania Supreme Court, in distinguishing Sokolow, observed in Lewis:

> *The factual circumstances of the instant case do not rise to the level of reasonable suspicion. The cash payment of $166 for the purchase of four one-way tickets and the short length of the trip to New York fall short of the suspicious behavior in Sokolow. Even when considered together, the facts articulated by the police officers in this case were no more indicative of a drug courier than an innocent traveler. The use of cash, rather than a credit card, for the inexpensive tickets was not unusual. The length of the trip to New York was concededly commonplace, unlike air travel of 20 hours for a trip with a duration of only 48 hours. . . . The use of a drug courier profile encourages the police officer to direct his attention to any individual whose behavior falls within an overinclusive set of characteristics that include innocent actions. A drug courier profile should serve only as a starting point of, and not as a substitute for, independent observation of an individual's behavior.*[26]

This observation should be especially significant when the target of such law enforcement action is a minority individual and the use of the "drug courier profile" device or tool may well be a means of concealing racial, national origin, or gender discrimination in the enforcement of our criminal laws.

Finally, in the area of consensual citizen encounters, consider the case of Joe Morgan, an ex-professional baseball player with the Cincinnati Reds, who brought a Section 1983 civil rights suit against federal agent Bill Woessner, Los Angeles police officer Clay Searle, and the City of Los Angeles, for harm caused to him in connection with an incident at Los Angeles International Airport in March 1988.[27] The suit against the federal agent was dismissed, but in a trial against the city police officer and the city of Los Angeles, a jury awarded Mr. Morgan $90,000 in compensatory damages and another $450,000 in punitive damages. The federal district judge found that the city police officer had acted unlawfully in detaining Joe Morgan and concluded that the only thing that linked Morgan to another black man the police suspected of carrying illegal drugs was that "both men were black."[28] Noting that Joe Morgan had told the city police officer that he was not with anyone else and that he wanted to be left alone, the appellate court observed:

> [W]hen a citizen expresses his or her desire not to cooperate, continued questioning cannot be deemed consensual. In this case, according to Searle himself, Morgan never consented or otherwise conveyed a willingness to cooperate with Searle. Rather, Searle testified that after he approached Morgan, Morgan indicated in no uncertain terms that he did not want to be bothered. Despite Morgan's unwillingness, Searle insisted that Morgan answer his inquiries and demanded that Morgan come with him.[29]

Against this factual and analytical backdrop, the Ninth Circuit Court of Appeals made this insightful observation:

> We know of no case in which a court has found a police–citizen exchange to be consensual where the citizen unequivocally expressed his or her desire to be left alone, and we decline to set such a precedent today. In short, we find that Morgan's unequivocal expression of his desire to be left alone indicates that the exchange between Morgan and Searle was not consensual.[30]

Further, the court concluded that Officer Searle stopped Joe Morgan for two reasons: 1) the tip of an African-American informant that he was with another man who looked just like him, a description which essentially made all black men suspect; and 2) the alleged fact that Mr. Morgan looked at the officers, turned, and walked away. The court concluded that no other court has "come remotely close to finding reasonable suspicion on such a slim set of observations."[31]

In referring to a "reality approach" to such encounters, it is interesting to note that the Ninth Circuit observed that Officer Searle testified that he believed that Mr. Morgan was not free to go.[32] Although an officer's subjective belief is ordinarily not relevant to the question of whether a citizen believes that he or she is free to go, it becomes relevant if there is reason to believe that the officer's belief was conveyed to the detainee. The Ninth Circuit also noted that Officer Searle did not advise Morgan that he was not under arrest and that he was free to go. Although an officer's failure to advise a citizen of his freedom to walk away is not dispositive of the question of whether the citizen knew he was free to go, the court held that it is another significant indicator of what that citizen reasonably believed.[33] Finally, the court held that "[s]tatements which intimate that an investigation has focused on a specific individual easily could induce a reasonable person to believe that failure to cooperate would lead only to formal detention."[34]

The dissent by Judge Nathaniel R. Jones in *United States v. Williams,*[35] a Sixth Circuit case, also graphically illustrates how the use of the "drug courier profile" may be abused and used in a manner reflecting racial bias and prejudice. Judge Jones noted:

> The district court found that the drug courier profile employed by the officers in the instant case led them to focus their attention on travellers who were: (1) young African-American males; (2) arriving into Cleveland from Detroit; (3) using the Greyhound bus system; (4) arriving in the late evening or early morning hours; (5) carrying no luggage; and (6) not met by family members or acquaintances. Factors two, three, and four are in and of themselves hardly suspicious and, more important, gave the officers no logical grounds for suspecting Williams and his companion above any of the other passengers who deboarded the bus that evening. . . . Nor did the government offer even a scintilla of evidence, statistical or otherwise, to rebut the entirely plausible, common-sense suppositions that many of those making the relatively short journey from Detroit to Cleveland would not be carrying luggage or would not necessarily have family or friends waiting to greet them. In short, the drug courier profile as used in this case creates the overwhelming impression that the officers singled out Terrance Williams primarily if not solely because he was a young African-American male, and

thereby seriously draws into question whether the officers' conduct does not run afoul of the protections guaranteed by the Equal Protection Clause against discriminatory treatment on the basis of race. . . . That Williams was a young African-American male not only influenced the officers' decision to trail Williams and his companion, but was explicitly relied upon by the district court in its determination that probable cause supported Williams' apprehension and arrest. This court as well as others continue to operate under the misapprehension that race plays less of a role in this Nation's treatment of its citizens, in particular through its law enforcement agents, than reality compels. The singling out of African Americans simply on the basis of race engenders and legitimates a negative stereotype of blacks, and undoubtedly is subject to the strictest scrutiny. The use of an immutable characteristic such as race to support a probable cause determination is clearly unconstitutional. For this court to permit law enforcement officers to cloak blatantly racist attitudes in a generic drug courier profile is nothing short of outrageous.[36]

CONSENT SEARCHES

Recent judicial decisions upholding traditional consent searches create another set of questions as to whether the evolving case law reflects reality. It is obvious that the consent required in the context of consent searches is far different from the free and voluntary action necessary to find a confession voluntary.[37] A critical analysis of the precedents over the past decade raises the question of whether some courts have found "consent" when there was, in fact, no consent. This in turn raises the question of whether the consent upheld by some courts is really only a charade in our war on drugs.

In *United States v. Felder,*[38] the court noted that this case was one of a series of "bus stops" in which members of the D.C. Metropolitan Police Department's Narcotic Interdiction Unit board buses stopping in Washington, D.C., in order to intercept drug smugglers coming from other cities.[39] Judge Stanley Sporkin concluded that he did not believe that a reasonable person would feel free to

leave under the circumstances of a "bus stop" in which officers boarded a narrow, cramped bus en route to another destination in order to randomly question passengers. Based on the totality of the circumstances and the officer's show of authority, Judge Sporkin found that a reasonable person would conclude that he was not free to leave the officer's presence. Judge Sporkin held: "Because the defendant was improperly seized by Det. Hanson, his subsequent consent to the search of his bag did not overcome the taint of the prior police conduct." [40] He then stressed a realistic approach to the required factual basis for finding genuine consent, stating:

Only when the subsequent consent is "the product of an intervening act of free will" can it "purge the primary taint of the unlawful invasion." Because such an intervening event was not present in this case, the defendant's consent to the search of his bag did not dissipate the initial taint of his improper seizure by the police.[41]

But more importantly, Judge Sporkin concluded,

[T]he record demonstrates that the defendant's consent was not voluntary. "Voluntariness is a question of fact to be determined from the totality of circumstances." . . . At the time of the questioning, the defendant was confined in his seat with two officers preventing his exit. . . . The officers had just made an announcement over the loudspeaker which suggested that they had assumed control of the bus. The Court is convinced that a reasonable person, innocent of any crime, would not have felt capable of saying "No" under these circumstances.[42]

More judges ought to have the courage to give evidentiary records such a realistic interpretation.[43] As Judge Sporkin so eloquently stated:

Our desire to overcome the scourge of drugs cannot over-ride the constitutional guarantees that generations of Americans have fought so hard to protect. . . . This case presents issues that go well beyond an isolated instance between an alleged dealer and a police officer. At stake here are the rights of a large segment of our populace. While I realize that the drug epidemic is of tremendous proportions, it cannot be said that everyone who boards an interstate bus must be deemed a suspected drug courier. I know of no precedent where a program as intrusive as this one has been upheld. No case has been made that the only way we can stamp out the drug scourge is for our local police to in effect "seize" buses engaged in interstate transportation in order to indiscriminately search travellers and their possessions. The police must not be allowed to initiate programs of this kind without taking into account the severe impact their actions might have on the constitutional rights of our citizens.[44]

It is important to note that, because of economic necessity, the most frequent users of interstate bus transportation are minorities and those in the lower socioeconomic status. The constitutional rights of these individuals are no less important than the constitutional rights of the more affluent and white Americans who are financially able to travel by airplane or privately owned vehicles.[45]

OBSERVATION POSTS AND ROADBLOCKS

In many urban communities, police officers frequently utilize observation posts and roadblocks as crime and traffic control methods. One familiar with these practices may well question whether these law enforcement techniques are applied in a manner which intentionally directs them at minorities, and thus reflects racial or national origin bias or prejudice against minorities, or which results in an unintentional adverse impact on minorities.

Observation posts are concealed locations from which police officers observe street activity, frequently through the use of high-powered binoculars. After observing alleged narcotics transactions, the observation post officers radio arrest team officers on the street, giving them descriptions of those individuals allegedly involved. Questions frequently arise as to the credibility of the observing officer: did he really see what he claimed he saw? In minority communities the use of the observation posts raises troubling questions. In challenging evidence garnered from such a post, will a minority defendant be unable to chal-

lenge the authority and veracity of a police officer? Also, is it possible that at a suppression hearing, the existence of the observation post will not be disclosed? That is, even if a defendant were to testify, law enforcement officers might well conclude that the defendant would be disbelieved or unable to discredit a police officer's testimony because the observation post location would be considered privileged law enforcement information which a court would not order to be disclosed.

Recently, some courts have become more concerned about the assertion of the "observation post privilege." In *United States v. Foster,*[46] the District of Columbia Circuit Court of Appeals held that a law enforcement officer could not refuse, under the cloak of such privilege, to answer the defense counsel's questions concerning the location from which the officer had made his observations of the defendant during the course of a drug sale. The court held that disclosure should be compelled where, without knowing the location, the defense counsel could not effectively probe the officer's ability to identify the defendant and the accuracy of the identification. In such circumstances, the government's claim that disclosing the observation post will destroy the post's future usefulness for detecting criminal activity must give way to the defendant's right to cross-examination at the trial where the effectiveness of that cross-examination could create reasonable doubt and result in the defendant's acquittal of the crime charged.[47] The appeals court thus reversed Foster's conviction because the lower court deprived the defense counsel of an opportunity to determine the observation post's existence.

In *Anderson v. United States,*[48] the court stated that the government would not be permitted to prevent public disclosure of the precise location of a concealed observation post if the defendant could show that application of this privilege would jeopardize the fairness of the proceedings. The court further observed that a defendant seeking disclosure of the location of a concealed observation post would be required to show not only that there are locations in the area from which a view would be impaired or obstructed but that there would also be some reason to believe that the officer was making his observations from such a location.[49]

In a close case concerning an observation post officer's credibility, a motions judge could require that the officer submit an affidavit for an in camera examination by the judge, and if after examination of the affidavit, the judge is satisfied that the officer could see what he claimed to have seen and that there were no obstructions, the judge could then seal the document for appellate review and refuse to allow the defense counsel to learn the precise location. On the other hand, if the contents of the affidavit reasonably suggest that cross-examination on the precise location could lead to the granting, of a motion to suppress or could raise a reasonable doubt as to identification at trial, then the contents of the affidavit must be furnished to the defense, unless the government dismisses the prosecution.[50]

The use of roadblocks in minority neighborhoods as a purported traffic control device also may be a guise or device intended to disrupt drug trafficking activities and to arrest solely minority defendants. For example, in *Galberth v. United States*,[51] the court concluded that the focus was on the use of a traffic enforcement technique to disrupt an open air drug market and for general crime deterrence.[52] The court held that the police could not use the roadblock tool for the purpose of detecting crimes relating to violence, drugs, and guns.[53] It held that the police must have individualized suspicion before they can seize someone for general law enforcement purposes.[54] The court also explicitly held that the police could not use the roadblock program to disrupt open air drug market activity, nor was the government's general deterrence interest substantial enough to outweigh the liberty interests of individuals stopped by law enforcement officials at such a roadblock.[55]

It is obvious that the unfettered discretion of police to stop all vehicles at such roadblocks can easily be used as a device to interdict drug traffic and other criminal activity and thus can be a source of injecting racial and national origin discrimination and gender bias into the criminal justice system. The use of roadblocks, for example, to focus on vehicles occupied by young white persons in an all-black neighborhood, based on the hunch that they were there to make narcotics buys, should not withstand critical constitutional analysis.[56] If the police targeted all sports cars or other expensive vehicles driven by young black males for special attention, on the assumption that the driver could not be earning enough money from legitimate employment to be the owner of the vehicle and thus must be a drug pusher or the driver of a stolen vehicle, such police conduct could present substantial constitutional issues of pretext and racial discrimination. The random stopping of motor vehicles driven by young black males because the vehicle is a Chevy Blazer, Honda Accord, or Toyota Supra, of the type frequently stolen, on the pretext of giving a citation for a minor traffic infraction for which tickets are not normally issued, or because the young black men are suspected of being involved in drug trafficking, should not pass constitutional muster. Conscientious judges must be alert to such practices and permit full development of the evidentiary record in such cases, and then not hesitate to rule that the police conduct was unlawful where racial and national origin bias or prejudice, or perhaps gender bias or prejudice, infected and influenced the law enforcement activity. Judges who are faithful to the principles of equal justice under law and equal protection for all persons must not allow such practices to taint and corrupt the fair and just administration of our criminal justice system.

THE PROSECUTOR'S ROLE

Under the doctrine of separation of powers it is frequently suggested that the judiciary should exercise no control over the prosecutor's decisions regarding who to indict and what charges to bring. However, this power of the prosecutor is not absolute. The prosecutor's decision in determining which cases to prosecute cannot be based on a defendant's race, sex, religion, or the exercise of a statutory or constitutional right.[57] The prosecutor's decision not to grant pre-trial diversion is subject to judicial review upon equal protection principles as well.[58] In *Federov v. United States,* the appellate court, en banc, observed that the government's decision to deny an arrestee admission into a pre-trial diversion program was a decision to prosecute and treated it as a claim of selective prosecution. While observing that a defendant bears a heavy burden, the court stated that a defendant has the right to make a prima facie showing that (1) others similarly situated were not prosecuted, and (2) the prosecution was improperly motivated because it was based on an impermissible consideration such as race or on a desire to prevent the exercise of constitutional rights.[59] Furthermore, a court has the authority and power to inquire into charging and plea bargaining decisions to determine whether a prosecutor is abusing his or her power to favor or disfavor individuals on the basis of their gender.[60]

Problems concerning prosecutorial bias on racial and national origin grounds have also occurred in the actual trials of cases and in arguments made to juries. Unfortunately, such prosecutorial misconduct has frequently surfaced in the prosecution of foreign nationals, thus reflecting discrimination on the basis of national origin. In *United States v. Doe*,[61] the United States Court of Appeals for the District of Columbia Circuit, in an opinion by Senior Circuit Judge Spottswood W. Robinson, III, held that the prosecution's offering of expert testimony during the trial that the local retail drug market had been taken over by Jamaicans was irrelevant and unfairly prejudicial in a prosecution in which two of the four defendants were of Jamaican descent. In addition, the court found the prosecutor's summation referring to the Jamaicans was improper. These matters resulted in the reversal of the convictions and the case was remanded for a new trial.[62]

Starting from the premise that the United States Supreme Court has declared that "[d]iscrimination on the basis of race, odious in all aspects, is especially pernicious in the administration of justice,"[63] Judge Robinson, citing *Batson v. Kentucky*,[64] noted that because of the risk that the factor of race may enter the criminal justice process, we have engaged in "unceasing efforts" to eradicate racial prejudice from our criminal justice system.[65] It is significant to note that, as applied to the issues raised by the two Jamaican defendants, Judge Robinson cogently observed:

> *We refuse to quibble, as does the Government, over whether the remarks about Jamaicans during Rawls' testimony referred strictly to race, for it simply does not matter. In legal theory, distinctions based upon ancestry are as "odious" and "suspect" as those predicated on race; in practical terms, appeals to either threaten the fairness of a trial. And the fact that only two of the three appellants are of Jamaican descent does not lessen the prejudicial impact on the third.*[66]

In this context he referred to other leading judicial precedent relevant to the subject of ancestry, noting that in *Hirabayashi v. United States*,[67] the Supreme Court stated, "[d]istinctions between citizens solely because of their ancestry are by their very nature odious to a free people whose institutions are founded upon the doctrine of equality."[68] Although Judge Robinson acknowledged that in some instances in a closing argument an unembellished reference to evidence of race simply as a factor bolstering an eyewitness identification of a culprit, for example, poses no threat to the purity of a criminal trial, he emphasized that the line of demarcation is crossed when the closing argument "shifts its emphasis from evidence to emotion. When that is done, it matters not whether the reference is to race, ancestry or ethnic background."[69]

Thus, prosecutors have an affirmative duty to make sure that racial and national origin bias, as well as gender bias and prejudice, do not enter into their charging decisions. In the course of the trial of the case, prosecutors must ensure that they do not consciously or unconsciously inject racial, national origin, or gender biases and prejudices into the trial of a case on its merits. Prosecutors also have an affirmative duty not to allow race, national origin, or gender to influence their plea bargaining decisions. Presiding trial judges must be vigilant in overseeing the trials of criminal cases to prevent bias and prejudice based on race, national origin, or gender from creeping into and infecting prosecutorial decisions and the conduct of the trial of cases. When such improper prosecutorial conduct does occur, as the judicial precedent above clearly indicates, a court has an affirmative duty and obligation to take appropriate corrective action, which could include the ultimate sanction of dismissal of the criminal charges.[70]

THE SELECTION AND COMPOSITION OF THE JURY

Much of the recent emphasis on the issues of racial and national origin bias and prejudice in the criminal justice system in the past decade has been on the selection and composition of juries and the use of peremptory challenges. Commencing with *Batson v. Kentucky*[71] in 1986, the Supreme Court and our federal and state appellate courts have given increasing attention to this issue in our criminal justice system.

Currently pending before the United States Supreme Court is a review of the decision of the Court of Civil Appeals of Alabama in *J. E. B. v. Alabama ex rel. T. B.*[72] The Court of Civil Appeals of Alabama held that the use by the State of peremptory strikes to eliminate men from the jury in a paternity action did not violate the Batson principle, concluding that Batson did not extend to gender-based strikes. Under equal protection principles, it seems that simple logic would dictate that the exercise of peremptory strikes solely on the basis of gender would constitute invidious discrimination not permissible in our legal system,[73] especially since the Batson progeny now emphasizes not only the right of the litigant not to have a juror excluded on the basis of race or national origin, but also the right of the juror not to be excluded on this basis.[74]

A recent case by the District of Columbia Court of Appeals is especially noteworthy as to the trial judge's responsibility in implementing Batson in a criminal case. Emphasis is placed on the responsibility of the trial judge not to accept the generalizations and conclusory justifications of a prosecutor for the strikes exercised, but rather to closely scrutinize and examine the reasons set forth and to determine whether those asserted reasons were equally applicable to the favored jurors whom the prosecutor did not excuse. In *Tursio v. United States,*[75] a three-judge appellate panel dealt with a case in which a Latino defendant was charged with second degree murder while armed in killing a black man, and in which the prosecutor excused a disproportionate number of white potential jurors in the exercise of his peremptory challenges. The venire from which the defendant's jury was selected contained fifty potential jurors; thirteen were white, thirty-seven were black, and none were Latino. The prosecutor used ten of his peremptory strikes and "passed" on the eleventh. He used nine of the ten to eliminate all the whites from the regular jury. Only one white was left: as an alternate. The government's primary witness was a black man; the defendant's two principal witnesses were white women who would have testified that the defendant did not match the description of the assailant they had seen at the time of the stabbing.

In this context, Judge John M. Fergren, writing for the majority, observed that the defendant had made a prima facie case immediately following the jury selection and, therefore, the trial judge should have made a searching inquiry at that time, rather than after the trial and verdict in connection with a motion for a new trial.[76] He observed that, in this case, statistics, combined with the racially-charged nature of defendant's trial, made the prima facie showing that the prosecutor was exercising racially discriminatory peremptory strikes quite compelling.[77] First, the prosecutor "used nine of ten peremptory challenges against whites, creating an all-black jury."[78] Judge Ferren pointedly observed: "Statistics are not, of course, the whole answer but nothing is as emphatic as zero."[79] He further observed that these numbers were particularly significant because the prosecutor used ninety percent of his peremptory challenges to strike a group—whites—that constituted only twenty-six percent of the venire.[80] He concluded that the racially-charged nature of the case itself also strengthened defendant's prima facie showing. Not only were the defendant and the victim of different races, but also their altercation arose out of a fight between Latino and black men. Because the defense was misidentification, the government's case turned on whether the jury would find the black witness more credible than the white witnesses. In addition, counsel in this case were of different races. The prosecutor was black; the defense attorney was white. The trial judge acknowledged the potential for racial bias in this case; he stated that "the animus between blacks and Latinos in the District was 'the strongest sort of prejudice [he'd] seen in [his] years around here.' "[81]

In this context, Judge Ferren stated that the trial court erred in accepting on the record the prosecutor's explanations when those same explanations were applicable to black jurors whom he did not excuse. Emphasizing that rigorous scrutiny is essential because the exclusion of even one black or one white member of the venire for racial reasons violates that prospective juror's rights under the Equal Protection Clause, the court found the trial court's inquiry too superficial to be meaningful. The court thus concluded that the defendant's prima facie showing of discrimination was so compelling that the trial court should have probed the prosecutor in detail about his different treatment of similarly situated jurors. The appellate court concluded that, on the record in this case, even had the trial court done so, it was "unlikely that the prosecutor, in light of his proffered reasons, could have rehabilitated his case for the peremptory strikes through further elaboration."[82] The conviction was reversed and the case was remanded to the trial court.

This case also raises the issue of whether the defendant was entitled to have any Latinos or Hispanic individuals on his jury. In another recent case in the Superior Court of the District of Columbia, a Jamaican defendant, who had not yet applied for American citizenship, but who was a lawful resident alien, filed a motion demanding a jury pro mediatem linguae, one-half Jamaican and one-half citizens of the United States.[83] He contended that under D.C. Code section 49-301, an English statute in force in Maryland on February 27, 1803, which permitted such a jury, was incorporated into the law of the District of Columbia and that it had never been repealed or replaced. The government

filed an opposition to that motion claiming that current provisions in the District of Columbia Code providing for juries superseded that law and cited *Clark v. United States*[84] for the proposition that the 1901 D.C. Code superseded prior law governing the selection of petit and grand jurors.[85] Government counsel also emphasized that District of Columbia law now explicitly required all jurors to be citizens of the United States.[86] This issue remains unresolved as the case was subsequently dismissed by the prosecutor after a motion's hearing on the issue of the reliability of certain pretrial identification procedures.[87]

SENTENCING

The suggestion of guidelines for sentencing offenders has been viewed in the past as a way of eliminating unwarranted discrimination and disparity in sentencing and as a way to assure equality in sentencing. However, notwithstanding this laudable goal, the rigidity of mandatory sentencing statutes and guidelines, like the federal guidelines, have now come to be viewed as having a disparate discriminatory impact on minority criminal offenders.[88] Equal protection arguments have been vigorously advanced concerning the disparate sentencing schemes for those involved with possession or distribution of crack cocaine versus powder cocaine, citing the absence of scientific conclusive proof that crack cocaine is 100% more potent and dangerous to its users than powdered cocaine.[89]

It is significant to note that Senior District Judge Louis F. Oberdorfer of the United States District Court for the District of Columbia in a recent case held the Federal Sentencing Guidelines, as applied to two aiders and abettors in a crack distribution case, to be cruel and unusual punishment in violation of the Eighth Amendment to the United States Constitution.[90] Instead of sentencing the two defendants to the mandatory sentences applicable to offenses involving crack cocaine, he sentenced the two defendants, Karen M. Blakney and Charles F. Campbell, within the sentencing scheme they would have faced in a powder cocaine case.[91] Ms.

Blakney had faced a ten-year mandatory sentence for aiding in the distribution of crack cocaine and Mr. Campbell had faced a twenty-year mandatory sentence for his role in assisting in the distribution of crack cocaine.[92] The court noted that they had merely received paltry compensation for acting as "cookers," converting powder cocaine into crack for two major drug traffickers.[93] It is fully anticipated that Judge Oberdorfer's decision will be appealed to the United States Court of Appeals for the District of Columbia Circuit.

The District of Columbia City Council may very well act in the near future in response to the criticism of mandatory minimum sentences for drug offenses. A bill introduced on March 1, 1994 provides for more flexibility in sentencing drug offenders and eliminates mandatory minimum sentences to reduce prison overcrowding. The bill gives judges more discretion in sentencing offenders, with greater emphasis on prevention and treatment programs and options, rather than incarceration. It appears that there are several members of the District of Columbia City Council seriously promoting this prospective legislation.[94]

Subsequently, another similar bill has been introduced.[95] Many constitutional lawyers and criminal justice practitioners are also attempting to persuade the House of Representatives to adopt more flexible provisions on sentencing in the federal crime legislation now under consideration by the United States Congress. The hope is that the final legislation which will emerge from the current Congress will restore to federal judges greater discretion in sentencing and eliminate those mandatory sentencing features which adversely impact on minority defendants and on women in our criminal justice system.[96]

Far more could be stated about the operation of our sentencing laws in America and reforms that are needed in the immediate future if we are to avoid having more individuals incarcerated in prisons per 100,000 population than any other [n]ation in the world. If we do not make some significant changes in our criminal justice sentencing policies and begin to provide alternatives to incarceration,

as well as meaningful prevention, education and skills training, and treatment programs, our criminal justice system will be far more costly than our welfare system or our health care system. It will bankrupt the [n]ation. But far more important than the financial burdens which will be imposed is the the loss of human talent and ability and the positive contribution many of these individuals could make to the quality of life in America. If we were able to develop and place into operation a system of social and community services which would develop each individual to his or her maximum capacity as a contributing member of our society, one could imagine how positively our criminal justice system might be impacted.

With reference to mandatory sentencing statutes and mandatory sentencing guidelines, it is my frank and candid view, after thirty-five years in the criminal justice system, that we need to reduce the number and extent of mandatory sentencing statutes. The public should look for protection and security by selecting judges who will impose appropriate sentences with due regard to all factors involving the individual offender balanced against the need to provide protection and security to all persons in the community. With reference to sentencing guidelines, they are and will remain necessary to protect against discriminatory and unwarranted sentences to the extremes. However, they should be discretionary rather than mandatory and judges should have the power to mete out sentences based on individualized considerations applicable to the person being sentenced. Furthermore, the defendant should have the right to appeal or to have a review of that sentence if it is in any way based on discriminatory factors of race, national origin, or gender, or any other arbitrary and capricious factors. Such a sentencing system may well be the best system for which we can hope. If we have judges appointed or elected who will take their judicial responsibilities seriously, who will be fully equalitarian in their dispensing of justice, and who will be always vigilant in the performance of their judicial duties, sentencing can only improve.

CONCLUSION

This review is intended to show the many stages at which racial, national origin, and gender bias and prejudice may enter into the criminal justice system and taint and corrupt the proper application of the principles of equal justice under law. The increasing diversity of our population further increases not only the need for our courts to dispense justice fairly and equally, but also the need for courts and the entire criminal justice system to be perceived by all persons in the United States as impartial and without bias or discrimination based on any grounds. To that end, all participants responsible for administering the criminal justice system should aggressively implement action to accomplish this imperative goal of cultural, gender, and racial neutrality. Only then will our justice system be respected by citizens and able to fulfill its role of rendering true justice equally to all.

NOTES

1. 392 U.S. 1, 30 (1968).
2. The Fourth Amendment reads:

> The right of the people to be secure in their persons, houses, papers, and effects, against unreasonable searches and seizures, shall not be violated, and no Warrant shall issue, but upon probable cause, supported by Oath or affirmation, and particularly describing the place to be searched, and the persons or things to be seized.
>
> U.S. CONST. amend. IV. The Supreme Court has stated that "no right is held more sacred, or is more carefully guarded, by the common law, than the right of every individual to the possession and control of his own person, free from all restraint or interference of others, unless by clear and unquestionable authority of law." Union Pac. Ry. Co. v. Botsford, *141 U.S. 250, 251 (1891)*.

3. See Adrienne L. Meiring, Note, Walking the Constitutional Beat: Fourth Amendment Implications of Police Use of Saturation Patrols and Roadblocks, 54 OHIO ST. L.J. 497 (1993).
4. See Randall S. Susskind, Note, Race, Reasonable Articulable Suspicion, and Seizure, 31 AM. CRIM. L. REV. 327 (1994).
5. See, e.g., *Florida v. Bostick*, 501 U.S. 429 (1991) (holding that a police–citizen encounter from which a reasonable person would have felt free to walk away does not amount to a "seizure" implicating the Fourth Amendment). The problem with this test is that judges, in applying an objective reasonable person test, may be applying a test reflective of the reasonable white male law-abiding citizen, rather than a test truly reflective of the reasonable African-American, Hispanic, or Asian-American citizen. The perceptions of this mythical reasonable person may not be the same as the perceptions of a reasonable minority citizen. Thus, this very test may incorporate a racial and national origin bias against minority citizens in our society. See Susskind, supra note 4, at 327–49. Perhaps our societal goal of eliminating racial and national origin bias would be better served by a subjective test which applies the perspective of the individual who is stopped by a police officer. This sort of test is utilized in our consent search jurisprudence. See generally *Schneckloth v. Bustamonte,* 412 U.S. 218 (1973) (discussing consent searches).
6. Such suits can be brought under 42 U.S.C. [sections] 1983 (1993).
7. 556 N.Y.S.2d 794 (N.Y.Sup. Ct. 1990).
8. Id. at 795. Drug enforcement activities frequently target African-American and Hispanic women as couriers; thus, the stereotyping may reflect both racial or national origin bias and gender bias at the same time.
9. Id. at 796.
10. Id.
11. Id. at 798 (citations omitted). The constitutional standard governing roadblocks is set forth in *Delaware v. Prouse,* 440 U.S. 648 (1979) (holding that random, suspicionless stops of automobiles for the purpose of checking licenses violate Fourth Amendment).
12. Evans, 556 N.Y.S.2d at 798 (citation omitted).
13. Id.
14. Id.
15. 446 U.S. 544, 557 (1980).
16. Evans, 556 N.Y.S.2d at 798.
17. 448 U.S. 438 (1980).
18. 460 U.S. 491 (1983).
19. 446 U.S. 544 (1980).
20. Evans, 556 N.Y.S.2d at 798–99.

21. Id. at 799.

22. See Susskind, supra note 4, at 334–38 ("[B]y condoning an ambiguous standard which legitimizes tools such as the 'drug courier profile,' courts permit almost any conduct to be evidence of suspicion. Law enforcement officers can determine whom to stop based on arbitrary criteria and then justify the stops later with almost any rationale.").

23. See *United States v. Thomas*, 787 F. Supp. 663, 676 (E.D. Tex. 1992) (unequivocally stating that law enforcement conduct intentionally predicated in any measure upon racial considerations offends this country's values of individual treatment and equal justice).

24. *United States v. Lewis*, 636 A.2d 619, 623 (Pa. 1994).

25. 490 U.S. 1, 8–9 (1989).

26. Lewis, 636 A.2d at 624. The court went on to comment that "the facile reliance on drug courier profiles is reminiscent of the generalized suspicions historically used to justify the general warrants of the British." Id. at 625.

27. *Morgan v. Woessner*, 975 F.2d 629 (9th Cir. 1992).

28. Id. at 633.

29. Id. at 636–37.

30. Id. at 637.

31. Id. at 638.

32. Id. at 637.

33. Id.

34. 670 F.2d 583, 597 (5th Cir. 1982) (en banc).

35. 949 F.2d 220 (6th Cir. 1991).

36. Id. at 222–23 (citations omitted) (emphasis added).

37. See, e.g., *Jackson v. Denno*, 378 U.S. 368 (1964); cf. *Mincey v. Arizona*, 437 U.S. 385 (1978) (statements taken while defendant was in the hospital, depressed almost to the point of coma, in great pain, and encumbered by tubes and needles, were involuntary and thus inadmissible even for impeachment purposes).

38. 732 F. Supp. 204 (D.D.C. 1990).

39. See also United States v. Lewis, 728 F. Supp. 784 (D.D.C. 1990).

40. Felder, 732 F. Supp. at 208.

41. Id. (quoting Wong Sun v. United States, 371 U.S. 471 (1963)).

42. Id. at 208–09 (citations omitted).

43. Under Supreme Court doctrine, the government has the burden of showing that an individual's consent was given freely and voluntarily. See *Bumper v. North Carolina*, 391 U.S. 543, 548 (1968). However, the cases do not require that an individual be told that he has the right to refuse to consent to a search. *United States v. Hall*, 969 F.2d 1102, 1106–07 (D.C. Cir. 1992). The absence of such advice is only one factor to be considered in the totality of the circumstances. Cf. In re J.M., 619 A.2d 497 (D.C. 1992) (discussing whether the war on drugs has caused courts to strain to find consent when a realistic assessment of the facts would show that the individual's consent was not given freely and voluntarily).

44. Felder, 732 F. Supp at 209.

45. The District of Columbia Circuit recently held that a suppression hearing is a "critical stage of the prosecution" affecting "substantial rights of the accused." *United States v. Hodge*, No. 93-3012, slip op. at 4–5 (D.C. Cir. March 24, 1994) (citing *United States v. Green*, 670 F.2d 1148, 1154 (D.C. Cir. 1981)). An accused should thus have the right at such a hearing to effectively cross-examine the governments witnesses and to call his own witnesses. Further, the court noted, while the Rules of Evidence do not generally apply to suppression hearings, see FED. R. EVID. 104(a): "[A]ny limitations on the right of cross-examination beyond the typical evidentiary rules limiting its scope to the subject matter of direct examination and to matters affecting witness credibility must be justified by weighty considerations." Hodge, slip op. at 4–5. The court emphasized that whether a consent to search was in fact voluntary and not the product of duress or coercion is a question of fact to be determined from the totality of all the circumstances, and noted that a court must evaluate the "environment in which [the exchange of communication] took place" (citing *Schneckloth v. Bustamonte*, 412, U.S. at 247). Finally, the panel clearly indicated that trial judges should not take a "crabbed" approach to allowing defense counsel to cross-examine government witnesses. Hodge, slip op. at 4–5. This is important because a broad latitude for cross-examination should enable skillful counsel to bring out improper biases and prejudices based on race or national origin in connection with such encounters.

46. 986 F.2d 541 (D.C. Cir. 1993).

47. See *Roviaro v. United States*, 353 U.S. 53, 60–61 (1957) (in a criminal trial the informer's privilege must give way when information sought is relevant and helpful to defense).

48. 607 A.2d 490 (D.C. 1992).

49. Accord *Carter v. United States*, 614 A.2d 913, 915 (D.C. 1992).

50. Cf. *Sturgess v. United States*, 633 A.2d 56, 62 (D.C. 1993) (upholding the use of a procedure which required sworn answers to defense counsel's questions in writing, with the informant's name expunged, as to exactly what the informant knew with reference to the essential aspects of the case, and suggesting that in appropriate circumstances an in camera examination by the judge may be sufficient inquiry as to whether or not there should be disclosure).

51. 590 A.2d 990 (D.C. 1991).

52. Id. at 992.

53. Id. at 991.

54. Id. at 998.

55. Accord *Taylor v. United States,* 595 A.2d 1007, 1009 (D.C. 1991) (holding roadblock intended to deter drug activity to be unconstitutional).

56. See Sheri L. Johnson, Race and the Decision to Detain a Suspect, 93 YALE L.J. 214, 245 (1983) (aptly noting that "stopping blacks in white neighborhoods and whites in black neighborhoods when their conduct alone does not justify the detention will discourage people from socializing or living outside their own racial group, possibly conveying social stigma and fostering stereotypes").

57. See, e.g., *Wayte v. United States,* 470 U.S. 598, 608 (1985) (discussing this principle); *Oyler v. Boles,* 368 U.S. 448, 456 (1962) (same); *United States v. White,* 972 F.2d 16, 20 (2d Cir. 1992) (same); *United States v. Allen,* 954 F.2d 1160, 1166 (6th Cir. 1992) (same); *United States v. Aanerud,* 893 F.2d 956, 960 (5th Cir. 1990) (same).

58. *Federov v. United States,* 600 A.2d 370, 377 (D.C. 1991).

59. Id.

60. The court in Redondo-Lemos held that once a prima facie showing of gender-based discrimination is made, as it deemed it occurred in that case, the trial judge must pursue an evidentiary inquiry. *United States v. Redondo-Lemos,* 955 F.2d 1296, 1303 (9th Cir. 1992). The court also stated:

> *[T]he Supreme Court has concluded that courts do indeed have the authority to inquire into charging and plea bargaining decisions to determine whether the prosecutor is abusing her awesome power to favor or disfavor groups defined by their gender, race, religion or similar characteristics. Even under these circumstances, however, the district court's authority to remedy apparently unconstitutional conduct is limited. It is not enough for the court to be convinced that the prosecutor's enforcement decisions have a discriminatory effect; it must also find that the prosecutor was motivated by a discriminatory purpose in the very case before it.*
>
> *Id. at 1301 (footnotes omitted); see also* State v. McCollum, *464 N.W.2d 44, 52 (Wis. 1990) (criminal prose-*

cution on charge of prostitution of female performers at a private party, but not their male patrons, violated equal protection principles).

61. 903 F.2d 16 (D.C. Cir. 1990).

62. Id. at 29.

63. *Rose v. Mitchell,* 443 U.S. 545, 555 (1979).

64. 476 U.S. 79, 85 (1986).

65. Doe, 903 F.2d at 21.

66. Id. at 21–22.

67. 320 U.S. 81, 100 (1943).

68. Id. This case dealt with an American citizen of Japanese ancestry. See also *Hernandez v. Texas,* 347 U.S. 475, 477–80 (1954) (improper reference to person as being of Mexican descent); *Korematsu v. United States,* 323 U.S. 214, 216 (1944) ("[A]ll legal restrictions which curtail the civil rights of a single racial group are immediately suspect."); *United States v. Hernandez,* 865 F.2d 925, 928 (7th Cir. 1989) (improper reference to "Cuban drug dealers"); *Fontanello v. United States,* 19 F.2d 921, 921 (9th Cir. 1927) (unwarranted references to "Italian" bootleggers); *Coreas v. United States,* 565 A.2d 594, 605 (D.C. 1989) (comment deemed to be calculated to arouse national origin bias against immigrant from El Salvador).

69. Doe, 903 F.2d at 25.

70. The concern for such bias and prejudice, however, is not limited to the conduct of the prosecutor. Bias and prejudice may also manifest themselves in the conduct of a defense counsel who endeavors to persuade a minority defendant to plead guilty and suggests that if the defendant does not plead guilty, counsel will be purposely ineffective in how he defends the case at trial for the defendant. See, e.g., *Frazer v. United States,* No. 92-55193, 1994 U.S. app. LEXIS 4173, at 11 (9th Cir. March 10, 1994). Thus, judges must also be vigilant in observing the conduct of defense counsel, especially where they are court-appointed, to make sure that they are not failing to render effective assistance of counsel because of racial, national origin, or gender bias or prejudice.

71. 476 U.S. 79 (1986).

72. 606 So. 2d 156 (Ala. Civ. App. 1992).

73. See *United States v. De Gross,* 960 F.2d 1433 (9th Cir. 1992) (holding that equal protection prohibits striking venirepersons on basis of gender).

74. See *Georgia v. McCollum,* 112 S. Ct. 2348, 2353 (1992) (individual juror possesses " 'the right not to be excluded from [a jury] on account of race' ") (quoting *Powers v. Ohio,* 499 U.S. 409, 424 (1991)); *Edmonson v. Leesville Concrete Co.,* 500 U.S. 614, 624 (1991) (holding that "exclusion on account of race violates a prospective juror's equal protection rights"). [Editors' Note: Since the preparation of this article, the Supreme Court has ruled that Batson applies to gender-based peremptory strikes! *J. E. B. v. Alabama ex rel. T. B.,* 114 S. Ct. 1419 (1994)].

75. 634 A.2d 1205 (D.C. 1993).

76. Id. at 1210–11.

77. Id. at 1210.

78. Id.

79. Id. (quoting *United States v. Hinds County Sch. Bd.,* 417 F.2d 852, 858 (5th Cir. 1969)).

80. Tursio, 634 A.2d at 1210.

81. Id.

82. Id. at 1213.

83. *United States v. Junior Brown,* No. M 17172 (D.C. Super, Ct. 1992).

84. 19 App. D.C. 295 (1902).

85. The government also argued that under the Sixth Amendment, a defendant has the right only to be tried by a jury that includes a representative cross-section of the community. To make this point, it cited *Taylor v. Louisiana,* 419 U.S. 522, 531 (1975) (holding that fair cross-section requirement is violated by systematic exclusion of women from jury panels, where women comprised 53% of the population) and *Lockhart v. McCree,* 476 U.S. 162, 177 (1986) (holding that "death qualification" of jury does not violate the fair cross-section requirement). The government further argued that this right does not require anything more than the inclusion of all cognizable groups in the venire and that it does not require that the petit jury itself include members of specific cognizable groups. Lockhart, 476 U.S. at 174–75.

86. See D.C. CODE ANN. [sections] 11-1906(b)(1)(B) (1993) ("An individual shall be qualified to serve as a juror if that individual . . . is a citizen of the United States.").

87. Thus, the trial judge did not have to rule on the pending motion. Our research has failed to disclose any decision in the District of Columbia Court of Appeals specifically addressing this issue.

88. See Gerald W. Heaney, Revisiting Disparity: Debating Guidelines Sentencing, 29 AM. CRIM. L. REV. 771, 781–82 (1992) (pointing out that in 1989, a higher percentage of blacks and Hispanics were sentenced to prison under the guidelines than those in pre-guidelines cases, whereas among whites the percentage decreased, and asserting that since an inner city minority is more

likely to have a higher criminal history category than suburban whites, mandatory sentences for the former group were necessarily higher).

89. See *United States v. Clary,* No. 89-167-Cr (4), 1994 U.S. Dist. LEXIS 2447, at 92 (E.D. Mo. February 23, 1994) (finding "no material difference between the chemical properties of crack and powder cocaine," and holding that the mandatory punishment under 21 U.S.C. [sections] 841 of 100 times greater for crack than powder cocaine, violates equal protection); *State v. Russell,* 477 N.W.2d 886, 891 (Minn. 1991) (Minnesota statute punishing possession of three grams of crack by up to 20 years in prison, while punishing possession of same amount of powder cocaine by up to five years, violates equal protection under the Minnesota state constitution). See generally, Samuel L. Myers, Jr., Racial Disparities in Sentencing: Can Sentencing Reforms Reduce Discrimination in Punishment?, 64 U. COLO. L. REV. 781 (1993).

90. *United States v. Walls,* 841 F. Supp. 24 (D.D.C. 1994).

91. Id. at 33.

92. Id. at 32.

93. Id.

94. See District of Columbia Mandatory–Minimum Sentences Amendment Act of 1994, Bill 10-595, introduced in the Legislative Meeting on March 1, 1994, by Councilmembers William P. Lightfoot and Harry L. Thomas, Sr. It is significant to note that this bill is being co-sponsored by six additional members of the City Council—Councilmembers Barry, Chavous, Mason, Nathanson, Cropp, and Chairman Clarke. Thus, eight out of the 13 members of the Council are sponsoring this proposed legislation.

95. District of Columbia Nonviolent Offenses Mandatory–Minimum Sentences Amendment Act of 1994, Bill No. 10-617. The purpose of this bill is to amend the Medical and Geriatric Parole Act of 1992, the District of Columbia Good Time Credits Act of 1986, the Prison Overcrowding Emergency Powers Act of 1987, and the District of Columbia Uniform Controlled Substances Act of 1981 to repeal mandatory minimum sentences as penalties imposed for nonviolent narcotic and abusive drug offenses and to eliminate disparities in penalties for crimes which involve forms of the single drug cocaine.

96. See Myrna S. Raeder, Gender and Sentencing: Single Moms, Battered Women, and Other Sex-Based Anomalies in the Gender-Free World of the Federal Sentencing Guidelines, 20 PEPP. L. REV. 905 (1993).

PART TWO

Crime Rates and Explanations

Today, the discipline of criminology[1] concerns itself with three major areas of study: (1) the origins and change of criminal law, (2) the causes (etiology) of criminal behavior, and (3) the administration of justice, including the community, police, courts and corrections. Although all of these areas receive a great deal of study today, until recently, criminology was concerned only with the causes of criminal behavior: Why did he or she do it? This question has been repeatedly asked by millions of people in their attempts to explain criminal behavior.

The usual range of explanations of criminal behavior includes the following:

1. The person chose to commit a crime through free will.
2. The person was born that way.
3. The person is mentally ill.
4. The person is from a "bad" family.
5. The person was influenced by a "bad" group of friends.
6. The person was forced to commit crime because of poverty or ethnic status.
7. The law itself or the criminal justice system is biased toward the person and his or her behavior due to his or her racial or ethnic status, class, or gender.

Many other explanations can be presented, but these generally cover the range of reasons noted by most of the public and many students of crime.

We might better visualize explanations of crime as emphasizing the following:

1. Personal characteristics of the criminal
2. Characteristics of the situation
3. Criminal's family life
4. Offender's social position as determined by ethnicity or race, employment, education, and so on
5. Offender's political position in terms of the definition of crime and the administration of justice
6. Offender's economic standing

The circles of explanations in Figure 2.1 provide a visual representation of these theories. These various emphases can also be identified as kinds-of-people, kinds-of-environment, and power/conflict explanations of criminal behaviors (Reasons 1975). Kinds-of-people explanations emphasize the biological or psychological characteristics of the criminal in explaining crime. Kinds-of-environment explanations stress the characteristics of the offender's family and community as major causes. Kinds-of-people and kinds-of-environment explanations focus on personal or social characteristics of criminals, whereas power/conflict explanations emphasize differences in power and economic control. Such

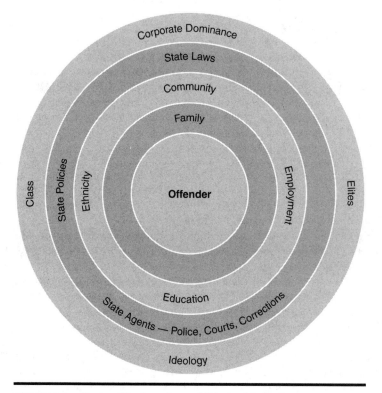

FIGURE 2.1   Circle of Explanations of Criminal Behavior

differences influence which behaviors will be defined as criminal through law making, and which people will be defined as criminal through criminal justice agents, including the police, the courts, and corrections institutions.

EXPLAINING CRIMINAL BEHAVIOR: A HISTORY

Knowledge is a social product, bound to a historical context and reflecting the events of an era. The explanations for criminal behavior, a specific form of knowledge, also emerge in a historical setting and are advanced by scholars and influentials who are responsive to the prevailing ideologies (Radzinowicz, 1966).

Demonology under Feudalism

Before the Age of Enlightenment and Reason in the seventeenth and eighteenth centuries, deviant behavior was largely explained through demonology; those who committed crimes were thought to be possessed by demons and driven by the devil. Various rituals and procedures were derived to determine guilt or innocence, all based on the assumption that other worldly powers were operating: Compensation for crime and for sin; trial by battle; trial by ordeal; testimony under oath; miraculous "signs" or omens indicating guilt or innocence all bespoke belief in a supernatural order (Vold, Bernard, & Snipes, 1997). For example, in a trial by battle, the innocent person would win through divine favor. Trial by ordeal, also based on demonological beliefs, has been described in the following terms:

> *It was popular among prosecutors because it eliminated the unpleasant chances of battle. The accused person, being bound hand and foot, was thrown into a pond. If he "swam," as it was expressed, he was taken out and dealt with as guilty. If he sank and drowned, his innocence was manifest and he was buried with all decency and respect. . . . A not unreasonable dissatisfaction was felt among the criminal classes, which at that time constituted the bulk of the population. (Block & Geis 1970, p. 424)*

The interpretation of trial by ordeal requires an understanding of the feudal society in which such a test was carried out. Under feudalism the dogma of the Church was the basis for criminal law. Thus, to swim or float indicated that one was rejected by the waters, which symbolized baptism. Baptismal "acceptance," as is evident, exacted a heavy price.

Classical School

With the decline of the feudal order and the emergence of trade capitalism during the Middle Ages, secular explanations for criminal behavior came to replace religious ones. More emphasis was placed on humans as calculating, free-willing actors who are masters of their fate. Rather than being driven by otherworldly forces, human behavior was seen as a product of choice. The historical stage was thus set for the emergence of the classical school of criminology in the eighteenth century. Such writers as Blackstone, Bentham, and Becarria helped to establish the basic beliefs of the classical tradition—that people are reasoning, rational beings who possess a will that regulates and controls behavior. Further, the will was free, in that there were no limitations to the choices an individual could make. Finally, for the classicists the fear of pain was the principle instrument used to control the will and was provided by punishment through the criminal code (Vold et al., 1997).

As a calculating, rational, free-willed actor, a human being selects that behavior that minimizes pain and maximizes pleasure. Given these primary ideas, the classical school held that punishments should be rationally fixed to outweigh the pleasure derived from the criminal act. If that is accomplished, then the human actor will not commit a crime. These classical-school ideas developed in response to the arbitrary, cruel, and oppressive nature of the existing criminal justice system. The school's adherents argued that such principles should be the basis of the penal code, and justice should be meted out equally, without favor or variation.

Although the notion of equal justice for all is an appealing doctrine, the practical application of this doctrine ran into disfavor in the French Code of 1791 due to substantial problems: The laws ignored individual differences and the significance of situational factors, treated first and repeat offenders alike, and viewed as purely rational decision makers the intellectually and emotionally disabled, minors, and others of diminished capability.

Neoclassical School

Such deficiencies in the law gave rise during the first half of the nineteenth century to the neoclassical school of criminology. These reformers modified the Doctrine of Pure Reason by noting exceptions such as incompetence and insanity and such mitigating factors as age, imbecility, or social situation. Although the neoclassical approach altered the concept of free will by noting individual and situational differences, this view was still based on the assumption that most behavior is rational, autonomous, and calculating. The assumption of rationality underlies much of our legal system today; the model of criminals receiving their just deserts reflects this reasoning. Nonetheless, this tradition recognized circumstances and conditions that reduced one's legal responsibility for one's actions. Such legal distinctions as necessity, self-defense, insanity, and juvenile delinquency became part of the definition of legal responsibility and the explanation of criminal behavior. Thus, for example, a child of seven or under could not have a criminal mind or intent (*mens rea*) because his or her reason was immature.

Increasingly, the notions of free will and rationality as the bases of human behavior were replaced by biological, psychological, and social factors as motivators of behavior. The scientific revolution in the seventeenth century profoundly changed attitudes toward custom and tradition. As Von Baumer states, "The Age of Science made the intoxicating discovery that melioration depends not upon change from within (St. Paul's birth of the new man), but upon change from without (scientific and social mechanics) (Von Baumer, 1964, pp. 249–250)." The classical school's emphasis on free will and the rational man was increasingly eroded in the nineteenth century. With further understanding of the role played by motives and other internal factors in human action, finer distinctions could be made regarding criminal responsibility. In fact, Mannheim (1960) views the history of criminal law as a history to exculpate offenders because of their general incapacity—for example, in children and the insane—to act with a guilty mind. During the enlightenment, the aim of reformers was to set the individual free by restricting law to maintain public order, not to control morality.

The Rise of Positivism

The upheaval in economic, social, political, and cultural life accompanying the Industrial Revolution gave impetus to a humanitarian movement, which aided in the rise of the social sciences. The French Revolution and Industrial Revolution had created rival classes and nations. The principles of individualism, science, and progress were espoused by the philosopher John Stuart Mill as a means of reforming European society. Agnosticism, science, and social service became the new "holy trinity," and the positivistic philosophy of Comte was used to create a better social order. Social reform and sociology became interrelated; the methods of inquiry of the natural scientists were applied to man and society. These changes signified the growing secularization of Western thought and culture: Human nature was believed to be rational and social, and humans were viewed as pursuing their own self-interest. Nature was a closed system with universal rules and, thus man could predict and understand nature. Faith in reason, science, and the future largely replaced faith in revealed religion.

The rise of positivism greatly influenced the structure of criminological thought. Positivism (1) denies free will, (2) divorces science and law from morality, (3) proclaims the priority of science and believes in the existence of invariable social laws, (4) emphasizes the unity of the scientific method for social and natural sciences, (5) emphasizes the criminal, (6) emphasizes quantitative not qualitative, research, and (7) holds causality and determinism as paramount concerns to be pursued through observation (Mannheim, 1960). The belief in the ability to use techniques of social control, such as the law, to create a better society produced much legislation for the purpose of guiding human morals. Thus, scientism and positivism as a panacea for human ills led to increasing overcriminalization of behavior and the belief that deviant behavior could be perfected through the use of the social sciences and the law. Begun in the work of criminologists Quetelet and Guerry, positivism emerged as the legitimate criminological perspective with Lombroso and the Italian school. Positivism established new trends in the study of crime, including (1) a focus on the individual criminal, (2) the motivation to do scientific studies of crime, (3) studies showing the priority of social influences in crime causation, (4) the establishment of international bodies and congresses, and (5) influence on the penal codes (Radzinowicz, 1966).

Early criminological positivism was immersed in the inherent pathologies of the criminal, using a medical model to emphasize diagnosis, prognosis, and treatment. Therefore, the goal was to change the nature of the criminal, and the search for the causes of criminal behavior became the "cause celebre" of criminological inquiry.[2]

THE BORN CRIMINAL

Students of crime, like many other citizens, have focused much of their time and effort on studying the criminal to find the causes of crime. This has led to many different explanations of criminal behavior, all looking for its causes within the people who are identified as criminals. In the early part of the twentieth century, such kinds-of-people theories held that some people were born criminals, and that the born criminal was the cause of crime. Specifically, crime was attributed to people of foreign races and other nationalities. The belief in the existence of innate differences between a criminal's behavior and that of a non-criminal reflected the era of social Darwinism, imperialism, and racist ideology. In the United States, the president of the California State Law Enforcement League epitomized the public concern in a 1925 article stating,

> *It is the law-breaking foreigners who we are talking about now. Schooled in low standards of morality, they seek to impose their European customs upon their newfound Land of Liberty. . . . Foreigners are predominant in all the big movements of lawlessness and these movements aim at anarchy. (Grant 1925)*

Grant was talking about Italian, Chinese, Polish and other "races" that were accused of creating crime waves. Such assumptions of born criminality and racial or ethnic inferiority led to the eugenics movement in the United States, in which many poor, nonwhites, and mentally disabled people were sterilized (Sheldon, 2001).

Although the scientific evidence against the born criminal theory is enormous, it remains popular in our ideology. Contemporary examples of the born criminal theory are found in the pseudoscience of psychology professor Rushton (1995), who argues that Blacks are innately inferior to whites in terms of IQ, and therefore, they have higher crime rates, particularly for violent crimes. Although it has been repeatedly criticized and scientifically discounted (see Pallone and Hennessy, 2000), this racist notion persists. The most recent, sophisticated, and well-publicized pseudoscientific argument of racial IQ inferiority was presented by psychologist Richard Herrnestein and political scientist Charles Murray in their book *The Bell Curve: Intelligence and Class Structure In America Life* (1994). The authors selectively use scientific research to present an argument that Blacks are innately inferior to whites. In analyzing education, employment, family, parenting, and IQ and other cognitive abilities, the authors use a pseudoscientific argument to attack affirmative action, economic and welfare programs, and employment opportunities for the disadvantaged, particularly Blacks. Herrnstein and Murray argue that the criminals are not at fault—they commit more crimes and are less involved in community and politics because it is in their genes! Although there has been widespread and valid criticism of this book as bad science; it became a bible for conservatives and racists, who used it to attack Blacks and the welfare state. Arguably, this book may have contributed to the drastic welfare reform in the 1990s and the anti-affirmative action movement. A more recent approach involves combining genetics and environment (Walsh, 2000).

ARE CRIMINALS PSYCHOLOGICALLY DIFFERENT?

One of the most widely accepted kinds-of-people positions today centers on the belief that those committing crime are psychologically different from the rest of us. A great deal of research and many rehabilitation programs are based on this assumption. Although such beliefs are quite compatible with the general ideology of corporatism (individualism and personal culpability), it presents somewhat of a dilemma for the offender. The offender is legally responsible for personal actions, but at the same time, he or she is treated for the malady that supposedly caused the deviant behavior through psychiatric or psychological methods such as casework, probation, and parole. We do not have a lot of good evidence supporting the assumption that criminals differ significantly from noncriminals psychologically. One criminology student describes the circular reasoning evident in such explanations as follows:

> The medical model has prompted a long and futile search for the psychological counterparts of germs and tumors. Unfortunately, there are no infected organs or disease entities that can be identified as the causes of deviant behavior. Instead we infer deviant personality types and emotional disorders from our observations of behavior. Then we use our psychological constructs to explain the very phenomena from which they are inferred in the first place. In short, deviance, including delinquency, is fundamentally different from physical illness. It has no existence apart from the judgments people make about particular kinds of behavior. (Balch, 1975, p. 117)

Despite the lack of supporting data for the psychological abnormality theory, except for small subgroups of offenders, it still receives a great deal of professional and public support. Since psychological positivism, like the biological approach, emphasizes the nature of the criminal, such an approach seems quite appealing, ideologically. Radzinowicz notes the ideological appeal of kinds-of-people explanations historically:

> This way of looking at crime as the product of society (kinds of environment) was hardly likely to be welcome, however, at a time when a major concern was to hold down the "dangerous classes." The concept of the dangerous classes as the main source of crime and disorder was very much to the fore at the beginning of the nineteenth century. They were made up of those who had so miserable a share in the accumulated wealth of the industrial revolution that they might at any time break out in political revolt as in France. At their lowest level was the hard core of parasites to be found in any society, ancient or modern. And closely related to this, often indistinguishable from it, were the "criminal classes."
>
> It served the interests and relieved the conscience of those at the top to look upon the dangerous classes as an independent category, detached from the prevailing social conditions. They were portrayed as a race apart, morally depraved and vicious, living by violating the

fundamental law of orderly society—that a man should maintain himself by honest, steady work. In France they were commonly described as nomads, barbarians, savages, strangers to the customs of the country. English terminology was, perhaps, less strong and colorful, but the meaning was fundamentally similar. (1966, pp. 38–39)

One of the problems with such assumptions as the existence of dangerous classes of people is that "official criminals," that is, those who are convicted, represent a small proportion of all those who commit most crimes. For example, most crimes are property crimes; however, the clearance rate is only about one-fourth arrests for all thefts committed. We know from research that the large majority of the population commits crime during their lives, from use of illegal drugs and underage use of legal drugs, to minor theft, gambling, simple assault, speeding, reckless driving, and so on. In other words, when we study convicted criminals, we are studying people who were caught, are repeat offenders, and so on—a small sample (for most offenses) of those who commit crime. Also, although psychological differences exist between some subgroups of these offenders and the general population, the extent to which these differences are unique to convicted offenders is not obvious. For example, institutionalized offenders tend to have high rates of learning disabilities and coping problems; however, most people who have these problems do not commit crimes and become incarcerated.

One of the major myths of the psychologically abnormal offender surrounds serial killers. Those who are hunting humans (Leyton, 1986) are often viewed as obviously psychologically ill. However, the diagnosis of psychological illness is usually *ex post facto*—it comes after the offenders have committed their heinous crimes. Most were not thought of as mentally ill until after they committed their crimes, but the nature of their crimes convinces us they must be "mentally ill." This is comforting ideology, but bad science. We cannot predict who will commit serial murders, because those people may appear to be just like "normal" people. We cling to our stereotypes of normality to divorce ourselves from the fact that serial killers may reflect larger social environments and forces at work.

Historically, the worst examples of serial killers and mass murderers are found in the genocide of Native Americans, the Holocaust, and the more recent examples of ethnic cleansing. Millions of innocent victims are murdered due to economic and ideological factors. We need to understand those large-scale events as existing on a continuum from the "individual who commits such acts to a whole nation or people who commit them. Through such analysis we will come to understand the role of ideology and socialization in creating such crimes" (Hughes, 1962). Therefore we must look at the relationship between the psyche of a nation and that of an individual. Rather than being divorced from each other, the individual and his or her society are very much interrelated—one's environment plays a major role in shaping one's mental condition.

THE BAD ENVIRONMENT

Although kinds-of-people explanations have predominated in positivist analysis, kinds-of-environment thought has increasingly gained influence in the twentieth century. Here, the explanation for criminal behavior lies in such factors as peer group influence, family, and community, including conditions such as poor housing, inadequate education, and unemployment. This approach to criminology began with the Chicago school of thought (Pfohl, 1994).

The notion that criminal behavior is learned from others is often advanced as a reason for crime. When parents warn their children not to play with "undesirables," they implicitly embrace the idea that their offspring will learn bad behavior. E. H. Sutherland, a major figure in North American criminology, formulated the *theory of differential association,* which emphasizes that criminal behavior, like noncriminal behavior, is learned. Although this theory has been criticized for its vagueness and difficulty in being tested, it has probably been one of the most influential theories in the twentieth and twenty-first centuries. This theory is evident in various policies in the criminal justice system and in crime prevention programs.[3]

What one learns or does not learn in the family has been a major explanation of delinquency and criminality. Parental laxity and permissiveness are often identified by the public as the causes of criminal behavior. Throughout the twentieth century and even earlier, students of crime observed that most criminals and delinquents have come from certain types of homes. The homes that official delinquent children come from are frequently characterized by one or more of the following conditions:

1. *Absence of one or both parents due to death, divorce, or desertion*
2. *Other family members are criminalistic, immoral, or alcoholic*
3. *Lack of parental control because of ignorance or illness*
4. *Home uncongeniality, as in domination by one family member, favoritism, oversolicitude, overseverity, neglect, jealousy, crowded housing conditions, or interfering relatives*
5. *Racial or religious differences, differences in conventions and standards, foster home, or institutional home*
6. *Economic pressures such as unemployment, poverty, or a working mother. (Vold et al., 1997)*

The significance of the family in explaining crime is apparent in various programs, policies, and practices in crime prevention and treatment. Big Brother, Big Sister, and Uncle programs, among others, are directed at youth who do not have certain family relationships. Of course, emphasis on family history and situation has also played a significant role in the determination of wardship in the juvenile justice system.

ECOLOGICAL THEORIES OF CRIMINAL BEHAVIOR

Ecological theories of criminal behavior focus on a community and the distribution of such homes and related characteristics. Here the distribution of crime and delinquency is mapped out within cities to identify the characteristics of communities with various crime rates. In lay terms, these are the places in the city where most crimes occur. In every city of substantial size are places where a large proportion of *official* crime takes place, and local citizens are aware of these places. Ecological analyses have generally found that an unduly high rate of official delinquency exists in areas of the city that are relatively poor and have a disproportionate number of ethnic and racial minorities, high unemployment, overcrowded population, poor housing, and higher incidences of problems in the home (Shaw & McKay 1972). The analysis of the distribution of official crime and delinquency has implication for programs, policies, and practices aimed at dealing with the problem.

A cursory look at arrest rates and the prison population in the United States attests to the fact that economic position, age, gender, and ethnic or racial status are related to officially recognized criminal behavior. Such observations have led to explanations emphasizing cultural differences between and among classes, ethnic or racial groups, youth, and adults. For example, Miller (1958) explains lower-class delinquency as a product of the "focal concerns" of the lower class—areas of major attention and involvement such as trouble, toughness, smartness, excitement, fate, and autonomy. He suggests that these "focal concerns" are distinctive to the lower class as part of their cultural system of values, separating them from the middle and upper classes. Therefore, the subculture characteristics of the lower class supposedly conflicts with that of the middle and upper classes.

As noted earlier, our home and community environments are ascribed by birth—we do not select our parents, family, or community conditions. Routine activity theory focuses on this reality by stressing that, in different neighborhoods and communities, the opportunities for legitimate and illegitimate behavior differ. Also, the chances of being victimized, becoming involved in illegal activity, being stopped by police, and being arrested and incarcerated are different in different communities. These are structured choices beyond our control (Lynch, 1996). One's environment is an important factor in explaining criminal behavior; analysis reveals that the structure and nature of inequality in different communities is found to significantly affect criminal behavior.

POWER/CONFLICT

Both the kinds-of-people and the kinds-of-environment theories of criminal behavior compare criminals and noncriminals in order to discover the correlates and ultimately the causes of crime. The power/conflict explanation differs from these traditional, positivistic approaches in its emphasis on the political economy of crime. This approach is concerned with such influences as class, a power elite, dominant ideology, and the role of the state in defining what is criminal and determining the emphasis of the criminal justice system.

Poverty, broken homes, and ethnic minority status are noted in most texts as significant causes of crime, but what can be said about the corporate executives who violate the law? These criminals do not live in poverty, and in most cases they have stable homes and family lives and are members of the majority ethnic group. This suggests that the relationship between crime and certain kinds of environments applies only to certain types of offenses (Wikstrom and Loeber, 2000). Again, we must become aware of the multitude of behaviors defined as criminal and realize that most of society's attention is focused on street crime and street criminals. The relationships we see among social class, ethnicity, family life, and crime are determined by a selective definition of crime. That is, the attention of law enforcement and the general public is focused on street crimes such as robbery, auto theft, and murder, which occur more frequently in the lower classes and oppressed ethnic and racial groups. However, such economic trespasses as fraud, price-fixing, and income-tax evasion—and such violent offenses as lack of standard safety maintenance in the workplace; systematic production of defective products; and poisoning of our air, water, or food gain little attention from the public or law enforcement.

The power/conflict approach emphasizes class, race, and gender bias in the process of defining what is criminal and in enforcing such laws. The overrepresentation of the lower classes and minorities in official crime statistics reflects both their disproportionate involvement in certain offences, and the differential enforcement and processing of these crimes (Greene and Gabbidon, 2000). If we pursued corporate theft and violence with the same vigor that we pursue street crime, the class and race of official criminals would be quite different (Cullen, Maakestad, & Covender, 1987; Clifford, 1998; Szockyi and Fox, 1996; Hills, 1988).

In the first reading in Part Two, social work professor Sherri Seyfried provides a grounded analysis of the effect of teachers on the life chances of black males. More specifically, she deals with the stereotypes and prejudices teachers may bring into the classroom and which may negatively affect young Black males. In a self-fulfilling prophecy, if all young Black males are viewed as criminal, gangsters, and thieves, and as aggressive and disinterested in education, then teachers will discipline them more often, have lower expectations for them intellectually, and create an environment in which they will fail and disproportionately become involved in the criminal justice system. Seyfried cites research that suggests that teachers' perceptions of student behavior and academic achievement indicate that regardless of social class, African American males are viewed more negatively than African American females or any other students. The teachers' perceptions of Black males' lack of social skills significantly influence student grade point averages.

Grounding her argument in social control theory, which emphasizes that commitment and bonding to legitimate institutions is important in staying out of trouble, the author emphasizes the need to change such stereotypes and labeling through collaborative relationships among teachers, social workers, families, and through the creation of positive self-concepts for young African American males. Reversing the negative stereotypes and labeling that create the conditions for failure is possible, and it should be a national priority. Seyfried offers an instructive analysis of the importance of our educational institutions in shaping the selves of African American male youth.

In the next reading, law professor Michael Tonry provides a critical analysis of the political motivation leading to the high rate of arrest and incarceration of racial minorities in the last two decades. Drawing from his well-known book *Malign Neglect: Race, Crime and Punishment in America* (1994), Tonry explains the increasing racial disparities in arrests, jailing, and imprisonment since 1980 as a product not of actual increased criminal behavior, but of the policies and practices of conservative Republican politicians. More specifically, he systematically points out that the war on drugs launched by the Reagan and Bush administrations has led to our current massive overrepresentation of racial minorities in prison. The harsh sentences and mandatory minimums of the war on drugs are not supported by most criminological research; however, they are a direct result of political opportunism and racism.

The use of the "race card" in the war on crime and the get-tough policies in the war on drugs were instrumental in helping Reagan and Bush get elected. The differential penalties and enforcement regarding illegal drugs, and the political use of Willie Horton (who committed murder after Michael Dukakis, Bush's opponent, granted him an early prison release), make apparent the politics of law making and the administration of justice. Tonry argues that white conservative politicians have used the race card by characterizing blacks as criminals and by directing the wars on crime and drugs to black communities, winning political victories on the backs of African Americans. Both in this article and in his book, Tonry has argued persuasively that the enormous racial discrepancies in arrest, jailing, and imprisonment are a product of ideology and politics, not of increased criminal behavior.

In "Latinos and Lethal Violence," Ramiro Martinez attempts to explain the Latino homicide rate, which is higher than that of whites and slightly lower than that of blacks, through analysis of measures of inequality. Rather than emphasizing kinds of people (i.e., Latino culture), Martinez looks at the nature of inequality in a variety of Latino communities in the United States in relation to whites, and inequality among Latino community members. What he discovers is that in areas where there is a high rate of absolute poverty among Latinos compared to whites, homicide rates are lower than in areas where there is increased inequality among Latinos. He explains that this is in part due to the fact that Latinos measure their self-worth and status in relation to other Latinos rather than in relation to the dominant white group. Further, the professional flight of middle- and upper-class Latinos out of barrios, followed by the flight of working class, helps us to understand urban Latino violence.

Some suggested policy implications are increased economic opportunities through labor market participation, school reform, and greater access to higher education. Here we encounter the previously discussed power/conflict model—How do we reduce structured inequity (Savolainen, 2000)? Martinez notes that unfortunately legislation in California such as Proposition 187 will marginalize more Latinos by singling them out for discrimination. This anti-affirmative action and anti-Spanish legislation attempts to marginalize minorities and will undoubtedly have a negative effect on Latinos. Martinez has provided an insightful and comprehensive analysis of homicide among Latinos from a structural kinds-of-environment approach.

In "Violence Against Gays and Lesbians," Reasons and Hughson address minority groups that are not usually addressed in criminal justice literature. The authors point out that violence against gays and lesbians has been increasing in recent years, and it is supported by both law and custom. Although hate-crime legislation has emerged in recent years to protect members of minority groups, this often does not include people who differ from the mainstream in their sexual orientation. Furthermore, sodomy laws and statutes prohibiting homosexual behavior still exist in a number of states. These laws provide both de jure and de facto means for prosecuting and persecuting gays and lesbians through the legal system. In the courts, a "homosexual panic defense" has been used to defend heterosexual males when they have committed crimes of violence against alleged gays or lesbians (McCoy, 2001). This defense is based on homophobia, not on science; nonetheless, in varying forms it has been successful due to the widespread nature of homophobia in American society. Finally, the military policy of "don't ask, don't tell" ensures that gays and lesbians will continue to be the subject of harassment and discrimination. Prominent politicians and religious spokespersons who would never expressly condemn racial minorities or women, will openly condemn gays and lesbians as evil, sinful, and bad. In 2000, the 5-to-4 decision by the Supreme Court in *Boy Scouts of America, et al. vs. Dale* further marginalizes and stigmatizes gays and lesbians. The decision by the majority of the court confirms it is legal to discriminate against gays and lesbians on the basis of the first amendment right of expressive association. Justice Stevens, in dissent with three other justices, observed that prejudice against homosexuality has a long history. In recent years, however, this prejudice has been reduced. Unfortunately, the court has legalized and institutionalized these prejudices in this decision (MacDougall, 1999).

Over the years, however, interaction with real people, rather than mere adherence to traditional ways of thinking about members of unfamiliar groups, have modified those opinions. For example, the American Psychiatric Association and the American Psychological Association removed homosexuality from their lists of mental disorders, and a move has been made toward greater understanding within some religious communities. Prejudices are still prevalent, however, and they have caused serious and tangible harm to countless gays and lesbians.

STUDY QUESTIONS_____

1. Compare classical, positivist and power/conflict explanations and solutions to crime.

2. Discuss how educational institutions influence the life chances of young black males.

3. How is the great increase in racial disparity in arrest, jailing, and imprisonment a product of political decisions, rather than of increased criminal behavior?

4. How is Latino homicide related to the nature and extent of inequality?

5. How has violence against gays and lesbians been supported by law and public policy?

NOTES_____

1. For an overview of criminological theory, see Vold, Bernard, and Snipes, 1997.

2. See Bohm and Haley (1999, pp. 66–67) for a further delineation of positivist theories.

3. We do not quarrel with the simple observation that behavior is learned. However, what is learned from one's associates is learned in a specific structural context. For example, one might discover that definitions learned in a ghetto or in a corporate suite favor violation of the law. Perhaps a more important question is, What are the social forces that produce both ghetto and corporate crime?

REFERENCES_____

Balch, Robert (1975). "The Medical Model of Delinquency," *Crime and Delinquency* (April):116–130.

Block, Herbert, and Gilbert Geis (1970). *Man, Crime and Society,* 2nd ed. New York: Random House.

Bohm, Robert, and Keith Haley (1999). *Introduction to Criminal Justice,* 2nd ed. New York: Glencoe McGraw-Hill.

Clifford, Mary (1998). *Environmental Crime.* Gaithersburg, Md.: Aspen.

Cullen, Francis, William Maakestad, and Gray Covender (1987). *Corporate Crime Under Attack: The Ford Pinto Case and Beyond.* Cincinnati: Anderson.

Grant, Edwin (1925). "Scum from the Melting Pot," *American Journal of Sociology 30*:641–651.

Greene, Helen, and Shaun Gabbidon (2000). *African American Criminological Thought.* Albany: State University of New York Press.

Herrnstein, Richard, and Charles Murray (1994). *The Bell Curve: Intelligence and Class Structure in American Life.* New York: The Free Press.

Hills, Stuart (1988). *Corporate Violence: Injury and Death for Profit.* Totowa, N.J.: Rowman & Littlefield.

Hughes, Everett (1962). "Good People and Dirty Work," *Social Problems, 10*:3–11.

Lynch, Michael (1995). "Class, Race, Gender and Criminology: Structured Choices and the Life Course." In *Race, Gender and Class in Criminology,* Martin Schwartz (Ed.). New York: Garland, pp. 3–27.

MacDougall, Bruce (1999). *Queer Judgments.* Toronto: University of Toronto Press.

Mannheim, Hermann (1960). *Pioneers in Criminology.* Chicago: Quadrangle Books.

McCoy, Scott D. (2001). "The Homosexual-Advance Defense and Hate Crimes Statutes: Their Interaction and Conflict," *Cardozo Law Review 22:*629–652.

Miller, Walter (1958). "Lower-Class Culture as a Generating Milieu of Gang Delinquency," *Journal of Social Issues, 14*:5–19.

Pallone, Nathaniel, and James Hennessy (2000). "Blacks and Whites as Victims and Offenders in Aggressive Crime in the U.S.: Myths and Realities." In *Race, Ethnicity, Sexual Orientation, Violent Crime: The Realities and Myths,* Nathanial Pallone (Ed.). New York: The Hawthorne Press.

Pfohl, Stephen (1994). *Images of Deviance and Social Control: A Sociological History,* 2nd ed. New York: McGraw-Hill.

Reasons, Charles E. (1975). "Social Thought and Social Structure: Competing Paradigms in Criminology," *Criminology: An Interdisciplinary Journal 13*:332–365.

Radzinowicz, Leon (1966). *Ideology and Crime.* New York: Columbia University Press.

Rushton, Phillipe (1995). *Race, Evolution and Behavior: A Life History Perspective.* New Brunswick, N.J.: Transaction.

Savolainen, Jukka (2000). "Inequality, Welfare State, and Homocide: Further Support for the Institutional Anomie Theory," *Criminology 38*:1021–1042.

Shaw, Clifford, and Henry McKay (1972). *Juvenile Delinquency and Urban Areas.* Chicago: University of Chicago Press.

Sheldon, Randall (2001). *Controlling the Dangerous Classes.* Boston: Allyn and Bacon.

Szockyi, Elizabeth, and James Fox (1996). *Corporate Victimization of Women.* Boston: Northeastern University Press.

Vold, George B., Thomas Bernard, and Jeffery Snipes (1997). *Theoretical Criminology,* 4th ed. New York: Oxford.

Von Baumer, Franklin L. (1964). *Main Currents of Western Thought.* New York: Alfred A. Knopf.

Walsh, Anthony (2000). "Behavior Genetics and Anomie/Strain Theory," *Criminology 38*: 1075–1108.

Wikstrom, Per-Olof, and Rolf Loeber (2000). "Do Disadvantaged Neighborhoods Cause Well-Adjusted Children to Become Adolescent Delinquents? *Criminology 38*:1109–1142.

African American Boys Are Getting Caught in a Spider's Web

But It Definitely Is Not Charlotte's Web!

SHERRI F. SEYFRIED
Chicago State University

African American male students are getting caught in a spider's web, but it definitely isn't Charlotte's web. E. B. White's best-seller, *Charlotte's Web,* is a children's story about an unlikely pair: Charlotte, a spider, and Wilbur, a shy pig that was the runt of the litter. To summarize the plot, Charlotte saves Wilbur from the butcher's block. However, the story is about much more than Wilbur's rescue. This is a story about social justice, humanity, belief, and the ability to look beyond an individual's physical appearance. The words that Charlotte spun into her web to describe Wilbur had a reifying effect (that is, perceptions and beliefs became reality) on how others perceived and responded to Wilbur. Toward the end of the story, Wilbur and others actually felt that he was a "terrific" and "radiant" pig. While *Charlotte's Web* is a fantasy, the story is compelling because it contains universal truths, the most dominant of which is that perceptions and expectations "create" reality. The societal perception of African American young men is anything but positive, and the discouraging educational statistics portray a grim reality that African American male students are headed towards a negative trajectory.

This reading first presents a statement of the problem and the ecological framework that guides my thinking about student–teacher relationships and academic achievement among African American students. Next a review of the literature regarding gender differences among African American boys and girls is provided. The reading concludes with implications for practice and policy.

THE PROBLEM

Why should we be concerned about how well African American boys are doing in school? We know that students who are at risk for school failure are also at risk for later drug use, delinquency, and violence (Dryfoos, 1990; Hawkins, Catalano, & Miller, 1992; Institute of Medicine, 1994; Maguin & Loeber, 1996). Youth that are ill prepared for work in today's economy will be attracted to illicit activity that promises quick money. In today's service-driven, technology-focused economy, jobs that offer benefits and competitive salaries require a college education. Youth, particularly minority youth, without a high school degree will be at a tremendous disadvantage. The jobs available to them will pay the minimum wage and will not offer benefits. Consequently, African American students who are bonded to school and who are also challenged to reach their potential will more than likely be those students that choose to stay in school and will be less likely to become involved in unhealthy, risky behavior. However, the data indicate that significant numbers of African American male students are at risk for school failure.

Data from a national study of over 25 million students found that African American boys are disproportionately represented among those students who receive corporal punishment, school suspensions and special education placements (Gregory, 1997). In another national study, inquiring about the reasons for early dropout, suspensions and expulsions from school were the most frequently reported motivations for early dropout among African American males (Jordan, Lara & McPartland, 1996). The data would suggest that African American boys may receive differential treatment in the classroom. If this is so, then interventions are needed to enhance teacher effectiveness with this population.

What is happening to African American boys in the classroom? What is the association between teacher perceptions of student behavior and academic difficulties? Does that relationship differ for African American boys and girls? There is evidence that teachers spend less time teaching those they view as troublesome (Brophy & McCaslin, 1992). Since more African American boys are viewed by teachers as having poorer social skills, do their higher rates of school failure result from their being viewed as troublesome? If this is true, then clearly school interventions which enhance teacher effectiveness are needed to promote the academic and social development of African American male students.

ECOLOGICAL FRAMEWORK

Charlotte's Web illustrates how the quality of reciprocal relationships can and does influence individual development. Wilbur and Charlotte shared a relationship that was mutually reinforcing. The quality of this relationship (largely due to Charlotte's reinforcement of Wilbur's positive qualities) also had a positive effect on how others perceived and then responded to Wilbur. The quality of the reciprocal relationships within our immediate environment (family, peers, teachers) has a profound effect on who we are. We also know that societal stereotypes (although more distant and abstract) can have an effect on self perceptions and how others perceive and respond to you, particularly if you are a member of the group that is being stereotyped. The ecological framework that guides my

thinking about the education of African American youth considers the quality of the student–teacher relationship to be central to achievement (Seyfried, 1994, 1998). We also know that student–teacher relationships can be (and often are) influenced by societal stereotypes, which have an indirect and more distant influence on achievement. The following section examines the literature related to teacher expectations, status characteristics, stereotypes, and labeling. Within the context of the learning environment the interrelationship between these concepts can create a "web" that can either "debilitate" or "promote" the academic potential of African American students.

Bronfenbrenner (1979) has developed an ecological framework that identifies the interconnected systems which influence human development. Bronfenbrenner (1989) believes that behavior occurs within *social contexts,* a series of nested systems. For the purposes of this article, attention is focused on the *mesosystem,* the interconnection between *microsystems* (the most proximal contexts, i.e. family, friends, school, work). More specifically, the focus here is with the association between teacher perceptions and student outcome. The teacher, representing the school system, brings with him or her personal values and expectations as well as professional values that are analogous with mainstream education. The student also brings a set of values and expectations regarding schooling that are influenced by the family environment. The degree to which student and teacher values, culture, and expectations are similar will influence the quality and character of the student–teacher relationship. Ultimately, however, it is the elementary grade school teacher's responsibility to provide classroom experiences which enhance and promote the academic potential of all students.

Teacher Expectations

Educational research has found that teacher expectations are associated with student outcomes (Babad, Inabar, & Rosenthal, 1982; Page & Rosenthal, 1990; Rosenthal, 1995; Rosenthal & Jacobson, 1968). Teachers with high expectations for student performance give students more feedback, are warmer, and present more challenging work (Rosenthal, 1973). Rosenthal further states that when students who are expected to do poorly in fact do well, some teachers do not reward their success. In one study the data suggest that this may be true (Seyfried, 2000). In Seyfried's study African American students with high achievement scores received lower grade point averages than their equally-high-achieving European American classmates. In this same study, teachers also perceived the African American males to be the most aggressive, followed by African American females, European American males and then European American females. As a response to teachers who are disinterested in their performance, perhaps, African American students (male students in particular) adopt "oppositional identities" (Beale-Spencer, Dupree & Hartmann, 1997; Graham, 1997; Ogbu, 1993). If this is so, then their behavior is understandable. Unfortunately, it is likely to perpetuate for them a vicious, downward cycle. The important point to note here is that teachers need to be aware of the impact their perceptions can have on student achievement.

Status Characteristics, Societal Stereotypes and Labeling

Status Characteristics. While the teacher expectation research has contributed to the body of knowledge which addresses the relationship between teacher expectations and student performance, this literature does not explain why teachers may form different expectations based upon race, gender or socioeconomic status. The status characteristics and expectation states theory (Berger, Rosenholtz, & Zelditch, 1980) provides a theoretical framework that addresses the relationship between status characteristics and performance expectations. This theory claims that evaluations of and beliefs about the performance ability of individuals are formed around external status characteristics such as race, ethnicity, gender, class, or age. When status characteristics are generalized, the expectation states theory suggests

that this is a consequence of the status characteristic functioning as a "diffuse" status. For example, to say that "All African American male teenagers belong to gangs, therefore the African American boys in this classroom will more than likely drop out of school and join a gang" illustrates the intersections of gender and race acting as diffuse status characteristics. Teachers that are more susceptible to biasing information produce negative expectancy effects that are evident in teacher behavior and student performance (Babad, Inabar, & Rosenthal, 1982). Interventions that enhance teacher effectiveness with African American male students are needed, for we know that the teacher's style of classroom management is related to student commitment and bonding to school (Harachi, Abbott, Catalano, & Haggerty, 1996; Hawkins, 1996; Hawkins & Catalano, 1992). African American boys that are engaged and involved in classroom activities will be motivated to stay in school.

Societal Stereotypes and Labeling. Most societal stereotypes involve the generalization of myths that are appropriated to individuals based upon status characteristics. Societal beliefs about the ability of African American boys are informed by negative stereotypes in the media which portray African American men as drug pushers, pimps, or gang bangers. Whether African American men choose to portray these images or not, societal stereotypes dictate how they will be perceived by other people (Beale-Spencer, Cunningham, & Swanson, 1995). Steele (1997) has found that for some youth, educational expectations may be dampened by societal stereotypes associated with ethnic status and potential for academic success. Unfortunately, many African American youth are distracted by the negative societal stereotypes which are imposed upon them and lose interest in education. They ask "Why should I get an education? There are few jobs for African American men, and regardless of how much education we get we are still viewed as thugs." African American boys without the support of family will be more vulnerable to societal stereotypes; therefore, for these students, it is essential that they experience positive, nurturing relationships with their teachers and other school personnel.

Many students that lose interest in school may be misdiagnosed and placed in special education classes, or they may be placed in vocational education classes, or they might drop out of school altogether. Once students are placed in special education classes, the effects of labeling have long-term damaging effects. Labeling diminishes self-reliance and denies the student's right to self-determination. The "reifying" effects of labeling limit the student's free will to make decisions and negate the student's efforts toward self-discipline.

I will never forget the experience I had when I was substitute teaching for a particular high school teacher that had all college prep classes except one. On this particular day, I was to sub for his vocationally oriented class. He told me that I would have difficulty with this class, for it was his least favorite class (he told me this not in the presence of the class). When I went to the class and introduced myself, a student immediately raised her hand and said, "You aren't going to like us—we're his least favorite class." She echoed the exact words that the teacher had told me. The student's statement indicated that it was important for her to know if I held the same low expectations for their performance as the classroom teacher. My response to the class was that "I expect to get along with you just fine." With that, the students looked at me with smirking smiles as if to say "Lady, are you for real?" They couldn't believe that I expected them to be responsible students. However, the class went well and the students adjusted very quickly to the expectations I had set for them. In fact I could tell they were proud to be challenged. Labeling encourages others to set limited expectations for the student's potential for performance and self-efficacy (Seyfried, 1997). Most importantly, once students are labeled it will be extremely difficult for them to realize their human potential as the reifying effects create the reality of their environment. Interventions are needed which enable the teacher to identify, acknowledge, and then promote the individual strengths and talent among students from diverse backgrounds.

More specifically, in order to be most effective those interventions must consider the unique social, academic, and developmental needs specific to gender and race.

GENDER DIFFERENCES AMONG AFRICAN AMERICAN STUDENT ACHIEVEMENT

Most mainstream research studies related to gender differences make no attempt to evaluate racial characteristics or ethnic status. However, Crick and Gropeter (1995), Harnish, Dodge, and Valente (1995), and Underwood, Kupersmidt, and Coie (1996) are examples of mainstream researchers who do consider racial differences in gender development. Even though racial characteristics are acknowledged in these studies, for the most part, the reciprocal influence of ethnic status and gender are not considered. Consequently, we know less about gender development among minority youth. Ethnic minority researchers recognize the salience of within-group examination of gender difference (Beale-Spencer, Brookins, & Allen, 1985; Beale-Spencer, Dupree, & Hartmann, 1997; Connell, Beale-Spencer, & Aber, 1994; Ford, 1992a, 1992b; Fordham, 1993; Gibbs & Merighi, 1995; Graham, 1997; Haynes, Comer, & Hamilton-Lee, 1998; Majors, 1998; Majors & Billson-Mancini, 1993; Pollard, 1993; Seyfried, 1994; Swanson & Beale-Spencer, 1997). The findings from this body of work contribute greatly to our understanding of African American youth development and, as a consequence, provide useful information for the design of culturally specific interventions with this group. Nonetheless, these researchers, with the exception of Seyfried (1994, 1998), have not explored the relationship between gender, teacher perceptions, and academic achievement among African American youths.

From an earlier review of the literature we know that teacher expectations and perceptions of student performance are directly related to academic achievement, but we know less about how teacher perceptions of student behavior predicts the academic achievement among African American boys and girls. In one ecological study of urban,

African American fourth, fifth, and sixth graders (Seyfried, 1994, 1998) it was found that teacher perceptions of social skills had significant influence on student grade point average. This was even true after controlling for ability, socioeconomic status and family environment. While socioeconomic status and family environment were related to each other, they were not related to those variables that were most closely associated with learning in the classroom. By far, teacher perceptions had more influence on grade point average than any other variable in the model. This was particularly true for the boys in the study. It was also interesting to note that there was a negative indirect correlation between gender, ability, teacher perceptions of social skills, and grade point average. This negative indirect effect meant that the boys in the study scored lower on the ability measure, which was associated with the teacher's perceiving the boys as having poorer social skills, which ultimately influenced the boys to receive lower grade point averages than the girls. This is particularly alarming in that the boys scored only slightly lower than the girls on the ability measure—basically they were of the same ability as the girls. I believe the relationship between ability, teacher perceptions, and grade point average is the part of the "web" or entanglement that catches African American male students. For we know that most ability measures (standardized achievement scores in this research) actually measure acquired knowledge. There are a number of factors which influence what one learns. Earlier we discussed the influence of teacher perceptions and expectations as one factor associated with student achievement. Could it be that the male students in this study have received different expectations which influence what they are able to learn? We must also consider the fact that perhaps the teachers interpreted the boys' slightly lower ability measures to mean that they are just not as smart as the girls, and responded to them as such. While this study was cross-sectional in nature, longitudinal research is needed to further investigate this hypothesis. Clearly, this study indicates that there is a connection between ability, teacher perceptions and grade point average, and that this re-

lationship had a negative outcome for the boys in this study. The findings from this study suggest that interventions are needed to enhance the quality of student–teacher relationships with African American preadolescent, male youth.

IMPLICATIONS FOR PRACTICE AND POLICY

Practice Implications

African American males are disproportionately suspended, expelled, or placed in special education classes (Gregory, 1997) and, as was mentioned earlier in Seyfried's work, it seems that African American male students are experiencing differential treatment in the classroom and are getting caught in a perilous web. Unless you happen to believe that African American boys (and African Americans in general) are as inherently devious and dim-witted as Herrnstein and Murray (1994), authors of *The Bell Curve,* would like for you to believe, then this data would suggest that African American male students are treated differently in the classroom. We know that students who are at risk for school failure are also at risk for violence, delinquency, and drug use (Dryfoos, 1990; Hawkins, Catalano, & Miller, 1992; Institute of Medicine, 1994; Maguin & Loeber, 1996). We also know that youth who are committed and bonded to school will more than likely stay in school. How do we enhance African American boys' commitment to school? We begin by addressing the school social worker's ability to enhance the quality of the student–teacher relationship.

Ecological Base of School Social Work. The unique quality of social work practice is the location of the social worker at the interface where an individual's coping behavior interacts with the quality and characteristics of the immediate environment (Germain, 1999). Germain states that the function of the school social worker places them at the interface between: (1) the parent and school, (2) the child and school, and (3) the community and school. Due to the school social worker's ability to work within and between each of these systems, the social worker's role is twofold: to enhance social competence and to enhance the competence-promoting qualities of the impinging environment (Monkman, 1999). Typically, social workers have had less involvement with competence building activities that occur at the student–teacher interface than with direct service to the student, bypassing the focus on the student–teacher relationship. I suggest a model of school social work practice which encourages teachers and social workers to form collegial, collaborative relationships. In this way social workers, in a nonthreatening manner, can provide teachers with assistance designed to enhance the quality of interactions with African American male students.

Reframing (Fine, 1992) is one technique that social workers may use with teachers to enhance the quality of student–teacher interactions. With reframing, the teacher is encouraged to respond to the motivation for student behavior and not the behavior itself. Usually when attention is focused on the behavior alone, negative consequences follow (i.e., the student is sent to the principal's office where he is punished in some way). Reframing is especially useful for teachers that do not know how to deal with the African American male student's "oppositional personality." For example, the student that tells the teacher he doesn't have time to deal with this "white man's stuff" is really saying, "I am afraid that if I do this work it's not going to get me anywhere. I see no future for Black kids like me." The teacher that has been trained in reframing would respond to the student's fear and not the defiance. Simply put, reframing helps teachers to see students as individuals with individual needs. Social workers with their knowledge of ecological systems, cultural diversity and professional obligation towards social justice are capable of providing teachers invaluable collegial assistance.

Possible Selves. While interventions are needed to enhance the quality of the impinging environment, in this case the student–teacher relationship, interventions are also needed to strengthen the cognitive development of African American students. Are African American students, boys in particular, able to see what it is they want to be when they grow up, and are their perceptions of what they want to be consonant with the achievement behaviors that are necessary to reach those goals? For many African American students it is difficult to associate the present with the future (Oyserman, Harrison and Bybee, 1998). As mentioned earlier, for African American students societal stereotypes, racism and discrimination obscure the possibility of who they want to become. Daphna Oyserman and her colleagues (1998) have developed a school-to-jobs program designed to improve academic and psychosocial outcomes by improving effort and reducing stereotype threat vulnerability. There are four components to the program. Youth are expected to: (1) conceptualize possible selves, (2) develop a repertoire of strategies to work toward possible selves, (3) increase their sense of connection to school, and (4) learn to obtain school and career relevant help and support from parents and community members. Oyserman reports that the initial findings from this program have been encouraging.

School social workers, by virtue of their professional orientation and function, are in a prime position to enhance the quality of student–teacher relationships and implement school-to-jobs programs. First, however, educational professionals, policy makers, and other professionals who are interested in the well-being of minority youth must see the merit in supporting such efforts.

Policy Implications

Healthy People 2000. The goal of Healthy People 2000 (U. S. Department of Health and Human Services, 1990) is to increase the high school completion rate to at least 90 percent. The promotion of academic success has been designated as a public health goal because there is evidence that students who are academically successful are less likely to become involved in health risk behaviors (Dryfoos, 1990). Healthy People 2000 states:

> *By addressing high school dropout rates as part of the nation's health promotion and disease prevention agenda, it may be possible to reduce unwarranted*

risk of problem behavior and improve the health of our young people (U.S. Department of Health and Human Services, 1990, p. 254).

The practice implications mentioned earlier would serve to promote those factors which facilitate the African American student's commitment and bonding to school, thereby encouraging them to stay in school. Moreover, interventions that enhance the quality of student–teacher relationships and also student self-perception will provide school districts with invaluable support towards reaching the goals of Healthy People 2000.

Link between Research and Policy.   Most importantly, policy makers should be aware of research which demonstrates: (1) the relationship between teacher perceptions and academic achievement of African American students (Seyfried 1994, 1998, 2000), (2) the relationship between teacher classroom management and student bonding and commitment to school (Harachi, Abbott, Catalano, & Haggerty, 1996), and (3) the success of jobs-to-school programs (Oyserman, Harrison, & Bybee, 1998). Federal agencies are more likely to fund programs that are based upon findings from empirical research.

CONCLUSION

African American male students are getting caught in a spider's web and, as the data indicate, they are not getting caught in Charlotte's web. Social scientists and educators have much to learn from Charlotte as she spins universal truths about social justice, bonding and commitment, belief, friendship, and the reifying effects of labeling and expectations. Perhaps this section from *Charlotte's Web* best captures the essence of E. B. White's classic children's fantasy:

> *Charlotte had written the word RADIANT, and Wilbur really looked radiant as he stood in the golden sunlight. Ever since the spider had befriended him, he had done his best to live up to his reputation. When Charlotte's web said TERRIFIC, Wilbur had tried to look terrific. And now that the web said RADIANT, he did everything possible to make himself glow (White, 1952, p. 114).*

Teacher perceptions and expectations have powerful, reifying effects on student behavior, and we know that this is particularly true for African American male students whose hopes and dreams have been diminished by the reality of racism, discrimination and societal stereotypes. We also know that teacher perceptions are related to academic outcome and teacher classroom management styles are related to student bonding and commitment to school. Is it a fantasy for us to believe that African American male students can be *radiant* and *terrific*? I don't believe it to be a fantasy. We just need the commitment and belief in the human potential of African American boys.

REFERENCES

Babad, E., Inabar, J. & Rosenthal, R. (1982). Pygmalion, Galatea and the Golem: Investigations of biased and unbiased teachers. *Journal of Psychology, 74*(4), 459–474.

Beale-Spencer, M., Brookins, G. K. & Allen, W. R. (Eds.). (1985). *Beginnings: The social and affective development of black children.* Hillsdale, NJ: Lawrence Erlbaum Associates, Inc.

Beale-Spencer, M., Cunningham, M. & Swanson, D. (1995). Identity as coping: Adolescent African-American males' adaptive responses to high-risk environments. In H. Harris, H. Blue and E. Griffith (Eds.), *Racial and ethnic identity: Psychological development and creative expression* (pp. 31–52). New York: Routledge.

Beale-Spencer, M., Dupree, D. & Hartmann, T. (1997). A phenomenological variant of ecological systems theory (PVEST): A self-organization perspective in context. *Development and Psychopathology, 9*(4), 817–833.

Berger, J., Rosenholtz, S. & Zelditch, M. (1980). Status organizing processes. *Annual Review of Sociology, 6*, 479–508.

Bronfenbrenner, U. (1979). *The ecology of human development: Experiments by nature and design.* Cambridge, MA: Harvard University Press.

Bronfenbrenner, U. (1989). Ecological systems. *Annals of Child Development, 6,* 87–249.

Brophy, J. E. & McCaslin, M. (1992). Teachers' reports of how they perceive and cope with problem students. *Elementary School Journal, 93*(1), 3–68.

Connell, J. P., Beale-Spencer, M. & Aber, J. L. (1994). Educational risk and resilience in African-American youth: Context, self, action, and outcomes in school. *Child Development, 65,* 493–506.

Crick, N. R. & Gropeter, J. K. (1995). Relational aggression, gender, and social-psychological adjustment. *Child Development, 66,* 710–722.

Dryfoos, J. G. (1990). *Adolescents at risk: Prevalence and prevention.* New York: Oxford University Press.

Fine, M. J. (1992). A systems-ecological perspective on home-school intervention. In M. J. Fine and C. Carlson (Eds.), *The handbook of family-school intervention: A systems perspective* (pp. 1–17). Boston: Allyn & Bacon.

Ford, D. Y. (1992a). The American achievement ideology and achievement differentials among preadolescent gifted and nongifted African-American males and females. *Journal of Negro Education, 61*(1), 45–64.

Ford, D. Y. (1992b). The American achievement ideology as perceived by urban African-American students: Explorations by gender and academic program. *Urban Education, 27*(2), 196–211.

Fordham, S. (1993). "Those loud black girls": Black women, silence, and gender "passing" in the academy. *Anthropology and Education Quarterly, 24*(1), 3–32.

Germain, C. B. (1999). An ecological perspective on social work in the schools. In R. Constable, J. P. Flynn, and S. McDonald (Eds.), *School social work: Practice, policy and research perspectives* (pp. 33–44). Chicago: Lyceum Books.

Gibbs, J. T. & Merighi, J. R. (1995). Young black males: Marginality, masculinity and criminality. In T. Newburn and E. A. Stanko (Eds.), *Just boys doing business?: Men, masculinities and crime* (pp. 65–80). New York: Routledge.

Graham, S. (1997). Using attribution theory to understand social and academic motivation in African American youth. *Educational Psychologist, 32*(1), 21–34.

Gregory, J. F. (1997). Three strikes and they're out: African American boys and American schools' responses to misbehavior. *International Journal of Adolescence and Youth, 7*(1), 25–34.

Harachi, T. W., Abbott, R. A., Catalano, R. F. & Haggerty, K. P. (1996). The effects of risk and protective factors on antisocial behavior and academic success in the early primary grades. Paper presented at the meeting of the Life History Research Society, London, October.

Harnish, J. D., Dodge, K. A. & Valente, E. (1995). Mother-child interaction quality as a partial mediator of the roles of maternal depressive symptomatology and socioeconomic status in the development of child behavior problems. *Child Development, 66,* 739–753.

Hawkins, J. D. (Ed.). (1996). *Delinquency and crime: Current theories.* Cambridge: Cambridge University Press.

Hawkins, J. D. & Catalano, R. F. (1992). *Communities that care: Action for drug abuse prevention.* San Francisco: Jossey-Bass, Inc.

Hawkins, J. D., Catalano, R. F. & Miller, J. Y. (1992). Risk and protective factors for alcohol and other drug problems in adolescence and early adulthood: Implications for substance abuse prevention. *Psychological Bulletin, 112, 64*–105.

Haynes, N. M., Comer, J. P. & Hamilton-Lee, M. (1998). Gender and achievement status differences on learning factors among black high school students. *Journal of Educational Research, 81,* (4), 233–237.

Herrnstein, R.& Murray, C. (1994). *The bell curve: Intelligence and class structure in American life.* New York: Free Press.

Institute of Medicine (IOM), Committee on Prevention of Mental Disorders. (1994). In P. J. Mrazek and R. J. Haggerty (Eds.), *Reducing risks for mental disorders: Frontiers for preventive intervention research.* Washington, DC: National Academy Press.

Jordan, W. J., Lara, J. & McPartland, J. M. (1996). Exploring the causes of early dropout among race-ethnic and gender groups. *Youth and Society, 28*(1), 62–94.

Maguin, E. & Loeber, R. (1996). Academic performance and delinquency. *Crime and justice: A review of research, 20,* 145–264. Chicago: University of Chicago Press.

Majors, Richard G. (1998). *An infrastructure for African-American males.* New York: The Urban Institute.

Majors, R. G. & Billson-Mancini, J. (1993). *Cool pose: The dilemmas of black manhood in America.* New York: Simon and Schuster, Inc.

Monkman, M. (1996). The characteristic focus of the social worker in the public schools. In R. Constable, J.

Flynn and S. McDonald (Eds.), *School social work: Practice and research perspectives.* Chicago: Lyceum Press.

Ogbu, J. U. (1993). Differences in cultural frame of reference. *International Journal of Behavioral Development, 16* (3), 483–506.

Oyserman, D., Harrison, K. & Bybee, D. (1998). Possible selves in the adolescent transition: The schools-to-jobs program. Poster presentation at the Society for Prevention Research, June.

Page, S. & Rosenthal, R. (1990). Sex and expectations of teachers and sex and race of students as determinants of teaching behavior and student performance. *Journal of School Psychology, 28,* 119–131.

Pollard, D. S. (1993). Gender, achievement, and African-American students' perceptions of their school experience. *Educational Psychologist, 28*(4), 341–356.

Rosenthal, R. (1973). *On the social psychology of the self-fulfilling prophecy: Further evidence for Pygmalion effects and their mediating mechanisms.* Module 53, 1–28. New York: MSS Modular Publications.

Rosenthal, R. (1995). Critiquing Pygmalion: A 25-year perspective. *Current Directions in Psychological Science, 4*(6), 171–172.

Rosenthal, R. and Jacobson, L. (1968). *Pygmalion in the classroom: Teacher expectations and pupils' intellectual development.* New York: Rinehart and Winston.

Seyfried, S. (1994). Academic achievement of black preadolescents: Factors associated with success. Unpublished doctoral dissertation, University of Illinois, at Chicago.

Seyfried, S. (1997). Does reliance on diagnostic labels help clients more than it hurts them?: NO. In E. Gambrill and R. Pruger (Eds.), *Controversial issues in social work ethics, values, and obligations* (pp. 25–38). Boston: Allyn & Bacon.

Seyfried, S. (1998). Academic achievement of African-American preadolescents: The influence of teacher perceptions. *American Journal of Community Psychology, 26*(3), 381–402.

Seyfried, S. (2000). Teacher perceptions, race, ability and grade point average: What's happening in the classroom? *School Social Work Journal, 24*(2), 1–19.

Steele, C. M. (1997). A threat in the air: How stereotypes shape intellectual identity and performance. *American Psychologist, 52*(6), 613–629.

Swanson, D. P. & Beale-Spencer, M. (1997). Developmental considerations of gender-linked attributes during adolescence. In R. D. Taylor & M. C. Wang (Eds.). *Social and emotional adjustment and family relations in ethnic minority families* (pp. 181–199). Mahwah, NJ: Lawrence Erlbaum Associates, Inc.

Underwood, M. K., Kupersmidt, J. B. & Coie, J. D. (1996). Childhood peer sociometric status and aggression as predictors of adolescent childbearing. *Journal of Research on Adolescence, 6*(2), 201–223.

U.S. Department of Health and Human Services, Public Health Service. (1990). *Healthy people 2000: National health promotion and disease prevention objectives.* Washington, DC: Superintendent of Documents, U.S. Government Printing Office.

White, E. B. (1952). *Charlotte's Web.* New York: HarperCollins Publishers.

Racial Politics, Racial Disparities, and the War on Crime

MICHAEL TONRY
Michael Tonry is Sonosky Professor of Law and Public Policy,
University of Minnesota. This article draws on Tonry's Malign Neglect:
Race, Crime, and Punishment in America *(1994).*

Racial disparities in the justice system have steadily gotten worse since
1980, primarily because of politically motivated decisions by the Reagan
and Bush administrations to promote harsh drug and sanctioning
policies that, existing research and broad agreement among practitioners
concur, could not significantly reduce crime rates or drug use. It is
difficult to imagine a persuasive ethical defense of promotion of policies
that were unlikely to achieve their ostensible goals but were foreseen to
have an adverse disparate effect on Blacks.

Racial disparities in arrests, jailing, and imprisonment steadily worsened after 1980 for reasons that have little to do with changes in crime patterns and almost everything to do with two political developments. First, conservative Republicans in national elections "played the race card" by using anticrime slogans (remember Willie Horton?) as a way to appeal to anti-Black sentiments of White voters. Second, conservative politicians of both parties promoted and voted for harsh crime control and drug policies that exacerbated existing racial disparities.

The worsened disparities might have been ethically defensible if they had been based on good faith beliefs that some greater policy good would thereby have been achieved. Sometimes unwanted side effects of social policy are inevitable. Traffic accidents and fatalities are a price we pay for the convenience of automobiles. Occupational injuries are a price we pay for engaging in the industries in which they occur.

The principal causes of worse racial disparities have been the War on Drugs launched by the Bush and Reagan administrations, characterized by vast increases in arrests and imprisonment of street-level drug dealers, and the continuing movement toward harsher penalties. Policies toward drug offenders are a primary cause of recent increases in jail and prison admissions and populations. Racial disparities among drug offenders are worse than among other offenders.

It should go without saying in the late 20th century that governments detest racial injustice and desire racial justice, and that racial disparities are tolerable only if they are unavoidable or are outweighed by even more important social gains. There are no offsetting gains that can justify the harms done to Black Americans by recent drug and crime control policies.

This [reading] presents data on racial trends in arrests, jailing, and imprisonment; examines the rationales for the policies that have produced those trends; and considers whether the adoption of policies known to have disparate adverse effects on Blacks can be ethically justified. First, the evidence concerning the effectiveness of recent drug and crime control policies that have exacerbated racial disparities is examined. Next, data on arrests, jail, and imprisonment trends are presented and demonstrate that racial disparities have worsened, but not because Blacks are committing larger proportions of the serious offenses (homicide, rape, robbery, aggravated assault) for which offenders were traditionally sent to prison. Finally, the reasons why recent policies were adopted and whether they can be ethically justified are considered.

CRIME REDUCTION EFFECTS OF CRIME CONTROL POLICY

There is no basis for a claim that recent harsh crime control policies or the enforcement strategies of the War on Drugs were based on good faith beliefs that they would achieve their ostensible purposes. In this and other countries, practitioners and scholars have long known that manipulation of penalties has few, if any, effects on crime rates.

Commissions and expert advisory bodies have been commissioned by the federal government repeatedly over the last 30 years to survey knowledge of the effects of crime control policies, and consistently they have concluded that there is little reason to believe that harsher penalties significantly enhance public safety. In 1967, the President's Commission on Law Enforcement and Administration of Justice observed that crime control efforts can have little effect on crime rates without much larger efforts being directed at crime's underlying social and economic causes. "The Commission . . . has no doubt whatever that the most significant action that can be taken against crime is action designed to eliminate slums and ghettos, to improve education, to provide jobs. . . . We shall not have dealt effectively with crime until we have alleviated the conditions that stimulate it."

In 1978, the National Academy of Sciences Panel on Research on Deterrent and Incapacitative Effects, funded by President Ford's department of

justice and asked to examine the available evidence on the crime-reductive effects of sanctions, concluded: "In summary, we cannot assert that the evidence warrants an affirmative conclusion regarding deterrence" (Blumstein, Cohen, and Nagin 1978). Fifteen years later, the National Academy of Sciences Panel on the Understanding and Control of Violent Behavior, created and paid for with funds from the Reagan and Bush administration departments of justice, surveyed knowledge of the effects of harsher penalties on violent crime (Reiss and Roth 1993). A rhetorical question and answer in the panel's final report says it all: "What effect has increasing the prison population had on violent crime? Apparently very little. . . . If tripling the average length of sentence of incarceration per crime [between 1976 and 1989] had a strong preventive effect," reasoned the panel, "then violent crime rates should have declined" (p. 7). They had not.

I mention that the two National Academy of Sciences panels were created and supported by national Republican administrations to demonstrate that skepticism about the crime-preventive effects of harsher punishments is not a fantasy of liberal Democrats. Anyone who has spent much time talking with judges or corrections officials knows that most, whatever their political affiliations, do not believe that harsher penalties significantly enhance public safety.

Likewise, outside the United States, conservative governments in other English-speaking countries have repudiated claims that harsher penalties significantly improve public safety. In Margaret Thatcher's England, for example, a 1990 White Paper (an official policy statement of the government), based on a 3-year study, expressed its skepticism about the preventive effects of sanctions:

Deterrence is a principle with much immediate appeal. . . . But much crime is committed on impulse, given the opportunity presented by an open window or an unlocked door, and it is committed by offenders who live from moment to moment; their crimes are as impulsive as the rest of their feckless, sad, or pathetic lives. It is unrealistic to construct sentencing arrangements on the assumption that most offenders will weigh up the possibilities in ad-

vance and base their conduct on rational calculation. (Home Office 1990)

Canada is the other English-speaking country that has . . . had a conservative government. In Brian Mulroney's Canada, the Committee on Justice and the Solicitor General (in American terms, the judiciary committee) proposed in 1993 that Canada shift from an American-style crime control system to a European-style preventive approach. In arguing for the shift in emphasis, the committee observed that "the United States affords a glaring example of the limited effect that criminal justice responses may have on crime. . . . If locking up those who violate the law contributed to safer societies then the United States should be the safest country in the world" (Standing Committee on Justice and the Solicitor General 1993). Six years earlier, the Canadian Sentencing Commission (1987) had reached similar conclusions: "Deterrence cannot be used, with empirical justification, to guide the imposition of sanctions."

There is no better evidentiary base to justify recent drug control policies. Because no other western country has adopted drug policies as harsh as those of the United States, a bit of background may be useful before I show why there was no reasonable basis for believing recent policies would achieve their ostensible goals. In drug policy jargon, the United States has adopted a prohibitionistic rather than a harm-reduction strategy and has emphasized supply-side over demand-side tactics (Wilson 1990). This strategic choice implies a preference for legal threats and moral denunciation of drug use and users instead of a preference for minimizing net costs and social harms to the general public, the law enforcement system, and drug users. The tactical choice is between a law enforcement emphasis on arrest and punishment of dealers, distributors, and importers, interdiction, and source-country programs or a prevention emphasis on drug treatment, drug-abuse education in schools, and mass media programs aimed at public education. The supply-side bias in recent American policies was exemplified throughout the Bush administration by its insistence that 70% of

federal antidrug funds be devoted to law enforcement and only 30% to treatment and education (Office of National Drug Control Policy 1990).

It has been a long time since most researchers and practitioners believed that current knowledge justifies . . . American drug control policies. Because the potential income from drug dealing means that willing aspirants are nearly always available to replace arrested street-level dealers, large-scale arrests have repeatedly been shown to have little or no effect on the volume of drug trafficking or on the retail prices of drugs (e.g., Chaiken 1988; Sviridoff, Sadd, Curtis, and Grinc 1992). Because the United States has long and porous borders, and because an unachievably large proportion of attempted smuggling would have to be stopped to affect drug prices significantly, interdiction has repeatedly been shown to have little or no effect on volume or prices (Reuter 1988). Because cocaine, heroin, and marijuana can be grown in many parts of the world in which government controls are weak and peasant farmers' incentives are strong, source-country programs have seldom been shown to have significant influence on drug availability or price in the United States (Moore 1990).

The evidence in support of demand-side strategies is far stronger. In December 1993, the President's Commission on Model State Drug Laws, appointed by President Bush, categorically concluded, "Treatment works." That conclusion is echoed by more authoritative surveys of drug treatment evaluations by the U.S. General Accounting Office (1990), the National Institute of Medicine (Gerstein and Jarwood 1990), and in *Crime and Justice* by Anglin and Hser (1990). Because drug use and offending tend to coincide in the lives of drug-using offenders, the most effective and cost-effective way to deal with such offenders is to get and keep them in well-run treatment programs.

A sizable literature now also documents the effectiveness of school-based drug education in reducing drug experimentation and use among young people (e.g., Botvin 1990; Ellickson and Bell 1990). Although there is no credible literature that documents the effects of mass media campaigns on drug use, a judge could take judicial notice of their ubiquity. It is not unreasonable to believe that such campaigns have influenced across-the-board declines in drug use in the United States since 1980 (a date, incidentally, that precedes the launch of the War on Drugs by nearly 8 years).

That the preceding summary of our knowledge of the effectiveness of drug control methods is balanced and accurate is shown by the support it receives from leading conservative scholars. Senator-scholar Daniel Patrick Moynihan (1993) has written, "Interdiction and 'drug busts' are probably necessary symbolic acts, but nothing more." James Q. Wilson (1990), for two decades America's leading conservative crime control scholar, observed that "significant reductions in drug abuse will come only from reducing demand for those drugs. . . . The marginal product of further investment in supply reduction is likely to be small" (p. 534). He reports that "I know of no serious law-enforcement official who disagrees with this conclusion. Typically, police officials tell interviewers that they are fighting either a losing war or, at best, a holding action" (p. 534).

Thus a fair-minded survey of existing knowledge provides no grounds for believing that the War on Drugs or the harsh policies exemplified by "three strikes and you're out" laws and evidenced by a tripling in America's prison population since 1980 could achieve their ostensible purposes. If such policies cannot be explained in instrumental terms, how can they be explained? The last section answers that question, but first a summary of recent data on racial trends in arrests, jailing, and incarceration.

RACIAL DISPARITIES IN ARRESTS, JAIL, AND PRISON

Racial disparities, especially affecting Blacks, have long bedeviled the criminal justice system. Many hundreds of studies of disparities have been conducted and there is now widespread agreement among researchers about causes. Racial bias and stereotyping no doubt play some role, but they are not the major cause. In the longer term, disparities in jail and prison are mainly the result of racial dif-

ferences in offending patterns. In the shorter term, the worsening disparities since 1980 are not primarily the result of racial differences in offending but were foreseeable effects of the War on Drugs and the movement toward increased use of incarceration. These patterns can best be seen by approaching the recent increases in racial disparities in imprisonment as a mystery to be solved. (Because of space limitations, jail data are not discussed here at length, but the trends parallel those for prisons. Between 1980 and 1991, e.g., the percentage of jail inmates who were Black increased from 40% to 48%.)

Figure 1, showing the percentages of prison inmates who were Black or White from 1960 to 1991, reveals two trends. First, for as long as prison population data have been compiled, the percentage of inmates who are Black has by several times exceeded the percentage of Americans who are Black (10% to 13% during the relevant period). Second, since 1980 the Black percentage among prisoners has increased sharply.

Racial disproportions among prison inmates are inherently undesirable, and considerable energy has been expended on efforts to understand them. In 1982, Blumstein showed that around 80% of the disproportion could be explained on the basis of racial differences in arrest patterns. Of the unexplained 20%, Blumstein argued, some might represent bias and some might reflect racial differences in criminal history or arguably valid case-processing differences. Some years earlier, Hindelang (1976, 1978) had demonstrated that racial patterns in victims' identifications of their assailants closely resembled racial differences in arrests. Some years later, Langan (1985) skipped over the arrest stage altogether and showed that racial patterns in victims' identifications of their assailants explained about 80% of disparities in prison admissions. In 1990, Klein, Petersilia, and Turner showed that, after criminal history and other legitimate differences between cases were taken into account, the offender's race had no independent predictive effect in California on whether he was sent to prison or for how long. There the matter rests. Blumstein (1993a) updated his analysis and reached similar

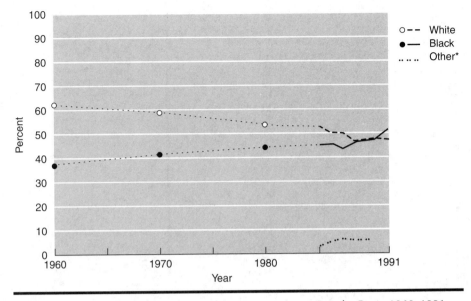

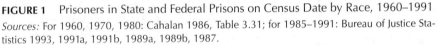

FIGURE 1   Prisoners in State and Federal Prisons on Census Date by Race, 1960–1991

Sources: For 1960, 1970, 1980: Cahalan 1986, Table 3.31; for 1985–1991: Bureau of Justice Statistics 1993, 1991a, 1991b, 1989a, 1989b, 1987.

* = Hispanics in many states, Asians, Native Americans.

conclusions (with one important exception that is discussed below).

Although racial crime patterns explain a large part of racial imprisonment patterns, they do not explain why the Black percentage rose so rapidly after 1980. Table 1 shows Black and White percentages among people arrested for the eight serious FBI Index Crimes at 3-year intervals from 1976 to 1991 and for 1992. Within narrow bands of fluctuation, racial arrest percentages have been stable since 1976. Comparing 1976 with 1992, for example, Black percentages among people arrested for murder, robbery, and burglary were slightly up and Black percentages among those arrested for rape, aggravated assault, and theft were slightly down. Overall, the percentage among those arrested for violent crimes who were Black fell from 47.5% to 44.8%. Because prison sentences have traditionally been imposed on people convicted of violent crimes, Blumstein's and the other analyses suggest that the Black percentage

among inmates should be flat or declining. That, however, is not what Figure 1 shows. Why not?

Part of the answer can be found in prison admissions. Figure 2 shows racial percentages among prison admissions from 1960 to 1992. Arrests of Blacks for violent crimes may not have increased since 1980, but the percentage of Blacks among those sent to prison has increased starkly, reaching 54% in 1991 and 1992. Why? The main explanation concerns the War on Drugs.

Table 2 shows racial percentages among persons arrested for drug crimes between 1976 and 1992. Blacks today make up about 13% of the U.S. population and, according to National Institute on Drug Abuse (1991) surveys of Americans' drug use, are no more likely than Whites ever to have used most drugs of abuse. Nonetheless, the percentages of Blacks among drug arrestees were in the low 20% range in the late 1970s, climbing to around 30% in the early 1980s and peaking at 42% in 1989. The number of drug arrests of

TABLE 1 Percentage Black and White Arrests for Index I Offenses 1976–1991 (3-year intervals)[a]

	1976		1979		1982		1985		1988		1991		1992	
	WHITE	BLACK	WHITE	BLACK	WHITE	BLACK	WHITE	BLACK	WHITE	BLACK	WHITE	BLACK	WHITE	BLACK
Murder and nonnegligent manslaughter	45.0	53.5	49.4	47.7	48.8	49.7	50.1	48.4	45.0	53.5	43.4	54.8	43.5	55.1
Forcible rape	51.2	46.6	50.2	47.7	48.7	49.7	52.2	46.5	52.7	45.8	54.8	43.5	55.5	42.8
Robbery	38.9	59.2	41.0	56.9	38.2	60.7	37.4	61.7	36.3	62.6	37.6	61.1	37.7	60.9
Aggravated assault	56.8	41.0	60.9	37.0	59.8	38.8	58.0	40.4	57.6	40.7	60.0	38.3	59.5	38.8
Burglary	69.0	29.2	69.5	28.7	67.0	31.7	69.7	28.9	67.0	31.3	68.8	29.3	67.8	30.4
Larceny-theft	65.7	32.1	67.2	30.2	64.7	33.4	67.2	30.6	65.6	32.2	66.6	30.9	66.2	31.4
Motor vehicle theft	71.1	26.2	70.0	27.2	66.9	31.4	65.8	32.4	58.7	39.5	58.5	39.3	58.4	39.4
Arson	—	—	78.9	19.2	74.0	24.7	75.7	22.8	73.5	25.0	76.7	21.5	76.4	21.9
Violent crime[b]	50.4	47.5	53.7	44.1	51.9	46.7	51.5	47.1	51.7	46.8	53.6	44.8	53.6	44.8
Property crime[c]	67.0	30.9	68.2	29.4	65.5	32.7	67.7	30.3	65.3	32.6	66.4	31.3	65.8	31.8
Total crime index	64.1	33.8	65.3	32.4	62.7	35.6	64.5	33.7	62.4	35.7	63.2	34.6	62.7	35.2

Sources: Sourcebook of Criminal Justice Statistics. Various years. Washington DC: Department of Justice, Bureau of Justice Statistics; FBI 1993, Table 43.

a. Because of rounding, the percentages may not add to total.

b. Violent crimes are offenses of murder, forcible rape, robbery, and aggravated assault.

c. Property crimes are offenses of burglary, larceny-theft, motor vehicle theft, and arson.

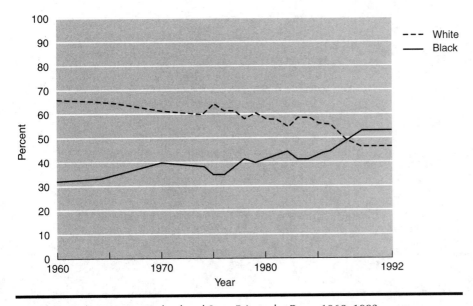

FIGURE 2   Admissions to Federal and State Prisons by Race, 1960–1992

Note: Hispanics are included in Black and White populations.

Sources: Langan 1991; Gilliard 1992; Perkins 1992, 1993; Perkins and Gilliard 1992.

TABLE 2   U.S. Drug Arrests by Race, 1976–1992

YEAR	TOTAL VIOLATIONS	WHITE	WHITE %	BLACK	BLACK %
1976	475,209	366,081	77	103,615	22
1977	565,371	434,471	77	122,594	22
1978	592,168	462,728	78	127,277	21
1979	516,142	396,065	77	112,748	22
1980	531,953	401,979	76	125,607	24
1981	584,776	432,556	74	146,858	25
1982	562,390	400,683	71	156,369	28
1983	615,081	423,151	69	185,601	30
1984	560,729	392,904	70	162,979	29
1985	700,009	482,486	69	210,298	30
1986	688,815	463,457	67	219,159	32
1987	809,157	511,278	63	291,177	36
1988	844,300	503,125	60	334,015	40
1989	1,070,345	613,800	57	452,574	42
1990	860,016	503,315	59	349,965	41
1991	763,340	443,596	58	312,997	41
1992	919,561	546,430	59	364,546	40

Sources: FBI 1993, Table 43; *Sourcebook of Criminal Justice Statistics—1978–1992,* various tables.
Washington, DC: U.S. Department of Justice, Bureau of Justice Statistics.

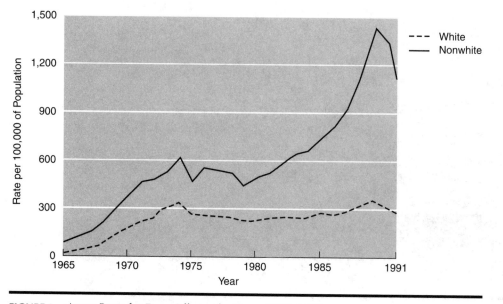

FIGURE 3   Arrest Rates for Drug Offenses by Race, 1965–1991
Source: Blumstein 1993b.

Blacks more than doubled between 1985 and 1989, whereas White drug arrests increased only by 27%. Figure 3 shows the stark differences in drug arrest trends by race from 1976 to 1991.

Drug control policies are a major cause of worsening racial disparities in prison. In the federal prisons, for example, 22% of new admissions and 25% of the resident population were drug offenders in 1980. By 1990, 42% of new admissions were drug offenders as in 1992 were 58% of the resident population. In state prisons, 5.7% of inmates in 1979 were drug offenders, a figure that by 1991 had climbed to 21.3% to become the single largest category of prisoners (robbers, burglars, and murderers were next at 14.8%, 12.4%, and 10.6%, respectively) (Beck et al. 1993).

The effect of drug policies can be seen in prison data from a number of states. Figure 4 shows Black and White prison admissions in North Carolina from 1970 to 1990. White rates held steady; Black rates doubled between 1980 and 1990, rising most rapidly after 1987. Figure 5 shows prison admissions for drug crimes in Virginia from 1983 to 1989; the racial balance flipped from two-thirds White, one-third non-White in 1983 to the reverse in 1989. Similarly, in Pennsylvania, Clark (1992) reports, Black male prison admissions for drug crimes grew four times faster (up 1,613%) between 1980 and 1990 than did White male admissions (up 477%). In California, according to Zimring and Hawkins (1994), the number of males in prison for drug crimes grew 15 fold between 1980 and 1990 and "there were more people in prison in California for drug offences in 1991 than there were for *all* offences in California at the end of 1979" (p. 89; emphasis in original).

Why, if Blacks in their lives are no more likely than Whites to use illicit drugs, are Blacks so much more likely to be arrested and imprisoned? One possible answer, which is almost certainly wrong, is that Blacks are proportionately more likely to sell drugs. We have no representative surveys of drug dealers and so cannot with confidence paint demographic pictures. However, there is little reason to suspect that drug crimes are more interracial than are most other crimes. In addition, the considerations that make arrests of Black dealers relatively easy make arrests of White dealers relatively hard.

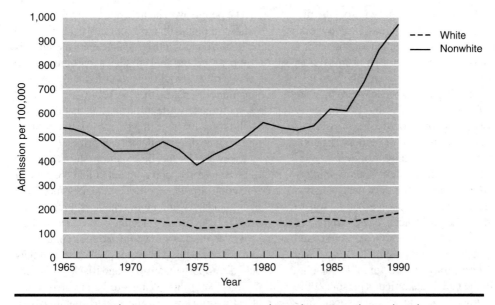

FIGURE 4   Prison Admissions per 100,000 General Population, North Carolina, by Race, 1970–1990
Source: Clarke 1992.

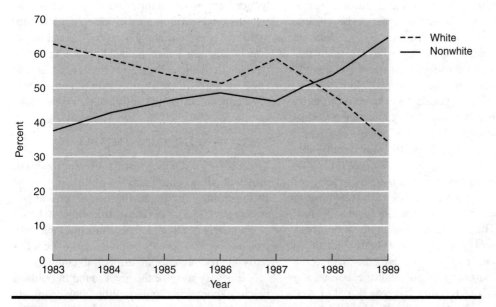

FIGURE 5   Percentage of New Drug Commitments by Race, Virginia, Fiscal Years 1983–1989
Source: Austin and McVey 1989.

Drug arrests are easier to make in socially disorganized inner-city minority areas than in working- or middle-class urban or suburban areas for a number of reasons. First, although drug sales in working- or middle-class areas are likely to take place indoors and in private spaces where they are difficult to observe, drug sales in poor minority areas are likely to take place outdoors in streets, alleys, or abandoned buildings, or indoors in public places like bars. Second, although working- or middle-class drug dealers in stable areas are unlikely to sell drugs to undercover strangers, dealers in disorganized areas have little choice but to sell to strangers and new acquaintances. These differences mean that it is easier for police to make arrests and undercover purchases in urban minority areas than elsewhere. Because arrests are fungible for purposes of both the individual officer's personnel file and the department's year-to-year statistical comparisons, more easy arrests look better than fewer hard ones. And because, as ethnographic studies of drug trafficking make clear (Fagan 1993; Padilla 1992), arrested drug dealers in disadvantaged urban minority communities are generally replaced within days, there is a nearly inexhaustible potential supply of young minority Americans to be arrested.

There is another reason why the War on Drugs worsened racial disparities in the justice system. Penalties for drug crimes were steadily made harsher since the mid-1980s. In particular, purveyors of crack cocaine, a drug used primarily by poor urban Blacks and Hispanics, are punished far more severely than are purveyors of powder cocaine, a pharmacologically indistinguishable drug used primarily by middle-class Whites. The most notorious disparity occurs under federal law which equates 1 gram of crack with 100 grams of powder. As a result, the average prison sentence served by Black federal prisoners is 40% longer than the average sentence for Whites (McDonald and Carlson 1993). Although the Minnesota Supreme Court and two federal district courts have struck down the 100-to-1 rule as a denial of constitutional equal protection to Blacks, at the time of writing, every federal court of appeals that had considered the question had upheld the provision.

The people who launched the drug wars knew all these things—that the enemy troops would mostly be young minority males, that an emphasis on supply-side antidrug strategies, particularly use of mass arrests, would disproportionately ensnare young minority males, that the 100-to-1 rule would disproportionately affect Blacks, and that there was no valid basis for believing that any of these things would reduce drug availability or prices.

Likewise, as the first section showed, there was no basis for a good faith belief that the harsher crime control policies of recent years—more and longer mandatory minimum sentences, tougher and more rigid sentencing guidelines, and three-strikes-and-you're-out laws—would reduce crime rates, and there was a good basis for predicting that they would disproportionately damage Blacks. If Blacks are more likely than Whites to be arrested, especially for drug crimes, the greater harshness of toughened penalties will disproportionately be borne by Blacks. Because much crime is intraracial, concern for Black victims might justify harsher treatment of Black offenders if there were any reason to believe that harsher penalties would reduce crime rates. Unfortunately, as the conservative national governments of Margaret Thatcher and Brian Mulroney and reports of National Academy of Sciences Panels funded by the administrations of Republican Presidents Ford, Reagan, and Bush all agree, there is no reason to believe that harsher penalties significantly reduce crime rates.

JUSTIFYING THE UNJUSTIFIABLE

There is no valid policy justification for the harsh drug and crime control policies of the Reagan and Bush administrations, and for their adverse differential effect on Blacks. The justification, such as it is, is entirely political. Crime is an emotional subject and visceral appeals by politicians to people's fears and resentments are difficult to counter.

It is easy to seize the low ground in political debates about crime policy. When one candidate campaigns with pictures of clanging prison gates and grief-stricken relatives of a rape or murder victim, and with disingenuous promises that newer,

4 Racial Politics, Racial Disparities, and the War on Crime

tougher policies will work, it is difficult for an opponent to explain that crime is a complicated problem, that real solutions must be long term, and that simplistic toughness does not reduce crime rates. This is why, as a result, candidates often compete to establish which is tougher in his views about crime. It is also why less conservative candidates often try to preempt their more conservative opponents by adopting a tough stance early in the campaign. Finally, it is why political pundits congratulate President Clinton on his acumen in proposing federal crime legislation as or more harsh than his opponents. He has, it is commonly said, "taken the crime issue away from the Republicans."

Conservative Republican politicians have, since the late 1960s, used welfare, especially Aid to Families with Dependent Children, and crime as symbolic issues to appeal to anti-Black sentiments and resentments of White voters, as Thomas and Mary Edsall's *Chain Reaction: The Impact of Race, Rights, and Taxes on American Politics* (1991) makes clear. The Edsalls provide a history, since the mid-1960s, of "a conservative politics that had the effect of polarizing the electorate along racial lines." Anyone who observed Ronald Reagan's portrayal in several campaigns of Linda Evans, a Black Chicago woman, as the "welfare queen" or George Bush's use of Black murderer Willie Horton to caricature Michael Dukakis's criminal justice policies knows of what the Edsalls write.

The story of Willie Horton is the better known and makes the Edsalls' point. Horton, who in 1975 had been convicted of the murder of a 17-year-old boy, failed to return from a June 12, 1986, furlough. The following April, he broke into a home in Oxon Hill, Maryland, where he raped a woman and stabbed her companion.

Lee Atwater, Bush's campaign strategist, after testing the visceral effects of Willie Horton's picture and story on participants in focus groups, decided a year later to make Horton a wedge issue for Republicans. Atwood reportedly told a group of Republican activists that Bush would win the presidency "if I can make Willie Horton a household name." He later told a Republican gathering in Atlanta, "there's a story about a fellow named Willie Horton who, for all I know, may end up being Dukakis's running mate." Atwood for a time denied making both remarks but in 1991, dying of cancer, recanted: "In 1988, fighting Dukakis, I said that I would . . . make Willie Horton his running mate. I am sorry."

The sad reality is that tragedies like the crimes of Willie Horton are inevitable. So are airplane crashes, 40,000 to 50,000 traffic fatalities per year, and defense department cost overruns. Every person convicted of a violent crime cannot be held forever. Furloughs are used in most corrections systems as a way to ease offenders back into the community and to test their suitability for eventual release on parole or commutation. Horton had successfully completed nine previous furloughs, from each of which he had returned without incident, under a program established in 1972 not by Michael Dukakis but by Governor Francis Sargent, a Republican.

Public discourse about criminal justice issues has been debased by the cynicism that made Willie Horton a major participant in the 1988 presidential election. That cynicism has made it difficult to discuss or develop sensible public policies, and that cynicism explains why conservative politicians have been able year after year successfully to propose ever harsher penalties and crime control and drug policies that no informed person believes can achieve their ostensible goals.

Three final points, arguments that apologists for current policies sometimes make, warrant mention. First, it is sometimes said to be unfair to blame national Republican administrations for the failures and disparate impacts of . . . crime control policies. This ignores the efforts of the Reagan and Bush administrations to encourage and, through federal mandates and funding restrictions, to coerce states to follow the federal lead. Attorney General William Barr (e.g., 1992) made the most aggressive efforts to compel state adoption of tougher criminal justice policies, and the Bush administration's final proposed crime bills restricted eligibility for federal funds to states that, like the federal government, abolished parole release and adopted sentencing standards no less severe than those in the federal sentencing guidelines. In any case, as the Edsalls' book makes clear, the use of crime control issues (among others including welfare reform and affirmative action) to elicit anti-Black sentiments from White voters has long been a stratagem of both state and federal Republican politicians.

Second, sometimes it is argued that political leaders have merely followed the public will; voters are outraged by crime and want tougher policies (DiIulio 1991). This is a half-truth that gets the causal order backwards. Various measures of public sentiment, including both representative surveys like Gallup and Harris polls and work with focus groups, have for many years consistently shown that the public is of two minds about crime (Roberts 1992). First, people are frustrated and want offenders to be punished. Second, people believe that social adversity, poverty, and a troubled home life are the principal causes of crime, and they believe government should work to rehabilitate offenders. A number of surveys have found that respondents who would oppose a tax increase to pay for more prisons would support a tax increase to pay for rehabilitative programs. These findings of voter ambivalence about crime should not be surprising. Most people have complicated views about complicated problems. For example, most judges and corrections officials have the same ambivalent feelings about offenders that the general public has. Conservative politicians have seized upon public support of punishment and ignored public support of rehabilitation and public recognition that crime presents complex, not easy, challenges. By presenting crime control issues only in emotional, stereotyped ways, conservative politicians have raised its salience as a political issue but made it impossible for their opponents to respond other than in the same stereotyped ways.

Third, sometimes it is argued that disparate impacts on Black offenders are no problem and that, because much crime is intraracial, failure to adopt tough policies would disserve the interests of Black victims. As former Attorney General Barr (1992) put it, perhaps in ill-chosen words,

"the benefits of increased incarceration would be enjoyed disproportionately by Black Americans" (p. 17). This argument also is based on a half-truth. No one wants to live in unsafe neighborhoods or to be victimized by crime, and in a crisis, people who need help will seek it from the police, the public agency of last resort. Requesting help in a crisis and supporting harsh policies with racially disparate effects are not the same thing. The relevant distinction is between acute and chronic problems. A substantial body of public opinion research (e.g., National Opinion Research Center surveys conducted throughout the 1980s summarized in Wood 1990) shows that Blacks far more than Whites support establishment of more generous social welfare policies, full employment programs, and increased social spending. The congressional Black and Hispanic caucuses have consistently opposed bills calling for tougher sanctions and supported bills calling for increased spending on social programs aimed at improving conditions that cause crime. Thus, in claiming to be concerned about Black victims, conservative politicians are responding to natural human calls for help in a crisis while ignoring evidence that Black citizens would rather have government support efforts to ameliorate the chronic social conditions that cause crime and thereby make calls for help in a crisis less necessary.

The evidence on the effectiveness of recent crime control and drug abuse policies, as the first section demonstrated cannot justify their racially disparate effects on Blacks, nor, as this section demonstrates, can the claims that such policies merely manifest the peoples' will or respect the interests of Black victims. All that is left is politics of the ugliest kind. The War on Drugs and the set of harsh crime control policies in which it was enmeshed were adopted to achieve political, not policy, objectives, and it is the adoption for political purposes of policies with foreseeable disparate impacts, the use of disadvantaged Black Americans as means to the achievement of White politicians' electoral ends, that must in the end be justified. It cannot.

REFERENCES

Anglin, M. Douglas and Yih-Ing Hser. 1990. "Treatment of Drug Abuse." In *Drugs and Crime,* edited by M. Tonry and J. Q. Wilson. Chicago: University of Chicago Press.

Austin, James and Aaron David McVey. 1989. *The Impact of the War on Drugs.* San Francisco: National Council on Crime and Delinquency.

Barr, William P. 1992. "The Case for More Incarceration." Washington, DC: U.S. Department of Justice, Office of Policy Development.

Beck, Allen et al. 1993. *Survey of State Prison Inmates, 1991.* Washington, DC: Bureau of Justice Statistics.

Blumstein, Alfred. 1982. "On the Racial Disproportionality of United States' Prison Populations." *Journal of Criminal Law and Criminology* 73:1259–81.

———. 1993a. "Racial Disproportionality of U.S. Prison Populations Revisited." *University of Colorado Law Review* 64:743–60.

———. 1993b. "Making Rationality Relevant—The American Society of Criminology 1992 Presidential Address." *Criminology* 31:1–16.

Blumstein, Alfred, Jacqueline Cohen, and Daniel Nagin. 1978. *Deterrence and Incapacitation.* Report of the National Academy of Sciences Panel on Research on Deterrent and Incapacitative Effects. Washington, DC: National Academy Press.

Botvin, Gilbert J. 1990. "Substance Abuse Prevention: Theory, Practice, and Effectiveness." In *Drugs and Crime,* edited by M. Tonry and J. Q. Wilson. Chicago: University of Chicago Press.

Bureau of Justice Statistics. 1987. *Correctional Populations in the United States, 1985.* Washington, DC: U.S. Department of Justice, Bureau of Justice Statistics.

———. 1989a. *Correctional Populations in the United States, 1987.* Washington, DC: U.S. Department of Justice, Bureau of Justice Statistics.

———. 1989b. *Correctional Populations in the United States, 1986.* Washington, DC: U.S. Department of Justice, Bureau of Justice Statistics.

———. 1991a. *Correctional Populations in the United States, 1989.* Washington, DC: U.S. Department of Justice, Bureau of Justice Statistics.

———. 1991b. *Correctional Populations in the United States, 1988.* Washington, DC: U.S. Department of Justice, Bureau of Justice Statistics.

———. 1993. *Correctional Populations in the United States. 1991.* Washington, DC: U.S. Department of Justice, Bureau of Justice Statistics.

Cahalan, Margaret Werner. 1986. *Historical Corrections Statistics in the United States. 1850–1984.* Washington, DC: U.S. Department of Justice, Bureau of Justice Statistics.

Canadian Sentencing Commission. 1987. *Sentencing Reform: A Canadian Approach.* Ottawa: Canadian Government Publishing Centre.

Chaiken, Marcia, ed. 1988. *Street Level Enforcement: Examining the Issues.* Washington, DC: U.S. Government Printing Office.

Clark, Stover. 1992. "Pennsylvania Corrections in Context." *Overcrowded Times* 3:4–5.

Clarke, Stevens H. 1992. "North Carolina Prisons Growing." *Overcrowded Times* 3:1, 11–13.

DiIulio, John J. 1991. *No Escape: The Future of American Corrections.* New York: Basic Books.

Edsall, Thomas and Mary Edsall. 1991. *Chain Reaction: The Impact of Race, Rights, and Taxes on American Politics.* New York: Norton.

Ellickson, Phyllis L. and Robert M. Bell. 1990. *Prospects for Preventing Drug Use Among Young Adolescents.* Santa Monica, CA: RAND.

Fagan, Jeffrey. 1993. "The Political Economy of Drug Dealing Among Urban Gangs." In *Drugs and the Community,* edited by R. C. Davis, A. J. Lurigio, and D. P. Rosenbaum. Springfield, IL: Charles C Thomas.

Federal Bureau of Investigation. 1993. *Uniform Crime Reports for the United States—1992.* Washington, DC: U.S. Government Printing Office.

Gerstein, Dean R. and Henrik J. Jarwood, eds. 1990. *Treating Drug Problems.* Report of the Committee for Substance Abuse Coverage Study, Division of Health Care Services, National Institute of Medicine. Washington, DC: National Academy Press.

Gilliard, Darrell K. 1992. *National Corrections Reporting Program, 1987.* Washington, DC: U.S. Department of Justice, Bureau of Justice Statistics.

Hindelang, Michael. 1976. *Criminal Victimization in Eight American Cities: A Descriptive Analysis of Common Theft and Assault.* Washington, DC: Law Enforcement Assistance Administration.

———. 1978. "Race and Involvement in Common Law Personal Crimes." *American Sociological Review* 43:93–108.

Home Office. 1990. *Protecting the Public.* London: H. M. Stationery Office.

Klein, Stephen, Joan Petersilia, and Susan Turner. 1990. "Race and Imprisonment Decisions in California." *Science* 247:812–16.

Langan, Patrick A. 1985. "Racism on Trial: New Evidence to Explain the Racial Composition of Prisons in the United States." *Journal of Criminal Law and Criminology* 76:666–83.

———. 1991. *Race of Persons Admitted to State and Federal Institutions, 1926–86.* Washington, DC: U.S. Department of Justice, Bureau of Justice Statistics.

McDonald, Douglas and Ken Carlson. 1993. *Sentencing in the Federal Courts: Does Race Matter?* Washington, DC: U.S. Department of Justice, Bureau of Justice Statistics.

Moore, Mark H. 1990. "Supply Reduction and Drug Law Enforcement." In *Drugs and Crime,* edited by M. Tonry and J. Q. Wilson. Chicago: University of Chicago Press.

Moynihan, Daniel Patrick. 1993. "Iatrogenic Government—Social Policy and Drug Research." *American Scholar* 62:351–62.

National Institute on Drug Abuse. 1991. *National Household Survey on Drug Abuse: Population Estimates 1990.* Washington, DC: U.S. Government Printing Office.

Office of National Drug Control Policy. 1990. *National Drug Control Strategy—January 1990.* Washington, DC: Author.

Padilla, Felix. 1992. *The Gang as an American Enterprise.* New Brunswick, NJ: Rutgers University Press.

Perkins, Craig. 1992. *National Corrections Reporting Program, 1989.* Washington, DC: U.S. Department of Justice, Bureau of Justice Statistics.

———. 1993. *National Corrections Reporting Program, 1990.* Washington, DC: U.S. Department of Justice, Bureau of Justice Statistics.

Perkins, Craig and Darrell K. Gilliard. 1992. *National Corrections Reporting Program, 1988.* Washington, DC: U.S. Department of Justice, Bureau of Justice Statistics.

President's Commission on Law Enforcement and Administration of Justice. 1967. *The Challenge of Crime in a Free Society.* Washington, DC: U.S. Government Printing Office.

President's Commission on Model State Drug Laws. 1993. *Final Report.* Washington, DC: U.S. Government Printing Office.

Reiss, Albert J., Jr. and Jeffrey Roth. 1993. *Understanding and Controlling Violence. Report of the National Academy of Sciences Panel on the Understanding and Control of Violence.* Washington, DC: National Academy Press.

Reuter, Peter. 1988. "Can the Borders Be Sealed?" *Public Interest* 92:51–65.

Roberts, Julian V. 1992. "Public Opinion, Crime, and Criminal Justice." In *Crime and Justice: A Review of Research,* vol. 16, edited by M. Tonry. Chicago: University of Chicago Press.

Sourcebook of Criminal Justice Statistics. 1978–1992. Washington, DC: Department of Justice, Bureau of Justice Statistics.

Standing Committee on Justice and the Solicitor General. 1993. *Crime Prevention in Canada: Toward a National Strategy.* Ottawa: Canada Communication Group.

Sviridoff, Michele, Susan Sadd, Richard Curtis, and Randolph Grinc. 1992. *The Neighborhood Effects of Street-Level Drug Enforcement.* New York: Vera Institute of Justice.

Tonry, Michael. 1994. *Malign Neglect: Race, Crime, and Punishment in America.* New York: Oxford University Press.

U.S General Accounting Office. 1990. *Drug Abuse: Research on Treatment May Not Address Current Needs.* Washington, DC: U.S. General Accounting Office.

Wilson, James Q. 1990. "Drugs and Crime," In *Drugs and Crime,* edited by M. Tonry and J. Q. Wilson. Chicago: University of Chicago Press.

Wood, Floris W. 1990. *An American Profile: Opinions and Behavior, 1972–1989.* New York: Gale Research.

Zimring, Franklin E. and Gordon Hawkins. 1994. "The Growth of Imprisonment in California." *British Journal of Criminology* 34:83–95.

Latinos and Lethal Violence
The Impact of Poverty and Inequality

RAMIRO MARTINEZ, JR.
The University of Delaware

Research on homicide proliferated during the 1980s. Despite this growth of knowledge, sociologists lack an understanding of both the patterns and causes of Latino homicide. The present study addresses this shortcoming by examining socioeconomic and sociodemographic predictors of Latino murders in 111 U.S. cities during 1980. Regression analysis supports an economic inequality interpretation of violence. Latinos' socioeconomic conditions were consistently linked to homicide, but sociodemographics also influenced murder. The conclusions stress the need for addressing the link between socioeconomic conditions and urban Latino homicide, paying special attention to educational attainment and economic inequality within the Latino population.

The link between economic conditions and homicide has long been a source of controversy among sociologists (see Bonger 1916; Parker 1995). One traditional view holds that increased poverty generates high rates of homicide because deprivation may encourage hostilities that escalate into violence (Bailey 1984; Parker 1989). Others disagree, contending that greater economic inequality is the mechanism whereby conflict and hostilities are reflected in criminal violence (Blau and Blau 1982; Harer and Steffensmeier 1992).

The case of Latinos[1] in the United States provides an opportunity to re-examine the debate. According to researchers on the Latino population, economic conditions rapidly worsened between 1970 and 1980 (Santiago and Wilder 1991). During this period, levels of Latino poverty increased in most metropolitan areas, and more than one-fifth of all Latino families lived below the poverty level (Santiago and Wilder 1991:511). While the highest levels of poverty were concentrated in the Northeast and Midwest—regions hit hard by deindustrialization—many urban areas in the Southwest also experienced high rates of poverty. Though some scholars contend that the economic status of Latinos is improving, Latino families feature prominently among the working poor (Bean and Tienda 1987). As but one example, Latino family income is 25 percent less than that of their Anglo counterparts. Though this difference could be due in part to a number of family characteristics (e.g., family size, levels of education, years of work experience, recency of immigration, etc.), little doubt remains, however, that Latinos are economically disadvantaged when compared to Anglos (Santiago and Wilder 1991).

While this body of research describes the socioeconomic conditions of Latinos, little attention has been paid to its link with violent crime, especially homicide. Thus, Latinos provide a particularly good case for investigating *how* social and economic factors impact homicide. The present study extends our understanding of both the patterns and causes of Latino homicide in the United States. This is accomplished by examining the impact of poverty and economic inequality on Latino homicide victims across 111 U.S. cities. A cross-sectional approach is used because longitudinal data are not presently fully available for Latinos in the United States.

THEORETICAL BACKGROUND

Inequitable distribution of economic resources is often thought to encourage high homicide rates in general and high homicide rates among minority groups in the United States in particular (Shihadeh and Steffensmeier 1994). Central to this long-standing subject of inquiry is debate on the impact of poverty versus economic inequality. For example, poverty is at the center of the work on absolute deprivation in the United States (Parker 1989). Low income and educational attainment correspond to higher rates of homicide, especially among minority group members, those most affected by social and economic deprivation (Bailey 1984; Sampson 1987). Parker (1989:986) notes:

> . . . *violence is one of the few options available to those without the economic means to deal with problems and crises of everyday life. Absolute deprivation may also produce emotional situations which escalate into violence . . . simply put, the absolute deprivation approach suggests that violence can occur among such individuals because everyday life is difficult.*

Others also link various measures of socioeconomic deprivation to high rates of homicides (Bailey 1984).

Still other researchers suggest economic inequality undermines the social status and economic resources of certain groups within the United States, especially minority groups (Blau and Blau 1982; Shihadeh and Steffensmeier 1994). Minority groups deprived of economic opportunity are part of a social structure with low education, poor wages, impoverished conditions, and a diminished professional occupation rate, relative to the dominant group (Anderson 1990). Central to this thesis is that feelings of alienation and frustration are particularly high in the disadvantaged minority group. One suggested response to social and economic deprivation is increased aggression, including high levels of homicide (see Blau and Blau 1982). According to this perspective, economic and racial inequality are viewed as the primary influence on criminal violence in urban areas. High homicide rates correspond to the economic advantage of one racial group over another racial group (Blau and Blau 1982; Land, McCall, and Cohen 1990).

Some researchers contend that the connection between inequality and violent crime is far from clear (Harer and Steffensmeier 1992; Shihadeh and Steffensmeier 1994). Shihadeh and Steffensmeier (1994) propose that a within-group measure of inequality is more consistent with relative deprivation theory, since feelings of deprivation emanate out of comparisons relative to fellow group members when seeking a referent for socioeconomic standings (see Merton 1957; Harer and Steffensmeier 1992). This approach, building on reference group theory, recognizes that within-group inequality is likely a better predictor of violence than either between-group or absolute measures because group members look internally for standards of comparison (see also Merton and Rossi 1968). Harer and Steffensmeier note:

> *People assess how well, or badly, they are faring economically not by comparing themselves with the population as a whole, but with particular reference groups with whom they share some status attribute (1992:1036) including education, occupation, age, sex, and race.*

Such is the case for Latinos. Research on youths and gangs demonstrates how Latinos use friends, family, and others in the Latino community as reference points (Horowitz 1983; Moore 1991). Linked to this notion, Moore (1991) notes many young adult gang men refer to other Latinos, including recent immigrants, as standards in economic and occupation comparisons. Youth gang members acknowledge others close by as referents for feelings about themselves, with few comparisons to the Anglo or Black communities (Horowitz 1983). Even research on labor markets shows that Latino workers, disproportionately represented in the secondary labor market, are likely to take other Latino workers close by as their reference point, not Anglos in the primary labor market force (Saenz and Anderson 1994). Therefore, it appears Latinos look within their community for standards of social and economic comparisons.

THE LATINO CONTEXT

Research on the Latino population has only recently emerged. During the 1970s increased demographic trends coupled with pronounced regional concentration heightened awareness of Latinos as a separate and distinct ethnic group in the United States (Bean and Tienda 1987). Rapid growth in population size alerted social scientists to an emerging group and fueled research on the Latino population (Bean and Tienda 1987). Taking advantage of Census Bureau data, scholars identified and examined the Latino population as never before. We now know more about the educational attainment, employment status, and household characteristics of the Latino population (Bean and Tienda 1987).

Unfortunately, owing to a number of difficulties in categorizing Latinos and perhaps biases against recognizing them as a distinct group, answers to seemingly straightforward questions about the incidence of violent crime among Latinos continue to elude researchers (Flowers 1990; Zahn 1987). Though homicide is reported to be the second and third leading cause of death among Mexican and Cuban Latinos respectively (Mercy

1987), little is known about the rate of homicide, our most serious crime, among the Latino population. Few studies examine the extent and causes of Latino killings, even in areas where large numbers of Latinos reside and are clearly identified (Flowers 1990).

The lack of knowledge is the result of the sparse research on Latinos and violence (Zahn 1987). A handful of studies provides comparisons of Black, white, and Latino homicides in specific cities (Beasley and Antunes 1974; Block 1985, 1993; Pokorny 1965). Others focus on Latino homicides in a purely descriptive manner in a single city (Laredo), state (Texas), region (the Southwest), or island (Puerto Rico) and ignore the correlates of Latino killings (see Mercy 1987; Rodriguez 1990; Valdez 1993; Wallace 1964).

Recent homicide research acknowledges the influence of Latinos but such studies are few in number and limited in scope (see Nelsen, Corzine, and Huff-Corzine 1994; Parker and Toth 1990). Though Nelsen and colleagues and Parker and Toth acknowledge the impact of Latinos on homicide in the United States, they restrict themselves to incorporating percent Latino population as one of many control variables shaping overall homicide, and do not directly examine Latino killings. Only Santiago (1986) probed the socioeconomic and sociodemographic factors shaping Latino murder but focused exclusively on the island of Puerto Rico.

Despite these limitations, some have attempted to place research on Latino violence within the general homicide literature (Zahn 1987). In a 1978 nine-cities sample, Zahn discovered the rate of Latino killings fell between Black and white homicide rates. Equally important is Zahn's speculation on the theoretical merits of using relative and absolute deprivation approaches to explain Latino homicide. After examining the socioeconomic characteristics of the Latino population, Zahn stresses absolute poverty does not affect Latino killings and suggests that future researchers pay closer attention to relative deprivation explanations of homicide. Unfortunately she did not directly test the impact of absolute and/or relative deprivation on Latino violence. Researchers have not yet investigated the social and economic determinants of Latino homicide across the United States.

The present research addresses these limitations by investigating the extent of Latino killings and the effect of several social and economic dimensions, especially poverty and economic inequality, on homicide. In particular, I examine the rate of killings and the socioeconomic determinants of Latino murder.

DATA COLLECTION

Data on the 1980 Latino homicide rate were gathered for 111 cities with at least 5,000 Latinos and one reported Latino homicide.[2] These data are drawn from Supplemental Homicide Report (SHR) information. Police agencies provide supplementary information on homicides, including details on victim and offender characteristics. The exact reporting procedures followed by individual agencies in submitting reports vary, depending on how each state processes Uniform Crime Report (UCR) data. In general, agencies submit monthly reports to either their state UCR coordinating agency or directly to the Federal Bureau of Investigation. Though some researchers contend that official police data portray an inaccurate image of crime in the United States, most acknowledge that homicide is the most reliably recorded index crime (Sampson 1987).[3]

A major advantage of the SHR is the detailed city-level information on each reported homicide. The SHR, for the first time in 1980, provided a separate ethnicity category (Hispanic, non-Hispanic, or unknown ethnicity), allowing a distinction by ethnic group in addition to traditional racial categories (white, Black, and Asian). To calculate homicide rates I use victim-level data rather than offender rates, since information on assailant ethnicity is missing for many cases.[4] While it would be desirable to examine Latino subgroups, e.g., Mexican, Puerto Rican, Cuban, and other Latino extractions, homicide data are not available for specific Latino groups, at least not from government statistics.[5]

Data for city characteristics were gathered from the 1980 U.S. Census[6] and merged with the SHR data. Cities are used as units of analyses because they are commonly used in aggregated and disaggregated analyses of homicide. In addition, detailed Latino-specific factors such as income, education, and others are available from published census reports at the city level permitting examination of Latinos across social units. Finally, cities may be considered homogeneous social units compared to SMSAs or states, since the latter encompass areas ranging from sparsely populated rural areas to densely populated cities (see Bailey 1984).

EMPIRICAL MODEL

The model utilized in this study examines measures of social and economic conditions used in previous research (Blau and Blau 1982; Harer and Steffensmeier 1992; Parker 1995; Peterson and Krivo 1993; Shihadeh and Steffensmeier 1994). Although researchers do not agree on what specific variables should be included, the model is essentially that of Peterson and Krivo (1993). Specifically, I use a modified version in which Peterson and Krivo's residential segregation measure is replaced by the immigration index proposed in this article.[7] The present research, also, appropriately employs Latino-specific measures of socioeconomic conditions rather than global indicators of structural conditions. This strategy is important because few scholars have combined group-specific measures of crime with theoretically guided group-specific measures of social and economic conditions (see Shihadeh and Steffensmeier 1994).

This research focuses on the impact of Latino poverty and economic inequality on homicide. Latino homicide rates are expected to change in relation to shifts in the poverty level. Cities with high rates of Latino poverty are hypothesized to also experience increased homicide.

Two measures of economic inequality, based on the distribution of family income, are used in the following analysis. Anglo-Latino income inequality is defined as the ratio of Anglo to Latino median family income. The income ratio allows us to control for differences across cities in average income, providing a measure of economic inequality in dollar figures between Latinos and Anglos. As the gap between Anglo and Latino income increases, the number of killings would be expected to increase. Second, Latino income inequality, as determined by the Gini coefficient, uses other Latinos as the reference point. This variable measures the extent to which Latino median family incomes are dispersed in each city relative to the average Latino income in that city. This objective measure of income inequality provides a relative interpretation with larger values indicating greater income distribution within our sample of Latinos. Thus, the former inequality income ratio compares Latinos relative to Anglos, and the latter controls for the range of income within the Latino population.

Other Latino economic conditions also are expected to impact homicide rates. Areas with low high school graduation levels would be associated with higher rates of homicide victims. In general, education is included to examine further the range of economic conditions within the Latino population, and it helps extend dimensions of Latino socioeconomic status.

A set of control variables are introduced to address the issue of demographic composition within the Latino population as well as circumstances unique to the Latino community. Percent Latino is included to account for the variation in size of the Latino population in each city. The percent Latino males age 15–24 is used to control for the high-crime prone population. The divorced population is included as a proxy for social disorganization. City population size is included because increases in size of the population increase opportunities for victimization. All four control variables are expected to positively influence the rate of Latino killings.

Two variables were also introduced to capture the unique demographic characteristics of the Latino population. A regional variable (Southwest) was included to distinguish cities in areas formerly belonging to Mexico and located in the southwestern United States. The southwest region

is defined as cities in Arizona, California, Colorado, New Mexico, and Texas, an area historically and numerically of Mexican origin. The main consideration is that Latinos, at least in this study, reside primarily in the Southwest and could differ demographically and/or economically from Latinos in other parts of the United States (Nelsen, Corzine, and Huff-Corzine 1994). A second demographic variable was included, as proxy, to account for the impact of Latino immigration on U.S. cities. The immigration index incorporates both percent foreign-born Latinos and proportion of the Latino community residing abroad (in 1975), including Puerto Rico. The rationale is that recent immigration could contribute to the homicide rate in varying ways across the United States. Cities with large influxes of recent Latino immigrants could be more likely to experience growing rates of killings than areas with an older and stable Latino population. In addition, the most recent Latino immigrants, presumably, have a lower socioeconomic status than U.S.-born Latinos.[8] Data for all independent variables were collected from the 1980 U.S. Bureau of the Census Reports.

OPERATIONAL DEFINITIONS OF VARIABLES

The Latino homicide rate was estimated as the number of reported Latino homicide victims per 100,000 Latinos in each city. This dependent variable presents for the first time a Latino-specific homicide rate across a large number of U.S. cities.

Poverty is measured as the percentage of Latino families living below the federal poverty levels. Economic inequality, as measured by income, was estimated in two measures: Anglo to Latino income is a measure of family income differences of Anglos and Latinos; within-group inequality, Latino to Latino, is defined in terms of the inequality (Gini coefficient) of income among Latino families.

A final indicator of Latinos' varying economic conditions is used: Education, operationalized as the percent of Latino high school graduates, examines the effect of educational attainment.[9] Four control variables were also employed: percent

Latinos in each city, percent Latino males age 15–24 years, percent divorced, and city population size (logged). Percent Latino accounts for the size of the Latino population in each city. Percent young Latinos controls for the population at greatest risk of being victimized. The proportion of divorced Latinos in each city is also a commonly used indicator of social disorganization. Population is defined as the population size (logged) in each city. Region was operationalized as a dummy variable coded "1" for cities in the Southwest and "0" for cities in other regions of the United States. Immigration is a z-score index capturing Latinos who are foreign-born or previously resided in Puerto Rico.

Ordinary least squares regression technique (OLS) is employed as the primary analytical tool and to diagnose collinearity among the explanatory variables (see Appendix).[10] Multicollinearity did not emerge as a serious problem in probing Latino homicide. At the bivariate level there was one instance of high correlation (> .60) when Anglo to Latino economic inequality overlapped with Latino poverty (r = .73). Therefore, Latino homicide was regressed separately on all variables except poverty and again on all variables except Anglo-to-Latino inequality. The results were similar to those in which both poverty and Anglo/Latino inequality are simultaneously entered. An additional test was conducted to test for multicollinearity. Specifically, I regressed each independent variable on all other independent variables. A high degree of collinearity exists if the R^2 is close to 1.0; however, none approached that threshold, thwarting the concern of serious collinearity. Residual plots and partial regression plots were also examined. Three outliers initially appeared (Houston, Miami and San Antonio). Equations were re-estimated eliminating one of the outliers for each equation. Afterwards, all outliers were deleted. The results were virtually identical. Thus, the regression results that follow are not distorted due to problems of multicollinearity.[11]

Yet another step was taken to address possible data concerns. These data are likely to be heteroscedastic—unequal variances because of the wide variation in rates of Latino homicide. Weighted least squares (WLS) regression corrects for this possibility and yields better estimates with the smallest sampling variance. A two-step weighting procedure provides the efficient estimates presented in the following analysis (see Greene 1993).

FINDINGS

This section begins by briefly highlighting the range of urban Latino homicide. Then, Latino killings are probed by directing initial attention to descriptive analysis. Finally, the full power of the data is harnessed by modeling Latino killings using OLS and WLS regression.

Since one goal of this research is to examine the rate of Latino killings, Table 1 illustrates the clear and dramatic range of urban Latino homicides across the United States. Supplemental Homicide Reports show that for 1980 Latino homicide-victim rates ranged from highs in Dallas (67.87) and Houston (64.13) to lows in Tampa (2.80) and San Francisco (1.19), with an average of 18 Latino killings per 100,000 Latinos in cities such as St. Louis and San Angelo. These initial findings confirm that understanding Latino homicides requires a closer look at the variation within the murder rate. The question is whether and how the range of Latino killings is linked to poverty and inequality.

The descriptive statistics are presented in Table 2. Most notable across the 111 U.S. cities is the high level of poverty and economic equality. Beginning with the three variables of primary interest, note that urban Latinos in this sample have a substantial rate of poverty (almost 19 percent) and a family income far less than Anglos. On average, Anglos earns $1.39 to every Latino dollar. Latino communities also exhibit strong variability within family income as measured by the Gini coefficient. For Latino inequality, the average income difference among urban Latino families is around two-thirds of the average Latino income. Economic inequality (as measured by income) exists not only relative to Anglos, but within the Latino population as well.

Table 2 further reveals the magnitude of Latino economic conditions. For example, less than half of the Latino population graduated from high school (45 percent). This feature stresses the

TABLE 1 Urban Latino Homicide Rates, 1980 (N = 111 Cities)

AVERAGE LATINO HOMICIDE RATE = 18.407			
Dallas, TX	67.866	Lakewood, CO	15.097
Houston, TX	64.128	McAllen, TX	14.769
Compton, CA	52.442	Worcester, MA	14.373
Hollywood, FL	47.370	San Mateo, CA	13.938
Fort Worth, TX	45.297	Aurora, IL	13.822
Galveston, TX	44.583	Pasadena, CA	13.768
San Bernardino, CA	43.596	Montebello, CA	12.781
Miami, FL	43.260	Ontario, CA	12.451
Chicago, IL	42.309	Irving, TX	12.335
Odessa, TX	38.310	San Diego, CA	12.314
Oceanside, CA	35.653	Whittier, CA	12.296
New York City, NY	35.388	Pico Rivera, CA	12.284
Long Beach, CA	35.697	Costa Mesa, CA	11.799
Lubbock, TX	33.673	San Jose, CA	11.404
Fresno, CA	33.157	Tempe, AZ	11.390
Miami Beach, FL	32.832	Arlington, VA	11.298
Bakersfield, CA	31.341	District of Columbia	11.190
Elgin, IL	30.734	Santa Ana, CA	11.031
Philadelphia, PA	29.617	Providence, RI	10.995
Wichita Falls, TX	27.153	Riverside, CA	10.905
Austin, TX	27.716	El Paso, TX	10.902
Stockton, CA	27.153	Waukegan, IL	10.789
Waco, TX	26.860	Escondido,CA	10.684
Midland, TX	26.826	Wichita, KS	10.231
Corpus Christi, TX	26.795	Laredo, TX	9.405
San Antonia, TX	25.367	Lorain, OH	9.208
Kansas City, KS	25.338	Torrance, CA	9.166
Denver, CO	24.906	Modesto, CA	8.935
Greeley, CO	24.213	Santa Monica, CA	8.717
Phoenix, AZ	23.129	Hialeah, FL	8.341
Albuquerque, NM	22.305	Oxnard, CA	8.338
Ventura, CA	22.297	El Monte, CA	8.213
Amarillo, TX	21.717	Glendale, AZ	8.025
Los Angeles, CA	21.097	Anaheim, CA	7.981
Tucson, AZ	20.684	Las Vegas, NV	7.785
Salinas, CA	19.625	Seattle, WA	7.778
Reno, NV	19.461	Sacramento, CA	7.711
Boston, MA	19.429	Huntington Beach, CA	7.445
Lawrence, MA	19.422	Springfield, MA	7.214
Alameda, CA	19.223	Harford, CT	7.153
Topeka, KS	18.860	Pomona, CA	7.066
Toledo, OH	18.799	Kansas City, MO	6.762
W. Palm Beach, FL	18.681	Santa Barbara, CA	6.067
St. Louis, MO	18.392	Garden Grove, CA	6.046
San Angelo, TX	17.799	Norwalk, CA	5.846
Victoria, TX	17.582	Inglewood, CA	5.604
Detroit, MI	17.313	Fremont, CA	5.445
Hawthorne, CA	16.988	Pasadena, TX	5.221
Cleveland, OH	16.865	Southgate, CA	5.135
Norfolk, VA	16.285	Monterey Park, CA	4.769
Ft. Lauderdale, FL	15.951	Alhambra, CA	4.116
Carson City, CA	15.779	Milwaukee, WI	3.834
Brownsville, TX	15.446	Oakland, CA	3.112
Arlington, TX	15.340	Tampa, FL	2.795
Chula Vista, CA	15.328	San Francisco, CA	1.188
Joliet, IL	15.271		

TABLE 2   Correlates of Latino Homicide: Descriptions, Means, and Standard Deviations

VARIABLE	DESCRIPTION	MEAN	STANDARD DEVIATION
Poverty	Percent of Latino families below the poverty line	18.980	9.541
Anglo-Latino income inequality	Ratio of Anglo to Latino median family income	1.387	.314
Latino income inequality	Gini index of family income inequality among Latinos	.377	.556
Education	Percent of Latino population older than 24 that graduated high school	45.453	12.216
Percent Latino	Percent of the total city population that is Latino	20.732	18.994
Percent Latino males, aged 15–24	Percent of Latino males aged 15 to 24	11.750	2.310
Percent Divorced	Percent of the Latino population older than 15 that is currently divorced or separated	6.948	1.819
Population (log)	Natural log of the total city population	5.230	.433
Region	Southwest = 1, Other = 0	.676	.470
Immigration	Index of foreign-born Latinos and Latinos living abroad in 1975	.022	1.820

educational hardship experienced by Latinos in U.S. cities.

Table 3 provides the OLS and WLS estimates for the model probing Latino homicides. I provide the OLS results for comparison but focus attention on the WLS findings.

The WLS results show that absolute deprivation, as measured by poverty, is related to Latino homicide. However, contrary to expectations, a larger poverty rate is associated with a lower homicide rate. This finding directly contradicts the absolute deprivation interpretation that suggests a larger poverty rate increases Latino homicide. In fact, just the opposite appears to occur for urban Latinos.

Turning to the other variables of theoretical interest, a leading predictor of homicide is Latino income inequality. A one standard deviation increase in Latino-to-Latino inequality is associated with a rise of more than one-third a standard deviation in the rate of Latino killings (b = .354). This finding confirms use of the disaggregation strategy because

it captures the uniqueness of the income distribution in Latino areas. As the income gap within the Latino population increases, the rate of killings increases as well. Economic inequality relative to other Latinos, not Anglos, is an important influence on homicide within the Latino community.[12]

One possible explanation for the Latino income inequality effect is that the Gini coefficient is more indicative of unequal resources than other deprivation measures in disaggregated homicide research. To the extent that Latino communities provide limited opportunities to associate with economically well-off Anglos and place more pressure on associating primarily with other Latinos, this could exert an influence on violence that tends to occur between Latinos.

In particular, note that educational attainment is the strongest predictor of homicide (b = .386). This finding suggests that increased education, as measured by high school graduation, has the most salient effect on decreased killings in the Latino population.

TABLE 3   Regression of All Cities on Social and Economic Factors, 1980

	OLS		WLS	
VARIABLE	*b*	β	*b*	β
Poverty	−.269	−.199	−.298	−.238***
	(.266)		(.090)	
Latino income inequality	.799	.336**	.806	.354***
	(.315)		(.111)	
Anglo-Latino income inequality	−4.361	−.106	−3.389	−.102
	(6.446)		(2.102)	
Education	−.399	−.379***	−.368	−.386***
	(.146)		(.046)	
Percent Latino	−.140	−.206*	−.125	−.207***
	(.083)		(.026)	
Percent Latino males, aged 15–24	.085	.015	.068	.013
	(.558)		(.173)	
Percent Divorced	−.347	−.049	−.215	−.032
	(.916)		(.287)	
Population (log)	8.469	.285***	7.497	.252***
	(2.843)		(.981)	
Immigration	−.402	−.057	−.286	−.045
	(.735)		(.237)	
Region	6.282	.229*	5.293	.207***
	(3.183)		(1.014)	
Constant	−25.906		−23.654	
R^2	.213		.203	
F	2.708**		21.790***	

Note: Standard errors in parentheses
*$p \leq .05$
**$p \leq .01$
***$p \leq .001$

Latino sociodemographic conditions played a significant role in homicide. High rates of Latino killings are more prevalent in cities with increased population size. A larger Latino population is related to less Latino killings. The fact that the Southwest region is positively related to the homicide rates is not surprising given that most Latinos live in this area.

In sum, several clear patterns emerge. Latino income inequality was a significant contributor to homicide. Further, educational attainment played an important role in the level of homicide. City population size also influenced the rate of Latino killings. Region of the country and percent Latino in each city also contributed to Latino homicide. Overall, the findings suggest that though Latino murders are primarily impacted by Latino education and income inequality, demographic factors are also significant contributors to levels of Latino homicide.

I also examined alternative measures of inequality. Balkwell (1990) extended measures of inequality by combining income information on five ethnic groups and weighting by the proportional representation of these groups in 150 SMSAs. As Messner and Golden (1992) and Harer and Steffensmeier (1992) point out, however, there appears to be no need to employ this weighting procedure in disaggregated homicide research because group-specific rates, when serving as the dependent variable, are standardized by the population size of the specific group. Despite this, I tentatively examined the Balkwell thesis. In this study it's plausible that reference points other than Anglos exist for Latinos, especially outside the Southwest. First, other groups (Anglo, Black, Asian, Native Americans) must exist if they are to serve as adequate points of reference. Information was collected on the number of Non-Latino whites, Blacks, Asians, and Native Americans in the present sample of 111 cities. The following distribution was discovered: almost 62 percent of the city population in this sample was white; close to 13 percent was Black; less than 1 percent was Native American, and a little more than 3 percent was Asian. It appears that Anglos are by far the largest group and the primary reference group across the 111 cities.

Indeed, Anglos were the largest group, net of Latinos, in almost every city (n = 107). In addition, recall that one criterion for inclusion in this study was that each city had at least 5,000 Latinos. Applying this same standard to Non-Latino whites, Blacks, Asians, and Native Americans, the following is discovered: In only 1 city did Anglos *not* meet the 5,000 minimum; 39 cities had less than 5,000 Blacks; 38 cities had more than 5,000 Asians; and 5 cities more than 5,000 Native Americans.

Finally, as a partial test of the Balkwell thesis, I included percent white, Black, Asian, and Native American into the equation and none of the variables was an important indicator of Latino homicide. The model fit, as judged in part by the R-square, was not significantly improved and, in fact, deteriorated. It appears that Anglos are by far the primary reference group across the 111 cities and the most useful point of economic comparison.

DISCUSSION AND CONCLUSIONS

This paper is the first comprehensive analysis of Latino homicide on a national basis. One purpose of this study is to expand earlier homicide research by examining the variation in Latino homicide-victim rates across U.S cities. Another is to carefully probe the link between Latino socioeconomic conditions and the incidence of homicide.

Overall, the results in this study reveal that disaggregating the homicide-victim rate and its correlates contributes to our understanding of the sources of killings among urban Latinos. The average Latino homicide rate (almost 20 per 100,000 Latinos) approaches the total African American homicide rate (27 per 100,000 African Americans) reported by Peterson and Krivo (1993:1012) and is twice the total 1980 U.S. homicide rate. This basic, though important, finding, highlights the need for Latino-specific measures in sociological research. Latino homicide is thus an important, largely unstudied, and generally underexamined social problem in contemporary U.S. society.

That economic inequality, not poverty, has a strong effect on Latino homicide is in line with an emerging body of literature (see Harer and Steffensmeier 1992; Shihadeh and Steffensmeier 1994). Steffensmeier and colleagues propose that researchers need to properly assess the effects of race-specific research, especially when conclusions stem from the importance of within-group inequality in explaining minority violence. Researchers should continue to focus attention on the impact of Latino inequality as a source of violence. It is possible that a large income gap within the Latino population creates a milieu in which a need to vent frustration at others results, usually at those in the Latino community, and with deadly consequences. Again, independent of other measures, the effect of Latino inequality, not poverty or inequality relative to Anglos, on homicide was strong and significant across the United States.

Furthermore, this analysis supports Blau and Schwartz's (1984) inequality hypothesis that economic inequality, rather than poverty, is responsible for high homicide rates. However, my findings differ from research proposing that pronounced economic inequalities *between* races leads to other types of conflict across communities (see Balkwell 1990). As demonstrated, intergroup inequality (Anglo-to-Latino) does not influence Latino killings. This finding is particularly noteworthy after taking into consideration prominent work on inequality and homicide (Balkwell 1990; Blau and Schwartz 1984). Note that the body of research discovering the impact of between-group inequality has typically analyzed total rather than group-specific homicide rates, and has analyzed general rather than group-specific predictors, in SMSAs not cities. For urban Latino's, emphasizing inequality relative to Anglos provides an incomplete and inaccurate picture of the influences on Latino homicide because aggregate measures would have masked the group-specific sources of violence. Perhaps the varying level of income inequality relative to Anglos is less meaningful since the persistent income gap among Latinos appears more immediate and widespread across the Latino community. This interpretation is speculative, but it highlights how determinants of Latino killings differ from those for total homicides or other group-specific killings (e.g., Black, Asian, Native American).

This is not to say that attention should be taken away from other social or economic sources of Latino homicide. Rather, the deprivation issue for Latinos is different than straight poverty or inequality relative to Anglos. Research by William J. Wilson (1987) provides a possible interpretation; namely, that the changing class structure in some urban areas, resulting from professional flight, followed out by the working class, leaving behind the most economically disadvantaged, is an important factor in understanding urban Latino violence. Alternatively, others argue that the Latino poor are not as concentrated in inner city barrios, relative to the underclass, and that the social structure for Latinos remains secure and stable (Moore and Pinderhughes 1993). Nevertheless, evidence exists that the income gap between middle-class and poor Latinos persists, and perhaps is widening, especially after considering the continuing growth in both classes (see Valdez 1993). As long as Latinos across the United States are concentrated in urban areas, characterized as part of the working poor, and continuously influenced by immigration, it will be difficult to reduce inequality. To illustrate, Perez and Cruz (1994) argue that inadequate levels of education and diminished job markets increase involvement in crime and violence for young urban Latinos. Coupled with the fact that the young and growing Latino population is constantly reinforced by economically and educationally disadvantaged immigrants in search of employment, the chances decline that Latinos will become more integrated, and, possibly, enable the less well-off to compete.

Perhaps enhanced economic opportunities fueled by school reform and greater access to higher education—intertwined with job training programs and economic growth—will reduce the income and educational attainment gap among Latinos. Sampson (1987) suggests that similar policies are more likely in the long run to reduce violence than alternatives seeking to increase incarceration levels. Unfortunately, legislation such as the recently passed Proposition 187 in California could tend to enhance the marginalization of Latinos by singling them out for discrimination. Such laws will likely decrease education, increase inequality, and make more violence likely.

Naturally, these conclusions are presented with some cautions. This paper encourages scholars to focus attention on a largely underexamined and mostly ignored population in the criminological literature. Clearly, it does not serve as a vehicle to propose or oppose any political agendas. This initial exploration sheds some light on an important social problem and raises questions about the patterns and causes of Latino violence.

In sum, little is known about Latino homicide, and this paper has not addressed every issue associated with Latino killings. It is, however, an important starting point. For the first time, it establishes a national Latino homicide rate and the socioeconomic factors that shape Latino killings. Future analyses will undoubtedly compare these 1980 findings to later time periods for greater clarity on the longitudinal impact of poverty and inequality. Still other studies might extend this area of research by exploring the impact of substance use within the Latino community, clarifying the link between drugs and alcohol to homicide (see Valdez 1993; Parker 1995). All of these issues are worthy of examination and should use this study as a foundation for future research on Latino lethal violence.

NOTES

1. Latinos are defined as persons whose national origin is Mexico, Puerto Rico, Cuba, or any other Spanish-speaking country (See Bean and Tienda 1987; Moore and Pinderhughes 1993). The term Anglo is used in the paper to refer to non-Latino whites (see Santiago and Wilder 1991 for similar usage of both terms).

2. A 5,000 Latino population size was used as a selection criterion (See Peterson and Krivo 1993:1006). Lowering the Latino population threshold led to unreliable homicide rates (e.g., Yakima, Washington, had a homicide rate twice as high as Dallas and Houston, Texas). After application of this criterion the number of Latino areas examined was 111 cities.

3. As best as I can determine, the SHR is the most reliable and consistent source of Latino homicide, although the UCR and Centers for Disease Control (CDC) also provide information on homicide. However, the UCR does not publish ethnic identification data for Latino victims. The SHR data are slightly less complete than the FBI's UCR data, the more commonly used source. In this analysis total homicide rates from both sources are highly correlated for the 111 cities examined (r = .96). The CDC reports were based on a special study using state-level death certificates in the Southwest and were not broken down beyond that level. Again, the SHR appears to be the only national source of Latino killings.

4. An examination of Anglo-Latino homicide differences, or any other racial/ethnic murder combination, is beyond the scope of this paper. A major reason is that the vast majority of homicides occur within ethnic groups (making the distinction between offender/victim arbitrary), at least in cases cleared with an arrest. In Texas, Rodriguez (1990:98) discovered 86 percent of Latinos were killed by other Latinos. Many other researchers also note the high rate of Latino on Latino murders in urban areas, e.g., Miami, Florida (85 percent); New York City (78 percent); and Chicago, Illinois (82 percent) (See Block 1993:301; Rodriguez 1987:82; Wilbanks 1984:159). Block (1985:112) also notes that from 1965 to 1981 approximately 12,876 homicides were recorded in Chicago. Even though a large number of Latino killings occurred during this time "too few interracial homicides (existed) for an analysis of monthly or even yearly patterns."

5. I thank Orlando Rodriguez at the Fordham University Hispanic Research Center for alerting me to published 1980 New York City Police Department homicide data (See Rodriguez 1987). Unfortunately, the police are not recording victims' ethnicity in the Greater New York-New Jersey metropolitan area (e.g., New Brunswick, Newark, Paterson, Clifton, and Passaic, New Jersey). For example, police agencies in New York and New Jersey failed to report a single Latino homicide victim to the SHR. Public health agencies also report similar missing data problems using death certificates collected at the state level (personal communication October 6, 1993, Lois Fingerhut, National Center of Health Statistics).

6. Census data were gathered from U.S. Bureau of the Census, County and City Data Book, 1988. U.S. Government Printing Office: 1988. U.S. Bureau of the Census, 1980 Census of Population: Volume 1 Characteristics of the Population, Chapter C General Social and Economic Characteristics. U.S. Government Printing Office: 1983. U.S. Bureau of the Census, 1980 Census of Population: Volume 1 Characteristics of the Population, Chapter B General Population Characteristics. U.S. Government Printing Office: 1982. Utilizing data from the 1980 Census establishes a baseline for future analysis of changes occurring in the 1980s.

7. In their original analysis, Peterson and Krivo also employed percent professional. This measure, at least for Latinos, created collinearity problems and other statistical inference problems with the educational deficiency variable. I opted to remove percent professionals because educational attainment is more closely related to homicide rates (See Balkwell 1990).

8. At the city level, data on recency of immigration by country of origin are not readily available (personal communication April 1995, Jorge Del Pinal, U.S. Census Bureau). To estimate a proxy for immigration I did two things. First, I examined a foreign-born variable. The Census Bureau provides data on the number of Latinos in each city born in a foreign country. This variable captures the bulk of Latinos born outside of the United States. However this does not adequately account for "immigration" in the Puerto Rican population. To garner an estimate on the number of Puerto Rican Latinos residing on the island, I incorporated the variable counting the number of Latinos living abroad in 1975, five years before the census was taken. Since both variables were highly correlated (r = .72), I created an index composed of both immigration proxies. The variables were transformed into z-scores and summed to compute the combined variable. This procedure avoids the possibility of counting persons twice. In the analysis that follows, both variables were individually introduced into the models, and then simultaneously incorporated, with similar results as the immigration index. Though not perfect, for the purposes of this paper, immigration is adequately addressed.

9. The unemployment rate was also added but this produced severe collinearity problems with several variables. The reader should note that, with the exception of the Puerto Rican population, Latinos are not characterized by high rates of joblessness but are disproportionately part of the working poor and working class, at least in 1980 (See Bean and Tienda 1987). Similarly, except for New York City and surrounding areas, Latino families are not significantly influenced by large numbers of female-headed households. However I did explore replacing female-headed households with the divorce rate and produced comparable results.

10. The use of OLS on the untransformed homicide rate raises several issues. After examining the skewness of the untransformed and logarithmic transformation homicide rates, and looking at kurtosis tests, several points emerged. First, the homicide distribution is not highly skewed. The natural value was modestly positively skewed, and, when transformed, became moderately negatively skewed. In addition, contrary to usual instance, the transformation seriously eroded the model fit as judged by both the large drop in the R-square and the F-test change from significant to nonsignificant. Based on interpretation ease and superior model fit, the untransformed dependent variable is preferred and used in the following analysis.

11. The issue of multicollinearity is further examined explicitly since it is a common problem inherent to ecological data (see Land, McCall, and Cohen 1990). First, although bivariate plots were examined and did not suggest that further transformations were necessary, I reestimated the model by introducing log transformations for each independent variable to check the linear assumption for each regressor. After comparing the kurtosis of each natural expression and log expression, the log expression of each variable was entered individually and in various combinations (e.g., log of A/L inequality and log of Latino poverty, etc). The results did not substantially change.

Next, I examined a number of possible interaction terms. Numerous interactions were looked at, including Anglo-to-Latino inequality, Gini coefficient, poverty, education, divorce rate, and the immigration index in various combinations. None was statistically significant.

Finally, Land and colleagues (1990) stress the need to be sensitive to Gordon's partialling fallacy, a statistical inference problem related to multicollinearity (see also Gordon 1968). Although poverty, Latino income inequality, and Anglo-Latino inequality have some conceptual overlap, each measure has a distinct and intrinsic meaning. To avoid inference problems, each of the three measures of poverty and inequality was individually entered and removed, and again, the following reported results did not appreciably change.

12. The ratio of Anglo-to-Latino median income is a fairly standard measure of intergroup inequality, although it is an imperfect one. Almost without exception, recent disaggregated homicide studies use a similar measure (white-to-Black median income) to, in part, capture majority relative to minority group inequality (see Harer and Steffensmeier 1992; Messner and Golden 1992; Peterson and Krivo 1993; Shihadeh and Steffensmeier 1994). However, I did reestimate the model using an alternative measure of Anglo-to-Latino inequality. A/L inequality was redefined as *relative poverty* by taking percent poor Latinos relative to percent poor Anglos, defined for both groups as those below the poverty line (e.g., percent poor Anglos/percent poor Latinos). This measure is not based on central tendency but rather the lower, deprived end of the income distribution. The results from this alternative specification had no effect on homicide when used in lieu of poverty and/or Anglo to Latino inequality.

REFERENCES

Anderson, Elijah
   1990   Streetwise. Chicago: University of Chicago Press.
Bailey, William C.
   1984   "Poverty, inequality, and homicide rates." Criminology 22:531–550.

Balkwell, James W.
   1990   "Ethnic inequality and the rate of homicide." Social Forces 69:53–70.
Beasley, Ronald W., and George Antunes
   1974   "The etiology of urban crime: An ecological analysis." Criminology 11:439–461.

Bean, Frank, and Marta Tienda
1987   The Hispanic Population of the United States. New York: Russell Sage Foundation.
Blau, Judith R., and Peter M. Blau
1982   "The cost of inequality: Metropolitan structure and violent crime." American Sociological Review 47:114–129.
Blau, Peter M., and Joseph E. Schwartz
1984   Crosscutting Social Circles: Testing a Macrostructural Theory of Intergroup Relations. New York: Academic Press.
Block, Carolyn R.
1985   "Race\ethnicity and patterns of Chicago homicide 1965–1981." Crime and Delinquency 31:104–116.
1993   "Lethal violence in the Chicago Latino community." In Homicide: The Victim/Offender Connection, ed. Anna Victoria Wilson, 267–342. Cincinnati, O.H.: Anderson Publishing.
Bonger, Wilhelm
1916   Criminality and Economic Conditions. Boston: Little, Brown and Company.
Flowers, Ronald
1990   Minorities and Criminality. New York: Praeger Publishers.
Gordon, Robert A.
1968   "Issues in multiple regression." American Journal of Sociology 73:592–616.
Greene, William H.
1993   Econometric Analysis. New York: MacMillan Press.
Harer, Miles D., and Darrell Steffensmeier
1992   "The differing effects of economic inequality on Black and white rates of homicide." Social Forces 70:1035–1054.
Horowitz, Ruth
1983   Honor and the American Dream. New Brunswick, NJ.: Rutgers University Press.
Land, Kenneth, Particia L. McCall, and Lawrence E. Cohen
1990   "Structural covariates of homicide rates: Are there any invariances across time and social space?" American Journal of Sociology 95:922–963.
Mercy, James A.
1987   "Assaultive injury among Hispanics: A public health problem." In Research Conference on Violence and Homicide in Hispanic Communities, eds. Jess Kraus, Susan Sorenson, and Paul Juarez, 1–12. Office of Minority Health, U.S. Department of Health and Human Services.

Merton, Robert K.
1957   Social Theory and Social Structure. New York: Free Press.
Merton, Robert K., and Alice K. Rossi
1968   "Contributions to the theory of reference group behavior." In Readings in Reference Group Theory and Research, eds. Herbert Hyman and Eleanor Singer, 28–68. New York: Free Press.
Messner, Steven, and Reid M. Golden
1992   "Racial inequality and racially disaggregated homicide rates: An assessment of alternative theoretical explanations." Criminology 30:421–445.
Moore, Joan
1991   Going Down to the Barrio: Homeboys and Homegirls in Change. Philadelphia: Temple University Press.
Moore, Joan, and Raquel Pinderhughes, eds.
1993   In the Barrios: Latinos and the Underclass Debate. New York: Russell Sage Foundation.
Nelsen, Candace, Jay Corzine, and Lin Huff-Corzine
1994   "The violent West reexamined: A research note on regional homicide rates." Criminology 32:135–148.
Parker, Robert Nash
1989   "Poverty, subculture of violence, and type of homicide." Social Forces 67:983–1007.
1995   Alcohol and Homicide: A Deadly Combination of Two American Traditions. Albany, N.Y.: SUNY Press.
Parker, Robert Nash, and Allison M. Toth
1990   "Family, intimacy, and homicide: A macrosocial approach." Violence and Its Victims 5:195–210.
Perez, Sonia M., and Steven Cruz
1994   Speaking Out Loud: Conversations With Young Puerto Rican Men. Washington, D.C.: National Council of La Raza.
Peterson, Ruth D., and Lauren J. Krivo
1993   "Racial segregation and Black urban homicide." Social Forces 71:1001–26.
Pokorny, Alex D.
1965   "Human violence: A comparison of homicide, aggravated assault, suicide, and attempted suicide." Journal of Criminal Law, Criminology and Police Science 56:488–497.
Rodriguez, Orlando
1987   "Hispanics and homicide in New York City." In Research Conference on Violence and Homicide in Hispanic Communities, eds. Jess

Kraus, Susan Sorenson, and Paul Juarez, 67–84. Office of Minority Health, U.S. Department of Health and Human Services.

Rodriguez, Salvador F.
1990   "Patterns of homicide in Texas: A descriptive analysis of racial/ethnic involvement by crime-specific categories." Ph.D. dissertation, Ann Arbor, M.I.

Saenz, Rogelio, and Robert N. Anderson
1994   "The ecology of Chicano interstate net migration, 1975–1980." Social Science Quarterly 75:37–52.

Sampson, Robert J.
1987   "Urban Black violence: The effect of male joblessness and family disruption." American Journal of Sociology 93:348–382.

Santiago, Anne M.
1986   "Socioedad encarcelada: Lethal violence in Puerto Rico." Report prepared for the Office of Research Coordinator, University of Puerto Rico at Mayaguez.

Santiago, Anne M., and Margaret G. Wilder
1991   "Residential segregation and the links to minority poverty: The case of Latinos in the United States." Social Problems 38:492–515.

Shihadeh, Edward S., and Darrell J. Steffensmeier
1994   "Economic inequality, family disruption, and urban Black violence: Cities as units of stratification and social control." Social Forces 73:729–751.

U.S. Bureau of the Census
1982   1980 Census of Population: Volume 1. Characteristics of the Population, Chapter B. General Population Characteristics. U.S. Government Printing Office.
1983   1980 Census of Population: Volume 1. Characteristics of the Population, Chapter C. General Social and Economic Characteristics. U.S. Government Printing Office.
1988   County and City Data Book. U.S. Government Printing Office.

Valdez, Avelardo
1993   "Persistent poverty, crime, and drugs: U.S.-Mexican border region." In The Barrios: Latinos and the Underclass Debate, eds. Joan Moore and Raquel Pinderhughes, 173–194. New York: Russell Sage.

Wallace, Samuel E.
1964   "Patterns of violence in San Juan." In Interdisciplinary Problems in Criminology, eds. Walter Reckless and Charles J. Newman, 43–48. Columbus, O.H.: Ohio State University Press.

Wilbanks, William
1984   Murder in Miami. Lanham, M.D.: University Press of America.

Wilson, William J.
1987   The Truly Disadvantaged. Chicago: University of Chicago Press.

Zahn, Margaret A.
1987   "Homicide in nine American cities: The Hispanic case." In Research Conference on Violence and Homicide in Hispanic Communities, ed. Jess Kraus, Susan Sorenson, and Paul Juarez, 13–30. Office of Minority Health, U.S. Department of Health and Human Services.

APPENDIX   Zero Order Correlation Martix (N = 111)

	1	2	3	4	5	6	7	8	9	10	11
Latino Homicide Rate (1)	1.000	.127	.169	.089	−.248	−.082	.026	−.087	.243	−.044	.016
Poverty (2)		1.000	.537	.733	−.586	.087	−.078	−.203	.214	−.013	−.265
Anglo-Latino income inequality (3)			1.000	.509	−.259	−.274	.055	−.054	.287	.047	−.222
Latino income inequality (4)				1.000	−.180	−.032	−.113	.132	.218	.316	−.446
Education (5)					1.000	−.285	.088	.539	−.019	.126	.022
Percent Latino (6)						1.000	−.290	−.331	−.218	.012	.326
Percent Latino males, aged 15–24 (7)							1.000	−.149	−.032	−.032	.074
Percent Divorced (8)								1.000	.144	−.063	−.252
Population* (9)									1.000	.001	−.258
Region (10)										1.000	−.290
Immigration (11)											1.000

*Natural logarithm

6

Violence against Gays and Lesbians

CHARLES E. REASONS
Central Washington University

QUENTIN HUGHSON
Kelowna, British Columbia

While the issues of women and the criminal justice system have become an increasingly significant area of both study and policy, issues surrounding gays and lesbians have largely been ignored. A review of the literature suggests this is largely an omission. In discussing sodomy laws and the homosexual panic defense, the discriminatory nature of the law becomes apparent. Significant in the history of the criminal justice system and the discipline of criminal justice is the predominantly macho, quasi-militaristic nature of the field. A discussion of the military policy regarding gays and lesbians is an example of institutional discrimination which fosters antipathy toward gays and lesbians in larger society.

In the last several decades, students of the law and criminal justice, legislatures, and criminal justice agencies have increasingly addressed issues of discrimination against racial minorities and women. Criminal law, human rights legislation, and public opinion have increasingly been used to reduce and suppress manifestations of racism and sexism. However, one minority group which is still struggling for protection is sexual minorities.

While the gay and lesbian movements have become increasingly mobilized to raise issues of discrimination and violence against sexual minorities, there are strong currents moving against such protection. There is evidence to suggest that violence motivated by homophobia and heterosexism is the most frequent, visible, violent and culturally legitimated form of hate crime in the United States (Jenness and Brood, 1997). Hate motivated violence against gays and lesbians or those presumed to be gays and lesbians is one of the fastest growing forms of hate crime in the United States. Such violence crosses racial, ethnic, religious, national and age boundaries. It appears that there is "open season" on sexual minorities in the United States.

The case of the gruesome murder of University of Wyoming political science major Matthew Shepard reveals the horror of gay-bashing. He was hung from a brick fence, beaten and unconscious, for eighteen hours. His skull was smashed with a blunt object and he appeared to have cigarette burns to his body and face. While this brought out a great outpouring of sympathy and condemnation, fundamentalist Christians and others on the far right do not want hate-crime laws extended to gays and lesbians (Fulwood III, 1998). While Matthew Shepard lay dying in a Fort Collins, Colorado hospital, a college homecoming parade passed nearby with a fraternity float carrying a straw-haired scarecrow labeled "I'm Gay" (*New York Times,* October 14, 1998).

VIOLENCE AGAINST GAYS AND LESBIANS

In its 1995 National Report, the National Coalition of Anti-Violence Programs (NCAVP) predicted an increase in anti-LGBT violence for 1996 based on the expectation of escalating anti-Lesbian, Gay, Bisexual, Transgendered rhetoric during the Presidential and Congressional elections, the fervor surrounding the possibility of the legalization of same-sex marriages in the United States and the possibility of the Supreme Court rendering a decision on Colorado's amendment 2. This prediction was based on the experience of NCAVP members that anti-LGBT violence increases when the community is used as a wedge in political arenas and the media (such as the controversy over gays in the military following the 1992 Presidential elections). Tragically, anti-LGBT violence rose nationally by 6% in 1996. A total of 2,529 anti-LGBT incidents were documented by NCAVP's fourteen national tracking programs. This increase in the total number of reported incidents sharply contrasts with the touted decreases in all forms of violent crime in most localities (in excess of 20% in some metropolitan areas).

Contrary to the conventional belief that most bias crimes are directed at property (such as graffiti and vandalism), a great majority of the violence against lesbians and gay men continues to be directed at individuals, while only 14% targeted property.

Across the nation, eight of the fourteen national tracking programs reported increases in incidents of anti-LGBT violence and six reported decreases. Documented incidents increased in Chicago (+16%), Cleveland (+64%), Columbus (+3%), Detroit (+29%), El Paso (+34%), Los Angeles (+55%), Minnesota (+4%), and Virginia (+206%). Documented incidents decreased in Massachusetts (–7%), New York City (–8%), Phoenix (–60%), Santa Barbara/Ventura (–40%), St. Louis (–10%), and San Francisco (–3%).

Intensity of Violence Increases

Not only did the number of incidents of violence increase, but the intensity and viciousness of the violence increased as well. This is clearly seen in the rise of the number of incidents that included assaultive offenses and the increasing severity of the resulting injuries from these offenses.

The number of incidents which included at least one assaultive offense rose from 39% in 1995 to 41% in 1996. These assaultive incidents resulted in injury or death to 867 victims in 1996.

The level of injury inflicted was often severe. Of the persons injured, 35% suffered serious physical injury (such as broken bones and permanent physical injury) or death. Another 58% of those injured required some type of medical attention, including 29% who received medical treatment in an emergency room or on an out-patient basis, 9% who were hospitalized, and 20% who needed, but did not receive, medical attention.

The severe level of injury is corroborated by the change in the most common weapons used: from primarily thrown objects in 1995 (such as bricks, bottles and rocks) to hand-held club-like objects in 1996 (such as bats, clubs, lead pipes and other blunt objects).

Another factor that confirms the escalating level of violence is the six year trend of increasing numbers of offenses per incident. An important measure of the overall severity of an anti-LGBT incident, offenses per incident indicates the number of individual crimes/offenses perpetrated in a given attack. Between 1995 and 1996 the national tracking programs reported a 1% increase in offenses per incident, from 2.17 in 1995 to 2.20 in 1996. This may only reflect a modest increase, but since 1991 the number of offenses per incident has increased nearly 50%.

Further pointing to the increase in intensity of the violence was the steep decrease in the number of incidents which involved only harassment, which is considered non-criminal behavior in most states. In 1995, 15% of the incidents reported involved only verbal/sexual harassment, while in 1996, merely 6% of the incidents involved only verbal/sexual harassment. In other words, 94% of the reported incidents were acts which constituted criminal behavior in most states.

Offenders

As the number of incidents increased, so did the number of offenders, with a 6% increase in the number of offenders from 4,211 in 1995 to 4,450 in 1996. More significantly, the ratio of offenders to victims increased 7% from 1.34 to 1.43 offenders to victims, indicating that the victims of anti-LGBT violence are usually outnumbered by the attackers.

Offenders were complete strangers in 41% of the incidents and clearly known in 37% of the incidents (including neighbors, landlords, family members, acquaintances and roommates), indicating that bias crimes are committed by a known person at nearly the same rate as by a total stranger.

The primary offenders continue to be teenagers and young adults, with 67% of the known offenders under 30 years of age, compared to 68% in 1995. The proportion of offenders under 18, however, increased significantly from 18% of known offenders in 1995 to 21% in 1996.

The number of female offenders is increasing from 418, or 12% of known offenders in 1995 to 596 or 15% of known offenders in 1996. In addition, the number of female victims increased nearly 6% from 853 in 1995 to 901 in 1996.

Anti-HIV Bias and Violence Increases

A total of 413 incidents were classified as motivated by fear and loathing of persons with (or perceived to have) HIV/AIDS, a 32% increase over 1995. Forty-five percent (45%) of these incidents involved both anti-gay and anti-HIV/AIDS bias, clearly demonstrating the continuing nexus between these two hatreds.

1996 Shows Few Safe Spaces for Lesbians and Gay Men

Neither home nor places of employment were safe spaces for gay men and lesbians. In 1996, 25% of all bias-related incidents occurred on a street or a public place, followed by 22% occurring in or around a victim's private residence, and 13% occurring in the workplace.

While the larger percentage of offenders were strangers to their victims (41%), landlords, neighbors and tenants (16%) and employers and co-workers (10%) together constituted over one-quarter of the bias-related incidents.

The highest number of incidents occurred during Gay/Lesbian Pride Month in June (301) and May (228); the least in November (182) and January (174). June being the month with the most incidents indicates that with visibility and media attention a backlash of hatred and violence often occurs.

While the overall number of bias crimes dropped 3% (381 to 368) in New York City in September 1998 compared to the previous September, bias crimes against gay men and lesbians rose 81% during the same period (Cooper, 1998). New York City Comptroller Alan G. Hevesi said too few officials have denounced anti-gay bigotry. This leads to a tolerence and acceptability of expressions of bigotry against gays and lesbians.

A 1997 survey of nearly 4,000 Massachusetts high school students found that 22% of gay respondents said they skipped school in the past month because they felt unsafe there, and 31% said they had been threatened or injured at school in the past year. This was five times the rate of heterosexual respondents.

Most Americans believe there is intolerance in their communities towards gays and that a violent attack like that against Matthew Shepard could happen in their communities ("Killing of Gay Stirs Concern, Poll Shows," 1998). While many college students are against racism and sexism, they are less sympathetic toward gays and lesbians (Bennett, 1998). Intolerance toward gays and lesbians is supported by current laws and practices.

Hate Crimes

While increasing attention is being given to hate crimes by criminologists (Martin and Chase, 1996), not all states have hate crime legislation, and not all hate crime legislation expressly provides for sexual orientation as a basis for such crime.

Senators Edward Kennedy (D-Mass.) and Arlen Specter (R-Pa.) introduced the Hate Crimes Prevention Act in the Senate on November 13, 1997, three days after President Clinton sponsored a first-of-its-kind White House conference on hate crimes. Clinton announced his support for the bill during his appearance at the conference.

The bill amends an existing federal hate crimes law to make it a federal crime to physically injure someone based on his or her sexual orientation, gender, or disability. The existing law covered hate crimes committed on the basis of a person's race, religion, or ethnicity.

The proposed revisions of the Hate Crimes Prevention Act would loosen restrictions on federal intervention, and add sexual orientation, gender, and disability to the categories covered. Besides the religious right, those opposed to the expansion argue against the incursion of the federal government into areas of criminal jurisdiction previously the exclusive domain of the state courts.

Subsequently, the federal law was changed to provide stiffer federal penalties than state penalties for persons convicted of crimes against someone who was targeted "because of his or her actual or perceived race, color, religion, national origin, ethnicity, gender, disability or sexual orientation."

However, the former law used the Constitution's sweeping 14th Amendment as the basis for its enforcement, enabling federal prosecutors to intervene in virtually all hate crimes based on race, religion or ethnicity. On the advice of legal experts, Kennedy and Specter used the Constitution's more restrictive "interstate commerce clause" as the basis for enforcing the Hate Crimes Prevention Act.

Many lawmakers, especially conservative Republicans, have long opposed adding 14th Amendment powers to civil rights laws, saying they take away powers from states.

STATE LAW: PROTECTING AND PROSECUTING GAYS AND LESBIANS

While forty states have some form of hate-crime legislation, only twenty-one include sexual orientation as a protected class (Fulwood, 1998). In the second most populous state in the country, New York, hate-crime legislation has been stalled in the State Senate for years. State Senate Majority Leader Joseph F. Bruna, R-Brunswick, says he is leery of creating a special class of victim (Herbeck and Michel, 1998). The concern about creating a new class of victim is also argued by fundamentalist Christian activists in their efforts to thwart federal legislation (Fulwood III, 1998). State legislation has emerged largely due to the efforts of gay and lesbian activists, in coalition with human rights organizations, and frequently spurred by a widely publicized hate crime (Jenness and Brood, 1997).

While some states are attempting to address hate crimes against gays and lesbians through legislation, other states continue to criminalize the sexual activity of gays and lesbians (Hare, 1997).

CRIMES WITHOUT VICTIMS: PROSECUTING AND PERSECUTING GAYS

"That utterly confused category" (Foucault [trans. 1990]: 23)

Within the United States, sodomy laws have been repealed in 24 states, struck down by state courts in at least 6 states; are extant in 5 states; and another 15 states still "prohibit some kinds of sex for consenting adults heterosexual or homosexual" (Harris, July 1997).

Five states (Arkansas, Kansas, Maryland, Missouri and Oklahoma) expressly (de jure) prohibit same sex relations, while fifteen states prohibit some kinds of sex for consenting adults heterosexual or homosexual. However, these prohibitions often are de facto discriminatory. For example, anal intercourse is prohibited for both heterosexuals and homosexuals; however, it weighs most heavily upon gays.

Sodomy statutes generally prohibit oral and anal sex, even between consenting adults. Some go much further. Michigan, for example, outlaws "gross lewdness" and "gross indecency." Penalties for violating sodomy laws range from a $200 fine to 20 years imprisonment. While most sodomy laws apply to both heterosexuals and lesbians and

TABLE 1   Status of Sodomy Laws

STATE	
Alabama	M 13A-6-65, Sexual Misconduct, 1 year/$2000 Does not apply to married couples
Alaska	repealed in 1980
Arizona	M 13-1411, Crime Against Nature (anal intercourse), 30 days/$500
Arkansas	M 13-1412, Lewd and Lascivious Acts, 30 days/$500
California	M 5-14-111, Sodomy, 1 year/$1000, same sex only Passed and signed into law by governor in 1977. [Has Anti-Hate Crimes Law, Q]
Colorado	repealed in 1976 [Civil rights Law, Anti-Hate Crimes Law, Q]
Connecticut	repealed in 1971 [Has Civil Rights Law, Anti-Hate Crimes Law, Q]
Delaware	repealed in 1973 [Has Anti-Hate Crimes Law, Q]
Dist of Columbia	repealed in 1993
Florida	M 800.02, Unnatural and Lascivious Act, 60 days/$500 [Has Anti-Hate Crimes Law, Q]
Georgia	F 16-6-2, Sodomy, 1 to 20 years Upheld as to homosexuals on the grounds that there is no fundamental federal constitutional right to "engage in sodomy." Bowers v. Hardwick, 478 U.S. 186 (1986). M 16-6-15, Solicitation of Sodomy, 1 year/$1000
Hawaii	repealed in 1973 [Has Civil Rights Law, Q]
Idaho	F 18-6605, Crime Against Nature, 5 years to life
Illinois	repealed in 1962 [Has Anti-Hate Crimes Law, Q]
Indiana	repealed in 1977
Iowa	repealed in 1978 [Has Anti-Hate Crimes Law, Q]
Kansas	M 21-3505, Sodomy, 6 months/$1000, same sex only
Kentucky	Struck down Commonwealth v. Wasson, 842 S.W.2d 487 (Ky. 1992)
Louisiana	F 14.89, Crime Against Nature, 5 years/$2000. Held unconstitutional by Orleans Parish Court, appeal pending. [Has Anti-Hate Crimes Law, Civil Rights Law, Q] Appeals Court threw out sodomy laws on basis of right to privacy, February 9, 1999
Maine	repealed in 1976 [HAD Civil Rights Law, repealed, see email; has Anti-Hate Crimes Law, Q]
Maryland	F 27-553, Sodomy, 10 years F 27-554, Unnatural or Perverted Sexual Practices, 10 years/$1000 Found not to apply to noncommercial, heterosexual activity in private. Schochet v. State, 1990. Sodomy laws ruled unconstitutional by Baltimore Circuit Judge, October 16, 1998, January 19, 1999
Massachusetts	F 272-34, Crime Against Nature, 20 years F 272-35, Unnatural and Lascivious Acts, 5 years/$100–$1000 Crime Against Nature applies only to anal intercourse. Unnatural and Lascivious Acts has been held not to apply to private consensual adult behavior. Commonwealth v. Balthazar, Supreme Judicial Court 1974. The ruling may also apply to a Crime Against Nature. [Has Anti-Hate Crimes Law; Civil Law, Q]
Michigan	750.158 (crime against nature, felony w/ 15-yr max) Invalidated by local trial court, Michigan Org. for Hum. Rts. v. Kelley, No. 88-815820 CZ

TABLE 1 *(continued)*

STATE	
Minnesota	M 609.293, Sodomy, 1 year/$3000 Minnesota's law also prohibits sex between humans and birds. [Has Anti-Hate Crimes Law; Civil Rights Law, Q]
Mississippi	F 97-29-59, Unnatural intercourse, 10 years
Missouri	M 566.090, Sexual Misconduct, 1 year/$1000, same sex only
Montana	07/02/97 repeal of its same sex only law banning "Deviate Sexual Conduct" with threats of 10 years in jail and a $50,000 fine.
Nebraska	repealed in 1978 [Has Anti-Hate Crimes Law, Q]
Nevada	repealed in 1993 [Has Anti-Hate Crimes Law, Q]
New Hampshire	repealed in 1975 [Has Anti-Hate Crimes Law; Civil Rights Law, Q]
New Jersey	repealed in 1979 [Has Anti-Hate Crimes Law, Civil Rights Law, Q]
New Mexico	repealed in 1975
New York	Struck down People v. Onofre 415 N.E. 2d 936 (N.Y. 1980)
North Carolina	F 14-177, Crime Against Nature, 10 years/discretionary fine
North Dakota	decriminalized in 1977
Ohio	repealed in 1974
Oklahoma	F 21-886, Crime Against Nature, 10 years A 1977 effort to repeal sodomy laws was met with a vote-delaying "chorus of giggles."
Oregon	repealed in 1972 [Anti-Hate Crimes Law, Q]
Pennsylvania	struck down Commonwealth v. Bonadio, 415 A.2d 47 (Pa. 1980)
Rhode Island	F 11-10-1, repealed in 1998 [Has Anti-Hate Crimes Law; Civil Rights Law, Q]
South Carolina	F 16-15-120, Buggery, 5 years/$500 "Abominable crime of buggery." no further definition in statute.
South Dakota	repealed in 1977
Tennessee	Struck down—appeal refused by state supreme court (1996) Jan. 26, 1996, Tennessee Appeals Court: Campbell v. Sundquist struck down that state's Homosexual Practices Act, ruling the state's same sex only sodomy law violated their right to privacy under Tennessee's Constitution, a right recognized in the 1992 case of Davis v. Davis in the earlier case, the Tennessee Supreme Court had established a state constitutional right to privacy, which gave Mr. Davis the right to prevent his ex-wife's donation to a childless couple of frozen embryos created using his sperm. It held that the Tennessee right to privacy included a right not to procreate. The ruling has not yet been appealed.
Texas	State v. Morales, 826 S.W.2d 201 (Tex. App. 1992), City of Dallas v. England, 846 S.W.2d 957 (Tex. Appl. 1993) review by higher court denied.
Utah	M 76-5-403, Sodomy, 6 months/$1000
Vermont	repealed in 1977 [Has Anti-Hate Crimes Law; Civil Rights Law, Q]
Virginia	F 18.2-361, Crime Against Nature, 5–20 years
Washington	repealed in 1976 [Has Anti-Hate Crimes Law, Q]

(continued)

TABLE 1   *(continued)*

STATE	
West Virginia	repealed in 1976
Wisconsin	repealed in 1983 [Has Anti-Hate Crimes Law, Civil Rights Law, Q]
Wyoming	repealed in 1977

Sources: Wintemute, Robert (1995). Sexual Orientation and Human Rights: The United States Constitution. The European Convention, and the Canadian Charter. Oxford: Oxford University Press [Appendix III]; OUT Magazine (November 1997). "News to You?" pp. 38–40; Harris, Jeff (email of July 1997). "Status of U.S. Sodomy Laws: July 1997" available online from the Queer Resource Directory.

gay men, they are primarily used against gay people. For example, some courts say sodomy laws justify separating gay parents from their children. Some cities use sodomy laws to arrest gay people for talking with each other about sex, in conversations which parallel those heterosexuals have every day.

While some states have Anti-Hate Crime laws, they do not necessarily include sexual orientation as a basis for hate crimes.

Sodomy laws were upheld in the case of Bowers v. Hardwick (478 U.S. 186, 1986). The Supreme Court upheld the state of Georgia's anti-sodomy law, based on an analysis which conflated behavior with identity.

Michael Hardwick was arrested in his bedroom and charged with sodomy when a police officer, who had gained admittance through a third party, found Hardwick engaged in oral sex with another man. Hardwick filed an action in federal court to have the law declared unconstitutional and was joined by an anonymous heterosexual couple who asserted "their rights were also violated by the law, which drew no distinction regarding the gender of the participants in anal or oral sex" (Leonard, 1991: 70–71). Leonard goes on to note how the heterosexual couple "were held by the district court to lack standing to challenge the law because they were in no immediate danger of prosecution" (ibid.: 72–73, footnote 24). Thus, the Supreme Court characterized the case as an answer to the question of whether or not 'homosexuals' had a fundamental right to engage in sodomy and, in doing so, narrowed the focus to 'homosexual acts' (which can

and do bear a remarkable resemblance to 'heterosexual acts'), rather than 'sodomy.' In his majority opinion, Justice White "asserted that if the Court applied the 'privacy of the home' theory to consensual sodomy, it would 'be difficult, except by fiat, to limit the claimed right to homosexual conduct while leaving exposed to prosecution adultery, incest, and other sexual crimes even though they are committed in the home' " (Leonard, 1991: 76). Thus, allowing homosexuals to engage in consensual sodomy in the privacy of the home would somehow open the floodgates to incidents of "adultery, incest and other sexual crimes" which, arguably, are more often perpetrated by those who identify as 'heterosexual' than by those who identify as 'homosexual.'

In contrast to Hardwick, Gryczan v. Montana No. 96-202 (July 2) shows a departure from the [pathologized?] decision of Bowers and in doing so, acknowledges the relatively quotidian quiescence of many queer lives. Gryczan struck down Montana's sodomy law with punishment of up to 10 years in prison and $50,000 in fines (ACLU Release, July 3, 1997). The Montana Supreme Court's decision in Gryczan, on the point of law and AIDS, states:

> The [sodomy] law was enacted almost 10 years before the first AIDS case was reported in Montana, and the presence of the ban has not stopped the disease from becoming the sixth-leading cause of death among middle-aged Montanans . . . (Anez, 1997)

However, the Montana legislature failed to vote to erase the law from the books. A bill that would have removed the law received a 50–50 vote by representatives, thus defeating the bill. In urging the defeat of the bill, Republican Representative Bob Clarke argued "the Supreme Court didn't say we had to take this law off the books. They just said it was unconstitutional. There is no harm in leaving the law in place" (House Defeats End to Ban on Gay Sex, February 14, 1999).

Gross Inequality

Mike Bowers, the former Georgia Attorney General who prosecuted the Hardwick case previously mentioned, was ... involved in a case which resulted in Bowers withdrawing a job offer he had made to Robin Shahar. Bowers made the initial offer after Shahar had "interned for him in 1990 but reneged after learning that the Emory University law school honors graduate intended to marry another woman in a Jewish ceremony." Bowers withdrew his initial offer in July 1991 in a letter to Shahar in which he stated, in part:

> *This action has become necessary in light of information which has only recently come to my attention relating to a purported marriage between you and another woman. As chief legal officer of this state, inaction on my part would constitute tacit approval of this purported marriage and jeopardize the proper functioning of this office. (Pettys, 1997)*

The Georgia court upheld the dismissal:

> *Judge Stanley F. Birch Jr., in a dissenting opinion joined by three other judges, said that claim rested on 'inference from Shahar's acknowledged homosexuality' ... that 'she is likely to violate Georgia's sodomy laws or would be unable or unwilling to enforce Georgia's sodomy or marriage laws.' (Lewis, 1997)*

Ironically, Georgia's anti-sodomy law was upheld and employment discrimination allowed based on moral grounds by a man who is also guilty of a criminal offense, adultery, a misdemeanor under Georgia's state laws subject to up to one year in jail. On June 5th, 1997, Bowers admitted to having had an adulterous affair for more than ten years while he was Georgia's Attorney

General (Pettys, 1997). Shahar asked the 11th U.S. Circuit Court of Appeals for a rehearing, based on Bowers' admission, but the court "ruled 9–3 that it was too late for Ms. Shahar to introduce the new information and said she could have asked for it six years earlier during the civil trial." The case has been appealed to the Supreme Court (Reuters, October 31, 1997 U.S. Supreme Court asked to consider lesbian firing By Mike Cooper [Appeal denied—see QL–12/31/97–]).

Bowers is also noted for his role in decisions such as those in which " ... public college newspapers could not refuse to publish anti-homosexual advertisements and with a ruling that the city of Atlanta could not include domestic partners in benefit plans" (Pettys, 1997). Bowers was seeking the Republican gubernatorial nomination in 1998 saying his campaign "would focus heavily on family values" (Pettys, 1997). One has to wonder what 'family values' Mr. Bowers is referring to ...

In spite of the above mentioned case, legal attacks continue upon the discriminatory nature of existing sodomy laws, with the American Civil Liberties Union announcing in 1998 a plan to challenge anti-gay sodomy laws on a state-by-state basis, beginning in Maryland (Taylor, 1998).

"In Maryland, we feel that the time is right to expose these laws," which "completely violate our rights and our privacy," said Michael Adams, staff counsel with the ACLU Lesbian and Gay Rights Project. Adams is heading up the court challenge along with Dwight Sullivan of the Maryland ACLU.

Adams and Sullivan are preparing a class-action lawsuit against Maryland on behalf of lesbian and gay male citizens in the state.

There are two laws dealing with sodomy in Maryland. The first deals with general sodomy (defined as anal intercourse or "buggery"), and the second with "unnatural or perverted sexual practices," including oral sex.

A 1990 court ruling in the case of Schochet v. State exempted heterosexual oral sex from the law, so long as it is "consensual, noncommercial," and conducted "between adults in the privacy of the home."

It is unclear whether or not the court's ruling also legalizes heterosexual anal sex, Sullivan said, but all forms of same-sex sexual activity, even consensual and private relations, remain illegal in Maryland and punishable by a maximum $1,000 fine and up to 10 years in prison.

While gay people are rarely arrested for consensual, private sexual relations, the Maryland sodomy laws are used against gay people in many ways, Sullivan said. Sometimes, they are used against gay parents in child custody and visitation cases. Often, the laws are used by police to justify undercover stings set up to arrest gay men for inviting men to engage in sodomy. In the summer of 1997, a series of Anne Arundel County police stings at 20/20 Books resulted in the arrest of more than 40 men on charges of soliciting for sodomy ("lewdness"). The names and home addresses of those arrested, including an Annapolis elementary school principal and a Navy spokesperson, were subsequently reported in local newspapers, including the *Annapolis Capital*.

On January 19, 1999, a Baltimore judge handed a victory to privacy and gay-rights advocates, ruling that Maryland's 80-year-old anti-sodomy law cannot apply to consensual acts.

The decision by Circuit Court Judge Richard T. Rombro extends his October ruling that homosexual oral sex could no longer be considered criminal by applying the same legal logic to anal sex as well.

"This is saying the government will not intrude in the bedroom," said Dwight Sullivan, a staff counsel for the American Civil Liberties Union, which had filed a class-action suit challenging the law on behalf of several gay men and lesbians.

State officials, who had offered no objection to the ACLU's argument to protect private, consensual anal sex, said the ruling was largely symbolic. They note that few Marylanders, if any, have been prosecuted for private sexual activity.

Yet ACLU officials argued that the old law posed a threat to privacy rights and left homosexuals vulnerable to job discrimination and unfair attacks in child custody cases.

The Maryland ruling follows a nationwide trend: Over the last couple of decades, anti-sodomy laws have been either repealed or ruled unenforceable by the courts in 31 other states. Sodomy remains illegal in Virginia and 17 other states, five of which only target homosexual acts. The U.S. Supreme Court ruled in a Georgia case in 1986 that anti-sodomy laws are constitutional (Arget Singer, 1999).

The Kansas Court of Appeals upheld the state law making homosexual sex a crime, citing the Bowers case in upholding the constitutionality of the statute ("Appeals Court upholds State Anti-Sodomy Law," 1998). The court noted that the city ordinance and state law did not make being a homosexual against the law; therefore, it does not discriminate. On the other hand, a superior court judge in Rhode Island declared a law forbidding oral and anal sex unconstitutional, because it discriminates against unmarried people (AP, April 25, 1998). Subsequently, the Rhode Island legislature repealed the statute.

On October 16, 1998, a Baltimore Circuit Judge ruled that the state's anti-sodomy law violates homosexuals' constitutional rights. The law prohibits oral sex between people of the same gender but not between heterosexual partners (Francke, 1998).

Military Injustice

It has only been until recently that it was a crime to be gay and in the armed forces; until 1993, there was a ban on gays and lesbians serving in the U.S. Armed Forces (de jure discrimination). President Clinton eliminated the ban under the "don't ask, don't tell" policy. Basically, homosexuals are to remain in the closet if they want to serve in the military. If they don't, they may be subject to investigation and discharge. The extreme is the death penalty as dramatically portrayed in *Any Mother's Son: The Dorothy Hajdys Story*.

Five years ago, Allen Schindler was murdered by shipmates in Japan for being gay. Allen was so brutally beaten that every organ in his body was destroyed. After uncovering the truth about Allen's terrible murder, his mother, Dorothy Hajdys, took on the Navy to bring his killers to justice. Her struggles and triumphs are depicted in *Any Mother's Son.*

Unfortunately, it appears some branches of the military are vigorously pursuing "suspected gays" in order to "out" them, according to a recent report. Military commanders routinely violate the Pentagon's "don't ask, don't tell" policy, according to the report, by aggressively investigating the private lives of military personnel suspected of being gay and failing to protect them from harassment.

The report charges that violations of the policy have become increasingly frequent each year since it was introduced by President Clinton in the face of considerable controversy in 1993.

The report describes what it calls "heavy handed and increasingly intrusive investigative tactics against suspected gays, including coercion and fishing expeditions." In addition, it said there is "no recourse or redress for service members asked, pursued or harassed" and that those who violate the policy are not held accountable for their actions.

Under the policy, commanders are allowed to begin an investigation if they receive "credible information" of homosexual conduct. But the report says investigations are often initiated based on nothing more than "belief or suspicion," rather than on "articulable facts."

These violations occur despite a promise by Secretary of Defense William Cohen to stop any "continued pursuits and prosecutions" under the policy (Freedberg, 1998). In a ruling by a federal judge (McVeigh v. Cohen, January 26, 1998), the Navy was found to have embarked on a search and "outing" mission of sailor Timothy R. McVeigh [not the convicted terrorist]. As the opinion notes:

The facts as stated above clearly demonstrate that the Plaintiff did not openly express his homosexuality in a way that compromised this "Don't Ask, Don't Tell" policy. Suggestions of sexual orientation in a private anonymous email account did not give the Navy a sufficient reason to investigate to determine whether to commence discharge proceedings. In its actions, the Navy violated its own regulations . . .

All that the Navy had was an email message and user profile that it suspected was authored by plaintiff. Under the military regulation, that information alone should not have triggered any sort of investigation. When the Navy affirmatively took steps to confirm the identity of the email respondent, it violated the very essence of "Don't Ask, Don't Pursue" by launching a search and destroy mission . . .

The subsequent steps taken by the Navy in its 'pursuit' of the Plaintiff were not only unauthorized under its policy, but likely illegal under the Electronic Communications Privacy Act of 1986 (ECPA).

In soliciting and obtaining over the phone personal information about the Plaintiff from AOL, his private on-line service provider, the government in this case invoked neither of these provisions [of ECPA] and thus failed to comply with ECPA . . .

The government knew, or should have known, that by turning over the information without a warrant, AOL was breaking the law.

Nothing has been produced before this court which would in any way suggest that his [McVeigh's] sexual orientation has adversely affected his job performance. Senior Chief McVeigh's place in the Navy might even be characterized by some to be the very essence of what was hoped to be achieved by those who conceived the policy. The plaintiff is no less an officer today than he was on January 5, 1998, the day before he was told of his imminent discharge from the Navy because of his sexual orientation . . .

As this Court stated in Elzie v. Aspin, 897F.Supp 1,3 (1995), it cannot understand why the Navy would seek to discharge an officer who has served his country in a distinguished manner just because he might be gay . . .

The Court must note that the defense mounted against gays in the military have been tried before in our nation's history—against blacks and women. Surely, it is time to move beyond this vestige of discrimination and misconception of gay men and women . . . *(emphasis added)*

Although four federal appeals courts have upheld the "don't ask, don't tell" policy, it will continue to be challenged.

In his July 2, 1997 opinion in Able v. Perry, Judge Eugene Nickerson of the Eastern District of New York struck down the military's "don't ask, don't tell" policy on gays as unconstitutional on equal protection and First Amendment grounds.

Nickerson's opinion points out that the military's primary justification for its proscription is that heterosexual disapproval of known homosexuals will disrupt "unit cohesion." The military has abandoned its previous explanations of why homosexuals were unfit to serve: they were security risks; they were more likely to spread infectious diseases; they suffered from mental illness. This is important because the current rationale, unlike its predecessors, correctly traces the source of dysfunction not to the homosexual but to the heterosexual. Noting this, Nickerson found that unit cohesion was "a euphemism for catering to the prejudices of heterosexuals," prejudices that he interpreted Romer to prohibit as a basis for state discrimination. In addition to striking down the prohibition on acts, he again struck down the speech prohibition, because, as the Second Circuit had stated, "a limitation on speech in support of an unconstitutional objective cannot be sustained." This was the first decision in the nation to strike down both the speech and conduct provisions of the Clinton policy on gays in the military.

The United States Supreme Court recently rejected, for the fourth time, a challenge to the "don't ask, don't tell" policy (Thomne v. Department of Defense, 98-91). It involved a Navy aviator who was honorably discharged for "homosexual admission." He had openly challenged the policy on the ABC news program *Nightline* in May 1992. He sued on the basis that the policy violated his free-speech and equal protection rights. The Supreme Court continues to refuse to hear a challenge to the constitutionality of the policy (Carelli, 1998). Nonetheless, some members of the judiciary have been outspoken in their criticism of the policy.

A veteran federal judge issued a stern challenge to President Clinton urging the president to "admit his mistake of judgment" and renounce the military's "don't ask, don't tell" policy.

"Renounce it because it is wrong, it is evil— as you surely know in your heart," declared U.S. 9th Circuit Court of Appeals Judge William A. Norris in Los Angeles.

The liberal jurist issued the unusual challenge in remarks at an evening ceremony at the Pacific Design Center, where he received a "Liberty Award" from the Lambda Legal Defense and Education Fund, a national nonprofit legal group working for full civil rights for gay men and lesbians. "Discrimination against lesbians and gay men as official governmental policy has emerged as the most intractable civil rights issue of the '90s," said Norris, 70, who is perhaps best known for his strong opinion in a 1988 case in which he said the military's ban on gays violated the U.S. Constitution's equal protection clause.

To be sure, other forms of discrimination, such as discrimination based on race or gender, persist as grave social problems in America, but at least they are no longer acceptable as official governmental policy. Regrettably, however, it continues to be acceptable for the government and government officials to promote hatred, fear and intolerance against gay men and lesbians.

Norris condemned "don't ask, don't tell" as a policy that "demands that gays and lesbians live a lie if they wish to serve in the military, and fight and die for their country. . . . I can think of no other instance in which the government passed a law whose very purpose is to force people to live a lie, to pretend that their true selves don't really exist."

In his address, the judge pointedly reminded Clinton of his recent commemoration of the 40th anniversary of the desegregation of the Little Rock, Arkansas, public schools, where speakers denounced the bigotry that had kept blacks in separate, unequal schools until then.

Norris said the "don't ask, don't tell" policy was equally worthy of condemnation. "It is also evil . . . Just as the racial policies of Gov. [Orval] Faubus were evil."

Norris predicted that the Bowers case and the "don't ask, don't tell" policy would eventually be buried in the "national cemetery of shame," along with earlier U.S. Supreme Court decisions that permitted slavery, segregated public facilities and authorized the mass incarceration of Japanese Americans during World War II (Weinstein,

1997). As long as the current policy exists in the military it will provide a basis for discrimination, harassment and hate-crimes.

HOMOSEXUAL PANIC DEFENSE: BLAMING THE VICTIM

A "homosexual panic defense" is one in which the accused attempts to defend their actions by pleading that a 'homosexual advance' induced a mindless and uncontrollable rage. Thus, 'my heterosexuality made me do it' and, in such cases, a 'normal' heterosexual identity is used to justify the accused's violent, often murderous, behavior. For example, as Lahey (1995) notes, "second year medical students in Canada are routinely taught that 'homosexual panic' is a mental disorder":

> Men whose unconscious homosexual strivings come to the surface (e.g., in the military or other situations of forced intimacy) may become acutely anxious and paranoid. In the midst of such panic, the individual in homosexual panic believes others are accusing him of 'forbidden' homosexual wishes and practices, and he may pick fights to prove his manhood. Such men frequently brawl in bar rooms with 'drinking buddies.' (25)

In the United States, Comstock (1992) summarizes the defense as follows:

> Typically the victim in such a case is a gay or purportedly gay man who is severely beaten or murdered. The theory of the defense is that the gay victim triggered a violent psychotic reaction in a latently gay defendant. The triggering action may have been merely a non-violent verbal or gestural solicitation by the victim. The solicitation caused the defendant to temporarily lose the capacity to distinguish right from wrong. Thus the defendant claims, like any defendant who successfully raises an insanity defense, he is absolved of responsibility.

This defense relies almost exclusively on anti-gay/lesbian biases of judges and jurors. The victim is placed on trial due to their sexual identity. A gay man making a sexual advance is equated with a sexual attack. Thus, the offender argues self-defense due to such a sexual advance. The sexual identity of the victim, not the physical threat

posed, becomes the justification for self-defense in these incidents. The absurdity of the defense is evident if we were to propose a "racial panic" or "gender panic" defense. If every woman murdered those who made sexual advances toward her under a "gender panic" defense, the gender ratio would be somewhat different!

In Canada, for example [R. v. Gilroy (1995) 5 years, manslaughter (Vancouver)], prosecutor Craig Dykes said Kenneth Gaspard, 35, died September 29 from multiple stab wounds inflicted by Gary Gilroy, 27. Gilroy met Gaspard in a gay bar and accompanied him home. Gilroy claimed he was having a shower when Gaspard launched an aggressive, unwanted homosexual attack upon him, provoking his very violent response.

In a homicide case, a successful defense of provocation reduces murder to manslaughter, which can carry a much lighter sentence. Ken Steffenson of the Gay and Lesbian Centre said the defense should not be available in cases of this type. "If a man can get off more lightly because he was propositioned by a gay person, the outcome means gay and lesbian people are being undervalued," he said.

"If the victim was a heterosexual female, all hell would break loose." Lawyer Barbara Findlay of the Canadian Bar Association's B.C. branch, said the so-called homosexual panic defense defies logic and is "the most appalling kind of institutionalized homophobia. The courts accept that the merest kind of advance by one man toward another is sufficient to enrage him so much that he justifiably kills him."

An autopsy indicated Gaspard received up to 60 stab and slash wounds, inflicted by six knives. In the United States (Comstock, 1992), an example of a judge's belief of a defendant's account of an incident in which the victim died is provided in *An Illinois Man . . . , Gay Chicago News*, Dec. 30, 1977, which goes as follows:

> An Illinois man, who confessed to slaying Frank A. Zedar, 23, in Tucson, Arizona in 1974, because Zedar reportedly made homosexual advances toward him, has been sentenced to from 5 to 10 years in prison. Robert E. Simpson, 27, who had been living in Rockford, Illinois, since the murder, confessed

to the slaying after he was arrested on a traffic charge in Champaign, Illinois. Simpson told police his conscience was bothering him and Superior Court Judge William E. Drake said he gave Simpson a relatively light sentence because the victim reportedly was the aggressor and Simpson "obviously had gone through a private torment for years."

Portland—The Maine Supreme Court has upheld the use of force in warding off a homosexual advance. The ruling came last month in the appeal hearing of Leland Philbrick, 23, who had previously been convicted of the second-degree murder of Charles Porterfield, 18. Philbrick claimed that Porterfield picked him up while hitchhiking. Philbrick said the younger man had put a hand on his knee and, when repulsed, became "aggressive." Philbrick then took a gun from his knapsack and shot Porterfield three times.

A man was acquitted of killing a Roman Catholic priest in Brooklyn, New York in 1987 using the homosexual panic defense.

In Hawaii, Stephen Bright was charged with murder for the beating death in 1997 of Kenneth Brewer, a gay man, at Brewer's Hawai'i Kai apartment. A Circuit Court jury convicted him recently of third-degree assault, a misdemeanor with maximum punishment of one year in prison.

Bright admitted beating Brewer but maintained he acted in self-defense to ward off Brewer's sexual advances. Friends and relatives of Brewer noted that the two men had met at Hula's Bar, a popular nightclub for gays, and contend Brewer would not have forced himself on a heterosexual man (Anti-Gay Violence, 1998).

Hawaii has no hate crime law and is the only state that does not collect statistics on hate crimes to forward to the F.B.I.

The 'deviance of homosexuality' which is alleged to have elicited these attacks pales in comparison to the deviance of heterosexuality used to legitimate these (among other) brutalities against those who are (or are perceived to be) 'deviant homosexuals.'

Again, 'my heterosexuality made me do it' but does this mean heterosexuality is deviant? Are all heterosexuals capable of such behavior? If so, should they be quarantined? Denied rights of kinship, inheritance and familial status so as to try and prevent them from forming demonic covens? As we all know, all heterosexuals are not alike and you can't judge them all by the actions of a limited few.

What these attacks show, however, is the difficulty in ascribing identity to an 'other.' In these cases of homosexual panic defense it is necessarily based on a rigid stereotype of masculine heterosexuality and it is the extreme attempt to achieve this unattainable ideal which motivates these crimes. Gay men are sought out in these instances by 'straight' men and are used as the ultimate means of disassociation from a homosexual identity. Yet, often, men who attack gay men have placed themselves in situations in which they are assured of meeting gay men. Often these attacks occur after the attacker alleges a 'homosexual advance' has occurred but these advances often occur in an intimate context.

The homosexual panic defense has no real basis in psychiatry. Those diagnosed with it in case studies demonstrate helplessness, passivity and inability to be aggressive (Comstock, 1992). The homosexual panic disorder is no longer expressly listed as a disorder in the Diagnostic and Statistical Manual of the American Psychiatric Association (Third Edition, 1987), although panic disorders remain. [Homosexuality, Ego-dystonic remains with reference to sexual disorder not otherwise specified, i.e., persistent and marked distress about one's sexual orientation.]

Comstock observes that it would be more appropriate to call it an acute aggressive panic disorder; however, this would not gain the same sympathy of jurors, judges and criminal justice personnel.

While the homosexual panic defense is increasingly in disrepute, a similar defense arises in the pleading of self-defense, i.e., the "homosexual advance" defense. That is, somehow the advances made by a gay man on a straight man must be met by violence. In October 1998, the Attorney General of New South Wales, Australia released a report on Homosexual Advance Defense. It points out that while homosexual advance defense is not a legally recognized defense, it refers to the use by men who are violent as a self-defense, provocation or diminished responsibility that their violence was caused by the sexual advance of the deceased. Therefore, it goes to blaming the victim for being murdered (victim-precipitated). Given the extent of homophobia, it is still a potentially useful defense strategy.

Parents of a slain gay man went along with a prosecutor's offer of a plea bargain in their son's 1996 murder in Virginia because they were told the defense would make a public inquiry into their gay son's sexual life at trial. According to the *Roanoke Times and World News,* the lead investigator said that "Unfortunately, even though we're in 1997, there was a fear that based on his lifestyle, a jury would believe he got what he deserved." Members of the legal profession may also be homophobic (Stryker, 1998).

In 1988, at a sentencing hearing for a defendant convicted of killing two gay men, Texas Judge Jack Hampton handed down a 30-year sentence rather than the life sentence requested by the prosecutor. His rationale? "I don't much care for queers cruising the streets picking up teenage boys . . . [I] put prostitutes and gays at about the same level . . . and I'd be hard put to give somebody life for killing a prostitute."

In 1987, Daniel Wan was beaten up outside of a bar in Broward County, Florida, by assailants who called him faggot, repeatedly kicking him and throwing him up against a moving car. He died from his injuries two days later. At a pre-trial hearing, Circuit Judge Daniel Futch jokingly asked the prosecuting attorney, "That's a crime now, to beat up a homosexual?" The prosecutor responded, "Yes, sir. And it's a crime to kill them." To that, the judge quipped, "Times really have changed." Although the judge apologized and maintained he was kidding, he was removed from the case (Stryker, 1998),

CONCLUSION

While strides have been made in the criminal justice literature to address the issues of subordina-

tion and discrimination against women and racial and ethnic minorities, gays and lesbians are largely ignored.

Gays are the subject of a significant amount of hate crime, and are criminalized in several states through sodomy laws. Furthermore, the policy of the United States military subjects them to witch hunts, invasions of privacy and continued oppression. The law, through the "homosexual panic" and "homosexual advance defenses," also uses homophobia as a basis for reducing the seriousness of violence against gays.

Gays and lesbians are minority groups in terms of a subordinate group whose members, because of physical or cultural characteristics, are disadvantaged and subjected to unequal treatment by the dominant group and who regard themselves as objects of collective discrimination. Like other minorities, "sexual minorities" have created their own sense of consciousness, carved out public spaces for the needs and activities of their vibrant and flourishing communities, and have secured private spaces within them for their families.

There has arisen a Queer legal theory (Valdes, 1993), which has connections with feminist theory, critical race theory and social constructionism (Namoste, 1994). Valdes (1993) outlines the three tasks of Queer legal theory as (1) to create a body of legal scholarship that is responsive to Queer life and identity; (2) to make the law accountable for its actual impact on the lives and fortunes of sexual minorities and (3) to join with Feminism and Critical Race Theory to strive to be liberated from subordination under law (Romonthan, 1996).

While there has been progress in some big U.S. cities in educating prosecutors and others on the fallacy of the homosexual panic and homosexual advance defense, much needs to be done. As long as it remains viable, it exposes gays to more violence. As one gay activist states: "It's OK to beat up gays as long as you say you were propositioned" (Comstock, 1992:99). That it remains open season on gays and lesbians is evident in the data on violence against them.

REFERENCES

Anez, Bob. July 2, 1997. Montana Overturns Ban on Gay Sex. Associated Press.

Anti-Gay Violence. October 13, 1998. *Honolulu Star-Bulletin.*

Appeals Court Upholds State Anti-Sodomy Law. April 26, 1998. *Wichita Eagle.*

Argetsinger, Amy. Md. Judge's Ruling Protects Private, Consensual Sex Acts. January 20, 1999. *Washington Post.*

Bennett, Lisa. Teaching Students to Face Their Anti-Gay Prejudices. October 23, 1998, p. A76. *The Chronicle of Higher Education.*

Carrelli, Richard. Gay Aviator Loses Court Appeal. October 19, 1998. *Associated Press.*

Comstock, G. Dismantling the Homosexual Panic Defense. 1992. *Law and Sexuality.* 2: 81–102.

Cooper, Michael. Reports of Anti-Gay Crimes Increase by 81 Percent. September 18, 1998. *New York Times.*

Elias, Robert. *The Politics of Victimization: Victims, Victimology and Human Rights.* 1986. New York: Oxford University Press.

Fletcher, George. *With Justice for Some: Protecting Victims' Rights In Criminal Trials.* 1996. Reading, Mass.: Addison-Wesley Publishing Co.

Foucault, Michel. *The History of Sexuality: Volume I.* 1980. New York: Vintage Books.

Francke, Caitlin. Homosexuals Win Challenge to State Sex Practices Law. October 17, 1998. *Baltimore Sun.*

Freedberg, Louis. Don't Ask Policy Reportedly Ignored. February 19, 1998. *San Francisco Chronicle.*

Fulwood III, Sam. Wyoming Death Spurs Debate Over Hate Crimes. October 16, 1998, p. 1. *Buffalo News.*

Fuss, Diana. *Inside/Out: Lesbian Theories, Gay Theories.* 1991. New York: Routledge.

Hare, Ivan. Legislating Against Hate—The Legal Response to Bias Crimes. 1997. *Oxford Journal of Legal Studies.* 17: 415.

Herbeck, Dan and Lou Michel. Viciousness of Beating Stirs Probe as Hate Crime. October 18, 1998, p. B-1.

Homophobia Often Found In Schools, Data Show. October 14, 1998. *The New York Times.*

Jenness, Valerie and Kendal Brood. *Hate Crimes: New Social Movements and the Politics of Violence.* 1997. New York: Aldine De Gruyer.

Killing of Gay Stirs Concern, Poll Shows. October 18, 1998. *The Buffalo News,* p. A-8.

Lahey, Kathleen. 1995. Submission on Bill C-41: An Act to amend the Criminal Code (Sentencing) and other Acts in consequence thereof. Prepared for Lesbian and Gay Issues & Rights Committee of the Canadian Bar Association–Ontario (copy on file with author).

Leonard, A. 1991. From Law: Homophobia, Heterosexism and Judicial Decision Making. *Journal of Gay and Lesbian Psychotherapy.* 1: 65–91.

Martin, Susan and Chevy Chase. 1996. Investigating Hate Crimes Case Characteristics and Law Enforcement Responses. *Justice Quarterly.* 13: 456–480.

Namoste, K. 1994. Queer Theory, Poststructuralism, and a Sociological Approach to Sexuality. *Sociological Theory.* 12: 220–231.

Pettys, Dick. June 5, 1997. Georgia Sodomy Law Advocate Admits Adultery. Associated Press.

Pettys, Dick. May 30, 1997. Lesbian Loses Georgia Court Case. Associated Press.

Roehr, Bob. July 16, 1998. Hate Crimes Hearing Before the Senate Judiciary Committee. *Bay Area Reporter.*

Romonthan, E. 1996. Queer Cases: A Comparative Analysis of Global Sexual Orientation-Based Asylum Jurisprudence. *Georgetown Immigration Law Journal.* 11: 1–44.

Stryker, Jeff. October 23, 1998. Asking for It: Judges and Juries May Go Easy on Gay Bashers Who Blame Their Victims. *Salon Magazine.*

Taylor, Jane M. January 2, 1998. ACLU Targets Maryland Sodomy Laws. *Washington Blade.*

Valdes, F. 1993. Coming Out and Stepping Up: Queer Legal Theory and Connectivity. *National Journal of Sexual Orientation.* 1: 1–34.

Weinstein, Henry. Judge Urges Repeal of Military's Gay Policy. October 17, 1997. *Los Angeles Times.*

Winer, A. 1994. Hate Crimes, Homosexuals and the Constitution. *Harvard Civil Rights-Civil Liberties Law Review.* 29: 387–397.

Wintemute, Robert. 1995. *Sexual Orientation and Human Rights: The United States Constitution, the European Convention and the Canadian Charter.* Oxford: Oxford University Press.

PART THREE

The Law

The law has become an increasingly prominent part of modern society as more and more aspects of our lives are regulated and controlled by laws. There are legal standards that regulate the production of the food we eat and the clothes we wear. Other laws regulate how and where our dwellings can be built, the type of materials that can be used, and how they are to be maintained. The whole area of family law penetrates our most intimate and private relationships, and we have labor relations standards at the workplace and administrative laws at school. Even at play, there are laws that regulate park use, field use, rink use, and what is appropriate behavior in each of these places. We have criminal laws at the federal and state levels, plus municipal laws that carry penal sanctions.

In order to begin, we must first consider just what we mean by law. When social scientists refer to the law, they usually have in mind a specific conceptualization or definition of the formal law (Reasons and Rich, 1978). Usually this definition focuses on the written rules produced by the state (the central authority in a society) for a specific territory or people (a jurisdiction). These formal laws also usually specify real or potential sanctions, which can be applied against those who violate the law. An essential part of this definition of the law includes a certain conceptualization of the state, since the state is the locus of most law-making and law-enforcement activity in society. As with the definition of law, social theorists have argued about how the state should be defined. Some, for example, have defined the state as the elected (or sometimes nonelected) officials who form the government in a particular society. Others have said that members of the government bureaucracy or civil service should properly be included in any definition of the state. Still others have pointed out the need to include the army, the police, and members of the various agencies in the criminal justice system in this definition.

Given the extensive role that these various groups play in the creation and implementation of law, we conceptualize the state in broader rather than narrower terms. Thus, following Chambliss and Seidman (1982), we will use a definition of the state that includes all those positions in government that are elected or appointed—such as senators and representatives at both the federal and state levels, as well as city council members—and public employees—such as the police, court reporters, teachers, firefighters, and nurses. This broad definition is necessary in order to emphasize the fact that laws are made and enforced by groups in addition to the elected officials of national, state, or local governments. Many institutions, such as schools and hospitals, as well as numerous state agencies, pass and enforce rules and regulations that have a direct impact on our lives, and therefore these institutions should be included in a definition of the state.

Questions about the law and about the nature and role of the state have spawned a rapidly growing area of interest for social scientists from a variety of disciplines. A number of important debates have emerged from the investigation. For example, where do laws come from, and, for that matter, why do we have laws at all? Why are certain things regulated by laws and not others? Why do laws differ historically and contemporarily within and among states? These and other questions have been the subject of much speculation for centuries and continue to generate considerable debate. Most of the research and writing in this area falls within one of two broad theoretical traditions: the order perspective and the conflict perspective. These two perspectives are described briefly in the following sections.[1]

THE ORDER PERSPECTIVE

One of the basic questions that has concerned social thinkers for many generations, has been the basis by which societies are able to continue operating. The question usually asked is, How is social order possible (see Simmel, 1965, pp. 337–356)? Order theorists have offered a variety of answers to this question. Thomas Hobbes, for example, believed that people are by nature aggressive and warlike, and that if they are left to their own devices, society would soon deteriorate into a war of all against all. Hobbes thought social order was possible only because of the existence of a centralized power or authority (the state) that intervened in human affairs. According to Hobbes, each individual citizen surrendered just enough autonomy to the centralized authority (which he called the "Leviathan") to keep the system going.

Hobbes's ideas about the nature of human beings and the role of the state form the basis of the order perspective. Human beings are seen as selfish and aggressive, and society is defined as necessary to control these undesirable human characteristics. At the center of this concept is the notion that people living in a society share common views of the world, have similar values, and generally agree on how society should operate. The law is thought to play a central role in the smooth functioning of the social system.

The order perspective assumes that the law reflects a broadly based consensus in society. Laws are believed to enshrine the most deeply held moral values of the people. The legal system is believed to provide fair and equal treatment for all members of society, regardless of class, sex, age, race, or religion. Whatever inequality exists is understood to be a reflection of the different values of contributions that different people make to the maintenance and functioning of society (Davis & Moore, 1945). Additionally, strict procedural rules govern the legal relations between individuals and the state. These rules are known as due process of law and are thought to form the basis of many of the rights and freedoms that exist in the legal and political system. In this conceptualization, the maintenance of equilibrium and balance ultimately underpin the behavior of law (Black, 1976).

Several schools of jurisprudence (the natural, cultural, and historical schools) reflect the ideas of the order perspective. Each school has identified a particular source for the law that is separate from and outside of the legal system. All of these schools, for example, have denied that the values of the lawmakers themselves have influenced the content of the law (Schur, 1969). On the contrary, these schools of legal philosophy suggest that the law and its agents (including enforcers and administrators) stand apart from society, forming a neutral body that can arbitrate in society's struggles and conflicts. Accordingly, judges are seen to epitomize the evenhanded, nonbiased, neutral stance advocated by this perspective. This point of view is widely disseminated by the media, educational institutions, and politicians. It is usually consistent with the prevailing view of equality of justice in a democratic society—until a highly publicized case, such as *Boy Scouts of America et. al. v. Dale,* (concerning gay scout leaders) places the administration of justice under scrutiny. It is at these times that the human side of the justice system is visible, and questions about the equality, impartiality, and fairness of the system emerge.

Within the order perspective are two basic theories: consensus theory and pluralist theory. Though these two theories are based on many of the same principles, there are important differences between them.

Consensus Theory

Consensus theorists view the law as merely the codification of mutually agreed-upon norms for the smooth functioning of society. The work of French sociologist Emile Durkheim (1858–1917) represents a major contribution to consensus theory. Durkheim believed that societies are founded on *social solidarity,* or cohesiveness. In his classic work *The Division of Labour in Society* (1933), Durkheim identified two types of social solidarity: mechanical and organic. Primitive societies, according to Durkheim, were founded on a shared morality (consensus), and co-operation in these societies was based on the shared beliefs and similar functions performed by people. Durkheim observed that societies based on this consensual, shared morality had *mechanical solidarity.*

In complex, stratified, and heterogeneous societies, as the division of labor increases, roles become more specialized, and people no longer share common bonds. Durkheim argued that as this happens, the common beliefs of mechanical solidarity are replaced by a collective conscience based on the interdependence of people performing dissimilar roles. Durkheim called this *organic solidarity.*

An order theory approach to law is reflected in the writings of the structural functionalists, whose work dominated sociology for a large part of the twentieth century. This theory posits that all social systems have "needs" (functional requisites) that must be met for their survival. For example, social theorist Talcott Parsons (1951) identified internal integration of the social system as necessary. This, he said, was accomplished through the maintenance of appropriate social and emotional relations among members of society. The agreed-upon legal system is particularly pertinent to fulfilling this societal need, according to Parsons, because laws inform people of what is appropriate behavior in different situations. Both old and new members of society could thus be socialized into accepting the already agreed-upon ways of doing things. According to Parsons, establishing a system of rules that everyone is to follow minimizes societal conflict. Obviously problems can develop if people aren't properly socialized and don't know the law, or if people fail to obey them. Problems can also arise if society fails to adequately enforce existing laws.

The heirs of the Durkheimian tradition (including the structural functionalists) have made many significant contributions to our understanding of social order, stability, continuity, and tradition. Their analyses of the functions of law have provided many insights into the role of law in various societies. However, the proliferation of laws in highly complex, stratified societies raises many serious questions that this approach does not adequately address.

Pluralist Theory

Pluralist theory, or pluralism, is a variant of the order perspective that addresses the problem of order in highly stratified, heterogeneous societies. Durkheim's notion of organic solidarity began to address this problem, but pluralist theory provides a more complex explanation. Although pluralist and consensus theories begin with similar assumptions about societal consensus, pluralists recognize the existence of conflict between competing interest groups within such societies. In complex societies with their plurality of interest groups, the law helps to keep disparate elements together and maintain social solidarity and order.

Although pluralist theorists recognize that conflicting interest groups may interpret and influence laws, they hold that consensus about the creation, implementation, and enforcement of law emerges in the end. Pluralists believe that although competing interest groups vie for power, the distribution of power will be decided by the neutral law and its agents for the better functioning of society. This theory depends on competing interest groups following the rules and regulations established to institutionalize societal conflict and produce a compromise, and on the belief that the legal system exists independently from the influence of specific groups or individuals and provides a neutral framework within which societal conflicts can be resolved.

Pluralists believe that the legal system is based on such notions as equality of law, fairness, natural justice, due process, and the one person–one vote method of electing representatives. These principles make up the "rule of law," which, according to pluralist theory, is the cement binding the various factions in society. According to pluralists, by adhering to the principles of the rule of law, the legal system and the state maintain their neutrality and act on behalf of society to maintain order and ensure its proper functioning.

The writings of Max Weber, particularly his analysis of the rise of capitalism and the development of legal–rational authority, have contributed greatly to the development of pluralist theory. According to Weber, because capitalism required predictability for the return of profit, contract and property law arose to form much of the basis of our current legal system. Contract law replaced feudal notions of fealty and subservience, whereas property law allowed the secularization of economic power by making it independent of one's birthright or social standing (Ritzer, 1996).

The abstract nature of formal rationality in modern western law was, for Weber, another necessary facet for the development of capitalist society and its legal system because it facilitated the separation of the legal system from the day-to-day divisions among classes, status groups, and political parties. The apparent independence of law, within its own rational logic, freed the law from capricious religious, political, or class influences. According to Weber, this provided the basis for legal domination by making it possible for the government to take whatever action it wished so long as this action could be justified by the rule-of-law doctrine. That is, as long as the government exercised power in accordance with the existing rules, it could claim that its actions were legitimate. This reflects precisely what Weber argued—that people accept the exercise of power as legitimate when clearly defined rules for its use are followed. Thus, we accept the decisions of our political leaders and accept the legislation that they pass as legitimate because we believe that they acquired their elected positions fairly and exercise power according to well-understood rules and regulations.

Weber detailed a historical change from power and authority based on tradition or charisma to that based on legal rights. Of particular significance to Weber was the rise of bureaucracies as important elements in the power struggle in societies. He saw such bureaucracies as increasingly reducing individual liberty and freedom, but viewed them as a necessary evil because they were the only practical means for organizing human conduct in large-scale, heterogeneous societies. Weber viewed such bureaucratic power as inevitable in both capitalist and socialist societies.

Weber saw society as a struggle between individuals and groups pursuing their own interests. He identified several sources of power used in the struggle between competing interest groups, including class, or economic power; status, or social power; and party, or political power. For example, Weber argued that status groups, consisting of individuals with certain social honor (lawyers and doctors, for example), have social power based on their standing in the community. He viewed one's voluntary associations, or party, as an important source of political power. In the American context, this could include a person's participation in formal political parties such as the Democratic Party, the Republican Party, the Reform or Green Party; or such associations as the Consumer's Association, the AFL-CIO, or the American Manufacturers' Association.

Social class was viewed by Weber as the basis of economic power. However, unlike many Marxist theorists, who accord social class a central position in their analysis of conflict in society, Weber and many contemporary pluralist theorists suggest that although competition and conflict do exist, no ruling class exists. Instead, they believe that a plurality of competing interest groups exists and that, since various interest groups can enter into coalitions around specific issues, no one group is able to dominate, and, by extension, no ruling class can develop.

Weber's historical analysis of the rise of capitalism and its attendant legal and bureaucratic forms contributed great insights into law. There is a rich tradition of research concerning the growth and nature of bureaucracies—particularly state agencies—and the laws surrounding such organizations. In fact, the area of administrative law, which concerns itself largely with bureaucracies, has been the fastest-growing area of law in recent years. The increasingly bureaucratized, formalized, and rationalized nature of capitalist states, such as the United States, confirms many of Weber's early insights. Their proliferation in the post–World War II world dominated by multinational corporations and the welfare state has led to increasing analysis of the interests that these bureaucracies serve. We live in a highly formalized and bureaucratized world, and the nature of benefits and costs to members of this society remains a crucial question.

THE CONFLICT PERSPECTIVE

The second approach to the question of the continuance of society is addressed by the conflict perspective. The conflict perspective is based on the idea that conflict and not consensus best accounts for the nature of social reality. Conflict theorists argue that an ongoing struggle occurs as competing groups vie for power. Although conflict theorists recognize that a certain amount of consensus is necessary to facilitate the continuation of social life and daily routines—for example, people generally obey traffic rules and rules

of etiquette—there is little consensus on more important moral, political, and economic issues related to the exercise of power in society.

Conflict theorists have argued that law is a legitimizing weapon of the highest order,
and that those who make, enforce, and administer laws are merely attempting to perpetuate the existing social arrangements (Chambliss and Seidman, 1982). These theorists have
sought to demystify the nature of laws by emphasizing that laws are human products and
state-created, not discovered in some supernatural realm beyond the influence and control
of ordinary mortals. The conflict perspective holds that participants in the legal system
have values, feelings, and biases that influence (sometimes subtly) their decisions. Thus,
instead of being a neutral framework for the collective interests of society, the law is seen
as an instrument of those in power, used to maintain their position and privilege.

There are two variants of the conflict perspective: Weberian conflict theories and
Marxist conflict theories. Some confusion arises because Weber's work has been used as
the basis for both pluralist and conflict theory explanations. However, Weber's theories
emphasize consensus, whereas Marx's emphasize conflict. Turk (1976, p. 276) presents an
example of a Weberian conflict theory. He argues for the conflict conception of law as
power, that is, as a set of resources whose control and mobilization can in many ways
generate and exacerbate conflicts rather than resolve or soften them. Conflict theorists
drawing on Weber's (1954) analysis have emphasized how the various sources of power
that Weber identified—class, status, and party—are used in the struggle between competing social groups. Unlike Marxist conflict theorists, however, Weberian conflict theorists identify economic or class power as only one form of power used in the struggle.

Marxist theories present a fundamentally different type of conflict theory. They emphasize the relationships among social classes and examine how these relationships are reflected in the creation and implementation of law. They argue that the state and its various
agents aid in the process of capital accumulation for capitalists and assist in the exploitation of workers. In its most manifest and obvious form—instrumentalism—the law represents a tool, or instrument, of class domination as it reflects ruling-class interests. In its
subtler form—structuralism—the law reinforces the existing structure of class arrangements and the dominant forms of inequality. Dialectical analysis, an attempt to overcome
some of the shortcomings of earlier Marxist approaches, emphasizes historical specificity
and the dynamic and constant tension that underlies social change. Dialectical analysis
focuses on the basic contradictions that characterize a specific society, and it examines
efforts directed at the resolution of the basic contradictions. According to Marxist analyses, the genius of the law in capitalist society rests, in part, on the fact that individuals are
conceptualized as legal and political equals despite the basic class inequalities that exist,
and which are a consequence of the capitalist mode of production (Ritzer, 1996).

This version of conflict theory is based on the work of Karl Marx. As both a historian
and an economist, Marx was devoted to studying the nature of capitalism, its growth, and
its subsequent transformation to socialism. Like Weber, Marx saw the rise of capitalism as
evidence of major shifts in social, cultural, and political relations. For Marx, each mode of
production—feudalism, capitalism, or socialism—entails different forms of economic and
social relationships. Under feudalism, lord–serf domination was secured through land
tenure and a system of laws justifying secular authority and dramatic differences in class
based on a system of religious beliefs (divine right of monarchs). Under capitalism,

master–servant domination is secured through wage labor and capital accumulation by state laws regulating labor and commodity markets.

According to Marx in The *Communist Manifesto,* the major classes are the owners of the means of production—the capitalists—and the wage laborers—the proletariat. History evolves through the struggle of classes and the resolution of contradictions that arise due to the inherently different aims of different classes. Such contradictions and the struggles to resolve them bring about change and ultimately transform capitalist societies into socialist societies. Marxian class analysis also recognizes that competition and conflict may exist between various segments of the same class, for example, between industrial capitalists and financial capitalists.

Although Marx gave prominence to the material basis of life and class relationships, he also emphasized the importance of ideas for capitalism. As both facilitator of the accumulation of profit and a standard-bearer of legitimacy, the law operates to mystify the basic inequalities of class relationships, according to Marx. Thus, we are all theoretically "equals"—legally, politically, and socially—and this is emphasized in popular belief and in our institutions: Some examples are the ideals of one person, one vote; blind justice; due process; natural justice; and the Constitution. However, legal equality belies the real material inequality found between different social classes. Workers free to sell their labor to the highest bidder find little consolation in their liberty when employers control the labor market, have a relatively large labor pool from which to draw, and determine the conditions of work. Thus, for Marx, law in the capitalist state both reflects and reinforces the dominance of the capitalist mode of production.

Marx saw the state as a product of capitalism and as a major facilitator for the private accumulation of capital. The state and its various institutions—political, legal, economic, educational, and so on—exist primarily to aid in the accumulation of wealth for capitalists at the expense of the other major class (the proletariat). Although Marx acknowledged the benefits of capitalism over the previous social formation—feudalism—he argued that the inherent contradiction between capitalists and workers would ultimately bring about capitalism's demise, the transformation of the capitalist state, and the rise of a proletarian state without class divisions. More specifically, since capitalism is based on accumulating private property and wealth, the major method for this accumulation is through exploiting the labor of workers. Profits of capitalists are based on the difference between the costs of production, including labor, and the price of the product. If a worker gets $300 per week in wages and produces $10,000 worth of goods each week, the profit is substantial, even considering other costs of production such as rent and machines. Therefore, the capitalist gains at the expense of the worker.

According to Marx, alienation arises when working people lose control over the purpose, process, and products of their labor. Marx saw alienation as including the lack of power over the production process; the separation of mental and manual labor; the intensification and rationalization of the production process, making for repetitive, specialized, and fragmented work; machine technology, which subordinates and further removes control from the workers themselves; and money, which gives people and social relationships an external, artificial character. Given the inherent class conflict in capitalist society, Marx argued that, based on their experiences in the workplace, workers will develop a sense of the objective situation in which they find themselves and work to change the structure of society.

Although Marx's work is more than one hundred years old, it has had a tremendous impact in the twentieth century, as can be seen in the revolutions in Russia, China, Vietnam, Korea, Cuba, Angola, and Nicaragua. Marx's basic concepts and method of analysis continue to be the basis for a great deal of analysis of law.

The theoretical perspectives discussed thus far are described in Table 3.1. The table lists several comparative issues, including each theory's stance on the role of the state, the origins of law, the operation of law, and the future of law. Within these perspectives, we have delineated two order theories—consensus and pluralist—and two conflict theory groups—Weberian and Marxist (both instrumentalist and structuralist).

TABLE 3.1   A Model of Order and Conflict Theories of Law

Order Perspective		*Conflict Perspective*		
CONSENSUS THEORY	**PLURALIST THEORY**	**WEBERIAN THEORY**	**MARXIST THEORY**	
			Instrumentalism	*Structuralism*
Role of the State				
State neutral (mere reflection of consensus)	State neutral (referee)	Theory of power. State is not central	State is instrument of ruling class—capitalists	State is relatively autonomous, but supportive of capitalism, not necessarily of individual
Origin of Law				
Custom codified	Consensus on rule of law, but interest groups compete (i.e., egalitarian ideology for the greatest good)	Law represents certain interests over others. Class, status, and party very important to law.	Needs of capitalist elite	Needs of capitalism of a social formation rule of ideology of law
Operations of Law				
Rational/logical. Based on societal needs	For greatest good, although it may work for one group—thus reform is needed	Systematic discrimination on basis of power differentials	For capitalist elite interests	For interests of capitalism as a social formation
Future of Law				
Necessary for maintenance of society in current form	Necessary for emerging rights of minorities, plus individual rights and group rights	Will increase with growth of conflicts and divisions	Will disappear with the state	Changes with the material and ideational conditions

THE ROLE OF THE STATE

As noted earlier, questions concerning the nature and role of the state are an important part of the analysis of the law. Theoretically, the concept of the state stands for various specific institutions that are connected to one another and thus make up the state: (1) the government, (2) the civil service, (3) the military and the police, (4) the judiciary, and (5) the subunits of central government (Miliband, 1969, pp. 49–67). Methodologically, the concept of the state is significant in underscoring the relationships among the various, seemingly unrelated, social institutions such as the polity, the economy, the family, and the educational system.

In the order perspective, the state is viewed as representing the will of the people. Thus the consensus theory emphasizes the fact that the state merely reflects the common consensus and morality (mechanical solidarity) in the legal sphere. The pluralist theory recognizes the divisions that may occur in society, but it views the state as a neutral referee overseeing the struggles of competing interest groups and acting for the collective good. This view is reflected in the notion of the rule of law—that we are a nation of laws, rather than of men and women. Epitomized by the independence of the judiciary and the principles of equity and fair procedure, the ideology of the rule of law suggests that laws are independent of our own particular interests and operate for the benefit of the entire society. Therefore, laws against common theft apply equally to the millionaire and the penniless unemployed, and laws against illegal mergers apply equally to multinational conglomerates and local family businesses.

The belief in the equality of law, both in its making and operation, is central to the order perspective. Although numerous studies indicate inequality in the law (see Box, 1981; Braithwaite, 1981; Michalowski, 1985; Brickey & Comack, 1986; and Reimund, 2001), order theorists assume either that these are exceptions to the basic justice and equality of law, or that the law guarantees only an equal start, after which individual differences take over. Although most laws may be evenly applied to all citizens, all citizens are not equals in terms of the economic, social, and political powers that affects one's legal standing. Therefore, many state agents such as police, judges, and lawyers may apply essentially the same standards to everyone, but not everyone is equally adept at meeting these standards. The laws themselves may represent specific partisan interest, thus biasing their "even," impartial application. For example, fine option programs can be applied equally to the poor, the middle class, and the rich, but more poor people will be unable to pay and will thus end up in jail or performing community service.

Weberian conflict theory does not emphasize the significance of the state in the analysis of law. The state is viewed as merely one of many sources of power. Therefore, Austin Turk (1976), in a classic article entitled "Law as a Weapon in Social Conflict," discusses how the law is used by various interest groups in power struggles, although Turk's article does not particularly reflect the functions and evolution of the capitalist state.

The significance of power in a variety of forms has been further addressed in the writing of French historian and philosopher Michel Foucault. In his book *Discipline and Punishment* (1977) Foucault argues that power is all-pervasive in the modern state and in a variety of social institutions. Law, in its various forms, merely represents the increasingly repressive nature of discipline in contemporary society, and it reflects the impersonal growth of bureaucracy and its various forms of power. Thus, the basis of modern institutions is power, as reflected in language and thought, not rationality or enlightenment, which in themselves reflect power struggles. The significance of Foucalt's work is in analyzing the manner in which the growth of organizations, professions, and the legal–rational and technical–scientific nature of society have created enormous power differentials between "ordinary people" and the experts. Rather than the manifest power of physical force, it is the power of language, knowledge, verbal and written skills, technical documents, official statistics, and a plethora of devices that render the general population increasingly reliant on officials and professionals for their physical, emotional, and intellectual well-being. Foucault's insights are confirmed in the literature on the professions and their power in influencing laws and matters related to their areas of expertise. For example, the role of medical doctors and lawyers, their language, their professional socialization, and their mystique has been analyzed in relation to their power in society (Larson, 1977).

The state has itself become an increasingly important interest group since World War II. This is evident in the role of the state on such issues as sexual, racial, and age discrimination. For example, affirmative action programs, legislation on equal pay for work of equal value, and human rights laws and tribunals show the active involvement of the state in these matters of social concern. Of course different states and different levels of the same state may end up on opposite sides of such issues. This conflict further emphasizes the fact that the state and its agents are active participants in the social struggles of our times and will reflect the interests of particular groups through legislation.

THE ORIGINS OF THE STATE AND STATE LAW

From Feudal Law to State Law[2]

In Europe, beginning roughly with the fifth century A.D. and continuing into the thirteenth century, a community order based on agriculture and caste prevailed. This community pattern—feudalism—can more accurately be defined as a social and economic system centered on land worked by serfs, workers who were bound to the land. Vassals who pledged fealty to overlords often held the land. Overlords were often titled members of nobility who ruled feudal states, conferring land holdings on vassals in return for military and other services (Chambliss & Ryther, 1975). Feudalism largely disappeared in medieval Europe due to a variety of historical forces, including external conquest, the growth of central governments, surplus population, the loss of serfs' rights to common land, and the rise of cities.

> In part as the legacy of the collapse of feudalism and in part as a consequence of the rise of institutions of capitalism which this collapse afforded, individualism as a generalized social movement emerged from a fact of institutional chaos to a social philosophy and a normative order and transformed, as it grew, the whole of Western society and its culture. Early or late, it came eventually to find social expression in religion as Protestantism; in philosophy as empiricism and idealism; in scholastic inquiry as deductive and inductive methods of natural science; in economy as new institutions such as private property, the market, entrepreneurship, rational accounting, and the re-division of labor along new social lines. (Kennedy, 1970, p. 20)

The feudal community based on shared responsibility was thus replaced by an emerging trade capitalism based on private property and bonded by a new ethic, that of individualism. Obviously, an economic system based on trade and markets required such things as

TABLE 3.2   Changes from Feudal Law to State Law

LEGAL FACTOR	FEUDAL LAW	STATE LAW
Unit of justice	Family	State
Jurisdictional ties	Blood	Territory
Basis of responsibility	Collective	Individual
Method of dispute settlement	Feud or compensation	State court procedures: civil and criminal

roads and standardized currency. Also, the developing merchant class had no warrior caste (vassals) available to protect its interests. A central authority would have to provide the force of arms necessary to defend private interests. Such needs, together with others, gave rise to the nation-state, formally institutionalized in Europe after the fifteenth century. With the establishment of the state, a transformation in law occurred, as outlined in Table 3.2.

Under the feudal system, the family, based on blood ties, was the basic unit determining and administering justice. With the demise of the feudal system, there emerged the nation-state, based on territorial ties, to determine and administer justice. Under feudal law, for example, if one took a person's life, the offender's kin, not the individual killer, would collectively be held responsible. Subsequently, the victim's kin might attempt to settle the debt by taking the life of any member of the killer's family, not necessarily the offender. This might precipitate a feud that could persist for some time. Another possible method of retaliation was extracting compensation from the offending family. Such compensation might be in the form of valued goods paid for the deceased. In the nation-state, by contrast, the killer is held individually responsible for the act and is punished by agents of the state. The nation-state does not allow for compensation as a means of resolving the harm, even if the family of the deceased should agree to a settlement. This is because criminal behavior is viewed as an offense against the nation-state and not just against and an individual.

Law versus Kinship

The laws that arose with the nation-state were in most instances unprecedented and in opposition to the customary order of feudal society. They represented a new social power of the state—and the new goals of an interrelated census, tax, and conscription system. The state's need for labor, an army, tax revenue, and a means of maintaining its bureaucracy gave rise to the census of citizens and the subsequent emergence of civil law. Among the first civil laws were those prohibiting homicide and suicide, which undermined the kinship system by establishing the individual as the property of the state (Diamond, 1971). Thus, the state grew in power and influence as a consequence of a new economic order of private property and the increasingly powerful interests of property owners.

What occurred politically between the fifth and thirteenth centuries to bring about such a dramatic change in legal systems? In addition to the economic changes discussed earlier, the political unification of heretofore separate feudal estates—largely due to civil wars among local military bands, the Danish invasion in the tenth century, and the acceptance of Christianity as the prevailing religion—greatly aided the rise of the nation-state. When William of Normandy became King of England in 1066, the Norman nobles replaced the

Saxons in the ruling hierarchy, and a system of common law emerged as the law for all English subjects. Subsequently, the state took the place of kin and no longer allowed private settlement of criminal cases.

> *English criminal law came about to protect particular interests, primarily those of the King. The criminal law placed the affairs of his subjects under his jurisdiction. The powerful land-holders and the church could no longer freely create and administer law in their own courts. Law that affected the nation was the King's law; the nation's interests were those of the King. (Quinney, 1975, p. 47)*

These changes in legal systems are related to changes in the nature of societies. In the stateless society, more emphasis was placed on compromise, as in the "give a little, get a little" theory of dispute settlement (Chambliss & Seidman, 1982, pp. 28–35). Such a means of resolving disputes usually occurs where an ongoing relationship between disputants is anticipated—in other words, in a small, homogeneous society where continuing close relationships are the rule, and compromise and negotiation are important. In complex, heterogeneous, stratified societies, however, the dispute-settling process determines that one party is right and one is wrong; that is, the winner takes all. Thus, in contemporary North America, the law and legal system are largely based on determining victims and criminals, right and wrong, victim and transgressor, based on the winner-take-all philosophy.

The development of this approach to conflict resolution is related to the extent of stratification in a nation-state.

> *The more economically stratified a society becomes, the more it becomes necessary for the dominant groups in the society to enforce through coercion the norms of conduct which guarantee their supremacy. (Chambliss & Seidman, 1982, pp. 33–34)*

Therefore, in our highly complex and stratified society one should expect the statistics on crime and the criminal justice system to disproportionately represent those in the lower classes. Furthermore, as society grows more diverse and complex, an increase in the number of formal agents of social control follows. The interests of the dominant and powerful segments of the nation-state will be those incorporated into and protected by the law and legal system. What arose with the nation-state was the development of a legal ideology to enhance and subsequently protect the interests of the emerging bourgeois class. As two legal scholars have noted,

> *This tendency is reflected in the importance accorded by lawyers and to legal training in all Western governmental structures and in all movements for social change which aim at seizing state power. (Tiger & Levy, 1977, p. 277)*

Understanding the Corporatist State and Corporatist Legality via the Dialectical Approach

Students of the state, such as O'Connor (1973), point out that the capitalist state's primary concern is aiding the capitalist in the accumulation of capital. Assisting in the functions of social control and legitimation are also important. As Panitch notes in *The Canadian State* (1977), the extent to which the state concerns itself with legitimation (appearing to operate on behalf of all classes) will vary among and within capitalist states over time. According to O'Malley (1983), who describes the rise of the corporatist state and corporatist legality in post–World War II capitalism, the corporate state is an interventionist state that plays a mediating role in a tripartite alliance with capital, organized labor, and government. It attempts to gain the cooperation of capital and labor for the "organic whole" of society. State regulation, based on legal–rational principles, seeks to maximize the rationality and coordination of production. The state attempts to remain a "neutral referee," with corporatist legality expressed in technical and administratively rational procedures that are established for the good of all. Through a variety of regulatory agencies, boards, commissions, and other bodies, the state presents itself as an arbitrator between the demands of the capitalists and those of labor.

The degree to which the state, through its particular agencies and agents, reflects an instrumentalist or structuralist analysis varies historically and cross nationally. A valuable aspect of dialectical analysis, in this context, is that although structural conditions provide limits to action, they do not predetermine it. Thus, the inherent contradiction between the capitalist drive for profit and labor's drive for material well-being may be played out quite differently in say, the 1990s than in earlier periods. For example, the relationship between the New York government and its employees or between the American Federal Employees Union and the U.S. government may vary dramatically as social, economic, and political factors change. In fact, treating all situations as equal masks differences in the actors involved, the critical issues of the moment, and the relative power wielded by various factions. Given the inherent contradictions of contemporary capitalism, the dialectical approach encourages us to look at how these contradictions are manifested in real events, at historically specific times, and among real actors.

One of the few legal scholars to build from earlier explanations, Chambliss (1986) suggests a dialectical analysis that views the creation of law as a process of resolving contradictions, conflicts, and dilemmas inherent in the social structure of a particular historical period. The starting point in such an analysis is a particular historical context and the passage of laws that attempt to address a particular contradiction or conflict. Rather than positing that laws have some supreme force or logic in and out of themselves, the dialectical approach emphasizes the fact that people create laws at a particular time to deal with specific issues and problems.

In the study of specific laws, some scholars (Chambliss & Seidman, 1982) suggest the need to go beyond instrumentalism or structuralism alone and approach the analysis of law dialectically. In recognizing the complexity of the state, with its bureaucracies and their contradictions, and the fact that people from all classes act and react to their social world, a dialectical approach appears to be more useful because it attempts to be sensitive to these various relationships.

> *People, we reiterate, make choices, respond to realities, and struggle against oppression. Those at the top act as a class to perpetuate their privilege; those sprinkled below do likewise. The contrary interests generate conflicts, in response to which the government becomes complex, interactive and ever-changing. In a word, it is dialectical. (Chambliss & Seidman, 1982, p. 316)*

The dialectical approach suggested by Chambliss and Seidman addresses the interaction, bureaucracies, status, and power evident in Weberian theory, as well as the Marxist concern with classes, contradictions, class struggle, and social change. Although the dialectical approach is ambitious in scope, it attempts to be more sensitive to the nature and complexity of society than other theories are. In some cases, either an instrumentalist account or a structuralist account of the origin of a specific law may be more consistent with the facts. However, dialectical analysis urges us not to rigidly prejudge history, especially the particular form that the class struggle has taken at different times.

The dialectical approach is a methodology by which we analyze and understand society historically and contemporarily. Both Karl Marx and his associate Friedrich Engles emphasized this way of understanding. Philosopher George Hegel presented in the early nineteenth century the notion that certain ideas emerge (thesis) and are contradicted by other ideas (antithesis), and from this contradiction new ideas emerge (synthesis). Hegel was an idealist; that is, he believed that ideas create material reality and are the dominant force in human life. Marx turned Hegel upside down, presenting a materialist analysis, which argues that concrete, everyday, objective conditions of material life (such as work and living conditions) constitute reality and establish the basis of various thought systems such as politics, religion, education, and law. Marx emphasized the material basis of life—that is, the way we produce and reproduce our daily necessities. Modes of production such as feudalism, capitalism, and socialism set the general boundaries for the nature of family life, work, leisure, politics, and religion. However, this is not an economic, linear determinism involving only one type of mode of production (capitalism) and only one type of political or family structure, with people's behavior determined by this external force. We have only to look at varying capitalist states such as South Africa, Canada, Brazil, the United States, and Sweden to find differing political and social practices. Thus, although capitalism is the dominant mode of production in all of these nations, the way their institutions—such as government, the family, education, and the legal system—are organized in each of them varies dramatically. Likewise, major differences exist between institutions in the socialist states of the People's Republic of China and Cuba, for example (Davis & Scase, 1985).

The real worth of the dialectical method is that it views individuals as not only influenced and shaped by social forces, but also as acting to shape and influence social institutions. This does not mean that we are free willed and can do anything—we act within definite parameters—but it does mean that we are not merely atoms being bounced around by social force fields. In nineteenth-century Canada and the United States, a few brave individuals fought for the rights of women, blacks, and native people, largely to no avail. They were executed by the state or lynched by vigilantes, ostracized, isolated, repressed, or ignored. During the twentieth century, particularly since World War II, people with essentially the same ideas have successfully reversed official (*de jure*) racism and sexism. One has to look at the particular historical circumstances of a given society to understand successes and failures in bringing about social change. This entails analysis not only of the individual biographies of the people involved, but also of the social history of the society and how the two relate.

> *The facts of contemporary history are also facts about the success and the failure of individual men and women. When a society is industrialized, a peasant becomes a worker; a feudal lord is liquidated or becomes a businessman. When classes rise and fall, a man is employed or unemployed; when the rate of investment goes up or down, a man takes heart or goes broke. When wars happen, an insurance salesman becomes a rocket launcher; a store clerk, a radar man; a wife lives alone; a child grows up without a father. Neither the life of an individual nor the history of a society can be understood without understanding both. (Mills, 1959, p. 3)*

Important to dialectical analysis is the notion of contradiction. Contradictions are inherent in society and differ in various modes of production. For example, under capitalism, profit is the major aim of those who own the means of production. The major source of profit is gained by paying workers less than the value of the goods they create or produce. This provides surplus value, which is the basis of profit. The drive for profit for the few who are owners is contradictory to the needs of workers to provide a decent living for themselves and their families. This fundamental contradiction may not produce constant conflict, but it helps to explain why conflict arises. Historically, the drive for profits (thesis) led to long hours and horrid working conditions for workers (antithesis), especially in early industrial capitalism—for example, in England. This led to conflict between workers and capitalists and eventually to the emergence of social legislation creating minimum wages and shorter work hours, reducing child labor, and establishing trade unions (synthesis). This new synthesis of legitimate trade unionism and social legislation did not eliminate the contradiction, but merely reduced the manifest conflict and institutionalized it in the form of labor relations.

The real material gains made by workers through unionization and the establishment of social legislation has led to increasing efforts by capitalists to replace workers with machines and advanced technology and with cheaper labor in other parts of the world (Rinehart, 1987). U.S. companies produce goods in other parts of the world, such as Asia and Latin American, where laxer working conditions are incentives for investment: low wages, minimal standards for environmental and health and safety and large tax concessions. This has led to deindustrialization unemployment in North America and a reduction in the quality of real material life of workers. In other words, becoming competitive in the international marketplace means wage freezes or rollbacks, reduced standards for working conditions and the environment, and the provision of tax incentives for foreign capital. Free trade is not necessarily "free" in its consequences (Reasons, 1994).

It is important in materialist dialectical analysis to be historically specific. One must look at specific states and people, and their lives at specific periods in history, to adequately analyze the nature of a situation. This approach avoids grand theorizing and broad generalizations devoid of specific concrete examples (Beire & Quinney, 1982). To view law dialectally is to integrate the various levels of social analysis into a meaningful whole. It is to take specific concrete people—such as judges, lawyers, and unionists—and understand their behavior and attitudes in relation to their particular community or country and its specific material and ideological conditions at a particular point in time. A dialectical approach incorporates aspects of all the previously mentioned perspectives and theories in an effort to explain a specific phenomenon. Why does there appear to be a consensus at a given time regarding a specific law? Why do certain interest groups emerge, and how do they reflect broader features of a society? Why does the state support certain crime-control policies and not others? Why do different segments of the state or of a social class disagree about particular laws and policies? All of these general questions must be grounded in a particular material and ideological reality (Milovanovic, 1988).

CASE STUDIES OF LAWS

Theft

A classic example of the role of dominant group interests in defining crime is the emergence of the law of theft (Hall, 1952). Prior to the fifteenth century, no legal conception of theft existed in the criminal law as we know it today. The legal concept of theft was established in the Carrier's Case of 1473, and it still flourishes in contemporary Western law. In the Carrier's Case, a transporter of goods took the wares he was entrusted with, converted them to his own use, and was subsequently charged with a felony. Prior to this case, taking goods entrusted to one was not theft. The burden was on those consigning commodities to others to find someone who was reliable and trustworthy. If merchants failed to find someone trustworthy, they could lose a large amount of goods. Thus, possession was ten-tenths of the law. However, in this case, the king's judges ruled the transporter guilty of theft, contrary to all legal precedent. Why the dramatic change?

In fifteenth century Europe, the commercial revolution was taking place, and the old feudal structure based on agriculture was giving way to a new order based on industry and trade. More significantly, the king was very involved in royal commercial activities, including trade, and could not allow such wrongdoings. Since the courts were subservient to the wishes of King Edward IV, this decision against the dishonest merchant should have been anticipated. Notwithstanding prior common law, the state's (i.e., the king's) interests were best served by expanding the definition of theft to better protect the commercial interests of the state and the new entrepreneurial class. As mentioned earlier, contemporary emphasis on theft as a working- or lower-class crime (i.e., a street crime) rather than a middle- or upper-class crime (i.e., a suite crime) continues this protection of dominant interests.

Rape and Witchcraft

While rape laws may be thought to be in the interest of all citizens, a historical accounting suggests otherwise. In fact, Diamond (1971) describes how rape laws were invented by the state for conscription purposes. A specific category of the king's women in Dahomey, England, were sent to local villages; men who had intercourse with them were charged with rape, and on summary trial, were punished by conscription into the army. Therefore, rape began as a *civil* crime. Such behaviors would have been dealt with differently under feudal law; however, the king needed soldiers, and this was one method to obtain them.

The emergence of rape laws in England reflects a sexist bias apparent in witchcraft laws. For some, the historical persecution and prosecution of witches portray a simple hatred of women and an attempt to maintain male hegemony. For example, the reasons given for the female nature of witchcraft reflected dominant male stereotypes. King James I explained in his *Demonologie* (1597), why women were twenty times more likely than men to be witches. His explanation is based on three conditions women are supposedly more susceptible to: curiosity, revenge, and greed due to poverty. Such a view was prevalent throughout the sixteenth and seventeenth centuries (Geis, 1979).

> *Suffice it to say that witchcraft charges, at certain times, and under certain conditions becomes a useful method for men to keep women inferior and in fear. (Geis, 1979)*

Though it is tempting to view witchcraft as another male chauvinist plot, it is necessary to go beyond the apparent sexism. Currie (1968) examines this phenomenon as it existed in Europe between roughly the fifteenth and eighteenth centuries. Although women were most frequently identified as witches in England, on the continent of Europe men were often found guilty of the practice. Further, although most witches in England were lower class, many on the continent were propertied. Why the difference in the sex and class of witches on different continents? In Great Britain, the center of an emerging and increasingly strong mercantile capitalism, law ensured the sanctity of private property. Thus, the state could not confiscate the property of witches. On the continent, however, due to the less dramatic decline of feudal order, property could be confiscated. Consequently, in Europe, there was a strong economic reason to identify men as well as women as witches, provided they held property. Accordingly, the witch-hunting business was a virtual industry on the continent. In Britain, during the same period of history, it was little more than a racket. Thus, what appears to be only sex-based discrimination may under closer examination reveal economic exploitation.

Witchcraft trials ceased in Great Britain when religion became a less powerful force in the state, medical practices improved, criminal procedures became fewer, and humans began to attribute disasters to something other than evil forces. Nonetheless, other forms of sexual discrimination and oppression emerged because the underlying conflicts remained unresolved.

While witchcraft laws and trials are only historic curiosities today, rape remains a significant social and political issue. Today's laws concerning rape are largely based on English common law. A major figure in defining legal approaches toward both witchcraft and rape was Sir Matthew Hale, a leading jurist of seventeenth-century England. His sexist bias was represented not only in witchcraft rulings, but also in rape cases. Rape laws arose to protect not women per se, but women as the property of fathers and husbands. From Hale emanated the long-standing cautionary instruction that rape "is an accusation easily to be made and hard to be proved, and harder to be defended by the party accused, the never so innocent" (Geis, 1979, p. 30). Although this is an often-quoted phrase, Geis (1979) shows it is entirely inaccurate. It has never been an easy charge to make, or difficult to rebut. This is particularly evident in the fact that the woman filing a rape charge often becomes the defendant when her character is put on trial.

Victimless Crimes

The elite class is also interested in maintaining social control via laws prohibiting victimless crimes such as pornography, obscenity, vagrancy, drunkenness, abortion, illicit drug use, gambling, and homosexuality. Drug laws in particular reflect class and racial interests. Other victimless offenses reflect class, moral, and economic interests. For example, vagrancy laws emerged in fourteenth-century England to supply labor for landowners. Subsequently, vagrancy laws were used to control criminal activities and "undesirable" elements in communities in England, the United States, and Canada (Chambliss, 1964). In recent years, such statutes have been attacked as unconstitutional and expunged, with other statutes substituted to control the underclasses.

Although drunkenness has been increasingly eliminated as a crime, historically it was established to uphold middle-class, rural, Protestant puritan beliefs about drinking. In fact, such interests led to the "noble experiment" of Prohibition (Gusfield, 1963). Previously, the temperance movement emerged during the post–Civil War period and continued on until the institutionalization of Prohibition in 1919. This was a time when immigrant workers —men, women, and children—were savagely exploited in the urban factory system. The image of alcohol-dependent workers seeking escape from toil was hardly comforting to the industrial elite. Thus, it is plausible to argue that Prohibition was more than a cultural victory for the Puritans. Rather, it was consistent with corporate industrial interests.

Juvenile Delinquency

Radio, television, newspapers, civic leaders, and criminal justice officials constantly remind us that juvenile delinquency is rapidly increasing and becoming a serious menace to society. However, if we look beyond the rhetoric of such assertions, we find that our contemporary problem of delinquency has a historical basis in the needs and values of specific dominant interests and their ideology of social control. Although legal distinctions based on age can be found in early Chinese society, our approach to juvenile delinquency today is based on English common law. The case of *Eyre v. Shaftsbury* in 1722 established the principle of *parens patriae,* wherein the king (i.e., the state) acts as a parent in the best interests of the child. Although such a principle appears humanitarian and benevolent, the facts of this case suggest other purposes. More specifically, the king had much to gain financially by managing the Earl of Shaftsbury's land, so the young earl was made a ward of the court (Venable, 1966). Subsequently, emphasis was placed on wealthy youth who were judged dependent or neglected and in need of "protection."

In the nineteenth century there emerged a "child-saving movement" in the United States and Canada that was interested in child welfare, education, reformatories, labor, and other youth-related issues (Platt, 1969). Many observers have characterized the anti-delinquency reformers as humanitarians who were disinterested citizens representing an enlightened and socially responsible middle class. Platt, however, argues that

> the child-saving movement was a coercive and conservatizing influence, that liberalism in the Progressive era was the conscious product of policies initiated or supported by leaders of major corporations and financial institutions, and that many social reformers wanted to secure existing political and economic arrangements, albeit in an ameliorated and regulated form. (1974, p. 336)

During the latter part of the nineteenth century, major cities in the United States were teeming with immigrants who were struggling with poverty, deplorable housing, and miserable living conditions. Juvenile crime, like other social problems, was viewed by the middle and upper classes as generally a product of the city, and specifically of the poor and working-class immigrants. As part of the "Progressive Era," women primarily of the middle and upper classes led the child-saving movement as an extension of the maternal role.

> For traditionally educated women and daughters of the landed and industrial gentry, the child-saving movement presented an opportunity for pursuing socially acceptable public roles and for restoring some of the authority and spiritual influence which many women felt they had lost through the urbanization of family life. (Platt, 1974, p. 371)

The progressive period was characterized by nativism and racism largely directed at the urban working class, which was mainly immigrant. The attempts to control the youth of this class paralleled other efforts at manipulation, such as birth control and eugenics. While their activities were legitimized as humanitarian, the child-savers reflected their class and ethnic position in society by working to maintain the status quo.

With the beginning of the juvenile court in the last decade of the nineteenth century in Chicago, a new era of social control emerged. Although the court initially concerned itself with juvenile acts that violated existing criminal statues, new "crimes" were to be developed that would greatly increase the scope of the court. These "status" offenses included vicious or immoral behavior; incorrigibility; truancy; roaming the streets; and frequenting such places as pool halls, bowling alleys, dance halls, and movies, among others. Such delinquent behavior was principally found among the working class and poor and is still falsely assumed to be a cause of subsequent criminality. The assumption by the child-savers was that "delinquent" behavior is correctable through treatment and rehabilitation. The new role of the social worker was to aid greatly in solving this "problem." It was more than coincidental that women were instrumental in both the child-saving movement and the rise of the social work profession. Each represented a traditional view of women's place in society. Advocates of probation and the social welfare profession, many of whom were women, also spearheaded Canadian delinquency legislation (Hagen & Leon, 1977). Established along with the definition of delinquency and separate court processing was a whole new set of occupations for an emerging profession.

Drug Laws

Opium and "The Yellow Peril."   The association of the "drug problem," specifically opiate addiction, with racism was particularly acute during the first few decades of the twentieth century. Opiate addiction was linked with the "yellow peril"—the stereotype of threatening Asian immigrants—and was felt to be incompatible with white morality and superiority. The issues surrounding the use of opium for smoking became part of a larger effort to stigmatize Asians as dangerous and insidious, to be condemned and isolated. "Anti-drug" became a rallying point for racists and nativists, who felt themselves to be in the throes of a life-and-death struggle with alien forces. Such racist appeals were significant in the definition of the drug problem in the United States.

The Chinese began to emigrate to the United States in large numbers in the 1850s. Two decades later, a serious crusade against opium use began during a period of economic depression. The press widely disseminated the imagery of opium-crazed Chinese who were supposedly a threat to "American" institutions. White members of the working class blamed their grim economic conditions on unfair competition with Chinese immigrant labor. As a specific ideology, the yellow peril rationalized the low wages and danger that often accompanied what was disparagingly termed "coolie labor." Thus, the yellow peril represented more than a symbol of cultural and racial bigotry. It was a specific ideology that diverted attention from the failure of the economic system, fragmented the working class, and preserved the interests of the higher circles (Helmer, 1975).

The English Opium Pushers.   The origin of widespread Chinese opium use began not in China, which became the most notable market for the drug, but in India in the state of Bengal, where the English became the dominant political power in the middle of the eighteenth century. It was in Bengal that the English established a monopoly over the opium industry and began to supply China. The command of this market was the basis of British opium policy throughout the nineteenth century.

The specific monopolist in the opium arrangement was the East India Company, as trade between Great Britain and China was its exclusive preserve. Pressured by British rulers, Indian landowners reluctantly converted more and more land to poppy production. The intention of course was to provide more opium profits for the East India Company and more tax revenues for the British crown. In the 1830s, the predictable happened—the vast shipments of opium to China began to glut the marketplace. The British responded by cutting the price. Between 1830 and 1839, opium prices averaged approximately 50 percent of those of the previous decade. Cheaper prices attracted more consumers, and thus the pattern was set for one facet of British colonialism that was to continue through the century—pushing opium on an international level. Although the trade was finally halted in 1917, local production emerged (Owen, 1934). Thus, the opium problem remained a colonial legacy in China, successfully controlled only with the coming of the Chinese Revolution in the latter half of the 1940s.

The "Mexican Menace."   The Federal Bureau of Narcotics was instrumental in the development of the Marijuana Tax Act of 1937. However, it is vital to understand the historical period within which this legislation emerged—the decade of America's deepest economic depression. As in the 1870s, markets collapsed, industrial production sagged, and unemployment was rampant. Once again, a specific ideology of drug control emerged. This time, opium and the yellow peril were replaced by marijuana and the "Mexican menace" (Reasons, 1975).

In 1928, the Benito Juarez Mutual Aid Society was founded as one of the first labor unions in California. It provided a storm warning for corporate agriculture and landowning interests in that state. Agribusiness in California was built on cheap Chicano labor, and the centrality of that labor was evident in growers' opposition to immigration quotas for Mexicans. However, the Great Depression meant a surplus of cheap labor, especially in urban areas such as Los Angeles.

In times of economic downturn, the propensity for scapegoating increases. The presence of Chicano workers as well as their use of cannabis as a peasant medicinal remedy produced no great moral crusades or legislative efforts when economic times were good. However, with the onset of the Great Depression, the Chicano labor force was cast as a threat to the growing legions of unemployed, and the use of marijuana became a symbol of evil. Users were supposed to commit violent crimes—including the shooting of police. Salvation from the menace required "repatriation" (deportation) and jail for the "enemy deviants" (Helmer, 1975). Thus, on a cultural level the marijuana menace was in part a nativistic phenomenon pitting Anglo against Chicano (Reasons, 1974).

DUAL LEGALITIES

Some of the previous examples provide evidence of how laws may criminalize certain races, women, and classes. One of the clearest historical examples is that of race and the law. It has been well documented that both in the colonial period and after the American Revolution, the legal institutions were expressly racist. In the major institutions of politics, employment, marriage, housing, schooling, criminal justice, and law making, non-whites were subject to discrimination (Bell, Jr., 2000; Kennedy, 1997).

In the following chart (Table 3.3) we provide some examples of the dual legality and rights denied during the history of the United States. It is only in our recent history that we have eliminated express (de jure) racism in the law. The articles in this section provide examples of the historical and current importance of race, class, and gender in the making and application of laws.

In the first article in this section, law professor Munger and sociologist Seron address the importance of class in the study of the law. They point out that although the sociology

TABLE 3.3   Racial Dual Legality (1492–1970)

FOR WHITES	FOR NONWHITES	RIGHTS DENIED NONWHITES
Declaration of Independence	Slave codes	Liberty
Bill of Rights	Head taxes for Chinese	Education
Civil War amendments	Japanese internment	Access to courts
Rights of property	Genocide of Native	Due process
Rights of contract	Americans	Religious freedom
	Jim Crow laws	Property ownership
	Lynchings	Employment
	Racist judicial decisions	Protection by law enforcement
	Discriminatory practices	Free speech

of law has provided a great deal of research, there needs to be more emphasis upon class analysis of the law, both in the application of the law and in the legal system and among lawyers themselves. Class can be studied objectively through social structural analysis or subjectively through narration of stories of people participating in the legal system. Although both class and law affect us in our everyday life, the authors argue that we shouldn't just emphasize the narrative, but should place that narrative within a more structural analysis of inequality in society. The authors also note how hierarchical and stratified the legal profession itself remains. Finally, they point out that social class is implicated in social change. That is, classes that are content with the way that inequality currently exists will be less likely to be agents of social change in the future. What the authors emphasize is that class at the structural level needs to be researched and considered in terms of law making and the administration of justice, both civilly and criminally. The persistence and importance of social class in our society must be recognized and considered among students of law and society.

In "Law and Race," Burns provides a brief but powerful comment on the nature of early racist codes regarding slaves, and overviews the racist decision in Dred Scott. Significantly, he points out that although after the civil war there were constitutional amendments purportedly "freeing the slaves," other legal barriers arose to Blacks via Jim Crow and related statutes and judicial decisions. Finally, he points out that while *Brown vs. Board of Education* began the process of eliminating Jim Crow laws, racism remains part of the fabric of the United States.

The O. J. Simpson trial gripped the nation as no other. Sociologist Olstead provides a penetrating analysis of race, class, and gender aspects of the Simpson trial. She points out that inequality based on race, class, or gender should not be viewed competitively but cumulatively. That is, the question isn't whether sexism is more evil than racism, but rather it is what happens when you are non-white, poor, and a woman. The cumulative fact of these forms of inequality become more oppressive. After a thorough discussion of the meaning of race, gender, and class, Olstead analyzes the O. J. Simpson case in terms of discourse analysis—what kinds of things were said in the media and elsewhere and what kinds of ideas or ideologies were distributed regarding race, class, and gender from this particular trial. She makes an excellent point that preconceptions about Blacks, class, and gender affected the way people interpreted the filtered presentations of the media. Likewise, media representations reflected these preconceptions and assumptions. In looking at the manner in which the trial was covered and the specific aspects of the case, she provides examples of how racism, genderism, and classism were evident in the O. J. Simpson case.

STUDY QUESTIONS

1. Compare order and conflict theory explanations of drug laws.

2. Identify the major changes in the law from feudal to state systems.

3. Through example, explain how there has been a dual system of law historically on the basis of race, gender, and class.

4. Drawing from the sociology of law, how does class influence the administration of justice?

5. How have the law and past U.S. Supreme Court decisions maintained racism?

6. After the Civil War, how were Blacks still subjugated legally?

7. Discuss how racism, genderism, and classism were evident in the O. J. Simpson trial.

NOTES

1. This discussion is based on theoretical distinctions found in "Theories of Law and Society," in *Law and Society: A Critical Perspective* by T. C. Caputo, M. Kennedy, C. E. Reasons, and A. Brannigan (Eds.). Toronto: Harcourt Brace Jovanovich, 1989, pp. 1–15.
2. The distinctions made here are based on Reasons and Perdue, 1981, pp. 331–335.

REFERENCES

Bell, Jr., Derrick (2000). *Race, Racism and American Law,* 4th ed. New York: Aspen Law and Business.

Black, D. (1976). *The Behavior of Law.* London: Academic Press.

Box, S. (1981). *Deviance, Reality and Society,* 2nd ed. London: Holt, Rinehart & Winston.

Braithwaite, J. (1981). "The Myth of Social Class and Criminality Reconsidered," *American Sociology Review 46:* 22–45.

Brickey, S. L., and E. Comack (1986). *The Social Basis of Law.* Toronto: Garamond Press.

Beire, Piers, and Richard Quinney (1982). *Marxism and Law.* New York: John Wiley & Sons.

Chambliss, William (1964). "A Sociological Analysis of the Law of Vagrancy," *Social Problems 12:*67–77.

Chambliss, William, and Thomas Ryther (1975). *Sociology: The Discipline and Its Direction.* New York: McGraw-Hill.

Chambliss, W., and R. Seidman (1982). *Law, Order and Power,* 2nd ed. Reading, MA: Addison-Wesley.

Chambliss, W. (1986). "On Lawmaking." In *The Social Basis of Law,* S. L. Brickey and E. Comack (Eds.). Toronto: Garamond Press.

Currie, Elliot P. (1968). "Crimes Without Criminals: Witchcraft and Its Control in Renaissance Europe," *Law and Society Review 3:*7–32.

Davis, H., and R. Scase (1985). *Western Capitalism and State Socialism.* Oxford: Basil Blackwell.

Davis, K., and W. Moore (1945). "Some Principles of Stratification," *American Sociological Review 10:*242–249.

Diamond, Stanley (1971). "The Rule of Law Versus the Order of Custom," *Social Research 38:* 42–72.

Durkheim, E. (1933). *The Division of Labour in Society.* New York: Free Press.

Foucault, Michel (1977). *Discipline and Punishment: The Origins of the Prison.* New York: Pantheon.

Geis, Gilbert (1979). "Lord Hale, Witches and Rape," *British Journal of Law and Society 5*:26–44.

Gusfield, Joseph (1963). *Symbolic Crusade.* Urbana, Ill.: University of Illinois Press.

Hagan, John, and Jeffrey Leon (1977). "Rediscovering Delinquency: Social History, Political Ideology and the Sociology of Law," *American Sociological Review 42*: 587–598.

Hall, Jerome (1952). *Theft, Law and Society,* 2nd ed. Indianapolis, Ind.: Bobbs-Merrill.

Helmer, John (1975). *Drugs and Minority Oppression.* New York: Seabury Press.

Kennedy, Randall (1997). *Race, Crime and the Law.* New York: Vintage Books.

Larson, M. S. (1977). *The Rise of Professionalism: A Sociological Analysis.* Berkeley: University of California Press.

Michalowski, R. (1985). *Law, Order and Crime.* New York: Random House.

Miliband, R. (1969). *The State in Capitalist Society.* New York: Random House.

Mills, C. Wright (1959). *The Sociological Imagination.* New York: Oxford University Press.

Milovonovic, Drogan (1988). *A Primer in the Sociology of Law.* New York: Horrow and Heston.

O'Connor, J. (1973). *The Fiscal Crisis of the State.* New York: St. Martin's.

O'Malley, P. (1983). *Law, Capitalism and Democracy.* Sydney: George Allen & Unwin.

Owen, David E. (1934). *British Opium Policy in China and India.* New Haven, Conn.: Yale University Press.

Panitch, Leo (Ed.). (1977). *The Canadian State.* Toronto: University of Toronto Press.

Parsons, Talcott (1951). *The Social System.* Glencoe, IL: Free Press.

Platt, Anthony (1969). *The Child Saviors.* Chicago: University of Chicago Press.

Quinney, Richard (1975). *Criminology.* Boston: Little, Brown.

Reasons, Charles (1994). "NAFTA and Inequality: A Canadian Perspective," *Constitutional Forum 5*:72–77.

Reasons, Charles E. (1975). "The Addict as a Criminal: Perpetuation of a Legend," *Crime and Delinquency 21*:19–27.

Reasons, Charles E., and Robert Rich (1978). *The Sociology of Law: A Conflict Perspective.* Toronto: Butterworths.

Reasons, Charles E., and William D. Perdue (1981). *The Ideology of Social Problems.* Palo Alto: Mayfield.

Reimund, Jeffrey (2001). *The Rich Get Richer and the Poor Get Prison,* 6th ed. Boston: Allyn and Bacon.

Rinehart, J. (1987). *The Tyranny of Work: Alienation and the Labour Process,* 2nd ed. Toronto: Harcourt Brace Jovanovich.

Ritzer, George (1996). *Classical Sociological Theory,* 2nd ed. New York: McGraw-Hill.

Rosoff, Stephen M., Henry N. Pontell, and Robert Tillman (1998). *Profit Without Honor: White Collar Crime and the Looting of America.* Upper Saddle River, N.J.: Prentice Hall.

Schur, E. (1969). *Law and Society.* New York: Random House.

Simmel, G. (1965). "How is Society Possible?," trans. Kurt Wolff. In *Essays on Sociology, Philosophy and Aesthetics,* Kurt Wolff (Ed.). New York: Harper.

Tiger, Michael E., and Madelein R. Levy (1977). *Law and the Rise of Capitalism.* New York: Monthly Review Press.

Turk, Austin (1976). "Law as a Weapon in Social Conflict," *Social Problems 23*:276–291.

Venable, Gilbert T. (1966). "The Parens Patrial Theory and Its Effects on the Constitutional Limits of Juvenile Court Powers," *University of Pittsburgh Law Review* (June): 892–914.

Law and Inequality:
Race, Gender . . . and, of Course, Class

CARROLL SERON
City University of New York

FRANK MUNGER
State University of New York

This [reading] discusses the concept of class in an important subfield, the sociology of law. Class, a pivotal institution of society, was central to the earliest studies of legal institutions and of law and inequality in particular. More recently, class has played a less important role. This [reading] argues for the continuing importance of class and provides examples of its potential use in contemporary sociolegal research. The first part reviews early work that employed class and instrumental models of the state. Grounded, anti-formal models of law provided a contrasting view. Following wider trends in the discipline, sociology of law turned from structural models to theories of law as an ideology, and most recently, as reviewed in the second part, to law as an element of consciousness and experience. While acknowledging the value of contemporary research that documents a deeply textured, paradoxical, and nuanced analysis of the role of law in society, the third part argues for theorizing the link between experience and context, including the role of social class, and presents a research agenda for a sociology of law, where the relationship between law and class is considered both as institution and experience.

The plain fact is that in a new stage of capitalism, class divides as ruthlessly as it did in the age of the Robber Barons.
—Richard Sennett,[1] 1942

INTRODUCTION

In this [reading] we review the ways in which class has been conceptualized and used to explain the role of legal institutions in society. Though always controversial in American social science, class is nonetheless central in thought and theorizing about society, including its legal institutions. In the past two decades, theories of class and social structure have been endlessly critiqued, and the importance of class as a research concept reduced to the point of near extinction. Class is only now beginning to be reconsidered—as one more anchor of personal identity like gender, race, and ethnicity. The contemporary turn from structural theory toward interpretive studies of experience emphasizes nuanced descriptions of actors' orientations to law in a particular context, but it has offered little to explain the interaction between individual agency and continuing patterns of political or economic hierarchy.

Understanding the structural foundations of class continues to be important in the postmodern world. Class describes an individual's position with respect to the central economic and cultural institutions of society and, in turn, relates that position to the social resources available to the individual. Just as new ways have been found to bring the state back in or to create a new institutionalism that acknowledges the importance of complex continuing patterns in social life—but purged of deterministic claims—so class must be reconceptualized. Indeed, our review of sociolegal research shows that class has continued to be an important, if largely implicit, concept not only making possible a clearer understanding of the distributive effects of economies but also providing a key to understanding power in contemporary society.

We show here that class, as a marker for the distributive effects of law, has been of great importance in sociolegal studies. In the 1970s, structural theories began to decline in importance. In the sociology of law, the importance of class was diminished still further by the weight of arguments of neo-Marxists and others that law is an ideological force, not a straightforward reflection of resource inequality or a simple instrument of domination.

The interpretive and postmodern turn in sociology is reflected in contemporary sociolegal research on legal culture and legal consciousness, and on narrative and discourse about law. The critique and decline of grand theory did not undercut interest in the concrete distributive consequences of law, the bread and butter of the field, but the shift did sever these studies conceptually from their roots in general theories of society. The second part of this [reading] describes the shift as well as the

conceptual limits of this paradigm: Agency alone will not provide an understanding of the group-life of a society or its institutions, or the ways in which class continues to form an important bridge between those contingencies that comprise elements of an actor's own understanding of action and those of which the actor is unaware.

Finally, the third part of the [reading] presents a research agenda for a sociology of law where the tension between structure and agency, class and law, frames the undertaking. Using recent studies as examples, we show why the institutions of class continue to explain dimensions of inequality and hierarchy and how incorporating a nuanced, agency-sensitive concept of class will contribute to the development of sociology of law and to class theory.

THEORY AND THE PROBLEM OF LAW AND INEQUALITY

The sociology of law has always drawn on theories prevailing in the discipline. Early sociology of law was shaped by mainstream theories, including conflict, structural-functional, and grounded theories of society (Dahrendrof 1959, Parsons 1964, Glaser & Strauss 1967). Conflict and structural-functional theories have been particularly influential in the sociology of law. Both were derived from nineteenth century social theory of industrial society in which class structure was understood as fundamental, as a source of both order and conflict. The purpose of the state was to make the differentiation of social roles at the heart of class structure work smoothly (structural-functional theory) or to contain the inevitable conflict that resulted from inequality created by class structure (conflict theory). Marxist conflict theory also viewed the state as an instrument of the ruling class or some combination of dominant classes (Marx & Engels 1950). In all of these theories of the class-state, the law legitimates authority, enabling the state to carry out its purposes (see Evans 1962). Almost all early sociology of law accepted this fundamental ordering of class, law, and the state. Weber's theory of legal formalism and the role of the legal profession in maintaining the authority of law has also been influential. It is not surprising, therefore, given the lineage of the theories dominating the early sociology of law, that economic class was universally and uncontroversially the measure employed in research on law and inequality.

A second perspective in the sociology of law was employed in studying inequality, but without connection to grand theory. Sociology of law shares with the discipline at large a body of research that begins with an anti-instrumental and anti-formal model of the relationship between law and inequality. Growing out of symbolic interactionism and inductive, grounded theory of society, law and inequality are explained as social processes marked by situation and context (Goffman 1956, 1961, Berger & Luckmann 1966).

Research within the sociology of law thus grew from widely shared theoretical perspectives within the discipline, and the contradictory premises of these perspectives, structural on one hand and antistructural on the other, contained the seeds of tensions that have driven debates within the field about the role of structure and class. Sociology of law has also been deeply influenced by intellectual traditions specific to legal scholarship, particularly liberal legalism. In contrast to conflict, stuctural-functional and grounded theories, liberal legalism is not a theory, but rather a "description of ideal practices on which law as we know it is said to depend" (Munger 1993:99). In this model of a sociology of law, social science helps policymakers achieve the law's ideals of fairness and equality. The influence of liberal legalism explains, in part, the tendency of American sociology of law to focus on description of legal problems rather than on theory development.[2]

Law and Inequality from the Top Down

Law and society scholars, finding the egalitarian pretensions of both liberal legalism and state theories of law an easy target, produced a vast literature exploring the inevitable gap between an ideal of equal justice on the books and the biases introduced by social organization into the law in action (Abel 1980). Class was often an important element of the explanation of the "gap," but it was rarely developed theoretically.

Numerous studies examined access to justice for persons of limited means. Research projects at the American Bar Foundation and elsewhere documented the legal problems of the poor. The poor, it was shown, made only limited use of lawyers and law, and a resources theory (Mayhew & Reiss 1969) was developed to explain the failure to act in terms of lack of knowledge, lack of material resources, or passivity in the face of oppression (Levine & Preston 1970, Curran 1977, Mayhew 1968).

Abel (1973) reviewed this literature and reframed its agenda in more general terms as a theory of the structure of dispute processing. While dispute processing theory and research has been criticized for failing to examine underlying social conflict (including class conflict) as well as the interplay and contestation that "socially constructs" all of social life (Kidder 1980–1981, Berger & Luckmann 1966), Abel's model provided a more precise conceptualization of the effects of structural inequalities on legal and prelegal conflict resolution than did any prior work (see also Felstiner, Abel & Sarat 1980–1981, Miller & Sarat 1980–1981).

Studies examined the stratification of the legal profession, especially in large cities (Smigel 1964, Handler 1967). Smigel's seminal study of the Wall Street lawyer, for example, documented the ways in which class and status intersected to create a closed world of elite, WASP law practice dominated and controlled by men. Class background and the privileges of status, as measured by such indices as membership in the Social Register, were of no significance for women, as Epstein's (1981) work made abundantly clear: Daughters of the elite were systematically denied entry to the Wall Street firms of their brothers. Epstein's work demonstrates how gender alters the effects of class on the stratification of legal practice. If gender was one key to exclusion from the professional elite, so was service to clients at the lowest extreme of the class structure, and several studies examined the careers and commitment of lawyers for the poor (Handler et al., 1978, Katz 1982).

Research showed the dependence of lawyers on the class structure of society. A market-dependence theory of the legal profession, linking professional organization and individual lawyer behavior to economic dependence on a capitalist market, profoundly influenced empirical research on both stratification and the role of the profession in society (Abel 1989). A more sophisticated theory of market dependence, combining literatures on the lawyer–client relationship, network analysis, and theories of mobility showed that lawyers in Chicago were stratified into two hemispheres of law practice defined by networks of professionals embodying distinct differences in clients, organization of practice, career lines, and values (Heinz & Laumann 1982).

A large body of research on the role of courts and adjudication (see Galanter 1986 for an extensive review), documented the gap between the promises of fairness and equality and the practices of the legal process. Research examined the stratified functions and effects of courts (Wanner 1974, 1975), their relationship to external social organization, and the construction of roles within the courts (Boyum & Mather 1986, Baum et al., 1981–1982, Kagan et al., 1977, 1978, Galanter 1986). Tracking social movements for reform of adjudication led to interest in the redistributive effects of judicial rationalization (Heydebrand & Seron 1990), mediation, and alternative dispute resolution [described at length by Menkel-Meadow (1984) and Galanter (1986) and extensively critiqued by Abel (1982)].

At the focal point of the literature on law and inequality is an article by Galanter, perhaps the most frequently cited in all of the earlier law and society research literature, which attempts to summarize the vast array of findings up to the mid-1970s (1975). The article presents a process model of the cumulative effects of disadvantage between those Galanter calls one-shot players in law and those he terms repeat players. The disadvantages stem from differences in knowledge, experience, material resources, and the social context of typical

pairings between one-shotters and repeat players. In addition, the differences in knowledge, resources, and organizational capacity are exacerbated by the institutional biases of legal process itself—unequal access to lawyers and ability to command their best efforts, the complexities of litigation that favor the knowledgeable and the rich, and the advantages of being able to "play for rules" in legislatures and before courts. In all but explicit terms, the article presents a comprehensive summary of the sociology of law research showing that the system of justice is thoroughly embedded in the class structure, and indeed the title of the article carries the message—"Why the 'Haves' Come Out Ahead." While Galanter presents a clear and powerful description, he does so, much as does the field itself, without developing a strong conceptual or theoretical scheme: In an article laced with evidence of inequality and hierarchy, the term 'Haves,' like social class itself, is neither defined nor theorized.[3]

Law and Inequality from the Ground Up

There is a second, anti-instrumental and anti-formal tradition of research and theory development in the sociology of law. In contrast to structural models of law and society, grounded theory gives much greater weight to agents' roles in constructing frames of reference.[4] For example, Blumberg (1967), Sudnow (1965), and Macaulay (1963) assume that the relationship between inequality and law can be understood primarily from the interactions among actors in the settings studied. Blumberg & Sudnow describe the construction of typifications through interaction between the regular participants in criminal court proceedings—the judge, prosecutor, and defense counsel. "Normal" crimes receive well-understood, routine treatment, based on typification of the defendant and the crime situation. Mutual commitments are made between court regulars about the expeditious disposition of cases that leave defendants, usually poor, out of the negotiation.

Macaulay's study of noncontractual relations in business has been highly influential in shaping this microsociology of law. Macaulay observed that sales transactions between businesses led to the establishment of continuing relations between sales personnel and the creation of sales practices based on mutual commitment established through long-term dealings (Macaulay 1963). The law, though technically applicable, was largely irrelevant to such practices when continuing relations developed between actors. The continuing-relations hypothesis, quite similar to observations on conflict resolution by anthropologists, makes understanding the effects of inequality considerably more complex, as Macaulay himself noted. Among his purchasing agents, continuing relations developed among relative equals, but not between large and small or among the very large businesses. Commenting on the generalizability of Macaulay's study, Yngvesson argued that continuing relations need not involve equals nor be based on trust, and they may involve coercion to prevent recourse to the law (1985, see also Macaulay 1966).

Reflecting on the implications of the line of research inspired by his study, Macaulay has suggested that continuing relations in the form of social networks, private associations, organizations, and informal groups break down formal structure and instrumental legal processes, rendering the state–society boundary meaningless. Sociology of law thus constructed from the ground up supports many of the impulses that led to rejection of class-structural theory of the state, including the claim that agency is more important than the invisible hand of class. Anticipating this turn in sociology of law, Macaulay has remained firmly committed to the importance of the role of social life in explaining the relationship between law and inequality (1984).

Legal Ideologies and Social Class

The failed social reforms and revolutions of the 1960s and 1970s fueled disillusionment with structural theories of law, in particular theories of class-instrumentalism. Empirical studies of contemporary and historical legal conflict by Marxist scholars pointed to a more ambiguous role for class in determining the long-run benefits and burdens im-

posed by law. A study of the court dispositions of participants in riots by African-Americans in Detroit in 1968 (Balbus 1973) showed that even in response to a serious episode of class and racial strife the courts followed conflicting imperatives. The findings of the study cast serious doubt on the ability of any one perspective, in particular class theory, to explain the behavior of courts even in the middle of a serious episode of class conflict. Similarly, studies by Hay (1975) and Thompson (1964, 1975) of the enforcement of repressive eighteenth-century English criminal laws showed that law aided class rule by being violent but also by seeming, and to a degree by being, just. Thompson concluded that the law displayed a "relative autonomy" from class control:

> It is true that the law did mediate existent class relations to the advantage of the rulers . . . On the other hand, the law mediated these class relations through legal forms, which imposed again and again, inhibitions upon the actions of the rulers. (1975:264)

The sociology of law was deeply influenced by the European Marxists and, neo-Marxists on the subject of legal ideology (Gramsci 1992, Hunt 1981, 1985). The concept of ideology provided a means of avoiding simplistic claims about mechanical class rule and false consciousness. The new challenge was to examine the politics of law—the playing out of class conflicts in contests about the meaning of law in a process that was class-biased but historically contingent. Instrumentalism, state-centered law, structural models of society, and ahistorical social science all came into question as ideology became the vehicle for explaining the relationship between law and social class.[5] Reviewing the literature on the study of law as ideology, Hunt cautioned "ideology is and will remain a difficult, slippery, and ambiguous concept" (1985:31), though it endures as a powerful lens for explaining the role and power of the legal form in social relations.

Some who have contributed to the growing body of research on legal ideology have assumed, as did most Marxist scholars, that legal ideology is a terrain of struggle, conflict, and indeterminacy, but also that ideology is related to "broader social forces rooted in economic, political, and other practices and to institutions" (Hunt 1985:32), that is, the reproduced patterns of social life that we have called structure. For example, Larson (1977) examined the historically contingent ways in which lawyers and other professionals secured a powerful class position by using ideological claims— merit, science, and service—coupled with political closure and control over access through university-based education and licensure by the state. Abel and his collaborators (1982) describe the rise of the politics and ideology of informalism in law and the reasons for its seemingly contradictory effect—extending the legitimacy and power of the state to new disputes and new parties. Both studies document the historically contingent impulses embedded in legal institutions with a view toward explaining their role in legitimating a structurally unequal, class-based society.

Studies like those of Larson and Abel that located legal ideology in an institutional structure have avoided a simplistic base-superstructure reading of Marx by emphasizing the complex and often contradictory functions of law in society, including the ways in which law constrains both the dominated and the dominating and the contingencies that mediate the law's effects. Some scholars have criticized the lingering instrumentalism and structuralism in such sociological studies of ideology (Harding 1986, Trubek 1984). Indeed, some scholars of legal ideology begin from altogether different premises.

As we show in the next section, a growing body of research focuses on interpretation, holding "that the *meanings of cultural and social forms* are constituted in their use" (Greenhouse 1988:687, emphasis added). The relationship between law and inequality is to be understood as the social and cultural processes by which things (genders, races, individuals, nations, and so on) come to be recognized as differentiable . . . from "the eye of the beholder" (1988:688). Because this perspective also holds that there are no intrinsically or historically prior differences, the interpretivist task is to study

only how some symbols of difference become "legitimate 'givens' of public life" while others do not (Sarat & Felstiner 1988, 1995).

Grounded sociological theory of law and inequality (described earlier) privileges agencies by emphasizing the sociological task of explaining the ways in which agents act and construct social meanings in the process. Interpretive theory in the sociology of law takes this one step further by being anti-institutional as well. Social difference—race, class, gender, or sexual preference— is explained entirely through the words, meanings, and language used by actors in the process of going about their business as citizens, employees, legal professionals, plaintiffs, or defendants. Interpretive explanations of difference are theoretically severed from any analysis of ongoing patterns of society outside the framework by which meaning is created for the actors being considered. There is no place for a classical sociological concept of structure in such an analysis, and in particular there is no room for analysis of relational inequalities such as class.

NARRATING THE STORIES
OF LEGAL EXPERIENCE

An emerging sociology of law employs interpretive methods to examine narratives and texts in order to understand legal ideology, legal consciousness, and law in everyday life. A constitutive theory of law attempts to understand the ways in which law forms identity and experience and is, in turn, constituted by the everyday interactions that give law meaning. Constitutive theory shares with Michel Foucault's (1977) description of cultural history a belief that culture determines the micro-distribution of power, thus decentering—but also largely determining—the allocation of power in society. As we noted in the first part of the [reading], some studies of legal ideology acknowledge the importance of the institutional dimension of action. Others, including those based upon constitutive theory, pursue the origins of meaning but not the dimension of social interaction that we term structure (Geertz 1983, Sarat & Felstiner 1995).

Narratives of legal consciousness are among the most common forms of interpretive scholarship employed on behalf of the constitutive perspective. Narratives have been used to demonstrate that power is contingent and specifically that power may not be determined by categories such as race, gender, or class. For example, the narratives of a welfare mother (White 1993), an African-American law professor (Williams 1991), a female defendant (Ewick & Silbey 1992), and parents of children with disabilities (Engel 1993) have been used to show that the expected hierarchies of wealth, race, or professional status can be subverted.[6]

In a recent review of this literature, Ewick & Silbey attempt to explain the contingent relationship between reproduction of the social order and narratives of legal consciousness (1995). They argue that there are limits to the power of narrative to subvert the existing social order because "[a]ll stories are produced and communicated interactively with a social context" (p. 211). While "narratives are likely to bear the marks of existing social inequities, disparities of power and ideological effects," yet, the "assumption that 'society' is an ongoing production that is created daily anew, rather than a fixed and external entity" is a reminder of the "dual capacity of reproduction and invention" (p. 222). Although they attempt to come to grips with the stability of "existing social inequities" and other patterns of social order that condition the timing, content, and interpretation of narratives, Ewick & Silbey's formulation of "reproduction and invention" offers no means of explaining such patterns other than the narratives themselves. Similarly, those who present narratives of the legal consciousness of the poor assume that such narratives, by themselves, provide a full understanding of law and poverty (see, e.g., Sarat 1990, Ewick & Silbey 1992, White 1991). Such studies collapse the distinction between idea and action. Put differently, by taking poverty to be what the poor say about poverty, such studies of narratives, methodologically and conceptually, abandon analysis of the social patterns or institutional practices and histories of poverty and law.[7]

Interpretive sociology of law is well illustrated by Sarat & Felstiner's observational study of lawyer–client interactions during divorce counseling (1995). Lawyer–client exchanges are interpreted to show how power "unfolds," "shifts," "permeates," and "moves" between lawyer and client in the process of defining, negotiating, and settling a divorce. For the lawyer, "interaction takes place in a familiar space and a space of privilege" symbolized by, for example, the office, law books, language, or rituals. But the lawyer's power over the client is "malleable." Sarat & Felstiner acknowledge that "structure" circumscribes and shapes "a limited reservoir of possibility defined by history and habit" (1995:23), but the outcome of the circumscription of possibility is rarely predictable or routine. From the interpretive perspective, inequality in power unfolds "in its use."

We are left to speculate: Are gender, race, class, or power so completely malleable? Is there no power in such differences to create inequality that shapes, or compels, or moves individual action or group interaction whether conscious or not? Does the power of class, gender, or race—difference—exist only as experience "in the eye of the beholder?" Is there no institutional and social history of the power of class, race, or gender beyond individual experience? As White has recently suggested:

> While the Foucaltian lens reveals the fluidity of power, it does not show how power can be congealed in social institutions in ways that sustain domination. It may be true that everyday interactions create and maintain social institutions, but this insight does not enable us to map those interactions against the institutional matrices they create. Nor does this insight show us how institutions constrain the circulation of power, channeling it to flow toward some social groups and away from others (1992:1505).

BRINGING CLASS BACK IN: AN AGENDA FOR THE SOCIOLOGY OF LAW

Our review of sociolegal research has shown that analysis of class has declined in importance and that the recent interpretive research on law and inequality has abandoned the institutional and social organizational perspectives of earlier research. The theoretical framework for class analysis employed throughout much of the twentieth century has been challenged by the emergence of a global economy, indeed a global society, in which local movements for human rights can be linked across continents by e-mail and fax, by changes in the organization of work, and by the rise of new cultural themes of consumerism and personal identity. The turn toward an interpretive sociology of law offers a nuanced and microsocial understanding of the asymmetry, paradoxes, and contradictory relations of once familiar experiences across a range of social institutions.

Nonetheless, interpretive research on law and inequality often inadequately addresses how individual lives are interwoven to become part of larger patterns, or why such patterns evolve and persist over time (Sewell 1992). Contemporary society—including the role of law in attorneys' offices, in public agencies, and in everyday life—does not emerge on a tabula rasa and cannot be explained exclusively by examining the interpretations of individuals outside of time and place. The limitation of an interpretive sociology, in particular the analysis of narratives, is in large part a limitation of method. While narratives may capture variation, improvisation, or resistance, by definition they cannot account for the institutional contexts of action, including the institution of class.

In this concluding part we focus our attention on the continuing importance of relative differences in institutional power and resources for the sociology of law. Economic class remains one important element of inequality. Economic class position, associated with employment (and unemployment), income, and ownership of economic resources, is a nearly universal part of social experience.[8] Because class is necessarily relational, everyone experiences inequality, difference, and almost universally, subordination in a fundamentally important aspect of social life.[9] Notwithstanding the continuing importance of economic class, in the late twentieth century, a group's position is defined only partly by its economic class endowments. Other sources of capital—cultural and symbolic—also create hierarchies, power, and subordination as well as opportunities for change.

The class theory of Pierre Bourdieu, to offer one promising example, examines the variation, improvisation, and even indeterminacy of agency without losing sight of group trajectories or the tendency toward reproduction of patterns in social relations (Bourdieu 1985, 1987, Bourdieu & Wacquant 1992). Groups are positioned by patterns in the distribution of endowments of capital. Bourdieu broadens the concept of capital to include the positioning power not only of economic relationships but also of cultural, social, and symbolic capital. Bourdieu's theory of agency considers the effects of a great range of resources while linking those resources to the societal processes that create or maintain them. The habitus, the interpretive context for action generated by a group's experience in society, is a system of "lasting, transposable dispositions which, integrating past experiences, functions at every moment as a matrix of perceptions, appreciations, and actions and makes possible the achievement of infinitely diversified tasks" (1977:82–83). Bourdieu's concept of class is flexible and empirical, providing a means of understanding both the positioning power of historical conjunctions of capital endowments for particular groups and the contingency of individual action.

While a theory of class such as Bourdieu's is complex and open ended, it offers a means of making more precise distinctions and observations about contemporary social relations. One consequence of failing to conceptualize class in more theoretical terms is to rely on even more problematic categorical descriptions by using holistic labels such as "working class American," "middle class family," "underclass African-American," or simply "poor," which are found in contemporary ethnographic studies of law and inequality. A theoretically informed concept of class, such as that employed by Bourdieu, will suggest specific institutional processes, generating inequality through endowments of capital and the formation of a habitus. Further, more precise concepts will make possible both comparison and extension of findings across studies. Herein lies the challenge—to build our understanding of the sources and continuity of social hierarchy while respecting the complexities of power and agency.

Class and Law in Everyday Life

Studies in the sociology of law reviewed in the first part of this [reading] include research on everyday encounters with legal institutions, documenting the ways in which law may (or may not) be mobilized by individuals of different class, race, or gender. The early studies of legal mobilization have been criticized because they seemed to provide only static portraits of individuals, a characteristic that has weakened categorical approaches to inequality. But the authors of many earlier studies were well aware of the dynamic and interpretive dimensions of action, conflict, and the assertion of rights that have become the focus of attention in more recent qualitative research. Findings of such studies offer guidance for contemporary sociolegal research attempting to link class and law in everyday life.

For example, research by Levine & Preston (1970) attributed a low rate of legal problem-solving among their low-income respondents to a lack of knowledge about rights and to lack of the legal competence often associated with higher income. Yet they considered that "subjects were probably experiencing powerlessness and a feeling of resignation in the face of circumstances about which they thought little could be done" (109) (compare Felstiner et al., 1980–1981). Mayhew & Reiss termed this perspective the personal resources theory, and they argued that it represented one aspect of their broader theoretical proposition that the role of law in everyday life is a product of the ongoing organization of social life and its institutional structure (1969).

The recent turn to research on legal consciousness can expand our understanding of the social organizational perspective. Studies of legal consciousness directly examine what was merely inferred from very thin data in the early studies—passivity or activism, legal competence, powerlessness, resignation, and the like. Studies of legal consciousness also have a direct bearing on institutional structure. The meaning of such concepts as employment, authority, market, and property are the foundation for the institutions that shape "legal contacts" (to employ Mayhew & Reiss' phrase) linking class to rights and justice (Sennett & Cobb 1972, Willie 1985, Hochschild 1981), to legal conflict (Crowe 1978, Baumgartner 1988), or to beliefs about entitlements (Newman 1988, Munger 1991).

While research on legal consciousness could fill a gap in our understanding of the relationship between meaning and structure, such studies often overlook any process that informants themselves do not describe. In some research the social organizational understanding of action, and specifically class organization, has been lost altogether. Few studies of legal consciousness examine the social organization of work, or more generally the class structure, as a source of the ideological matrix comprising legal consciousness.

For example, most recent community-based studies of legal conflict and dispute resolution pay only limited attention to class, for there is no systematic tapping of class experience as such unless class is mentioned by the subjects (Greenhouse et al. 1994). Such studies have focused on inductive discovery of the groups—social networks, neighborhoods, and families—whose interpretations shape disputes and legal conflicts. While some scholars pursuing these studies have suggested that the silence of their informants concerning class may itself have significance (see Greenhouse et al., 1994:185), there is no way to determine which aspects of the legal experience or consciousness described by means of the research are attributable to the effects of social class.

A more robust research agenda must attend to the social organizational elements deemed important for the formation of consciousness. As the focus and site of research in the sociology of law has shifted from formal legal institutions to the routines and events of everyday life that are only occasionally touched, if ever, by formal legal institutions, a broad invitation exists to explore beyond the outer edges of the narrative. Beyond the limits of narrative lie the patterns that connect the individual to jobs as well as to organizations, neighborhoods, families, associations, communities (with public authorities), and networks that enable or limit action, whether they are fully understood by their members or not. In these ongoing connections, class is the local embodiment of larger patterns shaped by property holding, market institutions, cultural preferences, and political organization, patterns that may be reconstructed locally, but as variations on themes that play more widely in society.

Class Hierarchy, the Economy, and the Legal Profession

Sociolegal research on lawyers has encompassed research on professional careers and on the social role of lawyers. In both lines of study scholars have examined the effects of class hierarchy, mapping the effects of social stratification on lawyers' careers and examining the effects of clients' wealth and power on lawyers' services. While the studies have been attentive to the effects of social hierarchies on professional stratification and differentiation, the research seldom considers lawyers in relation to class as an institution—namely the role of lawyers in the creation, maintenance, or changes in class organization. Further, both lines of inquiry began with studies of the external factors explaining the behavior of lawyers; more recently they have begun to take greater account of the ways lawyers themselves understand their careers and social roles. This shift from deductive to inductive research has enriched our understanding of the organization of professional work but has exacerbated the tendency of researchers to ignore the relationship between the profession and other institutions in society.

Studies of the career patterns of attorneys have closely paralleled the development of research on social stratification. The earliest work on lawyers' careers relied on conventional mobil-

ity models (Ladinsky 1963). Later research turned to network models to explain career patterns (Heinz & Laumann 1982, Nelson et al., 1992, Seron 1996).

Two recent studies of lawyers' careers draw on contemporary theory of class formation to examine how the organization of lawyers' work helps construct class differences. Contemporary theories of class formation (Bourdieu 1977, 1985) and agency (Sewell 1992) may help guide examination of the sources and significance of the social endowments possessed by lawyers and the development of their orientations as agents within a habitus created by class.

A second illustration of the potential contribution of the concept of class to research on professional careers is a recent study by Seron of New York City lawyers (1993, 1996). Reflecting a more grounded, inductive research tradition, Seron showed how lawyers are able to pursue a variety of adaptive strategies for reorganizing their work in response to changing economic pressures. Within a system of stratification among law practices created by market opportunities and lawyers' career endowments, lawyers demonstrate the possibilities for "regulated improvisation" (Bourdieu 1977:77) by a group for which the habitus of professional role is well defined. Seron's perspective could be extended. For example, contemporary research on the relationship between economic restructuring and reorganization within large law firms (Galanter & Paley 1991) would be greatly enriched by considering how lawyers form ideas about reorganizing large law firms and adapt to altered endowments of economic class capital and other forms of social capital implicated in market changes.

A large sociology of law literature considers the social role of the legal profession. Early research on the part played by the profession in promoting justice and ameliorating social inequality (Handler et al., 1978, Capelletti et al., 1975) found an easy target in the structural-functional theory which specified that the profession stabilized and legitimated the social order (Parsons 1964). Alternative theories suggested that a self-interested monopoly of professional knowledge (Freidson 1986,

Abbott 1988) or control of market position (Larson 1977, Abel 1989) motivated professional organizations and individual lawyer's behavior.

The relationship between lawyers and the evolution of major institutions of the society, including the class system, should be a prime area for continuing development of theory and research. A great deal of empirical evidence has been amassed to show the uneven distribution of lawyer's services, reflecting the market power of clients and professional self-interest. Yet this literature initially failed to consider the institutional questions raised by such findings—why social inequality persists and why it persists in particular forms (Currie 1971). Later research on the organization and the social role of lawyers partially addressed such questions by drawing on market dependency theory, which described the contribution of market pressure to the formation of professional organizations and the creation of a professional monopoly. But market dependency theory, by itself, does not account for the nature of economic hierarchy, or the complex relationship between class, the work of lawyers, and the production of professional culture (Nelson et al., 1992). Thus, in spite of decades of research showing that lawyers are influenced by client wealth and power, few broad theoretical attempts have been made to understand the role lawyers play in maintaining or transforming fundamental social institutions (Munger 1994).

Weber maintained that lawyers' commitment to law, irrespective of lawyers' class origins or class loyalties, is an important prop for legitimate authority in a plural society (1954), while, in contrast, Marx argued that the professions served the interests of those who held ultimate power—the capitalist class (1950). Heinz & Laumann's study of stratification among lawyers in Chicago raised questions about whether any significant core values are shared by all lawyers (1982). Their finding that lawyers are separated into two distinct hemispheres representing organizations and individuals, and subdivided further by types of practice within each hemisphere, suggests rather that lawyers' values vary considerably as a function of client influence (and by the class of the client).

The turn to grounded research on lawyers' work has also suggested that lawyers create culture, as well as reflect culture, when they serve their clients (Gordon 1982, Sarat & Felstiner 1995). For example, Dezalay & Garth conclude from their research on lawyers in international business transactions that lawyers are important carriers of legal and economic culture in the internationalization of trade and business relations (1995).

As grounded research continues to explore the interplay between professional work and the creation of social organization, economic change, or the control of conflict, class theory offers a means of looking beyond the situated lawyer to the normatively constructed habitus of professional life and to the institutional pressures and limitations imposed by the economic organization of society (see Simon 1988, Alfieri 1992, Bezdek 1992, Seron 1993, 1996). Contemporary qualitative research on the work of the profession should examine the conditions under which lawyers contribute to the reproduction or change in fundamental patterns in society such as markets and classes (Harrington 1985, Halliday 1987, Shamir 1993).

Class Structure and the Administration of the Law

By linking the internal practices of public and private organizations directly to the class structure of society, the theories of Marx & Weber posed a powerful hypothesis about the scope of social control.[10] Yet empirical research has increasingly demonstrated the importance of institutional, organizational, and professional practices as ends in themselves (Reichman 1989, Hawkins 1989, Heydebrand & Seron 1990). "Law from the bottom up" refers to the analysis of the practices of those who are the first-in-line (at the bottom of the authority ladder) to apply legal authority. Their practices do not merely alter the terms upon which law will be applied; they are the law (Cohen 1985, Massell 1968, Edelman et al., 1993, Macaulay 1963). The research has undermined to a considerable extent the Weberian master-narrative of organizational order (1995, Lempert 1991).

Such findings have made understanding the relationship of legal institutions to class structure both more difficult and more direct. To the extent that lower levels of officials, judges, police, prosecutors, and social workers are not controlled by higher level authorities, the structural theories of the state and class seem to lose their relevance. To the same extent, however, organizations may be permeated much more directly by class organization or culture and other influences on bureaucrats and functionaries, whose jobs are defined through a mixture of situational constraints and grass roots accommodations (Cohen 1985, Handler 1990). While innovation and change may come from the bottom, more often the effect is to permit routinization of decision-making according to locally generated norms about what constitutes a "normal" case or a "last resort" case. These typifications are subject to class, race, and gender biases (Sudnow 1965, Emerson 1981, Daly 1994).

Studies of social control suggest not only that class is a factor in the treatment of individuals but also that social control is organized quite differently to deal with different social classes. Through policing and welfare, the poor and especially the underclass experience a special kind of "government of the poor" (Simon 1993, Cohen 1985, Sampson & Laub 1993). In addition to a long line of studies showing that white collar crimes are treated relatively leniently (Sutherland 1955, Hagan et al., 1980, Shapiro 1987), Cohen argues that the "soft" technologies for social control—self-help, therapeutic guidance, education—are reserved for those who have greater social and economic capital (1985). Simon suggests that the disparity in class treatment is increasing because growing income differences, increasing numbers of permanently unemployed, and the Africanization and ghettoization of poverty in political discourse are contributing to a shift in emphasis from rehabilitation and reform of the poor to surveillance and control (Simon 1993, Feeley & Simon 1992).

"Loose coupling" (Hagan 1979) between and within the agencies of social control that is apparent from studies of crime control raises still broader questions about the relationship between class,

state, and society. Loose coupling between state agencies as well as extensive interpenetration of state and society often renders the state's attempts to regulate ineffective because power is shared among state agencies, private institutions, associations, and networks (Moore 1978, see especially Macaulay 1986). This state is not the class-state described by Marx, Weber, or Durkheim but is rather a more complex institution; it is dependent on the power of class but, absent special conditions, far less instrumental in its capacity. What implications do these findings have for the relationship between class structure and the role of the state's regulatory efforts over time?

Four research strategies are suggested by current work on the relationship between class, law, and the state. The first is to study the formation of the habitus of routine decision-making by the bureaucrats responsible for disposing of most of the state's business. Though the existing studies are revealing, they often do not approach their analysis of case decisions from the perspective of a wider set of cultural and institutional influences beyond the office setting.

Second, the state may be studied as a collection of concrete critical decisions and ongoing relatively stable processes. Calavita's study of the Immigration and Naturalization Service's handling of the bracero farmworker program shows that the theory that state bureaucrats are dependent on the resources of those with continuing access to the means of producing wealth must be supplemented with knowledge of the particular state managers involved in a particular decision (1992). The intersection of biography and the momentum of agency history exposes both the lasting dependencies between state and economy and their contingency.

Third, the state-class connection may be usefully considered in light of a nonfunctional systems theory articulated by Block (1987) to take account of surprising, counterintuitive patterns, for example, the strong response by law enforcement agencies to the savings and loan crisis (Calavita & Pontell 1994). Politics always creates an important contingency in law enforcement, especially in the United States (see Savelsberg 1994).

Finally, as sociology of law becomes more international and more global in its subject matter, the endowments of class, the links between societies, and the institutional response to change take on new complexities. Hierarchy, domination, and resistance are altered by the pressures of a global economy, the interactions between cultures, or simply by the power of modern communications that makes it possible to bypass the courts and even the nation state to assert claims for rights. The juxtaposition of the use of local, national, and international legal institutions reminds us that the relations of domination and exploitation take on new forms in a global society, forms that are often constituted in ways unfamiliar to western sociologists (Upham 1987, Winn 1994).

Class Mediation of Law and Social Change

Classic social theory placed law in an instrumental role. Law could both create and respond to social change; indeed, state capacity to respond to or manage the consequences of industrialization was a core concern of the theories of Marx, Durkheim, and Weber. The poignant ineffectiveness and contingency of legislation and litigation during America's civil rights era in the 1960s had an impact (Scheingold 1974, see Gordon 1984), but skepticism about the instrumental effectiveness of law is an older theme in American sociology of law, reflecting, among other sources, the influence of legal realism (Arnold 1935). Authors such as Handler (1978) and Rosenberg (1991), who amass evidence of the failure of social movements for legal rights, base their skepticism on theories about the direct effects of class and inequality on the state, and they challenge the liberal legal ideal of an effective, neutral, and responsive state. Handler and Rosenberg show that an imbalance in class resources combined with the inertia and bureaucracy of the state will nearly always defeat redistributive change (for an important critique of this view see Simon 1992).

An important locus of the relationship between law and change lies outside formal legal process. Sumner's claim that folkways always prevail over stateways was clearly wrong. Law directly influences ordinary life. The ways that it influences ordinary life are many—by contributing to the creation of social norms, by producing knowledge that becomes a foundation for action, and by direct enforcement of change. The effects of law vary, but they are not always marginal or inevitably invisible. Based on what we know about class differences in knowledge, moral decisions, values, styles of conflict resolution, and their interaction with gender and race, there is surely a class component to the social change that law can create. Now we have come full circle, because to understand such effects we must understand the context in which action is contemplated and undertaken in everyday life.

Michael McCann's study of the role of legal rights in the pay equity movement (1994) takes seriously the challenges of studying legal change and legal consciousness at the grass roots. He applies a discourse theory of legal mobilization in which "law is understood to consist of a complex repertoire of discursive strategies and symbolic frameworks that structure ongoing social intercourse and meaning-making activities among citizens" (1994: 282). Further, he argues that rights are "inherently indeterminate, pluralistic, and contingent in actual social practice (ibid)." While he also acknowledges the importance of institutional attributes such as social class and organizational or political context, his findings, like those in many recent studies that follow the turn to discourse and narrative, do not systematically locate the individuals interviewed in relevant group contexts—in the continuing patterns of association and experience that were either similar across all workplaces or unique to particular settings. Thus, McCann's study brings us back to the concerns with which we began this essay, namely, appreciating the connection between the larger institutional patterns of a class society and the role of law.

CONCLUSION

Research without a structural concept of class impoverishes our understanding of law and inequality. Underlying the reluctance of many to examine class is a generation-long skepticism about the concept of structure. The structure-agency problem goes to the core of sociological theory and method, and to what it means to conduct empirical research with conceptual rigor. A review of the literature in the sociology of law revealed swings between analyses that emphasized structure or agency. Just as earlier theory in the sociology of law tended toward a more instrumental view of social action, so contemporary theory tends to focus on the indeterminacy of action. While interpretive work presents an important critique of structural theory, structure and class have not gone away.[11] Class continues to describe an important aspect of social life, namely the powerful link between the lives of individuals and the economic organization of society that is beyond the control and often beyond the knowledge or full understanding of those individuals.

Our review of ways that more careful attention to the role of class might enrich the sociology of law leads to several suggestions for incorporating the concept of class into sociolegal research:

- The *experience* of class is a starting point. Biography—the experiences of individual and group through time—is fundamental.
- The relationship of class structure to the activities of members of a class is complex.

The direct effects of class structure are modified by the experience of race and gender, the roles occupied by individuals in complex organizations, and by the emergent and creative possibilities of social action.

- Research on class requires a comparative perspective.

Ultimately sociology studies the social group. Narrative and case-study methodology treat the subject as representative of a larger group. Identi-fication of the similarities and differences between sites and subjects should be made explicit, and class is one of the important dimensions on which narrative and case studies can be compared.

- The concept of class evolves through empirical research.

Class theory suggests possible connections between the experience of the situated individual and the group-habitus and the larger patterns of social life, but our understanding of class rests on discovery of the precise role of class and habitus through empirical research.

- The element of time is essential.

Both as situated experience and as a larger pattern in social life, class is best understood through biography and through community history. Class, so understood, is one important element in the accretion of particular routines, knowledge, and relationships that constitute the trajectory of a group through time. Out of these grow change and, equally, the tendency to reproduce the patterns of social life.

The turn to narrative studies in sociolegal research reflects awareness of the importance of context and agency. But in taking this turn, contemporary studies of law and society have sidestepped the capacity to explain the sources and significance of difference and inequality in terms that individuals themselves cannot employ. While biographies are individually experienced and understood, they are also shaped by history not only of the individual's making (Calavita & Seron 1992). As C. Wright Mills (1959) concluded, the promise of the sociological imagination lies in explaining the link between the meanings of the private lives of individuals and "the larger historical scene."

NOTES

1. As quoted in "Back to Class Warfare," The New York Times, December 27, 1994.

2. As a number of scholars have reported, in projects growing out of this model sociologists often played a second-class role to legal academics (see Simon and Lynch 1989, Skolnick 1965).

3. The lone effort to develop a general theory of law and inequality (Black 1976) also fails to do more than offer a set of unexplained categories. Black predicts a patterning of legal relationships according to the relative position of parties in the social order. For example, he predicts that the greater the social distance between two individuals, the more law will govern the relationship and the greater the likelihood of third-party intervention to resolve a dispute. Black's insistence that theory consider only observable behavior, not meaning or understanding from the actor's viewpoint, has been highly controversial. By providing a target for such criticism, Black helped to coalesce interest in the ideological analysis of the role of law and in interpretive theory.

4. An anthropology of law also played an important intellectual role in the development of sociolegal studies. Indeed, much of the work on dispute processing borrows heavily from anthropology (Nader 1969, Collier 1973, Moore 1978, Mather & Yngvesson 1980–1981, Merry 1982).

5. Feminist scholarship made a particularly important contribution by expanding the horizons of investigations, raising critical questions about method, and questioning whether there is even a distinction between theory and method (Menkel-Meadow & Diamond 1991). Within the sociology of law, feminist scholars have examined the entry of women into male bastions such as law practice (Epstein 1981, Menkel-Meadow 1989), courts (Cook 1978), and alternative dispute resolution (Menkle-Meadow 1984).

6. Although there are passing references to the working class, welfare poor, or the occupational status of the individuals' whose consciousness is described, these typifications are not carefully identified apart from the holism of oppressed consciousness, and there is often little or no systematic evidence of relevant group characteristics (Merry 1990, White 1991, Sarat 1990, Ewick & Silbey 1992, Alfieri 1992). Equally common are interpretive accounts that imply that social differences or power are completely dependent on contingencies that occur during social interaction (Abrams 1993, Sarat & Felstiner 1995).

7. Critical race scholars claim that (auto)biography, legal cases, personal experience, and historical chronicles are powerful forms of "storytelling in the law" (Lawrence 1992:2278), which permit the reader to live in the writer's world as she thinks about identity, law, and action (Williams 1991, Bumiller 1988, Engel 1991, Ewick

& Silbey 1992, Sanger 1993). For example, White (1991) writes about an African-American welfare mother who speaks up at a welfare hearing, contrary to her attorney's advice, a story that shows the possibility of autonomous action in spite of the repressive power of the context and the woman's own attorney.

8. As Rosemary Crompton remarks in the course of an exhaustive assessment of research on class, "although 'work' may possibly have declined as a significant source of social identity, work is still the most significant determinant of the material well-being of the majority of the population" (1993:18). Our point is somewhat broader, namely that work is not only an important source of material resources but also a relational position that places individuals in a hierarchy of authority as well as hierarchies of symbolic and material power.

9. Class is a system of relational inequalities created by the economy. Class is a relational inequality because, unlike height or talent, it exists through a social process which requires that some individuals acquire more benefits, including authority, status, and income, than others.

10. Instrumental and structural Marxism argued that in the last analysis law reflected class domination. Weber argued that law was upheld by an autonomous legal profession, but he also argued that legal authority existed in constant tension with the social hierarchies of class and status that distorted such authority. Much sociolegal research supports the existence of direct effects of class on legal institutions, and we have reviewed these in first part of this [reading].

11. Attempts to grapple with the structure-agency problem are in evidence across a variety of subfields, including the sociology of professions (Abbott 1988), comparative sociology (Orren & Skowronek 1994, Orren & Skowronek forthcoming; Somers & Gibson 1994), criminology (Savelsberg 1994), and organizations (Powell & DiMaggio 1991). The pivotal question is: "How [can] sociological theories which do accept the sui generis collective character of social arrangements . . . retain a conception of individual freedom and voluntarism?" (Alexander 1982).

LITERATURE CITED

Abbott A. 1988. *The System of Professions: An Essay on the Division of Expert Labor.* Chicago: Univ. Chicago Press

Abel RL. 1989. *American Lawyers.* New York: Oxford Univ. Press

Abel RL, ed. 1982. *The Politics of Informal Justice.* Vols. 1, 2. New York: Academic

Abel RL. 1980. Redirecting social studies of law. *Law Soc. Rev.* 14:(3)805–29

Abel RL. 1973. A comparative theory of dispute institutions in society. *Law Soc. Rev.* 8(2):217–347

Abrams K. 1993. Unity, narrative and law. In *Studies in Law, Politics and Society,* ed. A Sarat, SS Sibley, 13:3–35. Greenwich, CT: JAI

Alexander J. 1982. Positivism, presuppositions, and current controversies. In *Theoretical Logic in Sociology,* Berkeley/Los Angeles: Univ. Calif. Press

Alfieri AV. 1992. Disabled clients, disabling lawyers. *Hastings Law J.* 43:769–851

Arnold TW. 1935. *The Symbols of Government.* New Haven, CT: Yale Univ. Press

Balbus I. 1973. *The Dialectics of Legal Repression: Black Rebels Before the American Criminal Courts.* New York: Russell Sage

Baum L, Goldman S, Sarat A. 1981/1982. Research note: the evolution of litigation in federal courts of appeal, 1895–1975. *Law Soc. Rev.* 16(2):291–309

Baumgartner MP. 1988. *The Moral Order of a Suburb.* New York: Oxford Univ. Press

Berger P, Luckmann T. 1966. *The Social Construction of Reality: A Treatise in the Sociology of Knowledge.* Garden City, NY: Doubleday

Bezdek B. 1992. Silence in the court: participation and subordination of poor tenants' voices in the legal process. *Hofstra Law Rev.* 20:533–608

Black D. 1976. *The Behavior of Law.* New York: Academic

Block F. 1987. *Revising State Theory: Essays on Politics and Postindustrialism.* Philadelphia: Temple Univ. Press

Blumberg A. 1967. *Criminal Justice.* Chicago: Quadrangle

Bourdieu P. 1985. The social space and the genesis of groups. *Theory Soc.* 14:723–75

Bourdieu P. 1987. *Outline of a Theory of Practice.* Cambridge, MA: Cambridge Univ. Press

Bourdieu P, Wacquant LJD. 1992. *An Invitation to Reflexive Sociology.* Chicago: Univ. Chicago Press

Boyum K, Mather L. 1986. *Empirical Theories About Courts.* New York: Longman

Bumiller K. 1988. *The Civil Rights Society: the Social Construction of Victims.* Baltimore: Johns Hopkins Press

Calavita K. 1992. *Inside the State: the Bracero Program, Immigration, and the I.N.S.* New York: Routledge

Calavita K, Pontell H. 1994. The state and whitecollar crime: saving the savings and loans. *Law Soc. Rev.* 28:297–324

Calavita K, Seron C. 1992. Postmodernism and protest: recovering the sociological imagination. *Law Soc. Rev.* 26(4):756–71

Capelletti M, Gordley J, Johnson E. 1975. *Toward Equal Justice: a Comparative Study of Legal Aid in Modern Societies.* Milan: Guiffre/Dobbs Ferry, NY: Oceana

Cohen S. 1985. *Visions of Social Control: Crime, Punishment and Classification.* Cambridge, UK: Polity

Collier J. 1973. *Law and Social Change in Zinacantan.* Stanford: Stanford Univ. Press

Cook BB. 1978. Women judges: the end of tokenism. In *Women in the Courts,* ed. W Hepperie, L Crites, pp. 84–105. Williamsburg, VA: Natl. Cent. State Courts

Crompton R. 1993. *Class and Stratification: An Introduction to Current Debates.* Cambridge, UK: Polity Press

Crowe PW. 1978. Complainant reactions to the Massachusetts commission against discrimination. *Law Soc. Rev.* 12(2):217–35

Curran BA. 1977. *The Legal Needs of the Public: the Final Report of a National Survey.* Chicago: The Foundation

Currie E. 1971. Sociology of law: the unasked questions. *Yale Law J.* 81:134–47

Dahrendorf R. 1959. *Class and Class Conflict in Industrial Society.* Stanford: Stanford Univ. Press

Daly K. 1994. *Gender Crime and Punishment.* New Haven, CT: Yale Univ. Press

Dezalay Y, Garth B. 1995. Merchants of law as moral entrepreneurs: constructing international justice from the competition for transnational business dispute. *Law Soc. Rev.* 29(1):27–64

Edelman LB, Erlanger HS, Lande J. 1993. Internal dispute resolution: the transformation of civil rights in the workplace. *Law Soc. Rev.* 27(3):497–534

Emerson R. 1981. On last resorts. *J. Sociol.* 87:1–22

Engel D. 1993. Law in the domains of everyday life: the construction of community and difference. In *Law in Everyday Life,* ed. A Sarat, T Kearns, pp. 123–70. Ann Arbor: Univ. Mich. Press

Engel D. 1991. Law, culture, and children with disabilities: educational rights and the construction of difference. *Duke Law J.* 1991:166–205

Epstein CF. 1981. *Women in the Law.* New York: Basic Books

Evans W, ed. 1962. *Law and Sociology: Exploratory Essays.* Glencoe, IL: Free

Ewick P, Silbey S. 1995. Subversive stories and hegemonic tales: toward a sociology narrative. *Law Soc. Rev.* 29(2):197–226

Ewick P, Silbey S. 1992. Conformity, contestation and resistance: an account of legal consciousness. *New Engl. Law Rev.* 26:731–49

Feeley M, Simon J. 1992. The new prophecy: notes on the emerging strategy of corrections and its applications. *Criminology* 30:449–74

Felstiner WLF, Abel R, Sarat A. 1980/1981. The emergence and transformation of disputes: naming, blaming, claiming. *Law, Soc. Rev.* 15(3–4):631–54

Foucault M. 1977. *Discipline and Punish: Birth of the Prison.* New York: Pantheon

Freidson E. 1986. *Professional Powers: a Study of the Institutionalization of Formal Knowledge.* Chicago: Univ. Chicago Press

Galanter M. 1986. Adjudication, litigation, and related phenomena. In *Law and the Social Sciences,* ed. L Lipson, S Wheeler, pp. 151–258. New York: Russell Sage

Galanter M. 1975. Why the "Haves" come out ahead: speculations on the limits of legal change. *Law Soc. Rev.* 9(1):95–160

Galanter M, Paley T. 1991. *Tournament of Lawyers: The Transformation of the Big Law Firms.* Chicago: Univ. Chicago Press

Geertz C. 1983. *Social Knowledge: Further Essays in Interpretive Anthropology.* New York: Basic

Glaser BG, Strauss A. 1967. *The Discovery of Grounded Theory: Strategies for Qualitative Research.* Chicago: Aldine

Goffman E. 1961. *Encounters.* Indianapolis: Bobbs-Merrill

Goffman E. 1956. *The Presentation of Self in Everyday Life.* Garden City, NY: Doubleday

Gordon R. 1984. Legal thought and legal practice in the age of American enterprise. In *Profession and Professional Ideologies in America,* ed. G Geison, pp. 70–110. Chapel Hill: Univ. N Carolina

Gordon R. 1982. New developments in legal theory. In *The Politics of Law: A Progressive Critique,* ed. D Kairys, pp. 281–93. New York: Pantheon

Gramsci A. 1992. *Prison Notebooks.* New York: Columbia Univ. Press

Greenhouse CJ. 1988. Courting difference: issues of interpretation and comparison in the study of legal idealism. *Law Soc. Rev.* 22(4):687–707

Greenhouse CJ, Engel DM, Yngvesson B. 1994. *Law and Community in Three American Towns.* Ithaca: Cornell Univ. Press

Hagan J. 1979. Ceremonial justice: crime and punishment in a loosely coupled system. *Soc. Forces* 58(2):506–27

Hagan J, Huxter M, Parker P. 1988. Class structure and legal practice: inequality and mobility among Toronto lawyers. *Law Soc. Rev.* 22(1):9–55

Hagan J, Nagel I, Albonetti C. 1980. The differential sentencing of white-collar offenders in ten federal district courts. *Am. Sociol. Rev.* 45:802–20

Halliday T. 1987. *Beyond Monopoly: Lawyers, State Crisis and Professional Empowerment.* Chicago: Univ. Chicago Press

Handler J. 1967. *The Lawyer and His Community: The Practicing Bar in a Middle-Sized City.* Madison: Univ. Wis. Press

Handler JF. 1990. *Law and the Search for Community.* Philadelphia: Univ. Penn. Press

Handler JF. 1978. *Social Movements and the Legal System: A Theory of Law Reform and Social Change.* New York: Academic

Handler JF, Hollingsworth EJ, Erlanger H. 1978. *Lawyers and the Pursuit of Legal Rights.* New York: Academic

Harding S. 1986. *The Science Question in Feminism.* Ithaca: Cornell Univ. Press

Harrington C. 1985. *Shadow Justice: the Ideology and Institutionalization of Alternatives to Court.* Westport, CT: Greenwood

Hawkins K. 1989. "FATCATS" and prosecution in a reulatory agency: a footnote on the social construction of risk. *J. Law Policy* 11(3):370–91

Hay D, et al., eds. 1975. *Albion's Fatal Tree: Crime and Society in Eighteenth-Century England.* New York: Pantheon

Heimer C. 1996. Explaining variation in the impact of law: organizations, institutions, and professions. In *Fifteen Studies in Law, Politics, and Society,* ed. A Sarat. S Sibley. in press

Heinz JP, Laumann EO. 1982. *Chicago Lawyers: The Social Structure of the Bar.* New York: Russell Sage

Heydebrand W, Seron C. 1990. *Rationalizing Justice: the Political Economy of Federal District Courts.* Albany: SUNY Press

Hochschild J. 1981. *What's Fair?: American Beliefs about Distributive Justice.* Cambridge: Harvard Univ. Press

Hunt A. 1985. The ideology of law: advances and problems in recent application of the concept of ideology to the analysis of law. *Law Soc. Rev.* 19(1):11–37

Hunt A. 1981. Dichotomy and contradiction in the sociology of law. *Br. J. Law Soc.* 8(1):47–78

Kagan R, Cartwright B, Friedman L, Wheeler S. 1978. The evolution of state supreme courts. *Mich. Law Rev.* 76:961–1001

Kagan R, Cartwright B, Friedman L, Wheeler S. 1977. The business of state supreme courts. 1870–1980. *Stanford Law Rev.* 30:121–56

Katz J. 1982. *Poor Peoples Lawyers in Transition.* New Brunswick, NJ: Rutgers Univ. Press

Kidder R. 1980/1981. The end of the road: problems in the analysis of disputes. *Law Soc. Rev.* 15(3–4):717–25

Ladinsky J. 1963. *Career Development Among Lawyers: a Study of Social Factors in the Allocation of Professional Labor.* Ann Arbor: Univ. Microfilms

Larson MS. 1977. *The Rise of Professionalism: A Sociological Analysis.* Berkeley: Univ. Calif. Press

Lawrence CR. 1992. The word and the river: pedagogy as scholarship as struggle. *South Calif. Law Rev.* 65:2231–98

Lempert R. 1991. Dependency on the welfare state: beyond the due process vision. *Contemp. Sociol.* 20(1):84–86

Levine FJ, Preston E. 1970. Community resource orientation among low income groups. *Wis. Law Rev.* 1970:80–113

Macaulay S. 1986. Private government. In *Law and Social Science,* ed. L Lipson, S Wheeler. pp. 445–518. New York: Russell Sage Found.

Macaulay S. 1984. Law and the social sciences: Is there any there there? *J. Law Policy* 6(2):149–87.

Macaulay S. 1966. *Law and the Balance of Power: the Automobile Manufacturers and their Dealers.* New York: Russell Sage Found.

Macaulay S. 1963. Non-contractual relations in business: a preliminary study. *Am. Sociol. Rev.* 28:55–69

Marx K, Engels F. 1950. *Basic Writings on Politics and Philosophy,* ed. L Furer. Garden City, NY: Doubleday

Massell G. 1968. Law as an instrument of revolutionary change in a traditional milieu: the case of Soviet Central Asia. *Law Soc. Rev.* 2(2):179–228

Mather L, Yngvesson B. 1980/1981. Language, audience, and the transformation of disputes. *Law Soc. Rev.* 15(3–4):775–821

Mayhew L. 1968. *Law and Equal Opportunity: A Study of the Massachusetts Commission Against Discrimination.* Cambridge: Harvard Univ. Press

Mayhew L, Reiss AJ. 1969. The social organization of legal contacts. *Am. Sociol. Rev.* 34(3):309–18

McCann M. 1994. *Rights at Work: Pay Equity Reform and the Politics of Legal Mobilization.* Chicago: Univ. Chicago Press

Menkel-Meadow C. 1989. Feminization of the legal profession: the comparative sociology of women lawyers. In *Lawyers in Society: Comparative Theories,* ed. RL Abel, PSC Lewis, pp. 196–256. Berkeley: Univ. Calif Press

Menkel-Meadow C. 1984. Toward another view of legal negotiation: the structures of problem-solving. *UCLA Law Rev.* 31:754–842

Menkel-Meadow C, Diamond S. 1991. The content, method, and epistemology of gender in sociological studies. *Law Soc. Rev.* 25(2):221–38

Merry SE. 1990. *Getting Justice and Getting Even: Legal Consciousness Among Working Class Americans.* Chicago: Univ. Chicago Press

Merry SE. 1982. The social organization of mediation in nonindustrial societies: implications for informal community justice in America. See Abel 1982. 2:17–46

Miller R, Sarat A. 1980/1981. Grievances, claims and disputes: assessing the adversary cultures. *Law Soc. Rev.* 15(3–4):525–66

Mills CW. 1959. *The Sociological Imagination.* New York: Oxford Univ. Press

Moore SF. 1978. *Law as Process: An Anthropological Approach.* London: Routledge & Kegan Paul

Munger F. 1994. Miners and lawyers: law practice and class conflict in Appalachia. 1872–1920. In *Lawyers in a Postmodern World.* ed. M Cain, CB Harrington, pp. 185–228. New York: New York Univ. Press

Munger F. 1993. Sociology of law for a postliberal society. *Loyola Law Rev.* 27:89–125

Munger F. 1991. Legal resources of striking miners: notes for a study of class conflict and law. *Soc. Sci. Hist.* 15(1):1–33

Nader L. 1969. *Law in Culture and Society.* New York: Academic

Nelson R. 1987. *Bureaucracy, Professionalism and Commitment: Authority Relationships in Large Law Firms.* Chicago: Am. Bar Found.

Nelson R, Trubek D, Solomon RL. 1992. *Lawyers' Ideals/Lawyers' Practices: Transformations in the American Legal Practice.* Ithaca: Cornell Univ. Press

Newman K. 1988. *Falling From Grace: the Experience of Downward Mobility in the American Middle Class.* New York: Free

Orren K, Skowronek S. 1994. Beyond the iconography of order: notes for a new institutionalism. In *The Dynamics of American Politics: Approaches and Interpretations,* ed. LC Dodd, C Jilson, pp. 311–30. Boulder: Univ. Colo. Press

Orren K, Skowronek S. 1996. Forthcoming. Institutions and intercurrents: theory building in the fullness of time. In *Nomos: Political Order,* ed. R Hardin, I Shapiro. Vol. 37. In press

Parsons T. 1964. *Essays in Sociological Theory*. New York: Free

Powell W, DiMaggio P. 1991. *The New Institutionalism in Organizational Analysis*. Chicago: Univ. Chicago Press

Reichman N. 1989. Breaking confidences: organizational influences on insider trading. *Sociol. Q.* 30(2):185–204

Rosenberg GN. 1991. *The Hollow Hope: Can Courts Bring About Social Change?* Chicago: Univ. Chicago Press

Sampson R, Laub J. 1993. Structural variations in juvenile court case processing: inequality, the underclass and social control. *Law Soc. Rev.* 27(2):285–311

Sanger C. 1993. *Law as litany: teenage abortion hearings*. Presented at Annu. Meet. Law Soc. Assoc., Chicago

Sarat A. 1990. " . . . the law is all over:" power, resistance and the legal consequences of the welfare poor. *Yale J. Law Hum.* 2:343–79

Sarat A, Felstiner WLF. 1995. *Divorce Lawyers and Their Clients: Power and Meaning in the Legal Process*. New York: Oxford Univ. Press

Sarat A, Felstiner WLF. 1988. Law and social relations: vocabularies of motive in lawyer/client interaction. *Law Soc. Rev.* 22(4):737–69

Savelsberg JJ. 1994. Knowledge, domination and criminal punishment. *Am. J. Sociol.* 99(4):911–43

Scheingold SA. 1974. *The Politics of Rights: Lawyers, Public Policy and Political Change*. New Haven, CT: Yale Univ. Press

Sennett R, Cobb J. 1972. *The Hidden Injuries of Class*. New York: Vintage

Seron C. 1996. *The Business of Practicing Law: the Worklives of Solo and Small Firm Attorneys*. Philadelphia: Temple Univ. Press

Seron C. 1993. New strategies for getting clients: urban and suburban lawyers' views. *Law Soc. Rev.* 27(2):399–420

Sewell WH. 1992. A theory of structure: duality, agency and transformation. *Am. J. Sociol.* 98(1):1–29

Shamir R. 1993. Professionalism and monopoly of expertise: lawyers and administrative law, 1933–37. *Law Soc. Rev.* 27(2):361–97

Shapiro S. 1987. *Wayward Capitalists: Target of the Securities and Exchange Commission*. New Haven, CT: Yale Univ. Press

Simon J. 1993. *Poor Discipline: Parole and the Social Control of the Underclass, 1890–1990*. Chicago: Univ. Chicago Press

Simon J. 1992. "The long walk home" to politics. *Law Soc. Rev.* 26(4):923–41

Simon R, Lynch J. 1989. The sociology of law: Where we have been and where we might be going. *Law Soc. Rev.* 23(5):825–47

Simon W. 1988. Ethical discretion in lawyering. *Harvard Law Rev.* 101:1083–145

Skolnick J. 1965. The sociology of law in America: overview and trends. *Soc. Probl.* 12(4):4–39

Smigel E. 1964. *The Wall Street Lawyer: A Professional Organization Man?* New York: Free Press

Somers MR, Gibson G. 1994. Reclaiming the epistemological "other": narrative and the constitution of identity. In *Social Theory and the Politics of Identity,* ed. C Calhoun, pp. 37–99. Cambridge, MD: Blackwell

Suchman D, Edelman LB. 1995. Legal rational myths: lessons for the new institutionalism from the law and society tradition. *Law Soc. Issues* Nov.

Sudnow D. 1965. Normal crimes: sociologial features of the penal code in a public defender office. *Soc. Probl.* 12(3):255–76

Sutherland EH. 1955. *Principles of Criminology*. Philadelphia: Lippencott

Thompson EP. 1975. *Whigs and Hunters: The Origins of the Black Act*. New York: Pantheon

Thompson EP. 1964. *The Making of the English Working Class*. New York: Vintage Books

Trubek DM. 1984. Where the action is: critical legal studies and empiricism. *Stanford Law Rev.* 36:575–622

Upham FK. 1987. *Law and Social Change in Postwar Japan*. Cambridge: Harvard Univ. Press

Wanner C. 1975. The public ordering of private relations, part two: winning civil court cases. *Law Soc. Rev.* 9(2):293–306

Wanner C. 1974. The public ordering of private relations, part one: initiating civil cases in urban trial courts. *Law Soc. Rev.* 8(3):421–40

Weber M. 1954. *Max Weber on Law in Economy and Society*. ed. E Shils, M Rheinstein. Cambridge: Harvard Univ. Press

White L. 1993. No exit: rethinking welfare dependency: from a different ground. *Georgetown Law J.* 81:1961–2002

White L. 1992. Seeking " . . . the faces of otherness . . . ": a response to professors Sarat, Felstiner. and Cahn. *Cornell Law Rev.* 77:1499–511

White L. 1991. Subordination, rhetorical survival skills, and Sunday shoes: notes on the hearing of Mrs. G.

In *At the Boundaries of Law,* ed. MA Fineman, NS Thomadsen, pp. 40–58. New York: Routledge

Williams PJ. 1991. *The Alchemy of Race and Rights.* Cambridge: Harvard Univ. Press

Willie CU. 1985. *Black and White Families: a Study in Complementarity.* Bayside, NY: General Hall

Winn JK. 1994. Rational practices and the marginalization of law: informal financial practices of small businesses in Taiwan. *Law Soc. Rev.* 28(2):193–232

Yngvesson B. 1985. Re-examining continuing relations and the law. *Wis. Law Rev.* 1985(3):623–46

Law and Race in Early America

W. HAYWOOD BURNS

In 1855 white men sitting in the Kansas legislature, duly elected by other white men, passed a law that sentenced white men convicted of rape of a white woman to up to five years in prison, while the penalty for a black man convicted of the same offense was castration, the costs of the procedure to be rendered by the desexed.

The penalty of sexual mutilation appears at many points in the annals of American jurisprudence, Kansas in 1855 being but one of the more recent examples. What is special about the sentence of castration is that where it was in force, it was almost universally reserved for blacks (and, in some cases, Indians).

Apart from what this example reveals about the sexual psychopathology of white America, or at least of those in power, it graphically demonstrates the working of law in a racist society. The nexus between law and racism cannot be much more direct than this. Indeed, the histories of the African, Asian, Latin, and Native American people in the United States are replete with examples of the law and the legal process as the means by which the generalized racism in the society was made particular and converted into standards and policies of social control. Going beyond the Kansas example cited, a systematic analysis of racism and law provides keen insight into the operations of both.[1]

In early-seventeenth-century colonial America, blacks and whites often existed and toiled side by side in various degrees of bondage. Though there were gradations of unfreedom, there was, at first, no clearly defined status of "slave." As the century drew to a close, however, the social reality

and objective conditions changed sufficiently for the members of the colonial legislatures to recognize officially that the situations of the black person in bondage and the white person in bondage were diverging, with that of the black person becoming more debased. "Free choice" was hardly an issue for either whites or blacks who came in bondage to the New World. Still, there was a considerable difference in being, for example, an Irish indentured servant and a kidnapped African arriving in chains after the unspeakable horrors of the Middle Passage. There are vast differences between a societally enforced discrimination and an entire legal order founded explicitly on racism—a world of difference between "Irish need not apply," as reprehensible as that was, and statutory denial of legal personality, of humanity.

Black people were severed from much of their culture, language, kindred, religion, and all communication with the Old World of their fathers and mothers, from which they had been torn. The ugly sentiments of white racial superiority were beginning to sprout and rear their heads above the native soil. These facts, coupled with a growing understanding of the tremendous economic advantage to be gained from the long-term exploitation of black labor, brought about a social consensus (among whites) that sought to permanently relegate black people to the lowest stratum in a vertical relationship of white over black. This consensus found expressions and implementation in the form of laws passed in colonial legislatures that made slavery for black people both a lifetime condition and a hereditary condition. Thus, through the operation of law, in this case legislated societal racism, the institution of American chattel slavery was created and perpetuated.

With the advent of the detailed and oppressive colonial slave codes of the early eighteenth century, law played a consistent role throughout the period, up to and including the American Revolution. The Revolution, of course, produced a golden opportunity to do business other than as usual. It was, after all, a revolution fought in the name of liberty and egalitarian principles. It was an opportunity that was nonetheless missed or, perhaps better said, rejected. The revolution of Jefferson, Washington, and Madison was never intended to embrace the ebony throngs of captured and enslaved people in their white midsts. It was too much for the eighteenth-century white American mind to view these captured and enslaved people fully as people. It was too much for the Founding Fathers and the economic interests they represented to tamper with that amount of property—even for those who on moral, philosophical, or religious grounds opposed slavery.

Thus, the birth of the new order in the establishment of the Republic brought with it no new day for the African on American soil. In erecting the new state, black people were still consigned to be the hewers of wood, the drawers of water, for there enshrined in the fundamental law of the land, the new Constitution itself was the guaranteed continuation of the slave trade; the guaranteed return of fugitive slaves; and the counting of black persons as three-fifths human beings for purposes of taxation and political representation.

The pre-Revolutionary slave codes were more than ample models for the post-Revolutionary slave codes, which continued their detailed, oppressive harshness into the nineteenth century and into the new and expanding nation. The nineteenth-century slave codes provide an excellent example of law and state operating to impose a given social order. The slave codes legislated and regulated in minute detail every aspect of the life of a slave and of black/white interaction; assured white-over-black dominance; and made black people into virtual nonpersons, refusing to recognize any right of family, free movement, choice, and

legal capacity to bring a suit or to testify where the interest of a white person was involved. This legal structure defining a black person's place in society was reinforced by statutes requiring cruel and brutal sanctions for any black man or woman who forgot his or her place and stepped, or even tried to step, out of it.

Even in the so-called Free States there was ample borrowing from the statutory schemes of the slavocracy to enforce a societal (white) view of the black person's rightful station in life. Thus, northern states systematically resorted to legislative devices to impose their collective view on the lives of "free" blacks, restricting them in employment, education, the franchise, legal personality, and public accommodation.

The legal issue of the status of black people in pre–Civil War America came to a head in 1857 in the case of *Dred Scott v. Sanford.*[2] It proved to be one of the most important judicial decisions in the history of the black experience with the law. In that case, Dred Scott, a slave who had been taken to a free territory by his master, attempted to sue for his freedom based upon the theory that residence in a free state had made him free.

As Mr. Chief Justice Taney put it, "The question is simply this: Can a negro, whose ancestors were imported into this country, and sold as slaves, become a member of the political community formed and brought into existence by the Constitution of the United States, and as such become entitled to all the rights, and privileges, and immunities, guaranteed by that instrument to the citizen . . . ?"[3]

The Court's answer was, simply, "No." In ruling that Dred Scott, and by extension, any other black person, could not be a citizen under the Constitution, Taney went back to the founding of the Republic, examining what he declared was the public view of the black race at that point and tracing its history through time: " . . . [T]he public history of every European nation displays it in a manner too plain to be mistaken. [T]hey (the black race) had for more than a century before been regarded as beings of an inferior order, and altogether unfit to associate with the white race, either in social or political relations; and so far inferior, that they had no rights which the white man was bound to respect. . . ."[4] This ringing Taney dictum dashed the hopes of black people and abolitionists who had looked to the courts to resolve one of the most troubling questions of racial justice of the day. The majority's decision and its view of black people as inferior brought down a rain of criticism on the Court from the North and caused cries of joy to rise from below the Mason-Dixon line. It also set the stage for the oncoming War between the States.

Logically, the Civil War should have made a decided difference in this racial legal dynamic. It did not, for though slavery itself was destroyed by this cataclysmic confrontation, the racism and economic exploitation undergirding slavery remained very much intact. Thus, even after the Emancipation Proclamation, after the war and the Thirteenth Amendment, the South set out to win the peace, despite having lost the war. The states of the South, where well over 90 percent of the nation's black people then lived, countered the emancipation by putting in place a series of laws known as the Black Codes, designed to approximate as closely as possible, in view of the legal abolition of slavery, a white-over-black, master/servant society. This legal order governed movement, marriage, work relations, and most major aspects of the freedperson's life.

In fact, there are many ways in which the Black Codes very much resembled the pre–Civil War slave codes. Laws were instituted against vagabonds to curtail black men from moving away from the land. Sharecropping and the convict-lease laws were designed to keep the former slaves on the land. Unlike other statutes, the vagabond- and convict-leasing statutes were not racial in their terms; however, their purpose and effect were entirely clear. The southern economy was predicated upon a large, exploited black labor force; and except for the brief and bright interregnum of Reconstruction, the law and the state throughout the last years of the nineteenth century and the early years of the twentieth operated to preserve the old order and to wring maximum advantage from

white hegemony over an oppressed and economically ravaged black populace.

It was the law as well that played a crucial role in "the strange career of Jim Crow." In an uneven and nonsystematic way, culture and mores had provided for a separation of the races in many aspects of American life. For most of the nation's history, that was not even much of an issue because the presence of slavery took care of any need for social definition. However, during the late 1800s, states began to systematically codify separation of the races, *requiring* segregation literally from the hospital where one was born to the cemetery where one was laid to rest. Segregation no longer was open to local option, custom, and usage but was the state's legal order of the day. These developments occurred at the same point in time that an increasingly conservative Supreme Court was narrowing its interpretation of the Thirteenth, Fourteenth, and Fifteenth Amendment—the Civil War amendments. These trends culminated in the *Plessy v. Ferguson*[5] decision of the Supreme Court in 1896, in which "separate but equal" was approved as the law of the land, and the seal] of approval of the nation's highest court was placed upon our own American brand of apartheid.

The use of the legal system to create and protect a racially segregated society was coincident with government's manipulation of the law to disenfranchise black citizens. Beginning with the Mississippi constitutional convention of 1890, revising the state's constitution through a series of legal stratagems and artifices—and greatly aided by the extralegal depredations of lynch law—black people were stripped of the ballot and any real semblance of black political power. The poll tax, the literacy test, and the Grandfather Clause were legal devices employed in the service of this racist cause to desired effect.

As a result of state uses of the law in this fashion, black Americans entered the twentieth century segregated, sundered from full and free participation in American life, and politically powerless to do much about it. This situation largely obtained through this century, with minor indications of change and advancement from time to time but with no real major breakthrough in the wall of apartheid and powerlessness until the Supreme Court decision in *Brown v. Board of Education.*[6]

Brown and the struggle that followed in its wake—much of which involved use of the law to support and effect positive social change—obviously represent a highly significant advance in black Americans' quest for liberation. It would be an analytical mistake of considerable proportion, however, to view *Brown* as the end of explicitly racist legislation and court decisions, and the advent of civil rights laws as indicative of the end of the relationship among racism and the law and the state. For all our gains, America remains a country deeply infected by racism. Though this racism may not be as explicit or as obvious as it was in earlier times, it is present and no less real. Indeed, the last decade has seen a resurgence of racism in its most virulent as well as sophisticated forms.

NOTES

1. For good general treatment and historical overview, see Derrick Bell, Jr., *Race, Racism, and American Law* (Boston: Little, Brown, 1980); Derrick Bell, Jr., *And We Are Not Saved* (New York: Basic Books, 1987); Albert P. Blaustein, and Robert I. Zangrando, eds., *Civil Rights and the American Negro* (New York: Trident Press, 1968); John Hope Franklin and Alfred A. Moss, Jr., *From Freedom to Slavery* (New York: Alfred A. Knopf, 1988); Paul Finkelman, *Slavery in the Courtroom* (Washington, D.C.: Library of Congress, 1985); Thomas F. Race Gossett, *The History of an Idea in America* (Dallas: Southern Methodist University Press, 1963); Oscar Handlin, *Race and Nationality in American Life* (Boston: Little, Brown, 1957); A. L. Higginbotham, *In the Matter of Color,* vol. 1 (New York: Oxford University Press, 1980); Winthrop Jordan, *White Over Black* (Chapel Hill: University of North Carolina Press, 1968). Although this short essay focuses mainly on the history of black people and American law, a similar analysis would apply to the historical experiences of other persons of color in the United States.

2. 19 How.(60 U.S.)393 (1857)

3. *Id.* at 403.

4. *Id.* at 407.

5. 163 U.S. 537 (1896).

6. 347 U.S. 483 (1954).

Race, Class, and Gender
O. J. Revisited

RILEY OLSTEAD
York University

There are many reasons why the O. J. Simpson case has been and remains the focus of this and multiple other papers and discussions. Precisely because it has captured the collective attention of so many Americans, it continues to be worth analyzing and decoding. We have to wonder, even after the most conclusive and convincing arguments, what was so intriguing. In this analysis, I have chosen the O. J. trial as I view it as a defining moment wherein the entire country, and beyond, became involved in a process of creating new ways of understanding race, class and gender.

The O. J. Simpson trial must be viewed as an arena for discussions around our own social institutions. While O. J. Simpson was the officially declared defendant, in many ways the criminal justice system, along with other social institutions, was also "on trial." The trial raised questions such as "Is there room for a shift in paradigm in contemporary America, from a racist white-centric model to a meritocratic society in which African Americans, both male and female, are welcomed to compete alongside of whites?" and "How do we understand violence against women, and, more specifically, what location can women hold in American society today?" Also, the question was raised as to whether social institutions were, or could become, "color blind." Could the justice system work equitably for both African Americans and whites? The case looked at these and other important questions.

Even though the trial was opportune for raising questions that were central to the self-definition of Americans, many of those questions were left unanswered. In the end, multiple factors enabled the justice system to reassert itself as an instrument of and for white dominance. These developments are dealt with more clearly in the subsections on race, class and gender.

However, before any discussion can be launched in regard to race, class and gender, three points must be stressed. First, in no way should one form of inequality be positioned against another. That is to say, it is not useful to engage in a discussion as to "which group is most oppressed." Racism, then, cannot be said to be any worse than classism or vice versa. Clearly, the desire here is to search for a means by which race, class and gender discrimination can be eradicated. Second, an individual can experience one or many forms of discrimination. Therefore, an African American woman experiences a very unique form of racism, quite different than that experienced by an African American man. Third, as mentioned earlier, there are many other means by which individuals are excluded from privilege which will not be dealt with here. Issues around weightism and ageism, for example, are not being discussed. Individuals facing these types of bias are the "marginalized of the marginalized" in that their issues get very little treatment from most academics. Surely, this is an area which needs to be explored more fully.

In order to understand an analysis of the Simpson trial, we need to begin by examining what we mean when we talk about race, class and gender.

RACE

Race is a social construct and has been used as a means by which political and systemic abuses have been imposed upon certain groups while other groups benefit. It is a term that has, over time, become a component of daily discourse and what Gramsci[1] referred to as "common sense" (Miles: 1994). That is to say, we as a society do not often question our understanding of what race is.

In fact, we have not always understood ourselves in terms of racial divisions. The development of racial categories developed out of capitalism where the need for social stratification justified systematic inclusion and exclusion. That is to say, whites were instrumental in determining that they were the legitimate claimants to resources and services based on the fact that they were white. Consequently, *white* came to mean much more than a description of skin color. It came to mean that the individual, perceived as being white, ought be treated in specific, privileged ways. For nonwhites, certain phenotypical characteristics were attributed meanings in such a way as to create a system of categorization. By attributing negatively evaluated characteristics to the people sorted in those categories, racism was set in motion (Miles: 1993). Racism then, is a process of *signification,* or a representational process by which meanings are attributed to particular objects, features and processes, in such a way that the latter are given special significance, and carry or are embodied with a set of additional second-order features (cf. Potter and Wetherall: 1987).

Let us pretend for a moment that we are in a large group composed of multiple individuals from many different ethnic backgrounds. Signification occurs when we begin to differentiate between one another based on, say, skin color. All of the African Americans are requested to stand on one side of the room, while all the whites stand on the other. This exercise in segregation between African Americans and whites demonstrates, in highly simplistic terms, the way in which we impose meaning upon groups. We have collectively decided that there are real differences, distinguishable by skin color, that separate individuals in society. However, what if we were to have selected some other form of signification? Perhaps we could have chosen eye color. Our separation of groups would suddenly look much different. We must come to understand

that differences between groups only exist because, historically, dominant groups (whites) have singled them out as differences. We do not imagine ourselves in terms of "the green-eyed group" or the "brown-eyed group" and have instead focused our attention on skin color, language and accent, to name but a few. But why?

Robert Miles states that "the concept of racism refers to any argument which suggests that the human species is composed of discrete groups in order to legitimate inequality between those groups of people" (Miles: 1994, p. 49). Racism then, has long been utilized as a way in which individuals who are seeking power and resources enable themselves as a group to achieve privileges without obstruction from other parties. In looking at capitalism, for example, we have a supposedly "free market system" which operates in terms of "unharnessed competition." However, capitalism, the economic system, is always in need of an unemployed, marginalized group of workers (reserve army of labor) to provide labor in high production times and to drive competition for jobs up. In this way, the economic system creates, perpetuates and utilizes a social inequality (racism, for example) that ensures that a large group of individuals will be relegated to the ranks of the unemployed poor. As those groups remain on the periphery of the economic system, their relative poverty increases their inability to access resources. Both historically and contemporarily, only the group that capitalism privileges (whites) has been able to compete for resources. We must conclude, then, that capitalism does not encourage a "free" market at all but relies on discrimination in order to develop and grow. Capitalism attempts to disassociate itself from the social system of inequality and instead purports to be an economic system. However, both systems pursue the same end, and are undeniably intertwined. Capitalism doesn't just thrive on inequality—it depends on it.

It must be pointed out that racism has never been a static concept. It has been altered over time in order to meet the needs of various interests, and has come to be utilized by seemingly legitimate social institutions. As in the case of Nazi Germany, science largely qualified *race* as a means of distinguishing between certain groups. The Holocaust and genocide of millions of Jews and gypsies was a result of the embedding of radical racism in social institutions. Hitler's "final solution," the extermination of all Jews, was carried out under the institutional mandate of "social cleansing." While many today believe this event to be an anomaly, ethnic cleansing has happened more recently in East Timor, the former Yugoslavia and Kurdistan. However, more subtle forms of racial discrimination and violence also exist.

The more subtle forms of racism can often be identified at the institutional level. Institutional racism and individual racism are two distinct forms of racist expression. The latter involves one person's belief in the superiority of one race over another. Institutional racism, on the other hand, is systemic and involves such institutions as sports, family, the state, the justice system and the education system (Kendall: 1997). Institutional racism is a system of beliefs and behaviors by which a group defined as a race is oppressed, controlled and exploited because of presumed cultural or biological characteristics (Blauner: 1972). It is often difficult to recognize institutional racism because we begin to accept it as normal when it becomes embedded in the common patterns of our lives. As an example, most Americans may recognize that the system that existed in South Africa known as apartheid was a racist mechanism built into the state policy. However, those same people might not view Jim Crowism or the current ghettoization of African Americans as a means of apartheid. Reserve systems, apartheid and ghettoization are all forms of geographical/resource/social exclusion but are each treated in different ways based on the degree to which the dominant groups *perceive* them as racist. Some nation-states utilize force as a means of imposing divisions between groups, whereas other nations utilize more subtle, institutional forms of discrimination, and some, as in the case of the United States, use both.

In terms of the justice system, racism has always been present within the legal establishment. Take for example the famous Herndon Case in Georgia from 1932. Herndon, a young African American man, had been caught in possession of a pamphlet entitled *The Communists' Position on the Negro Question*. The court, at this time, dismissed a request by the defense to strike a juror based on the fact that he belonged to the Ku Klux Klan (Gordon: 1995). This case reveals a lot about the expression of institutional racism in the 1930s, and yet, while the character of the jury member and the consequent lack of concern on the part of the court seems outrageous to us today, racism continues to exist in equally overt, yet unacknowledged forms.

Take, for example, the beating of Rodney King case in 1991 (LaFountain: 1992). An onlooker recorded a videotape of the beating. Yet this evidence, along with the knowledge that at least twenty policemen watched as King was beaten, was not enough to convict the four white officers involved in the assault. One response to the acquittal by marginalized groups came to be known as "the L.A. riots." These events ultimately resulted in the death of fifty people, the majority of them African American and Latino (Cockburn: 1992). The way in which the "riot" was presented by media clearly underlined racist and classist assumptions. For example, it was reported that "parents [were] return[ing] home with bundles of Pampers, [and] packets of hamburger meat" (Cockburn: 1992). However, very few heard of the stripping of supermarkets by the affluent who loaded up their Volvos with T-bone steaks and escaped back to their homes (Cockburn: 1992, p. 19). The uprising was not portrayed as an act of community resistance to systemic inequalities. It was not seen as an organized and legitimate protest against real discriminatory practices. Instead, the media presented it as a "riot" and focused upon looting, vandalism and violence as opposed to poverty, racism and police brutality. And what of Rodney King?

The day after the trial President George H. W. Bush complained that he was "vexed" and "frustrated" by the verdict, presumably because he felt it necessary to make public display of symbolic concern regarding the lack of attention paid to the civil rights of Mr. King. Needless to say, the justice system was demonstrating its bias in favor of police with clubs and guns who "hunted black men with the audacity to drive around L.A. in their cars at night" (Cockburn: 1992, p. 19). While the "riots" located in South Central Los Angeles were sparked by the grotesque display of racism expressed in the verdict of the King trial, the rioters were also making a public statement of their own rejection of the *continuous* experience of racism within their community. An absence of jobs, services and hope for change in the area created the conditions in which residents felt compelled to take to the streets in a collective challenge to all institutions that denied access to essential services.

Infant mortality and poverty rates for African Americans living in American cities greatly exceed those of whites. In 1990 alone, 34 percent of African Americans living in large cities were living in poverty as opposed to 11 percent of whites (Cockburn: 1992). However, even though whites are generally aware of the conditions in African American neighborhoods, white people appeared surprised by the "riots." Whites collectively called for calm and understanding in an attempt to control and suppress African American anger.

However, this anger had been brewing for some time. The "riot" not only was a response to the poverty felt in African American communities, but was also a response to police discrimination towards African Americans. Two years before the "riot," Charles Stuart made headlines. Stuart claimed to have been shot, along with his pregnant wife, as they were leaving a birthing class. Stuart, a white man, described his assailant as a lone African American male. Within a matter of weeks, an African American man was arrested and Boston's mayor assigned more police officers to the Mission Hill District (the area in which the shootings occurred—an African American neighborhood) than had ever been assigned to any Boston community (Gomes and Williams: 1990). Several months after the murder Stuart's brother, Matthew, implicated Charles Stuart in the murder of his wife and unborn baby and then claimed that Charles had turned the gun on himself in order to have it appear that he was a victim of the same

gunman. After his brother's claims, Charles Stuart committed suicide. As it has been rightly noted, Stuart's "understanding of the potency of blaming an African American suspect was grounded in a long history of media popularization of the validity of the relationship between race and crime" (Gomes and Williams: 1990, p. 59).

However, it is not simply the influence of the media that perpetuates racism within the justice system. Rather, racism is continuously sustained by a dialogue among various social institutions. Many social institutions have similar agendas and, therefore, all work to support one another. Simply put, institutions are racist, and when they participate in advancing racism they are in fact building and reinforcing their own, as well as all, other institutional power. What does this mean in terms of changing institutions to equally meet the needs of *all* citizens?

The task on the part of the justice system is to remain neutral and provide an arena for the constitutional rights provided for in the Bill of Rights. The system has largely failed historically in terms of the provision of justice toward its peoples as a whole, as witnessed by the fact that it was not until the 1960s that most citizens became entitled to counsel and related constitutional rights at the state level. It must be clarified that the United States of America does not have a *justice* system, per se, but a legal system that has largely perpetuated the dominance of some over others.

CLASS

We have dealt only marginally with the issue of poverty and therefore have done an inadequate job of assessing issues surrounding class power in America today. Class has generally been overlooked in terms of current debates around the legal system. However, class is a means of subordination or a system of social inequality in which status is determined by the ownership and control of resources, the kinds of work people perform, and life chances[2] (Kendall: 1997). Social classes are often viewed as being on an economic continuum of social stratification—a hierarchical arrangement of large social groups based on their control over scarce resources (Kendall: 1997). In a real sense, once an individual is born into a social class, it is largely impossible for that individual to shift into another. This suggests that Americans live in a closed system and challenges the notion of individualism and meritocratism that is believed to be the foundation of a free and democratic nation. In this respect, we can imagine ourselves to have a caste system—a system of social inequality whereby one's status is permanently determined at birth based on the ascribed characteristics of one's parents (Kendall: 1997). However, there *is* a very small degree of social mobility, or movement between classes. This allows state agencies and others to claim that poverty is a result of laziness and stupidity, as opposed to obstacles within the system. As whites have generally monopolized the highest paid positions, including government, media and corporate positions, nondominant groups have been kept in low- and working-class positions. White Anglo-Saxon protestants account for 43 to 48 percent of all elites, whereas minorities account for only 3.9 percent (Gomes and Williams: 1990). The combination of the systemic racism that permeates every facet of the working community and the assumptions articulated through state policy in the form of welfare reforms and overall social spending cutbacks creates the perception that African Americans, Hispanics and others are inferior to whites.

I have spoken of apartheid earlier and have discussed how the white population in South Africa proclaimed the separation of the races a necessity. Apartheid was blatant in its racist intentions, whereas segregation in the United States has been achieved through subtler forms. Keeping African Americans poor has been another means of disguising the explicit nature of racist policies. White poverty creates a diversion from the ethnic identities of disadvantaged groups. To keep African Americans poor is, in and of itself, a form of oppression. However, it also has a secondary function—to hide racist discrimination by obscuring the connection between race and poverty. There are both poor African Americans and poor white people, however, the whites *are not poor because they are white*, whereas systemic racism is

very much operant in maintaining poverty amongst nonwhites. Whites who are poor are poor as a result of class, gender, mobility and other forms of discrimination. These multiple possibilities, which account for poverty, clearly outline the complexity of discriminatory forms. People who point to poor whites as being an indication of a lack of racism in America have bought into the myth of what I refer to as "discriminatory equity," the belief that the state discriminates equally against all of its subjects. And with this belief becoming quite common in "American common sense," we collectively move toward becoming a nation of Social Darwinists—those who believe that there exists a natural hierarchy among races of people where African Americans and other nonwhites are considered inferior to whites. This explanation for poverty denies that inequality exists, and therefore suggests that whites have earned white dominance and privilege as a group. *The Bell Curve,* for instance, uses similar arguments and has been given scientific legitimacy as it has been coauthored and promoted by members of the academe who utilized mock-scientific "evidence" to "prove" claims of African American inferiority (Herrnstein and Murray: 1994). *The Bell Curve* is an example of the move toward legitimizing blatant forms of racism by the right wing, but it is most significant that this kind of blatant racism is finding a foothold, once again, in our academic institutions.

Another means of disguising racism is to point to the few who seem to "make it." As an example, it is well known that Oprah Winfrey generates millions of dollars annually in revenues from Harpo! Productions. To suggest that all African American women are able to earn this kind of money is a direct insult to the multiple women who are caught in a system of poverty imposed on them by the state and other social mechanisms. However, conservative politicians enjoy pointing to individual success stories (the exceptions to the rule) such as Oprah Winfrey, Michael Jordan, O. J. Simpson and Eddie Murphy as evidence of the seemingly free society in which the American dream is available to those with the vigor to reach for it. African American people are expected to accept the success of individuals as illustrative of the equal opportunities for all. The "generalizability of 'blackness' is such that the success of one African American person heralds the death knell for institutional racism" (White: 1995). We must look at the larger social issues and maintain rigorous investigation of the systemic nature of inequality rather than allow the exception to influence our understanding of larger social issues.

As White (1995) suggests, there is an economy underlying race and racism. It is imperative that the interconnection between racism and the social economy be examined in order to determine the interrelationship of poverty, wealth, power and race. For example, though we often tend to believe that social institutions treat every individual the same, it has often been noted that one's class and ability to pay often opens greater opportunities for the wealthy, and generally closes doors to the poor. Because legal services, medical services, education and employment all rely upon the availability of money, many groups are unrepresented or underrepresented, fall ill, are uneducated and are unemployed as a result of their inaccessibility to funds to pay lawyers, doctors, teachers and to purchase the necessary attire for employment positions, for example.

Class is not simply a determination of the amount of money one possesses, but can be related to what Pierre Bourdieu calls cultural capital (1986). *Cultural capital,* in simple terms is status. Status is often achieved through an adherence to certain mannerisms, including manner of speech, posture, attire, gesture and therefore, self- presentation generally. The movie *My Fair Lady* (1964), for example, is about the transformation of Audrey Hepburn who plays a poor English woman, into a "proper English belle".[3] The transformation is only successful when Hepburn drops her Cockney drawl, changes her clothes, learns how to walk in a particular way and holds silverware in the manner employed by the upper class. That is, Hepburn is taught the components of cultural capital. Having given her substantial amounts of money would not have been sufficient in terms of elevating her social status; instead, she needed to adhere to those rules of behavior utilized by the wealthy in order to segregate groups by class. Cultural capital

is not a new concept to most, as it has often been understood through such comments as, "He has no class." or, "He is a classy man." Class, therefore, not only describes wealth or poverty but is also reflected in a system of behavior that has been claimed to be superior or inferior based on one's location in society. It must be added that, although they are unique concepts, class is similar to race as both are socially constructed and therefore one's class is never an adequate expression of group characterization. Nonetheless, these rules of behavior are means by which poor groups are excluded from jobs, schools and relationships. In a real sense, being white is an extremely powerful form of cultural capital, as it is perceived as being the ideal. Therefore, nonwhite groups are automatically excluded from achieving certain forms of cultural capital. In every way, whites exert an inordinate amount of power and control over wealth, and therefore power. Cultural capital is not simply an achieved status. Had Hepburn been an African American woman, her able handling of silverware would not have been an adequate distraction from the fact that she was African American. Status, class and race are all involved in an establishment in which whiteness ensures political, social and economic advantage.

GENDER

Often when we think of gender, we imagine the categories of *men* and *women.* However, these groups are, in fact, not gender categories but descriptions of one's sex. Gender, on the other hand, includes gays, lesbians, bisexuals and transgendered people. In fact, some people do not agree with classifications of gender and do not wish to classify themselves and others in any category or group. This resistance to being categorized is a way in which many people who have experienced homophobia and discrimination reject being "pinned down," identified and defined by those groups who would exploit those deemed sexually "different." It is important, however, to understand differences between sex and gender. We need to be able to make distinctions between various forms of oppression because they affect groups differently.

Certainly heterosexual women do not experience the same kinds of discrimination as lesbian women. Society distinguishes between the groups, so we must recognize the differing forms of systemic discrimination imposed upon them.

For example, the Supreme Court decision in *Baehr v. Lewin* suggests that same-sex partners may soon be entitled to marry in the state of Hawaii (Henson: 1993–1994). The institution of marriage, therefore, is closed to gays and lesbians. The act of marriage, then, is an exercise in privilege. The court system, in particular, has discriminated against nonheterosexual persons and thus has clearly demonstrated its disinterest in the welfare of many of the individuals for whom it claims to operate in the application of justice. However, looking at relations between men and women, social institutions have also displayed their preference for the establishment of male power over women. For example, the law has only recently acknowledged the criminality of marital rape by prosecuting husbands. Feminists have successfully argued that rape laws only serve to protect men's sexual access to female bodies rather than protect women's bodily integrity (Ryan: 1995). What does this say about the value of women's lives according to the state?

We have examined race, class and gender and have found that there are complex, often undefinable pressures, which keep individuals from achieving access to resources and services. We have learned that group discrimination over time is called *systemic inequality*. Further, we have examined several examples of systemic discrimination as it is found to exist within institutions. Let us now look in more detail at a specific case in order to understand how the media, capitalism, racism, classism and gender discrimination affect the social world.

CASE STUDY

On June 13, 1994, the bodies of Nicole Brown Simpson and Ronald Goldman were found at 875 South Bundy Drive in Los Angeles. (This examination focuses upon O. J. Simpson and Nicole Brown Simpson and does not examine the circumstances of Ronald Goldman, also found deceased at the home of Nicole Brown Simpson.) Investigators quickly claimed to have discovered blood stains at the residence and in the vehicle of O. J. Simpson—the retired football superstar and ex-husband of Nicole Brown Simpson. These bloodstains matched those found at the murder site. Nineteen previous complaints of spousal abuse against O. J. Simpson furthered the investigators's belief that they had discovered the correct identity of Nicole's murderer. On January 24, 1994, the murder trial of O. J. Simpson began. In late September of the following year, a jury composed of eight African American females, one African American male, two white females and one white male declared Simpson not guilty.

The People v. Orenthal James Simpson

We have spent time looking at some rather complicated issues around race, class and gender. In doing so, we have discovered that racism, classism and gender bias permeates all of society's institutions and, therefore, influences us all. In this respect, we all have a vested interest in seeing our institutions serve all of our needs equally, as opposed to serving the needs of white, middle/upperclass heterosexuals. As we look to the very popularized O. J. Simpson case, we can see the interplay between issues around race, class and gender. This case is an exceptional exemplar not only because it focused upon the three primary forms of discrimination examined within this particular discussion, but also because it was an event that for various reasons, ultimately drew much interest from the American public. In particular, the O. J. Simpson case was a forum for the discussion of issues of civil rights, democracy and justice, to name but a few. Most of the nation watched the proceedings eagerly as issues around inequality and discrimination were asked and answered. The trial proceedings came to be understood as an investigation into the truths of society, what democracy means and how Americans, as a nation should interact, understand one another and live.

Media

One of the important factors distinguishing the O. J. trial from other trials was its incredible popularity fueled by continuous exploitation by the mass media. Television coverage far surpassed that of the Super Bowl, the first day of the Gulf War and the landing on the moon. The first day of the trial had an audience of ninety-five million people in the United States alone (Gerbner: 1995, p. 562). Many suggest that televising the trial allowed unrestricted access to the proceedings and therefore upheld the foundation of democratic access. Yet others have continuously criticized the televising of such events. Christo Lassiter (1996), an Associate Professor of Law at the University of Cincinnati College says this:

> In the Anglo-American legal tradition, ideally, courts are elevated above the morass of public clamor, political crassness, personal bias, and petty idiosyncracies to perform the solemn task of deciding competing factual claims in accordance with objectively neutral law.
>
> (p. 934, emphasis mine)

However, the idea that there is such a thing as neutrality is a myth. We are continuously influenced by our own personal biases, suggesting that objectivity is indeed an ideal we will never reach. What needs to occur is a collective acknowledgment of our personal and institutional biases such that we can actively work to eradicate those mechanisms of inequality. A belief in objectivity benefits white upper- and middle-class heterosexual families. Interestingly enough, these people are very guarded against any attacks on the objectivity of institutions because they are aware, at some level, that a collective attack upon those institutions is a direct challenge to those instruments that maintain their own power.

When cameras were brought into the O. J. trial, the nature of the proceedings changed drastically. Once again, the media must be recognized as a white power structure that "creates" news more often than it reports it. De Certeau suggests that, "TV news needs be thought of not as informing the public, but as giving form to social practices" (Swenson: 1995, p. 75). Lassiter suggests that there are three primary effects of cameras in the courtroom. First, he suggests that "the trial, in reality, operates on a larger theme than the matter under charge; the judicial process is corrupted by a substitution of the solemn, calm, deliberate judgement of the finder of fact for the outrage of an inflamed public. Second, the adversarial system, designed for neutral and dispassionate judicial prosecution, transforms into an instrument of politically motivated persecution. Third, the public outcry leads to a political vice of judicial disposition against a disfavored minority" (Lassiter: 1996, p. 935). Lassiter is, of course, suggesting that the public is somehow unqualified to make decisions around what is just and unjust. Instead, he prefers that the largely white-male-dominated judicial system make decisions, regardless of whether that system has an anti-judicious mandate based on years of discriminatory decisions that only serve to reinforce their own group's power.

Second, Lassiter also wishes us to believe that the justice system is somehow apolitical and that it is tainted by an attempt to politicize. Really, Lassiter is one of those who eloquently professes the purity of the justice system even though his interest is in protecting the dominant community for whom the system serves. On the other hand, he shames those who speak out against the system—those who become angry at the continuous inequalities upheld by the courts in the name of justice. Nonetheless, Lassiter expertly proposes some very common concerns by those involved in dominant positions who feel themselves being challenged. Cameras, however, did not challenge the white-male privilege in the O. J. trial.

The influence of the media played such a major role during the trial that it can be said to have been an actor in the courtroom that controlled representation and identity of all of the players in the case. The African American community, in particular, assessed the reporting of the mainstream media, hoping that coverage would be fair and indiscriminatory. However, the media failed miserably and foretold of a continuing era of media exploitation of nondominant groups. The media played a major role in achieving social control over nondominant groups. But how?

To begin, the historical representation of African Americans, and in particular African American men, has focused on sports events, crime dramas, and "African tribal" movies. All of these represent the African American man as deviant, threatening, quaint, uncivilized and criminal. Good examples include African American men in football, who are still often kept from the so-called "thinking" positions of quarterback, coach and owner. Instead, African Americans are placed in positions that are considered to best utilize their abilities, such as being physical, aggressive and uncontrollable. Similarly, a recent introduction of the popular cop shows on television reveals that African Americans, or other nonwhites, are much more commonly pursued, arrested and incarcerated than whites (Kozol: 1992). Criminality, as television viewers interpret it, becomes defined by skin color. And, of course we have the *Shaka Zulu–Roots* phenomenon, which portrays African Americans as violent, irrational, bloodthirsty or as spectacles to amuse white audiences. Watching the struggles and triumph of individual African American characters generally legitimizes white beliefs that African Americans as a group are oppressed because they are lazy, ignorant, slow and underdeveloped. *Roots* tells us that oppression is a thing to be triumphed.

In short, the portrayal of African Americans on television restores racial inequality and social order. Furthermore, it reduces individuals to being perceived as an object, rather than as a real person. This objectification has enabled whites to show a general disinterest in discrimination because television promotes it as being innocuous, much in line with perceptions of talk shows and soaps. Judith Butler has stated that the television, in particular, is not neutral, as it is itself a racial form that reinforces the hegemony[4] of the dominant group in a most forceful way (1993). Therefore, when we view an African American individual on television, we immediately and uncritically perceive of that individual in terms of the continuous and normalized representation of African Americans through

the television medium. When, as in the case of the O. J. Simpson trial, we are presented with a question as to the guilt or innocence of an African American man, whites immediately presuppose a guilty verdict as a result of their intimate relationship with the television representation of the African American as criminal, along with previously held racist beliefs. Interestingly, a *USA Today* poll in September of 1994 found that 51 percent of African American respondents thought that television coverage would influence jurors against Simpson, while only 37 percent of whites felt it would have any persuasive effect (Sharkey: 1994). The irony here is that less whites than African Americans seem to believe that the media influences decisions within the courtroom, yet this same group had generally accepted, through evidence provided to them through the media, that Simpson's guilt was obvious. In a most clarifying statement, Richard Sherwin, author of "Law and the Myth of Self in the Mass Media," says that "our beliefs help to create what we see" (1995, p. 301). Sherwin is suggesting that our beliefs prior to the trial, more than the events themselves, will form our understanding of the events.

In the creation of meaning, what the media considers newsworthy is as important as what it does not. It seems as if American society has been presented with an all–African American lineup from which to gauge the meaning of social crimes. Issues of child sexual abuse, rape, sexual harassment and even murder are projected onto a community whose initial response is to gaze back into the projection, only to find themselves face to face with an African American male. As one African American media journalist suggested, it seems "extremely curious that [Clarence Thomas, Mike Tyson, Michael Jackson and O. J. Simpson] are being accorded far more media coverage than a cannibal like Jeffrey Dahmer" (Shipp: 1994, p. 15). And what of the alteration of O. J.'s picture by *Time* magazine? Simpson's skin was electronically darkened and his beard was enhanced to appear larger. Here we can see the "creation" of public fear and condemnation for African Americans, with artificially concocted, simulated and often unsubstantiated "truths" being presented by the media as the "American dilemma." Under such circumstances, where "African Americans make news as criminals at least twice as often as other groups" (Sharkey: 1994, p. 26), it is not the rape or violence which comes to be recognized as problematic, but the blackness of the assailant's skin.

Sports Heroes, Villains and Bench Warmers

It is important at this point to recognize the real power of our consumer society in terms of our comprehension of events televised. In a real sense, American society, its conventions, its belief systems and its worship of the commodity is primary to the O. J. Simpson case. As has been mentioned earlier, the media as an institution is very important because it controls and manipulates the information we receive. Also, we have examined the use of the television as a medium for the reracialization of African Americans on screen. Yet we have neglected to appreciate the transformation of O. J. and Nicole Brown Simpson from human beings to characters in a movie. O. J. in particular was used by the public to play a "position" much like that in a football game, in which certain groups found themselves invested in the "success" of O. J. while others "bet" on the other team. But who was the other team?

The methods of the media, in accordance with the methods of the court system, created a template or "game plan" wherein blackness was thrown into the ring with whiteness, maleness was pegged against femaleness, and democracy was challenged by the very freedoms it has claimed to uphold—those of free speech in the media, of individualism, women's liberation, racial equality, social mobility and, of course, the American dream itself! However, if we buy into this model and really believe that our adversarial court system is in fact interested in finding solutions to contemporary injustices, the whole trial process, including the media exposure it received, was a hoax. How can justice be achieved when we frame our decisions based on such binarisms—those which inevitably lead to a damnation of one por-

tion of society and an elevation of another group? For example, can men really be said to have "won" against women in terms of the not guilty verdict in O. J.'s trial? Certainly it seems that Nicole Brown Simpson's family and multiple feminists would suggest so. Yet this again is the great flaw of the justice system as we know it—the very fact that the adversarial system refuses to be self-reflexive, to consider itself as a potential defendant, to see itself as flawed. It seeks not to eradicate its own systemic racism and inherent mechanisms of inequality but rather serves up the issues of the nondominant as the main course for litigation, thus distracting our attention from the reasons that inequality exists in the first place! I am not necessarily criticizing the adversarial system per se, but rather the inability of that system to move beyond itself, so as to take stock of its own systemic mechanisms. While we have discussed many of the issues that were raised during the trial, it is most important to examine *what was not on trial;* this really leads us to an understanding of the larger impact of the O. J. case on societal consciousness, values and beliefs.

White male-dominated power was never challenged. Via the television screen, O. J. became the "fallen hero" for whom many African Americans rallied in support. Nicole Brown Simpson became the woman on whose body we imagined the historical and continuous assault of male battery against white women—but more specifically, African American male violence against white women. Nicole became a symbol for many women who saw her as the characterization of (white) female subjugation, silence and oppression.

And the absences spoke even louder—Where were the white men? They were, in fact, in charge of the proceedings as if they were puppeteers, negotiating the instruments of power, both in court and out, in order that their absence from the defendant docket be considered unextraordinary. The real presence of white men found its way into the trial in the form of somewhat discreet institutional forms. That is to say, even though Judge Lance Ito was the presiding judge, Marcia Clark, Johnnie Cochran and Christopher Darden were seen to be participants in negotiating the proceedings, they were acting in accordance with the white-male-dominated structures. In this respect, all of those who participate in the judicial system are, in a sense, controlled by the limitations and codes of conduct, methods and procedures as outlined by the dominant group. The establishment of such mechanism ensures the maintenance of white male power.

The American Bar Association's (ABA) Code of Professional Responsibility outlines that, "the duty of the prosecutor is to seek justice, not merely to convict" (section 3-1.1) (Schmalleger: 1996, p. 19). In examining the many tactics utilized by both the defense and prosecution during the trial, the fact that the system operates as an "adversarial" system suggests that, in fact, sides are taken with the intent to achieve either a conviction or acquittal—according to where one is standing. In fact, Frank Schmalleger, Director of the Justice Research Institute in South Carolina, suggests that the O. J. Simpson trial is important as it provides information around "tactics available to criminal defense attorneys, . . . challenges facing prosecutors and district attorneys, and . . . the everyday realities of American criminal justice practice" (1996, p. ix). When we consider the manipulability and the desire to manipulate the courtroom trial, how can it possibly be suggested that the ambition of any party is to seek justice above personal success, especially when personal reputations depend upon it? The adversarial system frames the antagonism between the defense and the prosecution, not between justice and inequity. Rather, these are potential end results of the presentation of the "facts" of the case. The achievement of a victory, in which evidence from one party is more convincing than that presented by the other, is often accomplished through highly artful measures. Therefore, the successful party is often that which has greater creative skills—hence the distinction between *factual* and *legal guilt*. Factual guilt deals with whether or not the defendant is actually responsible for a crime. Legal guilt, however, is established as a result of a convincing argument by the prosecution, oftentimes

achieved through inventive tactics. In this way, court proceedings are often disinterested in factual guilt. Because guilt is often "created" or "suppressed" according to the abilities of the defense and prosecution, it is the white-male structures that inform the proceeding. Nonwhite pressures within an environment such as the courts, then, are largely left impotent in the face of such a powerful and largely normalized institutional structure. However, there were instances where individual white men became the focal point of the trial.

The presence of men like detective Mark Fuhrman only enabled the white power structures to point to aberrant individuals operating within social institutions that "discredited an otherwise neutral forum." The courts and media then, found it useful to deter any criticism of their own camps by pointing to Fuhrman and condemning him as being a "lying, perjuring, genocidal racist. . . . The man thinks he's above the law" (Schmalleger: 1996, pp. 315–316). These kinds of comments were common and attempted to distract us from the institutionalized racism embedded in the legal system. Fuhrman was not an aberration, but a product of that system.

And where were African American women? As if the courtroom were attempting to model itself as a microcosm of society, African American women did not exist in the trial. Their absence spoke of a desire to "naturalize" the court proceedings, keeping the trial entirely inadequate in terms of representing all peoples equally. Some people, in response to this claim, have naively asked, "But African American women had nothing to do with the trial. Why should they have been represented?" To which I respond, "They should be represented to counter the very reason why the trial was about an African American man who may or may not have killed a white woman . . . for the very reason that the nation would not have "tuned in" and the media would not have been "turned on" if O. J. had been accused of killing an African American woman." African American women had a lot to do with this trial, and yet it was not until the jury, composed of twelve persons, eight of whom were African American women, came to their decision that they were noticed. And then the wrath fell upon them. White America had found its scapegoats, and even though all twelve jurors had to come to a unanimous agreement, the African American women were blamed for "letting a murderer go free." The condemnation of the apparently "African American" and "all-female" jury "supposedly provides evidence that blacks cannot 'do' science, that African American women do not 'receive' domestic violence. . . . This group of women is immediately transformed into a nation of potentially violent, certainly undereducated and uncivilized, blacks" (White: 1995, p. 50). Furthermore, African American women have been identified post–O. J. as a source of contempt, for within their lives, "morality, family values and "the work ethic"—the stuff of America's puritanical obsessions—dissolves" (Sharpley-Whiting: 1995, p. 42).

Domestic Violence

Domestic violence is also an issue influenced by the media. In particular, there has been an outcry by some media analysts who have calculated the number of times that Simpson was referred to as a *hero* in the mainstream press, alongside the number of references to Nicole Brown Simpson, and discovered that the more frequent references to O. J. as a hero reveals more about the misogyny (hatred of women) of the media than it revealed about O. J. himself. A *Time* magazine columnist wrote in July of 1994 that she had "not heard Nicole Simpson referred to as much of anything at all. A victim you say? She has become even smaller in death. . . . " (Sharkey: 1994, p. 25). Howard Kurtz of the *Washington Post* suggests that the coverage of the 1989 case "was a complete fumble" that occurred as a result of the media's desire to maintain "the good-guy image of this very popular sports star"(Sharkey: 1994, p. 25). Most interestingly, the Fairness and Accuracy In Reporting Group, a media watch group, reported that the media in general underreported domestic violence. This report, titled "Missing Voices: Women and the U.S. News Media (1992)" suggested that, "domestic abuse remains a gravely un-

dercovered story," and that when it is reported, the media "describe abuse in ways that mirror the batterers' own rationalizations" (Sharkey: 1994, p. 25). Once again, we are reminded that what the media does not publish is oftentimes equally as important as what it does present.

O. J. Simpson was brought to trial in 1989 on charges of domestic abuse, to which he pleaded no contest. The lack of media attention of the 1989 case tells much about the American position on wife beating and about abuse of women in general. Cornel West makes an important point when he acknowledges the lack of attention paid to the life of Eunice Simpson, O. J.'s mother, in terms of the domestic violence experienced throughout her life. No one has shown much concern around this and, therefore, the American people have also found little interest in issues of domestic abuse generally. There have also been reports of Nicole striking her maids, yet this information too has been ignored, suppressed and diffused by lack of exposure (Lerner: 1995). Can we, in light of this information, truly believe that domestic abuse is an issue in the United States? In keeping with the suggestion that the O. J. trial represented an assessment of America's most troublesome issues, domestic abuse seemed not to be one of them. While it seems that Nicole Brown Simpson had not been protected from her abusive husband prior to her murder, it appears as if the moment at which Nicole's life ended was also the moment when white America "put their foot down," so to speak. The trial spoke clearly to the issue of domestic abuse insomuch as it really said nothing at all. Its findings? In large part, Americans were told that African American men are still violent towards women, that white women are worth more than African American women (as the trial would not have captured the attention of the nation had O. J. murdered his African American wife) and that interracial marriages were tolerated but would, nonetheless, fail as a result of the inherent violence of blackness. As Renee White puts it, "the moral of the story was that even this most innocuous of black men was essentially dangerous" (1995, p. 51).

Looking back in history, we can find that there has been, and remains to be, a belief in the African American man as a sexual predator. In this way, race and sex have been overlapping ideologies that have defined the African American male since slavery. It has long been believed that African American men, in order to reverse their situations and regain power over white men, use violence against white women. Interestingly, this belief disregards the fact that white men have long since had a violent relationship with African American women. Hooks writes of the slave era that "the [white] master . . . forced his wife to sleep on the floor as he nightly raped a black woman in bed" (1990, p. 58). African American men have historically and contemporarily been defined as "rapists, eager to use sexual terrorism to express their rage about racial domination" (p. 60). Looking at various forms of popular culture, such as Madonna's video "Like a Prayer" or the more recent film *Secrets and Lies,* both present and reinforce, for millions of viewers, the belief that African American men are linked with violence against white women. This myth has continuously been reproduced and was crucial to the O. J. Simpson case. Hooks has said that:

> *Images of black men as rapists, as dangerous menaces to society, have been sensational currency for some time. The obsessive media focus on these representations is political. The role it plays in racist domination is to convince the public that black men are a dangerous threat who must be controlled by any means necessary, including annihilation.* (p. 61)

The trial was not so much interested in determining whether or not O. J. Simpson beat Nicole, but rather the primary focus was on the question as to whether or not O. J. had killed his ex-wife. In this way, it was taken for granted that O. J. was abusive to Nicole Brown Simpson. He was portrayed as the violent African American man that is so consistent with the myth that all African American men are threats to white society. In fact, it is not uncommon to find the term *black* as listed as a synonym in a thesaurus for the word evil (Corel WordPerfect Thesaurus: 1996). African Americans have been demonized and degraded by popular white imagery, and it would be naive to believe that these preformed assumptions did not play a large role in the Simpson trial.

While it is negligent to remove the feminist concerns around the lack of attention paid to the abuse of Nicole Brown Simpson, it is problematic to concentrate our collective concern around domestic abuse of white women without considering the domestic abuse of nonwhite women. The courts, on the other hand would have us believe that the *murder* of Nicole Brown Simpson was the only issue necessitating radical intervention, even though Nicole had made multiple calls to police throughout her relationship with O. J. What does this mean? It means that the courts did not want us to look at anything beyond O. J. If we collectively focused our attention on O. J. the individual, we would forget about systemic institutional abuses. We could not point fingers at the justice system, the police, the government, the media— all those who create the conditions for domestic abuse in homes across the nation. Murder is an event. Domestic abuse is a process. Intervention is more possible during a process than an event. So we focus on the event. We focus on the African American man, not the failures of the system. Whites in general, and the institutions that represent their interests are *still* considered neutral. In this way, white power was not challenged. Racism was not challenged, nor was domestic abuse.

O. J. . . . Running with the Ball

The trial was a production, like the dramas and comedy flicks that play out continuously on the television. As George Gerbner has commented, "the search for justice . . . was a spectator sport", with O. J. running with the ball (1995, p. 563). Our inability to see O. J. as anything other than that Heisman trophy winner of 1969 and Hall of Fame inductee in 1985 reinforced our desire to have him perform like a sports hero, undaunted by his seeming disabilities: his race and apparent lack of "white" education. It was a new game, a new kind of football field where money and fame could buy a Dream Team defensive line with a white "quarterback" to do all the strategic work (Shapiro). But it could not buy O. J. a different color of skin, nor could it rewrite the racist history that American naivete had long been denying. Because the trial failed to examine the relationship that social structures had with violence, it was certainly incapable of finding "Nicole's murderer," as it was looking in the wrong place altogether.

We must begin to make connections between the O. J. Simpson trial and previous trials which had really called attention to the inequities invested in the justice system. In the beating of Rodney King, South Central Los Angeles became enraged when the police officers were acquitted of the charges laid against them, even though the nation had watched video evidence of the police brutality over and over again. Even after the retrying of those officers, South Central and other districts remained outraged with the degree of blatancy to which the courts exercised racism. Was the O. J. trial a means to silence the unrest and vindicate the justice system? Certainly this is a possibility. Or the trial can also be imagined as a contemporary ritual, played out over the television, that mimics the rituals of American history since the invention of notions such as race and inequality. Perhaps the trial can be seen as a modern day lynching, the rope only metaphorically held over the African American man's head. After "the trial of the Century," O. J. can be said to have escaped a physical death, only to be victim to a social death. He is certainly no hero to the white community of Brentwood where he continued to live, and he has all but removed himself from the community of African Americans, some of whom refer to him as a *hero*.

The "lynching" of O. J. Simpson not only resulted from his rejection from white circles, but also culminated on the day of the civil trial in which he was charged with the duty of paying both the Brown family as well as the Goldman family monies for their losses. In this commodity culture, where the exchange of money speaks louder than any other voice, we all digested O. J.

as being the guilty African American man, beyond a reasonable doubt. As Lloyd DeMause suggests, "the operative group fantasy in the O. J. Simpson trial is identical to that of most early civilizations who practiced human sacrifice as a religious ritual . . . likewise in America today, a sinful nation, guilty for having indulged in too much pleasure . . . gathers before the TV set every night to watch the sacrifice of the football hero (O. J.) who stands in for all of us as guilty of sexual excess (womanizing exploits) and greed (high salary)" (DeMause: 1995, p. 392).

Class(ifying) O. J.

It is true that O. J. Simpson was not what you might call "any ordinary African American man." He was a sports hero, a legend in fact, and he was wealthy. The issue of class had much to do with the trial insomuch as the charade would not have gained so much momentum and coverage had O. J. not been able to afford the "props" for the televization of the drama surrounding the murders. The Brentwood mansion, along with Nicole's luxury apartment, the vehicles, the lawyers and the designer clothes were all provided by O. J. Ironically it was these explicit icons of success that helped fuel the massive attention by the media and public at large. Simpson was relatively successful at "playing the economic game. The way in which he acquiesced to the process of assimilation was rewarded by wealth and status" (White: 1995, p. 51). Simpson took control of the power and success he had achieved in order to defend himself against the same structures from which he had benefited. Apparently Simpson's wealth was simply a loan.

Great anger arose from many whites that felt Simpson was purchasing justice and was thus exercising an unfair advantage over the system. Regardless of the fact that *any* wealthy person would have utilized all resources possible in order to achieve an agreeable outcome, O. J. became the target for cries of "working the system" (White: 1996, p. 51). The irony of these kinds of claims has still not been realized. White polling participants felt that the L.A.P.D. was prejudiced and incompetent (Mixon et al., 1995), but it is a radical departure from the obvious to ignore that the justice system at large is fundamentally inequitable. Keeping this in mind, it is interesting that when O. J. assembled and funded the Dream Team, white public opinion was of anger and resentment. Even though people's differential access to legal representation has been a long proven fact, O. J. found himself the subject of charges of illegitimate maneuvering.

The attention paid to the amount of money utilized by O. J. was often an effective means of distracting Americans from the real issues at hand. The very fact that O. J. possessed a substantial amount of money became a source of controversy, not because he used it for his defense, but because he was African American and had used it for his defense. Some whites made it apparent that they felt taken hostage by a man who was using white money and therefore white power in order to disrupt white institutions. Claims around O. J.'.s "lack of blackness," his decision to live in a white neighborhood, marry a white woman and associate largely with white dominated groups annoyed many whites. O. J. became the undefinable black-skinned man who refused to "do blackness" as it has been defined and expected by whites. Instead, O. J. continues to be represented as an African American man who deceived the puritanical white clan, snuck in amongst them and looted, pillaged, brutalized their women, and stole their money and even their spiritual power. However, like the mythical tale of the fall of Lucifer, O. J. is then imagined to have been ousted from white-Heaven and hurled down to the fires of hell. In one climactic moment O. J., however, shifts the plot in seemingly unknown directions. Instead of perishing in hell, he builds himself a ladder made of the riches stolen from Eden and climbs all the way back to Brentwood. Shameful of having been revealed, O. J. retires to his mansion in an attempt to escape the scorn of the white angels who huddle closely nearby, recording his every move, commenting on the seriousness of his illegitimate residence in Heaven.

The issues surrounding class and the O. J. case can be satisfactorily called the *economics of racism.* Peniel Joseph's suggestion that, currently in the United States, race is being used by African Americans against whites in order to achieve special privileges is quickly gaining popularity (1995, p. 52). O. J. was presented as illegitimately utilizing class power in order to upset white legal dominance. This, in many ways, spelled out a definitive message for white America, that African Americans must be kept poor in order so that peace, justice and the American way are not challenged.

CONCLUSION

The O. J. Simpson trial revealed much about contemporary issues around American social institutions, civil rights and discrimination. Racism, genderism and classism, in particular, came to be highlighted by the trial and, in consideration of the vast audience it captured, it can be suggested that these issues really gave Americans a preview of future institutionalized thinking regarding inequality. It does not look very optimistic for nondominant groups in the United States. However, perhaps we can imagine the trial to be a stepping stone, a possible break from a decidedly oppressive and discriminatory past. We listen to the continuing preoccupation of white America with whether or not they think O. J. did it. What we must begin to ask is "Why is it we don't seem to care as much that the justice system 'did it,' that the police 'did it,' that white America 'did it' or, more importantly, that it is *still being done*? Interrogating white privilege is an important and necessary step to eradicating social inequalities. We must collectively apply pressure to those institutions which lead in the race to dominate nonwhite communities and we must be ever aware that, as Audre Lorde said, "the Master's Tools will never Dismantle the Master's House" (1984, p. 110). Perhaps we need to begin to look outside of mainstream institutions in order to find locations from which we, as a community of peoples—all peoples—can speak and be heard equally. This is my hope.

NOTES

1. Antonio Gramsci developed the concept of hegemony most fully in *Prison Notebooks,* written in the 1920s while he was imprisoned under the fascist regime of Benito Mussolini. In these writings, Gramsci defines hegemony as "the 'spontaneous' consent given by the masses of the population to the general direction imposed on social life by the dominant fundamental group; this consent is 'historically' caused by the prestige (and consequent confidence) which the dominant group enjoys because of its position and function in the world of production" (Gramsci: 1971).

2. Kendall suggests that *life chances* are the extent to which persons have access to important scarce resources (Kendall: 1997).
3. A more contemporary example might be *Pretty Woman* (1990) with Julia Roberts and Richard Gere.
4. *Hegemony* simply means the dominant perspective that is often times perpetuated by social institutions, and thereby becomes "common sense" for most people. Hegemony equates with social power.

REFERENCES

Blauner, Robert. *Racial Oppression in America.* New York: Harper, 1972.

Bourdieu, Pierre. "The Forms of Capital." *The Handbook of Theory and Research in the Sociology of Education.* Ed. J. C. Richardson. New York: Greenwood Press, 1986. 241–257.

Butler, Judith. "Endangering/Endangering: Schematic Racism and White Paranoia." *Reading Rodney King: Reading Urban Uprising.* Ed. Robert Gooding-Williams. New York: Routledge, 1993. 15–22.

Cockburn, Alexander. "Symbolic Injustice." *New Statesman Society.* V. 5, # 201. May 8, 1992. 18–19.

Corel WordPerfect Thesaurus. Ontario: Corel, 1996.

DeMause, Lloyd. "Shooting at Clinton Prosecuting O. J. and Other Sacrifice Rituals," *Journal of Psychohistory.* V. 22. Spring 378–393. 1995.

Foucault, Michel. *Power/Knowledge: Selected Interviews and Other Writings 1972–1977.* Ed. Colin Gordon, tr. Colin Gordon et al. New York: Pantheon, 1980.

Gerbner, George. "Cameras on Trial: The "O. J. Show" Turns the Tide." *Journal of Broadcasting and Electronic Media.* V. 39. Fall 1995. 562–568.

Gomes, Ralph and Linda Faye Williams. "Race and Crime: The Role of the Media in Perpetuating Racism and Classism in America." *The Urban League Review.* V. 1, #14. Summer, 1990. 57–69.

Gordon, L. "A Lynching Well Lost." *Black Scholar.* V. 25, #4. Fall 1995. 37–40.

Gramsci, Antonio. *Prison Notebooks.* New York: International Publishers, 1971.

Henson, Deborah M. "Will Same-Sex Marriages Be Recognized in Sister States?: Full Faith and Credit in Due Process Limitations on States' Choice of Law Regarding the Status and Incidents of Homosexual Marriages following Hawaii's Baehr v. Lewin." *University of Louisville Journal of Family Law.* V. 32, # 3. Summer 1993–1994. 551–600.

Herrnstein, Richard, J. and Charles Murray. *The Bell Curve.* New York: The Free Press, 1994.

hooks, bell. *Yearning: Race, Gender and Cultural Politics.* Toronto: Between the Lines, 1990.

Joseph, Peniel E. " 'Black' Reconstructed: White Supremacy in Post Civil Rights America." *The Black Scholar.* V. 25, #4. Fall 1995. 52–55.

Kendall, Diana. *Race, Class and Gender in a Diverse Society.* Boston: Allyn and Bacon, 1997.

Kozol, Jonathan. *Savage Inequalities.* New York: Harper Perennial, 1992.

LaFountain, Marc J. "Foucault and Rodney King: The "Rationality" of a Legal Beating." *Humanity and Society.* V. 6, #4. November 1992. 564–570.

Lassiter, Christo. "TV or Not TV—That is the Question." *The Journal of Criminal Law and Criminology.* V. 86, #3. Spring 1996. 928–1001.

Lerner, Michael. "After O. J. and the Farrakhan-Led Million March: Is Healing Possible?" *Tikkun.* V. 10, #6. 1995. 12–20.

Lorde, Audre. *Sister Outsider.* Freedom: The Crossing Press, 1984.

Madonna. "Like a Prayer." 1989.

Miles, Robert. *Racism.* London: Routledge, 1993.

Mixon, K., L. Foley and K. Orme. "The Influence of Racial Similarity on the O. J. Simpson Trial." *Journal of Social Behavior and Personality.* V. 10, #3, September 1995. 481–490.

My Fair Lady. Dir. George Cukor. With Audrey Hepburn and Rex Harrison. Fox, 1964.

Potter, J. and M. Wetherall. *Discourse and Social Psychology: Beyond Attitudes and Behavior.* London: Sage, 1987.

Pretty Woman. Dir. Garry Marshall. With Julia Roberts and Richard Gere. 1990.

Ryan, Rebecca, M. "The Sex Right: A Legal History of the Marital Rape Exemption." *Law and Social Inquiry.* V. 20, #4 Fall 1995. 941–1001.

Schmalleger, Frank. *Trial of the Century.* Upper Saddle River: Prentice Hall, 1996.

Secrets and Lies. Dir. Mike Leigh. Great Britain, 1996. 141min.

Sharpley-Whiting, T. Denean. "{White} Ladyhood and {Black} Womanhood Revisited: Legitimacy, Violence, and Black Women." *The Black Scholar.* V. 25. Fall 1995. 42–43.

Sharkey, Jacqueline. "Judgement Calls." *American Journalism Review.* V. 16, #7. September 1994. 18–27.

Shipp, E. R. "O. J. and the Black Media." *Columbia Journalism Review,* V. 33. November/December 1994. 39–41.

Sherwin, Richard K. "Law and the Myth of Self in the Mass Media." *International Journal for the Semiotics of Law.* V. 8, #24. 1995. 299–326.

Swenson, Jill Diane. "Rodney King, Reginald Denny, and TV News: Cultural (Re-)Construction of Racism." *Journal of Communication Inquiry.* V. 19, #1. Spring 1995. 75–88.

White, Renee, T. "The Economy of Race and Racism." *The Black Scholar.* V. 25, #4. Fall 1995. 49–52.

PART FOUR

Policing

The state has two major agents of social control, the military and the police. Prior to the emergence of the professional police force, the military and constabulary enforced the laws. In 1829, the London police force was created, providing the basic model of policing for contemporary American society.

With the spread of urbanization and industrialization and increasing class inequality, it became more difficult to rely on the constabulary system of enforcement. The disparities in income, wealth, and living conditions were becoming more visible, and resentment sharpened toward the military and constabulary based on their attachment to the propertied and wealthy class. Furthermore, social and political protest, in the form of "illuminations," was increasing. In these demonstrations, citizens would march in the streets and verbally attack policies or practices of the government or people in power. Citizens who supported the marchers' position would place lights in their windows to demonstrate support. If the windows remained dark, the house was subject to stoning. This and other forms of protest reflected an upsurge in the ideology of democracy and social justice. It was difficult to use the military to quell such disturbances because of mobilization and training problems, but most significantly, such force merely increased resistance to the government. Needless to say, the constabulary lacked the ability and legitimacy to control such situations. Thus, the professional police force arose to provide order.

WHY POLICE?

According to Silver (1967), the creation of the professional police force served a number of important functions:

- It relieved the propertied classes of the task of controlling "riots" (i.e., political protests).
- Ordinary citizens no longer had to perform basic police duties.
- The military did not have to be used for policing.
- It insulated the rich from the popular violence in the streets.
- It made the police rather than those in power the focus of animosity and attack.
- It separated constitutional authority from social and economical dominance.

The final point is particularly important, for the more legitimacy given to the law and its agents, the less likely that there will be collective action against such authority. The professional police came to be viewed as apolitical, neutral enforcers of the law, rather than as manifest representatives of the propertied and wealthy.

Essentially the same process of professionalization occurred in the United States. Increasing economic inequality and class stratification in urban areas, combined with riots, brought about the emergence of professional police in the United States (Parks 1970). New York City adopted the London plan in 1844, and subsequently other major urban centers created police forces so that by the early 1900s, most cities had professional controllers.

> *The paramilitary form of early police bureaucracy was a response not only, or even primarily, to crime per se, but to the possibility of riotous disorder. Not crime and danger, but the "criminal" and "dangerous classes" as part of the urban social structure led to the formation of uniformed and military organized police. Such organizations intervened between the propertied elites and the propertyless masses who were regarded as politically dangerous as a class. (Bordua and Reiss 1967, p. 276)*

FROM CONSTABULARY TO POLICE

Who dealt with offenders before the professional police arose? In early England, and subsequently in the United States, the military and constabulary systems preceded the emergence of the police as we know them today. The army or nobility under the king enforced the king's laws in early England and in its colonies in North America. In the reign of Edward I (1272–1307), the first official sheriffs appeared in the large towns of England. This policing was based on the system of constables, or reeves, appointed by noblemen to enforce laws in a local area and subsequently larger areas called shires; thus the office of "shirereeve" was created. These constables were charged with protecting property between sunset and daybreak. By the eighteenth century, there were increasing demands for more democratic participation in social institutions, including law. During this time, the night-watch system of constables spread in England, requiring civilians to patrol city streets "slowly and silently and now and then listen" (Parks, 1970, p. 85). It was difficult to compel citizens to take their turns at this graveyard shift, from 9:00 P.M. to sunrise, since many had day jobs. Although day watches arose in England with urbanization, they eventually gave way to the establishment of the professional police force in 1829.

Like England, the American colonies established the constabulary based on the collective responsibility of all able-bodied men. It was such a thankless job that as early as 1653 those who refused to serve were fined. They served only in the day, with a citizens' watch, or night watch, in the evening. The day constable basically responded to citizens' complaints of lawbreaking, whereas the night watch patrolled for fires, reported the time, and described the weather (Parks, 1970).

The constabulary worked in a consensually based, homogeneous community where most agreed on the rules and the need to obey them. However, with the heightened visibility of social, cultural, and economic differences in urban areas, the constabulary was to find social control increasingly difficult. Charles Reith observed that the basis for the constabulary was voluntary observance of the law. Such

> *can be seen to have never survived in effective form the advent of community prosperity, as this brings into being inevitable differences in wealth and social status, and creates, on this basis, classes and parties and fractions with or without wealth and power and privileges. In the presence of these divisions, community unanimity in voluntary law observance and the maintenance of authority and order must be found. (1952, p. 210)*

As explained in Part 3, until recently, the law and thus policing discriminated against nonwhites. There is a history of over four centuries of unequal protection and enforcement

(Kennedy, 1997). The police institution became an important factor in the maintenance of colonial rule, along with the military. For example, the Texas Rangers gained their notoriety through the control of Mexican Americans in that state. The legacy of colonialism in American policing is found in early slave patrols, in the treatment of Native Americans, and in the policing of the reservation, ghetto, and barrio, where an often hostile population viewed the police as an internal, domestic colonizer. As the Black writer James Baldwin noted,

> *The only way to police a ghetto is to be oppressive. None of the police commissioners' men, even with the best will in the world, have any way of understanding the lives led by the people; they swagger about in twos and threes patrolling. Their very presence is an insult, and it would be, even if they spent their entire day feeding gumdrops to children. They represent the force of the white world, and that world's criminal profit and ease, to keep the black man corralled up here, in his place. (1962, p. 65)*

Perhaps more has been written about police relations in communities of color than any other topic in the field of race and crime. Almost every urban riot since the turn of the twentieth century can be attributed to the behavior of police in African American and Latino communities (Report of the National Advisory Commission on Civil Disorder, 1967). The famous video of the beating of Rodney King in 1991, an unarmed African American man in Los Angeles, by a group of white police officers shocked white America since it brought the reality of police brutality into their homes. For many African Americans and Latinos, the video only recorded business as usual in communities of color. The subsequent acquittal of the officers by a nearly all-white jury ignited the largest urban rebellion of the twentieth century.

In another case, an unarmed West African immigrant was murdered by police in the vestibule of his New York City apartment. Diallo was riddled with nineteen bullets as he struggled to pull out his wallet to either show his green card or surrender his money to people he perceived to be robbers. The Rodney King case and video and the murder of Amadou Diallo are two cases that happened to gain international notoriety.

The police are the most visible representatives of the criminal justice system in the African American community, and public opinion polls consistently find that African Americans are less likely than whites to trust the police or believe that their communities are treated fairly by law enforcement. The police are suspected of harassing and brutalizing thousands of African Americans and Latinos each year. Many are shot under questionable circumstances. Most incidents do not make the mainstream papers, and cases against the police, no matter how much evidence points to their wrongdoing, almost never result in criminal charges. Police brutality cases and monetary settlements are occasionally won in civil court, however (Human Rights Watch, 1998).

The behavior of police in communities of color is the product of both individual prejudices and institutional racism. For decades, police work attracted individuals from working-class white ethnic groups, which often harbored prejudicial views of African Americans, Latinos, Native Americans, Chinese Americans, and most recently Southeast Asians. The Civil Rights movement highlighted the brutalities of police in their oppression of African Americans. The more radical Black Power movement that swept through major northern and western cities in the late 1960s and early 1970s popularized the image of police as an occupying force.

Throughout the 1970s and 1980s, a minor revolution occurred in major police departments throughout the country, and significant numbers of African American and Latino police officers were hired in rank and file and administrative positions. By the late 1980s, several major U.S. cities had African American police chiefs, and several cities had majority African American departments. Although the police community relations improved dramatically in these cities with the integration of police forces, charges of police brutality have not disappeared in these communities—evidence that it is institutional racism, not just the color and personal prejudices of the individual officer, that drives police behavior.

These efforts to recruit minorities and women have enhanced their representation in law enforcement. Nationally, blacks make up about 11 percent of all sworn officers, and other ethnic minorities constitute nearly 8 percent. Women, however, still make up only about 9 percent of all officers (Schmalleger, 2001). Women still have many barriers to face in a largely male and machismo occupation (Hoarr & Morash, 2000). They tend to have a higher educational level than their male counterparts and are better at diffusing potentially violent situations (Carter & Radelet, 1999). Twenty years of exhaustive research on the performance of women in policing shows that women police perform better than their male counterparts at defusing potentially violent situations, and they use excessive force less often than men do. Women officers build better community relations and respond more effectively to incidents of violence against women—crimes that account for as much as 50 percent of 911 calls to police.

This record stands in stark contrast to the dramatic underrepresentation of women in police departments. Women currently make up less than 10 percent of sworn police officers nationwide, and they are virtually absent from the higher policy-making ranks. Women police often encounter hostile workplaces, facing daily discrimination and sexual harassment on the job (National Center for Women and Policing, 2000).

In a study of 127 police-related lawsuits against the City of Los Angeles and against individual LAPD officers between 1990 and 1999 involving judgments or settlements exceeding $100,000, female officers' rate of involvement was much lower than that of males. No female officers were named as defendants in cases involving sexual assault, sexual abuse, molestation, or domestic violence. These cases alone cost the City of Los Angeles $10.4 million. The rate of killings and assault and battery was also much higher for male than for female officers (National Center for Women and Policing, 2000). Los Angeles is under a consent decree, and must have minorities and women on the police force. The scandal in the Ramparts police division further disgraced the department when it was revealed that several officers were implicated in drug deals, planting evidence, assault, and homicide in the Ramparts division of the Los Angeles Police Department (Cannon, 2000).

CRIME CONTROL AND DUE PROCESS MODELS

Law enforcement agencies are bureaucratic organization that, like other bureaucratic organizations, tend to substitute for the official goals and norms of the organization, policies and activities that maximize rewards and minimize strain for the organization. This goals substitution is made possible by

- An absence of motivation to resist pressure toward such goal substitution
- The pervasiveness of discretion among law enforcement officials
- The relative absence of effective sanctions to adhere to formal organizational rules

The extent to which such goal substitution exists depends in part on its visibility and who observes it.

Competing goals and demands are found in the crime control and the due process models of the criminal process. The crime control model emphasizes the repression of criminal activity as the agency's highest priority. Within this approach, there is an attempt to sanction as much criminal behavior as possible, including the searching out of crime through such means as patrolling and using undercover agents. Accused persons are assumed to be guilty, and speedy handling of cases is deemed necessary. The due process model, on the other hand, emphasizes the protection of the citizen from the power of the state through various procedural safeguards. The suspect is assumed innocent until proven guilty by the court. Although protection of the rights of the individual are formally required of law enforcement personnel, the informal norm is to process as many persons as possible in order to deter and suppress crime (Chambliss and Seidman 1971, pp. 272–74; Schmalleger, 2001).

POLICE VIOLENCE

As one might expect, most instances of police violence involve the use of the crime control approach. The underlying assumption is that police have to deal with crime in any way possible, including excessive force. From this perspective the use or threat of violence may be a deterrent without formally charging a person with an offense. Most cases of police brutality and excessive force are committed against the young, poor, and nonwhite, who are not as likely to pursue a grievance (Reis, 1968). The rate of civil rights complaints against the police are related to the proportion of nonwhites in a city and the degree of economic inequality (Holmes, 2000). From both an organizational and an individual standpoint, this is understandable, although not acceptable. The police are caught in the middle between the demands of the middle and upper classes for protection of property, and the demands of the poor for equal distribution of property.

> *The police are thus put squarely in the middle. The control of the disinherited, who are regarded as potentially dangerous, from the perspective of the police can be most efficiently accomplished through the arbitrary use of force and coercion. But these methods, when applied to the privileged, bring forth public criticism and censure. The simple and most often practiced solution is to adopt a dual standard. Crime-control practices prevail in dealing with the poor, and due process is observed in dealing with the privileged. (Chambliss and Seidman 1971, p. 359)*

The use of the double standard is significant in that street crimes such as robberies, muggings, and assaults are of top priority to community leaders, and thus pressure is placed on the police organization to produce arrests and suppress such crimes. Because such street crimes are disproportionately committed by the poor, nonwhite, and youth, these people are subject to the crime control model. However, the embezzler, income-tax cheater, antitrust violator, or manufacturer of unsafe cars is treated carefully according to the due process model (Pontell and Schichor, 2001).

The fact that these differing approaches are applied to different types of people committing certain types of crimes in certain areas of town explains why most citizens can honestly say they have no experience with police violence. However, many of the youth, poor, and nonwhites will just as honestly say that they have experienced police brutality. If you are raised in a middle-class neighborhood and continue to live your life in suburbia, it is likely you will not view police violence. Those who grow up and live in poorer, minority areas are more likely to have such experiences. There would most likely be a surge of protest if the surveillance and interrogations used in the poor, minority areas were used in suburbia.

Aggressive patrols, saturation patrols, stop and frisk incidents, and "broken-windows" policing of the poor and minority neighborhoods can create both antagonism in such neighborhoods and satisfaction in suburban neighborhoods (Oliver, 2001). This has raised the issue of how to "police the police." Besides civil suit; criminal charges, and internal review, some degree of civilian review has been increasingly advocated (Human Rights Watch, 1998).

HISTORY OF CIVILIAN REVIEW[1]

The Birth of Civilian Review

External review can be traced as far back as London in 1828. The first modern police department in London provided mechanisms for both internal and external review of citizen complaints about police misconduct (Landau, 1996). The movement for external investigation of complaints against the police gathered support in the 1960s. Two of the first civilian review procedures created in the United States were in Philadelphia and New York City.

In response to the demand of civilian rights groups, the Philadelphia Police Review Board was created on October 1st, 1958, by the executive order of Mayor J. Richard Dilworth. At first the board was highly disorganized. It had no funding and no clear mission statement of what it was supposed to do. In fact, during its first eight months, the board received few complaints and disposed of none (Walker and Wright, 1995a). In 1959, the board finally received some funding and was then renamed the Police Advisory Board (PAB). It wasn't until 1963 that the board obtained a full-time executive secretary and an office.

The PAB operated from 1958 to 1967. During this period, it recommended only punitive sanctions against police officers in 6 percent of the cases it reviewed. However, for much of its shaky existence, the board was not able to hold any hearings because of pending court decisions. The Philadelphia Lodge of the Fraternal Order of the Police had filed several lawsuits against the PAB. The opposition that the PAB faced from police unions proved to be too much for it to overcome. Inadequate staffing, lack of budgetary funding, and inability to hold hearings for almost three years led to the PAB eventually disbanding (Fyfe, 1985).

In New York City, the Civilian Complaint Review Board was established by Mayor Lindsay in July 1966. Its lifespan, even shorter than that of Philadelphia's review board, was only four short months. The Civilian Complaint Review Board was abolished by public vote in November 1966. However, it did receive 442 citizen complaints in that period, more than twice the number that had been reported annually to the internal review board (Perez, 1992). Just like the civilian review board in Philadelphia, it was not able to surpass the opposition of the rank-and-file police officer unions that openly opposed it.

The failure of civilian review in cities such as Philadelphia and New York discouraged the adoption of civilian review agencies throughout the country for a period of time. Efforts were renewed in the early 1970s, but in the face of bitter opposition by police, their unions, and political pressures, most civilian review mechanisms created during this period lasted only a short time. Police unions were effective in preventing civilian review boards from being created. Their opposition was successful in preventing the implementation of civilian review. These unions had enough political clout that they were actually allowed to help create the internal procedures for processing complaints and administering punishment for police misbehavior (Human Rights Watch, 1997).

Resurgence of Civilian Review

For over a decade it appeared as if police opposition would be successful in preventing the expansion of external review beyond that provided through conventional means such as county, state, or federal courts. Since 1980, however, citizen participation in the review process has been established in many major American cities. Throughout the 1990s, citizen review experienced its largest growth (Walker and Wright, 1995). Citizen review of the police has increased 74 percent since 1990, and it currently exists in thirty-six of the fifty largest U.S. cities. However, the largest increase in citizen review since 1990 has occurred among the second-largest U.S. cities, with a whopping 333 percent increase (Walker and Wright, 1995a).

Two factors have contributed to this growth. First, more public support is behind the creation of civilian review boards. The review boards in Philadelphia and New York City, by contrast, were created by executive order and did not represent a decision by a majority of the elected representatives. This made them politically and administratively vulnerable (Goldsmith, 1988). Incidents such as the Rodney King beating have drawn public attention to the police and have led the public to demand civilian review. Such incidents have helped organize the movement for civilian review. As Walker and Bumphus state, "a well organized demand for civilian review is probably a necessary condition for its establishment" (1991, p. 10). More elected officials, mayors, and city council members have also begun to support civilian review. Many have come to believe that civilian review is an appropriate method of handling citizen complaints about police misconduct (Walker and Bumphus, 1991). The second factor behind the creation of civilian review boards has been the apparent decline in the power of police unions in opposing such methods. Unions were the principal force behind the defeat of many earlier forms of civilian review, but as the rapid growth of civilian review in many cities illustrates, police unions have been increasingly unsuccessful in most cases. In fact, given that current civilian review boards have not been used as a major method of sanctioning police, police unions may be more accepting of them (Human Rights Watch, 1998).

Conclusions about Civilian Review

Although there is not yet adequate research on the implications and effects of civilian review, it is still possible to draw some tentative conclusions from this research. Advocates of civilian review believe that the involvement of citizens would produce a more independent and thorough method of review, which would lead to more complaints being sustained, which in turn would deter police from misconduct. This does not appear to be the case, however, and these claims made by civilian review advocates appear to be unfounded.

The independence of civilian review is somewhat questionable, since only one-third of all citizen review boards conduct their own independent investigations (Walker and Kreisel, 1996). Furthermore, around 27 percent of boards have police officers on the board. Are these boards really less biased than internal methods when the boards have such a high rate of police-officer participation?

Civilian review does not maintain a higher rate of sustaining cases than internal reviews do; on average, it has a much lower percentage of complaints sustained. The police internal affairs sustains complaints at more than twice the rate of civilian review (Human Rights Watch, 1998). The fact that internal review receives complaints from the police does not appear to be a significant enough factor to explain this large a difference. Therefore, civilian review does not appear to do a better job deterring police misconduct than internal methods.

Civilian review advocates argue that the involvement of citizens would open up the complaint process, based on the notion that citizens will be less intimidated if they can bring their complaints to civilians rather than to the police. Once again, this does not prove to be true. Most forms of civilian review require citizens to file their complaints with the police first. This means that most citizens who want to file a complaint against an officer are still initially being interviewed by police officers. Civilians may still be intimidated by the complaint process and hesitant to file their complaints.

Many of the arguments police use in opposing civilian review also tend to be unfounded. The argument that civilian review will be unduly harsh on the police has no factual basis. Civilian reviews end up being more lenient toward police officers than internal methods are (Griswold, 1994; Human Rights Watch, 1998). On the other hand, civilian reviewers also are not the kangaroo courts that police officers believed they would be. Perez (1992) found that most forms of civilian review actually gave police officers more procedural due process. Perez also concluded that the often-heard prediction that civilian review will cause poor morale and hamper aggressive policing is unfounded.

Persons opposed to civilian review point out that there is no need for it. They argue that we already have external checks on the police in the form of civil and criminal litigation. But this is another false assumption; a study conducted by Human Rights Watch (1998) found that local prosecutions of police officers are rare. Close working relationships between the police and the prosecutor, along with difficulties in convincing grand juries and trial juries that a police officer did not merely make an understandable mistake, make it unlikely that police will be prosecuted for misconduct. Human Rights Watch also found civil remedies to be ineffective: Most internal affairs staff believe that civil cases are not their problem and that settled suits do not indicate the guilt of an officer. The study also found that some internal affairs staff order investigations into such lawsuits only in order to assist the city in defending the officer.

Police have also argued that civilian review would only contribute to community hostility against police by focusing on police misconduct. This also does not prove to be true. Some studies demonstrate that the implementation of civilian review appears to help community perception of the police (Landau, 1996).

Civilian review does seem to have one very important benefit—it appears to have a positive effect on the public's attitude toward the police. Civilian review activists believe civilian review improves police and community relations by sustaining more complaints, which in turn deters police misconduct more effectively. Although it has been shown that this is not the case, apparently communities still believe that civilian review is more thorough and objective than internal methods. Whether these attitudes reflect reality or not may not be important. What civilian review bodies actually accomplish may not matter as much as what the public believes they accomplish. If the public believes that civilian review is achieving a greater amount of justice, and this has a positive impact on police–community relations, then civilian review may be worth its cost. However, there are ways to increase the effectiveness of civilian review (Human Rights Watch, 1998).

COMMUNITY POLICING

In the last few decades of the twentieth century, there emerged a new model of policing called community policing. This model has been contrasted with the political era of policing (1840s to 1930s) and the reform era of policing (1930s to 1980s). Community policing is characterized by community support, law and professionalism, broad provision of services, decentralization, use of task forces and foot patrol, problem solving, and focus on quality of life and citizen satisfaction (Miller and Hess, 2002).

Although efforts to improve police–community relations arose as a response to the conflicts of the 1960s (Reasons and Wirth, 1975), community policing emerged in the 1980s as a response to persistent problems and changing philosophies of policing, in part based on a problem-solving, social-work approach to policing (Oliver, 2001). Although community oriented policing has been embraced by the majority of police agencies, it has largely worked in more affluent, disproportionately white neighborhoods, whereas it is still difficult to effectively establish in poorer, nonwhite communities. Nonetheless, this approach, however defined, will continue to be embraced. It has much promise, but also some drawbacks, particularly in the use of aggressive patrol and saturation patrol in minority neighborhoods (Oliver, 2001; Walker, Spohn, & De Lare, 2000).

The first article in Part Four, "Driving While Black," by Katheryn Russell, discusses a "recent" issue in policing—racial profiling. Historically, being black or nonwhite has often criminalized one's behavior and provided a basis for suspicion, but since the 1970s, we have not expressly embraced this view. Nonetheless, as Kennedy (1997) notes in "Race, Law and Suspicion: Using Color as a Proxy for Dangerousness," police may still stop nonwhites based solely on their race. Russell points out that the United States Supreme Court has allowed such stops in *Whren vs. United States,* as long as there are lawful reasons for the stop, such as motor violations. High-profile cases and successful lawsuits have indicated that some departments and officers have routinely targeted blacks and other minorities. Russell observes that such stereotypes are part of a larger profiling of blacks as criminals when they walk in a neighborhood, idle their cars, stand in their own neighborhoods, or shop or ride buses. By using race as a proxy for criminality, police create more problems and resentment among those they are to serve.

The second article in this section traces how early police encounters with youth of color lead to their disproportionate arrest. In "Adding Color to a Black and White Picture," Darlene Conley focuses on police relations with youth of color in Washington State. This reading highlights the importance of research methodology in conducting race and crime research, particularly in the use of participant observation techniques. The study revisits a genre of research in which observational studies of police behavior were undertaken and in-depth interviews were conducted using actual citizens and officers, on both sides of the criminal justice system. However, observational studies of the police are expensive, time consuming, and politically charged. Police departments are reluctant to permit researchers to observe their daily behavior in the field. Furthermore, such studies are problematic since the mere presence of a researcher in the field influences the behavior of officers. Instead, much of what we learn about these encounters comes from the popular press, real-life videos shown on TV news, TV cop shows, or transcripts of police harassment cases.

Conley points out that "police reports do not capture the varieties of informal contact that the police have with communities of color that do not result in arrest." The only way to capture on paper what occurs at this stage of the juvenile justice process is through field observation and interviews. Conley and her colleagues participated in ride-alongs with police in their study of racial inequity in the Washington State juvenile justice system. By riding along with police, the researchers were able "to see the world through the eyes of the police" and examine how they frame or construct their reality. Police cited community fear of crime, the level of violence in communities of color, the prevalence of drugs, and alcohol and poverty as their reasons for treating youth of color differently.

The most important finding, however, centered around how the nature of police encounters and surveillance have changed since the classic police observational studies of Piliavin and Briar (1964) were undertaken. The present study took place in a state that is overwhelmingly white, but that arrests and incarcerates African American, Native American, and Latino youth at disproportionate rates. Data collected reveal different policing tactics for youth of various racial, ethnic, and class backgrounds. For instance, surveillance at shopping malls and the creation of "troublemaker files," complete with names and photos, was a strategy used to control youth of color in middle-class communities.

The last article in this part, "Boston Cops and Black Churches," describes an innovative program in Boston that involves the police and leaders of the African American religious community in a joint effort to improve police relations in minority communities and to reduce youth violence. The program represents a unique alliance, since the African American church has traditionally supplied the leadership and resources for movements protesting police violence. In this reading, Winship and Berrien examine the impact that the Ten Point Coalition had on the reduction of youth violence in the 1990s. In Boston, the youth homicide rate dropped 61.2 percent, exceeding the declines in other large cities, including New York, Los Angeles, Houston, Philadelphia, and Washington D.C. The authors argue that the Ten Point Coalition helped to reduce youth violence and improve the legitimacy of the police by allotting African American leaders more control over the judicial process.

Although police–minority community relations are problematic throughout the United States, racial tensions in Boston have historically been extremely high. Boston has been dubbed one of the most racist cities in the country. It was in Boston that the movement to integrate public schools through busing faced the most virulent and violent opposition by working-class whites. The racial tension escalated in 1989, when it became the site of one of the most highly publicized racial hoax cases of this century: Charles Stuart, a white man, murdered his pregnant wife and claimed that an African American man had shot his wife in a robbery. The case was widely publicized on the local and national news, and the Boston Police Department initiated a massive search for the assailant. The police used Gestapo-type search and seizure tactics that violated the civil rights of hundreds of African American males. It was later discovered that Stuart murdered his own wife, and his hoax once again evidenced the power of stereotyping African American males as criminals.

In the Ten Point Program, African American ministers assist the police with identifying the small percentage of youth who commit the majority of crimes in their community. In return, the police allot the ministers a limited role in determining the treatment of arrested youth and allow them to argue for leniency for certain youth and for stiffer sentences for youth involved in hard-core crimes. The authors argue that by providing the community a role in identifying the serious criminals, the community will be better able to understand the differential treatment of certain youth. The reading concludes that this strategy of community–police cooperation has contributed to the dramatic decrease in violent crime in Boston because the police, with the help of the community, can "concentrate on truly violent youth, rather than indiscriminately monitoring the innocent with the guilty."

STUDY QUESTIONS

1. Identify and discuss the important functions served by the creation of a professional police force.

2. Explain how the crime control and due process models of policing are related to issues of police violence, class, and race.

3. What are civilian review and community policing and how are they related?

4. Identify what "racial profiling" is, explain how it is evidenced, and discuss the negative consequences it produces.

5. Discuss the significance of participant observation techniques in researching race and crime.

6. What do we know about police use of excessive force, and how might we reduce it?

7. Discuss the Ten Point Program in Boston and how Boston cops and Black churches have created an effective program.

NOTE

1. This section is in part based on J. Reid, G. Kerlikowske, and C. Reasons, "Community Policing and Civilian Review Boards: A 'Natural' Combination?" Paper presented at the annual American Society of Criminology Meetings, Toronto, Ontario, November, 1999.

REFERENCES

Baldwin, James (1962). *Nobody Knows My Name.* New York: Dell.

Bordua, David, and Albert Reiss (1967)."Law Enforcement." In *The Uses of Sociology.* New York: Baer Books, pp. 275–303.

Cannon, Lou (2000)."One Bad Cop," *The New York Times Magazine,* October 1, pp. 1–5.

Carter, David and Louis Radelet (1999). *The Police and the Community,* 6th ed. Upper Saddle River, N.J.: Prentice-Hall.

Chambliss, William, and Robert Seidman (1971). *Law, Order and Power.* Reading, MA: Addison-Wesley.

Donziger, Steven R. (1996). *The Real War on Crime.* New York: Harper Collins.

Fyfe, James A. (1985). "Reviewing Citizens' Complaints against Police." In Fyfe, J. A. (Ed.), *Police Management Today: Issues and Case Studies.* International City Management, Washington, D.C.

Goldsmith, Andrew J. (1988). "New Directions in Police Complaints Procedures: Some Conceptual and Comparative Departures," *Police Studies 11*(2): 60–71.

Griswold, David B. (1994). "Complaints against the Police: Predicting Dispositions," *Journal of Criminal Justice 22*(3): 215–220.

Hoarr, Robin, and Merry Morash (1999)."Gender, Race, and Strategies of Coping with Occupational Stress in Policing," *Justice Quarterly 16:*303–336.

Holmes, Malcolm (2000)."Minority Threat and Police Brutality: Determinants of Civil Rights and Criminal Complaints in U.S. Municipalities," *Criminology 38:*343–367.

Human Rights Watch (1998). *Shielded from Justice: Police Brutality and Accountability in the United States.* New York: Human Rights Watch.

Kennedy, Randall (1997). *Race, Crime, and the Law.* New York: Vintage Books.

Landau, Tammy (1996)."When Police Investigate Police: A View from Complaints," *Canadian Journal of Criminology 38*(3): 291–315.

Mann, Coromae Rickey, and Marjorie Yatz (1998). *Images of Color, Images of Crime.* Los Angeles: Roxbury Publishing.

Miller, Linda, and Karen Hess (2002). *The Police in the Community.* 3rd ed. Belmont, CA: Wadsworth/Thompson.

National Center for Women and Policing (2000). Gender Differences in the Cost of Police Brutality and Misconduct: Content Analysis of LAPD Civil Liability Cases, 1990–1999.

Oliver, Willard (2001). *Community Oriented Policing: A Systemic Approach to Policing,* 2nd ed. Upper Saddle River, N.J.: Prentice-Hall.

Parks, Evelyn (1970). "From Constabulary to Police Society: Implications for Social Control," *Cataylst 6:*76–97.

Perez, Deanna (1992). "Police Review Systems," *MIS Report.* 24(8): 1–15.

Perez, Deanna (1994). *Common Sense about Police Review.* Philadelphia: Temple University Press.

Piliavin, Irving, and Scott Briar (1964). "Police Encounters with Juveniles," *American Sociological Review 70:*206–214.

Pontell, Henry, and David Schichor (2001). *Contemporary Issues in Crime and Criminal Justice: Essays in Honor of Gilbert Geis.* Upper Saddle River, N.J.: Prentice-Hall.

Reasons, Charles, and Bernard Wirth (1975). "Police–Community Relations Units: A National Survey," *The Journal of Social Issues 31:*27–35.

Reid, J., G. Kerlikowske, and C. Reasons (November, 1999). *"Community Policing and Civilian Review Boards: A 'Natural' Combination?"* Paper presented at the Annual American Society of Criminology Meetings, Ontario.

Reiss, Albert J., Jr. (1968). "Police Brutality—Answers to Key Questions," *Trans-action* (July/August): 10–19.

Reith, Charles (1952). *The Blind Eye of History: A Study of the Origins of the Present Police Era.* London: Farber and Farber.

Report of the National Advisory Commission on Civil Disorder (1968). Washington, D.C.: Government Printing Office.

Schmalleger, Frank (2001). *Criminal Justice Today.* Upper Saddle River, N.J.: Prentice-Hall.

Silver, Allan (1967). "The Demand for Order in Civil Disorder: A Review of Some Themes in the History of Urban Crime, Police and Riots." In *The Police: Six Sociological Essays.* David Bordua (Ed.). New York: John Wiley, pp. 1–27.

Walker, Samuel, and Vic Bumphus (1991). *Civilian Review of the Police: A National Survey of the 50 Largest Cities, 1991.* Department of Criminal Justice, University of Nebraska at Omaha.

Walker, Samuel, and Bill Kreisel (1996). "Variations of Citizen Review: The Implications of Organizational Features of Complaint Review Procedures for Accountability of the Police," *American Journal of Police 15*(3): 65–88.

Walker, Samuel, Cassia Spohn, and Miriam De Lone (2000). *The Color of Justice,* 2nd ed. Belmont, Calif.: Wordsworth.

Walker, Samuel, and Bonnie Wright (1995a). *Citizen Review Resource Manual.* Department of Criminal Justice, University of Nebraska at Omaha.

Walker, Samuel, and Bonnie Wright (1995b). *Civilian Review of the Police, 1994 National Survey.* Department of Criminal Justice, University of Nebraska at Omaha.

"Driving While Black"
Corollary Phenomena and Collateral Consequences

KATHERYN K. RUSSELL

Note: [Russell is] Associate Professor, Criminology & Criminal Justice Department, University of Maryland at College Park, A.B., 1983, University of California at Berkeley: J.D., 1986, Hastings Law School: Ph.D., 1992, University of Maryland.

INTRODUCTION: STATEMENT OF THE PROBLEM

In the public arena, issues of race continue to command center stage.[1] The ongoing debates and discussions have raised new questions, while not necessarily answering the old ones. Specifically, the recent dialogues have focused on the role that Blackness plays in today's society. Some assign Blackness a primary role, others believe it is secondary. Still others dismiss it as tertiary. These varied positions, ranging from "race has nothing to do with this" to "race has everything to do with this" have in some ways canceled out any meaningful discussion of racial issues. Each of the racial camps has been allowed to claim victory without giving any ground. The result: racial homeostasis.

This failure of movement is particularly troubling given that in the legal arena, Blackness itself faces increasing criminal penalty—both actual and perceived. One of the clearest examples is the phenomenon of "Driving While Black" ("DWB"). This expression has been used to describe a wide range of race-based suspicion of Black and Brown motorists.[2]

Once an offense known and discussed almost exclusively among African-Americans, DWB has risen from relative obscurity. Several factors are responsible for this. First, the United States Supreme Court decided *Whren v. United States,* involving a Fourth Amendment challenge to possible racial profiling in routine traffic stops.[3] The *Whren* Court held that earlier Supreme Court decisions "foreclose any argument that the constitutional reasonableness of traffic stops depends on the actual motivations of the individual officers involved.[4] The *Whren* decision thus made clear that, in the Court's eyes, traffic stops motivated by the racial prejudices of individual officers do not violate the Fourth Amendments's search and seizure guarantees, at least when there are other reasons for the stop.[5]

Second, during the same time period the Court issued this decision, there have been several high-profile incidents involving allegations of racial profiling. The case of Robert Wilkins, a Black attorney, is among the most notable.[6] Wilkins was traveling with family members, returning home from a funeral. Their car was stopped by a Maryland State Police officer and detained along a

Maryland interstate road. The officer told the driver (Mr. Wilkins' cousin) he had been speeding and then requested consent to search the vehicle. After consent was refused, the officers forced the occupants to wait until a narcotics dog was summoned to sniff the vehicle for drugs. No drugs were found and, almost one hour after they had been pulled over, the Wilkins family was allowed to continue on their journey. Following the incident, Wilkins filed a federal lawsuit, alleging constitutional and civil rights violations resulting from racial profiling practices by Maryland State Troopers.[7]

Another case involved a police shooting along the New Jersey Turnpike.[8] Four young men, three Black and one Hispanic, were traveling south on their way to a basketball camp. New Jersey state troopers stopped the van due to excessive speed. The police said that as they approached the vehicle from the rear it moved into reverse. The troopers responded with several rounds of gunfire, striking the van and its occupants 11 times.[9]

Third, in response to the Supreme Court's rollbacks and the escalating number of well-publicized race-based traffic stops, Congressman John Conyers introduced the "Traffic Stops Statistics Act."[10] The 1997 bill did not make it through Congress. In April of 1999, however, Conyers introduced an updated version of the earlier legislation.[11] The newer version has several additions, including a requirement that police collect data on gender and record whether the immigration status of occupants was questioned. The earlier bill was successful in placing a spotlight on the problem of racially-motivated traffic stops. The American Civil Liberties Union, for example, initiated a national campaign which highlighted DWB. It ran notices in national publications, including the *New York Times* and *Emerge* magazine.[12] The ad copy read, "Let me ask you something . . . Should 'Driving While Black' be a crime?" It also encouraged support for the Conyers bill.[13]

Finally, journalists have given increasing airtime to DWB.[14] As the number of DWB stories has increased, so has the numberer of DWB sto-

ries involving Black celebrities.[15] In turn, this media coverage prompted the call for stepped-up measures to address DWB.

The prevalence of DWB is unknown. Determining its breadth, however, is particularly important as a sociological phenomenon, given the role that cars play in American life.[16] This is particularly true for Blacks who have a historically unique relationship with their cars. During the era of Jim Crow, separate and unequal laws and racial discrimination by white business owners meant that Blacks could not secure hotel accommodations or eat in public restaurants.[17] This forced many of those Blacks driving long distances to sleep and eat in their cars.

The fact that the expression "DWB" has become commonplace is both heartening and depressing. The DWB short-hand indicates that this form of racial profiling has entered the public's vocabulary. Can it be a good sign that a questionable police practice is so firmly entrenched that it earns an acronym? The very fact that DWB has become so widespread that it has an acronym may mean that it has become an acceptable practice— the acronym makes DWB appear routine, normal and inevitable.

This Article explores DWB and related phenomena. Further, it considers how these problems affect criminal justice processing in particular and social policy in general. The discussion is divided into three parts. The first part considers ways in which Blackness has become a standard indicator of criminality. The second part provides an overview of the 1997 Traffic Stops Statistics Act. The final part evaluates the social fallout of DWB and its collateral consequences.

COROLLARY PHENOMENA: DWB'S KIN

In recent years, there has been mounting evidence that Blackness has become an acceptable "risk factor" for criminal behavior.[18] In all facets of life, Blacks report being stigmatized and labeled based on their race. As several high profile cases make clear, this labeling can have wide-ranging—even deadly—consequences. These cases point to the problem of determining what role race plays in interactions with law enforcement. At the same time, however, these examples indicate that in some instances the *perception* that race matters means that race matters. Further, individual cases can be explained, dismissed and justified. In their aggregate, the stream of anecdotal cases which suggest that Blackness can be equated with criminality has social consequence. A few examples follow.[19]

Walking While Black

Paul Butler, a Black professor in Washington, D.C., describes his experience of being stopped, questioned and hassled by police, as he returned home by foot one evening.[20] Butler details his ongoing "discussion" with Metropolitan police officers, who insisted that he show them identification before being allowed to continue on his way. Butler stood his ground, and the officers left only after a neighbor identified him.

Idling While Black

In December of 1998, Tyisha Miller, a nineteen-year-old Black woman, was shot and killed by Riverside, California, police after they responded to a call.[21] Miller's car had a bad tire late one night and she stayed with the car, parked at a gas station, while her friend got a ride home and called Miller's family. As her friend left, Miller rolled up the windows, turned up the car's heat and radio and tipped her seat back. When Miller's cousin and a friend arrived at the gas station to help, the cousin found Miller locked in the car, foaming from the mouth and unresponsive to shouts and banging on the window. A gun was in Miller's lap.

The friend called 911 to summon police help, reporting they could not wake Miller and that she had a gun in her lap. When the police arrived, Miller's cousin told them that Miller was in medical distress and again mentioned the gun. The po-

lice responded by breaking Miller's car window and shooting inside. Miller was struck twelve times in the head and back.

Police initially claimed that Miller shot at them and they simply returned fire. The four officers involved subsequently backed away from their initial story, and the police found no evidence that Miller had fired the gun. One of the more unsettling aspects of the case has been that, for many Blacks, it underscores the paradoxical threat of the police. Some even blame Miller's cousin for her death, claiming "You killed her! You called 911!"[22]

Standing While Black

This is the name Professor David Cole gives to the "crime" created by the ordinance at issue in *City of Chicago v. Morales.*[23] The controversial Chicago ordinance makes it a crime for gang members, or anyone who associates with them, to stand on a public street with no discernible purpose. It empowers police to stop anyone they "reasonabl[y] believe to be a criminal street gang member loitering in any public place with one or more other persons."[24] The *Morales* court observed that the vagueness of such an ordinance does not discourage arbitrary or discriminatory enforcement.[25] The ordinance is eerily reminiscent of a Georgia slave code statute which stated, "Any person who sees more than seven men slaves without any white person, in a high road, may whip each slave twenty lashes."[26]

Shopping While Black

In a widely-reported 1995 incident, three young Black men, shopping at a suburban Washington, D.C., Eddie Bauer store, reported being harassed and embarrassed.[27] An off-duty police officer, moonlighting as a store security officer, suspected that one of the youths, Alonzo Jackson, had stolen a shirt from the store. The youth, when questioned, told store employees that he had purchased the shirt at that store the previous day. His story was not considered credible and he was told he would have to *remove the shirt he was wearing* before he would be allowed to leave the store. The three youths filed a federal civil rights lawsuit against Eddie Bauer, alleging "consumer racism." After finding that the young men had been falsely imprisoned and defamed and that Eddie Bauer negligently supervised its security guards, the jury awarded $1 million in damages.[28]

. . . While Black

There are numerous other miscellaneous offenses which fall under the "While Black" umbrella. One example is "bus riding while Black." One such incident involved John Gainer, a Black music professor, at the University of Oregon. Based on a grainy enlarged photo of a different man suspected in a motel robbery, a mall security guard mistook Gainer for the robbery suspect and called the police. Police boarded the city bus Gainer was leaving on and asked him to exit the bus to answer questions. Soon after Gainer left the bus, however, police discovered the mistake. This was the second time in two years that police pulled Gainer off a city bus to question him about crimes he did not commit. The first time, after a series of mail thefts, a bystander saw Gainer closely scrutinizing mailbox numbers and called the police. Gainer, who is legally blind, told the police he was simply looking for a house to rent.[29]

The above anecdotes exemplify the extent to which society allows Blackness to be equated with criminality. Further, it is noted that there are numerous other ways in which Blackness has been targeted and criminalized, such as legislation enacted explicitly to address what is perceived as Black deviance.[30] Although some might argue that race-based police practices simply reflect crime rates, this view raises as many questions as it answers.[31]

A review of American history indicates that equating Blackness with criminality has long been a profitable enterprise. Professor Frederick Dennis Greene provides an interesting analysis of the parallels between the economics of the U.S. slave trade and today's prison system, as evidenced by the explosion in incarceration and prison construction.[32] In this mushrooming incarceration, Blacks are six times more likely than whites to be held in jail or prison.[33] This incarceration suggests that DWB and other "While Black" offenses are part of a much larger social problem.[34]

Mountains of anecdotes from the rich, famous and otherwise, have not resulted in a tangible, productive response to the problem of DWB. In order to move the debate beyond anecdote and personal narrative, it is clear that something more is needed. Enactment of the Traffic Stops Statistics Act has the potential to further transform the debate from an individual, micro-level issue, to a societal, macro-level concern. The next section details and critiques this legislative response to DWB.

RAY OF LIGHT?: THE TRAFFIC STOPS STATISTICS ACT[35]

For almost two years, the proposed Traffic Stops Statistics Act ("the Act"), offered a beacon of hope for altering the racial landscape of routine traffic stops.[36] The 1997 Act and its updated version would require record-keeping for each traffic stop. An officer who pulled over a motorist would have had to record an array of data for each traffic stop, including the race and age of the person stopped, whether a search was conducted and whether it produced contraband, whether a citation or ticket was issued and the legal basis for the stop.[37]

Not surprisingly, the proposed legislation and its state-level counterparts[38] have sparked a good bit of controversy and support. Police unions, for instance, have raised two main objections. First, such a law would place an undue burden on an already overworked police force. Second, such legislation would reverse years of police training designed to discourage officers from "seeing" race. The International Association of Chiefs of Police, the largest organization of police executives, opposes any such legislation.[39] The National Organization of Black Law Enforcement Executives, however, has voiced support for the Conyers legislation.[40]

Aside from objections raised by law enforcement, the bill's wording was problematic and its approach too narrow. First, it did not require any data about the police officer (e.g., age, race). Second, it would not have provided information on the location of traffic stops (e.g., city, state). As a result, the data could not be used to discern possible trends in DWB stops. Furthermore, the collected data were only to be used for research or data collection; the data would not be available for litigation purposes.

The failure to pass either federal or state legislation—or adopt other measures in their place—that would provide a picture of the role of race and traffic stops, leaves us where we started. The law's failure to respond proactively to the documented problem of DWB has several consequences. For one, the absence of a way to measure the breadth and scope of the practice forces reliance on anecdotes and lawsuits. As a result, a great deal of what has been learned about racial profiling in traffic stops has been filtered through civil actions, such as Robert Wilkins' case.[41]

The settlement in *Wilkins* revealed the degree to which Maryland State Troopers target Black motorists.[42] The terms of the settlement mandated the maintenance of computer records for all motorist stops. Along the Interstate 95 corridor, Black motorists, who comprise about seventeen percent of motorists, comprised *more than seventy percent* of the people stopped by the Maryland State Troopers between 1995 and 1997.[43] Amazingly, the racial imbalance in traffic stops persisted even after Troopers were notified that their stops were being monitored.[44]

The singling out of minority motorists represents an egregious, identifiable harm. There are, however, other, subtler outcomes which may sprout from these practices. The next section considers the possible fallout from society's failure to rein in DWB and DWB-related incidents.

COLLATERAL CONSEQUENCES OF FAILURE TO ACT

This Article has argued that DWB is part of a larger phenomenon which increasingly criminalizes Blackness. There are several potential outcomes from our continued failure to respond to the increased equating of Blackness with criminality. Two recent examples follow.

Legal Circumvention

In *United States v. Leviner,*[45] Federal District Judge Nancy Gertner issued a downward departure in the federal sentencing guidelines.[46] The reasoning behind the downward departure makes this otherwise unremarkable case remarkable. Alexander Leviner had several prior convictions before the subject of the case—being a felon in possession of a handgun. Under the guidelines, Leviner's criminal history classified him as a "Category V" offender, the second highest category.[47] After reviewing the record, Judge Gertner made two observations. First, that Leviner was Black. Second, she pointed out that most of his prior convictions were for motor vehicle offenses.[48] These factors led Judge Gertner to conclude that Leviner's priors were likely a result of DWB stops:

> *Motor vehicle offenses in particular, raise deep concerns about racial disparity. Studies from a number of scholars, and articles in the popular literature have focused on the fact that African American motorists are stopped and prosecuted for traffic stops, more than any other citizens. And if that is so, then it is not unreasonable to believe that African Americans would also be imprisoned at a higher rate for these offenses, as well.*[49]

It is unclear whether other judges have taken action similar to Gertner. It is known, however, that in other contexts federal judges have sought relief from harsh, racially disparate laws. The response of some federal judges to the federal crack statute provides one such example. Indeed, more than a few federal judges have balked at the disparity between crack and powder cocaine sentences and at their racially disparate impact.[50] Some judges have resigned in protest,[51] while others have apologized to defendants in advance of sentencing.[52]

Public Policy Fallout

A recent case involving the National Urban League illustrates another negative consequence of failing to address the DWB issue. In the fall of 1998, the Urban League withdrew from the Clinton Administration's "Buckle Up America" campaign.[53] The drive, which would make failure to wear a safety belt a primary traffic offense, would allow police officers to stop and ticket motorists for neglecting to do so. Citing concerns and fears that such a practice would result in increased racial profiling of Blacks, the Urban League withdrew its support.

The Urban League's response, though understandable, is problematic. This is especially true given that young Black and Hispanic motorists are *twice* as likely as their white counterparts to die in crashes due to failure to wear seat belts.[54] Furthermore, the failure to address the problem of seat belt use in Black and Hispanic communities increases the probability of not only higher mortality rates, but also increased auto insurance premiums and hospital costs for crash-related injuries. The Urban League's response indicates that the problem of DWB extends beyond the criminal justice system and impacts support for social policies. This stance has the potential for creating as much harm as it seeks to prevent. The Urban League's position symbolizes the tension between Blacks and the law enforcement community.

Other Responses

In addition to legal circumvention and public policy fallout, the DWB problem undoubtedly has additional ramifications. Moreover, the overarching issue of equating Blackness with deviance has a wide range of social costs. These include racial hoaxes,[55] anti-Black conspiracies,[56] lack of trust between police and Black and Hispanic communities and a more general racial alienation.[57]

CONCLUSION

This Article provides a brief overview of various ways that Blackness has been criminalized and associated with deviance. The discussion has primarily centered on DWB, and the host of legal, social and empirical questions raised by this recent phenomenon. It is argued that although DWB is among the most well-known crimes of Blackness, it is hardly the only one of its kind. In fact, the net which criminalizes Blackness has been cast far and wide.

It is, therefore, not surprising that the societal consequences of failing to address DWB and related phenomena, are grave indeed. The association of crime and deviance triggers a predictable cycle of events. First, it increases the probability that Blacks will be targeted for arrest. This in turn increases the probability that Blacks will be convicted and incarcerated for crimes.[58] Following logically, the enhanced likelihood of a felony conviction increases the likelihood of disenfranchisement.[59] Further, a felony conviction increases social marginality in many tangible ways, such as circumscribing employment possibilities (thereby increasing the probability of re-offending).

The impact of this goes far beyond those particular African Americans who have directly experienced racial targeting. As discussed above, it affects Blacks as a group and alters their response to the criminal justice system. As important, however, is the fact that criminalizing Blackness taints the image that every other racial group—whites, American Indians, Asians and Hispanics—have of Blacks. These images, which have historically materialized into racially-skewed criminal justice policy, regenerate the cycle.

NOTES

1. One salient example is President Clinton's 1997 initiative on race. *See President's Initiative on Race, One America in the 21st Century: The President's Initiative on Race* (1998). Another is the public debate following publication of Richard J. Herrnstein and Charles Murray's book, *The Bell Curve: Intelligence and Class Structure in American Life* (1994)

2. DWB has also been used to indicate "Driving While Brown"—the racial profiling of Hispanic motorists. Blacks and Hispanics, however, are not the only minorities who report being subjected to traffic stops on the basis of race. *See, e.g., Leslie Marmon Silko, Yellow Woman and a Beauty of the Spirit: Essays on Native American Life Today* 107–23 (1996) (describing the Immigration and Naturalization Service Border Patrol's detention and harassment of Native American motorists).

Racial profiling could be the result of an express police department policy, for example, where police department memoranda identify a particular racial group as part of its drug courier profile. It could also be the result of an informal, implied policy in which race is relied upon to determine whether stops are made. *See infra* notes 8–9 and accompanying text (discussing practices of New Jersey State Troopers). Racial profiling might also be the result of an individual officer's practices, based on stereotypes and prior experiences.

3. 116 S. Ct. 1769, 1772–73 (1996); *see also* Maryland v. Wilson, 117 S. Ct. 882 (1997) (regarding police conduct during routine traffic stops); Ohio v. Robinette, 117 S. Ct. 417 (1996) (same).

Though the U.S. Supreme Court has not expressly used the term "Driving While Black," it has appeared in decisions by lower courts. *See e.g.,* Washington v. Lambert, 98 F.3d 1181, 1188 (9th Cir. 1996) ("There's a moving violation that many African-Americans know as D.W.B.: Driving While Black," (quoting Henry L. Gates, Jr., *Thirteen Ways of Looking at a Black Man, New Yorker,* Oct. 23, 1995, at 59)).

4. 116 S. Ct. at 1774.

5. The Court did note, however, that selective enforcement of the law based upon race could be challenged under the Equal Protection Clause. *See id.* For detailed discussion and analyses of the *Whren* decision, see Angela J. Davis, *Race, Cops, and Traffic Stops,* 51 U. *Miami L. Rev.* 425, 432–38 (1997); David A. Harris, *Car Wars: The Fourth Amendment's Death on the Highway,* 66 *Geo. Wash. L. Rev.* 556 (1998): Carl J. Schifferle, *After,* Whren v. United States: *Applying the Equal Protection Clause to Racially Discriminatory Enforcement of the Law,* 2 *Mich. L. & Pol'y Rev.* 159 (1997); David A. Sklansky, *Traffic Stops, Minority Motorists, and the Future of the Fourth Amendment,* 1997 *Sup. Ct. Rev.* 271, 277–79 (1998); Craig M. Glantz, Note, *"Could" This Be the End of Fourth Amendment Protections for Motorists?:* Whren v. United States, 116 S. Ct. 1769 (1996), 87 *J. Crim. L. & Criminology* 864 (1997): Jennifer A. Larrabee, Note, *"DWB (Driving While Black)" and Equal Protection: The Realities of an Unconstitutional Police Practice,* 6 *J.L. & Pol'y* 291 (1997).

6. *See, e.g.,* Melba Newsome, *Power: The Usual Suspects, Vibe,* Sept. 1998, at 109.

7. The eventual settlement of the Wilkins case involved monetary damages and injunctive relief. *See* Davis, *supra* note 5, at 440. As Davis relates:

The Maryland State police consented to adopt a policy prohibiting the use of race-based drug courier profiles as a law enforcement tool. They further agreed that the policy would direct all Maryland State Police not to use a race-based profile as a cause for stopping, detaining or searching motorists traveling on Maryland roadways.

Id. (citing Settlement Agreement, Wilkins v. Maryland State Police, United States District Court for the District of Maryland, Civil Action No. MJG-93–468). For an interesting analysis of the Wilkins case and discussion of related issues, see Davis, *supra* note 5, at 438–42.

8. *See* John Kifner & David M. Herszenhorn, *Racial 'Profiling' at Crux of Inquiry Into Shooting by Troopers, N.Y. Times,* May 8, 1998, at B1. For an overview and critique of racial profiling on the New Jersey Turnpike, see John Lamberth, *Driving While Black: A Statistician Proves that Prejudice Still Rules the Road, Wash. Post,* Aug. 16, 1998, at C1.

9. During the past year, the New Jersey Attorney General's office investigated traffic stops made by 164 New Jersey Troopers. Investigators discovered that some troopers routinely falsified the race of the drivers they stopped. Further, the investigation revealed the practice of "ghosting." Some troopers may have used this scheme to hide the fact that they were targeting minority drivers for traffic stops. "Two state police supervisors said it was common practice for troopers on the turnpike to jot down the license plate number of white motorists who were not stopped and use them on the reports of blacks who were pulled over," David Kocieniewski, *Trenton Charges 2 Troopers with Faking Drivers' Race, N.Y. Times,* Apr. 20, 1999, at A23.

10. *See* H.R. 118, 105th Cong. (1997): *see also* Kevin Merida, *Decriminalizing 'Driving While Black,' Emerge,* Dec.–Jan. 1999, at 26 (noting John Conyers' introduction of the bill and discussing the bill's provisions): *infra* notes 35–44 and accompanying text.

11. *See* Traffic Stops Statistics Study Act of 1999, H.R. 1443, 106th Cong. (1999).

12. *See, e.g., Emerge.* Dec.–Jan. 1998, at 31.

13. The notice also includes the ACLU website, (http://www.aclu.org/forms/trafficstops.html) and encourages readers to complete a complaint form. *See id.*

14. *See, e.g.,* Timothy Egan, *On Wealthy Island, Being Black Means Being a Police Suspect, N.Y. Times,* May 10, 1998, at 12; Michael A. Fletcher, *Driven to Extremes: Black Men Take Steps to Avoid Police Stops, Wash. Post,* Mar. 29, 1996, at A1; Newsome, *supra* note 6; Hart Seely, *Black Males Say Its Normal for Police to*

Find an Excuse to Stop Their Cars and Hunt for Drugs, Syracuse Herald Am., Oct. 22, 1995, at A12.

15. A short roll call of names of well-known Black men who have been subject to "DWB" include: Marcus Allen, Le Var Burton, Calvin Butts, Johnnie Cochran, Christopher Darden, Miles Davis, Michael Eric Dyson, Al Joyner, Wynton Marsalis, Joe Morgan, Walter Mosley, Edwin Moses, Will Smith, Wesley Snipes, Blair Underwood, Cornel West, Jamaal Wilkes, Roger Wilkins and William Julius Wilson. *See, e.g.,* Katheryn K. Russell, *The Color of Crime: Racial Hoaxes, White Fear, Black Protectionism, Police Harassment, and Other Macroaggressions* 36 (1998).

For many Blacks, including the author, stories of DWB are part of family lore. As a child, I heard stories about racially-motivated traffic stops. One incident, involving my father's brother stands out. My uncle, who at the time drove a Lambourghini—a distinctive, rare sports car—was stopped by police. The office informed him that there had been a report of a stolen vehicle fitting his car's description. My uncle asked him the make of the stolen vehicle. The officer, apparently not sure what type of car my uncle was driving, could not answer.

16. *See, e.g.,* Harris, *supra* note 5, at 576 ("[N]o activity is common to more Americans than driving or riding in a car.").

17. *See, e.g.,* Katzenbach v. McClung, 379 U.S. 294 (1964); Heart of Atlanta Motel, Inc. v. United States, 379 U.S. 241 (1964).

18. For an interesting discussion of the historical and contemporary link between Blackness and criminality, see Tracey Maclin, *Race and the Fourth Amendment,* 51 Vand. L. Rev. 333, 333–36 (1998). Professor Maclin observes that "[t]oday, police departments across the nation . . . continue to target blacks in a manner reminiscent of the slave patrols of colonial America." *Id.* at 336: *see also* Charshee C. L. McIntyre, *Criminalizing a Race: Free Blacks During Slavery,* 167–88 (1993).

19. It is noted that while most of the DWB incidents referenced in this reading involve Black males, Black females also report being subject to race-based traffic stops. *See* Russell, *supra* note 15, at 36 (describing Black astronaut Mae Jemison's brush with police); *infra* note 28 (summarizing Lubbock, Texas incident involving Hampton University basketball coaches. Patricia Bibbs and Vanetta Kelso).

20. *See* Paul Butler, *'Walking While Black': Encounters with the Police on My Street, Legal Times,* Nov. 10, 1997, at 23.

21. *See* William Booth, *Calif. Police Shooting, Veiled in Gray, Becomes Black-White Issue, Wash. Post,* Jan.

10, 1999, at A3; Don Terry, *Unanswered Questions in a Fatal Police Shooting, N.Y. Times,* Jan. 9, 1999, at A8. The U.S. Attorney's office has announced that it will initiate an inquiry into whether Miller's civil rights were violated. *See U.S. to Investigate Killing of Teen-Ager, N.Y. Times,* Jan. 5, 1999, at A13.

22. Terry *supra* note 21, at A8.

23. *See* David Cole, *'Standing While Black.' The Nation,* Jan. 4, 1999, at 24. *See generally Chicago, Ill., Municipal Code.* § 8–4–015 (added June 17, 1992). *available in* <http://www.chicityclerk.com/legislation/codes/chapter8_4.html>: City of Chicago v. Morales, 687 N.E.2d 53 (Ill. 1997). For a discussion of the ordinance, see Cole. *supra.*

24. *Chicago, Ill., Municipal Code* § 8–4–015. The ordinance carries up to a $500 fine, six months imprisonment and 120 hours of community service. *See id.*

25. *See Morales,* 687 N.E.2d at 63.

26. J. Clay Smith, Jr., *Justice and Jurisprudence and the Black Lawyer:* 69 *Notre Dame L. Rev.* 1077, 1109 (1994) (quoting Georgia's Act of Dec. 13, 1792).

27. *See, e.g.,* Joann Loviglio, *Eddie Bauer Discrimination Case Goes to Jury in Greenbelt Court, Daily Rec.* (Baltimore), Oct. 8, 1997, at 19.

28. *See, e.g.,* Joann Loviglio, *Civil Rights Not Violated, But Eddie Bauer Told to Pay $1 Million in Shoplifting Case, Legal Intelligencer,* Oct. 10, 1997, at 4 (Alonzo Jackson was awarded $850,000 and the other young men awarded $75,000 apiece).

There have been other court cases which have alleged consumer racism. *See, e.g.,* Steven A. Holmes, *Large Damage Award to Black Whom Store Suspected of Theft, N.Y. Times,* Dec. 11, 1997, at A17 (citing case finding Dillard's department store engaged in systematic discrimination against Black customers, with federal jury awarding plaintiff Paula Hampton $1.56 million). Anecdotal incidents of racial discrimination while shopping abound. *See e.g.,* Patricia J. Williams, *The Alchemy of Race and Rights* 44–47 (1991).

In a recent case, two Black Hampton University basketball coaches were stopped and detained by police, in Lubbock, Texas. The coaches, in town for a game against Texas Tech, were arrested and charged with running a confidence game. It was later determined that the two had been mistakenly suspected. *See* Mark Asher, *Hampton Coach Decries Being 'Falsely Accused,' Wash. Post.,* Nov. 19, 1998, at E1.

29. *See Black Professor Mistaken for Robbery Suspect—Again.* Associated Press, Dec. 29, 1998; *cf. How about some common sense?.* The Bulletin, (Bend, Or.), Jan. 6, 1999, at A6 (editorial recounting these repeated mistaken police apprehensions of Gainer but arguing racism was not involved). For more examples of how Blackness has been used as indicia of criminality, see David Cole, *No Equal Justice: Race and Class in the American Criminal Justice System* 16–62 (1999).

30. *See, e.g.,* Dorothy Roberts, *Killing the Black Body: Race, Reproduction, and the Meaning of Liberty* 150–201 (1997). Roberts offers an incisive critique of how laws have been used to criminalize Black reproduction. The federal crack statute, which punishes possession of crack one hundred times more severely than powder cocaine, is another example of a law enacted partly due to racial fears. The bill was passed partly in response to the widespread fear that inner-city crack and its problems would spread to the suburbs. For a detailed discussion of the historical relationship between race and federal drug laws, see United States v. Clary, 846 F. Supp. 768 (E.D. Mo. 1994), *rev'd,* 34 F.3d 709 (8th Cir. 1994).

31. The argument is that Blacks are more likely to arouse police suspicion because Blacks are more likely to commit street crime. It is true that Blacks are disproportionately more likely to engage in street crime. Their rates of criminal involvement, however, do not approximate their encounters with the police. While Blacks are responsible for approximately one-third of all street crime, studies indicate that nearly half report having been watched or stopped by the police when they have done nothing wrong. *See e.g.,* Sandra Lee Browning et. al., *Race and Getting Hassled by the Police,* 17 *Police Stud.* 1. 3. 6 (1994) (finding that about 47% of Blacks and 10% of whites surveyed report being "personally hassled" by police: 66% of Blacks and 12.5% of whites report "vicarious hassling" by police (knowing someone who has been hassled by police)).

32. *See* Frederick Dennis Greene, *Immigrants in Chains: Afrophobia in American Legal History—The Harlem Debates Part 3,* 76 *Or. L. Rev.* 537, 562–65 (1997). Notably, increases in incarceration and prison construction are occurring despite the fact that since 1980 the total crime rate has generally decreased. *See Sourcebook of Criminal Justice Statistics*—1997, at 261 tbl.3.111.285 tbl.3.120 (Kathleen Maguire & Ann L. Pastore eds., 1998)

33. *See* Fox Butterfield. *Number of Inmates Reaches Record 1.8 Million. N.Y. Times.* Mar. 15, 1999, at A12 (Blacks six times more likely than whites to be held in jail and now make up over 40% of inmate population).

34. Professor Derrick Bell has argued that racial progress for Blacks is more likely to take place if the relief serves "the best interests of the country." Derrick Bell, *Race, Racism and American Law* 12 (3d ed. 1992).

In other words, such progress is more likely if the relief benefits more than just Black people.

35. H.R. 118, 105th Cong. (1997); *see also* H.R. Rep. No. 105–435 (1998), *available in* 1998 WL 105467 (discussing a later version of the bill). The version of the bill that passed the House in 1998 was known as the Traffic Stops Statistics Study Act of 1998.

36. Draft notes following the original Conyers bill state:

> *No American should have to live with the constant fear of an unwarranted pullover. African-Americans across the country are familiar with the offense of "DWB," driving while black. There are virtually no African-American males—including Congressmen, actors, athletes and office workers—who have not been stopped at one time or another for an alleged traffic violation, then harasssed with questions and searches. They may not receive tickets, but they do receive humiliation and more reason to distrust the justice system.*

(notes on file with author).

37. *See* H.R. 118.

38. Several states and jurisdictions have taken up this issue. For example, in California, A.B. 1264, a bill introduced by State Representative Kevin Murray, would have required annual record-keeping through the year 2003. *See* California Traffic Stops Statistics Act, A.B. 1264, 1997–98 Regular Sess. (Cal. 1997); *see also* Doc Anthony Anderson, III. *They're guilty of driving while being black or brown, San Diego Union-Tribune,* Dec. 24, 1998, at B7 (discussing origins of the bill).In contrast to the federal bill, A.B. 1264 explicitly mandated recording the *gender* of the person stopped. *See generally S. Comm. on Pub. Safety,* Committee Rep. for 1997 Cal. Assembly Bill No. 1264, 1997–98 Regular Sess. (Cal. 1998), *available in* Westlaw CCA Database (discussing features of California bill). In 1998, then-Governor Pete Wilson vetoed the bill. *See* Anderson, *supra.*

In April of 1999, the North Carolina legislature gave final approval to a bill which would mandate data collection for routine traffic stops. *See The State Requires Study of Highway Patrol Stops; N.C. House approves 'driving while black' bill, Morning Star* (Wilmington, N.C.), Apr. 8, 1999, at 3B. Rhode Island has similar legislation pending. *See* Traffic Stops Statistics Act of 1998, 8, 98–2434, Jan. Sess. (R.I. 1998). In addition, in at least two cities, San Jose and San Diego, California, law enforcement officials are voluntarily keeping race-based statistics on traffic stops. Julie N. Lynem & Marshall Wilson, *When Police Stop People for 'Driving While Black'; Cities move to track who is getting pulled over; San Francisco Chronicle,* Apr. 7, 1999, at A1.

39. *See* Kevin Johnson & Gary Fields, *Police chiefs resist race-related tallies, USA Today,* Apr. 8, 1999, at 7A.

40. *See id.*

41. *See supra* notes 6–7 and accompanying text.

42. *See supra* note 7; *see also* Russell, *supra* note 15, at 40–43: Lamberth, *supra* note 8.

43. *See* Russell, *supra* note 15, at 41–42.

44. This result raises the issue of what the impact of a bill such as the Traffic Stops Statistics Act would be. If the *Wilkins* case is any guide, the institution of a Conyers-like bill would do little to deter racial profiling, at least in the short-term.

45. Criminal No. 97–10260-NG, 1998 U.S. Dist. LEXIS 20323 (D. Mass., Dec. 22, 1998).

46. This decision has been widely reported. *See, e.g.,* Fox Butterfield, *Bias Cited in Reducing Sentence of Black Man, N.Y. Times,* Dec. 17, 1998, at A22; David Cole, *'Driving While Black: Curbing race-based traffic stops, Wash. Post,* Dec. 28, 1998, at A25.

47. *See Leviner,* 1998 U.S. Dist. LEXIS 20323, at *25. Category VI is the highest criminal history category under the Sentencing Guidelines. *See id.* Scores 10–12 are in category V. *See id.* at *25 n.17. Leviner's total score was 11. *See id.* at *25.

48. *See id.* at *26–28.

49. Id. at *33–34 (citations omitted). Judge Gertner sentenced Leviner to a 30-month term. *See id.* at *38.

50. *See* Russell, *supra* note 15, at 133 & 188 n.6.

51. *See id.*

52. *See, e.g., Judge Is Forced to Lengthen Sentences for Crack, N.Y. Times,* Nov. 27, 1995, at B5 ("[Judge Lyle Strom] who has bucked Federal sentencing guidelines in crack cocaine cases, arguing that they discriminate against blacks, reluctantly obeyed a higher court's instructions last week and used those guidelines to sentence two brothers. But in issuing the sentence [he] . . . apologized and told the brothers he would continue working to soften the guidelines.").

53. *See* Warren Brown, *Urban League Quits Seat Belt Drive; Group Cites Fears of Increased Police Harassment of Minorities. Wash. Post,* Dec. 11, 1998, at A14.

54. *See id.*

55. *See* Russell, *supra* note 15, at 69–93.

56. *See e.g., id.* at 145–46; Regina Austin, *Beyond Black Demons & White Devils: Anti-Black Conspiracy Theorizing & the Black Public Sphere, 22 Fla. St. U. L. Rev.* 1021 (1995). *See generally* Patricia A. Turner, *I Heard It Through the Grapevine: Rumor in African-American Culture* (1993).

57. *See, e.g.,* Vincene Verdun, *The Only Lonely Remedy, 59 Ohio St. L.J.* 793, 794 (1998) ("I put all [the racial slights] in [my] gunnysack, then and every time since then, until the sack got full. I threw all the hurt that comes from being black into the gunnysack, and then I moved on. But now, the gunnysack is full and heavy, and I sometimes get really tired of carrying it around. . . . You see, once the sack is full, any new weight that is picked up must be put somewhere else, so *it is stored in the heart, the mind, the kidneys, or somewhere.*" (emphasis added)): *see also* Russell, *supra* note 15, at 138–48.

58. Increasing incarceration of Blacks seems likely despite the fact that crime is on the decline. *See generally* Fox Butterfield, *Inmates Serving More Time, Justice Department Reports, N.Y. Times,* Jan. 11, 1999, at A10 (quoting observation of Frank Zimring, director of the Earl Warren Legal Institute at University of California at Berkeley, that "the changes in the American prison population are the result of a shift in policy, rather than any basic change in the nature of criminals or the crime rate"); Butterfield, *supra* note 33 (number of inmates at record high though crime rates have dropped for seven consecutive years; Blacks six times more likely than whites to be held in jail).

59. *See generally The Sentencing Project & Human Rights Watch, Losing the Vote: The Impact of Felony Disenfranchisement Laws in the United States* (1998). This report indicates that 13% of Black men (1.4 million) are disenfranchised due to criminal conviction for certain types of crimes. *See id.* at 1. Black men represent more than one-third (36%) of all persons ineligible to vote due to a felony conviction. *See id.*

Adding Color to a Black and White Picture

Using Qualitative Data to Explain Racial Disproportionality in the Juvenile Justice System

DARLENE J. CONLEY
Central Washington University

For more than three decades sociologists, criminologists, and other social scientists have debated why minorities, and specifically African Americans, are overrepresented in both the adult and juvenile justice system in this country. Unfortunately, decades of research have not brought us any closer to solutions or increased our understanding of why the problem persists. The hegemony of quantitative methodologies in disproportionality research has limited attention to the stages of the juvenile justice system that can be measured empirically and ignores what occurs before the stage of arrest. The data reported in this article are drawn from a larger study on minority disproportionality in the juvenile justice system in a western state, which combined both quantitative and qualitative techniques. The [reading] highlights participant observation data on encounters between police and youths of color. The qualitative data collected for the study demonstrate how information collected through interviews and field observations can be used to increase our understanding of the disproportionality dilemma.

For more than three decades sociologists, criminologists, and other social scientists have debated why people of color, and specifically African Americans, are overrepresented in both the adult and juvenile justice system in this country. Recent reviews of the research reveal that two thirds of the studies identify race as an important factor, whereas one third argues that race has no effect (Pope and Feyerherm 1992; Bridges, Deburle, and Dutton 1991).

Unfortunately, decades of research have not brought us any closer to solutions or increased our understanding of why the problem persists. Basi-

cally, the majority of researchers have demonstrated empirically that in juvenile justice, "race makes a difference." People of color, specifically African Americans and Hispanics, are more likely to be arrested, detained, tried and found guilty, and sentenced for longer periods of time than Whites. Explanations for why this happens differ. For some the reason is simple, "the system is racist." The vast majority of academics engaged in this research would argue that the reasons for the overrepresentation of youths of color in the juvenile justice system are complex. They struggle to identify the direct and indirect effect of variables other than race and ethnicity. Only a few venture so far as to charge that the system is racist (e.g., Wright 1990; Mann 1980, 1987, 1993); rather, most of these researchers carefully employ terms such as "extralegal" factors or "selection bias." The discriminatory treatment of minorities is referred to as "differential treatment," and the existence of institutional racism is seldom, if ever, mentioned. An increasingly smaller number of researchers argue that disproportionality is explained by the higher involvement rates of youths of color in serious and violent crime (Hagan 1974; Kleck 1981; Blumstein 1982; Petersilia 1983; Wilbanks 1987). Some of the findings from this group even suggest that people of color are actually treated more leniently at some stages (e.g., Petersilia 1983; Wilbanks; 1987).

Researchers should move beyond trying to settle the debate concerning whether or not race makes a difference. Instead, attempts to obtain greater understanding of the social processes involved in the construction of this problem should be undertaken. The question should not be whether or not race makes a difference, but how it makes a difference.

The hegemony of quantitative methodologies in disproportionality research has limited attention to the stages of the juvenile justice system that can be measured empirically. As a result, what occurs before and at the level of arrest is ignored. Yet what happens between youths of color and police at these stages is perhaps the most important factor contributing to racial and ethnic disproportionality. Encounters between police and youths of color shape perceptions and behaviors, yet they cannot be factored into a statistical analysis unless they result in arrest. Furthermore, what is recorded in the police report influences every other stage of the juvenile justice process. Because few observational studies of police and court proceedings are currently being undertaken, even the stages that are included in these analyses are reduced to artificial measures.

Quantitative analysis dictates that the social reality of these youths and their communities be reduced to a few variables, such as the instant offense, arrest rates, violent crime rates, and so on.

Unfortunately, by reducing these phenomena to single indicators, the richness of the social phenomena that they are attempting to describe is lost. For instance, none of the research has sought to describe the differences in race relations in the various communities where these studies have taken place. It can be assumed that the social reality of an African American youth growing up in a community in which the majority of persons in law enforcement are White is different from one growing up in a community with a more ethnically and racially diverse law enforcement population. Furthermore, does the presence [of] or increase in other "stigmatized" populations (e.g., Hispanics, Native Americans, Southeast Asians, and South Pacific Islanders) in the juvenile justice system influence perceptions of African American youths? And, are there different styles of policing in the various communities of color?

Qualitative research techniques can be used to address and provide answers to many of the issues that cannot be examined statistically. Some disproportionality studies are now employing qualitative research techniques (specifically in-depth interviews and focus groups) at the level of "discovery." However, most researchers merely use this data to guide questionnaire construction, to provide anecdotes to illustrate the key findings of their statistical studies, or to add a bit of color to what would otherwise be a Black and White picture.

This [reading] will highlight observational and interview data concerning police encounters with youths of color in a western state and demonstrate how qualitative data can be used to increase our understanding of the disproportionality dilemma. The data presented in this [reading] were collected as part of a larger study of disproportionality in the juvenile justice system of this western state. The first section of this [reading] briefly summarizes major findings from three decades of disproportionality research. The second section outlines the methodology used to gather data for the qualitative portion of the disproportionality study, and the third section highlights observational and interview data concerning police juvenile encounters and discusses how this data can be employed to understand social processes that contribute to the disproportionality dilemma. The final section discusses the implications of the findings from this study and suggests an agenda for future research.

PRIOR RESEARCH ON DISPROPORTIONALITY

Most of the research on disproportionality can be placed in one of two categories: (a) studies that debate whether or not disproportionality is caused by racial/ethnic bias or higher rates of involvement in serious crime by youths of color directly or indirectly; and (b) reviews that evaluate and assess the methodological rigor of previous studies. Furthermore, most of the research has focused on differences between African American and Whites and relatively few researchers have investigated differences between other racial/ethnic groups (Pope and Feyerherm 1992).

Of the earlier studies that argued against racial bias, perhaps the most noteworthy was by Terry (1967). After legal factors were controlled, he found the relationships between race and socioeconomic status and severity of disposition disappeared. His findings were supported by other studies conducted by McEachern and Bauzer (1967), Stephenson and Scarpitti (1968), Goldman (1963), Hohenstein (1969), Boyd (1976), Cohen and Kluegel (1978), Webb (1979), Kleck (1981), Blumstein (1982), and Hindelang (1982). These studies typically attributed higher incarceration rates of African American youths to the disproportionate involvement of youths of color in serious and violent crime.

Wolfgang, Figlio, and Sellin (1972), in a cohort study of 3,931 boys, reached the opposite conclusion—that racial bias did exist. Other studies that reached similar conclusions included Arnold (1971), Ferdinand and Luchterhand (1970), Thornberry (1973), Frazier and Bishop (1985), Bell and Lang (1985), Bortner, Sunderland, and Winn (1985), McCarthy and Smith (1986), Fagan, Slaughter, and Hartstone (1987), Krisberg et al. (1987), and Bishop and Frazier (1988).

Several researchers have reviewed many of these studies and assessed their methodological rigor. Many of what Zatz (1987) refers to as the first wave of statistical studies on disproportionality in the criminal justice system, because of selection biases and specification error, failed to demonstrate racial and ethnic bias empirically. Earlier analysis of juvenile disparity studies indicated that most were flawed in some way. Kleck (1981) suggested that studies finding evidence of discriminatory treatment were less methodologically rigorous than those that did not. Pope and McNeely (1981) suggested that past review of juvenile studies were problematic at best. Bishop and Frazier (1988) asserted that "analyses that focus on only one stage in processing—especially those that focus on dispositional outcomes—are likely to underestimate or altogether miss the influence of race" (p. 259). Pope and Feyerherm (1992) reexamined most of the studies relating to juvenile dispositional difference between African Americans and Whites and concluded that there was sufficient evidence to suggest that juvenile justice systems in various states may not be racially neutral. Although different methods of analysis were used in these studies (some used log linear, others used multivariate analysis or regression), regardless of what multivariate design was used, they all suffered from lack of methodological rigor. There does not seem to be any consistency in any of the studies. What is true, however, is that over the last three decades, the statistical methods used in studies have become increasingly more sophisticated. Unfortunately, the focus on the various techniques employed to analyze the data has resulted in more attention being paid to mathematical modeling than to addressing the problem and proposing solutions.

METHODOLOGY

The study reported in this [reading] combined both quantitative and qualitative methodologies to examine factors contributing to racial and ethnic disproportionality in the juvenile justice system in a far western state.[1] During the course of a year and a half, project staff traveled across the state, visiting juvenile courts and court personnel in six counties and collecting a representative sample of 1,777 cases at each major step in the juvenile justice system. A total of 170 in-depth interviews were conducted with court personnel, community leaders, defense lawyers, prosecutors, law enforcement officials, probation officers, judges, youth outreach workers, parents, and youths. Initial interviews were conducted with a reputational sample of key persons in the state's juvenile justice system and additional respondents were recruited through "snowballing," which is a technique through which additional respondents are selected from names of individuals suggested by individuals from the reputation list.

Researchers spent approximately 65 hours conducting participant observation with police officers in three of the counties with the largest populations of African Americans and Hispanics and another 60 hours was spent observing court proceedings and the plea bargaining sessions in these same counties. Researchers kept detailed field notes of police and court observations. Focus group interviews were held with youths in one of the correctional facilities in the state. To facilitate discussion, two of the focus groups comprised members from the same racial/ethnic group. One focus group consisted of African American males, another of Hispanic/Latino males, and the third was racially and ethnically mixed, including Whites, African Americans, Asians, Hispanics, and Native American youth. A total of 21 youths (7 per focus group) were interviewed.[2] Finally, researchers accompanied youth outreach workers in three counties and interviewed gang-affiliated youths, gang "wannabees," and other "at-risk" youths ($n = 20$). The following section will highlight data collected through the qualitative component of the research. More importantly, it will show how this type of data can be used to address questions that are not raised in quantitative studies.

The data collected from the quantitative component of the study showed that statewide, African American youths were severely overrepresented at every stage of the juvenile justice process. They were almost twice as likely to be arrested, 5 times more likely to be referred to juvenile court, 5 times more likely to be detained, 3 times more likely to be charged, 2.5 times more likely to be adjudicated, 11 times more likely to be sentenced to confinement, and 7 times more likely to be confined than their White counterparts. Statistically, Hispanics and Native American youths did not fare as badly and Asian/Pacific Islander youths were actually *under*represented at certain stages of the process.

Hispanics were overrepresented at every stage, except arrest and sentence to confinement. However, they were about twice as likely to be actually confined in a juvenile correctional facility.[3] Native American youths were twice as likely to be detained and three times more likely to be sentenced to and confined in correctional facilities.[4] Although youths of color represented only 15% of the state's youth population, they accounted for 39% of the total population admitted to the state correctional facilities.[5] Most of the previous research on disproportionality explains higher arrest rates for youths of color on higher rates of arrests for serious and violent crime. Although the stage of arrest was not found to account statistically for disparities at other stages of the system, the stages at which youths of color encounter the police (the stage before arrest and the stage of arrest) were the stages which youths of color, their parents, and community leaders most often identified in interviews as being most important in the production of racial disproportionality.[6]

"THE COPS ALWAYS BE IN MY NEIGHBORHOOD": WHAT HAPPENS BEFORE THE LEVEL OF ARREST

> The nature of the informal contact has more bearing on the alienation of African American kids from the police than anything else. Because in the eyes of the young African American youth, being stopped by the police is dissonant, you know, "disrespecting," calling him out of his name, already perceiving him as a gangster or a hood, and taking advantage of the obvious, you know, military and physical power that he has over him. (interview with community youth worker)

What occurs before arrest? Research by Pivilian and Briar (1964) and Chambliss (1973) provided qualitative accounts of how persons of color and other disadvantaged populations were victims of discriminatory stereotyping by police. We know that one of the most important areas where disparity occurs is at the level of police contact, because this contact frequently is not formalized through citations or arrest. Yet these encounters, or what Thomas and Znaniecki (1927) refer to as "definitions of the situation" (p. 68), shape the perceptions and behaviors of these groups toward each other. As one incarcerated youth stated in the African American focus group interview:

> Cops is more scared of Blacks. Because we just don't be caring, you know. The cops are everywhere. They've been messing with you so long, it's like, you know, fuck it, I don't care no more.

All of the other youths nodded and voiced agreement with that assessment. The impact of this surveillance was summed up by a youth outreach worker: "The kids say that if they are going to get harassed by the police, they might as well be doing something."

The only way that we have of capturing on paper what occurs at this stage of the juvenile justice process is through field observations and interviews. Although we already know a lot about the behavior of police in communities of color and we can safely conclude that most youths of color harbor negative perceptions toward the police, we still do not know much about the specific informal policing strategies that are carried out in particular communities over time. For instance, in our study we found that police handled youths differently at different times. At some times they might choose to ignore low-level drug dealing, at other times they chase the youths out of the areas, and at still other times they proceed with arrests. Two African American youths and one of the Hispanic youths complained during the focus group interviews that the police had ignored them several times when they were selling, but then would arrest them at another time for something that they did not do.

Interviews with both law enforcement officials and representatives from communities of color agreed that these areas are under heavier surveillance by the police. Observational data collected during ride-alongs revealed that police frequently stop and question youths of color walking down the streets of their neighborhoods or standing on corners. Both African American and Hispanic youths were called over to talk to police officers during ride-alongs. One African American focus group participant described the surveillance in the following way:

> They [police] going to be riding down the street real slow and if they know, they will call your name out on the loud speaker—that's messing with you.

Drug loitering laws in some of the urban areas enabled police to force youths "hanging out" on corners to disperse. However, the degree to which this happens differs across counties and changes over time. During certain periods of time, during the duration of our study, police, in various areas devoted more time to crimes involving gangs, whereas at other times and in other places, the focus was on individual crimes connected with drug, trafficking or alcohol abuse.

Another area where youths were increasingly watched and controlled was in shopping malls in predominantly White communities. This new surveillance strategy has emerged as a way of controlling the movement of middle-class African American youths who live in predominantly White communities. One NAACP activist explained that in one community,

> The kids would go to the mall and purchase the latest "sports" clothing that everyone was wearing. After buying the clothes, many of them would slip into public restrooms and change, so that they could walk around and show off their new clothes. Security officers and White patrons would assume that they stole the clothes or because they were wearing the same brands and colors, that they were members of drug trafficking gangs.

Youths who were identified as "gang affiliated" or "trouble makers" would be subsequently banned from the shopping center. In some cases, these incidents were handled by the shopping mall's internal security and at other times police were called in.

Surveillance techniques and informal practices were carried out differently in predominantly Hispanic communities. Through participant observation in one county, researchers noted that police would frequently stop cars with large numbers of Hispanic males inside or cruise down residential streets and shine spotlights on the faces of individuals sitting on their porches. The following scenario occurred during one ride-along in a county where Hispanics (primarily Mexican Americans) account for the largest percentage of youths of color:

> The police officer pulled over a car of young Hispanic males and told the driver to get out of the car and come sit in the back of the police car, while the officer ran a check on the youth's license. The officer noticed that the passengers were drinking cans of beer. He took the cans of beer and placed them behind the two rear tires of the car. He then told the driver to get back in his car and back up. The driver complied and crushed the cans and watched as beer squirted out behind the car. The officer did not give them a ticket or citation and told them that they could leave.

One Hispanic youth who participated in one of the focus groups provided an illustration of how the police handle minority youths informally:

> I got stopped one time, I was, my home boy got out and ran and I just stayed there, 'cuz I was kinda drunk, and I just stayed in there. I said, 'Fuck it, you know, I'm caught.' So [I] just started drinkin', kept drinkin'. The cop came, got me out of the, out of the um, the door, he just took me out, and just slammed me up against the car real hard and just started, kept slamming me like that. . . . I didn't think that was necessary, so I started cussin', being a little loud mouth. [He] pulled out his gun and shot right next to my ear, and I thought, you know, 'Damn! He's gonna kill me,' you know. I didn't really stretch it at the time 'cuz I was drunk, you know. I said, 'Fuck it, I'll be still.' He just left, I just left the car there and he let me go home. Oh, and he took the rifle that was sittin' next to me, he didn't take me to jail for that neither.

The above account illustrates how police use their discretion with youths of color. Police may assault, maim, and scare youths in poor neighborhoods without the fear of being held accountable. The youth claimed that the officer did not write anything down, thus there was no record of a stop.

LEVEL OF ARREST

> If you want to get arrested in America, all you have to do is dress up like a Negro. (quote from parent of an arrested youth)

This arrest stage is also often neglected in studies of disproportionality and disparity. However, researchers agree that this is the level where the selection bias that shapes statistical outcomes occurs (Morash 1987). Pivilian and Briar's (1964) classic study of the use of police discretion in the arrest and detention of youths is one of the few that focused on the juvenile justice system, and it found that decisions to arrest were based on the youths' group affiliation, age, race, grooming, dress, and demeanor.

One of the major criticisms of such studies is that the presence of an observer will influence the behavior of the police. In our own study, we found that although police were always conscious that observers were present, they tended to feel more comfortable with members of their own race/ethnicity and conversations opened up as the observer spent more time with the officer. Furthermore, we found that African American and Hispanic officers often held views different from those of their White colleagues and were more willing to share these views with observers from their own racial/ethnic groups. One African American police officer asserted that the police often misuse several laws. For example, "failure to disperse" and the "ordinance of obstructing and resisting arrest," he charged, are "basically catch-alls" that can justify arrests.

The construction of the gang label and stereotypes contributed to more surveillance, and this label is often applied at the point of arrest. One African American police officer who works with a special gang unit gave the following explanation for the disproportionate amount of attention paid to African American and Hispanic gang-related youths:

> Black, Latino, Mexican-style gangs are very easy to report. But it comes because of the way they announce themselves. It's sometimes through the style of clothes they wear. It's their whole agenda.

Other officials pointed to the disproportionate involvement of White youths in crimes that were not as visible to the community. Most research designs do not take into consideration the dynamic nature of policing activities. For instance, the attention that law enforcement and the media devoted to the so-called gang problem differed radically in different parts of the state at different points in time.

Still in another community, the police department, to support their claims that the "Bloods and Crips" were infiltrating the city, made a video, which combined footage of gang members from Los Angeles with pictures of local African American kids and crip graffiti in the background. We need to identify and trace the various ways in which the perceptions of actors involved in the administration of juvenile justice are shaped and manipulated.

IMPLICATIONS OF POLICE DECISION MAKING FOR YOUTHS OF COLOR

Future Research

To understand "how race makes a difference," it is important to focus on the first stage of the juvenile justice process—the stage where youths of color encounter police. It is this stage that shapes the perceptions and behaviors of youths of color toward the police, and what is recorded in the police report will continue to shape the responses of probation officers, prosecutors, judges, and correctional officers in subsequent stages. The perception of the police as to the dangerousness of the perpetrator defines what will happen to the youth. If the police officer perceives that the youth is not a threat, then the youth may not be arrested.

As Pivilian and Briar (1964) concluded three decades ago, "the stigmatization resulting from police apprehension, arrest and detention actually reinforces deviant behavior" (p. 206). In addition, they asserted that frequent negative encounters between police and youths innocent of wrongdoing could result in a self-fulfilling prophecy and youths of color might engage in deviant behavior because they are expected to. As one youth outreach worker was quoted earlier, "The kids say if they are going to be harassed by the police, they might as well be doing something wrong."

Future disproportionality research should incorporate more qualitative techniques to examine issues that cannot be answered statistically. For instance, future studies should address the role of the media on racial disproportionality. A common theme in all of the interviews with actors on both sides of the issue was that their perceptions of youths of color are largely shaped by the media. Furthermore, among leaders in communities of color, there is the perception that the media depicts crimes committed by White youths differently than those committed by youths of color.

Ethnographic accounts of life and race relations in certain communities can contribute to an understanding of the interaction between youths of color and actors in the juvenile justice system. Furthermore, such research should not be ahistorical. It is important to trace how the juvenile justice system in various communities has handled youths of color over time.

Finally, qualitative research can be employed to monitor the implementation and possible impact of future policies aimed at ameliorating disproportionality. Some researchers have recommended uniform guidelines for prosecutors and judges, thus restricting the use of extralegal factors such as school attendance and social background in decisions regarding detention of youths. Qualitative studies of neighborhoods would enable decision makers to better understand the youths. Several of the current wave of disproportionality studies have uncovered evidence which suggests that juvenile justice staff are detaining youths who they perceive as coming from dysfunctional families so that they can get needed services (e.g., medical care, counseling, prenatal care, etc.). However uniform guidelines have been vehemently opposed by prosecutors and court administrators, and in at least two states, they have argued that the numbers of youths of color who are detained will double or triple if they only consider the instant offense and prior record. Prosecutors have resisted uniform guidelines, arguing that the discretion would go by default back to the police.

Therefore, it is important to use in-depth interviews and participant observation to examine the possible consequences of recommendations such as uniform guidelines. It is not enough, for instance, to pinpoint the stage at which disproportionality occurs and to apply Band-Aids to one or two areas. Many of the policies that exacerbate disproportionality are not formalized practices (e.g., using detention to obtain social services for youths), and there is no doubt that other informal practices will emerge to take their place. Qualitative techniques should be used to study the implementation of new policies and to uncover new informal practices and policies that ultimately emerge when new guidelines are instituted.

NOTES

1. This study addressed three primary issues: (a) county differences in levels of ethnic disproportionality at each stage of the juvenile justice system; (b) case-level circumstances (e.g., characteristics of cases) contributing to disproportionality either independently at each stage of the juvenile justice process or cumulatively; and (c) the interpretations of juvenile justice officials, and others knowledgeable about juvenile justice, of the extensiveness and causes of racial and ethnic disproportionality.

This data analysis for the quantitative part of the project involved a series of multivariate statistical analyses of outcomes of cases at different stages of the juvenile justice process. The analysis of counties and county characteristics used multiple regression procedures, relying on ordinary least squares regression of logged dependent and independent variables. The analyses of individual case characteristics and the outcomes of the sample cases used a series of logistic regressions corresponding to the major stages of points of processing in the state juvenile justice system.

2. The participants for the mixed and Hispanic focus groups were selected by the correctional staff. The African American participants were recruited from a group enrolled in an African American history and life skills course.

3. Hispanic refers to an ethnic and not a racial category, which makes it problematic. One major problem, which is inherent in all of the disproportionality studies, is that an unknown amount of the Hispanic population is actually hidden in the White population because the category is treated as an ethnic group in the census and thus their race is frequently recorded as White (Mann 1993). The percentage of Hispanics who reported themselves as White when they had to choose *White* or *other* ranged from 20% to 70%. Furthermore, we have no way of knowing how the police determine race and ethnicity, and therefore the degree of error in arrest rates is inestimable and may not be random.

4. In the state in which this study was conducted, Native American youths are often handled through tribal courts and thus we were not able to include many of these cases in the sample.

5. Through multivariate analysis, it was shown that youths of color who were not attending school and those who came from single-parent households were more likely to be detained prior to adjudication, regardless of criminal history. Thus it was concluded that detention was the crucial stage that fuels disproportionality throughout the rest of the system. Furthermore, the presence of parents at hearings was an important factor in the outcome of hearings.

6. Rate of arrest for African American youths in this state was found to be lower than the national rate.

REFERENCES

Arnold, William R. 1971. "Race and Ethnicity Relative to Other Factors in Juvenile Court Dispositions." *American Journal of Sociology* 77:211–17.

Bell. D., Jr. and K. Lang. 1985. "The Intake Dispositions of Juvenile Court Decisions." *Journal of Research in Crime and Delinquency* 22(4):309–28.

Bishop, Donna M. and Charles E. Frazier. 1988. "The Influence of Race in Juvenile Justice Processing." *Crime & Delinquency* 25:242–63.

Blumstein, Alfred. 1982. "On Racial Disproportionality of United States' Prison Populations." *Journal of Criminal Law and Criminology* 73:1259–68.

Bortner, M. A., M. L. Sunderland, and R. Winn. 1985. "Race and Impact of Juvenile Deinstitutionalization." *Crime & Delinquency* 31:35–46.

Boyd, J. L. 1976. *Race of Inmate, Race of Officer, and Disciplinary Proceedings at a Federal Correctional Institution.* Washington, DC: U.S. Department of Health, Education, and Welfare.

Bridges, G. S., L. Deburle, and T. Dutton. 1991. "Treatment of Minority Youth in the Juvenile Justice System." Unpublished manuscript, University of Washington, Department of Sociology.

Chambliss, W. J. 1973. "The Saints and the Roughnecks." *Society* 11(1):24–31.

Cohen, L. E. and J. R. Kluegel. 1978. "Determinants of Juvenile Court Dispositions: Ascriptive and Achieved Factors in Two Metropolitan Courts." *American Sociological Review* 43(2):162–76.

Debro, J. 1975. "Institutional Racism in Federal Sentencing." Unpublished dissertation, University of California, Berkeley.

Fagan, J., E. Slaughter, and E. Hartstone. 1987. "Blind Justice? The Impact of Race on the Juvenile Process." *Crime & Delinquency* 33(2):224–58.

Ferdinand, Theodore N. and Elmer G. Luchterhand. 1970. "Inner-City Youth, the Police, the Juvenile Court and Justice." *Social Problems* 17:510–27.

Frazier, C. and D. Bishop, 1985. "The Pretrial Detention of Juveniles and Its Impact on Case Dispositions." *Journal of Criminal Law and Criminology* 76(4):1132–52.

Goldman, Nathan. 1963. "The Differential Selection of Juvenile Offenders for Court Appearance in New York: National Council on Crime and Delinquency."

Hagan, J. 1974. "Extra-Legal Attributes and Criminal Sentencing: An Assessment of a Sociological Viewpoint." *Law and Society Review* 8:357–83.

Hindelang, M. J. 1969. "Equality Under the Law." *Journal of Criminal Law, Criminology and Police Science* 60:306–13.

———. 1982. "Race and Crime." Pp. 168–84 in *Contemporary Criminology,* edited by L. D. Savitz and H. Johnson. New York: Wiley.

Hohenstein, W. F. 1969. "Factors Influencing the Police Disposition of Juvenile Offenders." In *Delinquency: Selected Studies,* edited by Thorsten Sellin and Marvin Wolfgang. New York: Wiley.

Kleck, G. 1981. "Racial Discrimination in Criminal Sentencing: A Critical Evaluation of the Evidence with Additional Data on the Death Penalty." *American Sociological Review* 46:783–805.

Krisberg, B., J. Schwartz, G. Fishman. Z. Eisikovits, E. Guttman, and K. Joe. 1987. "The Incarceration of Minority Youth." *Crime & Delinquency* 33(2):173–205.

Mann, C. R. 1979. "The Differential Treatment Between Runaway Boys and Girls in Juvenile Court." *Juvenile and Family Courts Journal* 30(2):37–48.

———. 1980. "Courtroom Observations of Extra-Legal Factors in the Juvenile Court Dispositions of Runaway Boys: A Field Study." *Juvenile and Family Court Journal* 31(4):43–52.

———. 1987. "The Reality of the Criminal Justice System." *Criminal Justice Research Bulletin.*

———. 1993. *Unequal Justice: A Question of Color.* Bloomington: Indiana University Press.

McCarthy, B. R. and B. L. Smith. 1986. "The Conceptualization of Discrimination in the Juvenile Justice Process: The Impact of Administrative Factors and Screening Decisions on Juvenile Court Dispositions." *Criminology* 24(1):41–64.

McEachern, Alex W. and Riva Bauzer. 1967. "Factors Related to Disposition in Juvenile Police Contacts." In *Juvenile Gangs in Context,* edited by Malcolm Klein and B. Myerhoff. Englewood Cliffs, NJ: Prentice-Hall.

Morash, M. 1984. "Establishment of a Juvenile Police Record: The Influence of Individual and Peer Group Characteristics." *Criminology* 22(1):97–111.

———. 1987. "The Changing Forms of Racial/Ethnic Biases in Sentencing." *Journal of Research in Crime and Delinquency* 24(1):69–92.

Petersilia, J. 1983. "Racial Disparities in the Criminal Justice System: A Summary." *Crime & Delinquency* 31(1):15–34.

Pivilian, I. and S. Briar. 1964. "Police Encounters With Juveniles." *American Journal of Sociology* 70:206–14.

Pope, C. E. and W. Feyerherm. 1992. *Minorities in the Juvenile Justice System.* Rockville, MD: U.S. Department of Justice, Office of Juvenile Justice and Delinquency Prevention, Juvenile Justice Clearing House.

Pope, C. E. and R. L. McNeely. 1981. "Race, Crime and Criminal Justice: An Overview." In *Race, Crime and Criminal Justice,* edited by R. L. McNeely and Carl E. Pope. Beverly Hills, CA: Sage.

Stephenson, Richard and Frank R. Scarpitti. 1968. "Negro-White Differentials and Delinquency." *Journal of Research in Crime and Delinquency* 4:218–30.

Terry, R. M. 1967. "The Screening of Juvenile Offenders." *Journal of Criminal Law, Criminology and Police Science* 58:173–81.

Thomas, W. I. and Florence Znaniecki. 1927. "The Polish Peasant." In *Europe and America.* Vol. 1. New York: Alfred A. Knopf.

Thornberry, T. 1973. "Race, Socioeconomic Status and Sentencing in the Juvenile Justice System." *Journal of Criminal Law and Criminology* 64:90–98.

Webb, G. L. 1979. *Conviction and Sentencing: Deception and Racial Discrimination.* Austin, TX: Coker Books.

Wilbanks, W. 1987. *The Myth of a Racist Criminal Justice System.* Belmont, CA: Wadsworth.

Wolfgang, M. E., R. M. Figlio, and T. Sellin. 1972. *Delinquency in a Birth Cohort.* Chicago: University of Chicago Press.

Wright. B. 1990. *Black Robes: White Justice.* New York: First Carol Publishing Group.

Zatz, M. 1987. "The Changing Forms of Racial/Ethnic Biases in 'Sentencing.' " *Journal of Research in Crime and Delinquency* 24(1):69–92.

Boston Cops and Black Churches

CHRISTOPHER WINSHIP

JENNY BERRIEN

In recent years, homicide rates in a number of large American cities have plummeted. Between 1990 and 1996, New York's rate dropped 58.7 percent, Houston's 54 percent, Los Angeles' 27.9 percent, Philadelphia's 17.7 percent, and Washington, D.C.'s 15.9 percent. In most, if not all of these cities, the precipitous decline in homicide rates derives from even sharper declines in youth violence. However, not all cities have been so fortunate. For example, in Baltimore, Phoenix, and Las Vegas, homicide rates have risen by 7.5 percent, 45.3 percent, and 103.8 percent respectively. A key question then is: Why has youth violence fallen so significantly in some cities but not in others?

Certainly, part of the decline in youth violence can be attributed to the robust economy, as well as to the nationwide decline in the number of youths aged 15 to 24, the most crime-prone age group. But these factors are present in almost all cities, and thus cannot explain the differences across the nation. Besides, similar declines in homicide rates did not occur in the mid and late 1980s when the economy was also strong. And the 7.7 percent drop in the number of youths aged 15 to 24, from 1986 to 1996, is too small to account for much of the improvement.

The dynamics of youth violence are complex, depending upon a myriad of factors that vary from city to city. But certain features of violence reduction in Boston stand out, yielding important answers as well as lessons for other cities. The drop in homicide rates in Boston has been the steepest in the nation. Between 1990 and 1996, Boston's

rates dropped 61.2 percent, from 152 homicides to 59. In 1997, the rate dropped further to only 43 homicides, a total decline of 72 percent from the previous high. By 1998, only 35 murders took place. Perhaps even more stunning is that, for the 29-month period ending in January 1998, Boston had no teenage homicide victims. Since that time (as of this writing) there have been four.

Boston is also unusual in that a group of ministers, the Ten-Point Coalition, is thought to have played a key role in reducing youth homicides. The media has already lavished attention on the coalition's work. *Newsweek* ran a feature story; *Time, Sojourners,* the *Weekly Standard,* the *New York Times,* the *Boston Globe,* and the *Atlanta Journal Constitution* have all run major stories on the ministers. PBS made the Ten-Point Coalition the subject of a documentary.

What we will explore is whether the coalition has, in fact, played a significant role in reducing youth violence in Boston. At first glance, the answer appears to be no. Crime rates have dropped dramatically in other cities without significant involvement from the clergy. The fact that only three ministers—Eugene Rivers, Raymond Hammond, and Jeffrey Brown—have been centrally involved, and that even they have not devoted themselves to the coalition full time, suggests that too little has been attempted by the churches for them to have played a substantial role in the crime reductions. And David Kennedy, a researcher at Harvard's Kennedy School of Government, has documented how new law enforcement policies and practices have led to more effective ways of dealing with youth violence. The assertion that the Ten-Point Coalition has been a significant player would seem to be, at best, good public relations.

We will argue, to the contrary, that the Ten-Point Coalition has played a critical role in Boston's sharp drop in youth violence. It has done so by changing the way the police (and other elements of the criminal justice system) and Boston's inner-city community relate to each other. In its intermediary role between the two parties, the Ten-Point Coalition balances the community's desire for safe streets and its reluctance to see its children put in jail. It has created what we will call an "umbrella of legitimacy" for fair and just policing.

THE BOSTON STORY

Boston has never been considered a violence-plagued city on the scale of Los Angeles or New York. But in 1990, 152 homicides occurred in Boston—a record high. The roots of this violence took hold in the late 1980s, when crack-cocaine found its way into Boston's inner city. As the crack market developed, so did turf-based gangs and gang violence. To protect their financial stakes in the booming crack-cocaine market, as well as to maintain "respect," the gangs increasingly turned to firearms. "Disrespect" was punished by violence. And a vicious cycle developed, in which individuals joined one gang to protect themselves from another gang. With firearms serving as the primary method of protection and retaliation, as well as being tools for spontaneous assaults, the frequency and severity of violence grew to a level never before seen in the Boston area.

Since Boston law-enforcement agencies had not previously dealt with turf-based violence and criminal gang activity, their initial response was inadequate. Up until 1990, the department denied that there was a "gang problem." Many current Boston police officers have vouched that the department simply had no policy for combating gang violence. Without an in-depth understanding of the problem or a plan of attack, police officers fell back on the aggressive, riot-oriented tactics of the

1960s. In addition, because homicide has traditionally been handled on a case-by-case basis, the police department aimed at making the "big hit" and arresting the "big player," rather than addressing the group-based nature of gang violence.

In 1988, the City Wide Anti-Crime Unit (CWACU), traditionally responsible for providing support across district boundaries, was permanently assigned to the most violent neighborhoods of Boston's inner city. In 1989, the police department declared that any individual involved in a gang would be prosecuted to the full extent of the law. Finally, the department had acknowledged the existence of a "gang problem."

But to what effect is another matter. According to one current police captain, the CWACU was expected to "go in, kick butts, and crack heads." A common attitude emerged within the force. They believed that "they could do anything to these kids" in order to snuff out their violent activity. This mentality produced, not surprisingly, highly aggressive and reportedly indiscriminate policing tactics.

COMMUNITY BACKLASH

Two scandals in 1989—the Carol Stuart murder investigation and the department's "stop-and-frisk" policy—alerted the community to the police's questionable tactics. Carol Stuart was a pregnant white woman who was murdered in the primarily African-American neighborhood of Mission Hill. Her husband, Charles Stuart, who was with her at the time of her death, claimed that a black male had murdered her. As a result of the accusation, the Boston Police Department scoured the Mission Hill neighborhood, looking for suspects. The community reported instances of police abuse as well as coerced statements that were later used as evidence against a black male suspect, William Bennett. But Charles Stuart himself was later identified as the alleged perpetrator of the crime, though he committed suicide before an investigation could be completed. The mishandling of the Stuart murder investigation and the dishonesty of the victim's husband created an atmosphere, especially within the African-American community, of extreme distrust of, and disillusionment with, the Boston Police Department.

The stop-and-frisk scandal intensified these sentiments. A precinct commander's description of the department's approach to prevent gun-related violence as a policy of "stop and frisk," *en masse,* outraged the black community and solidified the Boston public's suspicion of the police. There is some dissention within the police department about the extent to which their policy was really to stop and frisk all black males, indiscriminately, within high-crime areas—a policy also referred to as "tipping kids upside down." According to some officers, targeted individuals were either previously spotted performing some illegal activity or were known gang members. But officers also acknowledged that their approach was critically flawed in that it was often very difficult to "distinguish the good guys from the bad guys." In addition, some officers admitted that there were "bad-seed" cops who acted far too aggressively in certain cases. Accusations of "stop-and-frisk" tactics led to a court case in the fall of 1989 in which a judge threw out evidence acquired in what he considered an unconstitutional search and seizure.

Because of the bad press surrounding the Stuart case and the stop-and-frisk scandal, the CWACU was disbanded in 1990. However, it must be noted that the police department's aggressive street tactics seemed to work: Boston's homicide rates fell from 152 in 1990, to 103 in 1991, to 73 in 1992. But regardless of this success, most officers acknowledged that the department's aggressive searches dangerously inflamed the community.

The Boston press began to question the police department's ability to manage even routine policing activity. In 1991, the *Boston Globe* published a harshly critical four-part series, "Bungling the Basics," that detailed a succession of police foul-ups during the previous few years. A subsequent group of *Globe* stories reported serious failings in the department's Internal Affairs Division. The misguided investigations and questionable policing exposed by the press eventually led to the appointment of the St. Clair Commission, which was assigned the task of thoroughly reviewing Boston's police department and its policies.

At this point, the Boston Police Department began a desperately needed overhaul to deal with the negative publicity. "Bad-seed" cops were weeded out. The old and disbanded CWACU was transformed into a new unit, the Anti Gang Violence Unit (AGVU), which espoused a "softer" approach to violence prevention. The aggressive and indiscriminate—though admittedly effective— street tactics of the past were sharply curtailed. As a result, the short-term drops in homicides during 1991 and 1992 were followed by a sharp upswing in the homicide rate to 98 in 1993.[1]

The release of the St. Clair Commission's report in 1992 spurred further administrative changes at the highest level. The report cited extensive corruption within the department and recommended major changes. In 1993, Mayor Flynn resigned, and Police Commissioner Mickey Roach was replaced by the New York Police Department's Bill Bratton, who brought a new philosophy and a spirit of innovation to the Boston Police Department.

NEW POLICE METHODS

According to current Boston police officers, community policing tactics, which formerly "just existed on paper," were actively pursued under Commissioner Bratton. Many officers reported that the new administration was more open-minded, more willing to break away from traditional policing practices.

The newly organized Anti Gang Violence Unit looked for improved methods to manage gang violence. They targeted the areas where they had failed during the past few years. They were determined to employ "squeaky-clean" policing strategies in order to win back the community's trust. The AGVU also pursued an increasingly multi-agency approach to combat youth violence. Then, in 1993, the AGVU underwent an administrative change, becoming the Youth Violence Strike Force.

Other agencies within Boston's law-enforcement network were also being revamped. Workers in the probation department became disillusioned by the "paper-shuffling" nature of their jobs. Because of the dangerous levels of violence within certain Boston districts, probation officers had given up maintaining a street presence or making home visits. Consequently, the enforcement of curfew, area, and activity restrictions was entirely absent. Lacking enforcement, probation came to be viewed by law-enforcement officials as a "slap on the wrist" that had little effect in the battle against youth violence.

A strategy called "Operation Nightlight" was developed to make probation meaningful and effective. It began when three probation officers and two police officers ventured out in a patrol car on the night of November 12, 1992. During this first night, they made contact with several youths who were violating the terms of their probation. Youths suddenly became aware that they could no longer blatantly disregard the terms of their probation because their PO might show up at their house after curfew. Subsequently, Operation Nightlight became an institutionalized practice of Boston's law-enforcement agencies.

Inter-agency collaboration to address the issue of youth violence has now become standard procedure in Boston. The Boston Gun Project, a three-year program begun in 1995, brought together a broad interagency group, including the Police Department, Bureau of Alcohol, Tobacco, and Firearms, Probation Department, Boston school police, and Suffolk County District Attorney. Policy researchers (primarily David Kennedy and his associates at the John F. Kennedy School of Government) and key community members also played vital roles. The Gun Project coalition has attacked the problem both on the supply side, by cracking down on suppliers of illicit firearms, and on the demand side, by identifying high-risk individuals. These individuals, 1,300 in all, representing less than 1 percent of their age group city-wide, were responsible for at least 60 percent of the city's homicides.

In 1994, another program to reduce gun violence, "Operation Scrap Iron," was initiated. It attempted to identify smugglers who were illegally transporting firearms into Boston. Gun trafficking

within certain sections of the city was completely shut down by using such methods as "area warrant sweeps" in dangerous neighborhoods. In one housing project, the police arrested everyone with outstanding warrants in the area. Follow-up teams of street and youth workers offered their services to these areas once the police were gone. As one police officer noted, these strategies made sure that, "everyone was involved and brought something to the table."

By mid May 1996, the culmination of this collaborative work emerged with the implementation of Operation Cease-Fire. Operation Cease-Fire fully institutionalized inter-agency collaboration among Boston's crime-fighting agencies: Police, Probation, Department of Youth Services, Street Workers, and others. In addition, it involved key community members, primarily from faith-based organizations in the Boston area.

BIRTH OF THE TEN-POINT COALITION

Members of Boston's religious community were among the most vocal and publicized critics of the earlier aggressive tactics of the police department. Reverend Eugene Rivers, in particular, became a controversial figure during these years because of his harsh criticism of Boston's law-enforcement agencies as well as the city's black leaders. It is therefore quite remarkable that these religious leaders were later active participants in such law-enforcement initiatives as Operation Cease-Fire.

Boston's religious organizations did not begin working together until 1992. Until that point, most African-American clergy within Boston followed their independent agendas. Faith-based activity did not, for the most part, address the crisis of youth violence. Rivers did establish outreach programs for gang members and other community youth, but his differences with other clergymen made his effort a lone endeavor. A single tragic event finally instigated collaboration among Boston's African-American clergy. In May 1992, the Morning Star Baptist Church held a service for a youth murdered in a "drive-by" gang shooting. During the service, a shootout and stabbing occurred among several of the gang members. A melee ensued within the sanctuary.

The brazenness of the attack—within the walls of a church—captured the attention of the clergy, inciting them to action. They perceived that they could no longer effectively serve their communities by focusing solely on their own congregations. The community, with its troubled youths, had to become an extension of the church. Thus was the Ten-Point Coalition born, including some 40 churches, with Reverends Rivers, Hammond, and Brown as the key leaders. A "Ten-Point Proposal for Citywide Mobilization to Combat the Material and Spiritual Sources of Black-on-Black Violence," written by Rivers and a former drug dealer, Selvin Brown, was issued, calling upon churches to address the crisis of violence in their communities.

The creation of the Ten-Point Coalition marked the official beginning of Boston's African-American religious community's organized involvement in the youth-violence epidemic. As of 1992, relations between African-American community leaders and Boston's law-enforcement agencies were still strained. Rivers was constantly "in the face" of Boston law enforcement and viewed as a "cop basher" in police circles. He established a constant presence in the troubled neighborhoods of Dorchester and was in contact with the same kids as the Anti Gang Violence Unit. Rivers' aggressive advocacy for local youth, in and out of the courts, led to many confrontations with the AGVU. But this initial antagonism was eventually replaced by cooperation. A number of events, along with the new, improved policing approach, spurred the turnaround.

In 1991, Rivers' house in Four Corners, one of the most violent areas of Dorchester, was shot at for the first of two times. Though he and his family were not harmed, the incident reminded him, in the most literal sense, of the dangers of a solitary campaign against youth violence. Rivers increasingly sought allies in the religious community and in law-enforcement agencies.

The Ten-Point Coalition, and especially Rivers, had habitually and severely criticized the Boston Police Department. Now they sought to engage in constructive cooperation. In 1992, the coalition set up a "Police Practices Coalition" that monitored policing in the Boston area. Positive interactions with law enforcement increased, convincing the clergy that the department was indeed interested in reform. To acknowledge the department's progress, the ministers instituted a ceremony called the "Police Youth Leadership Awards," which would honor "good cops." These improved interactions between the African-American clergy and law enforcement were followed by other initiatives, and their relations have continued to evolve and expand in recent years.

THE MCLAUGHLIN MURDER

Today, inter-agency and community-based collaboration is the rule in Boston, and there is considerable trust between the police and the community. This progress was tested with the investigation of the McLaughlin murder. On September 25, 1995, a white assistant attorney general, Paul R. McLaughlin, was shot and killed on his way home from work at the commuter rail station in West Roxbury, a middle-class, predominantly Irish neighborhood in Boston. A well-respected prosecutor, McLaughlin had recently been working on a task force against gang members. His murder appeared to be a "hit" in retaliation for this work.

When the police department issued its description of the assailant—"black male, about 14 or 15 years old, 5 foot 7, wearing a hooded sweat shirt and baggy jeans"—there was instant concern among African Americans that such a vague profile could easily apply to many young black males. But immediate and reassuring responses from law-enforcement officials and community leaders helped to abate the potentially divisive nature of the vague description. The law-enforcement community had its own objective: Many suspected that McLaughlin was targeted mainly because he had prosecuted many gang members and wondered whether they were also in danger. The law-enforcement community therefore made it a priority to respond to the murder quickly and decisively.

So did leaders in Boston's African-American community. The executive committee of the Ten-Point Coalition publicly condemned the murder at a press conference the following day. Rivers cited the press conference as critical in preventing what he described as an "open season on black youth"—which he believed did occur during the Carol Stuart murder case. In the press conference, the clergy expressed sympathy for the McLaughlin family and placed a strong emphasis on bringing the city together to avoid the threat of severe polarization by advocating an aggressive, but fair, investigation of the murder.

This immediate and firm stance sent several important messages. First, the ministers emphasized that even a community characterized by historically antagonistic feelings toward the police would not tolerate the vengeful murder of a law-enforcement official. Thus the African-American youth in the community were told that the murder must not be interpreted as a kind of justifiable self-defense. And, by pledging their support for a fair police effort, the ministers emphasized that police aggression or harassment was unnecessary and would not be tolerated. In addition, the ministers' statement defanged the media. By taking a stand in support of police action, and by exhibiting trust in the department's approach, the black clergy made it less likely that the media would exaggerate or aggravate a tense situation. Finally, the coalition's stance indicated that, as a police source put it, the "clergy viewed them (the police) as a much different police force" by the time of the McLaughlin murder and were confident that the department would carry out a "professional investigation."

The improved police tactics were displayed during this particularly sensitive period. Commissioner Paul F. Evans spoke on a radio station with a large black audience soon after the murder to emphasize the limited value of the vague assailant description and to assert that an effective investigation depended on cooperation between the police and the community. The commissioner also joined the ministers at the Ten-Point Coalition's press conference to highlight police cooperation with the African-American community. Both the law-enforcement community's and black clergy's approach toward the McLaughlin murder illustrated the dramatic shift that had occurred in the relationship between these two groups since the late eighties and early nineties. (A convicted murderer, Jeffrey Bly, was indicted for the McLaughlin murder and is currently standing trial.)

BLACKS AND THE JUDICIAL SYSTEM

Something very unusual has happened in Boston: The black community and law enforcement are no longer at odds with one another. A moment's reflection on the general state of relations between African Americans and the judicial system will confirm just how unique such trust is. Many black communities in America's largest cities believe themselves to be at war with the local police. The metaphor of the police as an occupying military power is frequently invoked. The reasons for this perception are perfectly well known. The shooting in New York this past February [2000] of Amadou Diallo, an unarmed African street vendor, has again brought national attention to this problem.

Inner-city residents are often unwilling to support police activities, even though they are, to an overwhelming degree, disproportionately the victims of crime—and the crimes are frequently committed by their fellow residents. In his book, *Race, Crime, and the Law,* Randall Kennedy describes the growing alienation of black inner-city residents from the criminal justice system. He locates the origins of their resentment in the South and in the historical lynchings of blacks, offering as evidence, the following quotation from Gunnar Myrdal's 1944 book, *An American Dilemma:*

> The Negroes . . . are hurt in their trust that the law is impartial, that the court and the police are their protection, and indeed, that they belong to an orderly society which has set up this machinery for common security and welfare. They will not feel confidence in, and loyalty toward a legal order which is entirely out of their control and which they see to be inequitable and merely part of the system of caste oppression. Solidarity then develops easily in the Negro group, a solidarity against the law

and the police. The arrested Negro often acquires the prestige of a victim, a martyr, or a hero, even when he is simply a criminal.

Kennedy describes how this same dynamic is at work today:

It largely explains why many blacks rallied around the gang of boys who raped a white jogger in New York's Central Park, around Marion Barry, the mayor of Washington, D.C., who was caught red-handed smoking cocaine, around Alcee Hastings, the federal district court judge who, based on allegations of corruption, was ousted from office by the U.S. Senate (only to be subsequently elected to the House of Representatives), around Damian Williams and the other hooligans who gained notoriety when they were filmed beating a hapless white truck driver (Reginald Denny) in the early hours of the Los Angeles riot of 1992, and around Mike Tyson, the boxing champion, when he was imprisoned for rape.

The point is that excesses of the judicial system, both historical and present, have led inner-city minorities to view our criminal justice system as totally lacking in legitimacy. The result: Criminals are often seen as political dissidents and martyrs.

If Randall Kennedy's portrayal of inner-city minority residents' attitudes toward the criminal justice system is even somewhat accurate, it is hardly surprising that police have found it nearly impossible to deal with youth violence in our inner cities. When police are unlikely to receive cooperation from residents, the only option has been aggressive tactics that only further alienate community residents.

But why is the relationship between police and inner-city residents in such a chronically sorry state? Inner-city residents often have conflicting goals. On the one hand, they desire, as do all Americans, safe streets and neighborhoods. On the other hand, they do not want to see their children locked up. As Glenn Loury has noted, "The young black men wreaking havoc in the ghetto are still 'our youngsters' in the eyes of many of the decent poor and working class black people who are often their victims." Given these conflicting desires,

how are decisions to be made about whether a particular youth should be arrested or jailed? When should a youth be given another chance? What are the costs to the community versus the benefits to the youth of his not going to jail? When a youth gets into trouble, a terrible and difficult decision must be made. The youth may be allowed to remain in the community, potentially endangering its residents. Or the youth may be sent to jail, depriving him of his freedom and perhaps his future. Neither option is attractive to black parents.

But one thing remains clear: Most inner cities simply do not have institutions that can deal with this problem in a way perceived as just, both by the local community and the broader society. The police are too biased in favor of safer streets; social workers, street workers, and community organizers are too sympathetic to the kids. Community residents themselves frequently base their judgments upon who is in trouble and what the individual's relationship to them is. How is a decision to be made that is fair and just?

THE UMBRELLA OF LEGITIMACY

In Boston, the ministers of the Ten-Point Coalition participate in making decisions that are perceived to be fair and just. Through their involvement with at-risk youth and their intervention in situations where youth are in trouble with the law, they have projected a sense of fairness. Consequently, they have created an "umbrella of legitimacy" for law enforcement. This "umbrella" enables the police to do their job in a way that is in the best interests of the larger community and youth without an inordinate fear of public criticism.

If one were in search of legitimacy, there could perhaps be no better conferees than religious ministers. Ministers have a unique moral standing in society. They are expected to be fair and to protect the interests of the less fortunate. Amid the inner city, they and their churches are one of the last formal institutions committed to the welfare of their neighborhoods. Within the black community, especially, they are often looked to for leadership. In the case of Ten-Point, two of the three core ministers live in Boston's inner city; all three are well known for their extensive work with inner-city youth. These factors have lent Ten-Point considerable credibility in Boston's inner-city community.

The unique relationship between the police and Ten-Point is built on a number of implicit understandings, each of which potentially supports the legitimacy of the police: that youth violence needs to be dealt with as a criminal problem; that some kids need to be jailed both for their own good and the good of the community; that a small number of youths constitute this problem and that the ministers will help identify those youths; that the ministers will have a say in what happens to specific youths; that if police use indiscriminate and abusive methods in dealing with youths, the ministers will take the story to the media.

The first assumption is that, at least over the short run, youth violence must be treated as criminal. Yes, such factors as poverty, single-parent households, and inadequate schools contribute to youth violence. But the immediate problem will never be solved if law enforcement plays no role. Thus ministers have made it clear to at-risk kids that they have two choices. If they go straight, the ministers will help them to succeed in school, find jobs, and resist the peer pressure exerted by gangs. However, if they decide to participate in gang activities, the ministers will do their utmost to see them put in jail. The ministers make it clear that they are doing this both for the community's and the kid's own good. They are doing it for the community because the kid is a threat to its safety. They are doing it for the kid to save his future, even his life. If a kid is going to be involved in a gang, it is better that he be in jail than on the street.

Implicit in this "choice" is a second assumption—that some kids are sufficiently out of control that the only option is for them to be put away. It is not apparent that the ministers thought this in the beginning. Certainly, the police did not initially believe that the ministers would support the incarceration of certain individuals. Interviews with both police and ministers indicate that cooperation became possible at a single critical point—with the public acknowledgment by the ministers, most vocally by Rivers, that some kids were simply so out of control that they needed to be locked away. This did not mean that the police and ministers agreed on *which* kids needed to be put behind bars. But both parties now had the same definition of the problem, disagreeing occasionally on what should be done in particular circumstances.

A third assumption has been the understanding by both police and ministers that only a small number of youths cause most of the problems. Kennedy has estimated that this number is only 1 percent of the entire age group—1,300 youths. As Rivers his said, it only takes a few kids shooting off guns to terrorize a whole neighborhood. This is why standard stop-and-frisk procedures can be so oppressive. For the dozens of kids stopped, only one is truly part of the problem. An essential part of the informal agreement between Ten Point and the police has been that the ministers will help identify those kids who are the real problems. That is, they serve the police in a remote surveillance capacity. This not only makes police efforts more effective but increases their legitimacy by ensuring that they focus on malefactors only.

A fourth and related assumption is that the ministers have a nonofficial role in determining how different individuals should be treated by the judicial system. In some circumstances, this has meant that the ministers have contacted the police to request that certain kids be arrested. In such cases, the ministers will sometimes help police locate the kids. In other cases, it has meant that the ministers have appeared in court to argue either for leniency or for a stiff sentence.

Thus the umbrella of legitimacy allows the police to function more comfortably. The ministers enable the police to deal with the problem of youth violence without recrimination from the press or the community. The umbrella only provides coverage for specific activities, however, bringing us to the final assumption. When police focus on the truly bad youths, when they deal with these youths in a fair and just way, and when all this is done in cooperation with the ministers, their activities fall under the umbrella. Activities outside these boundaries fall outside the umbrella and will not be tolerated.

Our analysis suggests that Ten Point has become an intermediary institution between the police and the community. Black leaders now have some control over the judicial process and some say over who should be jailed and who let free. Ten Point helps adjudicate between the sometimes conflicting goals of having safe streets and keeping kids out of prison. Critically, because of the Ten-Point Coalition's involvement, the different treatment of different youths is more likely to be seen by the community as legitimate. Hard decisions are being made, but in a way that is seen as fair and just.

COOPERATION IS KEY

The police cannot be effective if their activities are not perceived as legitimate by the community. Communities want both safe streets and their youth out of jail. Choices need to be made—choices that are likely to be considered unjust by some subset of residents. In this environment, police action, no matter how beneficial, is often condemned as illegitimate.

The Ten-Point Coalition has evolved into an institution that addresses this situation. They have created what we have called an umbrella of legitimacy for police to work under. Freed of knee-jerk suspicion and benefiting from community cooperation, the police can concentrate on truly violent youth, rather than indiscriminately monitoring the innocent with the guilty. We believe that this new dynamic, which is unique among most major cities, has contributed to the spectacular drop in homicide rates in Boston.

The lesson of the Boston experience is this: In the struggle against crime, police cannot go it alone; they need the cooperation of community leaders. Such partnerships help reduce youth violence and, equally important, delineate what constitutes legitimate police behavior. Police strategies can only acquire true legitimacy within inner-city communities if the community supports appropriate police tactics while harshly criticizing inappropriate tactics. In these circumstances, churches and ministers are ideal partners. And, at the very least, the possibility that Boston has found an effective strategy for reducing youth violence, without severely and broadly compromising the civil liberties of its inner-city residents, is very exciting.

NOTE

1. The question of causality and timing here is complex. The most aggressive period of stop-and-frisk tactics ended in 1990. Yet the homicide rate continued to fall in 1991 and 1992. If one believes that the causal connection is contemporaneous, then this is evidence of a lack of a causal effect. However, if the causal effect of police enforcement lags, then this is evidence of a causal effect.

PART FIVE

The Courts

One of the basic principles of our democratic society is that we are governed by the "rule of law," which means equity, fairness, and impartiality in the application of the law. As we have seen earlier in this book, unequal justice existed for several centuries in the United States due to express *de jure* discrimination against women, racial and ethnic minorities, and the lower classes. Only in the second half of the twentieth century have we eliminated the express aspects of this discrimination. This is also true of the judicial system (Johnson and Wolfe, 1996).

HISTORY OF THE RULE OF LAW

Today the notion of the rule of law is an accepted principle in society. The law is to be administered impartially on the basis of long-established principles of equality and fairness that have developed through common law and parliamentary enactments. The idea that justice must not only be done, but also be visible to the public, suggests both the ideological and material aspects of the rule of law. The notion that individuals should be legally and judicially equal and free, however, is a relatively recent concept in the history of societies. Under feudal law, people had unequal standing before the law, largely based on inherited status and religious position. Lords, by right, controlled land, which was worked by vassals. This agrarian system based on land tenure was believed to be a naturally ordained way of life. The current taken-for-granted social and legal concepts of contract and property were the product of a social and legal struggle by the emerging merchant class against the feudal order. As Tigar and Levy (1977) point out in *Law and the Rise of Capitalism,* the growth of commerce, the spread of mercantile law, the systematization of agricultural production, and the bourgeois uprising between 1000 and 1200 A.D. were all reflected in the legal ideology of the bourgeois class—workers, proprietors, sellers, and buyers. Men would be freed from land tenure or other bondage based on either the authority of the church or their ascribed status. They would be free to pursue their own needs and wishes, particularly the accumulation of property. Ironically, this new-found freedom did not extend to women, who continued to be dominated by men and by laws made for and by men. For practical purposes, the freedoms gained during the bourgeois revolution applied to only half of the population. Bourgeois society remained essentially a man's world.

The monarchy and its aristocracy fell to the bourgeois revolutions between the seventeenth and nineteenth centuries. During this period, the old order of church, state, and monarchy was increasingly under attack for its restriction of freedom and the resulting inequality that existed. A new order was constructed based on concepts of equality, freedom, growth, and rational thought. Natural law, based on antiquated notions of the divine rights of kings and blood ties, was being replaced by classical jurisprudence, which emphasized individual rights and freedoms (Kerruish, 1991). Influential thinkers such as Hobbes, Rousseau, Smith, and Voltaire emphasized that the state must abide by the rule of law because people enter into a social contract giving power to the state only to the extent that this satisfies the needs of civil society. From these writers' work emerged the idea of the sacredness of private property and the duty of the state to ensure that the struggle for private property takes place according to predictable, rational–legal rules agreed on by subjects of the state (Berman, 1983). This led to the emergence of constitutional democracies, individual rights, the concept of private property, the right to vote, and the right to pursue self-interest within the rules of society (i.e., laws). In short, this established the supremacy of the rule of law. According to Fine,

> For the rule of law to hold good, the innocent must never be punished, specific privileges must never be conferred on anyone by name; rules must apply to all equally, justice must never be sold for private gain, the discretionary power of government to absolve people from the effects of law or to pardon them for their offenses must be limited; the law must provide for the security of the least of its members with as much care as for all the rest, and it must protect the poor against the tyranny of the rich! Most important of all, the law must protect private property, for the right of property is the most sacred of all rights of citizenship and even more important in some respects than liberty itself. (1984, p. 32)

Both the French and the American Revolutions were revolts against aristocratic, monarchical systems that were arbitrary and oppressive. The American Revolution and its subsequent legal documents, the Constitution of 1789 and the Bill of Rights of 1791, were heralded worldwide as the establishment of constitutional democracy, stripped of its monarchical aspects. These documents established the protection of private property, a representative federal form of government, and a set of restrictions on the government in terms of substantive and procedural guarantees of freedom of speech and freedom of the press.

French jurist Alexis de Tocqueville visited the new nation, America, and recorded his observations *On Democracy, Revolution and Society* (1980/1835). Democracy, according to de Tocqueville, could take two forms: (1) a state of society where there exists a general equality of rights and a similarity of conditions, thoughts, sentiment, and ideas, but no necessary connection with individual freedom or popular government; or (2) a form of government with a constitution whereby sovereign power is possessed by the numerical majority of citizens. The latter definition of democracy has been the one adopted in contemporary thought and practice.

With the emergence of constitutional democracy came major advances in individual rights and freedoms over the arbitrary abuse of power under monarchical regimes. The establishment of the rule of law, with its notions of equality and fairness for all citizens, signified the victory of the bourgeoisie over the old aristocratic ruling class. The famous English jurist A. V. Dicey (1885) identified three basic elements of the rule of law in constitutional democracies: (1) the absolute supremacy of law over arbitrary powers, particularly those wielded through government discretion, (2) all citizens are subject to ordinary law in ordinary courts, and (3) the rights of citizens are based on court decisions, not on abstract constitutional statements. Dicey held an elitist view of who is best qualified to make and administer law (Reasons, 1985), and his "view from above" was prevalent in nineteenth-century England. Early British parliamentary democracy meant democracy for the propertied and wealthy, and enslavement for the mass of the English working class.

The fact that early rights and freedoms very much benefitted the bourgeoisie has been documented by E. P. Thompson in *The Making of the English Working Class* (1976), where he takes the "view from below." That is, he documents the day-to-day harsh reality for the working class from the letters and writings of members of that class between 1780–1832. Others, such as Marx and Engels, have thoroughly documented the oppressive reality of early parliamentary democracy and industrial capitalism. However, as Thompson points out in *Whigs and Hunters* (1977), the rule of law was not entirely empty, and justice at times not only *appeared* to be carried out, but was carried out in fact. The periodic execution of an upper-class person and the pardon of a member of the working class was the exception to the rule, but it provided concrete evidence that no one is above the law and that there is a law common to all subjects (Hay, 1975). The final vestiges of the unequal application of the rule of law were eliminated in the recent, post–World War II movements for equality for minorities, women, and representatives of the disadvantaged. The history of the rule of law is paralleled by the history of the emergence of courts and the extent to which they provided justice for women, nonwhites, and the poor.

STATE LAW AND COURT SYSTEMS

As was discussed in Part 3 "The Law," the feudal community based on shared responsibility was replaced by an emerging trade capitalism based on private property and bonded by a new ethic, that of *individualism.* Obviously, an economic system based on trade and markets required such things as roads and standardized currency. Also, the developing merchant class had no warrior caste (vassals) available to protect its interests. A central authority would have to provide the force of arms necessary to defend private interests. Such needs, together with others, gave rise to the *nation-state,* formally institutionalized in Europe in the post-fifteenth-century period. With the establishment of the state, a transformation in law occurred, as is revealed in the following chart.

Changes from Tribal/Feudal to State Law

Legal Factor	*Feudal Law*	*State Law*
Unit of justice	Family	State
Jurisdictional ties	Blood	Territory
Basis of responsibility	Collective	Individual
Method of dispute settlement	Feud or compensation	State court procedures: Civil and criminal

Under the feudal system, the family, based on blood ties, was the basic unit determining and administering justice. With the demise of the feudal system, there emerged the nation-state, based on territorial ties, to determine and administer justice. For example, under feudal law, if one took a person's life, the offender's kin would be collectively held responsible, not the individual killer. Subsequently, the victim's kin might attempt to settle the debt by taking the life of any member of the killer's family, not necessarily the offender. This might precipitate a feud that could go on for some time. Another possible method of retaliation was extracting compensation from the offending family. Such compensation might be in the form of valued goods paid for the deceased. Within the context of the nation-state, by contrast, the killer was held individually responsible for the act and was punished by agents of the state. The nation-state does not allow for compensation as a means of resolving the harm, even if the family of the deceased should agree to a settlement. This is because criminal behavior is viewed as an offense against the nation-state and not just against an individual.

The nature of dispute resolution under the state system of justice includes what we take for granted as our state and federal court systems, both civil and criminal. Unlike in feudal, prestate society, conflicts are the property of the state to be dealt with through formal state process and procedure (Christie, 1978).

During the height of British colonization in the eighteenth and nineteenth centuries, the British imposed their political and social institutions, including their laws and courts and their justice system, on those colonized. This system was based on what is called common law, that is, the judicial decisions that were made over the centuries in England. Criminal or appropriate property, commercial and civil rights were all defined through judicial decisions (Johnson and Wolfe, 1996). After the American revolution, the revolutionaries established a statutory constitution, and the subsequent principle of statute law in the civil and criminal areas both at the federal and state levels. That is, the revolutionaries, upset about the arbitrary nature of British common law and judicial decisions, established the principle that citizens should be provided with statutes expressly stating rights and wrongs, rather than *ad hoc* and *ex post facto* criminalization through judicial decisions. Thus, today the United States and many other former common law countries have extensive statutes that explain appropriate and inappropriate behavior in various aspects of life. Of course, the statutes must be interpreted, and herein lies the role of the courts—to interpret statutes through the process of precedent and *stare decisis.* The notion of precedent or stare decisis means that what has been decided before should serve as a guide for current decision making. The importance of a decision depends on the level of court in which the decision is made. That is, when the United State Supreme Court makes a decision, that sets a precedent for all other courts in the United States (Schwartz, 1993). Since, unlike many other countries, we have a dual court system of federal and state courts, precedents can be set within both the federal and the state systems. The hierarchy of our courts, presented in Figure 5.1, shows that the federal system is separate from the state system, with the United States Supreme Court setting the precedents for both systems.

Criminal law is principally a state matter constitutionally; therefore, most crimes and most prosecution of crime occur in the state court system. Figure 5.2 provides an example of a typical state court system. Again, based upon the principle of stare decisis, a state's highest court sets the standards for lower courts in both civil and criminal matters.

Our courts are the most visible and open part of our legal institutions. Unlike the police and corrections, any day you can enter a courtroom in the United States and observe the proceedings. Whether civil or criminal matters are concerned, the basic principle of our democratic system is the openness of the adjudication of matters in the court. Therefore the courts are an open, public, and accessible institution (Murphy and Pritchett, 1986).

The court work group is basic to understanding how decisions are made within our courts. This work group includes the judge, district attorney, defense attorney, court clerk, witnesses, defendants, sheriffs, and the audience. As Neubauer discusses (1996), the relationships among members of the courtroom work group are important to understand when we look at court decisions. Our system is based on an adversarial model, with the judge being the arbitrator between the prosecution, or plaintiff, and the defense lawyer

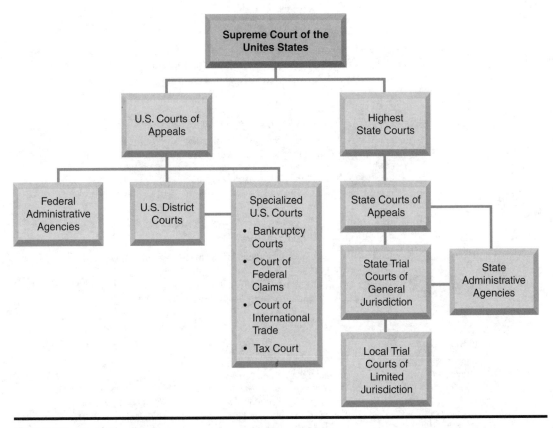

FIGURE 5.1   Dual Court System

for the defendant. Historically, as we have noted earlier, the legal profession itself has been largely male and white. In the last several decades, there has been a large influx of women and an increasing proportion of minority members into the legal profession (Neubauer, 1996). Nonetheless, the courtroom remains mainly a white-male bastion.

The United States is unique in the western democratic world in that major actors in its legal and criminal justice system are elected. This includes judges, district attorneys, and sheriffs, among others, with the most important actors being the judge and the district attorney or prosecuting attorney. Although judges and district or prosecuting attorneys are appointed in the federal system, they are elected in the state system. This of course, explicitly politicizes the judicial process. Although the judge holds the ultimate power within the courtroom, in recent decades district attorneys and prosecutors have gained increasing power, specifically through legislation tying the hands of judges in sentencing. Such laws as three strikes and you're out, mandatory minimums, and sentencing guidelines all limit the discretionary power of judges. This increases the discretionary power of prosecutors, giving them a lot more bargaining power in laying charges, obtaining plea bargains, and controlling the courtroom. Therefore, the discretionary power of judges has not been eliminated, but instead, some of it has been placed in the hands of district attorneys and

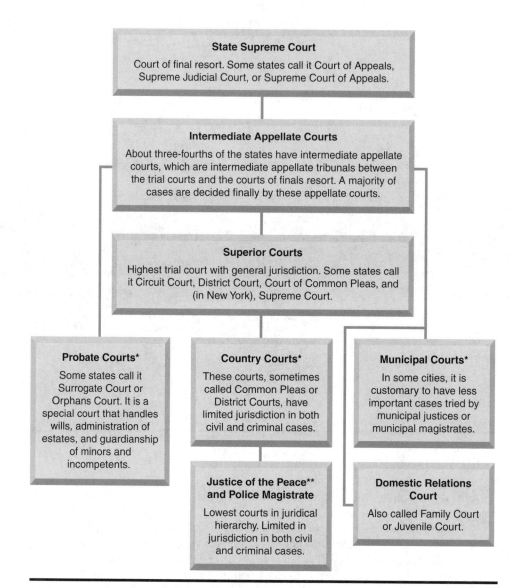

FIGURE 5.2   The Typical State Court System

*Courts of special jurisdiction, such as probate, family, or juvenile, and the so-called inferior courts, such as common pleas or municipal courts, may be separate courts or may be part of the trial court of general jurisdiction.

**Justices of the peace do not exist in all states. Their jurisdiction varies greatly from state to state when they do exist.

prosecutors who do not operate as much in the public eye. As will be evident from the readings in Part Five, nonlegal factors such as race, ethnicity, social class, and gender play a significant role in the decisions of the actors in the courtroom (Report of the Second Circuit Task Force on Gender, Racial, and Ethnic Fairness in the Courts, 1997; Fletcher, 1996;

Dershowitz, 1996). Fortunately, research on these nonlegal factors (Steffensmeir and De-muth, 2001) is being undertaken in several states. Some states have established standing commissions, such as the Washington State Minority and Justice Commission, to research and report on such issues. From the laying of charges to bail, plea negotiation, and sentencing, these factors remain significant (Fletcher, 1996). Although court procedures are no longer expressly discriminatory in law, there is evidence of *de facto* disparity and discrimination in the courts.

The first reading in Part Five, " 'Flotsam on the Sea of Humanity': A View from the Bench on Class, Race, and Gender," provides an unusual insight into the observations of a sitting judge. Due to judicial ethics, past practice, and notions of the rule of law, judges usually do not publicly present their ideas on such issues. Here, Justice Justin Johnson, writing as an intermediate appellate court judge serving the Superior Court of Pennsylvania, provides a critical analysis from his observations and experience of the importance of class, race, and gender in the court system. Although he is African American, Justice Johnson points out that he has the privilege of being male and a member of the professional class. Nonetheless, he has experienced racism and discrimination, and these experiences will continue because he cannot change his color.

Johnson begins by discussing three prominent women lawyers who were considered for the position of Attorney General of the United States. He notes that, although Janet Reno became the first female Attorney General of the United States, sexism was quite evident in the appointment proceedings. More specifically, Reno had no children or family to support, and therefore she was more attractive than the other two candidates who had to juggle a professional career and child rearing.

The next case that Johnson cites concerns a poor African American woman serving a minimum of six and a maximum of twelve years in a maximum-security women's prison as a result of attempting to shoplift $13.11 worth of cigarettes and a $17.99 pair of jeans. Johnson points out how the inferior status of being poor, black, and female contributed to this outrageous sentence.

In another case of a Black man on trial for rape, the prosecution used the race card by noting that the defendant was living in common law with a white woman. As the only Black judge on the Superior Court of Pennsylvania at the time, Johnson notes that if he hadn't experienced being singled out because of his race, the appeal of this Black man probably would have been ignored.

By contrast, the case of Judge Wachtler reveals that being a white male of upper social class means that, even if one is accused of extortion, blackmail, threat, kidnaping, and sexual harassment, one's trial can become a trial of the victim. This case also shows how the woman complainant can be minimized or denigrated, whereas the male accused receives sympathy from the press; the single mother who brought the charges against this influential Court of Appeals judge did not receive any sympathy.

Johnson concludes his critical analysis by citing Judge Leon Higginbotham, Jr., Chief Judge Emeritus of the Third Circuit Court of Appeals of Pennsylvania. In a letter he sent to newly appointed United States Supreme Court Justice Clarence Thomas, Higginbothem notes that Justice Thomas's place in history will be determined to the extent that he "provides a defense of the weak, poor, minorities, women, disabled, and the powerless." Higginbothem issued this public challenge to the new U.S. Supreme Court justice who ironically had been accused by Prof. Anita Hill of sexual harassment. In that case, Hill was characterized unkindly by the press, and to a great extent Justice Thomas was viewed as a victim. Nonetheless, Higginbothem was emphasizing that one should not forget one's own past and the history of discrimination against the poor, minorities, and women in general. Even if Thomas as an individual had overcome such potentially debilitating statuses, he should still be an advocate for those less powerful and less fortunate. Subsequent decisions by Justice Thomas, however, suggest that he is generally less sympathetic to the poor, disadvantaged, women, and minorities than those groups would like.

In the next reading, " 'Enough is Enough': Battered Women's Decision Making around Court Orders of Protection," Karla Fischer and Mary Rose provide an in-depth look at the decision making process of battered women when they seek court orders of protection. Based on a survey of 287 battered women and subsequent interviews with a subsample, we are given the perspective of the complainant regarding the court process. Often our research entails looking at statistics on outcomes, but this research provides qualitative data from women going through this process and gives a voice to the victim, someone who is not often addressed in the research.

Fischer and Rose first address the battered women's initial reason for obtaining court orders, and they discover that all of the women initially made a decision that they had endured enough abuse and wanted to exit the cycle. Domestic abuse is a manifestation of unequal power relationships and generally is cyclical in nature, in contrast to a more equitable relationship in which power is shared. Students of domestic violence agree that although such cycles are often evident, the decision to leave the relationship is a difficult one to make.

Fischer and Rose point out some of the barriers to obtaining orders of protection, including the fears that women who seek such orders have, such as the fear of having to call the police if the order is violated. Battered women also fear the actual court process, which is quite intimidating. As one observer notes, "if one set out by design to devise a system for provoking intrusive post-traumatic symptoms, one could not do better than a court of law" (Herman, 1992, p. 72). Those who have worked in the court system may not view it as trauma producing, but those who have had no prior experience with the courts—for instance defendants, witnesses, accused, or plaintiffs—often attest to the traumatic nature of this experience. In addition, many women who have had previous negative experiences with the law may be fearful of engaging with the courts again. Women also fear exposing their private problems to the public through an open forum. Finally, battered women justifiably fear retaliation from their partners. One of the most dangerous times for battered women occurs after they have left their partners; during this period, men disproportionately tend to murder or assault the women they have abused.

In spite of these fears, the final motivator, according to this research, is that battered women want a public record of this abuse, and they want their abusers to be forced to publicly acknowledge their crime in a court of law. They also want their abusers to recognize that society is intolerant of abuse and that the women they abuse are not willing victims. In this way, battered women gain some measure of control over their lives. As all the research on domestic violence shows, such violence is a form of power and control.

An order of protection gives a feeling of empowerment to the battered women. Many abused women emphasize the symbolic nature of this order, stating that it makes them feel better about themselves, gives them more control of their lives, and shows that they have started in a new direction. It also symbolizes the break of the cycle of domination and control by the abuser. In a thoughtful discussion of the implications of their research for the legal system, the authors point out that police officers, lawyers, judges, or other members of the legal system may be discouraged by the fact that women often drop their orders of protection (approximately 50 percent nationwide). However, from the viewpoint of battered women, the dropping of that order may reflect that they have already gotten what they have needed from it. The research encourages those in the criminal justice and legal systems to realize that they haven't failed if orders of protection are dropped or if the woman returns to the abuser. This is all part of a process, and from the viewpoint of the battered woman, it may be in her best interest to use only part of the legal system. Members of the courtroom setting and the police need to realize that they should be available to help at all times, even when women have not pursued the process to the extent that others would like.

The significance of social class and the sentencing of the traditional offender are addressed in the next reading, "Socioeconomic Status and the Sentencing of the Traditional Offender." The authors pursue conflict theory (see Part Three) to overview prior research and to interpret their own empirical investigation. Conflict theory presumes that those who have less power and are in the lower class will receive more severe legal sanctions than those who have more power and wealth. In reviewing the findings of thirty-eight sentencing studies, D'Alessio and Stolzenberg point out that, although results are mixed, the studies reveal sentencing disparities related to class, including differences in sentencing for first-degree murder and in applying the death sentence. The authors point out that most of the differences in findings among these earlier studies are due to problems in the research themselves. Firstly, the definition of socioeconomic status (i.e., class) varies in the research. Many of the studies also have problems with sample selection, which affects the outcome. Finally, earlier research did not include a disaggregation of data by type of offense.

In their own study of nearly 3,000 offenders committed to the custody of the Florida Department of Corrections, D'Alessio and Stolzenberg found the severity of the legal sanctions depends not solely on legal factors but also on the interaction between the offender and the offense. Contrary to popular belief, sentencing guidelines do not reduce disparity, especially in the sentencing of non–property offenders. That the nonlegal factor of socioeconomic status affects the sentencing of offenders should not be a surprise to any student of law and justice (Kairys, 1990). Money, or the lack of it, helps determine the type of justice you receive. In a fee-for-service legal system, the more money you have to spend, the better the lawyer you can hire, and the more research and investigation you can do on behalf of your defense. Recall also that the definition of crime itself is influenced by economics and politics; traditional common-law theft is criminalized, whereas white-collar and corporate theft, and violence for that matter, are generally not criminalized. As sociologist C. Wright Mills noted some time ago, "It is better to steal ten cents from 100,000 customers at the point of a corporation than to steal $10,000 from a bank at a point of a gun, and it is also safer" (Mills, 1956, p. 95). Observers of corporate and white-collar crime note that often the violence and economic costs of corporate and white-collar crime aren't even considered criminal, but instead are usually pursued, if at all, through regulatory law. Thus we do not see these individuals—whether they are legal entities, such as corporations, or members of an organization—in the criminal court. As in the Ford

Pinto and the Firestone tire cases, at most, the cases entail only civil action. Class, or socioeconomic status, thus affect the sentencing of the traditional offender, as well as the legal definition of the "traditional offense" (Reiman, 2001).

STUDY QUESTIONS

1. Define the "rule of law" and discuss its significance to constitutional democracies.

2. Identify the levels of our court system and the significance of the principles of precedent and *stare decisis.*

3. Who are the main actors in the courtroom work group, and how do politics play a role in their operation?

4. According to Justice Johnson, how do race, class, and gender affect justice in courts?

5. Discuss the decision to seek court orders of protection by victims and the significance of those decisions to the victim.

6. How does social class affect the sentencing of the traditional offender?

REFERENCES

Berman, Harold J. (1983). *Law and Revolution: The Formation of the Western Legal Tradition.* Cambridge, Mass.: Harvard University Press.

Christie, Nils (1978). *Conflicts as Property in the Sociology of Law: A Conflict Perspective,* C. Reasons and R. Rich (Eds.). Toronto: Butterworths.

Dershowitz, Alan M. (1996). *Reasonable Doubts: The Criminal Justice System and the O. J. Simpson Case.* New York: Touchstone.

Dicey, Albert Vern (1885). *Law of the Constitution.* London: Macmillan.

Fine, Bob (1984). *Democracy and the Rule of Law.* London: Pluto Press.

Fletcher, George P. (1996). *With Justice For Some: Protecting Victims' Rights in Criminal Trials.* Reading, Mass.: Addison-Wesley.

Hay, Douglas (1975). "Property, Authority and the Criminal Law." In *Albion's Fatal Tree.* D. Hay, P. Linebough, J. Rule, E. P. Thompson, and C. Winslow (Eds.). New York: Pantheon.

Herman, Judith (1992). *Trauma and Recovery.* New York: Basic Books.

Johnson, Herbert A., and Nancy Travis Wolfe (1996). *History of Criminal Justice,* 2nd ed. Cincinnati: Anderson.

Kairys, David (1990). *The Politics of Law: A Progressive Critique,* revised ed. New York: Pantheon.

Kerruish, Valerie (1991). *Jurisprudence As Ideology.* London: Routledge.

Mills, C. Wright (1956). *The Power Elite.* New York: Oxford University Press.

Murphy, Walter F., and C. Herman Pritchett (1986). *Courts, Judges and Politics: An Introduction to the Judicial Process,* 4th ed. New York: McGraw-Hill.

Neubauer, David W. (1996). *America's Courts and the Criminal Justice System,* 5th ed. Belmont, Cal.: Wadsworth.

Reasons, Charles E. (1985). "Ideology, Law, Public Opinion and Workers' Health." In *Law in a Cynical Society,* Dala Gibson and Janet Baldwin (Eds.). Vancouver: Carswell Company, pp. 262–282.

Reiman, Jeffrey (2001). *The Rich Get Richer and the Poor Get Prison,* 6th ed. Boston: Allyn and Bacon.

Report of the Second Circuit Task Force on Gender, Racial and Ethnic Fairness in the Courts (1997).

Steffensmeir, Darrell, and Stephen Demuth (2001). "Ethnicity and Judges' Sentencing Decisions: Hispanic-Black-White Comparisons," *Criminology 39:* 145–178.

Thompson, E. P. (1976). *The Making of the English Working Class.* London: Penguin.

Thompson, E. P. (1977). *Whigs and Hunters.* London: Penguin.

Tiger, Michael, and Murray Levy (1977). *Law and the Rise of Capitalism.* New York: Monthly Review Press.

Tocqueville, Alexis de (1980/1835). *On Democracy, Revolution and Society* (trans. J. Stone and S. Mennell). Chicago: University of Chicago Press.

Walker, Samuel, Cassia Spohn, and Miriam DeLane (2000). *The Color of Justice,* 2nd ed. Belmont, Cal.: Wadsworth.

Zatz, Marjorie S., and Edward L. Portillos (2000). "Voices from the Barrio: Chicano/A Gang, Families, and Communities," *Criminology 38:* 369–402.

"Flotsam on the Sea of Humanity"

A View from the Bench on Class, Race, and Gender

JUSTIN M. JOHNSON

On Wednesday, March 10, 1993, the Senate Judiciary Committee voted unanimously to endorse the nomination of Janet Reno to be the chief law-enforcement officer of these United States. That committee, which included women for the first time—thanks incidentally to the Anita Hill–Clarence Thomas contretemps—engaged in a two-day love fest before sending the nomination to the Senate floor, where the full Senate voted 98–0 to confirm her nomination as attorney general. She was sworn in last Friday.

A stranger to this country, who had not set foot on our shores until late February of this year, might mistakenly believe that Miss Reno's ascendancy to her new position was based solely on her admittedly excellent record as the chief prosecutor in Dade County, Florida. Those of us who are taking time to reflect upon the concept of class, race, and gender know differently.

My chief concern is directed toward the marginalized women at the lower end of the social scale. The Baird–Wood–Reno story, however, gives us a very current, sharply focused opportunity to see how gender can play a pivotal role when reviewing the qualifications of persons to fill the highest executive office within our federal justice system. I do not have to defend Zoe Baird's

Justin M. Johnson is an intermediate appellate court judge serving on the Superior Court in Pennsylvania (Suite 2702, Grant Building, Pittsburgh, PA 15219). This article is taken from remarks given before the Academy of Criminal Justice Sciences, 1993 Annual Meeting on March 19, 1993.

employment of undocumented aliens in order to assert that sexism pervaded the entire episode with both Baird and Judge Kimba M. Wood. Baird had admitted violating the law; arguably, that alone should disqualify her for such a high post. Judge Wood, however, had employed an alien for child-care at a time when it was legal to do so. She had paid all required taxes and filed all required forms. Because she chose to have a career, child care was a necessity. Her forced withdrawal as a nominee for attorney general clearly reflected the gender tilt imposed and maintained by the ruling male establishment. It is because her qualifications to the job were so outstanding that the tragedy of gender bias becomes more compelling. It is small comfort that the president finally turned to another woman, without children or a family to support, in hopes of finally filling the post.

We should not deceive ourselves that the unanimous confirmation of Janet Reno is anything more than a bright, shooting star across the heavens within a galaxy of bias, repression, and intolerance on matters of gender. With this as background, I would like to consider several cases from my own experience that may help to place the concept of class, race, and gender in a real perspective. The present position of this nation on matters of racism, sexism, and classism deserves our serious attention.

When I think of the interrelationship between these terms and, more particularly, their impact upon our system of criminal justice, one case with elements of all three quickly comes to mind. The

Pennsylvania Superior Court had occasion to consider an appeal involving a sentencing issue, where the defendant argued that her sentence on several petty-theft charges had been harsh and excessive.[1] The defendant, Cynthia Ellman, was a poor, African-American woman who had been caught shoplifting on three separate occasions.

Ellman had attempted to shoplift four packs of cigarettes on one occasion, and a carton of cigarettes on a second attempt, both at a Loblaw's grocery store in Erie County, Pennsylvania. She tried to shoplift a pair of designer jeans while on still another foray into a Value City discount store in a shopping mall in the same county. The full extent of her bounty, had she been successful in getting away from the store each time without being caught, would have been 16 packs of cigarettes and a pair of denim jeans with a total value of less than $32.00.

In Pennsylvania, we have recidivist provisions in our retail-theft statute; a third offense for shoplifting is classified as a third-degree felony, permitting a term of imprisonment of seven years.

This poor black woman was sentenced by a judge to two concurrent sentences of 2½ to 5 years of imprisonment on the separate attempts, to shoplift the cigarettes. Immediately following her sentencing on those charges, she was taken before another judge who had previously convicted her of shoplifting the flowered jeans, worth $17.99. The second judge sentenced Ellman to serve a term of 3½ to 7 years, the maximum permitted by law for a third-degree felony. This latter sentence was imposed to run *consecutively* to the other concurrent sentences of 2½ to 5 years. We end up with Cynthia Ellman serving a minimum of six and a maximum of 12 years in a maximum-security women's prison in Pennsylvania as a result of attempting to make off with $13.11 worth of cigarettes and one pair of jeans worth $17.99.

In imposing sentence on the attempted theft of jeans, the trial judge wrote on the guideline sentence form:

> *Def. is incapable of and unwilling to be rehabilitated. She is a career criminal unrepentant and surely as she stands before the court. She is flotsam on the sea of humanity, worthless and undeterred by any law. The only remedy of disposition which this court has at its disposal is incarceration—and for an extended period.*

Richard L. Nygaard, the state trial judge who wrote these words, finding the poor, African-American woman before him to be useless and without value, was subsequently appointed to the Third Circuit Court of Appeals by President Reagan in November 1988.

As a member of the three-judge state appellate panel that reviewed these judgments of sentence, I was unable to locate anything that I could characterize as an aggravating circumstance for sentencing purposes. At oral argument, I asked the attorney for the Commonwealth to support and defend the aggregate six to 12 years of imprisonment for the attempted theft of 14 packs of cigarettes and a pair of designer jeans. He replied that the sentence can be justified as necessary for the protection of the public." These are magic words found in our sentencing code to be applied as a general principle when choosing between probation, a fine, or partial versus total confinement. My response to the attorney then remains my response now: I am *one* member of the public who, on the facts set forth in the *Ellman* case, does not require quite so much protection.

It is entirely possible that Loblaw's grocery store could construct an argument that their self-interest might be advanced by imprisoning a person for a minimum of 2½ years for attempting to steal 14 packs of cigarettes worth $13.11. In the same vein, perhaps Value City might argue that 3½ years is a reasonable minimum period of incarceration for a third-time offender caught pilfering a pair of jeans worth $17.99. In my judgment, however, the victims in this case are not the retail stores that, not incidentally, recovered their merchandise and did not appear at sentencing, but Cynthia Ellman and the Pennsylvania taxpayers who are forced to maintain her in a maximum-security prison for a minimum of six years at considerable expense, all because of some attempted petty thefts by an admitted recidivist.

I mentioned that I was one of a three-judge panel that heard and decided this appeal. I found myself alone in believing that the sentence could not be squared with our sentencing guidelines in Pennsylvania. In their opinion affirming the consecutive sentences, my colleagues conceded that 3½ to 7 years' imprisonment for stealing $18 worth of merchandise is a harsh sentence for a crime that, if it had been Ellman's first offense, would be punishable by a maximum sentence of 90 days' imprisonment. They also acknowledged that the severity of the sentence was exacerbated by the fact that the Nygaard court ran it consecutively to the sentence imposed in the other shoplifting appeal. Over my dissent, the majority justified affirming the sentences with the following language:

> However, we note that Judge Nygaard, like Judge Pfadt, followed the legislative construct, consulted the guidelines, sentenced appellant in the aggravated range, and explained his reasons for doing so. Thus, if the sentence is harsh, it is so not because the trial court abused its discretion, but rather because the legislature has determined that recidivist retail theft offenders should be sentenced harshly. Accordingly, we cannot conclude that the court erred in imposing this maximum sentence.[2]

A visitor to Pennsylvania who would review everything that happened to this particular poor, black woman might conclude that class, race, and gender all were implicated and came together in some perverse way to seal Cynthia Ellman's fate.

Let me consider another incident from my own judicial experience that may illustrate aspects of racism, classism, and sexism from a slightly different perspective. I was member of a three-judge panel that was reviewing a conviction in a rape case, *Commonwealth* v. *Taliaferro*.[3] The major issue on appeal was whether trial counsel had been ineffective for failing to object to the D.A.'s reference to the defendant's common-law wife who was sitting in the courtroom during trial. Taliaferro was black. The rape victim was black. Taliaferro's wife was not a witness. She was white. She was dressed somewhat garishly, with uncoordinated blouse and stretch slacks. Taliaferro had already been tried once, resulting in a hung jury. At the first trial, the assistant district attorney, over the objection of defense counsel, had drawn attention to the wife. At the second trial, the assistant district attorney *again* drew attention to the wife, during cross-examination of the defendant. The assistant D.A. had asked, looking to the back of the courtroom: "Is this your wife in the back of the courtroom in the green pants and orange sweater?," pointing to the white woman for all jurors to see.[4] After Taliaferro answered the first question with a simple, respectful, "Yes sir, it is," the prosecutor went on, "and that's your common-law wife. You never had a ceremony with her or anything like that?"[5]

On post-trail motions, the trial judge admitted that there was no apparent reason for the questions, but declined to find error. On appeal, my colleagues wrote a proposed decision finding no ineffectiveness in defense counsel's failure to object to this line of questioning. I circulated a dissent that was joined by the third judge, thus becoming the majority view. The decision was filed reversing the judgment of sentence and granting a new trial. On petition for re-argument, the entire court voted to hear the case again, which meant that *seven* judges would decide the case, supplanting the decision of the three-judge panel.

After re-argument on our court, there were only two judges, including myself, joining Judge Brosky's plurality decision. One judge concurred in the result, and three judges dissented.[6] Judge Brosky found the cross-examination that invited the jurors to reflect upon class and race to be both irrelevant and prejudicial. Only two judges of the other six expressly agreed with him. The *en banc* court split four–three, on this issue!

When the *Taliaferro* case came before our panel back in 1983, I *knew* that the deliberate reference to the race of the defendant's wife was intentional, improper, and unjust. The incident reflected some of my own life experiences. I would suppose that some of my colleagues, who saw no legal harm and voted to affirm the conviction, in good faith were unable to see how a reference to a "common law" white wife of a black defendant could have any improper influence on the jury. Perhaps subconsciously, one or more of my colleagues may have believed that it was *wrong* for Taliaferro to be expecting regular "justice" when he would *dare* to come into the courtroom with a partner of another race!

To me, the assistant district attorney had deliberately and, let me say, malevolently tried to sway the jury by bringing to their attention that the black man on trial for rape was living, common law—God forbid—with a white woman: This improperly injected both class and race into the trial.

The matter was reversed and Taliaferro presumably got another trial. My concern in that particular case was not whether the defendant had, in fact, committed rape, but rather whether we would permit a conviction to stand where the prosecutor had deliberately injected racism and classism, and the trial judge either could not discern it or did not care enough to do anything about it, at that time.

I was then, as now, the only black judge on the Superior Court of Pennsylvania. What would have happened to Taliaferro's plea if, perchance, I or another like me who had *experienced* being singled out, had not been among those called upon to review Taliaferro's fate?

While gender appears to be the key limiting factor influencing the destiny of white women, there is evidence that race and racism remain the critical elements for a black male, even where gender is irrelevant and class has been overcome. Last month, a black United States member of Congress went on trial again, two years after a first jury had deadlocked along racial lines. The case, which involves federal bank fraud charges, is interesting because it appears to be the reverse of the Rodney King situation. Harold E. Ford was first tried in his hometown, Memphis, which is 55% black and where the congressman's family commands both respect and a powerful political machine. At the first trial, the jury of eight blacks and four whites was divided along racial lines after two and one half months of testimony. A mistrial was declared. A year later, the trial judge directed that the second

jury be picked from 17 rural west Tennessee counties where the population was about 18% black.

Congressman Ford appealed that order of court, which was upheld by the Sixth Circuit Court of Appeals. The Supreme Court declined to hear the case. In February of 1993, the Justice Department reversed the position it had held supporting the court's plan to select jurors from a predominantly white, rural section of the state and asked the court to reconsider the process. This led to the resignation of the United States Attorney in Memphis; two of his assistants asked to be removed from the case. Reconsideration was denied.

We all know that the white police officers in the first Rodney King case were able to have their trial transferred away from the county where the incident occurred, just as we all know that the jury that decided their fate did not contain any blacks. We also know that jurors either with prior police experience or related to people involved in criminal-justice enforcement were seated on that Simi Valley jury. In Congressman Ford's case, it appears that an intentional step was taken to ensure that the black defendant did *not* have an opportunity to be tried within his home community by jurors, among whom some may have been sympathetic to his cause.

Ford has contended through it all that the prosecution was racially and politically motivated. The fact that the then-acting Attorney General, Stuart M. Gerson, a Republican holdover from the Bush administration, finally decided to back the defendant's request does not detract from that contention. This case illustrates that even if one has the power, which appears to be a plus as far as class issues are concerned, and even if one is of the "correct" gender, that overriding issue of race can still be a trump card available to be played in any hand and in any game. Ford's status as a Congressman could not trump the fact that, in the final analysis, in too many parts of the system, he is still "just another nigger! "

If we look at the recent situation of Sol Wachtler and Jean Harris in New York—two separate incidents—we get a better appreciation of how class and gender can operate within the criminal-justice system, even where race may not appear to be a factor. The reaction by the media, and indeed the reaction of the justice system itself, to the escapades of Judge Wachtler point up the fact that class can play an important role in how an incident is handled.

Diane McWhorter pointed out in an Op-Ed item in the *New York Times*[7] that the case involving then-Chief Judge Wachtler was treated by the press, public opinion, and the legal system as a "tragedy." The judge was accused of extortion, blackmail, threatened kidnapping, and sexual harassment, but you would have been hard pressed to find a "victim." The victim appeared to be Judge Wachtler! The media had "no explanation" for his behavior outside of cancer or some other unfathomable disease. He received special treatment and was shielded from the public and the press when being chauffeured to and from arraignment. Presumably because of his "illness," he spent no time in a jail cell, but was accommodated first at a hospital and then at his home. It was stated that his conduct had to be the result of some unidentified medical condition, although this strange malady had escaped notice by his colleagues on the Court of Appeals. His fellow judges refused to suspend him, expressing "deepest sympathy for Judge Wachtler and his family." His delayed resignation was accepted "reluctantly but necessarily."

By contrast, the object of the judge's criminal actions, Joy Silverman and her 14-year-old daughter, did not receive any sympathy. One might speculate that had the wealthy Ms. Silverman not been an important Republican fund-raiser who could get the director of the FBI on the phone, this case might still be ongoing and Sol Wachtler might still be the highest judicial officer in the state of New York. I would venture that Cynthia Ellman, who is still working off her minimum six years for attempting to shoplift cigarettes and a pair of jeans, would gladly exchange places with Sol Wachtler. Yet that would not work, because—even if, by some miracle, she were to escape her poverty—she could not lay aside her race, or her sex. Even if she could travel from Erie, Pennsylvania, to Al-

bany, New York, to face the criminal-justice system of that state, our criminal-justice system would continue to see her as, and she would remain, "flotsam on the sea of humanity."

Of course, not everything that has resulted from the incidents involving Sol Wachtler has been bad. Less than a month ago, the same governor who belatedly commuted Jean Harris' sentence nominated Judge Judith S. Kaye to replace Wachtler and she will become the first woman Chief Judge of that state's highest court, the Court of Appeals, In New York, Judge Kaye will be responsible for running a system with 13,000 employees, including nearly 1,200 judges and a budget approaching one billion dollars. According the *New York Times,*[8] Judge Kaye will be one of five women serving as chief judges in the nation.

And what about Jean Harris? Here is a woman who certainly had both class and race going for her—or, at least, neither stood as an obstacle when she faced our criminal justice system some 12 years ago, following the slaying of Dr. Herman Tarnower, the author of the best-selling book on the Scarsdale Diet. However, her sex, and probably her age, 56, were a handicap. Jean Harris, the then headmistress of an exclusive girls' finishing school, was depicted as a woman scorned, who intentionally shot Tarnower after discovering some personal items belonging to a 37-year-old companion of Tarnower's in his bedroom. During her trial and throughout her incarceration, Harris was a model citizen. In prison, she taught and assisted her less fortunate sister inmates and was recognized by all as an outstanding role model. The New York governor rejected her applications for clemency three times and only approved her release after she had suffered a second heart attack in prison and was scheduled for surgery.

One can fairly ask whether Jean Harris would have to endure the length of incarceration placed upon her had she not been viewed as a vengeful female, much as Anita Hill was portrayed during the Clarence Thomas hearings 18 months ago. Last Friday, when interviewed on the "Today Show," Ms. Harris reminded us that, while it was good that she has finally been set free, there are many women more deserving of release than herself who remain in prison. Where class and race may of slight impact, gender and age can play a pivotal role in how the criminal-justice system treats its offenders. As Jean Harris reminds us, good fortune, grace, or pardon may sometimes shine on one who lacks only the "correct" gender, while bypassing or ignoring others less fortunate who lack the "correct" class, race, *and* gender.

Thus, if we look at Sol Wachtler as being white, male, and the highest judicial officer in the state, it should be fairly easy to predict the the criminal-justice system will afford him favorable treatment, even though it might not be done intentionally. By way of contrast, when we bring together the three factors possessed by Cynthia Ellman—not only is she both black and female, but without any resources and perceived as being in the lowest class of society—it is not surprising that the cumulative effect of the three "negatives" results in an excessive sentence for shoplifting, a sentence that in its implementation, I would regard as criminal.

I recognized that other factors, such as religion, geography, age, and national origin can influence the criminal-justice process. Certainly, anyone of these factors, if applied negatively within our society or within the criminal-justice system, would tend to aggravate the outcome for a defendant already saddled with the negatively perceived factors relating to race, class, and gender. It does seem reasonable to conclude, nevertheless, that the three factors of race, class and gender can have an overwhelming effect upon how decisions are reached in the justice system, and how we, as citizens, perceive whether justice has been done.

While I have mentioned two cases involving high-profile persons on the matter of gender, we cannot ignore the debilitating effect that our system of justice has on women in prison. During the 1980s, the number of women in both state and federal prisons tripled. Peter Applebome,[9] writing in the *New York Times,* placed the number at 90,000. The daily population of women in New York City's correction system went from 317 to 1,700 per day between 1980 and 1990. It has been suggested by a lawyer working with woman prisoners in Atlanta that children of prison inmates are five times as likely as most Americans to end up in prison themselves. About three-quarters of the women in state and federal prisons are mothers. Most have more than two children, Applebome's article[10] mentioned one recent study in which it was found that perhaps half the children never see their mothers while they are in prison. This is because female inmates, more often than their male counterparts, are likely to be the child's sole support, with no other adult figure to bring children to visit them.

The isolation and hopelessness that faces many African-American women in prison, arising in part from the effects of class, race, and gender was brought home for me during a visit to the women's prison at Goochland, Virginia, just outside Richmond. The poignancy that accompanies a consideration of how race, class, and gender can follow a marginalized person is seen in this experience. I was in Richmond attending a meeting of the Presbyterian Criminal Justice Committee. We spoke with Goochland inmates who participated in the M.I.L.K. Program (Mothers/fathers inside loving kids, sponsored by parents anonymous). One mother had been in Goochland for eight years. When started with M.I.L.K., her daughters were 11 and 12. Now they are 19 and 20 and bring their children (the prisoner's grandchildren) to visit four times a year. Another African-American inmate had been returned to prison for violating her probation. She had been originally convicted for shoplifting. When released on probation, she rejoined her family only to discover that there were no sheets for her children's beds. She issued a worthless check to buy sheets and found herself back in Goochland, this time for an extended stay of seven years. When she is released, she still will not have funds to buy sheets for her children's beds. She still will be black. She still will be poor. Unless the system changes its standards, we can predict only continuing tragedy for this woman, her children, and indeed our community.

I began my remarks by considering three white, woman lawyers, with identical gender and race, but with upper class status that went from Zoe Baird's top executive position as the $500,000 per year chief house counsel for one of the nation's largest insurance companies, through Kimba Wood, a highly respected federal district judge earning $129,000 per year, to Janet Reno, chief prosecutor for a Florida county earning perhaps $80,000 per year. All three of these women tried to scale the gender wall on their way to national public office; Miss Reno successfully got over it. We have also looked at some of the ways in which class, race, and gender affect the lives and fortunes of men and women, both blacks and whites, and persons from the highest reaches of our society as well as the marginalized and oppressed.

The concept can have supportive outcomes—witness Sol Wachtler—and it can have destructive results—witness Cynthia Ellman or the woman in Goochland prison with no sheets for her children. There is nothing accidental about the way class, race, and gender pervade every aspect of our criminal-justice system. Yet this is not surprising, since our justice system is simply another aspect, another piece, of the total United States socioeconomic system where negative forces like classism, racism, and sexism have always maintained a strong hold.

The problems facing our society do not appear to be lessening, even after the great society, promises of a kinder, gentler nation, and other broad schemes filled with hope and fanfare while delivering little. As we see the numbers of my people being placed behind prison bars ever increasing, and as we hear the politicians proclaim that the best solution to our problems must entail longer prison sentences, increased opportunities for infliction of the death penalty, and a drawing-in of those individual rights that many of us cherish and take for granted, it is not surprising that we might turn to our judiciary and ask: What role do you see yourself playing in promoting the rights of African Americans, other minorities, and the poor?

The crises in our criminal-justice system cry out for a response from all citizens. Society should no longer tolerate the preservation of a system of justice and corrections that offers neither justice to the accused and convicted nor safety to society.

Judge A. Leon Higginbotham, Jr., Chief Judge Emeritus of our Third Circuit Court of Appeals, wrote an open letter to Justice Clarence Thomas,[11] soon after Thomas became the 106th justice of the United States Supreme Court. This letter has received much deserved widespread attention and study. Judge Higginbotham predicted, in closing his letter to Justice Thomas, that no issue would determine Justice Thomas' place in history so much as his "defense of the weak, the poor, minorities, women, the disabled and the powerless."[12] He correctly reminded the new justice that "the fundamental problems of the disadvantaged, women, minorities, and the powerless have not all been solved simply because you have 'moved on up' from Pin Point, Georgia, to the Supreme Court."[13] He was challenging the justice to choose which principles he would serve.

Similarly, we might say that those problems that Judge Higginbotham delineated and we here consider have not been solved simply because a woman sensitive to these issues has now been installed as the Attorney General of these United States. Each of us must answer for ourselves. I was an attorney before I was a judge. I was a Christian before I was an attorney. My family experienced hardship before it enjoyed comfort.

Like Judge Higginbotham, I can say that, in my lifetime, I have seen African Americans denied the right to vote, denied opportunities to pursue a proper education, denied the right to work, to live, and to play where they choose. Like Judge Higginbotham, I have personally known racial segregation and discrimination. Some might argue that, as an intermediate appellate court judge, I have moved into a more favored class, which along with my maleness, is to my advantage, and to the advantage of my family. That may well be true. Still, I have been black all of my life. And *that* will not change. Will our attitudes?

NOTES

1. *Commonwealth* v. *Ellman,* 389 Pa. Super. 647, 560 A. 2d 825 (1989).

2. *Commonwealth* v. *Ellman,* Nos. 00752-00755-PGH 87, slip op. at 11 (Pa.Super. March 28, 1989).

3. 309 Pa.Super. 446, 455 A.2d 694 (1983).

4. *Ibid,* at 451, 455 A.2d at 696.

5. *Ibid.*

6. *Ibid,* at 451, 455 A.2d at 698.

7. Diane McWhorter, "The Real Tragedy of Judge Wachtler." *New York Times* (November 13, 1992).

8. Sarah Lyles, "Cuomo Picks Woman as New York's Chief Judge." *New York Times* (February 22, 1993).

9. Peter Applebome, "Holding Fragile Families Together When Mothers Are Inmates." *New York Times* (December 27, 1992).

10. *Ibid.*

11. A. Leon Higginbotham, Jr., "An Open Letter to Justice Clarence Thomas from a Federal Judicial Colleague." 140 U. Pa. L.Rev. 1005 (1992).

12. *Ibid,* at 1025.

13. *Ibid,* at 1026.

When "Enough Is Enough"
Battered Women's Decision Making Around Court Orders of Protection

KARLA FISCHER
Duke University

MARY ROSE
Duke University

Different reasons compel battered women to seek court orders of protection. Battered women decide to invoke the legal system by determining that they have had "enough." At this point women must often confront significant barriers to obtaining court orders, most of which involve symbolic and tangible fears. A number of motivations, however seem to counteract these fears. In addition, women may experience psychological benefits from orders by gaining some measure of control in their lives. A greater understanding of the factors involved in such decision making may assist legal authorities who deal with battered women.

Throughout my whole marriage, people would say to me, "that's enough, you've just had enough." But when is enough enough? I never knew . . . and when has he had plenty of chances? . . . Everybody else was going, "I wouldn't let it go that far, that's enough, come on, that's enough." And I would sit and cry and go "okay, but I, I just don't know, because I've got a family." It's just like no one knows, unless you're there in the situation . . . where was the drawing point. . . . It's different for me because he raped me, and that was it for me. I meant that, it's like he made up my mind for me pretty much. I mean, he just actually did something so bad that I was out.

As researchers in domestic violence (e.g., Berger, Fischer, Campbell, and Rose 1994) and

law (e.g., Mahoney 1991) struggle to draw some conceptual circle around abusive behavior, women in chronically abusive relationships engage in a parallel psychological process of identifying or rejecting the label of "abused" (cf. Browne 1991). The above sample narrative of a battered woman reflects an internal hesitation: Is this situation bad enough to justify leaving? This hesitation can often be the starting point in women's decisions to consider outside help for the escalating violence in their lives, and it may also signal an acknowledgment of the negative impact of violence on their own as well as their children's physical and emotional well-being (Kirkwood 1993).

The search for the invisible "enough" line compels battered women to confront the serious obstacles that stand in the way of a successful escape from an abusive relationship. These barriers to leaving, well-documented and described by other researchers, include the economic and practical difficulties of leaving, the social and psychological ties between the abuser and the victim, as well as fear of retaliation by the abuser (e.g., Browne 1987; Ferraro and Johnson 1983; Fischer 1992; Gelles and Straus 1988; Kirkwood 1993; Martin 1976; Pagelow 1984; Sullivan and Davidson 1991).

Women may leave battering relationships in a number of ways, one of which may necessitate the assistance of the legal system through a court order of protection. Although rooted in the factors connected to leaving the abuser, invoking the legal system involves an additional conscious decision-making process. In this article, we explore the different reasons that battered women choose to invoke the power of the law to enforce their decisions to leave their abusers. Illustrated primarily through narrative analysis, the themes that underlie battered women's rationales for seeking court protection teach us about the meaning and impact of the law in battered women's lives. We end by discussing the psychological benefits of obtaining an order of protection, which provides additional insight on the role of law in interventions in domestic violence.

BATTERED WOMEN'S INITIAL REASONS FOR OBTAINING COURT ORDERS

Our work with battered women who seek court protection orders began through a study of women's experiences with court orders, conducted by the first author in a medium-sized midwestern county court. Obtaining a court order of protection involves a two-step process. First, there is an "emergency," or *ex parte,* hearing; here, the victim is usually granted a short-term restraining order that does not require that the abuser be notified of the legal process. Next, the women must return to court to obtain a more permanent order; this occurs after the legal papers, including notice of the second hearing, have been served on the abuser. One piece of this research surveyed a large

sample of battered women ($n = 287$) who were waiting at the courthouse after their temporary orders had been approved and their paperwork was being processed. In a brief questionnaire, they were asked to report their reasons for obtaining the order and their expectations for what that order would do for them.[1] Their collective answers to this questionnaire suggest a complex portrait of victims: they are choosing to leave their abusers after fairly extensive periods of abuse, which they view as escalating. Although they harbor doubts that the order itself will evoke change in the abuser, instead expecting his pattern of abuse to continue, they have faith that the legal system will protect them from further violence.

Nearly all women acknowledged that they had had "enough," stating that one reason for obtaining the order was that they were "tired of the abuse" (92%). Most of these women equated that with making a change in their lives (87%). For the majority of battered women, the order of protection was a last resort, after other sources of help seeking had failed (75%). Smaller numbers targeted specifically the abuser's failure to seek help for either his alcohol or drug problem (45%) or for his violent behavior (53%). Many women also pointed to the role that others had in encouraging their decisions to obtain the order, citing family and friends (74%), the police (50%), or other public agencies (30%).

The women's perceptions of the place of the violence in their relationships seemed to be crucial to their decisions to invoke court protection. Walker (1979) argued that most battering relationships occur in a "cycle," where the abuse occurs after a period of tension building and is followed by a "honeymoon," where the couple reconciles and the abuser is apologetic for what he did. Gradually, cycles become more frequent and the abuse within them more severe. The women in our sample appeared to have enhanced sensitivity to changes in the abuse, including some perspective on its cyclical nature. The women had been in fairly long-term relationships (average of 7 years), where the abuse had been occurring for an extended period of time (4 years, on average). In addition, most women (66%) had at least one child by their abusers. The majority of women acknowledged that the abuse was becoming both more severe (60%) and more frequent (59%). About half the women (43%) believed that the physical violence was becoming worse, whereas many more (85%) targeted the emotional abuse as the source of the escalation. Many women also were concerned because they believed that the abuse was beginning to affect their children (50%) or that the batterer was assaulting the children (15%). Therefore, in spite of strong social and psychological connections to their long-term relationships, these women were able to recognize the escalating and expanding abuse in their lives. In choosing to invoke the law's protection as they left their assailants, they broke the cycle of violence that (at least in part) kept them trapped in these relationships.

The implicit message behind an order of protection, from those women who sought it, seems to be "I can leave you, and you can't hurt me for it." They believe the legal system will stand behind them and reinforce that message. At the time they made the decision to obtain the order, 98% said that they would stay out of this relationship permanently. Most (85%) were confident of their ability to provide financially for themselves and their children without his assistance. They felt their decisions to obtain the orders were good ones (91%), and expressed feeling more in control of their lives (98%) and the relationship (89%), even in the face of a nagging belief that the assailant would violate the order (86%). Their overall positive outlook can be best understood in the context of the women's faith in the criminal justice system to protect them, as nearly all (95%) reported feeling confident that the police would respond rapidly to violations of the order. Thus what seems to have changed for these women is not the threat of future violence in their lives, but the belief that some outside intervention would be available to them.

BARRIERS TO OBTAINING ORDERS OF PROTECTION

The reasons that these women offer at the moment they actually obtain their order are only one part

necessary to understand their decision-making process. The second piece of our research has been to examine this process more closely. In a second study, a subsample ($n = 83$) of the original population that completed the initial questionnaire was interviewed shortly after their hearing regarding their permanent orders.[2] The themes that emerged from these narratives speak to the simultaneous presence of a wariness of the legal system, with a desperate need for life-change.

Because women anticipated that they might need to enforce their orders, foremost on many women's minds was the perceived difficulty of calling the police. This act involved an emotional toll and corresponding guilt attached to the image of their abusers' arrest. Several women put this rather simply:

> It's hard to tell the police to take your husband away.

> I had a hard time even calling the police on him because I was so emotionally attached.

> I thought, I cannot put someone in jail. I just can't . . . women [should] not have so much control of putting the men in jail.

On the other hand, to imagine calling the police gave some women a sense of ultimate power and control. This was occasionally reflected in an unrealistic assessment of police response to violations of orders:

> . . . but, you know, just at any moment [e.g., if she runs into him], if I just pick up the phone and call the police and that's just (an) automatic warrant for his arrest. It's not my warrant, it's the judge and it's the attorney's warrant.

For one woman, calling the police at some possible future time invoked fear that escalated to the point where she had to drop her order:

> I spent money on it. I spent the time. I really needed it, but, you know, when you get something like that . . . you have to work with the law . . . you have to be the one to dial the telephone. See, and I'm a chickenshit. And I couldn't dial those 3 numbers [911] I didn't want to cause a scene. . . .

Fear of calling the police if the order was violated was often connected to perceived negative consequences to obtaining court protection. Some women specifically mentioned, for example, that they had to overcome their fear of leaving the relationship permanently because they knew that obtaining the order would signal the end of their relationship:

> I guess part of it that was real intimidating is because I knew that when I did this that there would be a divorce. I knew that I was sealing my divorce papers as I was doing this.
> . . . I mean, I kept telling myself I can do this on my own, I can raise the kids, take care of the house, and be all right as a person and manage without him. And then when it was really coming down to it, I guess I was scared. I mean, I know that I can do it. But it was like facing reality . . . [and] the prospect of being alone.

For other women, the fears that were associated with court protection were less symbolic and more tangible. It is not uncommon for perpetrators to threaten their victims if abuse is revealed (Browne 1987). In this sample, some women were afraid of retaliation from their abusers, either because of prior threats around police involvement or a belief that the order itself would escalate the abuser's violence. Women occasionally reported that their abusers saw themselves as "above the law"; for example, that "no order was going to do anything for him." As illustrated by the following narrative, these women often take pride in swallowing their retaliation fright and in choosing to invoke court protection:

> He had threatened to smash my face in if I ever called the police. . . . You know, for me to really go out and do it is real significant to me. To go out and really take the initiative to really do something for myself.

The last set of fears that appear to be barriers for battered women obtaining court protection pertain to their fear of the actual court experience. This fear is at least partly located in stereotypes that only people who have engaged in criminal behavior belong in court; in addition, women experience feelings of shame about why they are appearing before a judge. Women's common characterizations of their actual court experiences were "scary" and "intimidating":

> Custody was never an issue but I was so scared. I thought, "God, the judge is going to think I'm an awful person, too. . . . Please don't let him take my child from me."

> But just the process, the legal process is really frightening. And if somebody isn't frightened by that whole process, they must be really callous or used to it or something.

> I was scared to death. . . . I was embarrassed. I was so deeply hurt to think that my life had come to this.

In discussing their reactions to their court experience, women occasionally remarked that this fear of the court process can be so overwhelming as to cause a traumatic dissociative reaction. As Herman (1992) observed: "If one set out by design to devise a system for provoking intrusive posttraumatic symptoms, one could not do better than a court of law" (p. 72). For example, one woman in our study relayed:

> I could stand up there and start crying, you know, and I really didn't know if I was going to be able to handle it. . . . When I walked in there and I sat down, that was me physically in there, but that was not me. . . . I was not there that day. . . . I was scared to death.

For many women, fear of encounters with the legal system was the result of previous negative experiences with the law, sometimes involving police responses to prior orders of protection (which a minority of women in our sample—17%—had obtained). The common thread among these women's narratives was that the law, either in response to the battering itself or to violations of orders, failed to care about the violation of their rights and rarely imposed consequences on the abusers for their actions:

> . . . they don't care. . . . They treat women like property anyway. The cops' attitudes are basically like that because I called the police on him several times. . . . He knew the law's attitude, too. He knew that.

He was taken to jail. I went to the hospital, had the x-rays and he was home before I was. . . . It made me feel, as far as he was concerned, that the [previous order] was not protecting me. Because every time I called, I mean they turned around and let him right back out. . . . I don't care even that one day that I let him in to use the phone, he was still in violation the minute he threw my head against the wall. And what the cops put me through, it made me feel like, unless I was seriously almost dead, I wouldn't call them again.

In sum, one of the major barriers to obtaining orders of protection that battered women report is fear. Some of these fears are tangible, borne out of threats of retaliation from the abuser or previous negative encounters with the legal system. However, what emerged in many women's narratives was also a more symbolic sense of dread that surrounds the imposition of a public solution to what they consider to be a private problem. In other words, some women view their use of the law as representative of a failure to negotiate the relationship on their own. This view of courts as an arena for those who cannot "handle" a private, relational issue has been documented among other populations who use courts to settle disputes (cf. Merry 1990). Coupled with highly specific and reasonable fears, admitting to a perceived failure on the part of women in this study makes engaging the legal system an extremely difficult step to take.

Although part of their decisions, battered women's reports of the barriers we have discussed are obviously not complete obstacles to obtaining court orders. The decision-making process seems to be capped by a final motivating force or event, one that requires them to move beyond these obstacles and seek court protection in the face of what might be overwhelming fears for other battered women who do not make this choice.

THE UNDERLYING PROCESS OF DECISIONS: THE FINAL MOTIVATORS

Our earlier characterization of the initial reasons battered women reported as significant in their decision to invoke legal protection indicates that these women have been in fairly long-term relationships in which the abuse has been occurring for an extended period of time. They recognize that the abuse is escalating and beginning to have a negative impact on their children, and they feel like the court is their last resort to being able to successfully end the violence in their lives. Sometimes the frustration of invoking what they see as a last resort turns into resentment for needing to have a judge enforce what they believe to be an inherent right:

> I mean it seems to me that it's kind of silly that a person even has to have a piece of paper, you know, you start thinking about life, liberty and the pursuit of happiness, and it's like, you should be entitled to that anyway. . . . I mean it seems to me that legally anybody who comes to your house and you say, "Go away," if they don't go away, they should be arrested.

Consistent with this bitterness that they are not being given that which they are naturally entitled, some women emphasize the need to have the law act, in one form or the other, as a "loudspeaker." The law was deliberately chosen because it was the only form of communication to which the abuser would listen, guaranteeing that the message would be heard. As one woman said, who saw no alternative to this particular legal method:

> People like that, people like [my abuser], you, you can't handle outside the legal system. . . . There's no rules, and if he doesn't have rules that he has to follow then that opens me up to a lot of things for him to do.

The rules that women wished the loudspeaker of the law to communicate varied, but most centered around those illustrated by the following narratives. Women wanted their abusers to learn that society is intolerant of abuse, occasionally hoping that these messages would lead to change:

> I want him to find out . . . that it's not just me. Society takes it seriously. And you don't put up with it.

> . . . with the law being behind me and now he knows that the law is involved in our situation maybe that will help change his personality. . . . I think [obtaining the order] brought it to his attention.

It's . . . not only that I do not like it but that it's also not right. It's not legal. It's not only that it's not morally fair. . . . I have felt great comfort in that. To know that it's just not simply my choosing that it's not okay, but it really, really, isn't okay.

Presumably these women had to admit to themselves that they could not stop the abuse alone. They chose the law as an attempt to enhance the resources they needed, most pressing of which was to communicate the basic message that he is not allowed to abuse her. As important as it is for the loudspeaker of the law to send the message that abuse is not acceptable, it also seems that a critical factor for these women is that the message is in fact heard by the abuser.

Similar to the loudspeaker notion, some women expressed the motivating factor for seeking their order of protection as the need to have a public record of abuse. Part of this was an underlying desire to break the silence of abuse by "making someone else aware of my situation." These women believed that the legal papers on file at the courthouse, which detailed the abuse they had experienced, would speak for them and their efforts to stop the abuse if something were to ever happen to them.[3] A second narrative elaborates on the importance for those close to her to have the documentation that an order of protection allows:

I knew that in order to keep my own sanity and feel better and feel safe, that I needed to do something legally. That even though I did take a legal course of action, at least if it didn't stop, at least there is enough people around me that if something seriously, seriously happened to me because of him, that he was not gonna get away with anything. And the only way to do that is to go a legal route and have documentation. . . . There are laws to protect all of us. . . . I just knew I was in serious trouble with this guy and in order to feel safe I took the legal route.

Other women felt that the order served a more specific documentary purpose: proof to the police or other actors in the criminal justice system that they were serious in their conviction to end the abuse or the relationship. As one woman said, "[an order of protection] says, 'I'm not a willing victim.'" Their hope was that having an order of protection would bring about more effective police response:

That if anything happens, that if you call the police they'll be there right away because they know something else has happened before.

I was scared that it would happen all over again and that if it did that the police wouldn't respond. That was basically the biggest thing.

I just wanted to make sure that I was, had a fairly safe environment for myself and the kids . . . to where, if, if he were to try and to, you know, do some damage . . . at least I knew the police would come out. And somebody would believe me. Like, you know, I didn't fall down on the ice and do this to [my broken] arm.

These remarks indicate that having public documentation of abuse through an order of protection may lead to a concomitant heightening of women's expectations that the system will in fact protect them. When violations of orders are not recognized and punished, some women express outrage. For instance, one woman attempting to enforce her order of protection was angered by the unanticipated, uncooperative response she found in the State Attorney's office. Fearing for her safety, she informed the State Attorney that she had given his name to her family and stated: "I want my children to sue you when they don't have their mom."

Finally, many women mentioned in some way that what drove them to the law was the need to have some measure of control in their lives. This is supported by the quantitative findings (reported above), where women reported an enhanced sense of control over both the relationship and other aspects of their lives after they obtained the order. For some, this control took the form of a communication to the abuser that they had truly had enough and were transforming their personal territory into a safety zone:

Well he [the abuser] didn't think I'd do it, which I didn't because I, you know, I just felt too ashamed about it. I didn't want anyone to know . . . so I had to draw the line and show what I would do.

I knew at the beginning that I needed to do some-thing to get control again . . . to feel like I had a say or I wasn't going to put up with you doing this to me. I'm not going to put up with you coming to my house or calling my house or . . . being violent with me anymore or abusive or threatening or any of those things. . . .

Control . . . when it comes to your physical safety, to me, that's where you, like, draw the line. I mean, although maybe it's not more important [than emo-tional abuse], but somehow to me that was just a real simple decision to make. . . .

[The order] was something to hide behind. . . . it was my strength. I had control. I was calling the shots. Not that I was calling the shots, but it made, there, it was something in the middle, like a ref, like a coach or something, . . . "watch where you're stepping."

For these women, the core motivation to invoke the law seems to be a reclamation of what the abuse has systematically stripped from them: their control over their activities, their bodies, and their lives.

In addition to the need for control, we have identified other primary motivators to obtaining an order as the need for the law to act as a "loud-speaker" and the need to have a public record of abuse. These motivators often supersede any num-ber of barriers women face when deciding whether to seek court orders of protection. The barriers that were the most salient to the women in our study were the emotional costs of being forced to call the police to have the abuser arrested, a fear of re-taliation for seeking legal protection, fear of end-ing the relationship permanently, and perceptions of the scary and intimidating environment of the courthouse. Some women also needed to trust that the legal system would work this time, despite prior negative experiences.

Our vision of the process of obtaining a court order for battered women starts with acknowledg-ing that the abuse they have experienced is enough—enough to justify leaving and enough to require the assistance of the law. The process then involves moving past a number of specific fears about the public nature of court protection and rec-ognizing the presence of compelling motivators to

seek court protection. The end result is that women feel a need to have the legal system both approve and reinforce their decisions to leave their abusers. They see the legal system as a force larger than themselves and as having tangible power over their abusers, power they themselves have had stripped from them as a result of the abuse they suffered. Women who go through the difficult de-cision-making process to end abuse and seek legal protection often discover a number of psycholog-ical benefits beyond the practical assistance of a court order of protection.

THE FALLOUT FROM DECISION MAKING: THE PSYCHOLOGICAL BENEFITS OF AN ORDER OF PROTECTION

How can acquiring a piece of paper that prohibits the abuser from further derogating his victim with violence be psychologically meaningful to the bat-tered women who actually seek these court orders? The narratives of the women answering this ques-tion point, in different and indirect ways, to the symbolic value of that piece of paper. The order of protection becomes, for many women, a symbol of her own internalized strength; it represents the time she stood up to her abuser and told him, through the judge who signed her order, that she refused to "take it" anymore. As nearly all battered women are silenced about the abuse and the impact it has on their lives (Fischer, Vidmar, and Ellis 1993), the legal system becomes an enabling factor that al-lows them to find their own voices again.

To illustrate this aspect of the symbolic mean-ing of court orders of protection, consider the fol-lowing narratives:

Once I got the order I thought, it's time to start all over. When you go to court to get the order and you walk out with it in your hand, you feel like you have a little bit of power over your life again. Most abusers are bigger and stronger than you are, and the order gives you a little bit more an edge . . . it makes you feel as if you ate a can of spinach, like *Popeye*.

What I needed for myself was not to feel like a vic-tim anymore. After so long of just taking it and tak-ing it I needed to be able to show myself as much as show him that I was tired of being a victim. To me I still have the order of protection, because that feeling, of fighting back and speaking out, will never leave me. I still carry the order with me and, in my mind, it's still valid. [She dropped her order of protection the day after she obtained it.]

I mean it's like you're more confident. . . . It makes me feel like I've started, I mean, it's like I'm my old self again, before I got married. . . . I mean, you just, it's like your whole life is in this little fist right here. And it's like you open it up and . . . it's just like you're spreading your wings all over again.

It was significant because I put myself ahead of him . . . I let him run my life . . . as much as I resented it, I allowed it . . . and this is the first thing I did that I outwardly said, I'm more important than you are.

The orders may serve as a symbol for feeling better about themselves, as a turning point for change, or as a vision of a better life in the future. Woven through the text of these particular symbols were images of strength: that piece of paper becomes a psychological as well as legal victory, reflecting a determined woman rather than a weak, passive victim.

The legal system also more directly invokes the process of the reclamation of "voice." Voice, in this context, is intertwined with the function of the order of protection identified as a "loudspeaker." When battered women reported that the loudspeaker had worked, the end result was the benefit of feeling that the message had actually been received. Women repeatedly expressed that they felt as if they have constantly told him that they do not like the abuse, they are not going to stand for it, they want him to leave them alone, and that, in fact, he cannot abuse them. Whereas their voices were silenced or simply not heard, the force behind the legal paper communicated for them, in language to which the abuser was forced to respond:

It showed him just how serious I was about this: I'm not all talk and no show. It wasn't a control issue for me—I felt like I needed to make him understand how scared I and the kids were—He would not hear what I was saying, so I needed the law to say it for me.

You always have the idea about going back into the relationship and making it work. But how can you make it work when it hasn't been fixed? I want him to realize that he has not been fixed. I just want him to know that he has no right to do these things to me.

I think the order made him take note . . . he's real strict about following the law so if I sent him a legal paper then he's like, she's serious, I'm just going to leave her alone because I don't want to get into trouble.

Why might such a piece of paper, these judge-validated court orders, have such a powerful symbolic impact? The answer to this question returns us to the issue of the nature of battering relationships. When one pays attention to the relationship context of battering, a common thread involves a systematic pattern of domination and control by the abuser (Fischer et al., 1993). He typically accomplishes this by creating an ever-changing structure of rules that the victim must follow or be punished for violating. Over time he may need to do less and less to concretize the rules, as she may become so adept at survival that she self-censors her own and possibly the children's behavior in frantic attempts to avoid displeasing him. The abuser gets to define who she is, what she believes in, what her individual needs are. She is nothing unless he tells her that she is, and she has nothing unless he gives it to her. Her life and her self are completely socially constructed by him.

Intervention by the legal system interrupts this pattern of control and domination because it intervenes at the level of the relationship rather than the individual. An order of protection does not simply dictate that the abuser's behavior must change by stopping the abuse; it also structures other dimensions of the relationship, such as how and when the couple may contact each other, how and when visitation is to take place, and how property is to be temporarily divided. The battered woman, perhaps for the first time in a very long while, has the opportunity to have her vision for the structure of the relationship validated through the signature of a judge. Thus the order of protection comes to symbolize that all the relationship's rules can be broken: the batterer's hold over his victim through violence, the victim's silent compliance, and the batterer's power to define his victim no longer exist.

IMPLICATIONS FOR THE LEGAL SYSTEM

Throughout this article, we have described women's decisions to seek court orders of protection as a process that involves choosing to say "Enough!" along with a mix of fear, dread, and a strong desire for control and change. Although obtaining orders of protection may result in positive psychological outcomes, these outcomes result from intervening into a complicated relational context that the abuser has previously dominated. In short, both our quantitative and qualitative data suggest that women's decisions to pursue legal means are neither easy nor lightly undertaken. Instead, battered women encounter a difficult period of indecision and uncertainty about how best to draw lines and resolve conflicts with someone with whom they are still intimately connected. Women may emerge from this process with high hopes and great needs—making them extremely vulnerable—and this result has a number of implications for the legal system.

First, given that women have high expectations for protection, poor treatment by legal representatives can easily discourage women's attempts to gain control of their lives. In addition, Browne (1991) pointed out the difficult consequences of being labeled a "victim" in our society, and how fears regarding other people's responses often decrease victims' abilities to disclose their problems. Thus judgmental or blaming attitudes from authorities are likely to undermine women's motivations to move away from their abusive relationships. Battered women's self-blame and concerns about "how I must look" were common themes in our narratives, and it is of primary importance that legal personnel not exacerbate women's own (often exaggerated) sense of responsibility and shame for their situations.

Of course, vulnerability to the reactions of legal representatives also means that positive encounters are especially salient to victims. In fact, our narratives contained vivid and enthusiastic descriptions of police officers who were helpful or even instrumental in some women's lives. In an objective sense, these officers were simply doing their jobs. However, as we have described, many women perceive the legal system as a force far more powerful than themselves. Therefore, coming from such an authority, words of support for the woman and genuine condemnation for the abuser's actions may have significant impact. For instance, one woman described how a supportive police officer had given her a piece of paper with information about orders of protection months before she decided to seek one. She held onto this paper, underlining relevant sections, and came to view it as reassuring while she struggled to decide how to end the abuse in her life.

Finally, it is important for legal actors to understand that the needs of battered women may not always be consonant with legal mandates and frameworks at any given point in time. To the great frustration of judges and police, women will often drop their orders of protection (approximately 50% nationwide; see Kinports and Fischer 1993). Women described the humiliating difficulties they encountered as a result of dropping their orders:

> . . . he [the judge] didn't want to serve [the order] because the first two, the first one I dropped and then the second one he went through counseling and I dropped it again. So the judge says, "Well we're not gonna serve this third one because you've dropped these other. You didn't do anything."

> . . . [The judge] put a big guilt trip on me that if I had kept the last one he had gave me, I wouldn't have got hurt this time, and on and on. And he really just tore me up when I went back.

Nevertheless, in describing their reasons for dropping orders, most women simply say that the order had given them what they needed. If one assumes that what is needed in these relationships is not only cessation of violence, but also that the women have some measure of control, then it makes sense that an order might fill this need, without resulting in a permanent court-ordered separation between the woman and the abuser. Instead, the "loudspeaker" may have communicated the necessary message and, in essence, the woman feels safer. Understanding the larger context of decisions about orders of protection may reduce some of legal personnel's frustrations. Central in the context of court orders is that seeking them, just like leaving the abusive relationship, is not a single event, but a process that occurs over time. One woman in our sample stated these thoughts succinctly:

> You know, I don't really know how, though, to make it better or make the courts and the police understand that . . . even if we take [the abuser] back, it still doesn't give them the right to abuse us. And that, they can lecture us all they want, we're still going to take them back until we've had our fill of it. So if they'd just be there for us, and tend to the abuser and make him feel like a fool.

In short, what seems most important for authorities who interact with battered women is to understand that their primary function may be as communicators both to women and for women. Battered women need reassurance and support that they should not have to tolerate violence and emotional abuse in their lives. In addition, authorities will often need to send this message to the abuser, both directly or through deliberate and consistent response to women's requests for legal intervention. Rather than condemn women's decisions to drop court protection or return to the abuser as a step backward or a willingness to be abused, police and court officers can conceptualize this event as a necessary step in the process of leaving. Many women who dropped their orders felt that it was important to give him "one more chance" to behave, without the threat of jail. When the abuse begins again, they take what they have learned from vacating their court protection and try again. Indeed, battered women who had prior orders of protection are far less likely than first-timers to drop their orders (Fischer 1992). Finally, the legal system must be responsive to, and patient with, the complex process involved in defining "enough." Perhaps the greatest potential role for criminal justice personnel is to kick-start the intrinsic "enough" analysis by communicating to battered women each and every time they intervene that they are willing to do everything in their power to ensure that the abuse they have already endured is more than enough.

NOTES

1. These women sought court orders of protection from a midwestern, medium-sized urban county court between November 1990 and December 1991 with the assistance of the local battered women's shelter. Although women could obtain restraining orders without the shelter's assistance, more than two thirds of all orders filed in this county were clients (not residents) of the shelter. Two thirds of the research participants were White, slighty less than half were married, and three fourths lived in the urban area of the county. Participants had a mean age of 30.5 years, and most had at least one child (87%) that was fathered by the abuser (63%). Whereas there was great variability in socioeconomic status, the sample was predominantly poor and working class (30% received public assistance, and those who worked earned a mean monthly salary of $685). Participants' abuse histories suggested a fairly extensive pattern of physical, emotional, and sexual abuse, with 50% reporting injuries resulting from the abuse and 35% reporting being abused four times per week or more. These sample descriptives are fairly consistent with those reported in prior studies of orders of protection. Fagan and colleagues (e.g., Grau, Fagan, and Wexler 1984) concluded that women who sought orders of protection were younger, and typically in shorter, less violent marriages than other battered women. Horton, Simonidis, and Simonidis (1987) studied two samples of battered women who sought restraining orders, and reported that most victims were young (mean age of 30 years), married, receiving public assistance (50%), and had an average relationship length 5 years. Chaudhuri and Daly (1992), in a study of a small sample of battered women seeking court protection, reported that the participants had an extremely short relationship length (average 18 months) and were young, married, minority, and employed (80%). Our sample, therefore, reflects a somewhat more diverse population of battered women who seek restraining orders, particularly in terms of socioeconomic status and relationship length. Although abuse-history information reported from the other studies was sketchy, this sample may also represent a more severely abused group of battered women. The questionnaire that participants completed at the courthouse was developed after extensive pilot testing and each section demonstrated adequate internal consistency in the sample.

2. Participants for this study were recruited from a subsample of women in the larger study. Eighty-two percent of the sample available were successfully recruited for the study, which consisted of a 3-hour (on average) semistructured interview conducted by the first author and two trained research assistants. The interviews were audiotaped and later transcribed.

3. It could be argued that an . . . example of this appeared in the highly publicized O. J. Simpson trial. Evidence of Mr. Simpson's abuse of Nicole Brown Simpson came from apologetic letters he had written her, which she saved in a safe deposit box.

REFERENCES

Berger, Allison, Karla Fischer, Rebecca Campbell, and Mary Rose. Unpublished. "Defining Domestic Violence: How Battered Women Draw the Line."

Browne, Angela. 1987. *When Battered Women Kill.* New York: Free Press.

———. 1991. "The Victim's Experience: Pathways to Disclosure." *Psychotherapy* 28: 150–6.

Chaudhuri, Molly and Kathleen Daly. 1992. "Do Restraining Orders Help? Battered Women's Experience with Male Violence and Legal Process." Pp. 227–52 in *Domestic Violence: The Changing Criminal Justice Response,* edited by E. S. Buzawa and C. G. Buzawa. Newbury Park, CA: Sage.

Ferraro, K. J. and J. Johnson. 1983. "How Women Experience Battering: The Process of Victimization." *Social Problems* 30:325–39.

Fischer, Karla, 1992. *The Psychological Impact and Meaning of Court Orders of Protection for Battered Women.* Ph.D. dissertation: University of Illinois, Urbana-Champaign.

Fischer, Karla, Nell Vidmar, and Rene Ellis. 1993. "The Culture of Battering and the Role of Mediation in Domestic Violence Cases." *Southern Methodist University Law Review* 46:2117–73.

Gelles, Richard J. and Murray A. Straus. 1988. *Intimate Violence.* New York: Simon & Schuster.

Grau, Janice, Jeffrey Fagan, and Sandra Wexler. 1984. "Restraining Orders for Battered Women: Issues of Access and Efficacy." *Women and Politics* 4:12–28.

Herman, Judith. 1992. *Trauma and Recovery.* New York: Basic Books.

Horton, A., K. Simonidis, and L. Simonidis. 1987. "Legal Remedies for Spousal Abuse: Victim Characteristics, Expectations, and Satisfaction." *Journal of Family Violence* 2:265–79.

Kinports, Kit and Karla Fischer. 1993. "Orders of Protection in Domestic Violence Cases: An Empirical Assessment of the Impact of the Reform Statutes." *Texas Journal of Women and the Law* 2:163–276.

Kirkwood, Catherine. 1993. *Leaving Abusive Partners.* London: Sage.

Mahoney, Martha. 1991. "Legal Images of Battered Women: Redefining the Issue of Separation." *Michigan Law Review* 90:1–93.

Martin, Del. 1976. *Battered Wives.* San Francisco: Volcano.

Merry, Sally. 1990. *Getting Justice and Getting Even.* Chicago: University of Chicago Press.

Pagelow, Mildred D. 1984. *Family Violence.* New York: Praeger.

Sullivan, Cris and William S. Davidson. 1991. "The Provision of Advocacy Services to Women Leaving Abusive Partners: An Examination of Short-term Effects." *American Journal of Community Psychology* 19:953–60.

Walker, Lenore E. 1979. *The Battered Woman.* New York: Harper & Row.

Socioeconomic Status and the Sentencing of the Traditional Offender

STEWART J. D'ALESSIO
Florida State University

LISA STOLZENBERG
Florida State University

Conflict theory postulates that lower-class criminal defendants receive the most severe legal sanctions. The empirical literature testing the validity of the proposition, however, is equivocal. This study examined the sentencing of property, violent, and moral order offenders in a southeastern state with legally mandated sentencing guidelines. It was hypothesized that the severity of imposed legal sanction would depend on the interplay between an offender's socioeconomic status and offense type. Results from four different regression models indicate some support for this hypothesis. A significant inverse relationship was observed between socioeconomic status and length of sentence for manslaughter and the possession of narcotics. Findings also show that extralegal factors played a greater role in the sentencing of violent and moral order offenders while prior criminal record was more salient in the sanctioning of property offenders. Further offense-specific analyses are needed to shed light on the relationship between socioeconomic status and criminal sentencing.

INTRODUCTION

Scholars customarily have analyzed the functioning of the criminal justice system with a conflict paradigm that identifies "power" as the principal determinant in explaining sentencing disparities (Hills, 1971; Krisberg, 1975). Adherents of this paradigm generally take a static view of the sentencing process, emphasizing the unwavering impact of socioeconomic status (SES) on sentencing decisions (Chambliss and Seidman, 1971). More recent theorizing has questioned this static conception of SES by directing attention not only to

the interplay of SES and sentencing but also to the contextural factors that might mitigate this relationship (Benson and Walker, 1988). Wheeler, Weisburd, and Bode (1982) and Hagan and Parker (1985), for example, have argued that political scandals play a pivotal role in the sentencing decision. Others have pointed to the moral crusade against drugs as a salient contextual consideration (Peterson and Hagan, 1984).

The study reported here extended previous research on SES and sentencing in three important ways. First, it reduced the influence of random sentencing variation by examining sentencing practices in a state with legally mandated sentencing guidelines. Traditionally, judges have been afforded a substantial amount of discretionary latitude when determining severity of sanction. Consequently, a judge's sentencing decision may differ substantially from that of his or her peers even for identical cases (Kapardis and Farrington, 1981). Examination of sentencing decisions in a state with determinate sentencing reduces the influence of random variation and enables better modelling of the sentencing decision. Second, this study examined individual offense categories, a strategy that furnishes a more comprehensive picture of what factors are relevant in the sentencing of a particular offense. For example, factors that influence sentencing decisions for burglary may not be the same as those that predict sentence severity for rape. Third, the study explored several different regression specifications for each offense category, enabling a more accurate assessment of those factors that were consistently important in determining sentence severity.

PRIOR RESEARCH

The relationship between socioeconomic status and sentencing has been a topic of long-standing interest to social scientists. In their seminal work, Chambliss and Seidman (1971) demonstrated how the criminal justice system operates in the interests of existing power groups by affording upper-class criminal defendants the opportunity to circumvent the imposition of severe sanctions. Their proposition that "the most severe sanctions will be imposed on persons in the lowest social class" (1971:475) has undergone extensive empirical testing in recent years. While some studies have found a strong inverse relationship between a defendant's socioeconomic status and sanctions, others have not.

To show the breadth of the disparate findings, a comprehensive on-line search was undertaken of four abstracting indexes covering material published from January 1975 to December 1990 to identify those sentencing studies that specifically addressed the SES-sanction issue (see Table 1). These indexes included: *Sociological Abstracts, The Criminal Justice Periodical Index, U.S. Political Science Documents,* and *The National Criminal Justice Reference Service.* Citations from the articles finally selected for inclusion in Table 1 were used to identify any other SES-sanction articles that might have been indexed elsewhere.

An overview of the 38 sentencing studies reveals considerable variation in their basic characteristics and findings. The first column in Table 1 lists the author(s) of each study and the date of publication. An asterisk by the name of the author(s) indicates that the study found a significant inverse relationship between SES and severity of sanction. Column 2 denotes the observation periods, while column 3 lists the location of each study. Column 4 shows both the unit of analysis and the sample size used in each study. Control variables are listed in column 5. However, lack of space necessitated a partial listing of control variables for some studies. Column 6 and column 7 show the prior record variables and the SES measures, respectively. The most frequently employed prior record measure was prior convictions, while an offender's occupation was the most commonly used measure of SES. The dependent variables utilized in previous research are depicted in column 8. Several of the sentencing studies used either sentence length or a severity-of-disposition scale as their dependent variable. The remaining studies explored judicial decisions about whether to incarcerate an offender, sentence an offender to death, or carry out the death penalty against defendants already sentenced to die. The last two columns list the offense categories analyzed and the statistical methods employed.

Thirty-nine percent of the studies included in Table 1 reported a strong inverse relationship between an offender's socioeconomic status and severity of sanction. Judson et al. (1969), for example, compared differences in the rates at which blue-collar and white-collar offenders were sentenced to death for first-degree murder. They found that blue-collar defendants received the death penalty in 42 percent of the cases, in contrast to a

TABLE 1 Empirical Studies that Examine the SES-Sanction Hypothesis

STUDY	STUDY PERIOD(S)	LOCATION(S)	SAMPLE	CONTROL VARIABLE(S)
*Bedau (1964)	1907–60	New Jersey	Adults (232)	None
*Bedau (1965)	1903–64	Oregon	Adults (92)	None
Benson and Walker (1988)	1970–80	Midwestern state	Adults (189)	Act-Related, Actor-Related and Legal Process Variables, Age, Gender, Race, Watergate
Burke and Turk (1975)	1964	Indianapolis	Adults (3,941)	Age, Case Disposition, Offense Type, Race
*Carter and Clelland (1979)	1974	Southeastern metro-politan area	Juveniles (350)	Age, Charges, Counsel, Family Structure, Gender, Race
Chiricos and Waldo (1975)	1969–73	Florida, North Caro-lina, South Carolina	Adults (10,488)	Urbanization, Age, Race
*Clarke and Koch (1976)	1971	Mecklenburg County, NC	Adults (798)	Bail, Age, Offense Type, Counsel, Race, Arrest Promptness, Employment
Cohen and Kluegel (1978)	1972	Denver, Memphis	Juveniles (9,700)	Offense Type, Race, Present Activity, Court Location
*Croyle (1983)	1973–77	St. Louis	Adults (587)	Age, Gender Race, Offense Severity
*Farrell (1971)	5-Year Period	Large urban juris-diction	Adults (108)	Offense Severity
Hagan (1975a)	6-Month Period	Medium-sized city in western Canada	Adults (1,018)	Charge Alterations, Offense Severity, Plea, Counsel, Charges, Race
Hagan (1975b)	1973	17 cities in western Canada	Adults (754)	Offense Severity, Race, Demeanor, Charges, Probation Officer's Recommendation
*Hagan et al. (1980)	1974–77	10 federal districts	Adults (6,562)	Ethnicity, Gender, Age, Employment, Plea Bail, Charge Reduction, Charges, Offense Severity
*Hagan and Palloni (1986)	1973, 1975	New York District Court	Adults (3,077)	Offense Severity, Gender, Presence of Presentence Report, Plea, Race, Age
Hagan and Parker (1985)	1966–83	Ontario	Adults (226)	Defendant's Cooperation and Reputation, Counsel, Charge, Year
Holmes et al. (1987)	1976–77	Delaware County, PA; Pima County, AZ	Adults (684)	Age, Race, Bail, Plea, Counsel, Charges Charge Reducations
Jacobs and Fuller (1986)	1983	County in Maryland	Adults (514)	Gender, Race, Judge, Probation Officer
*Jankovic (1978)	1969–74	Sunsine County, CA	Adults (2,250)	None
*Judson et al. (1969)	1958–66	California	Adults (238)	Motive, Job Stability, Age, Defendant/Victim Relationship, Race

(continued)

Note: An asterisk (*) indicates support for the SES/sanction hypothesis.

TABLE 1 *(continued)*

STUDY	STUDY PERIOD(S)	LOCATION(S)	SAMPLE	CONTROL VARIABLE(S)
*Kruttschmitt (1980)	1972–76	Mid-sized county in northern California	Adults (1,034)	Age, Race
Lizotte (1978)	1971–72	Chicago	Adults (816)	Offense Severity, Race, Counsel, Bail
Lotz and Hewitt (1977)	1973	King County, WA	Adults (504)	Race, Gender, Marital Status, Offense Type, Bail, Probation Officer's Recommendation, Weapon
McCarthy and Smith (1986)	1982	Southeastern metropolitan area	Juveniles (186)	Days Detained, Gender, Offense Severity, Race
Miethe and Moore (1985)	1978, 1980	8 Minnesota counties	Adults (2,893)	Offense Severity, Weapon, Marital Status, Gender, Age, Race, Jurisdiction
Myers (1987)	1976–82	Georgia	Adults (15,270)	Race, Gender, Offense Type
Nagel and Hagan (1982)	1974–77	10 Federal districts	Adults (6,518)	Offense Severity, Age, Ethnicity, Gender, Charges, Employment
*Nienstedt et al. (1988)	1975–83	Maricopa County, AZ	Adults (545)	Race, Gender, Veteran, Age, Public Attorney, Residency Status
*Scarpitti and Stephenson (1971)	3-Year Period	Large eastern metropolitan county	Juveniles (1,210)	None
Terry (1967)	1958–62	Industrial midwestern community	Juveniles (246)	None
*Thomas and Cage (1977)	1966–73	Southeastern metropolitan court	Juveniles (1,522)	Offense Type
*Thornberry (1973)	1955–62	Philadelphia	Juveniles (3,475)	Offense Severity
Thornberry (1979)	1955–62	Philadelphia	Juveniles (9,601)	Offense Severity, Race
Unnever (1982)	1971	Miami	Adults (313)	Race, Offense Severity, Counsel, Bail, Charges, Gender
Weisburd et al. (1990)	1976–78	7 Federal districts	Adults (963)	Act, Actor, Legal Process, Gender, Age, Race, Judicial District
Walsh (1985)	1978–81	Metropolitan Ohio County	Adults (416)	Race, IQ, Age, Offense Severity
Wheeler et al. (1982)	1976–78	7 Federal districts	Adults (1,094)	Gender, Race, District, Offense Severity, Education, Impeccability Index, Counsel
Willick et al. (1975)	1962–64	Los Angeles County	Adults (490)	None
Wolfgang et al. (1962)	1914–58	Pennsylvania	Adults (439)	Race, Murder Type

TABLE 1 *(continued)*

PRIOR RECORD MEASURE(S)	SES INDICATOR(S)	DEPENDENT VARIABLE(S)	OFFENSE CATEGORIES	STATISTICAL METHOD(S)
None	Occupation	Executed/Commuted/Other	First-degree murder	Frequencies
None	Occupation	Executed/Commuted/Other	First-degree murder	Frequencies
Arrests	SES Index	Incarceration/No Incarceration, Sentence Length	White-collar crimes	Logit, Regression
Incarcerations	Occupation	Sentence Severity Scale	Traditional Crimes	Log-Linear
Court Contacts, Police Contacts	Social Worker's Assessment of Class	Sentence Severity Scale	Traditional, Status crimes	Correlation, Regression
Arrests, Convictions, Juvenile Incarcerations	SES Index	Sentence Length	13 Offense categories	Correlation, Regression
Arrests	Census Tract Median Income	Incarceration/No Incarceration	3 Offense categories	Crosstabs, GSK
Offense Record	Parental Income	Sentence Severity Scale	Traditional, Status crimes	Log-Linear
Convictions	Census Tract Median Income	Sentence Severity Scale	Drug, Sex offenses	Regression
Offense Record	SES Index	Sentence Severity Scale	Homosexual offenses	Chi-Square, Cramer's V
Arrests	Occupation	Sentence Severity Scale	Felonies	Correlation, Path Analysis
Convictions	Occupation	Sentence Severity Scale	Felonies	Correlation, Path Analysis
Convictions	Education	Sentence Severity Scale	White-collar, Traditional crimes	Regression
Convictions	Education	Incarceration/No Incarceration, Sentence Length	White-collar, Traditional crimes	Probit, Regression
Convictions	Occupation	Sentence Severity Scale	Securities violations	Path Analysis
Convictions	Employment	Sentence Severity Scale	Robbery, Burglary	Path Analysis
DWI Convictions	Income Index, Employment	Sentence Severity Scale	DWI	Regression
None	Occupation, Education, SES Index	Sentence Severity Scale, Likelihood of Incarceration	Felonies, Misdemeanors	Correlation
Convictions, Incarcerations	Occupation	Life/Death Sentence	First-degree murder	Partial Correlation
Years on Probation	Income, Employment	Sentence Severity Scale	Felonies, Misdemeanors	Regression
Arrests	Occupation	Sentence Length	Felonies	Correlation, Path Analysis

(continued)

255

TABLE 1 *(continued)*

PRIOR RECORD MEASURE(S)	SES INDICATOR(S)	DEPENDENT VARIABLE(S)	OFFENSE CATEGORIES	STATISTICAL METHOD(S)
Prior Record	Occupation	Incarceration/No Incarceration	Felonies	Chi-Square, Gamma, Path Analysis
Adjudications	Median Income of Postal District	Sentence Severity Scale	Delinquency	Path Analysis
Criminal History Scale	Education, Employment	Incarceration/No Incarceration, Sentence Length	Felonies	Regression
Arrests, Incarcerations	County Income Standard Deviation	Incarceration/No Incarceration, Split Sentence Severity, Sentence Length	White-collar, Traditional crimes	Weighted Least Squares, Regression
Convictions	Education	Incarceration/No Incarceration, Sentence Severity Scale, Sentence Length	White-collar, Traditional crimes	Regression
None	Education	Type of Sentence: Prison, Mixed, Probation	DWI	Logit, Tobit
None	Family Income, Occupation, Education	Sentence Severity Scale	Delinquency	Frequencies
Number of Offenses	Parental Occupation	Incarceration/No Incarceration	Felonies, Misdemeanors, Delinquency	Frequencies, Kendall's Tau B
Court Contacts	Parental Occupation	Sentence Severity Scale	Felonies, Misdemeanors, Status crimes	Correlation, Cramer's V
Prior Offenses	Census Tract Median Income	Incarceration/No Incarceration	Felonies, Misdemeanors	Frequencies
Prior Offenses	Census Tract Median Income	Sentence Severity Scale	Felonies, Misdemeanors, Delinquency	Log-Linear
Convictions	Employment, Occupation	Incarceration/No Incarceration	Drug offenses	Logit
Arrests, Convictions	SES Index, Occupation	Incarceration/No Incarceration, Length of Imprisonment	White-collar crimes	Logit, Regression
Prior Record Index	SES Index	Sentence Severity Scale	Sexual assault, Nonsex offenses	Partial Correlation, Eta2
Arrests, Convictions	Occupation	Incarceration/No Incarceration, Sentence Length	White-collar crimes	Logit, Regression
Convictions	Occupation	Sentence Severity Scale	Homosexual offenses	Frequencies
None	Occupation	Executed/Not Executed	Felony and non-felony murder	Frequencies, Chi-Square, Yules Q

5-percent rate for white-collar offenders. Similarly, Bedau (1964; 1965) found that occupational status was related strongly to whether an offender was executed. A study by Farrell (1971) showed SES discrimination in the sentencing of homosexual sex offenders. Farrell's findings were supported by the research of Croyle (1983). In an analysis of 587 drug and sex offenders, Croyle found a significant negative association between SES and severity of sentencing disposition. This pattern was maintained even when controls for age, race, and offense severity were introduced into the analysis.

Miethe and Moore (1985) assessed the impact of a new Minnesota determinate sentencing law on reducing sentencing disparities. They noted a significant inverse relationship between employment status and severity of sanction for the preguideline period. After the implementation of sentencing guidelines, however, that discrimination was no longer evident. Sentencing disparities related to socioeconomic differences also have been reported for juvenile offenders (Scarpitti and Stephenson, 1971; Thornberry, 1973; Thomas and Cage, 1977; Carter and Clelland, 1979) and federal offenders (Nagel and Hagan, 1982; Hagan and Palloni, 1986).[1]

Although these studies reported a strong inverse relationship between SES and sentence severity, agreement on the saliency of SES in sentencing is far from unanimous. Studies by Burke and Turk (1975), Hagan (1975a; 1975b), and Unnever (1982) found no evidence of SES discrimination in sentencing. Other more recent studies by Holmes, Daudistel, and Farrell (1987), Myers (1987), and Benson and Walker (1988) also have cast doubt on the validity of the Chambliss and Seidman conflict proposition. The inconclusiveness of the empirical literature, coupled with their own nonsupportive findings, prompted Chiricos and Waldo (1975) to conclude that the Chambliss-Seidman conflict proposition "will have to be abandoned, or at least modified" (1975:768).

Although the results of the sentencing studies listed in Table 1 are inconclusive regarding the validity of the Chambliss-Seidman proposition, this article argues that these disparate findings can be explained to a large degree by the methodological

weaknesses of previous research (Hagan, 1974; Hagan and Bumiller, 1983; Klepper, Nagin, and Tierney, 1983). Specifically, previous research on SES and sentencing has been limited in three respects. The first shortcoming relates to the operational definition of SES used in prior research. As Tittle and Meier (1990) noted, socioeconomic status has several interpretations. The orthodox Marxist position conceives of a capitalist society as polarized into two distinct groups: capitalists, who own the means of production and purchase labor, and workers, who do not own the means of production and consequently are forced to sell their labor for wages. Many studies that have examined the relationship between SES and sentencing have relied on such a two-class model of society (Carter and Clelland, 1979; Hagan and Palloni, 1986). However, several scholars have maintained that such a simplistic conception of society does not reflect present-day class divisions accurately (Klockars, 1980; Walsh, 1985). As Walsh aptly argued:

> *The lumping together of all individuals who occupy underprivileged social positions (with respect to their relationships to the means of production) into a homogeneous "lower-class" against which the "elite" and their agents of control are said to discriminate may be a serious misinterpretation of American class perceptions. (1985:63–64)*

Studies that conceptualize SES in categorical terms also are faced with the subjective decision of where to divide the social classes. The separation point is especially salient because the relationship between SES and other variables depends largely on where the division is made (Teevan, 1985). Moreover, valuable information is lost when a variable is dichotomized (Cohen, 1983). Although researchers do not appear to be overly concerned about the use of dichotomous or other categorical measures of SES, it seems obvious that consistent results are unlikely when such measures are employed.

Realizing the difficulties associated with categorical measures, many scholars have opted for more graduated measures of SES, such as occupation (Wheeler et al., 1982; Weisburd, War- ing, and Wheeler, 1990). Although they are an improvement over categorical measures, single- dimension continuous measures lack the necessary precision to represent an individual's status accu- rately in a pluralistic society. Consequently, this study used an eclectic continuous measure of SES based on the offender's income, education, and oc- cupation (Chiricos and Waldo, 1975).

Another explanation for the inconsistent find- ings reported in the literature involves inadequate control for sample selection bias. The criminal jus- tice system is often likened to a leaky sieve because at each stage of the judicial process a decision is made whether to continue prosecution of a case. It is quite possible that offenders whose cases are dis- missed early in the judicial process are systemati- cally different from those offenders who reach the final sentencing stage. Generalizations based on of- fenders sentenced to prison are problematic be- cause the exclusion of observations may bias parameter estimates (Heckman, 1979; Berk, 1983). Because several prior studies failed to include a correction for sample selection bias (Nagel and Hagan, 1982; Miethe and Moore, 1985; Walsh, 1985), there is a strong possibility that sampling bias may have adulterated their results.

A third explanation for the incongruous find- ings reported in the literature concerns the general failure of previous research to disaggregate by of- fense type. Combining different offense types in a single analysis is pervasive in the literature (Lotz and Hewitt, 1977; Wheeler et al., 1982; Weisburd et al., 1990), but some maintain that such a prac- tice masks sentencing differences within specific offense categories (McCarthy and Lindquist, 1985). As Chiricos and Waldo argued:

> ... when the crime is most serious and the threat to established interests most clear, there may be less margin for tolerance and sanctions may be rel- atively consistently applied—for all status groups. However, when the offense poses less of a generic threat, the sanction imposed may be more respon- sive to the symbolic threat generated by the defen- dant—thereby allowing for greater variance in sentencing by SES. (1975:768)

Although Chiricos and Waldo did not specify exactly what crimes pose the most serious threat to established interests, many Marxist scholars maintain that property offenses pose the most im- mediate danger to the state since the ownership of property is a requisite of capitalism. Jacobs (1978), for example, has maintained that property offenses, especially in contexts in which economic inequality is pronounced, pose a more serious threat to monied interests than violent offenses. Consequently, he has argued that property offend- ers will be sanctioned more severely than violent offenders. In a similar vein, Carter and Clelland (1979) contended that violations of moral order (mala prohibita) crimes pose a less endemic threat to established interests than do property offenses. Carter and Clelland explicated the Marxist posi- tion as follows:

> Yet, as we do, one could well infer from a Marxian perspective that juveniles who commit acts against property will be treated alike regardless of class position because acts against property must be uni- formly suppressed in a capitalist society since the sine qua non of capitalism is the private ownership of property. (1979:100)

Because crimes may differ in the degree of danger they pose to the established social order, there is reason to suspect that the saliency of an offender's SES on sentencing dispositions may vary within nonproperty offense categories. Re- cent research has suggested that this might be the case. For example, Farrell and Swigert (1986) re- ported evidence of differential treatment in the sentencing of violent offenders, while others have noted SES discrimination in the sentencing of DWI offenders (Nienstedt, Zatz, and Epperlein, 1988), drug offenders (Rhodes, 1991), and juve- nile status offenders (Carter and Clelland, 1979). If crimes differ in the degree of danger they pose to the established social order, then the failure of many previous studies to disaggregate by offense type may have suppressed the impact of SES on sentencing decisions.

In light of these considerations, the present study examined the impact of SES on sentencing outcomes for 12 specific offense categories in the state of Florida.[2] Controls were included for prior record, gender, age, race, and county urbanization. Further, a two-stage estimation procedure was used to correct partially for selection bias. It was hypothesized that extralegal factors play a greater role in the sentencing of nonproperty crimes.

DATA

The sample consisted of 2,760 offenders selected randomly from the admissions population of all adjudicated offenders committed to the custody of the Florida Department of Corrections during fiscal year 1985 (see Figure 1). The twelve offense categories examined were grouped into property, violent, and moral order offenses. Property crimes included burglary, forgery, fraud, larceny, unarmed robbery, and dealing in stolen property. Violent offenses were aggravated assault, aggravated battery, manslaughter, and sexual battery, while moral order crimes were represented by possession of narcotics and sexual offenses. However, before the analysis is described, a brief overview of Florida's determinate sentencing system is warranted since all offenders in the study were sentenced under legally mandated sentencing guidelines.

Sentencing Guidelines

During the late 1960s and early 1970s, Americans began to question the criminal justice system's ability to rehabilitate incarcerated offenders. Some studies found that, in general, rehabilitation programs had minimal effects on reducing recidivism (Martinson, 1974; Lipton, Martinson, and Wilks, 1975). In concert with reports asserting the failure of rehabilitation, Frankel (1972) demonstrated that indeterminate sentencing systems were inconsistent in the imposition of punitive sanctions. Further, repressive state control was highly probable within such sentencing systems (American Friends Service Committee, 1971). Because the benefits of rehabilitation seemed to be seldom realized and the potential for abuse was substantial, many people called for a return to the classical of

"just deserts" position on punishment. This viewpoint was expounded in several works that caught the public's attention, and it led to increased political pressure to initiate reform (Rawls, 1971; Morris, 1974; von Hirsch, 1976).

Sentencing reform eventually was manifested in the establishment of determinate sentencing systems throughout the United States. In Florida, for example, sentencing guidelines were implemented on 1 October 1983 in an effort to "eliminate unwarranted variation in the sentencing process by reducing the subjectivity in interpreting specific offense-related and offender-related criteria and in defining their relative importance in the sentencing decision" (Florida Sentencing Guidelines Commission, 1983:4). In addition to mitigating random variation in sentencing decisions, Florida's guidelines attempt to eradicate systematic variation related to race, gender, and social class. These guidelines provide judges with a sentencing range based on the severity of the conviction offense, the length and nature of the offender's criminal history, the degree of injury sustained by the victim, and the offender's legal status at the time the offense was committed. Deviations from the guidelines are permitted only for aggravating or mitigating circumstances, which must be described in writing by the sentencing judge. Legally mandated guidelines are considered more effective than voluntary approaches in achieving judicial compliance (Tonry, 1987).

Variables

An offender's prior criminal record was measured through five variables: number of prior misdemeanor probation sentences, number of prior felony probation sentences, number of prior felony sentences less than one year, number of prior felony sentences one year and over, and number of prior prison commitments. Because preliminary analysis revealed excessive multicollinearity among these variables, factor analysis was used to amalgamate them into a criminal history index (PRIORS).[3] Previous research has shown that composite measures of prior record have a stronger

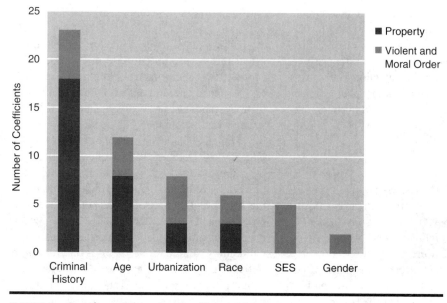

FIGURE 1   Significant Regression Coefficients (36 equations, P < .05)

impact on incarceration than single-dimension indicators such as prior arrests, prior convictions, or prior incarcerations (Nelson, 1989).

Extralegal factors such as age (AGE), gender (GENDER), race (RACE), and county urbanization (URBAN) also were included in the analysis. These factors have been shown to be important in determining severity of sanction (Myers and Talarico, 1987). An offender's gender was coded as 0 = female and 1 = male, while his or her race was defined as 0 = white and 1 = Black. Due to data limitations, Hispanic offenders were included in the white race category. To measure the urban/rural character of an offender's sentencing county, all 67 Florida counties were ranked individually in terms of population density, total population employed in non-agricultural labor, and total dollar value of all sales conducted within the county (Chiricos and Waldo, 1975). The lower the average score of these three rankings, the more urbanized the county.

Based on Chiricos and Waldo (1975) and Benson and Walker (1988), SES was operationalized as an indicator of relative position among de-

fendants. An offender's SES score represented a simple arithmetic mean of his or her three standardized scores for income, education, and occupation (U.S. Bureau of the Census, 1963; Nam and Powers, 1968; 1983). Offenders without a score reported for any one individual component of the SES index were assigned the average of the remaining components as their SES scores, while defendants without scores reported on any two individual components were assigned the score for the remaining component.

The dependent variable, prison sentence length, was coded in months. Life sentences or prison sentences greater than 600 months were recoded to 600 months to attenuate the skewness of the distribution and to quantify an individual's average life span more accurately. The recoding of these sentences to 600 months represents a realistic life sentence without parole since the average age of an offender in Florida's prison system is 29 years and the average life expectancy of an individual in Florida is 74 years (Florida Department of Health and Rehabilitative Services, 1985).

Analysis

The impact of an offender's SES on sentence length was assessed with ordinary least-squares (OLS) regression. If these regression coefficients are to be efficient and unbiased estimates of true population parameters, however, the problem of sample selection bias must be addressed. Logit regression was used to create a hazard rate variable (HAZRATE) from the entire population of offenders admitted either to prison or to community supervision during the period under observation (Keil and Vito, 1989; Erez and Tontodonato, 1990). This hazard rate variable attenuated bias by controlling for offenders who received a noninstitutional sanction (Heckman, 1979; Berk, 1983). Additionally, the hazard rate variable acted as a control for offense severity in the absence of a more direct measure (Myers, 1987). See Model 1 of Table 2.

In addition to the correction for sample selection bias, several regression diagnostic procedures were used to detect skewed distributions, aberrant observations, and heteroskedasticity. The assumption of normally distributed residuals was assessed by inspecting the histograms for each regression equation. Because many of the offense categories had residual distributions that were either kurtotic or skewed, a natural log of the dependent variable was taken. See Model 2 of Table 2. Besides this natural log transformation, a sensitivity analysis also was conducted for each offense category. All outliers more than three standard deviations from the mean were excluded from the analysis. See Model 3 of Table 2. To discern whether heteroskedasticity was present, a modified Glejser test was conducted for each equation (Goldfeld and Quandt, 1972). The results of this test revealed the presence of heteroskedasticity in the burglary, fraud, unarmed robbery, and possession of narcotics crime categories. The recommended solution for heteroskedasticity is a weighted least squares (WLS) procedure in which the number of heteroskedastic variables and the pattern of their residuals are used to create a weight (Hanushek and Jackson, 1977). The results of the WLS procedure are presented in Model 4 of Table 2.

FINDINGS

Table 2 reports the significant understandardized regression coefficients for the four regression models. It is clear from this table that the importance of SES differed across offense categories. Results show a strong negative relationship between an offenders' SES and severity of sanction for manslaughter. This relationship is statistically significant for two of the three equations estimated and is consistent with theoretical expectations. Although manslaughter is a legally conferred label, different motivational factors and contextual circumstances differentiate homicides (Daly and Wilson, 1988). First, manslaughter tends to be intraracial (Riedel, Zahn, and Mock, 1985) and intraclass (Zahn and Sagi, 1987; Hewitt, 1988). Second, the victim often instigates the crime (Wolfgang, 1966). Third, the offense pervades all social classes (Wolfgang, 1966). For these reason, one would expect more variation by SES in the sentencing of offenders convicted for manslaughter.

Socioeconomic status also was relevant in the sentencing of moral order offenders. As an offender's SES decreased, sentence length increased for possession of narcotics. Although this finding is consistent with theoretical expectations, one might argue that drug offenders should be sentenced similarly because of the instrumental crime associated with drug use. However, unlike their wealthy counterparts, lower-class offenders often support their habits through income-generating crime (Collins, Hubbard, and Rachal, 1985). As a result, they are often sanctioned more severely for their drug use because it is associated with property crime.

A strong relationship also was noted between county urbanization and the sentencing of moral order offenders. Like the research of Myers and Talarico (1986), this study found that drug offenders sentenced in rural counties received stiffer sanctions than those sentenced in more urban settings. In contrast, sexual offenses, which include crimes such as incest and sodomy, were treated with greater leniency in rural counties.

Contrary to expectations, there was little evidence of an SES effect for aggravated assault,

TABLE 2   Unstandardized Regression Results

OFFENSE CATEGORY	MODEL 1 Partial Correction for Sample Bias			MODEL 2 Natural Log of Dependent Variable		
	VARIABLE	*B*	SIG *T*	VARIABLE	*B*	SIG *T*
Property Offenses						
Burglary	HAZRATE	126.08	.002	AGE	0.02	.000
	AGE	2.62	.000	PRIORS	0.11	.000
	RACE	−22.73	.016			
Forgery	PRIORS	13.00	.000	PRIORS	0.26	.000
Fraud	PRIORS	12.76	.002	PRIORS	0.33	.000
				URBAN	0.02	.049
Larceny	AGE	0.42	.021	PRIORS	0.08	.011
				URBAN	0.01	.030
				AGE	0.01	.046
Robbery, unarmed	HAZRATE	498.86	.000	PRIORS	0.25	.000
	AGE	7.71	.000	AGE	0.02	.015
	RACE	−83.28	.000			
Stolen property	PRIORS	12.85	.000	PRIORS	0.30	.000
Violent Offenses						
Aggravated assault	P > .05			HAZRATE	2.62	.038
Aggravated battery	P > .05			P > .05		
Manslaughter	SES	−0.51	.039	HAZRATE	2.44	.006
				AGE	0.02	.027
Sexual battery	HAZRATE	−768.02	.028	HAZRATE	−4.91	.010
	PRIOR	89.46	.000	PRIORS	0.48	.000
	RACE	132.79	.022	RACE	0.69	.027
Moral order offenses						
Narcotics possession	AGE	1.97	.000	PRIORS	0.16	.004
				URBAN	0.01	.004
				SES	−0.01	.019
				AGE	0.01	.045
Sexual offenses	P > .05			HAZRATE	2.40	.022
				URBAN	−0.02	.033

aggravated battery, sexual battery, or sexual offenses. The data indicate, however, that Black offenders sentenced for sexual battery (forcible rape) received longer prison terms than white defendants. An offender's socioeconomic status also did not impact sentence length for any of the property offenses. Gender and county urbanization also played less of a role in the sentencing of property offenses.

The most apparent difference in the sentencing of violent, moral order, and property offenders concerned the impact of prior criminal history. Over-

TABLE 2   *(continued)*

MODEL 3 Sensitivity Analysis			MODEL 4 Weighted Least Squares				
VARIABLE	*B*	SIG *T*	VARIABLE	*B*	SIG *T*	R²	SIG *F*
AGE	1.18	.000	WHAZRATE	−61.52	.025	.09	.000
PRIORS	4.37	.000	WPRIORS	5.69	.008		
PRIORS	12.44	.000	N/A			.34	.000
HAZRATE	−180.28	.032	WPRIORS	8.85	.011	.31	.000
PRIORS	8.78	.000					
URBAN	0.67	.003					
PRIORS	2.72	.007	N/A			.07	.000
AGE	0.24	.020					
HAZRATE	−73.59	.001	WPRIORS	13.86	.001	.24	.000
PRIORS	19.25	.000					
HAZRATE	−78.26	.001	N/A			.27	.000
PRIORS	14.18	.000					
RACE	16.20	.002					
HAZRATE	82.60	.020	N/A			.08	.020
HAZRATE	−47.18	.027	N/A			.06	.014
GENDER	15.66	.019					
SES	−0.56	.018	N/A			.09	.016
HAZRATE	−768.02	.028	N/A			.20	.000
PRIORS	89.46	.000					
RACE	132.79	.022					
SES	−0.27	.004	WURBAN	0.37	.012	.18	.000
PRIORS	5.56	.009	WSES	−0.27	.008		
URBAN	0.30	.043	WAGE	1.60	.003		
HAZRATE	131.88	.016	N/A			.16	.001
GENDER	−86.16	.002					
URBAN	−1.23	.006					

Note: Nonsignificant coefficient estimates and related information are available on request from the authors.

all, prior criminal history was significant for more than 85 percent of the equations calculated for property crimes, as opposed to 26 percent for violent and moral order offenses. (See figure 1). This difference is rather striking and supports the research of Nelson (1989), who found that an offender's

prior criminal record was more closely related to incarceration for crimes that involved the theft of property.

Another finding that warrants attention is the influence of an offender's age on sentence length. Older offenders were consistently more likely to receive severe sanctions for property offenses. This linear relationship between age and sentence length was due primarily to the fact that age was correlated highly with prior record. Older offenders were more likely to have a serious prior criminal history. This strong positive association between age and prior record, however, was not constant for all defendants. There was substantial differences in the length and nature of criminal histories, especially among older offenders. Researchers scrutinizing the age-sanction relationship should be aware of prior record differences among older offenders and tailor their methodologies accordingly.

Table 2 also reports the largest R^2 for each offense category. All 21 of the regression equations for property offenses were statistically significant: burglary ($R^2 = .09$), forgery ($R^2 = .34$), fraud ($R^2 = .31$), larceny ($R^2 = .07$), unarmed robbery ($R^2 = .24$), and dealing in stolen property ($R^2 = .27$). In contrast, only 15 of the 19 equations for violent and moral order offenses were statistically significant: aggravated assaults ($R^2 = .08$), aggravated battery ($R^2 = .06$), manslaughter ($R^2 = .09$), sexual battery ($R^2 = .20$), possession of narcotics ($R^2 = .18$), and sexual offenses ($R^2 = .16$). Again, these findings indicate that more variation can be accounted for in the sentencing of property offenders than in that of either violent or moral order defendants.

DISCUSSION

In this analysis we examined sentencing dispositions for 12 offense categories in the state of Florida using four different regression models while controlling for SES, age, gender, race, county urbanization, and prior criminal record. The findings support the proposition that the severity of imposed legal sanction is not predicated solely on legal factors but instead depends on the interaction between offender and offense. The finding that SES and other extralegal factors played a greater role in the sentencing of nonproperty offenders is intriguing since many studies that were conducted in states with determinate sentencing reported little evidence of sentencing discrimination (Knack, 1982; Kramer and Lubitz, 1985, Miethe and Moore, 1985; Zatz and Hagan, 1985).[4] Several possible answers are suggested for our divergent findings.

One explanation, as discussed previously, relates to the methodological shortcomings of previous research. Because they neglected to use composite measures of SES (Unnever, 1982; Weisburd et al., 1990), aggregated offense categories (Miethe and Moore, 1985; Benson and Walker, 1988), and failed to include a correction for sampling bias (Jacobs and Fuller, 1986; Holmes et al., 1987), the findings of previous sentencing studies are somewhat suspect. Further, we found that our results changed when corrections for skewed distributions, aberrant observations, and heteroskedasticity were included in the regression analysis. When the hazard rate equation was estimated, for example, SES did not appear to affect the sentencing of drug offenders. However, estimation of the corrected regression equations revealed a substantial and consistent negative relationship between SES and severity of sanction for the possession of narcotics. Correction for heteroskedasticity also eliminated other puzzling findings. Two of the hazard rate equations for property offenses, for example, showed that age and race were the only significant predictors for burglary and unarmed robbery. Once we corrected for heteroskedasticity, however, only prior criminal record achieved statistical significance.

Organizational pressures also may provide some explanation for our findings (Peterson and Hagan, 1984). Prison overcrowding, caused partially by determinate sentencing, has become a major concern of the criminal justice system in Florida. The continually expanding prison population, coupled with an unwillingness to expend capital on increased prison construction, creates a quandary for the criminal justice system (Greenberg and Humphries, 1980). We premise that the increased discrimination observed in the sentencing of nonproperty offenders may serve a fuctional purpose because it contributes to an overall reduction in prison population levels. With inmate populations reduced, offenders who severely threaten established interests can continue to be sanctioned severely with minimal strain on the functioning of the criminal justice system. However, while such a thesis seems plausible, we are unable to assess exactly whether prison overcrowding is an important contextual consideration because no overcrowding variable was included in the analysis.

CONCLUSION

Sentencing research has yet to furnish a clear understanding of the relationship between SES and punishment. Some studies have found that SES has little or no impact on sentence severity, while other have reported evidence of a strong negative association. Although conflict theory treats the meaning of SES as static and unchanging, our results show that the impact of SES on sentencing dispositions is not constant but varies according to criminal offense. We also found little evidence that sentencing guidelines reduce disparity, especially in the sentencing of nonproperty offenders. Firm conclusions regarding the exact nature of the relationship between SES and severity of criminal sanction, however, must await further offense-specific research.

NOTES

1. Juvenile and white-collar sentencing studies are included in Table 1 to furnish a comprehensive review of the SES-sanction literature.
2. Hopkins (1977) and Reasons (1977) argued that only "within-class" SES distinctions can be made among offenders sentenced to prison for traditional crimes. Because of these commentaries, scholarly attention has focused on the sentencing of white-collar offenders (Benson and Walker, 1988; Weisburd et al., 1990). The examination of white-collar offenders is considered more advantageous for understanding the SES-sanction relationship because of increased SES variation among sentenced white-collar defendants. However, we question whether the examination of white-collar defendants provides an adequate assessment of the relationship between SES and sentencing since most people do not

have the opportunity to commit these types of crimes. At issue here is the distinction between censored and truncated samples. As Berk (1983:391) noted:

> When the selection process eliminates observations solely for the endogenous variable, one commonly speaks of censoring. When observations are missing in the exogenous variables as well, one commonly speaks of truncation. When a sample is truncated, as is the case when white-collar offenders are analyzed, estimation procedures, even if they include a control for censoring, will still yield biased and inconsistent estimates of structural parameters.

3. Variable means, standard deviations, correlation matrices, and factor scores for all offense categories are available on request from the authors.
4. See Rhodes (1991) for an important exception.

REFERENCES

American Friends Service Committee. (1971). *Struggle for justice: A report on crime and punishment in America.* New York: Hill and Wang.

Bedau, H. A. (1965). Capital punishment in Oregon 1903–1964. *Ore L Rev* 45: 1–39.

——— (1964). Death sentences in New Jersey. *Rutgers L Rev* 19: 1–55.

Benson, M., and Walker, E. (1988). Sentencing the white-collar offender. *Am Sociol R* 53: 294–302.

Berk, R. A. (1983). An introduction to sample selection bias in sociological data. *Am Sociol R* 48: 386–98.

Burke, P. J., and Turk, A. T. (1975). Factors affecting postarrest dispositions: A model for analysis. *Soc Prob* 22: 313–32.

Carter, T., and Clelland, D. (1979). A neo-Marxian critique, formulation and test of juvenile dispositions as a function of social class. *Soc Prob* 27: 96–108.

Chambliss, W. J., and Seidman, R. B. (1971). *Law, order and power.* Reading, MA: Addison-Wesley.

Chiricos, T. G., and Waldo, G. P. (1975). Socioeconomic status and criminal sentencing: An empirical assessment of a conflict proposition. *Am Sociol R* 40: 753–72.

Clarke, S. H., and Koch, G. G. (1976). The influence of income and other factors on whether criminal defendants go to prison. *Law & Soc R* 11: 57–92.

Cohen, J. (1983). The cost of dichotomization. *Appl Psychol Meas* 7: 249–53.

Cohen, L. E., and Kluegel, J. R. (1978). Determinants of juvenile court dispositions: Ascriptive and achieved factors in two metropolitan courts. *Am Sociol R* 43: 162–76.

Collins, J. J.; Hubbard, R. L.; and Rachal, J. V. (1985). Expensive drug use and illegal income: A test of explanatory hypotheses. *Crim* 23: 743–64.

Croyle, J. L. (1983). Measuring and explaining disparities in felony sentences: Courtroom work group factors and race, sex, and socioeconomic influences on sentence severity. *Political Behavior* 5: 135–53.

Daly, M., and Wilson, M. (1988). *Homicide.* New York: Aldine de Gruyter.

Erez, E., and Tontodonato, P. (1990). The effect of victim participation in sentencing on sentencing outcome. *Crim* 28: 451–74.

Farrell, R. A. (1971). Class linkages of legal treatment of homosexuals. *Crim* 9: 49–68.

———— and Swigert, V. L. (1986). Adjudication in homicide: An interpretive analysis of the effects of defendant and victim social characteristics. *J Res Crime* 23: 349–69.

Florida Department of Health and Rehabilitative Services. (1985). *Florida vital statistics.* Tallahassee: Office of Vital Statistics.

Florida Sentencing Guidelines Commission. (1983). *Florida sentencing guidelines manual.* Tallahassee: Supreme Court of Florida.

Frankel, M. (1972). *Criminal sentences: Law without order.* New York: Hill and Wang.

Goldfeld, S.M., and Quandt, R. E. (1972). *Nonlinear methods in econometrics.* Amsterdam: North-Holland.

Greenberg, D. F., and Humphries, D. (1980). The cooptation of fixed sentencing reform. *Crime Delin* 26: 206–25.

Hagan, J. (1975a). Parameters of criminal prosecution: An application of path analysis to a problem of criminal justice. *J Crim Law* 65: 536–44.

———— (1975b). The social and legal construction of criminal justice: A study of the pre-sentencing process. *Soc Prob* 22: 620–37.

———— (1974). Extra-legal attributes and criminal sentencing: An assessment of sociological viewpoint. *Law & Soc R* 8: 357–83.

———— and Bumiller, K. (1983). Making sense of sentencing: A review and critique of sentencing research. In *Research on sentencing: The search for reform,* ed. A. Blumstein, J. Cohen, S. E. Martin, and M. H. Tonry. Washington, D.C.: National Academy Press.

———— Nagel-Bernstein, I. H.; and Albonetti, C. (1980). The differential sentencing of white-collar offenders in ten federal district courts. *Am Sociol R* 45: 802–20.

———— and Palloni, A. (1986). 'Club fed' and the sentencing of white-collar offenders before and after Watergate. *Crim* 24: 603–21.

———— and Parker, P. (1985). White-collar crime and punishment: The class structure and legal sanctioning of securities violations. *Am Sociol R* 50: 302–16.

Hanushek, E. A., and Jackson, J. E. (1977). *Statistical methods for social scientists.* New York: Academic Press.

Heckman, J. J. (1979). Sample selection bias as a specification error. *Econometrica* 47: 153–61.

Hewitt, J. (1988). The victim-offender relationship in convicted homicide cases: 1960–1984. *J Crim Just* 16: 25–33.

Hills, S. L. (1971). *Crime, power, and morality: The criminal law process in the United States.* New York: Chandler.

Holmes, M. D.; Daudistel, H.C.; and Farrell, R. A. (1987). Determinants of charge reductions and final dispositions in cases of burglary and robbery. *J Res Crime* 24: 233–54.

Hopkins, A. (1977). Is there a class bias in criminal sentencing? *Am Sociol R* 42: 176–77.

Jacobs, D. (1978). Inequality and the legal order: An ecological test of the conflict model. *Soc Prob* 25: 515–25.

———— and Fuller, M. (1986). The social construction of drunken driving: Modeling the organizational processing of DWI defendants. *Soc Sci Q* 67: 785–802.

Jankovic, I. (1978). Social class and criminal sentencing. *Crime & Soc Jus* 10: 9–16.

Judson, C. J.; Pandell, J. J.; Owens, J. B.; McIntosh, J. J.; and Matschullat, D. L. (1969). A study of the California penalty jury in first degree murder cases. *Stanford L Rev* 21: 1297–1497.

Kapardis, A., and Farrington, D. P. (1981). An experimental study of sentencing by magistrates. *Law and Hum Behav* 5: 107–21.

Keil, T. J., and Vito, G. F. (1989). Race, homicide severity, and application of the death penalty: A consideration of the Barnett scale. *Crim* 27: 511–31.

Klepper, S.; Nagin, D.; and Tierney, L. (1983). Discrimination in the criminal justice system: A critical appraisal of the literature. In *Research on sentencing: The search for reform,* ed. A. Blumstein, J. Cohen, S. E. Martin, and M. H. Tonry. Washington, D.C.: National Academy Press.

Klockars, C. R. (1980). The contemporary crisis of Marxist criminology. In *Radical criminology: The coming crisis,* ed. J. Inciardi, Beverly Hills: Sage.

Knapp, K. A. (1982). Impact of the Minnesota sentencing guidelines on sentencing practices. *Hamline L Rev* 5: 237–56.

Kramer, J. H., and Lubitz, R. L. (1985). Pennsylvania's sentencing reform: The impact of commission-established guidelines. *Crime Delin* 31: 481–500.

Krisberg, B. (1975). *Crime and privilege.* Englewood Cliffs, NJ: Prentice-Hall.

Kruttschnitt, C. (1980). Social status and sentences of female offenders. *Law & Soc R* 15: 247–65.

Lipton, D.; Martinson, R.; and Wilks, J. (1975). *The effectiveness of correctional treatment: A survey of treatment evaluation studies.* New York: Praeger.

Lizotte, A. J. (1978). Extra-legal factors in Chicago's criminal courts: Testing the conflict model of criminal justice. *Soc Prob* 25: 564–80.

Lotz, R., and Hewitt, J. D. (1977). The influence of legally irrevelant factors on felony sentencing. *Social Inq* 47: 39–48.

Martinson, R. (1974). What works? Questions and answers about prison reform. *Pub Interest* 35: 22–54.

McCarthy, B. R., and Lindquist, C. A. (1985). Ambiguity and conflict in sentencing research: Partial resolution through crime-specific analysis. *J Crim Just* 13: 155–69.

McCarthy, B. R., and Smith, B. L. (1986). The conceptualization of discrimination in the juvenile justice process: The impact of administrative factors and screening decisions on juvenile court dispositions. *Crim* 24: 41–64.

Miethe, T. D., and Moore, C. A. (1985). Socioeconomic disparities under determinate sentencing systems: A comparison of preguideline and postguideline practices in Minnesota. *Crim* 23: 337–63.

Morris, N. (1974). *The future of imprisonment.* Chicago: University of Chicago Press.

Myers, M. A. (1987). Economic inequality and discrimination in sentencing. *Soc Forces* 65: 746–66.

——— (1986). Urban justice, rural injustice? Urbanization and its effect on sentencing. *Crim* 24: 367–91.

——— and Talarico, S. M. (1987). *The social contexts of criminal sentencing.* New York: Springer-Verlag.

Nagel, I. H., and Hagan, J. (1982). The sentencing of white-collar criminals in federal courts: A sociolegal exploration of disparity. *Mich L Rev* 80: 1427–65.

Nam, C. B., and Powers, M. G. (1983). *The socioeconomic approach to status measurement.* Houston: Cap and Gown Press.

——— (1968). Changes in the relative status level of workers in the United States, 1950–1960. *Soc Forces* 47: 158–70.

Nelson, J. F. (1989). an operational definition of prior criminal record. *Journal of Quantitative Criminology* 5: 333–52.

Nienstedt, B. C.; Zatz, M. S.; and Epperlein, T. (1988). Court processing and sentencing of drinking drivers: Using new methodologies. *Journal of Quantitative Criminology* 4: 39–59.

Peterson, R. D., and Hagan, J. (1984). Changing conceptions of race: Towards an account of anomalous findings of sentencing research. *Am Social R* 49: 56–70.

Rawls, J. (1971). *A theory of justice.* Cambridge: Harvard University Press.

Reasons, C. E. (1977). On methodology, theory and ideology. *Am Sociol R* 42: 177–81.

Rhodes, W. (1991). Federal criminal sentencing: Some measurement issues with applications to pre-guideline sentencing disparity. *J Crim Law* 81: 1002–33.

Riedel, M.; Zahn, M. A.; and Mock, L. F. (1985). *The nature and patterns of American homicide.* Washington, D.C.: National Institute of Justice.

Scarpitti, F. R., and Stephenson, R. M. (1971). Juvenile court dispositions: Factors in the decision-making process. *Crime Delin* 17: 142–51.

Teevan, J. J. (1985). Socioeconomic status is significantly related to . . . *Soc Perspect* 28: 241–47.

Terry, R. M. (1967). Discrimination in the handling of juvenile offenders by social-control agencies. *J Res Crime* 4: 218–30.

Thomas, C. W., and Cage, R. J. (1977). The effect of social characteristics on juvenile court dispositions. *Social Q* 18: 237–52.

Thornberry, T. P. (1979). Sentencing disparities in the juvenile justice systems. *J Crim Law* 70: 164–71.

——— (1973). Race, socioeconomic status and sentencing in the juvenile justice systems. *J Crim Law* 64: 90–98.

Tittle, C. R., and Meier, R. F. (1990). Specifying the SES/deliquency relationship. *Crim* 28: 271–99.

Tonry, M. H. (1987). *Sentencing reform impacts.* Washington, D.C.: Office of Communication and Research Utilization.

Unnever, J. D. (1982). Direct and organizational discrimination in the sentencing of drug offenders. *Soc Prob* 30: 212–25.

U.S. Bureau of the Census. (1963). *Methodology and scores of socioeconomic status.* Working paper number 15. Washington, D.C.: U.S. Government Printing Office.

von Hirsch, A. (1976). *Doing justice: The choice of punishments.* New York: Hill and Wang.

Walsh, A. (1985). Extralegal factors in felony sentencing: Classes of behavior or classes of people. *Sociol Inq* 55: 62–82.

Weisburd, D.; Waring, E.; and Wheeler, S. (1990). Class, status, and the punishment of white-collar criminals. *Law and Social Inquiry* 15: 223–43.

Wheeler, S.; Weisburd, D.; and Bode, N. (1982). Sentencing the white-collar offender: Rhetoric and reality. *Am Sociol R* 47: 641–59.

Willick, D. H.; Gehlker, G.; and Watts, A. M. (1975). Social class as a factor affecting judicial disposition. *Crim* 13: 57–77.

Wolfgang, M. E. (1966). *Patterns in criminal homicide.* New York: Wiley.

——— Kelly, A., and Nolde, H. C. (1962). Comparison of the executed and the commuted among admissions to death row. *J Crim Law* 53: 301–11.

Zahn, M., and Sagi, P. (1987). Stranger homicides in nine American cities. *J Crim Law* 78: 377–97.

Zatz, M. S., and Hagan, J. (1985). Crime, time, and punishment: An exploration of selection bias in sentencing research. *Journal of Quantitative Criminology* 1: 103–26.

PART SIX

Corrections

In the 1980s, the National Association for the Advancement of Colored People (NAACP) announced that there were more African American males in prison than in college in the United States. People of African descent are the most imprisoned people in the world. According to a report by the Bureau of Justice Statistics (BJS) that appeared in the *Wall Street Journal* in 1998, African American males have a 28.5 percent chance of going to state or federal prison in their lifetimes, and Hispanic males have a 16 percent greater chance. On the other hand, whites have only a 4.4 percent chance of going to prisons in their lifetimes (Bureau of Justice Statistics, 1998). If the percentage of minorities in prison continues to increase at the same rate that it did from 1980 to 1993, almost two out of three young African American men and one out of four Hispanic men nationwide between the ages of eighteen and thirty-four will be in prison by the year 2020 (Donzinger, 1996). Los Angeles lawyer and activist Marilyn Mackel refers to prisons as the modern day equivalent of "slave ships" (Shelden, 1999, p. 20).

Most of the readings in earlier parts of this book examine the social processes that contribute to the overincarceration of people of color in general, and African Americans in particular. Those articles trace how institutional racism is embedded in the various organizations comprising the criminal justice enterprise, which fuels higher arrest, prosecution, and incarceration rates for African Americans and other minorities. Institutional racism is manifested through the differential policing of minority communities and racial profiling; differential application of laws to different minority groups—specifically drug laws; inadequate access to legal defense and bail; institutional barriers blocking African Americans from participating in juries; persistence of prejudicial beliefs, attitudes, and behaviors of prosecutors, judges, probation and correctional staff; and the perpetuation of negative images of African Americans and Hispanics and other minority groups by the media and popular literary culture for over two centuries. For most of U.S. history, socioeconomic status and gender have exerted a dominant force in determining who went to prison and who didn't (Shelden, 2001). However, in the last two decades, the exponential growth of the African American and Hispanic populations in these institutions has made class a less important and visible variable. In fact, as we shall see, the variable of gender exerts less influence over who goes to jail, if the person is African American.

The readings in Part Six examine how inmates of color are treated once they are siphoned into the correctional system, and how the growing incarceration of African Americans and other people of color has impacted the internal operations and daily life in U.S. prisons. These readings address such questions as, What are the consequences of the disproportionate incarceration of African Americans and other people of color? Why should the public be concerned about the overincarceration of African Americans? What are the social, political, and economic consequences of this phenomenon?

There are, of course, ethical and moral reasons for opposing a society that unfairly imprisons growing numbers of nonwhites and the poor. First, the existence of a criminal justice system which systematically treats one group of people unfairly threatens to undermine the legitimacy of our democracy.

Second, the cost of maintaining such a system imposes an enormous economic burden on taxpayers. America has the largest system of incarceration in the world, with a prison population of over two million. The population in state and federal prisons has quadrupled over the past twenty-five years, and spending at the state level has doubled over the last decade. It is estimated that total prison expenditures in the U.S. exceed $100 billion annually, and during the past twenty years, expenditures on crime control have increased twice as fast as military spending (Shelden, 1999).

However there is a more selfish motive for being concerned with the growth of the prison system and the disproportionate incarceration of people of color and the poor: The nation's prisons are powder kegs. Race riots in prisons are far more dangerous than race riots that occur in outside society, and the prison riots that have occurred in this century have lead to hundreds of deaths of inmates and correctional staff, as well as tortures, rapes, and mutilations.

What happens in these institutions inevitably impacts the outside society because the majority of inmates will eventually be released. Individuals who work in prisons must also function in outside society, and their daily experiences spill into their outside lives. The majority of female prisoners have children who live and are supported by people on the outside. The incarceration of a parent is often a contributing factor to future criminal behavior by their offspring. Finally, as the criminal justice enterprise grows, it employs more people and becomes a more integral part of the U.S. economy. What happens behind the walls of these institutions will impact all sectors of the economy.

HISTORY OF RACE AND CORRECTIONS

A racist joke goes, "What do you call a white man with 1,000 Black men? A warden." Unfortunately, there is truth in this joke. The disproportionate incarceration of African Americans is not a new phenomenon. What is changing are societal attitudes and state policies toward the discrimination and oppression of African American's and other people of color. These changes have been brought on by the Civil Rights movement, world opinion, and the empowerment of African Americans in society. Until the middle of the twentieth century, African Americans and prisoners in general were not able to mount any serious opposition to the system of oppression.

Scholars have argued that formal prisons were not important as a form of social control during slavery since "plantation justice tended to siphon Blacks out of the state punishment system" (Adamson, 1983, p. 556). After the Civil War, however, convicts were leased out to plantations, profit-making corporations, mining companies, railroad contractors, and quarries on a long-term basis (Owens, 1977). Many researchers have argued that the convict-lease system enforced on African American inmates provided a cheap source of labor after slavery was abolished in 1865.

In 1870, African Americans comprised 33 percent of the prison population in the United States, in 1880, they accounted for 40 percent, and in 1939, they comprised 44 percent, according to the U.S. Bureau of the Census (Owens & Bell, 1977). Sociology scholars of that period argue that criminal activity among African Americans was considerably higher than among whites during this era (e.g., see Myrdal, 1944; Du Bois, 1902; Johnson, 1941; and Sellin, 1928). Other scholars question the accuracy of this argument, given the vast amount of evidence for fabricated crimes such as rape to justify lynchings. In addition, African Americans were frequently arrested for political crimes of resistance, including failing to abide by segregation laws, protesting theft of their property, protesting sexual assaults, engaging in verbal arguments with whites, and trying to exercise the right to vote (National Research Council, 1989).

Owens and Bell (1977) argue that until the middle of the twentieth century, African American inmates accepted their confinement and punishment in prisons without much united resistance against the system. They explain that although the conditions and treatment in prisons was considered inhumane, there was little opposition because (1) the courts had a hands-off policy with respect to penal conditions and issues, and (2) the institutions were located primarily in rural areas and thus functioned in relative isolation, and the guards were all white. As Conley and Debro point out in their article on Black Muslims (see Reading 16),

> Blacks in the past had been seen by prison authorities as persons who "did their own time" and did not complain about the injustices of the prison system even though it was openly discriminatory. (2001, p. 4)

Until the second half of the twentieth century, the vast majority of African Americans resided in the southern states. Prisons, like other major institutions in the South, were segregated along racial lines. However, the distribution of the African American population across the nation shifted dramatically between 1940 and 1950, close to one-half of the population migrated to the North and to far western states. This demographic shift made racial segregation more difficult and expensive to maintain in all institutions, including penal institutions.

After World War II, the United States assumed the role of leader of the free world in the international community, and the nation's image as a democracy that guaranteed equal rights and treatment for all people regardless of race, religion, or economic status had important political and economic implications. The United States began to extend its markets, and, along with its allies, engaged in various international military conflicts in Southeast Asia and Latin America. As a result of this increasing global involvement, racial segregation and the inhumane treatment and exploitation of certain groups came under close international scrutiny, and the hypocrisy of the United States was frequently exposed by opponents of U.S. economic and military policies.

In the late 1950s, the Civil Rights movement began to gain momentum and gave impetus to the plethora of social movements of the 1960s and 1970s that argued for the rights of disenfranchised populations. Many African American and white social activists were catapulted into the criminal justice system because of their participation in civil rights activities. Most of the major African American leaders spent some time in jail—including Martin Luther King, Jr., Stokely Carmichael, Medgar Evers, Ralph Albernathy, Malcolm X, H. Rap Brown, Huey Newton, and Angela Davis—and they wrote about the inhumane prison conditions (Owens & Bell, 1977). Although the movement for prison reform in this country had been introduced in the nineteenth century, it did not make serious inroads and become a major public issue until this time period.

The first article in Part Six, by Darlene Conley and Julius Debro, is a historical piece on the rise of the Black Muslim movement in prisons in California. Debro was one of the few African Americans working as a correctional officer at San Quentin in the 1960s when the philosophy espoused by the Nation of Islam began to gain influence among young African American inmates in correctional facilities across the United States. The emergence and rapid spread of this movement had important consequences for the prisoners' rights movement of the 1960s and 1970s.

Although the Nation of Islam had limited success in convincing African Americans to abandon Christianity in the general society, the strict discipline of the faith, the doctrines of Black pride and economic self-sufficiency, and the centrality of white racism as an explanation for the plight of African Americans quickly attracted a following among incarcerated African Americans. The most famous recruit, Malcolm X, converted to Islam while serving time in prison. Even the founder of the Nation of Islam, Elijah Muhammed, had spent time in several prisons.

The Nation of Islam preached racial pride and described a history in which African Americans were kings and rulers, and African nations reign supreme. In a society that disparaged everything connected to African American people and Africa, the ideology of the Nation of Islam was especially attractive to a new generation of African Americans who had never been taught anything positive about their history and who had been convinced that African Americans could not make important strides toward political and economic freedom without the support, guidance, and money of "well-meaning" whites. Whereas the Civil Rights movement had sought to achieve equality through integration and cooperation with whites, Black Muslims preached separation from whites and rejected the ideology of nonviolent resistance. The Black separatist ideology of the Nation of Islam was quickly adopted by the new generation of Black political activists, and it influenced the emergence of groups such as the Black Panthers.

This new, unfamiliar movement, which referred to whites as "blue-eyed devils," frightened white Americans; they feared that Black Muslims would incite large numbers of African Americans to violence. When African American inmates began to join this movement, prison officials became frightened of these inmates who were meticulously groomed, articulate, and practiced a military style of discipline by abstaining from alcohol, drugs, tobacco, and sex. In the 1960s and 1970s, the African American prison population was rapidly increasing and these institutions were still overwhelmingly administered by whites who were beginning to recognize the vulnerability of their numeric minority status in prisons.

The African American and Hispanic prison population in California has grown to over one-half of the total state prison population. Despite policies to the contrary, racial segregation was routinely practiced in California institutions during the 1960s and 1970s. Conley and Debro quote one inmate protestor who wrote to the associate ward of Folsom Prison in 1961:

> *You deny us the opportunity to learn skilled jobs, so that you can keep us doing your menial work. The sad fact is, then, prison work seems to appeal to bigots and ignorant persons, for in a segregated setup it allows them to have a field day to vent their evil passions.*

This letter started the first organized complaint at Folsom. Prison officials ignored the concerns of inmates, and violence erupted after a group of African American inmates attempted to integrate the cafeteria. Ironically, Black Muslims did not initiate these protests, since their doctrine preached segregation. Officials, however, reacted by dispersing the Black Muslim inmate population at Folsom to different facilities throughout the state.

Debro and Conley argue that the early suppression of the Black Muslim movement from 1952 to 1967 within the California prison system gave rise to a "much more militant movement," which resulted in conflicts between Black Panthers and other Black Nationalists at San Quentin and Soledad Prisons. The authors' views proved prophetic because they preceded the eruption of the nation's largest prison riot in Attica, New York, on September 9, 1971. Close to 1,500 inmates seized one of four cellblocks and its adjoining yard and took about forty guards and civilian workers as hostages. About 85 percent of the rebels were African Americans and Puerto Ricans, and many of their demands centered around the racist behavior of the all-white prison guard staff and the suppression of the Islamic faith. Other inmate demands included humanitarian changes such as the provision of more than one shower a week; the washing off of bugs from food; an increase in wages from twenty-five cents to a dollar per day; the inclusion of nonpork meals for Muslims and Jews; and freedom of religion. The rebellion lasted until September 13, when an assault force of 1,000 state troopers, prison guards, and National Guardsmen burst into the prison and killed thirty-two inmates and ten hostages, and wounded over 300 inmates. A total of forty-two people died at Attica. Ironically, the state troopers and guardsmen killed many more inmates and guards than did the prisoners themselves (Silverman and Vega, 1996).[1]

The Attica riot and government siege were televised for four days and forever changed the correctional system. It heightened public awareness of the importance of dealing with racial conflict behind bars. In the decades since the Attica uprising, the numbers of African Americans among the ranks of correctional officers and prison administrators have gradually increased, but prisons continue to be dominated by white males. In addition, the prisoners' rights movements, both inside and outside of prison walls, have lead to increased public acceptance of nonmajority religions such as Islam and Native American religions, and they have lead to the incorporation of cultural events and ethnic history into prison programs.[2]

In the late 1980s, politicians and victim rights organizations shifted attention away from prison reform and rehabilitation and began to advocate for tougher crime laws, longer sentences, and returning to prisons as instruments for punishment. Advocates of this movement created a fantasy world in which "society could lock' em up and throw away the key." Many states passed "three strikes and you're out" legislation, which would impose life sentences without parole for career criminals. Once incarcerated, the individuals comprising our prison populations are virtually forgotten by the outside world until they are released or there is a prison riot or uprising. What happens behind prison walls rarely attracts the attention of the media or sympathy of the general public,[3] and American prisons still remain powder kegs. In contrast to the days of Attica, inmates organize into gangs along racial and ethnic lines for survival and protection; thus racial and ethnic conflict of new dimensions and heightened importance occurs within prison walls. Although racial segregation is technically illegal, many prisons still separate inmates along racial lines in order to prevent racial violence.

Despite the changes brought on by the Civil Rights movement and uprisings at Attica and other facilities, whites still constitute the majority of correctional officers and administrators. Based on data from the American Correctional Association (ACA), in 1995, over 70 percent of correctional staff employed in the state prisons were white, and approximately 60 percent of those employed in the Federal system were white (*Sourcebook of Criminal Justice Statistics*, 1997).

Laura Fishman's and Richard Turner's article "Race Matters within the Vermont Prison System" takes a look at the current state of race relations in prisons in Vermont and how people of color (African Americans, Latinos, Native Americans, and Asian Americans—ALANA) adapt to incarceration in what the authors refer to as a *sea of whiteness.* In contrast to Conley's and Debro's article, Fishman and Turner focus on Vermont, a state in which the number of incarcerated minorities is still relatively small. Despite being dubbed the "whitest state" in the United States, people of color are still disproportionately overrepresented in Vermont's correctional facilities. Nonwhites represent less than 1 percent of Vermont's total population, but 6.7 percent of its prison population. Despite major increases in the numbers of minorities employed in corrections since Attica, there are still several areas in the country where prison staffs are still overwhelmingly white and rural. Fishman and Turner refer to the "domination of whiteness" in the prison system.

Under this domination of whiteness, ALANA inmates suffer from feelings of "diminishment, vulnerability, invisibility, and degradation." Little had changed since the Attica days when one inmate wrote,

> The prison population—nearly all nonwhite—comes from urban areas, but the prisons are out in rural, out of the way places. They're like isolated plantations where residents have never seen a black man who wasn't a prisoner. (Richard X. Clark, The inmates' spokesman tells what happened inside the prison during the fateful days of the Attica Rebellion. (Levitt, 1973, p. 47)

For Asians and Native Americans, the scarcity of staff and other prisoners who look like them presents yet another hardship that prisoners endure. Their anxiety of being in a "sea of whiteness" is often translated into fear, since many Asians are immigrants whose initial encounters with whites in their native Vietnam were under warlike conditions.

Although correctional facilities throughout the United States are becoming "browner," the Vermont situation of white domination and isolation is not an anomaly in this country. Increasingly overcrowded urban facilities are transferring prisoners and renting space for them in rural institutions outside of their home states. For example, the District of Columbia sent inmates across the country to rural Walla Walla, Washington, and Honolulu, Hawaii, has sent Asian Pacific inmates to prisons on the mainland that are located in predominantly white and rural areas.)[4]

Although the issue of race is central to any discussion of the criminal justice system, the role of class is relegated to a subordinate position in most contemporary research. Mainstream social science theories tend to deny the existence of a class-based system in American society divided into two basic classes of the "haves" and "have nots," or the bourgeoisie and the proletariat.[5] Radical and critical criminologists and social scientists, however, maintain that there is a ruling class that owns and controls the means of production, and that our laws are designed to protect their interests. Mainstream social science theories that dominate the field, however, maintain that laws are made by people through the political process, and these laws protect the interests of all citizens regardless of socioeconomic status.

Historically, most societies have used prisons to regulate and control the most powerless and politically threatening classes—the poor and the ethnic, religious, political, and sexual minorities. In the United States, prisons have been almost exclusively reserved for the poor and working-class males, and they have always imprisoned a disproportionate number of African Americans, Native Americans, and persons from the most recent, darker-skinned immigrant groups.

For decades, social scientists have debated which variable is more important—race or class—for predicting level of oppression. Although the authors of the previous readings in Part Six would agree that the disproportionate incarceration of people of color is partially fueled by their disproportionate concentration in the lowest socioeconomic groups in the society, they focus on the role that institutional racism plays as the direct variable causing the overincarceration of people of color. These authors recognize that people of color have fewer economic resources at their disposal and thus are often unable to post bail or attain adequate legal defense, but they also insist that poor whites are not subjected to the racial bias of police, prosecutors, and judges. In addition, these scholars point out that the economic status of people of color is a consequence of institutional racism. Thus they conclude that race is more important than class as factors in oppression.

Most of the readings in this book have dealt primarily with male prisoners. Twenty years ago, however, African American revolutionary Angela Davis asserted that "sufficient attention has not been devoted to women in prison" (Davis, 1971, p. 109). Whereas the role that class plays in the criminal justice system is blurred by the variable of race, the role of gender has been rendered virtually invisible. Ironically, gender is the strongest predictor of criminal behavior in all societies, since most crimes are committed by young males. The last article in Part Six draws attention to the debate of female criminality and the treatment of African American women.

Like their African American brothers, African American women have always been overrepresented in the nation's correctional facilities. However, the arrest and incarceration rates of women of all races remained at constant levels until the mid 1970s. (*Sourcebook of Criminal Justice Statistics,* 1997).[6] However, as a result of the war on drugs in the mid 1980s, the number of African American women in state prisons on drug-related charges soared 828 percent from 1986 to 1991 (*Young Black Americans in the Criminal Justice System: Five Years Later*). Not surprisingly, although white female inmates reported higher levels of injection drug use than either their African American or Hispanic sisters (42 percent for white women compared to 24 percent for African American women and 4.6 percent for Hispanic women), African American and Hispanic women are more likely to be apprehended and imprisoned as a result of their drug use (Collins, 1997).

Until the 1970s, most research on gender and crime in the United States highlighted the relative advantage that women faced in the criminal justice system. Chivalry tended to filter white women out of the prison system (Johnson, 1995; Klein & Kress, 1976). Freda Adler's landmark book *Sisters in Crime* noted the changing nature of crimes committed by women and predicted that "as women gain greater equality with men, the male-dominated judicial process will likely treat them with less deference and impose more stringent sanctions; the condition of being a woman in a man's world will carry less protection" (Adler, 1979, p. 10). Whereas chivalry tended to filter white women out of the prison system, Adler's prediction has always been reality for women of color, long before the feminist movement emerged, and male chivalry has never worked in favor of African American and Latina women. Visher theorizes that police officers held "behavioral expectations of black females that were contradictory to the behavioral expectations of women who were deserving of chivalrous treatment" (1983, p. 6).

"The Children of Female African American Prisoners" focuses attention on the unintended and often forgotten victims of the criminal justice system—the children and families of incarcerated women. Catherine Fisher Collins's article presents a picture of this problem at the aggregate level. At the time that this article was written, there were estimated to be 56,000 children of female inmates.

According to a national survey of imprisoned women in the United States, the majority are young women of color and single mothers (American Correctional Association, 1990). The war on drugs and its imprisonment of tens of thousands of addicts and street-level drug dealers has impacted women of all races, but it has had an especially crippling effect on low-income African American communities where women are most often the sole support of their families.

Drug addiction, AIDS, and the war on drugs has forced an entire generation of aging grandparents, often living at the poverty level, to assume financial and legal responsibility for the children left behind. Thousands of other children have been pushed into the overburdened foster care system and have become the responsibility of the taxpayers. How many of these mothers, once released, will be able to assume financial responsibility for these children? How many female inmates will be released terminally ill from AIDS and leave behind homeless orphans? What will happen when the aging grandparents caring for these children become disabled and die, removing the fragile extended family safety net?

Fisher Collins maintains that the enforced separation of children from their imprisoned mothers will no doubt have negative repercussions for these children. In a society where African American and other minority children are disproportionately poor, unhealthy, and live in communities plagued by violence, their enforced separation from their mothers will make their survival even more difficult. Finally, the added stigma of having a parent behind bars will undoubtedly increase the odds of these children being caught in an intergenerational cycle of crime and incarceration.

STUDY QUESTIONS

1. Identify the current extent of incarceration of nonwhites and the reasons for wanting to reduce this amount.

2. Historically, how has corrections been a part of slavery and the subjugation of African Americans?

3. Discuss the rise of the Black Muslim movement in prison, its significance for African American inmates, and the response of correctional officials.

4. How do people of color respond to the "sea of whiteness" in Vermont, and how does their situation reflect that of the nation?

5. Discuss the impact of the war on drugs on African American women and their children.

NOTES

1. State officials lied about the carnage and claimed that "knife-wielding inmates" killed many of the victims. Families of survivors and inmates filed a federal lawsuit in 1974. In September 2000, a federal judge awarded an $8 million settlement to the survivors of Attica and their families. No appeal.
2. Racial and ethnic conflict did not play a prominent role in the New Mexico Prison riot which occurred in the 1980s. This riot was the bloodiest to date and centered around inhumane treatment and torture of prisoners of all races by both white and nonwhite correctional officers.
3. The prison uprisings and takeovers that occurred in the 1980s and 1990s have received considerably less media attention since Attica, and the Marion facility in Illinois remained in lock down status for years after it endured inmate unrest.

4. Furthermore, as the privatization movement grows, in which private for-profit corporations are chosen to operate correctional facilities, it is likely that these corporations will not be required to hire individuals who are representative of the inmate population in terms of race and ethnicity, and to provide training that will enable their staffs to become culturally competent. Thus Fishman's and Turner's study has a great deal of relevance for policy makers in other states.

5. The mainstream social science theorists present an alternative depiction of social stratification which argues that the middle-class is a dominant force in the United States; that technocrats who administer the machines of the owners of production and common stockholders actually control corporate decisions; and that political power is not always determined by economic elites, but can be influenced by the middle class and poor through political interest groups and voting.

6. The rate of sentenced female inmates in state and federal institutions per 100,000 persons in the population was 5 per 100,000 in 1970, 10 per 100,000 in 1979, and 54 per 100,000 in 1997 (*Sourcebook of Criminal Justice Statistics,* 1997).

REFERENCES

Adamson, Paul (1983). "Punishment After Slavery: Southern State Penal Systems, 1865–1890," *Social Problems, 30:*555–569

Adler, Freda (1975). *Sisters in Crime.* New York: McGraw-Hill.

Collins, Catherine Fisher (1997). *The Imprisonment of African American Women.* London: McFarland & Company.

Conley, Darlene, and Julius Debro (2001). "Black Muslims in California Prisons: The Beginning of a Social Movement for Black Prisoners in U.S." Original manuscript.

Donziger, Steven R. (1996). *The Real War on Crime.* New York: HarperCollins.

Davis, Angela (1971). *If They Came in the Morning: Voices of Resistance.* New York: New American Library.

Du Bois, W. E. B. (1902). "Crime and Our Colored Population," *The Nation: 75:*499.

Johnson, Greg (1941). "The Negro and Crime," *Annals of the American Academy of Political and Social Science 217* (September): 93–104.

Johnson, Paula C. (1995). "At the Intersection of Injustice: Experiences of African American Women in Crime and Sentencing," *Journal of Gender and Law 4*(1):2–76.

Klein, Dorie, and June Kress (1976). "Any Woman's Blues," *Crime and Social Justice 5:*34–49.

Levitt, Leonard (Ed.) (1973). *The Brothers of Attica.* New York: Links Books.

Myrdal, Gunnar (1944). *An American Dilemma: The Negro Problem and Modern Democracy.* New York: Harper and Brothers.

National Research Council (1989). *A Common Destiny: Blacks and American Society.* Washington, D.C.: National Research Council.

Owens, Charles E. (1977). "Looking Back Black," In *Blacks and Criminal Justice,* Charles E. Owens and Jimmy Bell (Eds). Lexington, Mass.: Lexington Books, pp. 7–15.

Owens Charles E., and Jimmy Bell (1977). *Blacks and Criminal Justice.* Lexington, Mass.: Lexington Books.

Sellin, Thorsten (1928). "The Negro Criminal: A Statistical Note," *Annals of the American Academy of Political and Social Science 140* (November): 52–64.

Shelden, Randall (1999). "The New Apartheid," *The Critical Criminologist* (Fall): 1–5.

Shelden, Randall G. (2001). *Controlling the Dangerous Classes.* Boston: Allyn & Bacon.

Silverman, Ira, and Manuel Vega (1996). *Corrections: A Comprehensive View.* Minneapolis/St. Paul: West Publishing Company.

Visher, Carol A. (1983). "Gender, Police Arrest Decisions, and Notions of Chivalry," *Criminology 21:*5–28.

Black Muslims in California Prisons

The Beginning of a Social Movement
for Black Prisoners in the United States

DARLENE J. CONLEY

JULIUS DEBRO

The Civil Rights movement and the numerous other social and human rights movements that followed had a tremendous impact on the views and activities of Black inmates and led to an important revolution behind walls. The most important movement, however, was the Black Muslim movement. This movement, perhaps more than the Civil Rights movement, played a pivotal role in politicizing Black prisoners. It was the ideology of the Nation of Islam and the Black Muslims that gave rise to the separatism philosophy of the Black Power movement, which gained hegemony in the African American community in the late 1960s and 1970s. Although the civil rights movement and the ideology of equality and integration challenged the existing social order in the American correctional system, it was the Black Muslim movement that was viewed as a serious political threat that could undermine the entire system.

The state prison system in California underwent a radical change in its population in the late 1960s. In 1945, approximately two-thirds of all male felons in prison were white, one-eighth were Chicano, and less than one-sixth were Black. In 1964, more than one-half were white, one-sixth were Chicano, and more than one-fourth were Black. In 1970, nearly one-half of all prisoners within the state system were either Black or Chicano.[1] Despite changes in the racial population,

the techniques for dealing with prisoners remain essentially the same as they were twenty years earlier when the system was based on confinement and isolation from conventional society rather than on rehabilitation of the offender.

When the Black Muslim movement began in the California prison system in the fifties, California administrators attempted to handle the problem by identifying and isolating those persons who were considered leaders in the movement. The isolation and segregation of Muslims gave the organization the publicity it needed to recruit members not only within the institution, but from the community as well.

This reading will attempt to show that the administrative responses to the activities of Muslims resulted in further recruits for the movement and contributed to an increase of violence by inmates as well as by the administration. This reading traces the history of the movement within California prisons from its initial inception in 1958 to 1970, with particular emphasis on efforts by the administration, first to curtail the Muslim movement and, finally, to accord it a certain form of legitimacy. However, to fully explain the significance of the treatment of Black Muslim inmates in the prison system, it is necessary to briefly review the history and ideology of the emergence of the Nation of Islam, the religion that gave rise to this movement.

THE HISTORY OF THE NATION OF ISLAM AND THE RISE OF THE BLACK MUSLIM MOVEMENT IN THE UNITED STATES

The Nation of Islam was founded in the 1930s by a Black man named Elijah Muhammad. It was loosely based on the doctrine of Islam, but preached that Blacks were a superior race that had lost their dominant position in the world. Like traditional Islam, the women were obligated to cover their heads and assume a subordinate role in the family. All Muslims were encouraged to abandon their surname and take the last name *X* because the religion reminded Blacks that their last names were a remnant of slavery forced on their ancestors by their respective slave owners.

The religion began to gain momentum in the 1950s and it was during this period that the religion attracted its most famous recruit and spokesman, Malcolm X. In later years, heavyweight champion Cassius Clay announced his conversion to the Nation of Islam and changed his name to Mohammed Ali.[2]

Although the Nation of Islam had great difficulty competing with Christianity among the general society, it had a special appeal to incarcerated Black males. In contrast to the various Christian denominations, which preached religious repentance and submission and obedience to the U.S. justice system to prison inmates, the Nation of Islam preached Black pride and resistance to white oppression. The U.S. criminal justice system represented an arm of white-dominated society, which sought to oppress and destroy Black males. It provided inmates with a strategy for changing their lives and gave them a political ideology that promised hope for the Black race. The Black Muslim faith rejected the "pie in the sky" promise of Black Christianity and encouraged its members to improve their lives on earth.

The Nation of Islam required converts to abstain from tobacco, alcohol, drugs, and sexual activities. Membership required strict discipline and insisted that inmates engage in prayer several times a day, be immaculately groomed, and adhere to a strict diet of pork and sweet potatoes, two important staples of traditional Black cuisine. The African tradition of music and singing in church was considered a distraction to worship and music was eliminated from religious services. Inmates were also required to pursue educational opportunities available to them in prison and seek other avenues that could lead to self-improvement.[3]

This new religion and the activities of its adherents frightened white prison officials. The ideologies of Black superiority and racial separatism were diametrically opposed to the philosophy of the Civil Rights movement, which preached racial equality and integration. Whereas the Civil Rights movement preached nonviolent resistance, the Black Muslims voiced a philosophy of self-defense. Many whites interpreted the popular slogan, "By any means necessary," as a call to commit violent acts upon the white society.

THE MUSLIM MOVEMENT WITHIN THE CALIFORNIA PRISON SYSTEM

The first official contact with Muslims occurred at San Quentin in early 1958 when a Black male prisoner was observed preaching to other Blacks in the yard. The institution was not fully aware of the significance of this small gathering of Blacks. However, it began to collect information concerning the Muslims, based on the information obtained from the first preacher. Additional information was gathered primarily from other law enforcement agencies. This material proved to be highly inflammatory in nature.

One police group, which must remain anonymous, indicated that the Muslims had embarked not merely on a campaign of vilification of white police authorities but one of organized efforts at murder also. The chief of police stated that the Muslims' victims had been police officers. He further indicated that the Fruit of Islam (a highly trained cadre of Muslim males) would kill any policeman when the opportunity presented itself, no matter what the circumstances. The chief ended his memorandum to all police and law enforcement agencies with this quote:

> The men of these groups are extremely dangerous, further they are a type of fanatic and are willing to die for their cause, content if they take a Caucasian preferably a police [sic], with them.

The late Chief Parker of the Los Angeles Police Department made a request that the organization be declared subversive. Other organizations within law enforcement felt that groups of Muslims should be banned as a possible threat to security.

These allegations made by law enforcement agencies within the community began to create problems for those persons working within the institution. Institutional personnel did not know how to respond to the rising militancy of the Black inmates who were beginning to embrace the Nation of Islam.

The first official response by the Department of Corrections, which labeled the Muslims a management problem, occurred in 1958.[4] An administrative bulletin indicated that the Reception and Guidance Center (persons preparing social evaluations) should look for indicators of Muslim affiliation. If the inmate was identified as a Muslim, then the extent of his participation was to be evaluated and recorded in his file. All staff members were urged to collect and evaluate information concerning the group in the interest of "intelligent management and departmental security."[5] This document was sent to all of the institutions with a further note requesting each institution to forward reports of Muslim activities to central headquarters in Sacramento. The number of prisoners with Muslim affiliations was extremely small; however, at that time it was not known how many people were actually identified as belonging to the Muslim faith.

In 1960 another bulletin summarizing the teachings of the religion was issued by the Department of Corrections.[6] The bulletin cited the beliefs of the Muslim—that the Black man is a true descendant of "original man" and will rise to rule the world; Caucasians are devils; the Caucasian race and Christianity and Judaism are doomed; the Black man will rule America; and so

on.[7] The memorandum indicated that the organization was being investigated by the Federal Bureau of Investigation and other law enforcement agencies for evidence of criminal activity.[8]

The Department of Corrections now had clearly taken the position that the organization was a cult rather than a religion and that it should be discredited within the institution. This memorandum was used as the basis of banning within prisons such well-known Black publications as the *Pittsburgh Courier,* the *New York Amsterdam News,* and the *Los Angeles Herald Dispatch* because they carried columns written by Elijah Muhammad. The department indicated that these publications were carrying articles advocating racial segregation and superiority of one race over another, thus creating a danger to the safety and security of the institution.

Black inmates were becoming openly rebellious and much more radical than ever before. Prison officials believed that if Muslims were allowed to practice their beliefs within prison, it would create a greater division between Blacks and whites and eventually lead to race riots within the institutions. Prison authorities had seen Blacks in the past as persons who "did their own time" and did not complain about the injustices of the prison system even though it was openly discriminatory. Now Blacks were beginning to unite in a curious kind of way and prison officials did not quite know how to deal with the problem.

The prison climate generally reflects what is going on in the general communities from which its members are obtained. During this period, the Black revolution was just beginning in the United States. That is, the movement was changing from a rather conservative status-oriented posture to a more militant one focusing on the basic social and economic issues confronting the masses of Black people. Malcolm X, an ex-convict and a Muslim, was considered the most eloquent spokesperson for the new movement. Muslims continued to enter prisons at a rapid rate from the outside community and, as they were assigned to various prisons, they brought with them their conceptions of what the Muslim faith was all about.

The first organized complaint occurred in early 1961 at Folsom Prison when a group of Black inmates attempted to integrate the segregated mess hall [cafeteria]. Segregation has existed in various forms within the prison system since the initial opening of San Quentin in 1852, despite policy statements to the contrary. Folsom Prison has always been one of the most notorious for its racist, segregationist policies. In early February of 1961, an inmate sent a letter to the Associate Warden at Folsom:[9]

We the Afro-American population of this institution are wondering exactly, if anything, is being done in regards to the ugly and evil segregated policies of this institution?

As you know, California likes to boast about having one of the most enlightened penal systems in the world. There is some evidence to support this claim, however Folsom prison is the only institution in the state of California that is still segregated in the very same manner that it was in 1898.

. . . With each passing day our people of this institution are being taken undue advantage of by persons who feel that it is their duty to use their authority to persecute and intimidate those who will not cooperate and help them earn their pay.

. . . You deny us the opportunity to learn skilled jobs, so that you can keep us doing your menial work. The sad fact is, then, prison work seems to appeal to bigots and ignorant persons, for in a segregated setup it allows them to have a field day to vent their evil passions. The Afro-Americans are persecuted while imprisoned, and they emerge bitter and full of resent[ment] and hatred, not good ingredients for a successful assimilation into society.

Yet you wonder why your penal system is a failure.

We do not believe that the Governor is aware of the inhuman and barbaric methods that goes [sic] on behind these huge granite walls, and we cannot believe that the officials of this prison would want to see how men can react when they are being taken undue advantage of and everyone turn[s] their head in another direction.

There is a lot of discontent because of this deplorable thing called segregation.

This prison is a powder keg and it is subject to blow up and you can be assured that those who have
turned their heads on us will be the very first to be replaced with competent and unbiased persons.

The care and rehabilitation of prisoners is a complex problem in itself without compounding it with the evils of racial segregation.

I personally feel that Folsom should get out of the segregation business completely.

Since prison would seem to be the last place for "White only clubs," what do you think, sir?

The Associate Warden answered the letter:

Please be advised that you have been misinformed about the policies of this institution.

We do not have any racial segregation policy or rules in this institution and any man, no matter what his color, race, or religion, is eligible for all of the programs that are available here.

We will certainly remember your complaint, however, and if any segregated practices are brought to our attention, we will take appropriate action.

The answer by the Associate Warden made no mention of the fact that the dining room was segregated and no attempts had been made to alter the situation. The reply from the Associate Warden was widely distributed among the Black inmates at Folsom. On the last day of February, this same inmate sent a letter to the Warden:

Dear Sir:

We the Afro-American prisoners of this institution have a petition to Governor Brown in regards to the segregated policies of this prison.

For we cannot and will not believe that Gov. Brown is an active and supporting partner in racial segregation.

Folsom [P]rison is the only penal institution in the state of California that still enforces racial segregation, and we, the Afro-Americans, are at a great disadvantage from a rehabilitation standpoint, for racial segregation prevents the very rehabilitation that a stay in prison is supposed to produce.

We are segregated as a breed apart in living quarters, eating facilities and we are also segregated as far as job placements are concerned. We are definitely not classified according to our qualification, but are according to the color of our skin.

According to the Captain, there is no segregated policy in this institution, however, there has never been an official announcement to this effect, and there are rumors that we the Afro-Americans would rather be segregated.

I most emphatically assure you that no survey has ever been taken to determine what we would prefer, and there is also a rumor that there would be trouble should integration ever come to Folsom. Personally we do not think so, that is if it is put to the men in an intelligent manner, as a new ruling. We feel that the majority of men would abide by it.

Very frankly, sir, it all boils down to this,

The officials make the rules and control this prison, or the prisoners make the rules and control the officials. There has been no serious trouble in this prison in almost 30 years.

And you can be assured that there was no serious trouble in other California [p]risons when they were integrated, there will not be any in Folsom because the [m]ajority of the inmates appreciate the shows, the sports, the canteen and their radios, but these are all privileges, not "rights."

We feel that the care and rehabilitation of prisoners is a complex problem itself without compounding this any longer with the evils and unfairness of racial segregation.

This letter apparently was not answered by the Governor's office because within the next few days, the prison erupted in violence. On March 2, 1961, at breakfast, several Blacks sat on the traditionally white side of the dining room. At the noon and evening meals, the percentage of Blacks integrating the dining hall increased. This continued through March 3 with certain white inmates refusing to enter the dining halls. On that morning, 47 inmates, including the prisoner who had written the letters, were transferred to another institution. The writer of the letters was labeled a troublemaker, even though he had chosen an orderly manner in which to protest. Other inmates were labeled Muslims or agitators, despite the fact that the Muslims preached segregation rather than integration of the races. Despite the fact that segregation in the dining room was voluntary, when Blacks tried to integrate, the administrators felt that this was sufficient conduct to label the transferred inmates as "agitators." The authorities indicated that the "agitation" was in some way connected with a petition for a Writ of

Habeas Corpus, which had been filed by ten Muslims, eight of whom were transferred.

Integration by Blacks continued until violence broke out in the dining room between Blacks and whites. On March 4, a group of ten inmates met with the warden and it was decided that a section at the back of the mess hall be set aside for integration. Few if any persons sat at those tables. The warden and his staff were firmly convinced that the incident was caused by the agitation of the Muslims within the prisons. The warden gave an official statement to the press indicating that officially there was no segregation but convicts had, of their own accord, segregated themselves in the mess halls. The warden indicated that Blacks, led by Muslims, staged sit-ins in sections usually occupied by whites. He further added that "Muslims" aggressively tried to create incidents. Additional press releases indicated that Walter Dunbar, Deputy Director of the State Department of Corrections, issued a statement to the press:

> *The removal of 24 Black Nationalist Muslims from Folsom to another institution was to prevent violence. . . . Some of these colored people are trying to take over. We are now seating these people to our liking, not to theirs.*

These statements concerning Muslims tended to inflame not only white prisoners within the institutions but the administrators and other workers throughout the prison system as well. Each institution became acutely aware that Blacks now constituted a potential threat to the system. What the authorities failed to consider was that there was another group within the prison system that called themselves Afro-Americans and they were in no way affiliated with the Muslims.

The findings of the Civil Rights Division of the Attorney General's Office regarding the incidents at Folsom indicated that the outbreak of violence was not the direct result of Muslim activity. They further stated:

> *that the tendency of Folsom authorities to label all Negroes opposing segregation as Muslims is a serious error. Justifiably or not, Negro prisoners at Folsom believe there is a widespread discrimination*

there, not only in the refusal of the authorities to enforce integration in the main dining rooms, but in job and classification opportunities. We do not assert the foregoing as a fact and have not been able in our brief inquiry to establish the truth or falsity of the charges. We do believe it is significant, however, that Negro inmates believe the foregoing to be factual.[10]

Even though this report had in essence cleared the Muslims, the damage had been done in terms of labeling all Blacks who were concerned with integrating prisons or who caused trouble within the prison as Muslims. Persons within prison who happened to have literature concerning the Muslims were also given the label "Muslim" and information concerning their Muslim affiliation was placed in their personal files.

During 1961, 111 known Muslims had been identified and so labeled. However, they were well dispersed throughout the system. Forty-two were at Folsom, 24 at San Quentin, 3 at Duel Vocational Institute, 4 at Vacaville, 11 at Soledad, 25 with the Division of Adult Paroles, and 5 with the California Youth Authority. Yet one year later, one out of every twenty institutionalized Black male felons was identified as a "Black Muslim."

Previous writers of sociological thought ignored the Black inmate because he was often not considered a definite part of the prison inmate culture. Only a few writers even indicated that members of different ethnic groups might experience a different set of problems in prison and develop an inmate culture with special features.[11] Blacks can only be considered as sharing one thing in common with other groups in prison and that is a mutual dislike for the whole system of the administration of criminal justice because they are acutely aware that police brutality and harassment occur repeatedly in Black communities;[12] that from arrest to sentencing, they have been denied equal justice; that procedures such as bail and fines have been perverted to perpetuate institutional racism.[13] They know that their deterioration began at birth and in most cases, the family structure reflects complete instability. The inmate often is the product of a broken home and his lifestyle from birth until arrest has been one of utter frustration against the system.[14]

Compared to other Black inmates, those identified as Black Muslims were:

1. More often committed for a violent offense with the exception of homicide
2. In a younger age category
3. A returnee from parole, with a prior commitment record
4. An escapee from jail
5. Under life sentence
6. Committed from the Los Angeles area

INSTITUTIONAL RESPONSE TO MUSLIM MOVEMENT

The Muslims were seen by those who ran the prisons as a threat to the orderly management of the institution. Extensive pressure was being applied to those persons identified as Muslims. Black inmates who were considered leaders were locked up in adjustment centers and segregation units. Wardens and superintendents decided to deal with the Muslim movement in the same ways they had dealt with violence in the system in the past. Correctional officers who hated Blacks before the Muslim movement now had reason to hate Blacks more than ever. Not only could they now hate the Black simply because he was Black, but they could hate him because he embraced the Islam faith as well. The authorities used any excuse for disciplinary action if the individual was a Muslim. Based on the information as they read it, the institution concluded that Black Muslims had more violence potential than other Black inmates within the institution.[15] The Department of Corrections stated that

[T]o allow the preaching of racial superiority and enmity would be tantamount to inviting open violence, the teachings of the Muslim cult are heavily flavored with a concept of race hatred that contemplates violence as the ultimate solution to the problem. The cult further preaches segregation, which is against Departmental policy.[16]

The above statement indicated that the prisons were not segregated when, in fact, they still were to a certain degree.

Prison administrators saw the Muslim movement as the beginning of a violent racial revolution. Within the prison structure, as well as in the general community, people associate race and crime. Blacks are always seen as being more criminal than whites.[17] The crimes of Blacks within the California prison system are more assaultive than those of whites. Blacks commit more homicides, robberies, assaults, and auto thefts proportionately than members of other groups.[18] Blacks within the prison system were easy recruits for the Muslim movement because they needed an escape mechanism from the many hours and years spent in the system. For the first time, Blacks within prisons were beginning to unify around a common cause. The Muslim movement was the first organized Black movement on a national scale since Marcus Garvey and his "Back to Africa" crusade of the United Negro Improvement Association between 1916 and 1925.[19]

From 1962 to 1967, the Black Muslim movement experienced the greatest suppression within the system. In February, 1962, a Black Muslim was killed on the Adjustment Center yard at San Quentin by a white guard as he attempted to break up a fight between another Muslim and white inmate. There were approximately twenty inmates on the yard at the time of the shooting. Shots had been fired on the yard on each of the three days prior to the incident. A fight would start, the guard would fire a shot and the fight would be over. On this day, the fight started, the guard fired a shot, but the fight continued. The Muslim minister went over to break the fight up and was killed. Perhaps the death could have been avoided—if the guard had not been afraid of Muslims.

It was customary at San Quentin to assign one guard to walk the "cat-walk" and observe the inmates during their exercise period in the yard. The guard was not assigned to the Adjustment on a regular basis and, as a result, did not know the inmates housed within the center. Nor was he familiar with the many problems within the center. His only understanding of what normally happened was from other guards or from the reputation of inmates. Thus, the guard came to his job with preconceived

notions of how dangerous the Black Muslim inmates were within the Adjustment Center.

The death of the inmate at San Quentin immediately escalated the problem of the Muslims within the system. Blacks, whether they were Muslims or not, unified because of the shooting. Black inmates refused to go to work, and for many days the situation was very tense. The Muslims now had a cause and became more and more vocal because of the obvious suppression of the movement.

Prior to the Muslim movement, Blacks within prisons were easily isolated in mind and body from the rest of the inmate population. There were neither common beliefs nor acceptance of Blackness by the inmates. Most inmates wanted nothing to do with the concept of "Black"; even portraits in cells of Black inmates indicated a preference for white models.[20] The movement for Black identity therefore was a new concept that had to be dealt with, not only by Blacks, but by prison officials as well. Blacks began to isolate themselves within the prison, but this time for different reasons.

Daniel Glaser noted that isolation of Blacks from officers at Milan Federal Prison was due simply to a lack of communication by Blacks with whites in the community and that this was a consequence of segregation in their neighborhoods and schools.[21] Previous studies had indicated that inmates as a group were far from being an integrated social body.[22] Black Muslims were becoming unified within the prisons and prison authorities interpreted this as a conspiracy, which would ultimately lead to violence.

Prisons have always been expected to keep inmates quietly and securely confined, and to a large degree a prison's success is measured by absence of trouble in the form of escapes, riots, or physical violence. Prison administrators have worked out two principal kinds of solutions. One is to keep inmate society as unorganized as possible, and the second is to prevent individuals from joining forces. To this end, psychological isolation is substituted, to the fullest extent possible, for physical isolation. This permits inmates to work and to participate in prescribed activities, but it minimizes the danger of violence, revolt, or riot. To facilitate the state of disorganization or anomie, administrators always admonish inmates to "do your own time."

The response of the institutions to demands by prisoners has traditionally been coercive. Coercion *per se* is not repression, but it tends to dehumanize those against whom it is used, thereby fostering the growth of repressive patterns of domination.[23] The prison administration fears the implications of prisoners' demands, even if they are only asking for minor concessions. The easiest and most efficient response to an unpleasant situation has been to lock up those persons involved, or to lock up the entire institution for a "cooling-off period." Most of the Muslims were locked up in segregation units where they remained for long periods of time without being allowed to return to the main prison population. Despite this practice, Blacks were beginning to unify within the prison. And to the prison officials, unification meant an eventual attack against prison rules and regulations if efforts were not made to contain the movement.

Blacks were not "doing their own time" because they were agitating against whites and the system and demanding the constitutional right to practice their religion. It was quite obvious that the Department of Corrections would continue to try to suppress the movement as much as possible. Therefore, it became necessary for the inmates to petition the courts for redress. The institutional argument within the courts was that the Muslims preached segregation and hate against the white man, thus creating a management and discipline problem.

Courts have indicated over and over that they lack general supervisory powers in the areas of management and discipline within the prison. Judge Soboloff indicated in one of the Muslim cases that the maintenance of discipline in prison is an executive function with which the judicial branch will not interfere.[24] Subsequent Muslim cases were also thrown into the discipline/management category.[25] Most courts and institutions discounted the argument that there was a denial of religious freedom because it was sincerely believed that the Muslims practiced a cult and not a religion. Therefore, the Muslims were treated as a management problem.

It is clear that the prison's first responsibility is to protect society from those persons who are incarcerated for the commission of a crime and that this protection extends until such time as the person is released from the institution and returned to the community. In addition to the prison's role as protector, it is also charged with the responsibility of rehabilitating the offender. Both the protection and rehabilitation of the offender could not be accomplished if Blacks were allowed to embrace the religion of Islam. Muslim activities were seen as a threat to the orderly management of the prison, thus preventing the prison from doing its job.

Sociologists assert that prisons are *total institutions;* that is, "a place of residence and work where a large number of like-situated individuals, cut off from the wider society for an appreciable period of time, together lead an enclosed, formally administered round of life."[26] Not only are they total, but they are coercive as well. Coercive organizations, such as prisons, must maintain total control of their subjects in order to run the institutions in such a way that the managers can tell the community that they are indeed rehabilitating the offender. The Muslims posed a threat to this totality of institutional control. Thus the two could not coexist.

A former Adult Authority Board member indicated that there was a basic layer of ignorance throughout the department regarding minority problems. Administrators did not even remotely understand that minority problems could exist. Having no knowledge of such problems, administrators flatly stated that the Muslim problem was not a minority problem. Since the Adult Authority is charged with term setting, I asked what the policy was regarding Muslims who appeared before the Board. I was told that the Board initially took the position that the Muslims were the concern of the Department of Corrections. If the rules were violated, then this must be regarded by the Board initially as an infraction, regardless of the cause of the violation. The policy of the Board during the early sixties was that you could not appear before the body unless, prior to seeing the Board, you had six months without a violation. This rule excluded many Muslims because once the institution had identified them, it was extremely difficult to exist in prison for six months without having a rule infraction. This six-months rule was eventually changed so that the Board saw prisoners when their Board date came up, regardless of infractions. The Board finally took the position of not denying a person his parole simply because he was a Muslim.

MUSLIMS, PRISON, AND THE COURT

The courts finally ruled in *Cooper v. Pate* on June 20, 1967, that the blanket refusal to permit Black Muslim inmates to attend organized religious services conducted by a recognized minister of their faith constituted religious discrimination.[27] Additionally, the court stressed that it was up to the authorities to select the time and place for services, the number of persons admitted, and the number of guards necessary to maintain proper order and discipline.[28] This was a landmark case relating to prisons within the country. The decision was handed down in the State of Illinois; however, there were similar Muslim cases pending in the federal courts within the State of California. From the decision of the court in *Cooper v. Pate,* it appeared to be rather clear that the courts were moving in the direction of legitimizing the Muslim religion and that it would only be a short time before California courts would make a similar ruling.

In early 1967, the Department of Corrections established a "Race Relations Task Force" to study the Muslim question. In May of 1967, a "Muslim and Extremist Survey" was undertaken. The result of this survey indicated that there were a minimal number of incidents directly attributable to Muslims but that a larger number of "episodes" were directly traceable to institutional rules. The survey concluded that there was good reason to believe that "hoodlums" rather than Muslims per se constituted the real problem. The task force further noted that the elaborate identification procedure that had been established by the Department of Corrections had little value and that the minimal results obtained were not worth the expenditure of staff time. The final recommendation of the Task Force was that the Muslim religion should be recognized and the reporting of Muslim affiliation discontinued.

The recommendations of the task force were implemented in a Director's memorandum issued in November of 1967.[29] It recognized the Muslims as a religious body and allowed them the same rights as members of other religious faiths. Despite this memorandum, however, the recording of a religious affiliation with the Muslims still continues in a large percentage of the prisons.

Muslim ministers had not entered the institutions to any appreciable degree by the beginning of the 1970s. San Quentin invited a minister from the San Francisco mosque and he held services each Saturday for approximately eight months before writing to the institution indicating that it was with regrets that he must stop his services. This minister first spoke to the employees of San Quentin. They were impressed because, as one administrator stated, his replies were based on self-pride for the Black man and respect for others. The administration indicated that it had previously believed that Black Muslims preached that Islam was based on self-pride and no respect for others.

Once the movement was given an air of legitimacy at San Quentin, there was, according to one official, a noticeable change in the attitude of the Muslim inmates. The chapel was open for the inmates and they had their religious meetings once a week without difficulty. However, the prisons have not given the kind of support to the Muslim movement that it has given to other religious programs within the institution. A ruling was handed down by Judge Zirpoli in the U.S. District Court for Northern California in *Northern v. Nelson*[30] in July of 1970 that required the institutions to allow prisoners to receive the newspaper *Muhammad Speaks* and to make available at least one copy of the *Holy Koran* in each institution. The ruling also ordered prison authorities to pay Muslim ministers for their services when they visited the institutions.

The court order should not have been necessary. These changes should have taken place within each institution as soon as the director issued his memorandum recognizing the Muslims as a legitimate religion. The *Holy Koran* should have been ordered, just as the Bible or other religious material is ordered, as a matter of course. Prison personnel should have responded to Muslims' need for additional literature. Librarians, school educators, and other administrators within the prison should have routinely ordered sufficient copies to ensure that the Muslims had adequate reading material concerning their religion.

Once Islam was recognized as a religion, the institution quieted down somewhat. However, Muslim religious programs are still monitored or "supervised" by the administration. Persons charged with the duty of overseeing religious services maintained written reports at some of the institutions. Subtle forms of harassment were still used. I.D. cards were checked before entering Muslim services, and in some cases, I.D. cards had to be surrendered when Muslims entered the chapel for religious services. Names of all inmates attending services are also kept. Some comments of the administrative staff at one institution regarding Muslim religious services are quoted as follows:

> *I can recall no other religious meeting of any faith [that] went to such great lengths to advocate the destruction of our present system of democracy.*

> *In my opinion, the Muslim group is expounding a vicious racial attack and that such messages are highly out of order.*

> *I consider myself very tolerant, yet the speaker got to me in his talk in making many derogatory and insulting remarks about Christians. I wonder why I should voluntarily subject myself to this verbal venom directed against a religious group.*

> *Although the meeting was orderly, it was my feeling that the speaker took too much liberty in propagating hatred toward this country, the institution and the Caucasian race.*

> *There is still no real immediate problem though mass paranoia cannot be ruled out and there remains the potential for social destructive behavior.*

These comments were made by decision-makers within the institution who were in a position to make recommendations regarding job assignments, cell assignments, degrees of custody, transfer, and finally, release. Yet most of these decision-makers cannot or will not see that Muslim services, whether or not they have religious content, are a form of release for the individual, allowing him to vent his hostility toward the system.

CONCLUSION

In looking at the Muslim movement, one should not conclude that, if given legitimacy by the Department of Corrections prior to the court decisions, there would not have been violence within the prison institutions. While the Muslims did not openly advocate violence, they attracted persons to whom violence was a way of life and who would not hesitate to resort to violence again if they were frustrated in any way. There will always be persons who will use a movement for their own personal gain and their response will in no way reflect the ideology of the movement.

The prison failed because it was unwilling to grant the Muslim movement any degree of legitimacy. The Muslim movement could have been given legitimacy as a religion at a much earlier stage, thus eliminating the problem and expense of litigating in court.

It should not be necessary for the courts to tell the prison system to change. The prison system should change because there is an impelling desire to try things that are different and that will, to some degree, decrease the violence within the institution, even though in some cases this will entail an initial escalation of violence to bring about the change. Prisons have always been expected to keep inmates quietly and securely confined. To a large degree, a prison's success is measured by absence of trouble in the form of escapes, riots, or violence. Escapes are somewhat easy to contain. Violence within prisons continues to escalate at a very rapid rate within California prisons. Most of the violence has involved racial confrontations between inmates. African Americans see themselves as being an oppressed minority, both in the general community and in the prison. African Americans respond to injustices in a different kind of way than they did years ago. The response to in-equality today is much more militant and unified.

The African American prisoner sees racial dis-crimination each and every day within the prison; he sees it in cell assignments, eating facilities, job assignments, vocational training, and school as-signments. Although prison authorities may claim no segregation exists within the prisons, African Americans believe that it does exist and this con-tributes to their dissatisfaction. African Americans know that when violence breaks out within the walls and alliances are formed, they are formed along racial lines. The African American prisoner must stand alone while other groups form alliances.

The threat of violence reinforces the belief that African Americans must create a primary group based exclusively on race. The Muslims were such a primary group. There is an interaction that exists between a majority of African Ameri-cans within prison that has never existed in the wider community. The prison administration re-sponded to the Muslims in a violent repressive way because there was a fear that rising national-ism among African Americans within the prison would carry over into the larger community and lead to conflicts within the larger society.

Years ago, Black inmates unified around the program of the Muslims. Today, they are unifying around the program of the Black Panthers. The na-tionalism of the Muslims is somewhat tame com-pared to that of the Black Panthers today. The Panthers today were the Muslims of the early six-ties. The Muslims were seen as a cult or sect whose primary purpose was to create racial strife and whose method of operation was unlawful and violent. The Panthers are seen as a militant group that has created racial strife and will defend itself if attacked by others. Both the Panthers and the Muslims stress self-defense as one method of dealing with the power structure. Both organiza-tions have been the objects of close scrutiny by po-lice forces. Both organizations have attempted to build racial pride in elements of the Black com-munity. Both identify closely with prison inmates, and leaders of both organizations have been in prison. African American inmates today identify very closely with the Panther organization or are at least sympathetic to the movement.

The prison has responded to the Panthers in the same ways it responded when the Muslims first began. It has locked up those persons in Adjust-ment Centers and Segregation Units who have been identified as Panthers. Isolation is not the final solution to the problem, for when these inmates are eventually released, they return to the community with more hostility than when they went into the prison. Huey Newton has indicated that the

> *Walls, the bar, the guns, and the guards can never encircle or hold down the idea of the people. . . . The prison operates with the idea that when it has a person's body it has his entire being. They put the body in a cell, and seem to get some sense of relief and security from that fact . . . when the per-son in jail begins to act, think, and believe the way they want him to, and then they have won the bat-tle and the person is then "rehabilitated."*[31]

Black prisoners are now determined to fight insti-tutional racism within the prison. Prisons have not responded to the needs of African Americans in the past and if they do not respond in the future, violence will continue to escalate.

We must refocus our thoughts and begin to deal with the African American prisoner in a some-what different manner than the white prisoner. African American prisoners bring into the prison all of the hostility and frustration they have acquired in the community. They must have an outlet to vent these hostilities, and quite often it is done by joining groups such as the Panthers and the Muslims. Dras-tic changes must be made in our prisons if we are going to bring about changes in attitudes.

At Soledad in 1970, eight people were killed—two correctional officers and six inmates. Most of the deaths have been linked to racial strife within the prison. It began in Soledad on January 13, 1970, when a white guard shot three Black in-mates to death on the exercise yard of the maxi-mum security facility at Soledad. From there, the violence escalated throughout the system moving outside into the community. George Jackson, a Black militant, was accused of pushing a white guard over the railing, resulting in his death. Jackson was transferred to San Quentin and ultimately was killed in an attempted escape from the Adjustment Center. Jonathan Jackson, his brother who was in the community, tried to rescue prisoners on trial at the Marin County courthouse. He was killed along with a judge, a guard, and another inmate. Angela Davis was accused of supplying weapons for the attempted escape and was held in jail for over a year prior to her trial on the charge. Davis was subsequently acquitted of the charge.

Soon afterward, the riots at Attica occurred, resulting in more than thirty-five deaths of inmates and correctional officers. We must begin to reassess our role in prison administration and concern ourselves with prisoner rights. We must think in terms of immediate changes within the system rather than long-term changes in order to counteract the racism that exists in prisons. African Americans must be represented on the prison staff in proportion to the inmate population. The President's Commission on Correctional Manpower and Training indicated that Blacks within prisons make up a large percentage of the total prison population, but that only eight percent of correctional employees are Black.[32] Only three percent of all top and middle-level administrative personnel in prisons throughout the country are Black.[33] Our first priority should be to hire more Blacks and Chicanos as staff members within the prisons. Minority members should be brought in at the middle-management level so that inmates will have visible symbols always present and not feel that prisons are an all-white institution.

We must stop recruiting retired military men for positions as correctional officers. Although it is true that they are easier to work with and that they follow orders, their patterns are well set and they are very rigid and cannot easily adapt to changing situations without resorting to the use of a gun, a club, or tear gas. Most often these men have strong racist attitudes that are nearly impossible to change.

Wardens and superintendents of prisons should not have to serve long apprenticeships before attaining positions of leadership within the system. The longer a person remains in a system, the more difficult it is for him or her to change. Although it is true that custody runs the prison, treatment should have top priority in all of our institutions.

It is abundantly clear that prisons are becoming the spawning ground for Black revolutionaries within this country. It is also clear that within prison systems throughout the country, there has been, in the past, a unanimity of thought among top-level administrators against movements such as the Muslims and the Panthers. Perhaps if a Black administrator is present in the prison institutions, there may be an opportunity for the institution to attempt to work out a meaningful program for the Muslim without resorting to systematic isolation because of a difference in ideology. We must not wait until the courts compel changes within the institution. If one warden or one superintendent had allowed the Muslims to have a place of worship within his institution, we probably could have saved millions of dollars in courtroom litigations and prison administrative time.

The Muslim movement is no longer a moving force within the prison system. It has been replaced by a more militant movement that threatens to disrupt the entire prison system if alternative ways of dealing with Blacks are not provided. Changes within the system must occur at a much more rapid rate if we are going to return to the job of rehabilitating the offender.

NOTES

1. Department of Corrections, Characteristics of Felon Population in California State Prisons by Institution, A report prepared by the Research Division (Sacramento: Department of Corrections, 1970), p. 1.

2. Malcolm X with Alex Haley, *The Autobiography of Malcolm X.* (New York: Ballantine, 1964).

3. Ibid.

4. Department of Corrections, Administrative Bulletin No. 58/16, Sacramento, California, February 25, 1958.

5. Ibid.

6. Department of Corrections, Administrative Bulletin, *Muslims,* Sacramento, California, October 10, 1960.

7. Ibid.

8. Ibid.

9. Assembly, State of California, House Resolution No. 144, Regarding Acts of Violence at Folsom State Prison, March 28, 1961.

10. Ibid.

11. Sheldon L. Messinger, "Issues in the Social System of Prison Inmates," *Issues in Criminology,* (University of California, Berkeley, 1969), p. 140.

12. President's Commission on Law Enforcement and Administration of Justice. *Task Force Report: Report of the National Advisory Commission on Civil Disorders* (Washington, D.C.: U.S. Government Printing Office, 1967), p. 158.

13. Ibid.

14. Julius Debro. The Negro Offender (unpublished Master's thesis). San Jose State College, CA, 1968, p. 191.

15. Department of Corrections, *Characteristics of Felon Population-State Prisons of Ethnic Groups and Black Muslim Membership* (a report prepared by the Research Division, Sacramento: Department of Corrections, 1962), p. 1.

16. Department of Corrections, Information Bulletin, March 3, 1961.

17. Marvin Wolfgang and Bernard Cohen, *Crime and Race* (New York: Institute of Human Relations Press, 1970), p. 3.

18. Department of Corrections, *California Prisoners* (a report prepared by the Research Division, Sacramento: Department of Corrections, 1968), p. 66.

19. Department of Corrections: *The Muslim in Prison* (Washington, D.C., 1961).

20. Eldridge Cleaver, *Soul on Ice* (New York: Dell Publishing Co., 1968), p. 8.

21. Daniel Glaser, *The Effectiveness of a Prison and Parole System* (New York: Bobbs-Merrill Company, 1969), pp. 81–82.

22. Donald Clemmer, *The Prison Community* (New York: Rinehart, 1958), p. 118.

23. Philippe Nonet, "The Jurisprudence of Law and Order" (unpublished manuscript, Center for Study of Law and Society, University of California, Berkeley, 1970), p. 8.

24. *The Autobiography of Malcolm X* (New York: Grove Press, Inc., 1964), p. 183.

25. Ibid, p. 183.

26. Ervin Goffman, *Asylums* (New York: Doubleday and Co., 1961), p. xiii.

27. Cooper v. Pate, 382 Fed 2d 518 (7th Cr. Ct. of Appeals—April, 1967)

28. Ibid.

29. Department of Corrections, Religious programs (an Administrative Bulletin issued to Wardens, Superintendents, Deputy Directors and Staff Members (Sacramento: Department of Corrections, 1967).

30. Northern v. Nelson, No. C-69 279 AJZ (D.C. N.D. Cal, 1970)

31. Levitt, L. (Ed.), *The Brothers of Attica.* "The Inmates' Spokesman Tells What Happened Inside the Prison During the Fateful Days of the Attica Rebellion" by Richard X Clark (New York: Links Books, 1973).

32. Ibid.

33. Ibid.

BIBLIOGRAPHY

Caldwell, Wallace F. *Black Muslims Behind Bars,* Washington State University, Pullman, Washington, December 1966.

California Peace Officer, *The Muslim Movement,* Allen P. Bristow, Assistant Professor of Police Science and Administration, Los Angeles State College, May-June 1961, p. 21.

Cleaver, Eldridge. *Soul on Ice.* New York: Dell Publishing Co., 1968.

Clemmer, Donald. *The Prison Community.* New York: Rinehart Co., 1958.

Cooper v. Pate, 324 Fed 2d 165 (7th Cir. 1963).

Cooper v. Pate, 382 Fed 2d 518 (7th Cir. Ct. of Appeals—Apr. 1967).

Department of Corrections, *California Prisoners,* Research Division, Sacramento: Department of Corrections, State of California, 1968.

———, *Characteristics of Felon Population in California State Prisons by Institution,* Research Division, Sacramento: Department of Corrections, State of California, June 30, 1970.

———, *Characteristics of Felon Population State Prisons of Ethnic Groups and Black Muslim Membership,* Research Division, Sacramento: Department of Corrections, State of California, November, 1963.

———, *Inflammatory Inmate Groups,* Administrative Bulletin No. 58/16, Sacramento: Department of Corrections, State of California, May 18, 1961.

———, *Integration,* Progress Report. Sacramento: Department of Corrections, State of California, March 29, 1961.

———, *Islamic Literature,* Administrative Bulletin No. 61/40. Sacramento: Department of Corrections, State of California, April 4, 1961.

———, *Muslim Cult in Prisons,* Information Bulletin. Sacramento: Department of Corrections, State of California, March 3, 1961.

———, *The Muslim in Prison,* a Study of the Institute of Criminological Research, Department of Corrections, Washington, D.C., 1961.

———, *Muslims,* Informational Memorandum. Sacramento: Department of Corrections, State of California, October 10, 1960.

———, *Religious Programs,* Administrative Bulletin No. 67/82, Sacramento: Department of Corrections, State of California, November 20, 1967.

———, *Rules,* Sacramento: State of California, 1960.

———, *Special Procedures for Muslim Inmates,* Administrative Bulletin No. 58/16. Sacramento: Department of Corrections, State of California, May 18, 1961.

Fonder, Philip S. *The Black Panthers Speak.* New York: J. B. Lippincott Co., 1970.

Glaser, Daniel. *The Prison Community.* New York: Rinehart Co., 1969.

Goffman, Ervin. *Asylums.* New York: Doubleday & Co., 1961.

Magida, A. *Prophet of Rage: A Life of Louis Farrakhan and His Nation.* New York: Basic Books, 1996.

Northern v. Nelson (recent case, citation not available, U.S. Federal Court, Northern District of California, *IIC-69* 279 AJZ, July 1970).

Schafer, Stephen. *Theories in Criminology.* New York: Random House, 1969.

Wolfgang, Marvin, and Bernard Cohen. *Crime and Race.* New York: Institute of Human Relations Press, 1970.

X, Malcolm, with Alex Haley. *The Autobiography of Malcolm X.* New York: Grove Press, Inc., 1964.

Department of Justice, *Disturbances at Folsom State Prison,* Re: House Resolution No. 144. Sacramento: Office of the Attorney General, State of California, March 28, 1961.

Race Matters within the Vermont Prison System

Reactions of Prisoners of Color to Racism and Imprisonment

LAURA T. FISHMAN

RICHARD C. TURNER

INTRODUCTION

People bear all they can and, if required, bear even more. But if they are black in present-day America they have been asked to shoulder too much. They have had all they can stand. . . . Turning from their tormentors, they are filled with rage.
— Grier and Cobbs

It is not easy to be African American, Latino, Asian, or Native American within the U.S. prison system, especially within a virtually all-white prison system. This observation runs through the accounts of African American, Latino, Asian, and Native American prisoners (i.e., ALANA prisoners) imprisoned within Vermont's correctional facilities. Regardless of ALANA prisoners' social backgrounds, attitudes, values, and lifestyles, they embark on a new life once they enter Vermont prisons. Incarceration demands that they become socialized into a system whose structure, values, and regulations dominate every aspect of their lives. Within the prison system their status as "free" individuals is terminated. This transformation demands that ALANA prisoners cope with (1) the "usual" series of mortifications, degradations, and dehumanizing events that are rendered to all prisoners,[1] and (2) the process of reconciling two stigmatized roles; that is, being a person of color and being a prisoner.

This reading is about ALANA prisoners and the adjustments that they have and have not made to living in Vermont's virtually all-white prison system. A detailed examination will show the extent to which ALANA prisoners perceive they are living in a prison environment dominated by whites whom they believe to be racist.

There is evidence that what has been described as the dual systems of oppression (racism and the "pains of imprisonment") can and does affect Vermont ALANA prisoners. As people of color, as with white prisoners, they find themselves constantly confronted with their debased and stigmatized status as prisoners. But as people of color, ALANA prisoners also suffer the additional burdens of prejudice and mistreatment that befall anyone with darker skin. An African American prisoner, incarcerated in a Vermont prison, illustrates this point:

> They [correctional staff] just didn't care. They don't care about nobody. So they don't care about the white or the Blacks. But most of all they don't care about the Blacks. Like I said, they love themselves first. And they hate Blacks. But you're a prisoner here so they're going to put everyone in the same category. But if it's a white or a Black, they're going to go for the white first.

There has been a national shift in our thinking about race and imprisonment. We are beginning to recognize that imprisonment, especially when coupled with race, produces so many stresses that the coping abilities of ALANA prisoners are challenged to the extreme. Race carries with it a tremendous stigma and has a tremendous impact on a prisoner's ability to cope. A second shift, a consequence of investigators' forays into various prisons, is the contention that "race matters within U.S. prison settings."[2] There is some evidence that ALANA prisoners receive differential treatment from that afforded the general prison population. Differential treatment includes excessive surveillance by prison staff, a disproportionate number of disciplinary reports, increased time served in segregation, and disrespectful treatment by both prison staff and white inmates.

Implicit here is the distinction between the attitudes and behaviors of one racial group toward another. It is reasonable to expect that ALANA prisoners who are at the bottom see differential treatment within the context of race relations and therefore see these forms of treatment from a different perspective than those at the top. How ALANA inmates in Vermont perceive race relations is the substance of this reading. Accordingly, the term *race relations* refers to how members of different racial groups interrelate (see Genders and Player, 1989).

In this reading I focus on how relations within the Vermont prison systems are influenced by the experiences of imprisonment per se and by the identities and pre-prison experiences that ALANA prisoners bring with them from the outside community. Secondly, I present the ALANA prisoners' assessments of race relations in two Vermont prison systems by considering (a) the extent to which ALANA prisoners identify race relations as problematic and (b) how they utilize coping devices to ameliorate the "pains" of perceived prejudice and discrimination.

Finally, using qualitative data based on interviews and focused sessions with ALANA prisoners, I address the ways in which "race matters"

within the Vermont prison systems.[3] The ways in which the patterns of interaction between different prison groups is shown to be influenced by race as well as by the organizational features of the prison system. This reading also describes the racism that the ALANA inmates encounter within the Vermont prisons and the extent to which these encounters affect their daily lives.

Types of Vermont Prison Systems

The analysis in this reading is based on two Vermont correctional facilities (Fallsburg State Correctional Facility and Belmont Regional Correctional Facility) and how they structure the interactions that can occur between ALANA prisoners and white prisoners and prison staff.

The Fallsburg State Correctional Facility (Fallsburg State) is a traditional medium-security prison for convicted felons from throughout the state. The facility has various security levels ranging from long-term offenders in need of maximum-security and medium-security to those in need of short-term higher security detention. Fallsburg State also has a sexual offender program and a violent offender program.

As one of the four community-based correctional facilities in Vermont, the Belmont Regional Correctional Facility (Belmont Regional) serves as a medium-security facility for both detainees and convicted offenders. The Belmont Regional is also intended "to provide a bridge" for prisoners to re-enter the community. The security levels therefore vary according to whether prisoners are on work release, extended furlough, or weekend passes. As a result, there is a continual turnover of inmates, creating an atmosphere of instability and crisis.

Within both facilities, the administration and staff are overwhelmingly white, with most of the staff drawn from the rural areas of Vermont. Unlike other U.S. prison systems, Vermont's is dominated by whites.

The racial breakdown of the U.S. prison population has altered considerably since the 1960s. Recently, an increasing number of correctional facilities have not only gotten bigger but also have gotten "browner." A similar trend is occurring in Vermont. The incarceration rate for racial minorities has increased so rapidly that the local media concluded that there is now a disproportionate number of ALANA prisoners in all the correctional facilities.[4] An informal census of Vermont's prisons shows that almost 6.7 percent of the state's prisoners are members of racial minorities, whereas census figures show that less than 1 percent of Vermont's general population is nonwhite.

METHODOLOGY

This reading is based on data gathered from in-depth, unstructured interviews with ALANA prisoners incarcerated at the two designated Vermont correctional facilities. Correctional staff who knew the racial identity of the prisoners informed the prisoners of our presence within the facilities and the purpose of our visits.

Each facility provided a list of ALANA prisoners. However no one ever contended that these lists were inclusive. Therefore, sample size inaccuracies may occur for two reasons. First, the inmate population at the Belmont Regional Correctional Facility was in continual flux. Consequently, staff found it difficult to recall all racial minority inmates who were still housed in the facility as well as ones who had been released, paroled, or transferred to other facilities. In contrast, the Fallsburg State's prison population was far more stable because the majority were serving extensive sentences. Even though the turnover was less rapid, staff still failed to provide an accurate list of minority prisoners. Second, neither the Native American nor the Latino prison population were easily identifiable. Many did not disclose their racial membership and attempted to merge quietly into the white prison population. These prisoners could successfully "pass" because they did not possess easily identifiable physical and cultural characteristics.

After the final lists of ALANA prisoners were compiled, we made arrangements to interview all the listed ALANA prisoners. The interviews were administered in prison offices, meeting rooms, or lawyer–client visiting rooms.

At the beginning of each interview session, confidentiality was assured. Prisoners also were informed about the broad goals of the study and about elements of our own history. All prisoners became aware of some commonalities between us and them. For instance, we too, belong to a racial minority. We, too, had lived in several predominantly African American and Latino inner-city neighborhoods. We, too, came to the interview with a great deal of familiarity with crime, courts, and prisons. Thus they understood that we would share the worlds in which they lived to a greater extent than most university professors.

All the prisoners except five agreed to take part in the research. We were impressed by the seriousness and thoughtfulness with which they approached the questions and by the ways in which they sought to offer a dispassionate view of their experiences. Although some prisoners glossed over relevant events to present a more favorable picture of themselves, there is no reason to suppose that they had a vested interest in lying about their encounters with differential treatment within a historically white prison system. The main focus of the sessions was on the various aspects of the prison system, not on their prior criminal conduct.

All interview sessions were focused and in-depth; each lasted no less than two hours and sometimes as much as three. An interview guide was used to ensure that the same basic topics were covered during each session. The main body of the interview guide consisted of open-ended topics on subjects related to recent experiences with racial prejudice and discrimination. Prisoners were encouraged to speak freely. They were allowed to discuss questions out of sequence and to digress to other topics. The unstructured, qualitative interview permitted ALANA prisoners to speak in their own terms, to present their accounts of everyday events, and to include much information about their social contexts and relationships. Their accounts reveal much about the racial practices and structures of Vermont prisons. Each interview was unique, of course, but together they identified broad patterns of interaction between the ALANA inmates and the Euro-American staff and prisoners. The composite of interviews also illustrated the shared ways of coping with prejudice and discrimination.

Another source of data evolved from our initial contacts with the ALANA prisoners at Fallsburg State. Small groups of prisoners began to meet informally with us. Occasionally four to six of us sat together and participated in spontaneous discussions about past and present events. These discussions provided important insights into the meaning that various events held for the prisoners, as well as a comparison of racial differences in defining issues of paramount concern.

A final source of important data was the more formal focused sessions held at the two prisons. Between fifteen and twenty prisoners attended these "rap sessions." Often we began with the prisoners' complaints about how they were treated as persons of color. In the course of each session, they would share specific information about the colorations of racism within their facility and the possible means of coping with differential treatment based on race. At times, we were passive participants in these discussions. At other times we directed the discussions into areas that interested us.

Because there has been no previous study of race relations within virtually all Euro-American prison systems, this research is an exploratory case study. The major purpose of this paper is to describe how racism is manifested within two Vermont prison systems and to recommend ways to ameliorate the "pains" of racism. To accomplish these goals, the data collection and analysis proceeded simultaneously, and an understanding of the phenomenon was constantly revised as more data was collected. Information from the data sources was subjected to rigorous comparisons, cross-checking, and validation with respect to ALANA prisoners' perceptions of how racism affects their daily lives within the Vermont prison

setting. Thus, much of the analysis presented here is a product of this process.

A PROFILE OF ALANA PRISONERS

All of the ALANA prisoners who participated in this study did so voluntarily. The total number of participants included in the final study population was thirty-seven men and two women. Of these, fifteen men and two African American women were incarcerated at Belmont Regional; nine men were African Americans, five Latinos, and three Native Americans. African Americans dominated the ALANA prison population and Latinos were overrepresented when compared to their presence in the nonprison Vermont population.

The Latinos' fluency in English varied; most, however, were bilingual. Only two of Mexican descent did not speak any English and therefore were not included in the sample population. The majority of Latinos came from Puerto Rico. Three came from the Dominican Republic and Colombia. In contrast, the three Asian prisoners were first generation immigrants (from Cambodia and Vietnam); two spoke English haltingly, one spoke very little English.

Typical of prison populations, the study population was young. Three-fourths were under thirty years of age. In contrast to the African American, Latino, and Asian population, two of the three Native Americans were over the age of thirty.

Whatever their race, most of the ALANA prisoners were poor, badly educated, under- or unemployed, and not part of stable households.

Most of the African American inmates either had completed high school or had received a high school equivalency diploma. On the other hand, the majority of Native Americans, Asians, and Latinos had not finished high school.

The majority of ALANA prisoners, regardless of racial group, were chronically unemployed or employed infrequently and for short durations. The majority of jobs were seasonal. The older ALANA prisoners were more likely to be steadily employed in unskilled and semi-skilled jobs. The two African American women were homemakers and received some form of governmental assistance. Ten of the men got money by petty crime or drug dealing.

In contrast to the white incarcerated men in the Vermont prisons, most of the African American and Latino prisoners had lived in large urban areas (e.g., New York City, Boston, and Chicago) before settling in Vermont. Almost all were relative newcomers to the state. They reported that they had resided in Vermont for one month to two years before being arrested. Only a few were native to Vermont. In turn, all the Asian prisoners indicated that they were recent immigrants to Vermont. Only one had resided in Burlington for as long as two years. Lastly, all the Native Americans were born in Vermont and either resided within small urban areas or the rural areas of the state. None claimed to live with the Abenaki community.

This background of marginalization strongly suggests that most of the study population paid a price for being poor and nonwhite. The price was the use and abuse of drugs. A sizeable number, especially the African Americans and Latinos (no Asians reported that they used drugs), consumed drugs; the drug of choice tended to be either cocaine/crack or heroin. All the Native Americans spoke about abusing alcohol prior to their imprisonment.

According to most of the prisoners incarcerated in both facilities, they were charged with a variety of crimes against persons, ranging from simple assault, aggravated assault, sexual offenses, robbery, and homicide. Many claimed that their involvement in these crimes was drug-related. Only a few were charged and convicted solely for possession of drugs, drug dealing, or other nonviolent crimes.

Almost all ALANA prisoners imprisoned in Belmont Regional were serving short sentences. Those who had been in prison for less than two years and had sentences of less than forty-eight months were considered short-sentenced, newly-entered inmates. The long-sentenced, newly-entered inmates had been in prison for less than two years but had sentences of more than forty-eight

months and were most likely to be at Fallsburg State. Four men were transferred to Fallsburg State while the field research was in process. The few remaining inmates who were being detained due to lack of bail were mainly incarcerated at Belmont Regional.

It is not surprising that most men at Fallsburg State, and a few at Belmont Regional, had extensive criminal histories and reported that they had spent time in prison prior to their current incarceration.

Finally, the ALANA prisoners' accounts revealed that they appeared to bring their knowledge and criminal identities with them as they moved their residences from distressed inner-city communities to Vermont. Given this, a sizeable majority appeared to have been tied rather closely with the slum drug subcultures in their communities. The values, norms, and lifestyles of this subculture were imported first to Vermont and then to the Vermont prison systems.

The Clash of Various Cultures

The experience of imprisonment for most ALANA men and women was based on their encounters with prison systems in which African American and Latino prisoners were the dominant racial groups. For most, Vermont was an "unusual" experience that did not match their previous prison experiences. For instance, a significant number of African American and Latino prisoners were previously imprisoned in the New York State prisons in which 85 percent of the state's prison population was African American and Latino. All noted that they brought with them to the Vermont prison experience a sense of race relations as experienced primarily within urban inner-city communities and out-of-state prisons.

According to the accounts of ALANA prisoners, the very structure of the Vermont prison system—its walls and bars, its rigid hierarchy, its whiteness—is designed to reinforce a relevant image of the power of the white system of oppression. This system—including staff and inmates—is overwhelmingly Euro-American. The common, "usual way of doing business" has been rural and "white" in orientation. A prisoner at Belmont Regional illustrates this point:

> When I got here I was in awe. I walked inside and I didn't see anybody of color. This is going to be a major problem. And it was. Especially the country boys because they're the ones usually telling the Black jokes and they are the most ignorant on the subject.

The distinct racial and cultural identities and lifestyles that ALANA prisoners bring with them are highly influential in shaping their subsequent adaptations to a predominantly Euro-American and rural prison life. And the major components of these cultural identities and lifestyles are crucial to understanding the kinds of adaptations forged by ALANA prisoners in response to a system that they immediately perceived as racist. As one African American male points out:

> These white boys come from here and they are thrown in jail for sexual assault. We come from the ghetto and we rob for money and steal and sell drugs. We're different. They just rob because they get drunk. We rob because we have to eat. When I was fourteen years old, my mother was not able to feed us so I robbed to eat.

Almost all the ALANA prisoners felt culturally distinct. They brought their own lifestyles, interests, and activities, which often clashed with those of the white, rural prison population. This is not unusual in our society where ALANA culture and social experiences have clashed with white culture and social experiences throughout history.

The African Americans and Latinos were largely an urbanized group. They had a metropolitan smartness that they continually contrasted with the perceived dull, rural mentality of both their white custodians and fellow prisoners. As one African American male said:

> We have the streets and the book education. We come from Boston and New York. We're more advanced. Our school system is more advanced. The people from the farm country do not have as much education. They work the land.

They do more primitive crimes like sexual crimes. These are the sex offenders. They have a primitive

mentality. They are only concerned with taking care of their physical needs.

Racial identification was the primary axis of life for most African Americans and Latinos with the deprivations of incarceration being subordinate to this concern. It was this racial perspective that has its origin in the inner-city ghetto cultures.

What is clear from the accounts of African Americans and Latinos, especially those who were ghetto dwellers, is that they share common understandings that they use to define themselves as distinctly African American or Latino. In turn, they view themselves as possessing a cultural frame of reference distinct and in opposition to that of whites. This frame of reference includes beliefs and practices that provide a defense against racism; it excludes certain white cultural traits as inappropriate and includes oppositional practices to keep whites at a distance. The many themes of this perspective are subsumed under a code-of-the-streets that is employed to maximize surviving such circumstances of life among the ghetto poor as lack of jobs that pay a living wage, the stigma of race and the fallout from rampant drug use and drug trafficking, and the resulting lack of hope for the future. Thus this oppositional culture and its code-of-the-streets create a unique way of moving, gesturing, talking, and thinking that can be viewed as irrational and frightening by whites.

As a consequence of incarceration within this virtually white prison system, a theme recurs in the ALANA prisoners' reports. This message, which they have heard since early childhood, consistently extols white identity and culture; it stresses that the ALANA prisoners' languages, culture, food, and habits are inferior and should be changed to those of the Anglos. This perceived domination by whites has resulted in their feeling that they are incarcerated in an environment controlled by a "white" structure that they cannot change and that threatens to destroy their oppositional cultural frame of reference.

To combat feelings of powerlessness, exclusion, and absence of control over the conditions of their existence, most attempted to maintain a strong identification with such components of their cultural identities as (1) the code-of-the-streets, and (2) their racial heritage. According to these prisoners, the street cultural orientation amounts to a set of informal rules governing interpersonal public behavior, including violence. At the heart of these rules is the issue of respect, loosely defined as being treated "right" or granted the deference one deserves. Respect also is an active concept that must be earned in order to achieve deference. One young African American man observed:

> Respect means that you treat guys the way you wanted to be treated. To give respect, you do not put your hands on people. I see the way I am treated by other people. I know when I get respect. Like a CO talks to me before he accuses me . . . I'm in my unit. I can go down to booking. I can make a phone call when I need to. I get free phone calls. I get respect and clout. If an argument breaks out and they know that I can control it, the brothers respect me and listen to me.

Not only in the street culture, but here in the Vermont prison systems, respect then can be viewed as almost an external entity that is hard-won; because it is easily lost, it must be constantly guarded. The rules of the code in fact provide a framework for negotiating respect.

Not only "on the streets" but within the prison community, material objects play an important and complex role in obtaining "respect." For instance, within the constraints of material deprivation, sneakers, gold jewelry, and pressed pants not only reflect the inmates' taste but also a willingness to possess things that may require defending. As recalled by a Latino prisoner from New York City:

> I'm new in the neighborhood. They want to see if I can stick up for myself. If they came after me and I run, I get no respect. They can come up and say that they like my sneakers. Then they can say my sneakers are their size. I can get beat up for my sneakers. And they then keep doing it. But if I fight, they say that the kid has got heart. He's not afraid. I get respect. They do not mess with you any more. Eventually, I can hang with them and they can mess around and joke with me.

Violence will win respect. And to maintain respect, inmates reported that they must continually show that they are not someone to be "messed with" or "dissed" (disrespected). Any slight can be considered disrespectful. One African American said:

> You give respect, you get it. First there's a confrontation between me and a mutant [i.e., a white prisoner]. I will try to make him afraid of me. But I try to tell him "not to push it" and to get out of my face. We have a couple of clashes and then this guy knows that he is not going to stomp me. Then he comes up to me and says, "You're from New York. I have a Black friend." First I use influence but I will stomp on them when necessary. Whenever I'm totally disrespected, when a white guy gives it, I do what I've done for years. I assault him.

What is suggested here is that one's bearing must send the unmistakable if sometimes subtle message to the next person that one is capable of violence when the situation requires it.

Relevant here is the strong belief that manhood is to be displayed on a daily basis. Manhood is related to respect. For many African Americans and especially Latinos, manhood and respect are flip sides of the same coin. Manhood means taking the prerogatives of men with respect to white prisoners. It implies a physicality, a confrontative attitude toward authority, nerve, and ruthlessness. Both require a sense of control, of being in charge, of taking no "crap" from anyone, of being a "stand up" person, and of pushing the authorities to the limit.

These findings are consistent with observations made about the exaggerated importance of manhood and respect among prisoners of color in other prisons in our country. Given this, many ALANA prisoners concurred that the Vermont prison system, like any other prison system, attacked inmates' sense of self-worth while mortifying their "moral identity." Manhood and respect, as a consequence of the onslaught on feelings of self worth, become seriously jeopardized; they become major issues in confronting the intersection of the dual structure of oppression.

In contrast, those inmates who are Black Muslims became hypersensitive to issues of respect based not only on their dual discredited status but also on their religion. Central to their adherence to the Muslim religion in the face of the onslaught of multiple oppressions is the notion of respect as tied to both the street code and the Muslim religion. The core aspects of their notions of "respect" tend to focus on both manhood and the daily adherence to Muslim religious practices, traditions, and beliefs. For instance, a Muslim recalled:

> I'm a Muslim and in their eyes, it's a Black thing. See that guy there, I give him half my food at chow because he is a Muslim and they won't respect his rights to get certain foods.

Two Native Americans reported that issues of respect were central to their lives within these facilities. However, as with the Muslims, they, too, perceived that issues of respect were defined by their group, the Abenakis, and by the Abenaki religious beliefs and ways of living. They expressed a strong commitment to Abenaki ceremonial practices that affirm their spiritual connection. Practicing their religious beliefs and their way of life becomes central to a sense of respect. One man struggled to reaffirm his heritage as a way to gain respect by encouraging aggressors to cease bothering him. A Native American asserted that:

> I'm proud of my heritage. I have a whole family tree. I can go back to the 1600s to Chief Greylock's wars. I've done some research on my family. I love it. The more I hear about it, the more I demand that these people respect me as an Abenaki.
>
> I respect my heritage and I expect that others will know that I come from a group who fought. We built our reputations on being fighters. We were respected.

The Native Americans also indicated that they perceived any sign of disrespect as an attack on their Indian manhood; they also searched for methods to undermine the ongoing onslaught by searching for means to be respected as prisoners and as Native Americans.

The Southeast Asians reported that they were more exposed to the stresses and strains of survival; that is, dealing with the daily constraints of language, which prevented them from adequately accommodating what they considered a disorienting and strange world. One Asian spoke repeatedly about his fears and anxieties, which centered around living with "tall, giant-like white men with long hair and tattoos." He was terrified. Incarceration had forced him to encounter a deep-seated fear of "Americans with long hair and tattoos." He reported that he acquired this fear in his homeland as a young boy. And all the Asians expressed a generalized fear of being treated in a hostile manner as well as fear that they would be unable to avoid hostility because of their status as Asians. For them, issues of respect were minor to the exigencies of survival.

To conclude, for the African Americans and Latinos especially, their search for self-identity becomes one of striving for respect. Nathan McCall's recollections in *Makes Me Wanna Holler* (1994: 52) about the importance of respect for young inner-city Black males are relevant here:

> *The whole emphasis in the streets . . . was rooted in respect. . . . For as long as I can remember, black folks have had a serious thing about respect. I guess it's because white people disrespected them so blatantly for so long that blacks viciously protected what little morsels of self-respect they thought they had left. . . . It was universally understood that if a dude got disrespected, he had to do what he had to do.*

RACISM: AN EVERYDAY EXPERIENCE

On the street, I deal with racism on a daily basis and here I deal with it all the time. It's just part of getting up and putting my clothes on. It's there, the racism.
—*African American prisoner at Fallsburg State*

The theme that recurred throughout all ALANA prisoners' accounts is that Vermont prisons were oppressive, not only because they were prisoners, but also because they were members of racial groups. Above all, for ALANA inmates, "corrections" meant an atmosphere charged with racism, regardless of which Vermont prison they encountered. Given this, life for ALANA prisoners in virtually all-white prisons is one of multiple oppressions.

Vermont correctional facilities for the most part are located in the rural areas of the state. These prisons are run predominantly by white people who have worked as staff or officers for many years. When ALANA prisoners enter these "white" prison communities, they immediately become aware of the domination of "whiteness." An African American shared his first observations about being a Black person in a predominantly white institution. "Everything, everywhere I look, everywhere I turn, right, left, is white." Another inmate, an African American raised in Chicago, said:

> When I first came here, I experienced cultural shock. I could not adapt to the "whiteness." I was not being understood. I'm Black. I don't forget this and everyone is white. I did not feel comfortable. I feel a constant tension here.

As this example shows, the initial days and weeks were trying times for most ALANA prisoners, reminding them constantly that they were prisoners of color in a white world. Most expected differential treatment; they expected whites to victimize them. As one African American prisoner, who had been imprisoned in both facilities, said:

> I expect any kind of treatment that they offer. But they can't make me feel worse off than what I feel right now. They don't treat a Black person the way a human should be treated. As a human being. So they treat me different from the whites. I don't expect any different. My father already told me. Don't expect nothing from white people. Don't expect any good. And if they show you any good faith, don't act like you cherish it too much.

Among African Americans and Latinos there appeared to be some consensus that while "on the streets" they developed a sensitivity to discrimination and victimization. So in their view, when they confronted establishments such as the Vermont prison system where whites control everything, what else were they to think but that the system was racist? Should they, for example, assume that if they were to come in conflict with white prisoners that their side would be heard without preju-

dice? Thoughts such as these instilled feelings of fear, and for some ALANA prisoners these fears were overwhelming during their first weeks of incarceration. A sense of vulnerability was another consequence felt by ALANA prisoners now placed in such close and intimate proximity to whites. They also feared there would be no place "to hide" or be safe within these virtually white environments. Most of the African American and Latino prisoners who were recently relocated to Vermont brought their concerns for safety from the inner-city ghettos. Within those communities, the concern for safety typically focuses on the potential dangers that stem from street life or even from participation in drug subcultures. As they assumed risks and looked danger square in the face, many recalled they had acquired the view of pervasive victimization, which gave rise to a view of life as a "jungle." They imported this view into the prison environment along with suspiciousness of one's environment and the motives of others in this predominantly white culture. One young African American, a native of New York City, discussed the lack of safety in both Vermont facilities:

> I do not feel safe here. I felt safer in Belmont Regional. There I could point out who belonged to the Klan. It was a smaller population of officers. They have no unity and they are busy stepping on each other and cutting each other's throats. They will tell you who is a Klansman. Here [Fallsburg State] they have a sense of unity. They appear to have folded up their sheets. You can't see who they are. You don't know who is coming at you.

To deal with the issues of fear, anxiety, and survival, most African American and Latino prisoners came to the Vermont prison situation with some skills for coping. The concern for safety in the ghetto, along with the economic insecurity, gave rise to a strong peer group orientation that was a source of mutual aid and affection frequently given the status of kinship as in "brothers" and "sisters," or in the status of "homies" (homeboys and homegirls).

For entirely different reasons, the Asians also reported that their initial encounters with the "whiteness" of the prison environment aroused disturbing emotional feelings, especially feelings of fear and anxiety. Although most of them barely spoke English, they all perceived themselves as strangers to the issues of inequality that, in turn, set them up for feelings of vulnerability. None of them entered the prison environment with any of the skills for coping that other prisoners of color had developed "on the streets." They feared intimidation and violence. An Asian inmate, native to Vietnam, related that:

> I'm still afraid of the men [white prisoners] with long hair who are so tall and have very loud voices. My people do not speak with loud voices. My people do not show they are angry. These tall men get really angry. I am afraid.

Finally, according to the Asians, the resulting disorientation and helplessness were especially disconcerting and unpleasant because they must, out of necessity, learn to live in this strange culture. One Asian inmate observed that it was not a problem of loss of identity but a problem of confusion. The biggest problem was to quickly figure out how to survive within this environment of "whiteness."

The Prison Administration as a Symbol of Malign Neglect

Running through the ALANA prisoners' accounts was the observation that discrimination and prejudice was an everyday experience and that racism was everywhere. Racism was inescapable. These prisoners reported that the pervasiveness of racism was reflected in the perceived dominance of the Vermont Department of Corrections and in the ability of each prison's administration to maintain cultural oppression. Such control ensured that the white culture and way of doing things had ascendancy over ALANA culture and way of doing things. For many of these prisoners, this exemplified the whites' inability to "see" people of color as individuals. This section examines the various ways in which prisoners saw their needs as people of color ignored by the prison administrations. These findings suggest that the failure of the Ver-

mont prison system to recognize the needs of ALANA prisoners and to create policies that adjust for these needs can be translated into "pains of imprisonment" unique to prisoners of color.

First, as typical of any prison system, there is a vast number of rules and regulations that extend into all areas of prisoners' lives. These rules cover access to legal materials, correspondence, medical services, dress codes, disciplinary hearings, meals, schedules, length of hair, sanitation, contact with family, library use, and so forth. Many of these rules could and did arouse hostility among all inmates simply because they did not make sense or were seen as irritating gestures of authoritarianism that restrict inmates' ability to make choices.

According to ALANA prisoners' accounts, however, other rules and regulations failed to recognize or incorporate the particular needs of an ALANA prisoner population. For instance, an important concern for many ALANA prisoners was separation from their families and friends who are often out of state. This "pain of separation" was frequently profound. For instance, visiting for the prisoners at Fallsburg State was restricted to a specified number of visiting hours and days of the week. Due to work constraints or the difficulties of traveling such long distances, many families will come to visit—but not at the specified visiting times. Some families will visit when they are able to pull everything together to make these visits, for example, when they can afford to rent a car, get a day off from work, and so forth. These families are generally turned away if they are not visiting on the specified days. Many of these men indicated that the administrations make no attempt to be flexible. That is, they generally do not permit any visits except at the permitted visiting hours, even when their relatives are at the gates. Sometimes these relatives do not speak sufficient English to understand why they cannot visit whenever it is convenient for them. A Latino man, native of Boston, illustrated this point:

> My people came here at 3:40 p.m. to see me. I was told that they came at 3:40 and they were not allowed to see me. They do not speak English. They

do not know or understand why they cannot just come to visit. They discriminated. My people are not white. Some inmate had a visitor on Saturday and Sunday. They made an exception to the rule for him. They could be more flexible. They came all the way up here and had to spend the night in a motel and drive back the next day. It was the first time they come.

Second, according to most African American inmates and a few Latinos imprisoned in both prisons, the educational curriculum was not racially diversified; it continued to reflect the topical interests of the white population. They cited that both prison libraries suffered from a lack of material about people of color. One Latino indicated that, "We cannot get a Spanish newspaper to read." Others reported that the only way they could read about African Americans was by ordering their own books and then sharing these books with other African Americans. Within this context, those who were incarcerated at Belmont Regional did note that one of the Learning Center's teachers did attempt to introduce multicultural books and magazines into the library and classroom sessions. But all of them concurred that this effort remained a pebble in an ocean of neglect. Others revealed that within classroom sessions, they generally were taught and read about the history of the dominant group as well as about its customs, culture, and achievements. A few reported that within these readings the symbols of who were the "good" guys were usually the dominant group, whereas the symbols of the "bad" guys were likely to be people of color.

And some revealed that very little was done to educate all inmates about the contributions of persons of ALANA descent to the development of our society. This African American man, incarcerated at both facilities, observed that:

> This is not a place for Blacks. We didn't even get a special meal for Martin Luther King Jr.'s holiday. We can't even watch Black programming. If we vote for a TV show and it's a Black show, we're going to be out-voted.

And still another reported an additional neglect in the educational process:

Most of our brothers and sisters do not get their needs met by this prison. Many of them are lacking an adequate education and nothing is done for them. Even when it was Martin Luther King Day, we had forty white guys making fun of the "I Had a Dream" speech. I almost flipped.

It is clear from these accounts that the failure to include a multicultural education with culturally diverse books and magazines increases these prisoners' feelings of diminishment, invisibility, and degradation.

Another "pain" reported to be inflicted on ALANA prisoners was the administration's failure to abide by their constitutional rights to practice their religion. The most vocal group, the Muslims, voiced their frustrations with the many ways in which their religious needs were left unmet. A common complaint was that both prison staff and prison administrations did not understand the Islam religion nor did they appear to make any attempt to educate themselves. At both facilities, many staff, for instance, considered the knit skull caps, known as *Kuffi,* which the Islam religion requires men to wear, to be "hats" and therefore were forbidden by prison policy to be worn in parts of the buildings. Nor had they been given the same opportunities for religious worship enjoyed by what they term the Euro-American-supported religions. For instance, an African American Muslim said:

> We don't have a service. We have to make our own service. There is no subscribed place to make daily prayer. As far as Christianity goes, they have a meeting every week. They have a lot of meetings. They get to use the visiting room. We should have call outs for services. There are four or five of us. There is even a white brother who wanted to look into Islam. We can run our own services.

Nor was it understandable why they were not able to hire Muslim ministers on the same basis as Catholics and Protestant clergy were hired. And lastly, the Muslim prisoners informed me that they not only needed a time and a place to practice their religion daily but they also had religiously prescribed diets. They had repeatedly requested special foods; although there was no catering to

Muslim diets, an Orthodox Jew received catered Kosher food.

> For Ramadan, which is a month-long Muslim holiday, I'm supposed to get a full meal after sunset each night. But all they give me is a care package. I can't do that every night for a month. I get stuck eating cheese. I had to raise heck to get the boss to let my Koran in. They bring hundreds of Bibles into the facility but I'm not allowed my Koran.

At Fallsburg State, another group of religiously distinct individuals, the Native Americans, contended that their First Amendment rights to the free exercise of their religion must be adhered to even it if meant the correctional system must modify its structure, procedures, and tolerance of cultural differences. They did agree that the denial of their religious practices could not be completely attributed to racist harassment but more likely to the administration's ignorance and reluctance to make any changes. They stressed their need to participate in sweat lodge ceremonies.[5] According to Grobsmith (1994), attending sweat lodge ceremonies has become the single most important and widespread religious activity among Native American prisoners. Other prison systems have constructed sweat lodges and found it beneficial not only for Native Americans to enact their religious practices but also beneficial for other prisoners and staff. The Native Americans included in his study population contended that the sweat lodge would provide a unity of cultural and religious expression in prison, despite the varied tribal affiliation and racial composition of the prison population.

One could argue that such arbitrary denial of prisoners' dietary and religious needs is difficult to justify in light of the benefits reported by prison officials who have allowed such practices. For instance, participation provides the opportunity for others to understand Native Americans' heritage and it improved the prisoners' attitudes and subsequently lowered rates of disciplinary actions.

Other African American and Latino prisoners not of the Muslim persuasion noted that another "pain" imposed on them was the administration's failure to recognize their special meal needs by incorporating their ethnic food into the general prison menus. For example, many of them observed that the cafeteria food reflected Euro-American customs. Over and over, these prisoners contended that the white prisoners were not deprived of their culturally valued foods but ALANA prisoners were. An African American reported the failure of the administration to provide soul food:

> We don't get the types of food we're accustomed to eat like rice, lentil peas, fried chicken, fish, potatoes, potato salad with paprika, kale.

Complaints that their customary foods were not integrated into the menus were made by both African Americans and Latinos. Repeatedly they asserted that not only must they endure the "pains of imprisonment" and enforced intimacy with "rednecks and Klansmen" but they were also forced to share with the "superior race" its food habits.

One unmet need listed by those in the study population consisted of the inability to wear some of their traditional clothes, which made up their customary wardrobes "on the streets":

> There is a dress code here. It fits the needs of the whites. Coming from New York City, we're used to wearing hoods, big shoes. They feel threatened when we wear them. We cannot wear doo-rags. Our doo rags are a form of hat. The whites can wear a scarf. They only allowed me to wear one pair of sneakers. What Black man only has one pair of sneakers?

Another unmet need was the absence of traditional hygienic supplies. At the commissaries, they were not able to buy "Black-oriented" products for hair maintenance and for hygienic purposes. One African American complained that the administration and the correctional staff did not understand the importance of these products:

> I asked for a doo rag and to be able to wear one. It's a hair covering to keep my hair in place. The administration denied this request. The girls gave us some stockings to wear. They flipped when they saw us with them on. They just don't understand why we need it. I have very dry skin. Most Blacks

have dry skin and we need to use cocoa butter lotion. We're denied that.

Another African American indicated:

> I wanted a brush. One that fits our texture hair. They cut off the commissary carrying Afro picks. The white guys get brushes. They cut off ours but not theirs.

Finally, the two African American women incarcerated at Belmont Regional were bewildered that they were denied straightening combs. Most African American women perceive straightening combs as essential to the management and care of their hair.

The Asians and a few Latinos (especially those detained by the federal government at Fallsburg) reported that the language barriers were another "pain" with which they had to cope. Not only did the Asians complain about the indifference that existed concerning their inability to speak English but so did some African Americans and Latinos. Their complaints stressed the necessity for the administrations to find out about the language needs of Asians and Latinos and to develop programs to address those needs. They consistently pointed out that there seldom were translators available to convey to the non-English-speaking prisoners the essential information about how the various prisons function, their rules and regulations, and the culture of the prison system. There were no rule books in the languages of the Asian and Spanish-speaking populations. They also reported that most announcements made on the public system were made in English. The combination of the lack of services with the scarcity of Spanish-speaking and Asian-speaking correctional personnel set up these non-English-speaking prisoners to violate rules and regulations, or so the ALANA prisoners contended.

Finally, African Americans and Latinos incarcerated at Fallsburg State were more likely than the ALANA prisoners imprisoned at Belmont Regional to point out the "pain" of unequal access to prison jobs. They observed that when prison administrations ordered their priorities, a certain predictable outcome occurred that usually favored white prisoners and reinforced the relative disadvantage of ALANA prisoners. One way in which this process became apparent was by the allocation of labor within the two prisons. That is, the Vermont prison system recreated the poverty cycle experienced "on the streets." Prisoners of color were denied the good prison jobs and the valued vocational assignments—a situation not unlike what they traditionally experienced "on the streets."

Many prisoners of color complained about exclusion from the more prestigious work assignments that were usually reserved for the white inmates. According to these inmates, the "best jobs are kitchen work, the print shop, library, and some outdoor jobs." One African American recalled his job situation at Belmont Regional:

> They discriminate very much. They don't give Blacks any job assignments. I've seen it happen. A Black guy gets assigned to the kitchen for six months and a new guy comes in and he goes right to the kitchen. I've seen Black guys get passed over for jobs two or three times by guys just coming in. I've heard remarks about how they don't want Blacks washing their clothes. That's ridiculous.
>
> I can honestly say that I've never seen a white person cleaning the bathroom or mopping the floor. They give those jobs to the Black people.

Other inmates said that the unequal assignment of jobs meant that they received the worst job—the lowest paying, the most menial, and the least interesting. The accounts revealed that it was highly conceivable that those African American and Latino prisoners incarcerated in the Vermont prisons who were more politically aware did not want these less desirable jobs, known by many of these prisoners as "plantation work" or "slave labor."

To conclude, the findings presented here suggest that the prison community is synonymous with the "white power structure." In turn, most prisoners of color reported that some "pains of racism" stem from this "white power structure." They therefore believed that these "pains" indicated a system that not only excluded them and made them invisible but also continually reinforced the notion that they counted for nothing. Subsequently, the perceived white domination resulted in feelings of rage against a "white" structure that disempowered them because they were people of color. Feelings of rage, powerlessness, exclusion, and an absence of control over the conditions of their existence constituted estrangement—a feeling they had known "on the streets" in the larger society but which was clearer, sharper, and more intense within the Vermont prison system.

RACE RELATIONS WITHIN THE PRISONERS' SUBCULTURE

Only certain people there are racist. Most of them I got along with. I played ball with them and I played a few card games with them. I look at these whites for who they are and I accept them for who they are. I've made some friends here.

When I first came here, I did hear a lot of inmates say "niggers" on several occasions. I got into a few fights over some racial matters. One guy said to me, "What are you doing nigger?" He ripped up the things on my bed. I felt mad. I beat him up. He gave another Black guy some trouble. He started little things. He wanted that Black guy to go to the hole.

—*African American male incarcerated at Belmont Regional*

All ALANA prisoners described the Vermont prison environments as very tense because race relations were a major problem. This tense interracial climate stemmed from the prisoners' daily interactions with the white staff and the white inmates. Racism was one of the dominant features of prisoner relationships within the various prisons. The findings of this study indicated that not only the prison staff but also many of the white prisoners brought their racist attitudes with them into the prison milieu. They also shared the biases of the rural white population in the towns where they resided prior. In these areas, as in the larger U.S. society, people of color were viewed as being of a lower racial caste.

In numerous accounts, it was noted that both the African American and Latino prisoners believed that these racist attitudes were based on ignorance. The major source of any racial knowledge

for most of the white prisoners was from the culture of their communities (mostly small-town Vermont) as well as the media. Most of the prison population had little direct interaction with persons of color prior to their incarceration. And, therefore, most were ignorant about the histories and cultures of different racial groups.

Most ALANA men and women also came into the prison community with their baggage of distrust, suspicion, and hostility. Many held firmly to negative racial stereotypes and prejudicial attitudes about white prisoners, views they learned before they came to these prisons. In the eyes of the majority of ALANA prisoners, white prisoners were believed to be racist, weak, politically unaware, not too intelligent, and "rednecks" imbued with bigotry. This quote conveys some additional racially stereotypical views:

I'd say that in spite of what I've seen on the television, white people are physically nastier than Black people. I knew a white guy here. He was here for thirty days and he never took a shower. I've seen a guy who had bugs in his beard. One guy never did anything but shit in the yard. I called them "woodchucks." I see them get up and not wash and go eat breakfast. These whites come from the hills. These "woodchucks" live crazy. On the TV they only show Blacks in rat-infested apartments. But these whites are dirtier.

I thought that white people were better. They had more than me. They had new cars and sneakers. I believed that all white people were like that. As I grew older I see how nasty and dirty they are. We were forced to live like that but whites do it because they must like it.

In addition, they felt free to share with me some other views of most white inmates. Not only were the white prisoners perceived of as physically dirty but they also were described as not brushing their teeth or pressing their pants. As noted by a Latino, they were perceived of as uncouth and sexually deviant:

There is a guy here who used to strip naked. The white guys would cheer him on. He was Ready Turner. He had a lack of respect for his own self.

And his friend stuck candy up his ass, then dropped it out and ate it. I went to prison in the '70s and if you had done a sex crime, you could not go to population. Here it's accepted. They're right here with us. They call them snappers. It's the cool thing to be.

These stereotypical beliefs pervaded the interview sessions. All of the prisoners, however, denied that they expressed their prejudicial attitudes within the public arena.

A striking feature of their accounts was that no ALANA prisoner expressed open hostility toward all whites. Almost all indicated that they had some close associates among the white prisoners and that some of the white inmates treated them with respect. The ALANA prisoners reported that they sometimes hung out with whites, played basketball, lifted weights, and played cards with them, as this African American commented:

> We all have to live together. Some whites do not go out of their way to avoid Blacks. When we play ball, some whites are with us. There is a certain bunch known as nigger haters, but the majority, we accept.

And some others noted that there were whites with whom they were willing to hang out occasionally. These men were termed the "wannabees." One African American incarcerated at Fallsburg State explained, "We call him a 'wannabee.' He wants to be Black." Still another provided an additional insight:

> They think that they have a certain coolness when they hang with us Blacks. They want to be around us as much as possible because of the way we talk, the way we dress, and 'cause they emulate the hip hop.

Historically, the Vermont prison has been a virtually all-white prison system. As the population of inmates of color increases, there is a concomitant pressure from the white inmates to put the ALANA prisoners "in their place" as inferior and subordinate. There is also a demonstrated need, expressed by some white inmates, to retain a dominance in the prison system; this dominance is measured by who has greater access to the few available privileges.

To relegate the ALANA prisoners to a status more inferior than that of "inmate," white staff and prisoners used the following techniques: (1) verbal aggression in the form of racially stereotypical remarks directed to ALANA prisoners, (2) disrespect of ALANA prisoners by exclusion from the white prisoners' groups and cliques as well as a minimum of interaction with them, (3) white inmate domination of prison privileges, and (4) scapegoating ALANA prisoners by setting them up for verbal and sometimes physical confrontations, which would then commonly set them up to receive disciplinary reports. From accounts provided by ALANA prisoners, it was clear that the relations between them and the white prisoners were permeated by attitudes of racial prejudice and discrimination.

Although attempts had been made to control racial slurs as well as the racially stereotypical beliefs of the correctional staffs, this did not appear to be the case for the inmate population. According to most ALANA prisoners, racially derogatory language was used repeatedly by the white inmate population. Racial slurs, racial epithets, and racial name-calling were commonplace within both prison systems. For example, pejorative words such as *nigger, spic, slanted eyes, chop suey,* and *dirty Injun* were used by many white inmates:

> I was scared coming here. Since I am Native American, I thought I heard everything that could be said about Native Americans. In the last two years, it has been worse here than "in the street." Inmates call me "no good Indian," "scraw," "half-breed." I get upset.

Both incarcerated African American women cited the racial taunts that they must endure daily— *black bitch, coon, Aunt Jemima, black whore, nigger bitch, buckwheat,* and so forth.

Many ALANA prisoners clearly recalled being offended by the naivete of the white prisoners. Both African American women remembered being offended by the other female inmates who wanted to touch their hair or who asked offensive questions about whether brown skin became suntanned or who wanted to know the size of African American men's genitals. For these ALANA prisoners, the ignorance was a frequent, painful experience.

At Belmont Regional, African Americans mentioned that they had found racial insults written on the walls or the doors to their rooms. For instance, an African American man reported that, "In the house you get more attention from the inmates than the guards. And so you get more name-calling. Somebody is always writing something on the wall like 'No spooks' or something like that."

Several ALANA inmates discussed how they became fully aware of what it meant to be a prisoner of color within an almost all-white prison. The awareness came from not only the racially derogatory language but also the racist joking. One West Indian, who wore a Rasta hat, noted:

> They commented on my hat. It's a new one. One guy said that it looks like a popcorn bag. Later some other prisoners came over and continually made fun of my hat. They feel like all Black people are their toys. They make you look like you're nobody.

A few African Americans suggested that white inmates perhaps may not realize how offensive and troubling racist jokes could be; others may tell such jokes intentionally because they know the jokes caused pain.

Racially offensive language, naive questions, and racist jokes disparaged racial minorities and were utilized as a quick and efficient way to put ALANA prisoners in their place as culturally and racially despised. This bigotry was bad enough on the streets, the ALANA prisoners reported, but "on the streets," they could walk away from it; inside the prison walls, such language kept them constantly wrapped up in a controlled atmosphere of racism. There simply was no place to hide from it.

Some African Americans and Latinos offered another reason for the ceaseless barrage of racially offensive language at both facilities. They reported that the white prisoners perceived them as a threat to their physical security. According to them, the white prisoners felt threatened by any form of African American and Latino solidarity. Because both racial groups came from inner-city ghettos and

adhered to a similar "street" code, the white inmates assumed there was a racial solidarity. This supposed solidarity created not only fear among the white inmates but also respect. Members of the study population indicated that the white inmates saw African Americans and Latinos as men who remained "clean," maintained their honor and dignity, were loyal, and generally did not exploit one another. Interesting enough, this was exactly how the Latinos and African Americans described themselves.

The anxieties and fears of many ALANA prisoners about being "dissed" (disrespected) centered around the television sets located in each wing of the cell blocks. The issue of television was of less concern to those at Fallsburg State because many of them had earned the privilege of having their own television set in their cells. But even at Fallsburg State as well as at Belmont Regional, the choice of programs was generally determined by which racial group was in the majority at any particular time. Therefore, the white inmates frequently dominated which programs were viewed. Repeatedly, the ALANA prisoners complained that they rarely saw a drama or comedy that was oriented to people of color, or basketball or programs that focused on issues of concern to them. Altercations, both verbal and physical, arose to establish which race would control the televisions.

Finally, less frequently but nevertheless reported by a significant number of ALANA prisoners, was the complaint that white prisoners set them up to receive disciplinary reports (DRs). Setting them up could occur by taking advantage of an Asian's difficulties in understanding the language; insisting that some Black prisoner whom no one could identify had violated a rule; and picking fights with a prisoner of color and calling for an officer's help when the designated inmate responded physically. An African American woman described the following incident:

> There was this one girl who gave me a problem when I first came here. I would ask her a question and she would go off on me. Don't ask me shit. So I felt like she wanted to fight me or something. So I said, "You know, I'm very civil to you and I

appreciate if you be civil to me. But you seem like you want to fight me, and if you do, then let's go. Let's get it out of the way." Apparently she had a little more pull in here as far as the inmate code of honor goes, and she got her little friends together, and they all wrote statements on me, and got disciplinary reports and I got put in the hole for five days. I had not been here that long. I had been in the hole for five days and I had been with the unit for two days.

The possibility of intimidation and violence increases for ALANA prisoners when they are incarcerated in prison systems historically accustomed only to white prisoners. Racially motivated assaults might not be a daily occurrence but they are frequent enough to be ordinary events. At Belmont Regional, the African American prisoners observed that the Asian prisoners were the most frequent targets of the white inmates. One Asian recalled:

> I was afraid when I came here. They [white inmates] have the long hair. And sometimes they speak too loud. When I look at them they are big people with long hair. In my country we have short hair. . . . They beat me up. The long haired one beat me up. They look at me like a small person and they do not like me. So they beat me up.

The ALANA prisoners observed that correctional officials seldom interfered in disputes that were verbally or physically abusive. And white prisoners were seldom the recipients of disciplinary reports when they initiated a hostile encounter with ALANA prisoners. One African American woman said:

> They [white inmates] call us niggers, black bitch, coons. All kinds of shit. And when we go after them we're the ones that hit the majors. It's not the sex of these girls. They don't care about that. I told them I'm tired of you guys coming after me and Della. When I go to argue in here, they come immediately. But these girls can talk any kind of way they want, they can taunt me whenever they want and they get away with it.

This issue of "malign neglect" on the part of correctional officers strongly suggested to some

ALANA prisoners that there existed a white inmate elite that was practically exempt from custodial control.

Consequences: Issues of Respect and Violence

Although there was agreement within the study population that racial intolerance rarely escalated to the point of physical aggression, almost all ALANA prisoners reported a high level of verbal aggression directed at them by both correctional officers and white inmates. They reported that they immediately became fearful and defensive; fearful that someone would be openly hostile to them, and defensive because they had to be constantly prepared for hostility.

Most ALANA prisoners came to the virtually all-white prison environment with a profound distrust of whites. They knew they must be on guard to protect themselves against hurt. And they must be able to withstand mistreatment from both the officials and the white inmates. If they did not protect themselves, they would find prison life unbearable.

For instance, racially derogatory remarks were a form of dissing. To those invested in the "street" code, these words became serious indications of the other person's intentions. Consequently African American and Latino prisoners, and to a lesser extent Native Americans, became very sensitive to advances and slights that could well serve as warnings of imminent physical danger.

Another aspect of the "street" code that comes into play is that they are more concerned about the threat of "injustice" at the hands of a peer than at the hands of the staff.

The prison experience of racism, as the interviews concurred, not only was very painful and stressful but also had a cumulative impact on ALANA inmates (see Feagin and Sikes, 1994). The findings presented here suggest that the cumulative impact on an ALANA prisoner of repeated personal encounters with racial hostility was greater than the sum of these encounters. These experiences were likely to be stored not only in individual memories but also in ALANA stories and group recollections. As a result, a broad racial consciousness and a sense of group solidarity was reinforced.

Furthermore, to defend themselves, the ALANA inmates responded to potential harm by wearing a "veneer of toughness" to convince both the correctional staff and inmate population that they were something they were not. Central to wearing a "tough veneer" was the ALANA prisoners' use of this veneer to turn the "disrespectful" actions of the whites into a heightened respect for them. To achieve this valued respect, most concurred that they must always express a willingness to respond to racial aggression with verbal or physical aggression. One Latino noted his willingness to stand tall:

> And we almost got in a fight. You know I fight for my people. I'm Puerto Rican one hundred percent. I'm no ninety percent. I'm one hundred and ten percent. I'm not ashamed to say that I'm Puerto Rican. I'm Puerto Rican and that's it. If I hear somebody say something at work, I stand up. I'll say, "Listen, I'm Puerto Rican. What's the problem? Do I look like a bad person?" If necessary, I will fight.

An African American man illustrated the defensive style used by many:

> I be trouble for them. When they first see me, I project that I'm going to be trouble. I do not talk to these guys. I has a lot of anger. They felt this when I came here. I be the kind of guy that burn mattresses. I'm just trying to do my time and get out of here.

This focus on "being respected" and on being "treated with respect" was even more important within the prison setting when ALANA prisoners found themselves to be a "true minority of small numbers." And in turn, the need to be respected may become yet further exaggerated in a historically white prison system. In such systems, they are forced on a daily basis to publicly encounter various forms of racial harassment reinforcing their debased status as people of color. A few African American men mentioned that the issue of respect most often emerged when there were no other avenues by which to achieve identity and power.

Manliness or machismo for an ALANA prisoner was tied to his need to keep his "respect" intact. As one Latino said, "So what else do we have?"

Within this context of manliness and machismo, both African American and Latino men adhered to similar attitudes and values surrounding violent solutions to the problem of being "dissed" (disrespected). They appeared to agree that the various forms of violence were the best defense available, as explained by this Latino:

> Five or six white guys surrounded me. They kept calling me "spic" and other kinds of names. I said, "You guys want a piece of me?" I got ready to fight. A brother came by and said, "He has heart." I was respected. I'm used to this. I do not show fear. I fight. If you show any fear, they are always on your back.

There were many scenarios that pushed the willingness to fight into actual fighting. Most ALANA prisoners asserted that they cannot be seen as walking away from a fight. Generally, it was not enough to present oneself as rough and tough to be respected. Very often, among ALANA peers, it was quite acceptable to appear "tough" until one was tested, but then that presentation must transform itself into action or the individual will quickly lose "respect."

A few men noted that because prison restricts movement, the interchanges could escalate to violence even if one of the participants wanted to retreat. In some cases, these men contended if they had been separated from abusive and threatening comments or actions, these incidents would never have occurred. For instance, this African American related how he reacted to white inmates directing racial slurs at him:

> I can't do anything here. On the streets, someone calls me nigger, I can hit them and not get caught. Here if I punch someone, not only do I go to the hole but I get DRs.

To sum up, the interview sessions revealed that ALANA men and women often quickly resorted to unscheduled explosions of rage. Many reported that they resorted to violent behavior because: (1) they wished to appear to others as "tough" and (2) they were to be treated with respect; that is, with deference as persons of color, not as prisoners of color who deserved to be despised, degraded, and humiliated. Aggression was a way of communicating to the racist white staff and inmates—not just the men and women in the immediate incident—that they were not to be messed with or treated in a racist manner. The assumption therefore was that a "tough" aggressive demeanor was necessary for survival in prison, and that an aggressive image was a positive and worthwhile attribute of one's public personality which must be consciously cultivated.

CONCLUSION

The experiences of ALANA prisoners within the historically white Vermont prisons was not encouraging. There was consensus among the ALANA prisoners that the Vermont prison system was a racist institution for the following reason: The organization and activity patterns of ALANA prisoners and white administrators, correctional officers, and inmates were strikingly negative or antagonistic.

The world of ALANA prisoners was dominated by both the "pains" of imprisonment and racism. Daily encounters with overt racism did not make ALANA prisoners feel safe or certain that they could deal with the two systems of oppression; that is, the oppression directed at them as prisoners and the oppression directed at them as members of racial minorities.

This research provides some important insights into aspects of this racially oppressive environment. According to most ALANA prisoners, the racism was institutionalized in that the various prisons intentionally or unintentionally distributed resources unequally, maintained unresponsive and inflexible structures, and generally ignored the racial victimization of the ALANA prisoners. As some noted, this racial oppression existed along with the "white power structure's" indifference to the existence of differential treatment accorded by staff to inmates.

Differential treatment generally occurred on a daily basis within the various facilities. And to ALANA prisoners, differential treatment was treatment which primarily benefited the Euro-Americans. For instance, a few argued that it was to be expected that the Asians' language needs were summarily ignored. There also was no meaningful curriculum in the prison schools; the major monetary resources for maintaining books in the prison libraries continued to benefit the Euro-Americans. The best or most desirable prison jobs and the few vocational training programs continued to be dominated by the Euro-American inmates. Within this context, then, the economic needs of ALANA prisoners were overlooked. They, as "on the streets," were the last to be hired and the first to be fired. The special needs for visiting relatives and friends were ignored. Lastly, the issue of the constitutional rights of Muslims and Native Americans to practice their religions was only partially addressed by the administrations. Christian groups, however, continued to be welcomed into the prison communities. In contrast, those who adhered to the Islamic faith or to the religion of Native Americans encountered hostility or indifference when requesting the presence of their religious leaders to hold services or classes.

These findings strongly suggest that the Vermont correctional model, which has always been based on the Eurocentric male system, must be vigorously examined. Clearly, for instance, those ALANA men and women who must go to prison must have equal access to vocational programs. This makes sense because both whites and ALANA inmates need to be economically self-supporting during their incarceration as well as on their release. Visitation programs should reflect the fact that most families of ALANA prisoners reside out of state and therefore face unique difficulties traveling to various Vermont prisons. The educational curriculum needs to include the study of various ALANA cultures, history, community issues, and public services. The ALANA prisoners reported that they needed validation of their experiences and culture.

The findings also revealed that ALANA prisoners were more likely to accuse administrators of "malign neglect" than staff or inmates. That is, many ALANA inmates stated that although administrators more strongly endorsed integration and even support for ALANA concerns, they were more likely to ignore the needs of ALANA prisoners. There appeared to exist a general apathy among administrators toward racial outbursts and racial tensions that existed between ALANA inmates and the officers or white inmates.

Underlying this lack of response and apathy, ALANA inmates observed the pervasiveness of covert racism. Because of its elusive nature, however, covert racism easily could be ignored by those who had never experienced it and denied by those who contributed to it. What made this stressful was the denial of legitimacy to the perceptions and experiences of injustice experienced by ALANA prisoners.

Moreover, all ALANA prisoners were exposed to recurring humiliation of a sort most white people do not recognize. The prisoners pointed out that administrators were more likely to treat them in subtle racially demeaning ways whereas both the white staff and inmates directed not-so-subtle forms of racial prejudice and discrimination at them. Overt racism, "open and up-front" racist behavior, included daily racial insults, stereotyping, over-surveillance, and verbal and physical racially related victimization. All these forms subjected ALANA prisoners to embarrassment, humiliation, and loss of respect. Many indicated that smoldering hostilities were waiting to erupt. An important consequence of both "malign neglect" and racial tensions was a prisoner subculture dominated by racial polarization and conflict. As the number of ALANA prisoners has increased within these prisons, the racial polarization and conflict among prisoners has intensified and continues to do so.

NOTES

1. The major deprivations of imprisonment were identified by Gresham Sykes as the loss of liberty, the loss of possessions, the loss of autonomy, the loss of privacy and the loss of heterosexual relations (Sykes, 1958).
2. The literature on prisons consistently points out that not much has changed within today's prisons. Race does matter. The variable *race* has been noted as having an effect on the inmates' social process (Irwin, 1970; Jacobs, 1977; Carroll, 1974).
3. In this reading, the term *racism* is generally used in the broad sense as utilized by Feagin and Sikes (1994).

It refers not only to the prejudices and discriminatory actions of some white bigots but also to institutionalized discrimination and to the recurring ways in which white people (in this case correctional staff and white inmates within the Vermont prison system) dominate people of color.
4. See *Burlington Free Press, Rutland Herald, Vermont Times,* spring, 1995.
5. Sweat lodges are small, tentlike saunas that are essential to the Native American religious practices. Their purpose is to cleanse and purify both the body and the spirit.

BIBLIOGRAPHY

Adler, Patricia A. 1985 *Wheeling and Dealing: An Ethnography of an Upper-Level Drug Dealing and Smuggling Community.* New York: Columbia University Press.

Aguirre Jr., Adalberto and David V. Baker 1995 *Sources: Notable Selections in Race and Ethnicity.* Guilford, CT: The Dushkin Publishing Group, Inc.

Allen, Walter, Edgar G. Epps and Nesha Z. Haniff, editors 1991 *College in Black and White: African American Students in Historically Black Public Universities.* Albany: State University of New York Press.

Benjamin, Lois 1991 *The Black Elite: Facing the Color Line in the Twilight of the Twentieth Century.* Chicago: Nelson-Hall Publishers.

Carroll, Leo 1974 *Hacks, Blacks, and Cons: Race Relations in a Maximum Security System.* Prospect Heights, IL: Waveland Press, Inc.

Cohen, Stanley and Laurie Taylor 1972 *Psychological Survival: The Experience of Long-Term Imprisonment.* Hammondsworth, Middlesex, England: Penguin Books Ltd.

Feagin, Joe R. and Melvin P. Sikes 1994 *Living with Racism: The Black Middle-Class Experience.* Boston: Beacon Press.

Flanagan, Timothy J. editor 1995 *Long-Term Imprisonment: Policy, Science, And Correctional Practice.* Thousand Oaks, CA: Sage Publications, Inc.

Fleming, Jacqueline 1984 *Blacks in College: A Comparative Study of Students' Success in Black and in White Institutions.* San Francisco: Jossey-Bass Publishers.

Genders, Elaine and Player, Elaine 1989 *Race Relations in Prisons.* Assistance by Valerie Johnston. Oxford: Clarendon Press.

Goodstein, Lynne and Doris Layton MacKenzie, editors 1989 *The American Prison: Issues in Research and Policy.* New York: Plenum Press.

Grobsmith, Elizabeth S. 1994 *Indians in Prison: Incarcerated Native Americans in Nebraska.* Lincoln: University of Nebraska Press.

Haas, Kenneth C. and Geoffrey P. Alpert 1995 *The Dilemmas of Corrections.* Prospect Heights, IL: Waveland Press, Inc.

Irwin, J. 1970 *The Felon.* Englewood Cliffs, NJ: Prentice-Hall.

Jacobs, J. and L. Kraft 1978 "Race Relations and the Guard Subculture." *Social Problems* 25(3) p. 304–318.

Jacobs, J. 1977 *New Perspectives in Prisons and Imprisonment.* Ithaca: Cornell University Press.

Johnson, Robert and Hans Toch, editors 1982 *The Pains of Imprisonment.* Foreword by Christopher S. Dunn. Prospect Heights, IL: Waveland Press, Inc.

McCall, Nathan 1994 *Makes Me Wanna Holler: A Young Black Man in America.* New York: Vintage Books.

Merlo, Alida V. and Joycelyn M. Pollack 1995 *Women, Law and Social Control.* Needham Heights, MA: Simon and Schuster Company, Allyn and Bacon.

Peterson, Marvin W., Robert T. Blackburn, Zelda F. Gamson, Carlos H. Arce, Roselle W. Davenport and James R. Mingle 1978 *Black Students on White Campuses: The Impact of Increased Black Enrollments.* Ann Arbor, MI: The Institute for Social Research, The University of Michigan.

Sykes, G. M. 1958 *Society of Captives: A Study of a Maximum Security Prison.* Princeton, NJ: Princeton University Press.

Tonry, Michael 1995 *Malign Neglect: Race, Crime, and Punishment in America.* New York: Oxford University Press.

Willie, Charles V., Michael K. Grady and Richard O. Hope 1991 *African-Americans and Doctoral Experience: Implications for Policy.* New York: Teachers College Press.

18

The Children of Female African American Prisoners

CATHERINE FISHER COLLINS

In order to fully understand the serious problems for African American children when their caretaker is imprisoned, we must first gain some insight into the social and health status of these children.

HEALTH AND SOCIAL STATUS OF AFRICAN AMERICAN CHILDREN

In general, African American children are the most vulnerable citizens of this nation. This vulnerability is heightened by their mother's arrest and subsequent imprisonment. In 1986, when prisons were overflowing with African American women, the social and health status of the children of these prisoners was deplorable. In *Ebony* magazine's 1986 article "Crisis of the Black Family," black children were compared to their white counterparts. This article states that black children are twice as likely to

1. Die during the first year of life;
2. Live in institutions;
3. See a parent die;
4. Suffer low birth weight; and
5. Be born prematurely;

three times as likely to

1. Be poor;
2. Have their mother die at childbirth;
3. Live with a parent who is separated from the other parent;
4. Be murdered between five and nine years of age;

5. Be placed in an educable mentally retarded class; and
6. Die at the hands of a known child abuser;

four times as likely to

1. Be murdered before one year of age or as a teenager; and

five times as likely to

1. Be dependent on welfare.

Further, in 1988 more than half of all African American children (15 million children under age 18) lived with one parent. These children represent more than 50 percent of the African American childhood population living with a single parent, as compared to 19 percent of white children (Schmolling, 1992, p. 5). Equally important are the numbers of African American children living in poverty. In 1990 the poverty rate for African American children was 31.9 percent compared to 10.7 percent for whites. In the same year infants and toddlers were poorer than the rest of the population. When compared to prime adults (ages 25–64) who lived in poverty and whose rate was 8 percent, and those 65 and older whose rate was 13 percent, the rate for infants and toddlers was an astonishing 20 percent (U.S. General Accounting Office, April 1994, p. 6). Still even more disturbing was the increase since 1980, which went from 1.8 million to 2.3 million children (p. 7). Poverty rates for these children correlate closely with the rates in many areas of the South and Southwest where more African American women have been herded into prison cells.

Poverty is based on the ability (or lack thereof) to purchase those needed services to maintain adequate health status. To this end, these same African American children are also twice as likely as whites to be inadequately immunized (*USA Today*, 1993, p. 15A). Additionally, one of the most serious and devastating illnesses to impact African American children has been the AIDS epidemic. As Table 1 shows, the AIDS virus has had a severe effect on African American children.

In the United States the increase in drug usage by African American women in inner-city communities has resulted in a deplorable impact on African American children, our most vulnerable U.S. citizens. Parental drug exposure has had a serious impact on children who are in foster care. Mothers of many of these children are abusing cocaine at an alarming rate. Between 1986 and 1991 cocaine abuse increased from 17 to 55 percent, respectively (U.S. General Accounting Office, April 1994, p. 2). Further, in a 1991 survey of state prison inmates by the Bureau of Justice, it was reported that women used more drugs and used them more frequently than men. This report stated that about 54 percent of women used drugs in the month before their arrest, and one in four females reported committing their offense to get money to buy drugs (p. 7). The impact of drugs on minority females was very significant. Of Hispanic women 4.6 percent reported injecting drugs, as did 42 percent white and 24 percent black women before admission to prison. The number of children affected

may be underestimated because most medical personnel rely on the mother's self-reporting (as in the 1991 Survey of State Prison Inmates) of drug use, as well as other clinical tests. Furthermore, testing during birth will only detect recent drug use. Therefore, the effect on these vulnerable children, whose health status is already poor, is further compounded by placement in a foster care system.

Some of the health problems noted in the GAO (April 1994) study include behavioral problems, cardiac defects, low birth weight, and development delay (p. 10). Another result of the substance abuse has been an increase in the number of AIDS-infected infants. In Buffalo, New York, alone, there were 56 infants born to AIDS-infected mothers in 1992. These predisposing factors, coupled with maternal separation due to incarceration, have placed African American children at even greater risk. These now very vulnerable citizens, who have not developed the coping skills and defenses needed to deal with change, are now placed, if lucky, in the care of the inmate's extended family. According to the above-mentioned 1991 survey of state prisons, "three quarters of all women in prison had children. . . . An estimated 25,700 female inmates had more than 56,000 children under the age of 18. The racial/ethnic distribution were black—69 percent, Hispanic—72 percent, and white—62 percent" (p. 6). If the inmate's family, many of whom also live in poverty, are unable to care for the children, these youngsters become wards of the state (foster care) and their vulnerability is heightened even more.

THE IMPACT OF MATERNAL SEPARATION ON AFRICAN AMERICAN CHILDREN

African American children's vulnerability has never been a primary concern to those in charge of their destiny: white America. From the time of the birth of the first African American slave child they have been treated with disrespect (then seen as property sold into slavery), and today continue to die at alarming rates before their first birthday. The African American infant mortality rate in the United States in 1990–91 was 18 percent, with

TABLE 1   Cases of Children with AIDS in the United States, by Race and Age, June 1996

	BLACK	WHITE	HISPANIC
Under 5 years	3,539	877	1,313
5–12	662	437	390
13–19	1,165	895	2,175
Total	5,366	2,209	3,878

Source: U.S. Department of Health and Human Services, Surveillance Report, Midyear Edition, Vol. 8, No. 1, p. 13.

Third World countries like Malaysia (15 percent) and Kuwait (14 percent) doing better than African American infants (*USA Today,* December 1993, p. 15A).

African American children did not have a healthy start in the past and today so many external factors determine their fate. Years ago they, like all slaves, were considered to be the property of the slave owners, and thus, their value was set by their physical worth. In the case of African American children, their teeth set their value, while the mother's breasts and the father's weight were determinants of their worth. To separate the African American child from its family members was of little consequence then or now. Today, the lack of concern for the well-being of African American children is of minor consequence in the criminal justice system: evidenced by the disparity that exists between white and black sentencing patterns. Plagued by maternal substance abuse, and—if they survive a life of poverty—to be separated from the one stable force in their life can be very traumatic for a child.

The ideal nuclear family, where the mother has total child-rearing responsibilities, does not lend itself to the African American mother whose racial oppression has denied her family sufficient resources to support their needs. Fortunately, for survival of motherhood and its nurturing role, responsibilities had to be shared by the extended family members. For the children of African American prisoners, the extended family is their only hope. Of the previously mentioned 56,000 children of incarcerated women in 1991, it was reported in the Bureau of Justice Statistics Special Report that the grandparents of these children (57 percent black, 55 percent Hispanic, and 41 percent white) were the primary caretakers while the mother was imprisoned. While the biological mother is the ideal provider, without collective responsibility shared by the prisoner-mother, sisters, grandmothers, great-grandmothers, and other relatives, the survival of the inmates' African American children would not have occurred. Today more than 3.3 million children live with grandparents, a 41 percent increase since 1980 (*Good Housekeep-*

ing, July 1994, p. 181). However, there are those African American children whose mother lacks the benefits of a grandmother or an extended family. These children are subjected to the individual state's foster care system. In the last five years alone this system—for young children under 5 years of age—has increased nationally from helping 280,000 in 1986 to trying to care for 429,000 in 1991. The three states with the largest number of children in foster care (New York, Pennsylvania, and California) also have the largest increase in numbers of incarcerated African American females. Thus it appears that the increase in the foster care population correlates with the 1986–1991 increase in female incarceration in these states. In most instances neglect, caretaker absence, or incapacity were the reasons for the placement of young children in New York and California.

In spite of the poor health and social status of African American children, there is very little written about their psychological and social conditions while their mothers are incarcerated. However, a number of studies have examined in general the impact of maternal separation on the family (Swan, 1981; Bresier and Lewis, 1983; Baunach, 1982; Datesman and Cales, 1990; Henriques 1996). Most of these studies argue that there are serious consequences when children are separated from their mother.

Erik Erikson's developmental theory posits that infancy is when children develop a sense of trust that is the basis for *all the other* relationships that children will develop during the rest of their life. This trust is developed from the "nurturing, concerned, and positive interaction that occurs between a living parent . . . which is . . . sensitive, consistent care they are given" (Lisner, 1983, p. 135). Patricia Lisner also cites that when infants are raised in an "inconsistent environment in which their needs are only sporadically met [they] may develop a sense of mistrust towards the world and the individuals in it" (p. 135).

There are also those who feel that children "who lack affection may manifest a greater tendency to develop self-destructive and delinquent behavior that imperils not only the child, but other people as well" (Huie, 1992, p. 23). Further, it is felt that children who fail to bond through the nurturing process may grow up without caring or feeling toward others, or even a conscience. Thus, these children, whom we entrust into the care of foster parents or extended family members, may experience bonding or nurturing deprivation. This could lead the child to crime-ridden streets, to be a prime candidate for the influences of gangs, drugs, miseducation, and the vicious wheel of misfortune.

AFRICAN AMERICAN CHILDREN AFFECTED BY THEIR MOTHER'S INCARCERATION

The number of children in jeopardy grows with every arrested or incarcerated female prisoner. According to the Center for Children of Incarcerated Parents at Pacific Oaks College in Pasadena, "the population of children of imprisoned parents has soared from 21,000 in 1978 to 1 million in 1990, and could reach 2 million by the year 2000" (Huie, 1992, p. 22). Again, of the 56,000 children of incarcerated women, 69 percent were children of African American female inmates. As you will note in Figure 1, the majority of the children affected in New York State by maternal separation are African American.

With the previously mentioned social and health factors facing African American children in general, the separation from the one parent, in most cases, can be devastating to the children.

In the American Correctional Association's 1990 survey of state facilities it was reported that the characteristics of the respondents (4 percent of 43,000 female inmates, or 1,720) to their survey were reasonably representative of the female prison population. Some specific characteristics that added to the study's validity included the following:

1. 57 percent were minorities between ages 25–29;
2. 62 percent lived alone with 1–3 children;
3. 48 percent of their children lived with a mother or grandmother; and
4. 37 percent had never been married.

These survey results are consistent with the findings of other studies and surveys previously mentioned.

PREGNANT INMATES

Pregnant inmates are entering the jailed population in what appears to be record numbers. According to the 1990 American Correctional Association study, the Northeast has the largest number of pregnant inmates on intake (Figure 2), while the South has the highest number of children born in prison (see Figure 3).

Unfortunately, the races of the study subjects—pregnant women—were omitted. However, from the data previously presented we can safely speculate that since the majority of imprisoned

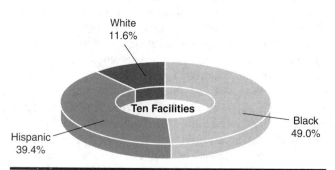

FIGURE 1   Women with Children in New York State Prisons, by Race and Ethnicity, 1992

Source: Collins Survey of State Prisons, 1992.

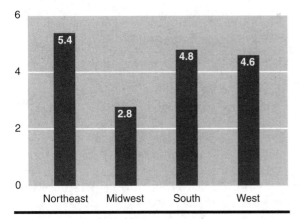

FIGURE 2   Inmates Who are Pregnant at the Time of Intake in Local Jails, in Percentages
Source: Reprinted from ACA, *The Female Offender,* 1990, p. 17, with permission from the American Correctional Association.

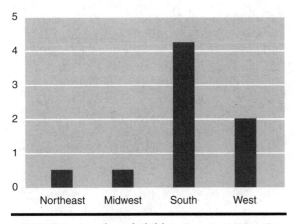

FIGURE 3   Number of Children Born to Women in Jail
Source: Reprinted from ACA, *The Female Offender,* 1990, p. 17, with permission from the American Correctional Association.

women are African American, they would constitute the largest number who are pregnant and give birth while incarcerated. Also at the state level, prisoners are entering at various degrees of pregnancy. In 1991, 6.1 percent of the 25,700 inmates were pregnant at the time of admission; 5.2 per-

cent of white, 6.7 percent of black and 5.9 percent of Hispanic inmates (U.S. Department of Justice, Bureau of Justice Statistics, Survey of State Prison Inmates, 1991, p. 10).

With her pregnancy being a major factor, the female inmate's unborn fetus is placed in serious jeopardy. The primary cause of this jeopardy can be attributed to the attitude of prison authorities who see them on a regular basis: first, as unworthy of motherhood, and second, as a drain on limited prison resources, requiring such attention as special diets, vitamins, and prenatal visits.

PARENTAL CONTACT WITH CHILDREN

The criminal justice system has been very unresponsive to the needs of its inmates' children. A survey by James Boudouris (1985) of 50 states, representing 57 institutions and 15,337 prisoners, was compared to the findings of the Collins 1992 survey of 44 states, representing 52 institutions and 14,192 incarcerated females. This comparison revealed virtually no change in parental services provided (see Table 2).

Certainly, there should be some attempt to satisfy the emotional and psychological needs of African American women in relation to their children. However, we have failed once again to build needed programs that will foster closer parent–child

TABLE 2   Comparison of Parental Services in State Facilities, 1985, 1992

	BOUDOURIS STUDY 1985	COLLINS STUDY 1992
Prenatal classes	53	44
Furloughs	45	31
Overnight visits with children	17	14
Conjugal visits	5	9
Community facilities for mother and child	5	8
Prison nurseries	1	1

relationships. Here are a few models that are known to work:

1. Mothers and Their Children (MATCH) which provides a child-centered environment;
2. TALK program, which helps to facilitate mother-child bonding; and
3. Prisoner Mother-Infant Care program, a network of halfway houses for low-risk female prisoners and their children to live together while serving out their sentences (Huie, 1992, p. 23).

In New York State's Bedford Hill Prison, one of the few that still allow some inmates who give birth while incarcerated to keep their infant up to one year, Herman Tarnower's mistress, Jean Harris, recognized the need and established parenting classes for mothers and soon-to-be mothers. She also ran a prison program promoting more visits between inmates and their children (*Buffalo News*, October 5, 1994). It is unbelievable that a murderess—who received clemency after 12 years—and not the prison officials would have expanded existing or established additional parenting classes to meet inmates' needs; Harris saw the need and turned her skills to this prison deficiency. She is commended for this effort.

When these programs, such as those attributed to Harris's efforts, are not available for the African American female prisoner, she must draw upon one of the African American strengths: the ability to delegate and distribute the mother's role to other family members, most often the grandmother. This one custom has been the salvation for most African American children. Without the help of the extended family members, most children of prisoners would become wards of the state and be placed in the foster care system. If the mother is blessed with relatives who are willing to take on the responsibility of her children, upon release the mother can reclaim her children without too much hardship. However, if she loses her parental rights, the judicial system is unfriendly to her when she requests the return of her children. This mother must then approach a system that on one hand wants the mother to have control of her children, but on the other hand sees her as unfit and not worthy to be a mother.

No one can argue the fact that children suffer when their mother or family is unable to provide the economic resources to purchase appropriate health care. When African American mothers are separated from their children, whose health status is questionable, they are known to develop psychological behaviors similar to those encountered due to a loss through death (Flowers, 1987, p. 159). Likewise, the children have been known to experience serious psychological consequences due to the separation from the one caretaker who provides nurturing and loving support. Children who are lucky enough to be cared for by the extended family have a much better chance of being reunited once the mother is released from prison. However, very few of the children who are placed in the foster care system are returned to the mother without a struggle upon her release.

If a child is born while the mother is incarcerated, poor or no prenatal care can severely jeopardize the health status of the unborn infant. If the infant survives the birth and reaches a certain age, the child is then separated from a mother who has in most cases bonded with the infant. When this nurturing of the prison mother is removed, once again, this vulnerable African American child is placed in jeopardy. Once again, both infant and parent experience extreme psychological disturbances.

There are many arguments, pro and con, as to why the child should not be separated from the mother. However, the judicial system has not fully explored or implemented options (for example, parole upon birth) that might better benefit both the child and the inmate mother. Nor has the system fully implemented inmate vocational and parenting classes, which help to meet the needs of those mothers who will be returning to their communities and children. If the criminal justice system does not provide opportunities for the inmate to learn while incarcerated, when she returns to a hostile, poverty-stricken environment—where it is easier to sell drugs than to get an education—she will return to prison: the ever-turning, revolving door.

REFERENCES

Baunach, P. J. "You Can't Be a Mother and Be in Prison . . . Can You? Impacts of the Mother-Child Separation" In Barbara R. Price and Natalie Sokoloff, *Criminal Justice System and Women.* New York: Clark Boardman (1982), 155–169.

Boudouris, J. "Prison and Kids, Program for Inmate Parents." *American Correctional Association.* College Park, Md., 1985.

Bresler, Lewis, and Diane Lewis. "Black and White Women Prisoners' Differences in Family Ties and Their Programmatic Implications." *Prison Journal* 63, no. 2 (1983): 116–123.

Buffalo News, October 5, 1994; November 13, 1994; January 19, 1995; September 11, 1995; September 25, 1996.

Datesman, Susan, and Gloria Cales. "I'm Still the Same Mommy: Maintaining the Mother/Child Relationship in Prison." *The Prison Journal* 63(2) (1983): 142–154.

Flowers, B. Ronald. *Women and Criminality: The Women as Victim, Offender and Practitioner.* Westport, Conn.: Greenwood, 1987.

Good Housekeeping. "Grandmothers in Place of Mothers." (July 1994): 181.

Henriques, Zelma. "Imprisoned Mothers and Their Children: Separation-Reunion Syndrome Dual Impact." *Women and Criminal Justice,* vol. 8 (1) 1996:77–95.

Huie, Virginia. "Moms in Prison: Where Are the Kids?" *The Progress.* (April 1992), 22–23.

Lisner, Patricia A. *Pediatric Nursing.* Albany, N.Y.: Delmar, 1983.

Schmolling, B. *Human Services in Contemporary America.* Florence, Ky.: Wadsworth, 1992.

Swan, L. Alex. *Families of Black Prisoners: Survival and Prayers.* Boston: G. K. Hall, 1981.

U. S. Department of Justice, Bureau of Justice Statistics Special Report. Survey of State Prison Inmates 1991. "Women in Prison," by Tracy Snell.

U. S. General Accounting Office. "Foster Care, Parental Drug Abuse Has Alarming Impact on Young Children." Washington, D.C.: GAO/HEHS-94-89 (April 1994).

USA Today. (1993), 15A.

Index

Credits:

Reading 1, "Gender, Class, and Race in Three High-Profile
  Crimes: The Cases of New Bedford, Central Park, and
  Bensonhurst" by Lynn Chancer, is reprinted by permission
  of Anderson Publishing Co., Cincinnati,
  www.andersonpublishing.com, and Lynn S. Chancer.
Reading 2, "Permeation of Race, National Origin, and Gender
  Issues from Initial Law Enforcement Contact through
  Sentencing: The Need for Sensitivity, Equalitarianism, and
  Vigilance in the Criminal Justice System" by Arthur L.
  Burnett, is reprinted with the permission of the publisher,
  Georgetown University, and American Criminal Law
  Review, © 1994.
Reading 3, "African American Boys Are Getting Caught in a
  Spider's Web: But It Definitely Is Not Charlotte's Web!" by
  Sherri F. Seyfried, is printed by permission of Sherri F.
  Seyfried.
Reading 4, "Racial Politics, Racial Disparities, and the War on
  Crime" by Michael Tonry, is from *Crime & Delinquency,*
  Vol. 40, pp. 475–494, copyright © 1994 by Sage
  Publications, Inc. Reprinted by permission of Sage
  Publications, Inc.
Reading 5, "Latinos and Lethal Violence: The Impact of
  Poverty and Inequality" by Ramiro Martinez, Jr., is reprinted
  from *Social Problems,* Vol. 43, No. 2 (May, 1996),
  pp. 131–146, by permission. Copyright © 1996 by The
  Society for the Study of Social Problems. Reprinted by
  permission of Florida International University.
Reading 6, "Violence against Gays and Lesbians" by Charles
  E. Reasons and Quentin Hughson, is from the *Journal of
  Offender Rehabilitation,* Vol. 30-1/2, 1999, pp. 137–159.
  Copyright © 1999 by The Haworth Press, Inc., Binghamton,
  NY. Reprinted by permission of the publisher.
Reading 7, "Law and Inequality: Race, Gender . . . and, of
  Course, Class" by Carroll Seron and Frank Munger, is
  reprinted, with permission, from the *Annual Review of
  Sociology,* Vol. 22, © 1996 by Annual Reviews,
  www.AnnualReviews.org, and with permission from Carroll
  Seron and Frank Munger.
Reading 8, "Law and Race in Early America" by W. Haywood
  Burns, is from *The Politics of Law: A Progressive Critique,*
  3rd edition, by David Kairys. Copyright © 1998 by David
  Kairys. Reprinted by permission of Basic Books, a member
  of Perseus Books, L.L.C.
Reading 9, "Race, Class, and Gender: O. J. Revisited" by Riley
  Olstead, is printed by permission of Riley Olstead.
Reading 10, " 'Driving While Black': Corollary Phenomena
  and Collateral Consequences" by Katheryn K. Russell, was
  originally published in Vol. 40:3 of the *Boston College Law
  Review,* 1999. Reprinted by permission of the publisher.

Reading 11, "Adding Color to a Black and White Picture:
  Using Qualitative Data to Explain Racial Disproportionality
  in the Juvenile Justice System" by Darlene J. Conley, is from
  the *Journal of Research in Crime & Delinquency,* Vol. 31,
  pp. 135–148, copyright © 1995 by Sage Publications, Inc.
  Reprinted by permission of Sage Publications, Inc.
Reading 12, "Boston Cops and Black Churches" by
  Christopher Winship and Jenny Berrien, is reprinted with
  permission of the authors from *The Public Interest,* No. 136
  (Summer 1999), pp. 52–68. Copyright © 1999 by National
  Affairs, Inc.
Reading 13, " 'Flotsam on the Sea of Humanity': A View from
  the Bench on Class, Race, and Gender" by Justin M.
  Johnson, is from *Social Justice,* Vol. 20 (1994), pp. 140–149.
  Reprinted by permission of Social Justice
  (SocialJust@aol.com).
Reading 14, "When 'Enough Is Enough': Battered Women's
  Decision Making around Court Orders of Protection" by
  Karla Fischer and Mary Rose, is from *Crime & Delinquency,*
  Vol. 41, pp. 414–429, copyright © 1995 by Sage
  Publications, Inc. Reprinted by permission of Sage
  Publications, Inc.
Reading 15, "Socioeconomic Status and the Sentencing of the
  Traditional Offender" by Stewart J. D'Alessio and Lisa
  Stolzenberg, is reprinted from the *Journal of Criminal
  Justice,* Vol. 21, pp. 61–77, 1993, with permission from
  Elsevier Science.
Reading 16, "Black Muslims in California Prisons: The
  Beginning of a Social Movement for Black Prisoners in the
  United States" by Darlene J. Conley and Julius Debro, is
  printed by permission of Darlene J. Conley and Julius
  Debro.
Reading 17, "Race Matters within the Vermont Prison System:
  Reactions of Prisoners of Color to Racism and
  Imprisonment" by Laura T. Fishman and Richard C. Turner,
  is reprinted by permission of Laura T. Fishman, Ph.D.,
  Sociology Department, University of Vermont, and the
  Vermont Department of Corrections, 103 S. Main St.,
  Waterbury, VT 05671-1001, 802-241-2265.
Reading 18, "The Children of Female African American
  Prisoners" by Catherine Fisher Collins is from *The
  Imprisonment of African American Women: Causes,
  Conditions and Future Implications* © 1997 Catherine
  Fisher Collins by permission of McFarland & Company,
  Inc., Publishers, Box 611, Jefferson, North Carolina 28640.
  www.mcfarlandpub.com. Orders: 800-253-2187. Figures
  18.2 and 18.3 in this reading are reprinted from *The Female
  Offender,* published by the American Correctional
  Association, Lanham, MD.